ḤIDDUSHIM

CELEBRATING HEBREW COLLEGE'S CENTENNIAL

ḤIDDUSHIM

CELEBRATING HEBREW COLLEGE'S CENTENNIAL

Edited by MICHAEL FISHBANE,
ARTHUR GREEN, and JONATHAN D. SARNA

BOSTON
2022

Library of Congress Control Number: 2022932975

ISBN 9781644698563 (hardback)
ISBN 9781644698570 (Adobe PDF)
ISBN 9781644698587 (ePub)

Book design by PHi Business Solutions
Cover design by Ivan Grave

Published by Academic Studies Press
1577 Beacon Street
Brookline, MA 02446 USA

press@academicstudiespress.com
www.academicstudiespress.com

Contents

Introduction

דברי ברכה

Opening Blessing

I am, by temperament, a deeply nostalgic person. I love hearing and telling family stories, looking at old photographs, lingering over letters, postcards, and aerograms (remember aerograms?) that have gathered over the years. And so, the occasion of the Hebrew College Centennial—including the publication of this wonderful collection of essays—has been a delightful opportunity to reflect and remember—to learn more of the "family lore," to discover and dust off some of the gems in our institutional archives, to witness the abiding tenderness and devotion with which so many alumni speak of their time at Hebrew College.

But, of course, milestones like this are more than an opportunity to reminisce. A Centennial is an invitation to reflect on the last century of teaching and learning at Hebrew College, to ask ourselves what has changed and what has endured, to explore accomplishments and share ongoing struggles, to articulate our aspirations for the next one hundred years.

I am deeply indebted to all those who have enthusiastically embraced this invitation by contributing to this Centennial Volume. I offer my profound thanks to the faculty and alumni whose learning and loving voices fill this collection; to Shana Burstyn, who gracefully held all the pieces of this volume in its early stages; and to Rabbi Shani Rosenbaum, whose skillful, steady hand helped guide this project to completion and whose sensitive touch is evident throughout. Above all, I want to thank Hebrew College rector, Rabbi Arthur Green, PhD, and esteemed Hebrew College alumni Dr. Michael Fishbane and Dr. Jonathan D. Sarna, for conceiving and creating a beautiful volume that is not only a testament to the rich history of Hebrew College over the last hundred years, but a stunning tribute to the vitality of Hebrew College today.

The first piece in this volume, written by Rabbi Dan Judson, PhD, traces the evolution of the College since its founding in 1921, highlighting key inflection points and underscoring the ways in which the College has adapted to dramatic shifts in the landscape of Jewish life in Greater Boston, Israel, and North America. Several alumni memoirs, spanning many decades, fill out the historical picture, and bring the various periods of the College's development vividly, personally, and poignantly to life. Reading these essays, one cannot help but be humbled by the magnitude of the events and existential challenges that have faced the Jewish people over the last century and have formed the unfolding context of the College's educational work.

Responding creatively to these changing realities has been a vital part of the College's mission throughout its history, precisely because Hebrew College has never been an institution committed to academic scholarship in a vacuum. It is an institution that stands at the nexus of the academy and the community, at the meeting place of scholarship and culture, learning and leadership, Torah and life. The teachers and students of Hebrew College, in all its eras, have shared an intense sense of being part of something larger—of engaging in *study for the sake of service* to the Jewish people and to the world. This sensibility has expressed itself differently in different periods, but the fundamental impulse—to engage in deep and rigorous learning that is creative, generative, and generous—has been at the heart of Hebrew College's ethos since its inception.

One hears a powerful expression of this sense of purpose in the words of Dean Eisig Silberschlag: "From its incipient days, the Hebrew College reflected a thorough commitment to Jewish culture. [Culture is] an elusive entity—a derivative of the Latin word *colere* which means to till, to improve one's field or garden through labor." As Rabbi Judson writes, "For Silberschlag, culture is intellectual farming. Actual farming explores the potential of the earth, while intellectual farming, 'embraces the vast potential of the universe.'"[1]

Echoes of the same impulse can be heard in the arresting remarks delivered at a Hebrew College Board meeting a year later by Lou Newman, upon his retirement as director of the Boston Bureau of Jewish Education. Newman cites as coauthor of these words Dr. Susan Shevitz, then a faculty member at Brandeis University and today a member of the Hebrew College Board of Trustees.

> Every eighteen-year-old should know about the basic challenge of existence. It is that the world does not appear to us with its meaning or purpose as given. It is an ever-continuing, challenging puzzle. Humankind, however, is irremediably limited in its capacity to solve this puzzle. Every way of life, therefore, every religion, every philosophy, and every articulated "style" that is at

---

1 See Daniel Judson, "A Home for Jewish Learning in 'The City on the Hill': The History of Hebrew College" on page 11 of this volume.

> all appealing, is a subjective imposition of some meaning upon the universe. Because there are always the unknowns behind the beginnings and the ends of life and of the world, no solution to the problem of meaning is complete. Yet, for the thinking person who would rescue existence from alternating absurdity and tragedy, it is an absolute necessity to make a considered, subjective choice. Whether called philosophy, religion, or lifestyle, the choice is what a person bets his life on … The Jewish educator's task is to make clear, with the purpose of convincing, how Judaism enables one to respond to the unceasing challenge of being alive.[2]

While the semantic field and pedagogic focus may shift at various points from the collective to the individual, from the creation of culture to the construction of personal lives of meaning, there is a shared sense of urgency that reverberates across the generations at Hebrew College. As Silberschlag, Newman, and Shevitz all suggest, the academy must not speak only to itself. It must have a purpose that points beyond itself. It must till, it must improve, it must "respond to the unceasing challenge of being alive."

The scholarly essays contained within this collection are a living embodiment of this orientation to the academic enterprise. Deeply rooted in texts ranging from the Bible to the Talmud to midrashic literature to the Hasidic masters, they give voice to a Torah that is at once intellectually rigorous and emotionally resonant. Sometimes poetic, sometimes prayerful, sometimes playful—the voices in these pages are insistently honest about the spiritual search, exquisitely sensitive to the challenges of being alive, and consistently serious about, in the words of Rabbi Arthur Green, "building a bridge between the study of the Jewish past and the construction of the Jewish future."

This brings us back to the name so aptly chosen for this collection, *Ḥiddushim*: The Hebrew College Centennial Volume. The word *ḥiddushim* comes from the Hebrew root meaning innovation or renewal. In the world of traditional Torah study, a *ḥiddush* is a new insight into an ancient text that emerges in the living dialogue between study partners, around the tables of the *beit midrash*. The Babylonian Talmud, B. Eruvin 3b, goes so far as to teach that "*ein beit midrash be-lo ḥiddush*." There is no house of study without a new idea.

---

2 Louis Newman, "Selections from His Words and Writings," in *Studies in Jewish Education and Judaica in Honor of Louis Newman*, ed. Alexander M. Shapiro and Burton I. Cohen (New York: Ktav Publishing, 1984), 213.

The title *Ḥiddushim* refers, on one level, to the specific, innovative works of scholarship collected and contained within this Centennial Volume. But, at this significant milestone in the life of Hebrew College, the word *ḥiddushim* also speaks to the enduring value of creativity and renewal that lies at the heart of our educational mission.

In response to the well-worn arguments in contemporary Jewish life about which is more important—tradition or innovation, continuity or change—Hebrew College has insistently and emphatically said, "Yes." It is *through* deep literacy that we give rise to intellectual, spiritual, and cultural creativity. It is *through* Jewish education that we give birth to a vibrant Jewish future. It is *through* the interpretive tradition, the enduring process of faithful innovation, that Torah is continually revealed. Whether as individuals or as a collective, it is through our continued capacity for learning, growth, and renewal that we remain most fully alive.

At the deepest level, this commitment to *ḥiddush* flows from the conviction that every human soul is an utterly new and unique reflection of the divine image. Human diversity is sacred and woven into the very fabric of creation. "There is no *beit midrash* without a new idea" because every *beit midrash* is filled with living, breathing human beings who bring their own insights and experiences to the process of inquiry and discovery. Every individual has something distinctive and meaningful to contribute, and what takes place around the tables of the *beit midrash* is not only a battle of ideas but a meeting of souls, an encounter of whole human beings.

In this context, Torah becomes a continual process of co-creation, in which every member of the community is a valued partner. It is essential to elicit the creative contributions of everyone in the room—not only as an act of hospitality, but because each person's unique voice is needed for the fullness of the community to unfold, and for the fullness of Torah to emerge. Qualities of empathy, curiosity, humility, and respect must be actively cultivated, and the process of learning becomes one of *ḥevruta*, of friendship, of learning to know—and to not know—together.

A Few Words in and about Hebrew

It is not an accident that we have chosen a Hebrew word—*ḥiddushim*—to convey our commitment to this process of continual renewal. It is, indeed, not an accident that among all the shifts and changes the College has undergone in its one hundred years, the Hebrew language remains a constant thread through the work we are doing together, core to our vision and, of course, our very name.

השפה העברית פותחת לנו שער לשייכות יותר עמוקה, יותר מלאה, יותר מתמידה לעם היהודי, לתרבות ולספרות היהודית, למסורת היהודית בכל מקום ובכל דור. השפה העברית היא מפתח רב ערך שפותח לנו שערים ומזמין אותנו פנימה, לתוך השיחה היהודית גם ברחבי ארץ ישראל וגם סביב לשולחנות של בית המדרש.

ברחבי ארץ ישראל, העברית השותפת מאפשרת קשר הרבה יותר עמוק ורחב לא רק עם ההסטוריה של המקום אבל גם עם המציאות החיה של המקום ועם האנשים החיים בו.

בשיר של יהודה עמיחי שנקרא "תיירים," המשורר כותב על תיירים שמבקרים בארץ. "בקורי אבלים הם עורכים אצלינו" מתחיל השיר. "יושבים ביד ושם, מרצינים ליד הכותל המערבי, וצוחקים מאחורי וילונות כבדים בחדרי מלון." עמיחי מזכיר לנו שלהיות תייר זה לעמוד ולהסתכל מבחוץ, ממרחק בטוח. בסוף השיר הוא מזמין אותנו להתקרב, ולראות אדם חי, שקנה פירות וירקות לביתו.

השפה העברית מאפשרת לנו להתקרב, להכיר, להרגיש שייכות לא מר-חוק, לא מבחוץ, לא כתיירים, אלא שייכות מבפנים. אני רוצה להדגיש את אותו הדבר לא רק בקשר למציאות החיה של החברה הישראילית, אלא גם למציאות החיה של עולם בית המדרש של התורה שבכתב ושבעל פה, של השיחה והשירה והתרבות והמסורת היהודית בכל דור ובכל מקום. השפה העברית מזמינה אותנו פנימה, ונותנת לנו מקום ליד השלחן -- בכל מקום של לימוד וחידוש תורה, לא כתיירים שמסתכלים מבחוץ, אלא כבני בית.

לפני כחמש עשרה שנה הייתי בארץ עם קבוצת נוער אמריקאים ויש-ראלים ביחד. אחת מהעמיתים הישראילים היתה בחורה אתיופית ותוך כדי שיחה על שיר של דן פגיס, שהוא בעצמו ניצול שואה, דברנו על הקשר שלה לחוויה של יהודי אירופה. אני זוכרת אותה חושבת בשקט, מסתכלת עלי, ואז אומרת: "בתוך עמי אנוכי יושבת." מילים מהתנ"ך, מספר מלכים ב.

המילה שנשארה איתי אחרי כל השנים האלו זאת המילה הפשוטה: "בתוך."

אני מקווה שבשבילינו ובשביל התלמידים שלנו, השפה העברית תמשיך לגרום לפתיחת שערים, להזמנה פנימה, לעודד אותנו לא להתבונן מבחוץ, אלא לשבת בתוך.

In our generation, rabbinic education, and Jewish education more broadly, is in no small measure about the retrieval of a rich, spiritually, culturally, and emotionally resonant Jewish language. It is about helping students speak as insiders to the textual tradition. At Hebrew College, an important part of this process, particularly for future rabbis, cantors, and educators, is about acquiring comfort and fluency in the Hebrew language. The process of Hebrew language acquisition is much more than a technical undertaking for our students. The Hebrew language is both a deep well of memory and meaning, and a doorway into the Jewish conversation across time and space. Our students understand this, and they devote themselves to the study of Hebrew—many of them intensely, over several years—because they long to open that doorway and enter fully, participants in an ancient and enduring dialogue, empowered to be both inheritors and innovators, prepared to lovingly invite others to enter as well.

In our generation, there are—and there must be—many different doorways to Jewish life. Our work at Hebrew College is grounded in the faith that every doorway offers an opening—to deeper learning and growth, to compassion and creativity, to a heightened awareness that we are each part of a greater whole.

As we move beyond our centennial year and onto a shared campus with other mission-aligned partners, our new home will be a vibrant communal hub, physically embodying multiple doorways to Jewish life. It is a privilege and a blessing for me to lead this beloved and venerable institution into the next century, as we continue to meet people at all of those doorways—inviting them into the complexity, beauty, and depth of an interpretive tradition that has been carried on for millennia, welcoming them as active and creative participants in the ongoing and unfolding dialogue through which Torah is forever revealed and renewed.

Bi-vrakha,

Rabbi Sharon Cohen Anisfeld
President, Hebrew College

Message from the Editors

It is with a great sense of honor and delight that we present to you this collection of essays by alumni, faculty, and Israeli friends of Hebrew College. The centenary of this venerable institution, a mainstay of the greater Boston Jewish community that has also achieved a national and international reputation, is indeed an occasion for celebration.

As Daniel Judson's historical survey will show you, both the College and the American Jewish community have been through vast upheavals in the course of these hundred years. The founders of *Beit ha-Midrash le-Morim* in 1922 could not have begun to imagine what Jewish life looks like today. They knew only that they were dedicated to shaping and strengthening the Jewish future in uncertain times, and understood that this needed to begin with Hebrew literacy and a solid foundation in Jewish learning, neither of which was to be taken for granted in the post-immigrant generation. In that sense, it may be said that they and the present leadership of Hebrew College have a great deal in common.

The volume before you is divided into three sections. The first is devoted to the institution itself: Boston Hebrew Teachers College/Hebrew College. The historical essay is followed by a series of personal memoirs, written by alumni of various years and programs offered by the College. This is followed by the longest section, essays in Jewish thought, literature, and history, by scholars who study a wide range of the Jewish people's experience and creativity. The essays are arranged in chronological order of the subjects under consideration. The final section is a group of essays in areas of Jewish education, a special focus of this institution throughout its history.

We hope you learn from these essays and enjoy reading them. May they stimulate the ongoing growth of your own Jewish education, a process that continues throughout life and across the generations. May Hebrew College celebrate many more milestones in the years ahead!

We want to take this opportunity to express our thanks to Rabbi Sharon Cohen Anisfeld, president of Hebrew College, for the enthusiastic and supportive response she offered to this idea from the moment it was suggested to her.

Profuse thanks go to Rabbi Shani Rosenbaum, who served as managing editor of this project during her final year in our rabbinical program and worked *me-'al u-me'ever,* far beyond the call of duty, in putting it together.

Michael Fishbane
Arthur Green
Jonathan Sarna

Section I

MEMORY AND HISTORY

CHAPTER 1

A Home for Jewish Learning in "The City on the Hill": The History of Hebrew College

Daniel Judson

The Prime Minister of the still new country of Israel arrived in Boston in 1951 on a mission to encourage people to buy Israel bonds. As his motorcade paraded through downtown Boston, an estimated 300,000 people came out to greet him. In the evening he spoke to a sold-out Boston Garden crowded with 18,000 people. But before the parade and the crowds at the Garden, David Ben Gurion came to speak at a small institution in Roxbury, MA that had a deep commitment to Zionism and the Hebrew language. Surveying the students and faculty assembled in the auditorium, Ben Gurion told them that of all the places in America where he was scheduled to speak, it was Hebrew Teachers College that he was most looking forward to visit.[1] Decades after the visit, a student remembered that the auditorium on that day was overflowing and cheering as the Dean of the College accompanied Ben Gurion down the aisle: "Ben Gurion concluded his brief and stirring comments with *anachnu rotzeim etchem* (we want you); we responded with spirited song and dance which spilled over onto Crawford Street."[2]

Hebrew College, originally Hebrew Teachers College, was founded in 1921 as part of a wave of institutions established to train teachers. Some of these were independent colleges of Jewish studies—Baltimore Hebrew College, Spertus

1 For Ben Gurion's visit to Boston and Hebrew College, please see: "300,000 Jam Downtown to Cheer Premier," *Jewish Advocate*, May 17, 1951, 1; "Hub Opens Heart to Ben Gurion: 18,000 Pack Garden for Salute to Israel Launching Big Bonds Drive," *Jewish Advocate*, May 17, 1951, 1; "Report of the Dean," Hebrew College Board Minutes, May 22, 1951, Hebrew College Archives; "The Family Remembers," *Hebrew College Bulletin* 5, no. 4 (June 1974): 27.

2 "The Family Remembers," *Hebrew College Bulletin* 5, no. 4 (June 1974): 27.

College of Judaica in Chicago, and the Cleveland College of Jewish Studies were all founded in this period.[3] Other teacher training programs opened as part of existing institutions, like at Hebrew Union College, the Jewish Theological Seminary, and Yeshiva University. The creation of so many Teachers Colleges reflected a number of historical factors. Central among them was the influence of Samson Benderly and other Jewish educators who pushed to modernize Jewish educational methods in supplementary schools.[4]

This period in American Jewish life was one of transition. The doors to immigration were closing and the Americanized children of immigrants were now the preponderance of students. The traditional European style Talmud Torah was losing favor in an American context. Modern methods of teaching Jewish studies were necessary. However, there was a dearth of teachers who had the requisite skills to teach Jewish studies according to the new pedagogic ideas, so institutes of training needed to be established.

Alongside the need for better educators was the embrace of Hebrew language and Zionism. The Balfour Declaration, as well as the devastation to world Jewry from World War I, inspired a growing American Jewish commitment to Zionism. Each of the training institutions would adopt some form of Aḥad Ha'am's cultural Zionism. This movement saw the Hebrew language as the organic connection between the individual and the Jewish community. Teaching Hebrew would inspire a commitment to Jewish identity and inoculate Jewish youth against assimilation.[5]

At Hebrew College, as its very name would imply, modern Hebrew would be primary to the institution. In the early years of the College students took classes in spoken Hebrew, Hebrew literature, and Hebrew grammar as well as courses in Bible, Talmud, Jewish history, codes, and education. Even in the non-Hebrew specific courses, the language of instruction was primarily Hebrew. "The aim was to make spoken Hebrew an everyday experience, while in school

---

3 For more on independent colleges of Jewish Studies, see Gary Schiff, "Between Freedom and Responsibility: The Independent College of Jewish Studies," in *Freedom and Responsibility: Exploring the Challenges of Jewish Continuity*, ed. Rela Geffen and Marsha Edelman (Hoboken, NJ: KTAV, 1998), 301–319; Walter Ackerman, "A World Apart: Hebrew Teachers Colleges and Hebrew Speaking Camps," in *Hebrew in America: Perspectives and Prospects*, ed. Alan Mintz (Detroit, MI: Wayne State University Press, 1993); Louis Hurwich, "Hebrew Teachers' Colleges in the United States: Digest of Survey," *Jewish Education* 22, nos. 1–2 (Winter-Spring 1950–1951): 73–96; and Oscar Janowsky, ed. *The Education of American Jewish Teachers* (Boston, MA: Beacon, 1967).

4 See Jonathan Krasner, *The Benderly Boys and American Jewish Education* (Waltham, MA: Brandeis University Press, 2011).

5 See Ackerman, "A World Apart," 109–110, for description of Aḥad Ha'am's influence on Hebrew Teachers Colleges.

and thereafter."[6] One of the highlights of the year was "Hebrew Week," a city-wide event, which culminated in the dean of Hebrew College giving an address in Hebrew and a student reading a Hebrew poem by Bialik.[7] With such a central focus on Hebrew language and culture as core to its vision of Jewish revival, it is no wonder that a figure like Ben Gurion was drawn to Hebrew College as a kindred spirit in the project of Jewish flourishing.

While the devotion to Hebrew was central to the College, Hebraism was only part of Hebrew College's broader understanding of Jewish culture. From its earliest years, Hebrew College promoted all aspects of Jewish life. Its first building included a theatre where the Masada Student Organization put on plays by Shalom Asch and Shalom Aleichem. The College held Shabbat and Holiday services, it had a dance troupe of "Palestinian" dancers, it had a museum, a gymnasium, an orchestra, a library, and it held evenings devoted to Hebrew poetry, Zionist thinkers, and rabbinic scholarship, as well as holding Purim balls and monthly dances. It embraced seemingly all aspects of Jewish life and culture. The first president of the College, Leon Medalia, wrote that above all other goals, the central purpose of the College was "to create high standards of Jewish culture in America."[8]

In this commitment to culture, the College has displayed a great degree of continuity over the century. In 1954, the College published its three primary objectives, the first of which was "to impart to students a thorough comprehension of Jewish culture and appreciation of its wisdom, its morality, and its beauty."[9] In 1979, the College defined its educational mission as having graduates who "have developed an appreciation and love for the entire range of Jewish culture and for the values inherent in it."[10] As part of its 2011 mission statement, the College continued to stress the importance of Jewish culture: "We embrace music, literature and the visual and performing arts as sources of inspiration and as vital modes of Jewish discovery and expression."[11]

---

6 Louis Hurwich, *Memoirs of a Jewish Educator: Louis Hurwich and the Story of Boston's Jewish Education* (Boston, MA: Bureau of Jewish Education of Greater Boston, 1999), 147. Just to underscore the institution's commitment to Hebrew, Hurwich originally wrote his memoirs in Hebrew, and the Hebrew version was published by the Bureau of Jewish Education in 1960.

7 "'Hebrew Week' in Boston," *Jewish Advocate*, May 11, 1922, 8. See also "Fine Program to End 'Hebrew Week,'" *Jewish Advocate*, June 21, 1928.

8 Leon Medalia letter to Louis Kirsstein, February 6, 1922, Hebrew College Archives.

9 "Objectives and Range of Activities," *Hebrew College Course Catalogue, 1954*, 10, Hebrew College Archives.

10 "Handbook for the Long Range Planning Committee of the Board of Trustees," November 1979, 19, Hebrew College Archives.

11 "Mission Statement," Hebrew College website, hebrewcollege.edu/about/mission-statement, accessed June 27, 2021.

Eisig Silberschlag, an acclaimed Hebrew scholar and a figure deeply entwined with the history of the College for over thirty years, first as a professor and then as Dean, wrote that, "From its incipient days, the Hebrew College reflected a thorough commitment to Jewish culture—an elusive entity—a derivative of the Latin word *colere* which means to till, to improve one's field or garden through labor." Culture, Silberschlag continued, is intellectual farming. Actual farming explores the potential of the earth, while intellectual farming, "embraces the vast potential of the universe."[12] For a century, the College has been engaged in intellectual farming. Its basic mission has remained relatively unchanged. It is committed to teaching teachers, teenagers, and Jewish adults by embracing and celebrating a broad sense of Jewish culture within an academic environment.

"Carrying Out the Old Message of the Jew into the New Americanism": The Founding of the College

Leon Hurwich, the founder of Hebrew College, traced the College's origins to a summer job he held in 1917. Hurwich had just completed his Masters in Jewish Communal Work from Columbia University when he reached out to Morris Waldman, the new head of Boston's Federated Jewish Charities (the precursor to what is now Combined Jewish Philanthropies), to inquire if he could work for the Federated during the summer. Waldman agreed and gave Hurwich the task of surveying all Sunday and Hebrew schools to see how many pupils they had, what method they were using to teach Hebrew, how much they charged, and so forth.[13]

Leon Hurwich was a remarkable figure. He attended the famed Volozhin Yeshiva as a child but left after discovering Zionism and a love of modern Hebrew. He immigrated to America as a teenager to avoid being conscripted into the Russian army and settled in the lower east side. He was set to become an engineer but his love of Hebrew (he would raise his children in Boston speaking only in Hebrew to them) got him interested in Jewish education. Ultimately his fluency in modern Hebrew, Yiddish, and English made him ideally suited to navigate the different parts of the Jewish community. His students would later remember his kindness above all traits: "He was like a father to all of us, he knew every one of us by our names, our parents, what they did, our brothers and sisters . . . . He would raise our coat collar and button our top button as we left in

---

12 *Hebrew College Bulletin* 12, no. 4 (June 1982): 15.
13 Hurwich, *Memoirs*, 22–23.

the cold winter nights on our way home ... and he participated in our [Shabbat] services, not as a teacher or a Dean, but as a fellow Jew."[14]

When Hurwich arrived in Boston to carry out the school survey, his first encounter was with a principal of a Hebrew school who viewed the Federated as the enemy and Hurwich as a potential spy. Hebrew schools at that time received no help from Federated leaders and felt looked down upon in their efforts to train children. Hurwich's survey would become the turning point in Jewish education in Boston as it would galvanize the broader Jewish community to support Jewish education.[15] Hurwich found that 1,529 students attended Hebrew schools in Boston, and 1,800 pupils attended Sunday schools. At the time, Hebrew schools and Sunday schools were entirely separate endeavors. Hebrew schools taught Hebrew language and culture, and Sunday schools covered bible stories and holidays and were taught in English. Given Hurwich's interests, it was primarily to the Hebrew schools that he directed his attention. He had a range of proposals to improve the schools including creating an association of Hebrew schools, increasing teacher salaries by twenty-five percent to make teaching a more attractive profession, and adding extracurricular activities. The Federated Jewish Charities, which had previously allocated no money to Jewish education, committed to a $30,000 annual allotment ($608,000 in today's money) to carry out Hurwich's plans for improvement.[16]

Another of Hurwich's findings from his survey was the lack of high-quality Hebrew teachers. Many of the schools were using young people, fifteen- to seventeen-year-olds, as assistant teachers because of the lack of qualified teachers. One of central problems in attracting teachers, besides the low pay, was that qualified Hebrew speakers were no longer coming to America because of the immigration restrictions, which had begun in 1914 and would become permanent in 1924. While immigration restrictions are usually not seen as central to the founding of Hebrew College, it is a dominant theme in much of the discussion leading up to its opening.[17] The problem though was not only the lack of immigrant teachers, according to Hurwich; even if there were a supply of such teachers, American-born teachers needed to be trained because only they could relate to Americanized Jewish youth. "Being foreign born," he explained, "[the immigrant teacher] cannot fully appreciate what goes on in the soul of the American child, an understanding which can only be gained by those who lived

14 *Hebrew College Bulletin* 12, no. 4 (June 1982): 21.

15 Hurwich, *Memoirs*, 35–36.

16 Ibid., 35–72.

17 Ibid., 96.

and breathed the same atmosphere in which their prospective pupils now live and grow."[18]

As a response to the need for teachers, Hurwich proposed a Hebrew Teachers Training School, which would focus on teaching the young assistant teachers and as well be open to new graduates of the Hebrew schools. This was not the first call for teacher training. In 1913, a small group had created the Jewish Educational Society, which opened a Normal School for teacher training. It quickly attracted 130 students, but just as quickly failed, and was no longer operative by the time Hurwich entered the scene.[19] Hurwich proposed a two-year program with a curriculum of Bible, history, and Hebrew with some education courses taught by professors at nearby universities. Significantly, at a meeting of Boston-area Hebrew schools, it was decided that the lack of teachers was such a pressing need that Hurwich was empowered to fund the Training School out of the education allotment from the Federated Charities. This marks the beginning of a crucial relationship, as the College would be reliant on Federation funding throughout its history.[20]

The first year of the Training School attracted twenty-one students, which would become forty-eight students two years later. But the need for educators remained high and Hurwich believed that the Training School's two-year, part-time program was not sufficiently serving the need of Hebrew schools. He proposed a four-year, full-time program. Bolstering his hopes of attracting students was the fact that Hebrew schools were bursting with students and the lack of teachers meant that salaries for Hebrew school teachers were higher than public school teachers.[21] Hurwich envisioned a budget of $30,000 ($389,218 in today's money), which would go for staff salaries, paying for a building, and student subsidies to offset tuition for students in need. Tuition was set at $200 ($2,594 today) yearly. Hurwich was blunt in his financial assessment, "The cost of the Institution will by no means be little, but the community loses infinitely more by lulling itself into the belief that matters will take care of themselves."[22] Hurwich's plan was accepted by the Bureau of Jewish Education and The Federated Charities, as well as a wider group of committed educators led by the clergy of Temple Israel in Boston.[23]

---

18 Louis Hurwich, "First Hebrew Teachers College to Be Dedicated," *Jewish Advocate*, August 18, 1921, 1.

19 Untitled Speech by Leon Medalia, May 10, 1917, Hebrew College Archives.

20 Hurwich, *Memoirs*, 86.

21 Ibid., 122.

22 Hurwich, letter, April 6, 1921.

23 Hurwich, *Memoirs*, 121–124.

One of the first steps for the new Institution was the acquisition of a building to house a full-time program. Hurwich learned that a bank had recently foreclosed on an orthodox shul in Roxbury. Because the building was in disrepair, the bank agreed to sell it to the Bureau of Jewish Education for $8,000 with just $300 as a down payment. The newly organized College bought a building before it even had a staff and students.[24] This optimism should be understood in light of the explosive growth of Jewish institutions in Boston (as well as the whole country), which made the purchase and refurbishing of a building seem a relatively safe choice. In the 1920s the synagogue-center model of Mordecai Kaplan who envisioned the synagogue as a social as well as a spiritual center took hold in Jewish life. No less than four massive institutions were constructed in Boston at this time—Temple Israel, Temple Ohabei Shalom, Mishkan Tefilah, and Kehillath Israel—all of which still stand today and all of which were built with exorbitant budgets for the time. Just the first phase of Temple Israel's construction alone would cost $5.5 million in today's dollars.[25] The cost of these institutions bespoke a Jewish community, which felt itself more materially secure than at any previous point in history. This is not to suggest the College did not struggle to raise money for its new enterprise, but the College came about precisely at a time of philanthropic largesse.

Having successfully bought a building and raised money for the initial budget, the founders of Hebrew College sought an educator to carry out their plans. Dr. Nissan Touroff, who would become the first Dean of the College, was raised in Minsk in a traditional home before moving to Moscow where he was an aspiring artist. When the Jews of Moscow were expelled in 1891, he needed to find another profession and entered the Hebrew Teachers' Institute of Vilna. He received his doctorate from the University of Lausanne in Switzerland writing on the philosophy of education. He had also become an ardent Zionist, and contributed articles to the major Hebrew newspapers of the time including *Ha-Shiloaḥ* edited by Aḥad Ha'am. The Ḥovevei Ẓion organization offered him the job of being principal of the girls' gymnasium in Jaffa, which he accepted in 1907. He spent twelve years in Palestine overseeing schools and becoming superintendent of all Palestinian schools during World War I. He was also one of the founders and first editors of *Ha-Aretẓ*, a daily newspaper still publishing today.[26]

---

24 Ibid., 126.

25 For full analysis of the Jewish construction boom of the 1920s see Dan Judson, *Pennies for Heaven: The History of American Synagogues and Money* (Waltham, MA: Brandeis University Press, 2018), 148–156.

26 "Heads Hebrew Teacher's College," *Jewish Advocate*, September 1, 1921, 5.

Dr. Touroff negotiated what would be a substantial annual salary of $5,000 ($72,642 by today's standards) with the newly established Hebrew Teachers College Organization—the equivalent of the Board—making him one of the highest-paid Jewish educators in the country. His tenure at the College turned out to be relatively brief, as he resigned in 1926 and took a position at the newly established Jewish Institute of Religion in New York. Colleagues said Dr. Touroff did not easily accommodate to American mores, but he was also someone of enormous passion and charisma beloved by students and faculty. When he spoke, Hurwich wrote, "A flame was lit in the heart, a holy flame, steady and full of love for the Torah, the people and the spiritual world of the people."[27] After he left the College, he was spoken of with a religious fervor, "Dr. Touroff [was] the prophet carrying out the old message of the Jew into the new Americanism. He believed in taking the best from the new land, so different from anything the Jew has known, and adding it to that store of wisdom and culture that the Jew has paid for so dearly throughout the ages."[28] Dr. Touroff represented for the fledgling institution an ideal combination of academic credentials, professional accomplishment, a commitment to Hebraism, Zionism, and the totality of Jewish life and culture.

Touroff's successor, Dr. Samuel Perlman, had a remarkably similar background. Dr. Perlman received rabbinic ordination in Minsk, but left observance for secular education and Zionism. He received his doctorate from the University of Berne in Switzerland before moving to Palestine where he worked in education. He gained renown as a Hebrew scholar and worked with Vladimir Jabotinsky on a historical Hebrew atlas, which was used in schools throughout the world. On a trip through America, Bialik himself said Perlman's Hebrew style placed him in a class by himself.[29] Because of immigration restrictions however, Perlman was initially denied a work permit, and leaders of Boston Jewry travelled to Washington, D.C. to plead for a special exemption from the Committee on Immigration. Perlman was eventually granted a work permit but he had to leave his wife and child behind for his entire stay in Boston.[30]

The College's extensive efforts to secure an academic leader of Perlman's renown reflected how crucial the College considered its academic reputation. Simply educating young Jews was not sufficient for its goals; the founders of

---

27 Hurwich, *Memoirs*, 134–135.

28 "Hebrew Teachers College Means of Jewish Culture," *Jewish Advocate*, October 10, 1929, 6.

29 "New Dean of Hebrew College is Known as an Outstanding Hebrew Scholar," *Jewish Advocate*, April 15, 1926, B4.

30 Hurwich, *Memoirs*, 151.

the College wanted to create an institution that would raise the status of Jewish scholarship in the non-Jewish world. "Professors of Harvard are already looking with interest upon the organization of the Hebrew Teachers College," wrote Medalia in those early years. "The Hebrew Teachers College's continued growth and increased contact with non-Jewish graduate schools of Education can only tend in one direction, namely—to create more respect for the Jewish education in the minds of non-Jewish educational experts."[31]

"A Real Hebrew Centre": The First Decade

The College opened its doors in 1921 with thirteen men and women of differing ages and backgrounds. Classes were held on Sundays through Thursdays with weekday classes beginning at 4:00 p.m. to allow students to attend either high school or college. On top of classes, students were expected to do several hours of homework a day. Classes ran for ten months of the year, except for the "weak lambs" (students who struggled with the coursework) who needed to work through the summer.[32]

One important aspect of the College is that from its inception it was open to women and men for studying together. This was little remarked upon at the time; among the myriad contemporaneous documents about the College there is not a word written about the College's open stance towards coeducational learning. But Hebrew College would have been one of the only institutions in Boston where men and women would have been engaged in serious study of Jewish sources on equal footing. The encouragement of women's learning in Teacher Institutions was not, however, unique to Hebrew College. Jonathan Krasner notes that in New York, Samuel Benderly similarly encouraged women to train as teachers, "because he, like many of his counterparts in secular education, believed that [women] were on average more nurturing and temperamentally better suited than men to teach [young children]."[33] The commitment of the College to teach and empower women should properly be given its place as an important stage setting for the broader movement of Jewish feminism. Feminist scholars like Paula Hyman and Anne Lapidus Lerner were both products of a Hebrew College education.

---

31 Leon Medalia letter to Louis Kirskstein, February 6, 1922, Hebrew College Archives.

32 Hurwich, *Memoirs*, 134–135.

33 Krasner, *The Benderly Boys*, 104.

By the second year of the College, the number of students had quickly grown to fifty. The majority of the new students were American-born and came with little Jewish education compared with European-born students. The faculty felt that a preparatory high school program was needed to allow students with limited backgrounds to prepare for the College program. This was the beginning of the Prozdor High School program, which is still part of the College today.[34]

That same year, the College bought a significant collection of Jewish books, which became the basis for the Hebrew College library. Rabbi Louis Epstein, who led Congregation Kehillath Israel in Brookline, was vacationing in Germany and met a Jewish bookseller who offered 3,000 volumes for $500 ($7,615 in today's terms). The volumes were in Hebrew, German and Yiddish, and were added to a small collection of existing books. This created, at the time, "the only real Jewish library in New England."[35] Over time, the library would grow to 90,000 volumes and maintain significant collections of Hebrew literature and American Judaica.

The College's initial success encouraged the Board to embark on an ambitious plan to build a new building attached to the existing structure at a cost of $75,000 ($1.142 million).[36] As Dean Touroff explained, "The new building under construction is to be very much more than merely an educational institution.... We are going to make our new building a real Hebrew centre in the community."[37] The new building included a large gymnasium with showers, locker rooms, and a removable stage with seating for 500 for plays, concerts, and High Holiday services. It also housed a library as well as a museum, which would highlight the flora and fauna of Palestine. To literally top it all off was a roof garden for open-air music concerts.[38]

As noted above, the creation of a Hebrew Centre was well in keeping with the trend in American Jewish life, influenced by Mordecai Kaplan, to build centers that served social and physical as well as intellectual and spiritual needs. And the College believed it important for its students to have such a well-rounded

---

34 Ibid., 141–142.

35 "Gives 3000 Volumes to HUB [*sic*] College," *The Jewish Advocate*, September 21, 1922, 1. As Professor Jonathan D. Sarna reminded me, Harvard University and the Boston Public Library had larger Jewish collections at the time, but Hebrew Teacher College's library, unlike the others, was owned and managed by Jews.

36 "Hebrew Teachers College will Campaign for $75,000 for Additional Building," *Jewish Advocate*, February 21, 1924, 1.

37 "Hebrew Teachers College Preserves Jewish Culture," *Jewish Advocate*, September 25, 1924, 17.

38 "Hebrew Teachers College in Immediate Need of $20,000," *Jewish Advocate*, October 16, 1924, A2.

experience. For young immigrant students, the College would be their second home and a place to eat, socialize, and play. Because some of the students came from poor families, the College even had physicians and nurses to provide care for students knowing that they would not get it at home.[39] The College also believed that students needed more than simply classroom learning; they needed to be immersed in the cultural aspects of Jewish life—drama, music, poetry, dance—as well. But the Centre model also reflects the College's commitment beyond its students to be a Centre for the Boston Jewish community. The construction of a library, museum, gym, and theatre were meant to place Hebrew College at the center of New England Jewry and establish a commitment that the College would continue throughout its history of seeing itself as the public center of Jewish culture as well as a training ground for students.

The College's centrality to New England Jewry can be seen in speeches preserved from a conference held at the College to raise $5,000 ($74,150) from communities outside of Boston. At issue was the need of the College to diversify its funding so it was not totally reliant on the Boston Federation (still known at this time as the Associated Jewish Philanthropies). The Federation had reduced its annual allotment to the college by $7,500, so the College was forced to quickly find alternative revenue sources. Jewish leaders from Boston as well as central Massachusetts, Maine, New Hampshire, and Rhode Island converged on the College to discuss a plan for Jewish communities outside of Boston to pay a portion of the College's budget. The conference highlighted two broad issues that would remain ongoing issues throughout its history. The first was the reliance on Federation funding and the need to diversify the revenue base beyond the Federation and tuition from students. The second was the extent to which the College was a local institution as opposed to a New England institution. In later years this issue would be a tension between being perceived as a local institution versus a national one.

Henry Yossell of Lynn, MA outlined an aggressive plan that would ultimately pass where each community in New England, which benefitted from the College, would be assigned a fee—Worcester, $1,000; Providence, $750; Springfield, $750, and so forth. He argued:

> Only up to a few short years ago, most people thought that America was barren soil for Jewish learning. We lacked faith in our ability to continue the tradition of Jewish learning in this,

39 See "Ninth Meeting of the Board of Trustees of the Hebrew Teachers College," March 24, 1930, Hebrew College Archives.

> our new country of adoption.... Then the Hebrew Teachers' College came.... At first, the constructive influence of the Hebrew Teachers' College was felt only in Boston. It did not take long, however, and we who live in other communities found out that a new light began to spread in Jewish life, that a great school was organized and that that school was ready to serve and to guide all other schools outside of Boston whenever guidance is needed.[40]

By 1927, the College would reach the high point of its early years. It had almost 200 students enrolled in the College coming from all over Boston. Some students travelled over an hour each way to study at the College five days a week. Evening lectures were frequently held on modern Hebrew literature or Zionist thinkers, as well as musical concerts and even plays by a Hebrew Dramatic Society. The curriculum for students was intensive. They studied Bible with commentary, Mishna and selections of Talmud, Jewish history, codes (Jewish law), education and of course Hebrew—Hebrew literature, Hebrew grammar and spoken Hebrew were all studied.[41] At the end of the year students contributed Hebrew essays to a *Sefer ha-Shanah* (Yearbook). "The tone of seriousness, the quality of maturity and the elegance of Hebrew style, characterizing all the contributions ... stamp this book as a splendid achievement in Hebrew education on American soil."[42] A local newspaper article about the book paints a rich picture of the students and the mission of Hebrew College at this time:

> at the Hebrew Teachers College, modestly concealed on Crawford Street, Roxbury, there attend about two hundred students who are consecrating their young lives and giving the flower of their youth in order to gain a thorough knowledge of our people's literary heritage. While others fritter away their time in self-indulgence, or generally in some stupid, inexplicable manner feel themselves above a knowledge of Hebrew, these young

40 "New England Jewish Communities Rally to Support of Hebrew Teachers' College of Boston," April 6, 1930, Hebrew College Archives. See also "Rally to Call of Hebrew College," *Jewish Advocate*, April 11, 1930, 1.

41 Hurwich, *Memoirs*, 147; "Malden First to Pay Its Hebrew College Quota," *Jewish Advocate*, April 29, 1930, 4.

42 "'Sefer Hashanah' or the First 'Year Book' of the Students of Hebrew Teachers College," *Jewish Advocate*, December 3, 1925, A3.

> students are willing to forgo even the very fragrance of their youth to acquire an intimate fellowship with the ideals and lore of their ancestors.[43]

As Frank Manuel, a student at both Hebrew College and Harvard who would go on to become a distinguished professor, put it, "I found Hebrew Teachers College more stimulating than Harvard College."[44]

The culmination of this period in the life of the College came in March 1927, when the State of Massachusetts granted a charter to the College enabling it to "award the degree of Bachelor, Master and Doctor of Hebrew Literature, of Hebrew Laws and of Jewish Education … and to award certificates of efficiency to persons qualified to teach in Jewish religious schools."[45] President Medalia spoke at a celebration, saying that the granting of the charter "surpasses the hopes and the dreams of the most optimistic … early pioneers and builders of this college."[46] For Medalia, the charter represented crucial recognition by the non-Jewish world of the importance of the College. The College had, as it were, made it. Its mission to spread Hebrew learning was seen by the outside world as an act worthy of official sanction.

"This Sum is For My Son's Tuition": The Depression and the 1930s

The Hebrew College Board meeting on October 9, 1929 was a relatively mundane affair. It was reported that 140 students had signed up with more registrants expected. There was a discussion of purchasing a private collection of 1,500 volumes on social work to be added to the library at a cost of $4,500, and the Dean of the School negotiated a salary raise of $1,000 a year to $7,000.[47] It was Dean Perlman's bad luck to negotiate a raise just two weeks before the crash of the stock market. He would never see that raise, and the next Board meeting was anything but relatively mundane.

---

43 Ibid.

44 Arthur Goren, "Ben Halpern: At Home in Exile," in *The "Other" New York Jewish Intellectuals*, ed. Carole Kessner, (New York: New York University Press, 1994), 77.

45 "The Charter," April 15, 1927, Hebrew College Archives.

46 Leon Medalia, "Hebrew Teachers College Celebration by the Students of the Right to Confer Degrees," April 4, 1927, Hebrew College Archives.

47 "Seventh Meeting of the Board of Directors of the Hebrew Teachers College," October 9, 1929, Hebrew College Archives.

Like so many Jewish and non-Jewish institutions at the time, the crash of the stock market put the College in existential peril. The Associated Jewish Philanthropies, which had already been running behind in its campaign, had been planning a fund drive, which was now seen as unlikely to succeed. The College was asked by the Federation "to state what it considered the absolute irreducible minimum" upon which it could survive. On the positive side, the library purchase of books went ahead.[48]

The impact of the Depression was particularly felt in the field of Jewish education. Across the country, paying for Jewish educators was at the bottom of priorities for the Jewish communities and for individual families. "The Great Depression had a devastating effect on Jewish education, virtually wiping out many of the gains of the previous two decades… . Layoffs at schools and educational agencies were de rigueur, while the salaries of those who remained were cut and sometimes unpaid for months at a time."[49]

This was in part Hebrew College's fate as the Board reported in early 1931 that salary payments were in arrears, and every effort needed to be make up the deficit, including selling library books.[50] By the end of the year, the College was asking all faculty to take a voluntary 5% pay reduction, it was late with mortgage payments, and it had approximately $14,000 in unpaid bills.[51] And yet the College hung on through the Depression and in some respects even thrived. In 1932 the College had its largest number of students: 172. Students came despite significant concerns about graduates not having jobs because so many Hebrew and religious schools were suffering.[52]

The College credited the large registration in part to the commitment of many local Hebrew schools, which ran small advanced Hebrew classes, despite losing money on them, so that a sufficient number of young people could pass the College entrance Hebrew exams. The parents of students were also praised for their dedication during such difficult economic times. Louis Hurwich, who had stepped into the role of Dean after Dr. Perlman went back to Palestine, spoke movingly of the commitment of parents to send their children to HTC:

---

48 "Minutes of the 56th Meeting of the Executive Committee of the Bureau of Jewish Education and the 8th Meeting of the Board of Trustees of the Hebrew Teachers College," November 29, 1929, Hebrew College Archives.

49 Krasner, *The Benderly Boys*, 160.

50 "Fifteenth Meeting of the Board of Trustees of the Hebrew Teachers College," March 9, 1931, Hebrew College Archives.

51 "Nineteenth Meeting of the Board of Trustees of the Hebrew Teachers College," November 26, 1931, Hebrew College Archives.

52 "Annual Meeting of the Corporation of the Hebrew Teachers College," January 15, 1933, Hebrew College Archives.

> Very few among the parents belong economically to the middle class. All others struggle hard for a mere living. . . . In one case, a father of a student appeared at the office and said, "I have been unemployed for the last eight months. I owe for several months' rent, groceries and for what not. But here is $5 on account of my son's tuition fee." [Hurwich] refused to accept the money, stating that under the circumstances [the father] had better use the sum for some pressing need and that his son is entitled to free tuition. Tears appeared in the father's eyes. He stated his regret over his inability to give more. "This sum however," he said, "I scraped together for my son's tuition fee. I beg you to take it all. I shall feel very badly if you refuse." The sum was accepted. A gleam of light appeared in the man's eyes, and thereby a family epic, which it is hoped will be repeated on many happy occasions, has been created.[53]

At the height of the Depression, the College even began a number of new ventures, which would become significant in its history. One program was a three-year extension course for adults, "for the purpose of initiating what may become known as the minimum knowledge of things Jewish required of any intelligent Jewish adult." The course was created in recognition of the fact that so many adult Jews had no Jewish education. "The main aim of the course shall be to give the individual a general understanding of the Jewish past, Jewish spiritual creations and to fit the individual to participate intelligently in the present community activities."[54] Seventy students signed up for the program. Courses were offered in general Jewish history, Jewish customs, and multiple levels of Hebrew. The program was a historical precursor to Me'ah, a two-year course of study for adult learners, which was also aimed at providing Jewish literacy for adults and would become a hallmark of the College in the 1990s until today.

Another significant program started during the Depression was the creation of the New England Women's Association of the Hebrew Teachers College. The Association's primary mission was to raise money for the college. Women's philanthropic auxiliary societies were common for Jewish institutions at this time. The National Federation of Temple Sisterhoods supported Hebrew Union

---

53 "H.T.C. Has Largest Registration in Its History," *Jewish Advocate*, October 4, 1932: 3.

54 "Twenty-third Meeting of the Board of Trustees of the Hebrew Teachers College," July 1, 1932, Hebrew College Archives.

College with significant scholarship aid even before World War I (which it still provides today under the name of the Women of Reform Judaism), and the Women's Religious Union of the United Synagogue (today the Women's League of Conservative Judaism) supported the Jewish Theological Seminary. Such organizations allowed for women's leadership to be exercised in an essential aspect of the institution.[55] The Association was founded in 1932 and immediately 100 women joined for a small annual subscription. In 1933, the Association crucially raised $1,250, which was used to pay down the mortgage. The president of the College said the Association "was of invaluable service to us financially and of great moral support."[56] The Association would go on to serve the College in innumerable ways. A 1941 article details the following:

> The New England Women's Association of the Hebrew Teachers College gives scholarships to able and needy students; it conducts a student lunchroom to help keep the students health at par; it adds hundreds of books to the library yearly to be used by students and others; it pays off a college mortgage through its life memberships; and it endeavors to bring the importance of higher Jewish education before the community.[57]

The Women's Association would also commit itself to adult Jewish education specifically for women. It created a Women's School for Jewish Studies, which ran adult classes on various themes often related to Zionism and Hebrew.[58]

By the middle of the decade, the College was thriving with ever-increasing numbers of students and had gathered an impressive collection of faculty. Jacob Newman was a Talmud professor at the College who produced for his students the first translation of Talmudic tractates into modern Hebrew with an explanatory Hebrew commentary.[59] The translation of Talmud into modern Hebrew for pedagogic means suggests a great deal about the spirit of the College at this time—a mix of Jewish tradition, Hebraism, and pedagogy.

---

55 David Ellenson and Jane Karlin, "Mothers and Sons, Sisters and Brothers: Women of Reform Judaism and Hebrew Union College-Jewish Institute of Religion," in *Sisterhood: A Centennial History of Women of Reform Judaism*, ed. Carol Balin, Dana Herman, Jonathan Sarna, and Gary Zola, (Cincinnati, OH: Hebrew Union College Press, 2013).

56 "President's Annual Report," January 15, 1933, Hebrew College Archives.

57 "Reception to Members of Hebrew College Women's Association," *Jewish Advocate*, January 17, 1941, 8.

58 "Women's School for Jewish Studies," *Jewish Advocate*, November 13, 1942, 6.

59 "Publication of Talmud to be Celebrated," *Jewish Advocate*, February 24, 1944, 1.

Professor Newman passed away unexpectedly and was succeeded in 1943 by Nahum Glatzer who spent four years as the Rabbinics teacher at the College. Glatzer had an international reputation, ultimately publishing over 60 books and becoming the authoritative biographer and editor of the writings of Franz Rosenzweig.[60]

One faculty member who joined in 1932 would become associated with the College for almost four decades. Eisig Silberschlag was the professor of Hebrew Literature before becoming Dean of the College in 1947. He oversaw the College's move from Crawford Street to its new home on Hawes Street in Brookline in the 1950s. Silberschlag was an internationally renowned Hebrew poet, translator and literary critic. Born in Poland in 1903, he emigrated to America in 1921 but returned to Europe to pursue his PhD at the University of Vienna. He then taught at the Teachers Institutes of both the Jewish Theological Seminary and the Hebrew Union College before coming to Boston.[61] He had an enormous range—his book of Hebrew essays, *Tehiyyah u-Teḥiyyah ba-Shirah* (Search and Rebirth in Poetry) was the first book in Hebrew to deal with German, French, and English nineteenth-century poets. His work of original Hebrew poetry, *Aleh Olam be-Shir* (Rise, World, in Song), which he wrote in 1943, won the Louis Lamed award given annually to the best Hebrew book in America. He wrote a well-received work of criticism in English about one of his major influences, Saul Tschernichowsky, who like Silberschlag, blended Zionism, Jewish tradition, and world literature in his work.[62] He was also a master of Greek and Latin and was perhaps best known for his translation of Aristophanes comedic plays into Hebrew, which won the Tel Aviv Prize in 1965.[63] Silberschlag's massive erudition and genuine love for Hebrew profoundly shaped the College for decades. After his passing, a faculty member wrote, "Despite the changing mores and modern demands, an institution takes on and holds to the sensitivities of all the 'temporary' guides of its destiny. Part of the glitter of our Hebrew College belongs forever to Eisig Silberschlag."[64]

---

60 "Biography," Nahum Norbert Glatzer Papers, Brandeis University Archives.

61 "Dr. Silberschlag Joins Hebrew Teachers College Faculty," *Jewish Advocate*, September 16, 1932, 5.

62 Eisig Silberschlag, *Saul Tschernichowsky: Poet of Revolt* (Ithaca, NY: Cornell University Press, 1968).

63 "Prof. Silberschlag Translates Greek Masters into Hebrew," *Jewish Advocate*, January 16, 1947, 7.

64 "Eisig Silverschlag," *Jewish Advocate*, October 13, 1988, 12.

"Give My Special Regards to Mr. Hurwich and all the Teachers": The War Years

While the College grew in both students and programs throughout the 1930s, it retained the feeling of a second home for its students. When the War years came, the deep attachment between students and the institution becomes clear in a fascinating trove of letters sent to Hebrew College from students and alumni who served in the War. Hebrew College soldiers served all over the world and sent letters back to the College registrar describing some of their experiences. Hebrew College in turn would send a Hebrew College Bulletin with information culled from the letters about how soldiers were doing. According to one soldier, the bulletin was "a wonderful tonic for our lonely spirits."[65] The letters from the soldiers reveal nothing of battles nor even the difficulties of being a soldier. Instead we learn something about Jewish life in the army—Shabbat services, Passover observance, Ḥanukkah celebrations—and very often the soldiers used their Hebrew College background to help lead ritual and programs.

For example, a soldier stationed in San Francisco reported:

> On the Jewish front, we are kind of busy this month. We have resumed a Saturday morning Service (The Torah Reading is … a new job for me) and are preparing for Chanukah. Our monthly Oneg Shabbat promises to be a great success. Our services are gaining popularity and attendance these days. We have reached a fairly good medium for our program, considering that we have no chaplain there. The services are recited at half and half Hebrew and English with a good amount of congregational participation. I relate a few talmudic or other folk tales and present a reading. Then, after the religious service there is an informal discussion (always successful) led by us or a guest chaplain or doctor. Our subject matter varies with the events of the day and the speaker's specialty. Occasionally (often enough), I conduct one on Zionism, a "Jewish" literature, etc. Of course, our singing is as important as ever and very popular.[66]

---

65 "The Family Remembers," *Hebrew College Bulletin* 10, no. 4 (June 1980): 28.

66 Letter from unidentified soldier to Hebrew College Registrar, December 6, 1944, Hebrew College Archives.

A soldier stationed in Fiji wrote, "My religious activities continue to keep me pleasantly occupied.... A recent project of mine has been to arrange with Shapiro's Book Store to send the boys who request them (and many do), some gold 'Mogen Davids' (religious tokens) which they can attach to their Dog Tag chains."[67] Sergeant C. Jack Hurvitz wrote from China that he was working for the one and only Jewish chaplain in the China theatre of operations.[68]

Soldiers also wrote about some of the deeper questions affecting them. Harvey Schrier, for example, stationed in Virginia, reflected on how lonesome and bereft he felt without connection to other Jews. He committed himself "... to make up for [my] lack of ... participation in real Zionist work by assuming a larger share in the revitalizing of dormant Jewish culture."[69]

Another solider in the Pacific wrote about his work as a lay chaplain and giving comfort to a Jewish soldier who found out his mother had died:

> I had ... my first test as a religious lay leader. A fellow who had just received notification of his mother's death came to the office looking for some religious consolation. There was nothing in the way of verbal sympathy we could adequately express, for he had already witnessed much death during two brief army periods. What he wanted was some religious method of expressing his sentiments. What we did might appear superfluous, but they were utilized to serve the end. Firstly at the following large service, we arranged for the memorial prayer to be chanted, we organized as many daily services as we could, I showed him the portions he should read and ... I had a memorial ("Yahrzeit") candle lit in his mother's honor.[70]

Soldiers also wrote with enormous affection for Hebrew College, the place where they had spent countless hours learning. The College in turn printed a regular list of its soldiers, proud of their "children" fighting for their country. Like many American Jewish institutions at the time however, the board minutes and bulletins from the era reflect almost no mention of the Shoah and the devastation of World Jewry. Safely harbored in Boston, Hebrew College simply carried on.

---

67 Letter from "Lammie[?]" to Hebrew College Registrar, May 15, 1944, Hebrew College Archives.

68 "Sgt. C. Jack Hurvitz," *Hebrew College Bulletin*, February 16, 1944, 1.

69 Letter from Harvey Schrier to Hebrew College Registrar," August 25, 1944, Hebrew College Archives.

70 Letter from "Lammie[?]" to Hebrew College Registrar.

One of the projects that happened during the War was the creation of Camp Yavneh, the College's summer camp for over sixty years. The force behind the creation of Yavneh was Louis Hurwich's wife Leah who had run a summer camp in the Catskills and would become the founding Director. The goal of the camp was "to get greater depth in our students' knowledge and to create a really warm religious attitude in our student body." When the Hurwichs began pursuing the idea, they had a problem in that a summer camp devoted to Hebrew study had never existed. Hurwich sent a query to leading Jewish educators all over the country asking for their opinion on the endeavor. He received eighteen replies encouraging him to try, although many doubted its feasibility. The Associated Jewish Philanthropies made their support conditional on Hurwich finding twenty people to contribute $1,000 each. At the end of his campaign, he had thirty-seven initial contributors. Hurwich found an existing camp on sixty acres in Northwood, NH and bought the property for the bargain price of $18,000.[71]

By 1947, in just its third year of operation, the camp reached its maximum capacity of 104 students. But it was the educational vision of the camp that was the true highlight for Hurwich and his cofounders. Students were fully immersed in Hebrew and Jewish life. Every morning had a prayer service (boys and girls sitting separately), followed by a flag ceremony where the American and Israeli flags were raised (students recited Psalm 137 before the founding of Israel, and "Ha-Tikvah" afterwards.) The morning was spent entirely in Hebrew lessons and the afternoon spent in sports and other camp activities. Saturdays were spent praying, eating, singing, and studying Torah in observance of the Sabbath. More than any particular program though, it was music and joy, which marked the experience for many. Hurwich wrote about the last day of camp in 1947 in reverential tones:

> The meal was over but the campers remain seated. Physical hunger was met but there was still a desire of the soul and this was met by song. No one told the campers what to do. Melodies followed in an unbroken chain. The songs were surcharged with a joy over a grand yesterday and a glowing tomorrow. It was an achievement, Hallelujah, and all of it in Hebrew, charged with memories. The counselors sang as one with the campers, feeling as one big, dearly loved family.[72]

---

71 Hurwich, *Memoirs*, 233–247; *Excerpts From Minutes of Board of Trustees of the Hebrew Teachers College Regarding the Hebrew Teachers College Summer School and Camp*, Hebrew College Archives.

72 Ibid., 242.

Hurwich saw Yavneh as a kind of Zion in America. Campers were transformed not just intellectually but like Zionist pioneers, they were physically changed as well: "All [campers] had a deep tan and muscles that had been strengthened by daily exercise in swimming and games. Most campers gained in weight, some as much as 15 pounds and some attained an inch in height."[73] Yavneh was a response to what Hurwich perceived as a crisis in Jewish education that had always been a challenge in America but was greatly exacerbated by suburbanization, "the whole process of Jewish education [is] anemic and this, in turn, is ruining the very vitals of Jewish studies ... generations of children are lost to us as conscious Jews." At Yavneh the problem of assimilation was countered by immersion: "Instead of wrestling with an indifferent environment, we decided to create an environment that would be our own. Instead of competing with general education for the spare time of the child, there would be no competition at all. The total child and all of his time would be left to our disposal.... The summer vacation became a gold mine for Jewish education!"

"The Blessings of Assimilation": The Move to Brookline, the 1950s–1970s

When Hebrew College was established, Roxbury, alongside the neighboring area of Dorchester, was one of the centers of Boston Jewish life. Second-generation Jewish families had moved there from the more crowded urban areas of the North and West End. By the 1930s, there were 70,000 Jews living there. But by the 1950s, demographics were changing. Roxbury's Jewish population was almost halved between 1945 and 1955.[74] Jews were moving to the suburbs. By the end of the 1940s, the majority of students now came from the wealthy suburbs of Brookline and Newton. And so the College decided to move with the Jewish population.

In the fall of 1951, The College purchased a two-story building that previously served as the home of the Gordon Divinity School, but was originally built as an estate. The College purchased the building for $90,000 after receiving approval from the Associated Jewish Philanthropies. As a beneficiary organization of the Associated, it was the College's primary financial supporter. The

---

73 Ibid., 242.

74 Paula Hyman, "From City to Suburb: Temple Mishkan Tefila of Boston," in *The American Synagogue: A Sanctuary Transformed*, ed. Jack Wertheimer (Hanover, NH: Brandeis University Press, 1987), 186–187.

Associated made clear that the College needed itself to raise all funds related to the purchase of the building, and needed to raise the funds privately, as it was concerned that a public campaign for the College would inhibit its own annual campaign. Nathan Friedman, a member of the College Board, stepped forward and with other members of his family donated $50,000 towards the purchase. As a result of his generosity, the new building was named after Nathan and his wife Sadie.[75]

Similar to the purchase of their first building, the College's procuring of a suburban property was part of a broader trend in Jewish life. Jews were moving to the suburbs, and Jewish institutions—synagogues and JCCs—were moving with them. As the title of an extensive 1959 front-page article in the *New York Times* put it simply, "Judaism on Rise in the Suburbs." The article noted the large number of synagogues that were taking over old firehouses, banks, and churches, not to mention the vast number being built from scratch.[76] The move from city to suburb though was not entirely without complications.

As alumna Paula Hyman wrote in her article on Congregation Mishkan Tefila's similar move from Roxbury to Newton, the transition from city to suburb, "has been characterized as a virtually automatic process accompanying geographic, social and cultural mobility." But such moves are always, "conscious and deliberate, rather than automatic and reactive," and thus provide an opportunity to examine a number of crucial questions including the impact of the departure on the urban neighborhood it left.[77]

In the case of Mishkan Tefilah, the congregation promised it would continue to provide services in Roxbury as well as financially enable its Roxbury members to be involved in the Newton synagogue. Neither of those promises held. Hebrew College similarly had plans to have part of the high school program remain in Roxbury, but within a few years the College had no presence there. Given the significant issues that would ultimately lead the Jewish community to leave Roxbury-Dorchester, it is unlikely that Hebrew College's move significantly changed the trajectory of Jewish life there, but it certainly did not impede the process of suburbanization.

Regardless of what it left behind, the College's move to the suburbs was a resounding success in terms of attracting students and programs. By the late

---

75 "Special Meeting of the Board of Trustees," *Hebrew College Board Minutes*, November 7, 1951, Hebrew College Archives; "Dear Fellow Trustees," *Hebrew College Board Minutes*, October 17, 1951, Hebrew College Archives.

76 "Judaism on the Rise," *The New York Times*, April 5, 1959, 1.

77 Hyman, "From City to Suburb," 185–187.

1950s and into the 1960s, the College was in many respects at the height of its institutional strength. Hundreds of students attended Prozdor (the Hebrew high school), and around 100 students were part of the undergraduate and graduate programs, which offered a master in Jewish education degree as well as a bachelor of Jewish education and a bachelor of Hebrew literature.[78] On top of this, the College created branches in New Haven, Providence, Springfield and Hartford specifically for working teachers to take classes and receive academic credit. But the academic programming was only the beginning. The College's library had evolved into a significant institution unto itself. It had 30,000 volumes with fifty Hebrew manuscripts printed in the sixteenth century and one incunabula, that is, a manuscript printed in the fifteenth century.[79] A Hebrew College Alumni Association was organizing programs, the Women's Association continued to flourish, a division of adult education was established, a Hebrew Teachers College Press published selected works, the museum held small exhibits of Jewish art, and cultural programs like the annual book festival and Israeli music festivals were ongoing. In short, the College was a vital center for Jewish life.

Central to that vitality was the extraordinary faculty assembled by the college and the *heimish* (warm) culture the faculty created. Many of the faculty were European transplants who had studied in *yeshivot* in their youth. They were also Zionists who were deeply committed to Hebrew and personally involved in local and national Zionist and Hebrew organizations. The faculty were not just academic teachers, they were beloved figures who consciously acted as role models for a Jewish life that integrated intellectual vibrancy with a deep appreciation for tradition and personal humility.

Dr. Jacques Mikliszanski arrived at the College in the forties as professor of Halakhic Literature. He was born in Warsaw to a family of rabbis. He received rabbinic ordination at the Mir Yeshiva before moving to Paris to get his doctorate in international law. He fled to America ahead of the Nazi invasion, and taught at Dropsie College amongst other institutions before coming to Hebrew College, which would be his home for over two decades. He taught Talmud, Jewish history, Jewish philosophy, and *halakhah* to generations of students. Dr. Mikliszanski was a nationally known figure in Hebraist circles. He wrote regularly for American Hebrew newspapers including *Ha-Do'ar*. He also published a number of scholarly works including: *A Sourcebook for the History of*

78 "Handbook for the Long Range Planning Committee of the Board of Trustees," November 1979, 17, Hebrew College Archives, 17.

79 "Brookline Home for Hebrew Teachers College," *Jewish Advocate*, November 22, 1951, 1.

Halakha and *A History of Hebrew Literature in America*.[80] Students remembered Dr. Mikliszanski's amiability, "the ever-present twinkle in his eye ... and his gentle, wry sense of humor."[81]

Dr. Joseph Steiner was also a Polish immigrant. He received his doctorate from the University of Lemberg before moving to Palestine in 1939. He came to Hebrew College in 1948 as a professor of Hebrew Literature and would retire as a professor emeritus in 1972. Like other faculty, Steiner was passionate about Hebrew and was known as the "Hebrew Voice of Greater Boston" for his weekly Hebrew radio show. Steiner published hundreds of essays on Zionism, nationalism and Hebrew literature as well as editing a Yiddish weekly and authoring a book in English on the Middle East.[82] His students said, "He was as soft-spoken and gentle in his teaching as he was hard hitting in his writing." When he would read poetry with his students, "Dr. Steiner would become animated, his voice would occasionally tremble as his index finger would punctuate the air for effect. We can still see it: we are in armchairs, books open to Agnon, and Dr. Steiner peering through his glasses, clears his throat, and says, '*Tov, namshich*' (good, let's continue)."[83]

Dr. Mordecai Wilensky was a beloved professor of Jewish History for thirty-four years. He was also raised in Poland and studied at the Yeshiva of Kobryn in his youth. He was a Zionist from an early age and moved to Palestine where he would ultimately get his doctorate in philosophy from Hebrew University. Dr. Wilensky wrote a weekly Hebrew column in the *Jewish Advocate* and was a leader in the Histadrut Ivrit (Hebrew Organization). Wilensky's most well-known work was a study of arguments between Hasidism and their opponents, *Ḥasidim u-Mitnaggedim: Le-Toldot ha-Pulmas she-Benehem ba-Shanim 1772–1815* (*Ḥasidim* and *Mitnaggedim*: A Study of the Arguments between Them in the Years 1772–1815).[84] Wilensky's other work that drew attention was in an entirely different field and concerned the sixteenth-century controversy over the readmission of Jews to England. Wilensky argues in his work that Baptists, because of their understanding of the need to separate church and state, were the most vigorous proponents for the readmission of Jews. In an unusual turn of events for a scholar of Jewish history, Wilensky's research caught the attention of advisors to Governor Jimmy Carter who was running for president, and Wilensky visited the president to discuss his work and was given a special invitation

---

80 "Obituaries: Prof. J.K. Miklaszanski, Scholar, Hebrew Writer," *The Jewish Advocate*, January 6, 1983, 19.

81 "The Family Remembers," *Hebrew College Bulletin* 12, no. 4 (June 1982): 21.

82 "Hebrew Scholar to Speak on Poet June 5," *The Jewish Advocate*, May 26, 1977, 7.

83 "The Family Remembers," *Hebrew College Bulletin* 12, no 4 (June 1982): 24.

84 Mordecai Wilensky, *Hasidim u-Mitnaggedim* (Jerusalem: Mossad Bialik, 1990).

to Carter's inauguration.[85] Upon his retirement, the College created a scholarship in his honor noting his boundless energy, sharp wit, and vital interest in each of his students. An editorial in the local newspaper written by a former student said that it was inconceivable that anyone else could teach Jewish history at the College. Not that other teachers did not have the intellectual capabilities to teach it, but Dr. Wilensky quite simply was Jewish history.[86]

The senior librarian of the College during this period was Dr. Joseph Marcus, a rabbi and scholar. "[Dr. Marcus] was in love with the Torah, the Jewish people, the Hebrew language and Eretz Yisrael."[87] In his scholarly work, Marcus was noted for having discovered part of the book of Ben Sira in Hebrew amidst the fragments from the Cairo genizah.[88] His primary scholarship was in the field of medieval poetry. But like many of the faculty, Marcus is remembered not just for his intellect but for his warmth:

> We loved Dr. Marcus because he was self-effacing and gentle. We respected him because his life and acts were a model for all of us to follow. Dr. Marcus knew the taste of every single student at the College as far as books were concerned ... he would quietly sit behind a student with a new book in his hand, waiting for the boy or girl to look up from their studying in the library to present them with the book as he said, "this book just came in, I think it is just what you like to read."[89]

Marcus had a boundless love of books and Jewish scholarship. His daughter recalled when her father was dying that he told her not to worry, he was looking forward to meeting his "friends," that is, to meeting the great Hebrew teachers and scholars of history in the world-to-come. "Ben Sira is surely waiting to thank me for finding part of his original Hebrew manuscript," he said.[90]

Dr. Marcus oversaw a large expansion of the library's collection, but some of this growth was sadly due to the Shoah. All of the books and manuscripts, which

---

85 See Mordecai Wilensky, "The Literary Controversy in 1656 Concerning the Jews' Return to England," *Proceedings of The American Academy of Jewish Research* 20 (1951): 357–393; "Book Brings Inauguration Invitation to Professor," *The Jewish Advocate*, January 13, 1977, 18.

86 "Dr. Wilensky to Retire," *The Jewish Advocate*, May 22, 1980, 7; "Mordecai Wilensky, Teacher," *The Jewish Advocate*, June 5, 1980, 12.

87 "The Family Remembers," *Hebrew College Bulletin* 9, no. 4 (June 1979): 23.

88 Joseph Marcus, "A Fifth MS. of Ben Sira," *Jewish Quarterly Review* 21, no. 3 (January 1931): 223–240.

89 "The Family Remembers," *Hebrew College Bulletin* 9, no. 4 (June 1979): 23.

90 Ibid., 24.

the Nazis plundered from Jewish communities, were given to Jewish institutions across the world. The main inheritors were the National and University libraries in Israel, but certain American libraries including Hebrew College were designated "heirs" by an international commission of scholars. Eisig Silberschlag remembered going to a warehouse in Brooklyn where he spent hours, "selecting hundreds of books in the field of liturgy and Hasidism, and secular literature of the 18th, 19th and early 20th century. They [the books] had been placed in cartons and makeshift shelves—silent witnesses of horrors perpetrated on their owners. But I also remember the bittersweet joy of giving these books a new home and a new readership in Boston."[91]

The flourishing of the College in the post-war era not only reflected the talent of the faculty but was also enabled by the demographic shift of the Jewish community to the suburbs. This period saw the establishment of hundreds of new suburban synagogues across the country, most created with the express aim of educating Jewish youth. Each of those synagogues would need Jewish educators, and so there was plenty of demand for Hebrew College graduates. The founding of the State of Israel was another factor in the College's strength. The creation of the Jewish State would further establish Zionism as the civic religion of Jews across denominations—a belief central to Hebrew College's ethos. Jewish studies programs at secular colleges, which would come to eclipse Hebrew College's academic standing, were only beginning to be established, and so the College was still seen as a center of academic Jewish learning.[92] And Hebrew College's intensive commitment to Hebrew still had an audience of willing students. High school students travelling every day to Hebrew College from around Boston to spend three to four hours of time learning entirely in Hebrew would go out of fashion by the 1970s, but this was still an era where such demands were met with a willing supply of students.

There is probably no better indication of the success of Hebrew College during these times than noting the number of Jewish scholars who were launched into their careers by attending Hebrew College. This list includes notable individuals such as: Arnold Band, Michael Fishbane, Ben Halpern, Paula Hyman, Anne Lapidus Lerner, Jonathan Sarna, Isadore Twersky, and Ilan Troen, to name just some of the scholars produced by the College. These scholars were all at the top of their respective fields of Jewish studies, and all were path-breaking in significant ways.

---

91 Ibid.

92 A sign of this impact can be seen in the anxiety of Hebrew College Board members about the future of the College upon learning that Brandeis was going to offer a Bachelor of Arts degree in Hebrew literature. *Hebrew College Board Minutes*, May 24, 1950, Hebrew College Archives.

The most famous speech ever given at Hebrew College testifies as well to the vitality of that period in Jewish life. In 1966, Gerson Cohen, a visiting professor of history at the Jewish Theological Seminary where he would soon be named Chancellor, was invited to be the College's graduation speaker. His talk, "The Blessings of Assimilation," was an eloquent argument affirming that change and adaptation, what he termed "healthy assimilation," have been central to Jewish survival and growth. While not denying assimilation is a problem, he argued that "Throughout Jewish history, there have been great changes in law, in thought, and in basic categories of expression, reflecting the need of Jews to adapt themselves and to their way of life to new conditions. This assimilation ... was not the consequence of a desire to make things easier, but the result of a need to continue to make the tradition relevant."[93] While Cohen's speech is cited by Jewish historians as one of the more significant twentieth-century essays, it is rarely associated with the place it was delivered. But Cohen's words were directed at Hebrew College teachers who he said had been trained with an authentic sense of what is healthy assimilation because they had learned the middle path of being both teachers of Judaism and social critics. The College's middle path of upholding both the academy and tradition, as well as its commitment to both Zionism and American values, were essential to its success in this period.

"The Acid Test of Our Community's Commitment": Hebrew College in the 1970s–1990s

By the late 1970s the College found itself in dramatically changed circumstances. Some of the same demographic changes, which had encouraged its growth, were now threatening its existence. While suburbanization was initially a positive force for the College, the Jewish community continued to disperse to suburbs well outside the city. As one of a number of studies the College commissioned to analyze its situation stated it, "Bringing high school age students to our campus entails significant hardships for parents who reside beyond the 128 Beltway [the highway encircling Boston] and fewer each year appear prepared to commit themselves to these hardships."[94] The College opened up branches

93 Gerson Cohen, "The Blessings of Assimilation," in his *Jewish History and Jewish Destiny* (New York: JTS Press, 1997), 152–153.

94 *Handbook for the Long Range Planning Committee of the Board of Trustees*, November, 1979, 9, Hebrew College Archives.

in a number of outer suburbs to try and reach more families, but the branches proved unsuccessful. A 1981 analysis suggested that Prozdor was losing roughly $187,000 annually because of the diminishing number of students.[95]

The problems for the College, though, went well beyond decentralization. The previous era's growth in religious school jobs turned around entirely. Because Hebrew schools had reduced the amount of time students spent in school, synagogue jobs became part-time. There were less than ten full-time educational jobs in all Boston area synagogues combined, and all of these positions were paid less than $12,000 regardless of experience.[96] Alongside the reduction of Hebrew school jobs due to fewer students, synagogues also began hiring less qualified people for the jobs that remained. Under the guidance of Benjamin Shevach who ran Boston's Bureau of Jewish Education, synagogues had been obligated to hire graduates of the College or equivalent schools for Hebrew school positions. In the 1970s the Bureau no longer operated as a central authority and synagogues were free to hire college students, further reducing the number of positions available for Hebrew College graduates. The reduction in jobs meant a commensurate drop in the numbers of people seeking to become professional Jewish educators.

Another issue was the massive growth of Jewish studies departments. Hebrew College was previously one of few places for studying Judaism at an undergraduate or graduate level. By 1981, there were an estimated 800 Jewish studies professors at universities around the country and students were choosing to study Judaism at "regular" universities. One internal document noted bitterly that because universities required no prerequisite knowledge to take Jewish studies courses, it obviated the need for any serious learning during the high school years. Thus students were not coming to study as undergraduates at Hebrew College, nor did they need to come to the Prozdor High School to prepare for Jewish studies courses.[97]

An additional issue was that even the students who did come were coming on a part-time basis. The College offered a Masters in Jewish Education and Masters of Hebrew Letters, but this program was quite small; it hovered around twenty students in the 1970s, and these students generally worked while taking classes. The high school program was a supplemental program. But the biggest concern for the college was the undergraduate situation. The College had agreements

---

95 *A Needs Assessment of Boston Hebrew College: A Report Presented to the Hebrew College Study Committee by the Center for Jewish Community Studies*, May 1981, 38, Hebrew College Archives.

96 *Handbook*, 8.

97 Ibid.

with many of the local universities, and students would do a dual degree between Hebrew College and a nearby university. But as the tuition costs at universities went up, fewer students could afford to come to Hebrew College as a second institution. A study of the College's problems in 1978 found that:

> The $600 Hebrew College tuition fee, even when reduced partly by scholarship grants, is frequently the "straw that breaks the camel's back" when added to the $5000-$7000 cost at general universities. [Hebrew College tuition] is enough to prevent some students from coming to us. Because of rapidly rising university costs, an increasing portion of university students have to work to help offset these costs. Qualified potential students tell us that when they get through with university requirements and time spent on the job, they have no time for Hebrew College.[98]

The feeling in the College was that the 1950s and 1960s represented "the days of glory" for the institution and there was much interest in trying to return the College to its former place. The number of students was actually greater in the 1970s and 1980s than in "the glory days"—there were 144 undergraduate students in 1979, versus just 83 in 1956. However, the students in 1956 were primarily full-time Hebrew College students who saw the other institution they attended as their secondary school, whereas in 1979, the story had entirely flipped and Hebrew College was seen by undergraduates as the less significant institution.[99]

One solution the board envisioned was to work with its accreditors and the state to change its charter to allow it to grant BA undergraduate degrees. Students could come to Hebrew College as full-time students without needing to attend another university. Students would take general humanities courses as cross-registrants at other schools, but they would be full time at Hebrew College. "We would have a core of full-time students who would give their complete attention to their studies at Hebrew College (since we would have much greater leverage over their progress). Their presence is likely to have a positive effect on the attitude of the entire student body and on the morale of the faculty."[100] That the student body and faculty needed significant morale-boosting is another indication of where the College was in this period. The plan to be a full-time undergraduate

---

98 "Re: Becoming the Primary Institution for a Portion of our Student Body," November 14, 1978, Hebrew College Archives.

99 *Handbook*, 17.

100 Ibid., 3.

institution had actually been floated in the 1960s but had previously been shut down by the Combined Jewish Philanthropies (CJP) as overly ambitious. The same fate awaited this endeavor. Despite the endorsement of the faculty and the Board, the College was unable to convince the Federation and other stakeholders of its feasibility.

The last significant issue facing the College was its relationship with CJP. The College's budget was heavily reliant on their Federation allocation. The College received tuition from students, as well as scholarship aid from the Women's Association, but the Federation accounted for roughly two-thirds of the total budget (in 1979, CJP allocated $506,605 out of a total budget of $767,705). And like any dependent relationship, it could at times be quite fraught. The College complained that while their total allocation was increased every year, those increases did not nearly keep pace with inflation. The costs of building upkeep and cost-of-living adjustments alone created more expenses for the College even if no new programs were added.

While the Federation was the "life-blood" of the College, it became clear that the College would need to seek philanthropic resources on its own to survive. This was not a straightforward proposition as the College could not be seen as competing for donors with the very Federation it was dependent upon for allocations. One report concluded though that the key to the future of the College was an attitude shift on the part of the Board. The Board thought of the College as an agency of the Federation, and therefore the responsibility of the Boston Jewish community to fund. But the Board needed to think in broader terms, as "partners in the promotion of excellence at a dynamic college or university," and one with national and not just parochial aims. The report recommended to unwind the relationship with the Federation to some degree, and to raise the endowment by $10,000,000 over ten years.[101]

It would take some years, but the College would ultimately shift away from its reliance on the Federation and develop its own philanthropic sources. This shift involved significant tensions as it meant the College needed to raise money for itself in an unprecedented way. However, it did allow for the College to chart its own path. Programs, which were beyond the scope of the Federation, like the creation of a rabbinical school with national aspirations, became possible when the College was on its own.

Despite the changing relationship between the College and the Federation, one of the most successful elements of the College at this time was a partnership

---

101 *Handbook*, 56.

between the two organizations. The Me'ah program began in the early 1990s and quickly become a centerpiece of the College.[102] Perhaps not surprisingly, in all of the reports issued to save the College in the 1980s, creating an adult education program where participants spend 100 hours in a serious, academic study of Judaism did not make any of the prospective solutions. The program started with two classes in 1994, and just a few years later hundreds of students were enrolling every year. The program was such a success the College tried to bring it to other cities, including New York. In 1997, it received a large grant to create an online version of Me'ah for a national audience, making it one of the first attempts at Jewish education on the internet.[103]

The success of Me'ah reflected a number of factors. Boston is an academic hub, so a program with an academic bent taught by professors from the Boston-area colleges was very much part of the communal ethos. But the program was not strictly academic; it was taught from a critical perspective, but it was also very much an attempt to connect students with their Jewish identities. Barry Shrage, the head of CJP, brought to his role an unusual commitment to the power of Jewish learning to solve the problems of intermarriage and assimilation highlighted in the 1990 National Jewish Population Survey. The survey was met with a seismic reaction and galvanized the Jewish community around the issue of Jewish continuity. For Shrage, at the heart of the problem of continuity was Jewish illiteracy, and Me'ah represented a strategy towards solving the problem:

> We [the Jewish people] had no trouble becoming totally literate in English, and becoming Ph.D.s and doctors and lawyers—in one generation, a miracle occurred. It's because our grandparents valued it. At the same time, modernity seemed to be telling the Jewish people that Jewish learning and values were secondary, old-fashioned. Turning that around is a matter of helping an entire generation understand that this can't happen without meaning in their lives. That's what Meah [is] about.[104]

For David Gordis, the president of the College in the 1990s, the success of Me'ah and the possibilities of bringing it to a national audience reflected his own belief

102 For the full history of Me'ah, see the article by David B. Starr in this volume, "Growing Up Jewish: Me'ah and American Jewish Adulthood."

103 "Hebrew College to Introduce Course into Cyberspace," *The Jewish Advocate*, March 20, 1997, 4.

104 "Shrage Marks 10 Years With CJP," *The Jewish Advocate*, September 11, 1997, 1.

in the College's need for expansion and greater prominence. Towards that end, he established an Institute of Jewish Policy Studies whose aim was to "stimulate creative thinking on issues facing American Jews and formulate strategies that precipitate change and growth in Jewish life."[105] The Institute would bring Hebrew College's voice into national conversations and it would over its years of existence sponsor significant conferences on peoplehood, Jewish continuity, and the future of synagogues. Gordis also revived plans to have undergraduates at Hebrew College studying on a more full-time basis; he hoped to triple the number of undergraduate students through a partnership with Boston University (a plan that, like its predecessors, did not come to fruition). But there were two decisions by Gordis that would have the most significant impact on the life of the College.

The first decision was another move for the College. In 1995, Gordis announced a plan for the College to purchase land in Newton from the Andover Newton Theological Institute, the oldest graduate school for theological studies in America, and create a new campus. A number of reasons sparked the move. The Brookline building had become outdated for a modern institution and had no space for growth and minimal room for parking. Geographically, although just a few miles from the old building, the new building was more convenient for Jews to gather from surrounding Boston suburbs. But also, from the very beginning, the move was about a partnership with the Protestant seminary.

The partnership with a Christian seminary was somewhat controversial at the time. One editorial in *The Jewish Advocate* called it a "disaster" and railed against the notion of joint educational programs between Christian and Jewish organizations.[106] Another article quoted Barry Mesch, the provost of HC, dispelling concerns that having Jewish students living in student housing with Protestant seminary students would lead to inter-dating and intermarriage.[107] But Gordis understood that a shared campus would allow the College to be seen as bold and visionary in meeting the needs of a twenty-first-century Jewish community. Responding to concerns that the Jewish identity of Hebrew College would become watered down because of its association with Andover Newton, he said, "The mission of Hebrew College is to prepare our students to participate in a pluralist community. Hebrew College will continue to do its own thing. But peripherally, we will also serve as a source of Jewish knowledge to [Andover

---

105 "Incoming President David Gordis: A Bold Vision for Hebrew College," *The Jewish Advocate*, September 10, 1992, 1.

106 David Neiman, "The Move is a Real Disaster," *The Jewish Advocate*, March 23, 1995, 15.

107 "Moved Approved: Hebrew College Board Ok's President Gordis' Plan," *The Jewish Advocate*, April 6, 1995, 1.

Newton], so they can learn about authentic Judaism from an authentic Jewish community.... We will not become watered down to make a pareve [bland] mixture of something ecumenical."[108]

The College would move into its new Campus in 2001 after a fundraising campaign unprecedented in the College's history, but one that also left the College in significant debt. The campus was designed by the world-famous Israeli architect Moshe Safdie and included a two-story library wing, a cafeteria, a social hall/event space, and three stories for classrooms and offices. The new campus, far grander than its Brookline incarnation, would ultimately be financially unsupportable, and less than two decades after moving into the building, the College has plans to be on the move again.

The College's partnership with Andover Newton Theological School would prove to be as valuable and creative as Gordis suggested. Under the aegis of Danny Lehmann, who succeeded David Gordis as president of the College, a deep relationship was established with students frequently taking courses at the other institution and faculty co-teaching courses from both faith perspectives. A group of students would establish an interfaith dialogue group called Journeys on the Hill, which would be important to the cultures of both institutions in creating an ongoing container for relationship-building between the students. Andover Newton closed its doors in 2018 as the numbers of liberal Christians interested in studying for the ministry dwindled. But the spirit of pluralism and interfaith dialogue has taken root in the College and is seen as a central pillar of its present mission, expressed in part through the creation of the Miller Center for Interreligious Learning and Leadership.

David Gordis's other bold decision as president of the College was the creation of a new rabbinical school. The rabbinical school would be pluralistic and outside the bounds of any denominational setting. Given the seeming monopoly over rabbinic education that the movements had in America, the creation of a new rabbinical school was a risky endeavor. Where would graduates of a non-denominational school find jobs given that most synagogues belonged to one of the denominations, and, to make matters worse, those denominations forbid the hiring of non-denominational rabbis? Who would come to a school that was five years, full-time study that did not have the same scholarship capacities as the denominational schools? Despite these very real questions, the rabbinical school would emerge to challenge the primacy of the denominational schools and become core to the Hebrew College project.

---

108 Ibid.

A Rabbinical School for the Twenty-First Century: Hebrew College Today

At first blush, the creation of a rabbinical school would seem to be discontinuous with the cultural, Zionist orientations of the College's founders and leaders. But this impression would be mistaken. As noted previously, the College always had a broad conception of Jewish culture, which encompassed a religious viewpoint.[109] In fact, the idea that the College might serve as a rabbinic training ground was actually part of the College from the very beginning. In 1922, Leon Medalia, the first president of Hebrew College, wrote a fundraising letter to Louis Kirstein, the chair of Filenes and the most significant Jewish philanthropist in Boston. Medalia listed the "potentialities" of the College—those things that he hoped the College would soon accomplish. At the top of his list was his belief that the College would be a feeder for rabbinical schools—The Jewish Theological Seminary and Hebrew Union College.[110] In the 1940s, Hebrew Union College, believing that the College was excellent preparation for the rabbinate, offered an annual scholarship of $450 to any Hebrew College graduate who pursued rabbinic studies at HUC.[111] Throughout its history, the College was seen as a potential training ground for rabbis, and numbers of graduates went on to rabbinical school.

The present success of the Rabbinical School of Hebrew College was to some degree a matter of fortuitous timing. The creation of a pluralistic school happened just as the denominational structures of Judaism were weakening. A 2015 study of Boston Jewry found that the numbers of Jews who claim to be a member of one of the liberal movements has shrunk to historic lows, while the numbers of Jews who say they are "Just Jewish" or nondenominational continues to rise.[112] This would be in line with trends in the Christian world, where the weakening of denominational boundaries, particularly among mainline sects, has been seen for many years. The rise of independent *minyanim*, which have been particularly successful among young, urban Jews, have further weakened the movements.[113]

---

109 Shabbat services were held in the 1920s and 1930s in the first building, and some professors encouraged daily prayer services to be held before classes started in the 1950s. See *Hebrew College Bulletin* 12, no. 4 (June 1982): 22–23 for a brief description of morning prayer.

110 Leon Medalia letter to Louis Kirstein, February 6, 1922, Hebrew College Archives.

111 *Hebrew College Catalogue, 1946–1947,* 19 Hebrew College Archives.

112 Cohen Center for Modern Jewish Studies, Brandeis University, *2015 Greater Boston Jewish Community Study*: https://bir.brandeis.edu/bitstream/handle/10192/33150/GreaterBostonJewishCommStudy2015.pdf?sequence=1&isAllowed=y.

113 See Elie Kaunfer, *What Independent Minyanim Can Teach us About Building Vibrant Jewish Communities* (Woodstock, VT: Jewish Lights Publishing, 2010).

The disruptive nature of the internet and the creation of enormous amounts of on-line Jewish content has also meant Jews are not reliant on denominations as resource creators. All of these factors have made it easier for people thinking about the rabbinate to choose Hebrew College over a seminary affiliated with a movement.

But it is not solely timing that accounts for the success of the Rabbinical School. The hiring of Arthur Green, first as the founding dean and then as rector, created a vibrant intellectual and spiritual vision for the College. Green had already been for many years moving between academia and rabbinic education. He had started the Havurah movement in the 1960s, been a professor of Jewish studies at Brandeis University and the University of Pennsylvania, served as president of the Reconstructionist Rabbinical College, and is widely considered one of the most significant Jewish theologians of his era. Green's scholarship on Hasidism, beginning with his acclaimed biography of Naḥman of Bratslav, would serve as the backdrop for forming an institution that incorporated his neo-Hasidic thinking.

Green articulated two central ideas, which animated the school. Students were meant to be deep learners of tradition. They would spend significant time in traditional *ḥevruta* (partnership) learning in the *beit midrash* (study hall). Second, students needed to take seriously their own spiritual quest. Reacting against some of the professionally oriented training of previous generations of rabbis, Green envisioned a school where students' spiritual lives were as attended to as their intellectual lives. In creating learned and spiritually minded rabbis, Green believed Hebrew College could respond to the many Jews who struggled with spiritual questions but were not finding answers in synagogues that lacked either spirituality or Jewish depth.

The newest president of Hebrew College and its first female leader, Sharon Cohen Anisfeld, has brought her own formidable talents to this undertaking. Serving for many years as the Dean of the Rabbinical School before becoming president, Cohen Anisfeld's rich and poetic writings and sermons, as well as her sense of a relationally oriented Judaism, attract to the College many students and supporters. Under Cohen Anisfeld's leadership, the College is poised to move forward into a new era.

"Sweet and Proud and Strong": Looking to the Future

The second century of the College approaches with hope as well as notes of caution. The Rabbinical School has grown to become one of the main training grounds for American rabbis today. But financial challenges remain for the College. Training Jewish clergy is a costly endeavor. The closing of Andover Newton Theological School because of the paucity of liberal Christians interested in ministry could be an ill harbinger for liberal Jewish seminaries.

In 2004, a Hebrew College Cantorial School was created along similarly pluralistic lines as the Rabbinical School. The field of Jewish music has become a site of growth and diversity but the role of the Cantor in synagogues is in the process of transition. There is hope that a revamped program that includes the possibility of training simultaneously as a rabbi and a hazzan will enrich the program.

The School of Jewish Education, which has been part of the College for a century, also finds itself at a crossroads. The number of students interested in pursuing a Masters of Jewish Education has dropped across all institutions. As synagogues have gotten grayer and commit less hours for Hebrew school, full-time jobs in the field of Jewish education have diminished. Further, rabbis and individuals with graduate degrees in Jewish studies are sometimes competing for Jewish education jobs, which has further complicated the job market. The Masters of Jewish Education program is working on responding to this changing Jewish landscape.

The community education aspect of the College has, however, seen dramatic growth in recent years with a large population of adult learners taking College classes. The College has diversified and broadened its offerings with classes offered in Jewish history, Jewish environmentalism, social justice, *mussar* (moral teachings), interfaith understanding, Bible, Talmud, on and on. There is a series of classes offered specifically for parents as well as for young adults. The profusion of classes bespeaks a renaissance of Jewish learning. While some trends in American Jewish life, like synagogue membership, are in decline, the increase in Jewish learning reflects a continued hunger for knowledge and connection. Responding to these needs has been part of the College's mission for a century.

***

Theodore White is one of the College's most well-known alumni. He simultaneously attended Harvard and Hebrew College, graduating from the College in 1936. He would become nationally known as a foreign correspondent for *Time* magazine during World War II, and then as an author of numerous books on presidential elections. To celebrate the College's fiftieth anniversary, he published a short reflection on his experience at Hebrew College:

> Once upon a time only yesterday, there lived in a place called Boston, Massachusetts, a community of Jews who were once so

> sweet and so proud that they took upon themselves the lighting of the candles of the tradition in a strange land.... They felt that no matter what other Jews were doing anywhere else in the Land, it was up to them in Boston, to teach their children of their past so their children could pass on to their grandchildren the same lessons, the same songs, the same culture that had made Jews sweet and proud and strong for two thousand years. I am sure they had no idea of what they were trying to do; and perhaps even now they have no idea how spectacularly they succeeded.[114]

Fifty years on from these words, the College remains a place to transmit the sweet Jewish culture of the past into the future.

114 *Hebrew College Bulletin* 5, no 4 (June 1975): 19.

CHAPTER 2

Four Men Entered an Orchard

Arnold J. Band

Sometime in the fall of 1953, four young men were ushered into the office of Eisig Silberschlag, then President of the Boston Hebrew College in Brookline, Massachusetts. These four were Walter Ackerman, David Weinstein, Arnold Band, and Yitshak Twersky. We were congratulated for being the first group of American-born and trained instructors to teach at Hebrew College, whose instructors since its founding in 1921 had been European-born and trained. In his usual mildly ironic tone, Silberschlag evoked the famous midrash of the four great *tannaim* who entered the orchard of Torah learning. We realized, of course, that we were not the equals of these famed scholars, yet appreciated the literary reference. I write these words as the last living member of this group, sixty-six years after the event.

Often, when we met, we reminisced about that moment. We discussed that period and increasingly became aware that our meeting with Silberschlag, as important as it was in the life of Hebrew College, really lacked historical depth. After all, we were still in the first decade of the two events that have shaped Jewish life since then: the Holocaust and the establishment of the State of Israel. These two events and their implications were not part of the discussion that day, or, for that matter in the academic life of the college. It wasn't as if we had no meaningful Jewish associations outside the college. Ackerman and Weinstein had already served in the American army while Twersky and I, somewhat younger, were active in Zionist groups not affiliated with Hebrew College.

We never really discussed the ideological underpinnings of the "Hebraism" of the Hebrew College, either its origins or its implications. We were, of course aware of the development of modern Hebrew since the middle of the nineteenth century. We read with reverence Bialik and Mendele and Agnon among many other modern writers. But we knew little of the *tarbut* movement, which emerged in Poland and Lithuania in 1921, how its ideology differed from that of the speakers of Yiddish, with which most of our parents had some familiarity. In general, for most English speakers, the term "Hebrew" was an interesting substitute for the term "Jewish." It was simply more dignified, suggesting some vague connection with the Christian world of the general population. For most Jewish families, however, Hebrew language learning was a problematic experience reserved for boys who had to be prepared for their bar mitzvahs, after which they would abandon their Hebrew studies and turn to other passions of adolescents. The Hebraism the four of us embraced at Hebrew College, by contrast, was clearly meaningful to us and shaped our careers.

But it is also obvious that this Hebraism does not exist today, only two generations after that meeting in 1953. In describing the career paths of this group, we might arrive at some understanding of what happened to this Hebraism, what happened to all the Hebrew colleges throughout this country since then.

Before presenting the brief CV of each of us four, it is helpful to call attention to several features in our lives:

1) We all grew up in the Dorchester-Roxbury districts of Boston, where Hebrew College was also situated in those days. Those two neighborhoods were mostly occupied by Jews at that time. Today, there is little to no Jewish residence there.
2) We were all enrolled at the Boston Latin School between the seventh and twelfth grades, where we were subjected to a demanding high school curriculum.
3) We all attended Harvard University in addition to our studies at the Hebrew College and were awarded PhDs from that prestigious institution. None of us, however lived in the dormitories at Harvard, but traveled to Cambridge with our brown bag lunches. Our Harvard experiences were consequently diluted.
4) All of us spent some time during summers at Camp Yavneh, the Hebrew-speaking camp sponsored by Boston Hebrew College. The camp was founded in 1944 by Louis Hurwich, then the dean of Hebrew College.

Walter I. Ackerman (1925–2008)

Of my three Hebrew College colleagues, "Ackie" was the closest and maintained with me the longest, most intense friendship. I first met him in 1949 when he returned from his army service in Europe and resumed his studies both at the Hebrew College and Harvard. He also spent two years, 1950 and

1951, in Israel, first at the Hebrew University, then as an associate director of the youth village at Ben Shemesh. We both lived in Los Angeles between about 1960 and 1973, when he moved to Beer Sheva to join the faculty at the Department of Education at the Ben Gurion University. I had moved from Boston to Los Angeles in 1959; there I joined the faculty at UCLA where I worked until my retirement in 1996. From 1962 to 1973, Ackie and I were both in Los Angeles, and after he moved to Beer Sheva, I would visit him during my many trips to Israel. Our friendship continued until his last years in Jerusalem, where he died in 2007.

Though we would work in different fields, Ackie in education and I in literature, I felt that we had so much in common that I wrote a joint intellectual biography of the two of us named "Confluent Myths" for a festschrift in his honor published by his university where he had a distinguished career as a professor of education and dean of humanities. Many of the ideas presented there inform this present article.

A listing of Ackie's activities and biography spans eight pages of a Google search, and is overwhelming in its array of teaching positions in both Los Angeles and Beer Sheva; a variety of administrative projects in both Jewish and general education in the United States and Israel. He served as Director both at Camp Yavneh of Boston Hebrew College (1952–1959) and at Ramah Camps in California (1960–1970) and Canada (1972–1973); as Dean of the University of Judaism (1964–1970); as Chairman of the Department of Education at Ben Gurion University (1973–1976); and as Dean of the Faculty of Humanities and Social Sciences at Ben Gurion (1974–1977). When you add to these positions an impressive publication record (over eighty articles and two books), and his service on dozens of committees, you must come to the conclusion that Ackie was one of most formidable figures in Jewish education in the second half of the twentieth century.

David Weinstein (1927–1986)

My friendship with "Doch" began at the waterfront at Camp Yavneh where he was the head of the waterfront and I was for a short period a swimming instructor. Though a versatile athlete, Doch's real passion was the teaching of the Hebrew language. To found this passion on a professional basis, he did his graduate studies at Harvard under the direction of the famous linguist I. A. Richards, with whom he published his well-known primer, *Hebrew through Pictures,* followed by a reader. Subsequently he participated in editing a pocket edition of the famous *Ben Yehuda Hebrew Dictionary*. He served as Registrar at Hebrew College between 1957 and 1964.

Weinstein's major achievement was his twenty-year period as president of the Chicago College of Jewish Studies (later called Spertus College of Jewish Studies) from 1964 to 1984. Throughout his tenure in Chicago, he pursued many consortium arrangements with other institutions of higher education in the entire Chicago region. Some of these worked; some did not. In a sense this pursuit of cooperative arrangements with other academic institutions was the opposite of the insular ideology of the Hebrew colleges created in this country in the 1920s, and was probably the wisest administrative choice at the time. Spertus grew and remains until today one of the few Hebrew colleges left in the United States.

Isadore Twersky (1930–1997)

My friendship with Isadore Twersky (calked "Ickie" then) began in the late 1940s when we were both students at Hebrew College (he was a class ahead of me), and at Camp Yavneh. Unlike Ackie and Doch, who were from families similar to mine, Twersky was the son of a Hasidic Rabbi, the Talner Rebbe, who was established in Roxbury only a few streets away from Hebrew College. Later in his life, when he was already the professor of Jewish history at Harvard, he became the Talner Rebbe himself and led a congregation situated in Brighton.

As a boy at Camp Yavneh Ickie stood out for his rabbinic learning, far superior to that of the rest of us, and his daily pious practices. In fact, far from the fellows in our bunk, he was the one who maintained the practices of a pious Jew. He prayed with *tefillin* every morning, and also prayed the *minḥah* and *ma'ariv* service by himself. He wore a *tallit qatan*, which I had never seen before. I assume we became friends because I joined the small group of students at camp who studied Talmud many mornings with Rabbi Yisrael Wind of Yeshiva University. I was the only non-Orthodox member of that group. Back in town we met at Hebrew College and I would visit him to play ball at his home in Roxbury, which had a Hasidic *shtibel* built into its first floor. While we never discussed this, the difference in our modes of living were significant.

Ickie and I both spent the academic year 1949–1950 at the Hebrew University in Jerusalem on scholarships provided by the Alumni Association of Hebrew College. While our academic interests were different, we took several classes together with Gershom Scholem and Yitshak Baer. Since we lived fairly close to each other, I visited him often. On one occasion we hiked together throughout the Galilee.

Upon our return to Boston we rarely met, since we had both graduated from Hebrew College and embarked on different studies at Harvard, he in history and Jewish philosophy with Prof. Harry Wolfson and I in comparative literature with a specialization in Greek literature. Our social lives, furthermore, were radically different. The friendship, however, always remained and whenever I visited Boston from Los Angeles where I lived after 1959, I would visit him at his home in Brookline.

Twersky's career at Harvard was indeed distinguished. He inherited the Littauer chair in Jewish studies from his mentor, Harry Wolfson, and taught there until his death in 1997. The variety of appreciative articles published by his students upon his death is truly impressive; he trained thirty students, some of whom occupy significant positions in the academic world. They published a memorial volume after his death. His two main scholarly works, *Rabad of Posquieres: A Twelfth-century Talmudist* and his magisterial *Introduction to The Code of Maimonides*, were widely praised. It is clear that Twersky became one of the leading Judaic studies scholars in the second half of the twentieth century, as well as a revered community leader in his position as the Talner Rebbe.

Arnold J. Band (b. 1929)

Since I am the one left of the four young men who studied at Hebrew College and began to teach there in the 1950s, I write in both sadness and joy. Sadness, since I have lost these good friends; joy, since I can write this reflection in our names.

Like Ackie and Doch, I came from a lower-middle-class family of no distinction. My mother came to Boston from Berdichev as a baby in 1893, knew little Yiddish, and spoke English with a decided Boston Irish accent. My father, a Lithuanian Jew, had studied at the Ponevezh Yeshiva in the town of his residence, immigrated in 1906, but studied little Talmud after that. I was the fourth child in a family of four. The house was kosher, but maintained little observance of any of the standard Jewish daily practices, or Sabbath and holiday observance. I had never witnessed *birkat ha-mazon* or *havdalah* before my days at Camp Yavneh. My Jewish upbringing was hardly different from that of most Jewish boys of my age in Dorchester.

The one crucial difference was the Beth El Hebrew School on our street, which both my brother and I attended. Since I excelled at Hebrew school, my teachers persuaded my parents to send me to the Boston Hebrew Teachers College in Roxbury, which changed the course of my life. I rapidly advanced in the high school department there and finished the four-year course in two. In addition to the study of Hebrew texts, I was introduced to the two major Jewish events of my adolescence: the Holocaust and the struggle for the State of Israel.

At the same time, I, like my friends, attended the Boston Latin School. There I was exposed to world literature and languages: Latin, Greek, and French. The trip to Latin School brought me daily into the Back Bay of Boston, in many ways its cultural heart. My daily trip for six years was home to Latin School to Hebrew College, and finally home again. My involvement in the world of Hebrew College was intensified when I was invited in 1946 to attend the College's Hebrew camp, Yavneh, in New Hampshire. With the exception of the years I spent abroad, I worked at Yavneh between 1946 and 1958, mostly as a teacher. As mentioned above, I spent 1949–1950 in Israel; throughout 1952 and 1953 I studied at the University of Paris on a Harvard fellowship. During the late 1950s I wrote my doctoral dissertation in comparative literature on "Aristophanes and the Comedy of Issues" under the direction of Eric Havelock.

Upon receiving my doctorate in June 1959, I was offered two university positions, one in classics in Kansas, the other in Hebrew literature at UCLA. The choice determined the course of my career. In June 1959, I left Boston for Los Angeles to begin at UCLA, where I was appointed assistant professor of Hebrew literature in the Department of Near Eastern Languages. I taught there until my retirement in 1994. During the 1960s and 1970s, departments of Jewish studies were created in many other universities throughout North America, which obviously generated a new challenge for the Hebrew colleges, since students could now study Hebrew and other areas of Jewish studies in their universities and not only at a Hebrew college. This growth led to the creation the Association for Jewish Studies in 1969, first housed at Brandeis University. I was a member of the small organizing committee, which formed the Association, and served as its third president, from 1972 to 1974. The Association, which had at its first annual conference at Brandies with only 39 attendees, now has about 2000 members and meets annually in different cities in North America.

UCLA, like many other universities, was eager to grow academically in the 1960s and 1970s. In 1969 I was invited to form a comparative literature program (later a department), which I chaired for its first ten years. In 2019 we celebrate its fiftieth year; during this period we awarded 230 PhDs, 26 of which were granted to my students. In 1994 I organized the Center for Jewish Studies, which celebrated its twenty-fifth year in 2019.

My publications during this period were varied and numerous. In 1963 I published a collection of Hebrew poems, *Ha-re'i bo'er ba-esh*. My major study of the writings of S. Y. Agnon, *Nostalgia and Nightmare*, appeared in 1968. My translation of the Hasidic tales of R. Naḥman of Bratslav was published in 1978. About 100 of my articles on various topics in modern Jewish literature, some in English and some in Hebrew, were collected in two volumes: *Studies in Modern Jewish Literature* (2003) and *She'elot nikhbadot* (2007). For my research I was granted two awards, one from the Guggenheim Foundation and the other from the National Endowment for the Humanities, and I was admitted as a member to the American Academy of Jewish Studies. In recent years two of my students, William Cutter and David Jacobson, published a collection of scholarly articles, *History and Literature* (2020), in my honor.

In 1953, when the four young men met with Eisig Silberschlag, they were all American-born, but their parents, like their own Hebrew teachers, had been born in Europe. It would not be an exaggeration to state that Hebrew College itself, though opened in Roxbury in 1921, was really founded in Europe. Its Hebraism, taking after the European *tarbut* school movement, was mostly a transplant, from Eastern Europe to Boston, or in other cases, New York, Philadelphia, Baltimore, Chicago. On the other hand, after the initial period of absorption of massive immigration, Israel became a major source for Jewish education in a wide variety of areas: programs, courses, textbooks, and teachers. The Hebrew colleges are no longer the main source of Hebrew teachers for the many institutions sponsored by the American Jewish community for its own needs. The Jewish student today has a wide choice of study options, from Birthright trips to full Jewish studies programs in many universities. Unlike 1921, the Hebrew colleges of 2021 are now only one player in a vast and growing field of Hebrew and Jewish education.

CHAPTER 3

Girsa de-Yanquta, or Hebrew in the Afternoon: A Memoir of the Prozdor in Worcester[1]

Ira Robinson

What came of it was everything.
—Phillip Roth[2]

It is evident to me that the road that led me to my life work as a scholar of Jewish studies began in earnest in an afternoon Hebrew school housed in Congregation Beth Israel, a Conservative synagogue in Worcester, Massachusetts. I grew up there, quite oblivious to the serious decline in manufacturing jobs that caused the city's population to decline some twenty percent from its peak of 203,486 in the 1950 census, shortly before my family moved to the city, to a nadir of 161,799 in 1980, shortly after I left the city for good.[3]

The story of my Hebrew education is worth telling not for any significance I might have as a scholar, but rather because it illustrates a path to fluency in the Hebrew language and the Judaic tradition that existed then, and does not exist at present in the same way. Beth Israel Hebrew School was a path that did not carry me to this fluency alone. A number of others, like Alan Mintz, the late distinguished scholar of Hebrew literature, trod it together with me.[4]

---

1 I would like to thank Professor Jonathan Sarna, whose suggestion that I write this memoir stemmed from a conversation at his Shabbat table.

2 Phillip Roth, *Operation Shylock: A Confession* (New York: Simon & Schuster, 1993), 312.

3 "Worcester, Massachusetts," Wikipedia, https://en.wikipedia.org/wiki/Worcester,_Massachusetts, accessed June 18, 2020.

4 Alan Mintz, "Hebrew: a Memoir," in *What We Talk about When We Talk about Hebrew (and What It Means to Americans)*, ed. Naomi B. Sokoloff and Nancy E. Berg (Seattle, WA: University of Washington Press, 2018), 211–225.

At present, the royal road to fluency in the texts of the Jewish tradition passes through Jewish day schools, most of which are under some form of Orthodox sponsorship. Afternoon Hebrew schools, which supplemented general education in the American public schools, have declined precipitously from their position as "the overwhelmingly dominant form of Jewish education in the United States" for most of the twentieth century.[5] But just as I was not conscious at the time of the global economic decline of Worcester, I was only barely conscious that Jewish day schools might be viable alternatives to my educational path. There was (and still is) an Orthodox day school in Worcester under the auspices of Chabad, but I did not then identify as Orthodox. On the contrary, I identified with Conservative Judaism and had the vague idea that I would one day become a rabbinical student at the Jewish Theological Seminary, as had others who graduated from my Hebrew school. So the Lubavitcher yeshiva was not for me, though ultimately Chabad in Worcester did become an influence in my life. The possibility of enrolling in Boston's Modern Orthodox Maimonides School, which did have a very few students from Worcester in my time, was never brought up with me by my parents, and I certainly had no inclination to go there. Possibly because some of my cousins went to a private school, Worcester Academy, my parents did briefly flirt with the idea of sending me to a distinguished Episcopalian private school relatively near Worcester, St. Mark's. However, they balked at the then still compulsory Christian chapel attendance. So it was the Worcester public school system for me, supplemented by afternoon Hebrew school at Beth Israel.

Congregation Beth Israel was founded in 1924, and, like many Conservative synagogues in that era, started out as Orthodox. In 1939, Beth Israel built a synagogue building on Pleasant Street in Worcester's West Side, a fairly prosperous residential area far away from the old Jewish immigrant district on the East Side. In 1959, Beth Israel erected a larger, more impressive synagogue of modern design in that same area, with a separate wing for the Hebrew school.[6] It is this 1959 building that housed my memories of growing up Jewish. That is where my affair with Hebrew in the afternoon began.

The Beth Israel Hebrew School in my time was presided over by a remarkable educator, Zvi (Harry) Plich (1893–1982). Mr. Plich was in my memory a formidable figure and not in mine alone. Here is how Mr. Plich is described by Alan

---

5 Jack Wertheimer, *Schools That Work: What We Can Learn from Good Jewish Supplementary Schools* (New York: Avi Chai Foundation, 2009), 3.

6 Joseph Klein and Howard Borer, "Worcester," in *Encyclopaedia Judaica*, ed. Michael Berenbaum and Fred Skolnik, 2nd ed. (Detroit, MI: Macmillan Reference USA, 2007), vol. 21, 213–214, https://link-gale-com.lib-ezproxy.concordia.ca/apps/doc/CX2587521092/GVRL?u=concordi_main&sid=GVRL&xid=c205344e, accessed June 4, 2020.

Mintz: "Mar Plich as we called him . . . . His ideological devotion to Hebrew was implacable; this was a stern allegiance that brooked no contradiction."[7] Mintz eventually expressed his respect for Mr. Plich by dedicating one of his books to his memory.[8]

Mr. Plich was also on my mind when I wrote the following in the "Acknowledgements" section of my 1980 doctoral dissertation at Harvard:

> מכל מלמדי השכלתי. I have been truly fortunate over the years to have had many dedicated and talented teachers who succeeded in nurturing my love of Judaism and in giving me the tools with which to explore its sources and understand its history. In particular, I would like to thank Mr. Harry Plich, of Worcester, Massachusetts, for giving me the strong foundation in Hebrew studies during my elementary and high school years which made all else possible. In a very real sense, Mr. Plich's dedication to the highest principles of Jewish education gave me my start in this field.[9]

I also dedicated an article to him shortly after he passed away.[10]

Joel Baker, a somewhat younger contemporary who attended Mr. Plich's school and went on to become president of Congregation Beth Israel, reminisces about Mr. Plich with great respect, and some trepidation as well:

> In my family, Mr. Plich is certainly a legend. When he was first in Worcester, he taught my uncle who is my father's younger brother, so he taught two generations of my family. There is a plaque in the shul with a likeness of Mr. Plich and I have always said when I walk by, it talks to me in his voice telling me to get back to class.[11]

As a young man, before he came to head the Beth Israel Hebrew School, Zvi Plich's devotion to Zionism, the Jewish people, and the Hebrew language led him to leave his home in the Russian Empire and become a *ḥalutẓ* in *Ereẓ Yisra'el*

---

7 Mintz, "Hebrew," 213.

8 Mintz wrote in his dedication: "To the memory of my teacher Harry (Zvi) Plich (1893–1982)." See Alan Mintz, *Hurban: Responses to Catastrophe in Hebrew Literature* (Syracuse, NY: Syracuse University Press, 1996), 5.

9 Ira Robinson, *Abraham ben Eliezer Halevi: Kabbalist and Messianic Visionary of the Early Sixteenth Century* (PhD diss., Harvard University, Boston, MA, 1980), iv.

10 I wrote in my dedication "In memory of Zvi Plich, educator, lover of Torah and Israel." See Ira Robinson, "Halakha, Kabbala, and Philosophy in the Thought of Joseph Jabez," *Studies in Religion* 11, no. 4 (1982): 389.

11 Email from Joel Baker to the author, June 5, 2020.

prior to World War I. He was thus a member of that influential cohort of Jews coming to the Land in that era that was collectively known as the Second Aliyah. Like many Jews who came to Ottoman-ruled Palestine at that time, he found himself unable to stay, and he left *Ereẓ Yisra'el* for the United States. There he began teaching Hebrew school to earn a living while studying engineering. However, he never got his college diploma. World War I intervened and he volunteered as a soldier in the Jewish Legion, a military unit within the British Army that participated in the British conquest of Palestine. While he never spoke of his military exploits in my hearing, he did once mention being in the same bunk as Yiẓḥaq Ben-Zvi (1884–1963), the future second President of Israel.

Another salient fact we students knew about Mr. Plich was that he had studied medicine in Belgium, and would have graduated medical school there in June 1940.[12] The German invasion of France, Belgium, and Holland in May 1940 prevented his graduation and he probably counted himself lucky to be able to return to the United States, where he became the Principal of the Beth Israel Hebrew School no later than 1948.

We can catch a glimpse of Mr. Plich's intellectual milieu in Worcester at this period from the pen of his younger colleague and friend, Rabbi Baruch Goldstein (1923–2017).[13] A survivor of the Holocaust, Rabbi Goldstein married and moved to Worcester in 1948. He met Mr. Plich for the first time at a *ḥug ivri*, a Hebrew-speaking circle of fifteen or twenty couples that met once monthly "for discussions, lectures, and socializing, all in Hebrew."[14] It seems reasonable to assume that many of the members of this *ḥug ivri* were Hebrew teachers, whether at the Beth Israel Hebrew School or at the rival Ivriah School, a community Talmud Torah founded in 1927, which ceased to exist in the 1980s.[15]

Mr. Plich used the social connection the Worcester *ḥug ivri* created to recruit Rabbi Goldstein as a teacher in his school and Rabbi Goldstein describes the Beth Israel Hebrew School under Mr. Plich's leadership in some detail:

> [T]he Beth Israel Hebrew School offered an intensive educational program beginning with a kindergarten class for [public

12 Mintz, "Hebrew," 213.

13 Stacey Dresner, "Rabbi Baruch Goldstein, Former Rabbi at Congregation Beth Israel, Dies at 94," *Western Massachusetts Jewish Ledger*, June 15, 2017, http://www.wmassjewishledger.com/2017/06/rabbi-baruch-goldstein-former-rabbi-at-congregation-beth-israel-dies-at-94/.

14 Baruch G. Goldstein, *For Decades I Was Silent: A Holocaust Survivor's Journey Back to Faith* (Tuscaloosa, AL: University of Alabama Press, 2015), 139.

15 Klein and Borer, "Worcester." The Ivriah School did not have a strong public presence in the 1960s, so that Alan Mintz, whose father had received his Hebrew education at the Ivriah School, was unaware of its existence in his boyhood. Mintz, "Hebrew," 212.

> school] first graders that met once a week on Sunday mornings. The Hebrew School program consisted of a six-year curriculum of study designed for children who attended public school. It began with second grade and ended with seventh. Classes met four days a week, Sunday through Wednesday, for two-hour sessions each day. The curriculum consisted of Hebrew language, *tefillah* [prayer], Jewish history, *Ḥumash* [Torah], the early prophets, and Jewish holidays and customs. It was an intensive curriculum, indeed, considering that the students met only eight hours a week.[16]

Rabbi Goldstein adds a description of the model lesson he taught the Hebrew School's fifth grade in 1949 in order to be hired as a teacher. The lesson covered *ḥumash*, Jewish history, and Hebrew grammar. He taught it basically in Hebrew, though, as he stated, "I had to supplement many explanations in English."[17]

Rabbi Goldstein's detailed description of the Beth Israel Hebrew School's curriculum and schedule stemmed from 1949. The curriculum was most likely coordinated with that of nearby Boston's Bureau of Jewish Education,[18] and was recognizably the same in the years I studied at the school in the late 1950s and early 1960s.

It is perhaps self-understood that many, if not most students of the Beth Israel Hebrew School ended their Hebrew education with the end of the six grade curriculum, around bar mitzvah age (bat mitzvah did exist at Beth Israel but not in as prominent a way as it would later become). However for those who wished to continue their Hebrew education, Mr. Plich and his faculty offered high school students an advanced Hebrew curriculum, coordinated with Boston's Hebrew Teachers College, known as Prozdor. As I recall, neither I nor my parents had any doubt or hesitation about my continuing in the Prozdor.

So for my high school years I spent some serious time with my Hebrew studies with Mr. Plich and his colleagues as my teachers. They, but particularly Mr. Plich, put their heart and soul into turning an assorted cohort of Jewish teenagers into budding Hebraists, and with some success. Of course, we as a group were never quite as serious in our studies as our teachers would have liked. I recall Mr. Plich as a man often frustrated by his students, who were not always capable of mustering the sort of concentration and attention, after a full day of

---

16 Goldstein, *For Decades I Was Silent*, 140.

17 Ibid.

18 Mintz, "Hebrew," 212.

public high school, that the sacredness of the task of studying Hebrew required. "You are eating my heart out," he would often say to us with feeling.

In fact, Mr. Plich, like his contemporary, the Montreal Yiddishist educator Shloyme Wiseman (1899–1985), movingly described by his former student, David Roskies, understood that North American Jewish teachers—Hebraist and Yiddishist—were tasked with the nearly impossible utopian goal of, in Roskies's words, "creating a maximalist culture of *yiddishkayt*" and of "keep[ing] alive the longing for a more total and more beautiful *yiddishkayt*."[19] We, their students, were not always completely up to that utopian task, though it does have to be said on our behalf that we were there in Mr. Plich's Prozdor classroom, while most of our Jewish friends from high school were not.

The Prozdor curriculum, as I recall it, was a more advanced version of the Beth Israel Hebrew School curriculum. We did a lot of Hebrew language, including grammar on a fairly advanced level, whose intricacies I only semi-comprehended at the time. This study of *diqduq* nonetheless gave me in the end a fairly good sense of the structure of the Hebrew language. We also read Modern Hebrew poetry and prose, though, as Alan Mintz correctly recalls, we did not really speak or read the Hebrew of contemporary Israel.[20] As well, we studied a lot of Bible, including extensive sections from the Torah, the Prophets, and the Writings.

Yiddish language and literature were not touched. It was only considerably after my graduation, when I began to study Yiddish, that I discovered in a casual conversation with Mr. Plich that he maintained a deep love of Yiddish literature, particularly the works of Yehuda Leyb Perets.

We also did not do much rabbinics—Talmud and commentaries—in Prozdor. There was, indeed, some rabbinic literature in the curriculum, mostly Mishnah, and occasionally Gemara. I think that Mr. Plich, our teacher for that subject as for much else, taught these subjects under a sort of mild protest. "I am not a talmudist," I recall him once saying. Most certainly there was no effort to give Prozdor students any sort of coherent understanding of the Aramaic language and its grammatical structure, the way there was with Hebrew. I was able to partially fill that gap by studying with Rabbi Hershel Fogelman (1922–2013), the Lubavitcher rabbi of Worcester and the principal of its day school.[21] I was

19 David Roskies, "Yiddish in Montreal: the Utopian Experiment," in *An Everyday Miracle: Yiddish Culture in Montreal*, ed. Ira Robinson, Pierre Anctil and Mervin Butovsky (Montreal: Véhicule Press, 1995), 31.

20 Mintz, "Hebrew," 213–214.

21 Menachem Posner, "Rabbi Hershel Fogelman, Trailblazing Educator, Builder of Communities," Chabad.org, July 4, 2013, https://www.chabad.org/news/article_cdo/aid/2261879/jewish/Rabbi-Hershel-Fogelman-Trailblazing-Educator-Builder-of-Communities.htm, accessed June 16, 2020.

unaware at the time that Rabbi Fogelman had the distinction of being the very first Chabad emissary in North America, sent in 1942 by the then Lubavitcher Rebbe, Yosef Yitsḥak Schneersohn (1880–1950), to establish a Chabad school in Worcester. It was Rabbi Fogelman who took the time out of what must have been an extremely busy schedule to introduce me and some of my friends to the textual study of Gemara and Hasidism.

The other place I was exposed to the study of Hebrew, and particularly of rabbinic texts, was Camp Yavneh, a Hebrew-speaking summer camp in Northwood, New Hampshire that was affiliated with Boston's Hebrew Teachers' College. For a student of Hebrew, one of Camp Yavneh's decided advantages, as Alan Mintz points out, was exposure to the use of Hebrew on an everyday basis.[22] Certainly the campers spoke English among themselves, but nonetheless they utilized Hebrew for much communication, from the *ḥadar okhel* three times daily to the *agam* and the *migrash ha-sport* on a daily basis.

No less impressive was the study aspect of Camp Yavneh. Campers had more hours of exposure to Hebrew education during the weeks of camp than during the school year, and this meant that subjects for which there was little or no curricular time in the ordinary school year could be attempted. What most impressed me on a personal level was my first extended exposure to the literature of biblical commentary. I had certainly studied Torah before, but never with Rashi. Studying Torah with Rashi opened up whole new vistas for me. Since at that period in my life I was much taken with reading (and writing) poetry, I recall when that when reading Rashi for the first time, I literally felt like the protagonist in Keats's poem "On First Looking into Chapman's Homer":

> Then felt I like some watcher of the skies
> When a new planet swims into his ken;
> Or like stout Cortez when with eagle eyes
> He star'd at the Pacific—and all his men
> Look'd at each other with a wild surmise—
> Silent, upon a peak in Darien.[23]

It was in a Camp Yavneh classroom that I first heard the Aramaic term *girsa deyanquta*,[24] helpfully explained by my teacher in Hebrew as the sort of youthful

---

22 Mintz, "Hebrew," 214.

23 John Keats, "On First Looking into Chapman's Homer," Poetryfoundation.org, https://www.poetryfoundation.org/poems/44481/on-first-looking-into-chapmans-homer, accessed June 17, 2020.

24 Lewis Glinert, *The Joys of Hebrew* (New York: Oxford University Press, 1995), 86.

study that lasts a lifetime. That the teacher saw fit not merely to introduce the term but also to emphasize it to the class indicates to me, in retrospect, that he saw that the studies we were undertaking at Camp Yavneh were our *girsa de-yanquta*. Indeed, this was so for me.

My four summers at Camp Yavneh (1964–1967) helped me, like it helped Alan Mintz and many others, gain facility in Hebrew, greatly supplementing what we studied in Prozdor. This is obviously how it was supposed to work. Thanks to the Prozdor program in Worcester, carefully overseen by Mr. Plich, combined with the concentrated summer study program at Camp Yavneh, I graduated able to intelligently read a wide range of Hebrew texts. As I found out when I first went to Israel, in the summer of 1968 with Camp Ramah, I was able to speak an understandable Hebrew. Most difficult of all, I was even beginning to be able to write in that language.

The only tangible object I retain from that period of my life is a set of *Miqra'ot Gedolot* on Torah I won in a Hebrew essay contest at Camp Yavneh in 1965. The inscription in the first volume of the set, accompanied by a photo of all the winners (see figure 1), indicates that the topic of the essay was "*mashber ha-ḥurban u-tequmat Yavne*" (the crisis of destruction and the rise of Yavneh).

This *Miqra'ot Gedolot* was the first set of books I owned that related to traditional Jewish learning, and here, too, Camp Yavneh seemed to set the tone for the further development of my religious life. As Alan Mintz recalls, the campers at Camp Yavneh included an admixture of teenagers from Orthodox homes as well as campers coming from backgrounds similar to mine: traditional and more or less identified with Conservative Judaism.[25] At Camp Yavneh, the rhythm and regularity of the compulsory *shaḥarit* prayers (*minḥa* was available but optional and only attended by the strictly Orthodox) became a part of who I was becoming as a Jew.

I graduated from Prozdor after four years with two ceremonies. The first was in Worcester, where the local graduates were celebrated. Later, we all travelled to Brookline, where the Worcester cohort joined the Brookline students, many of whom I knew from Camp Yavneh. I was set to begin the next phase of my life, college.

It is a tribute to the Hebrew education that I received at the Beth Israel Hebrew School and the Worcester Prozdor that, when I was accepted at Johns Hopkins University for the Fall of 1969, I automatically assumed I would enroll in classes at Baltimore's equivalent of Boston's Hebrew Teachers College, the Baltimore

---

25 Montz, "Hebrew," 214–215.

Hebrew College (later to be renamed Baltimore Hebrew University), as well as at Johns Hopkins. I was, after all, the educational product of a dual system of education. There was elementary school and Hebrew school; there was high school and Prozdor. They all went together. Why not college and Hebrew College? Ultimately, in 1973 I graduated with a BA from Johns Hopkins University and a BHL from Baltimore Hebrew College.

The path through which I acquired my Hebrew education in Worcester, Massachusetts in the mid-twentieth century is no longer available in the same way to Jewish children there. Congregation Beth Israel is still there in the same building I recall, but the intensive Hebrew school program I went through is no more. There is no longer a branch of the Hebrew College Prozdor in Worcester. When Mr. Plich passed away in 1982, the Congregation named its school the "Zvi Plich Hebrew School" in his memory.[26] However, at some point that name was dropped.[27] The present iteration of the congregational school is the Rimon Religious School that has a curriculum considerably removed from the intensive language and text-based learning I experienced.[28]

After I left Worcester, there were two attempts to create a community Jewish day school in the city. A Solomon Schechter Day School, that was identified with Conservative Judaism, and that was housed at Congregation Beth Israel, was founded.[29] Somewhat later there was an attempt to establish another school known as the New Jewish Academy of Worcester.[30] Neither institution lasted. For parents of Jewish children looking now for a school offering their children intensive exposure to Judaic texts in Worcester, Massachusetts, there remains Chabad's Yeshiva Academy, the school that was founded in 1942 by Rabbi Hershel Fogelman, then barely twenty years old, who had been sent by his *rebbe* to start a school for Jewish children in Worcester, MA.[31]

---

26 "Our History," Beth Israel, https://www.bethisraelworc.org/our-history1.html, accessed June 17, 2020.

27 Joel Baker states, "I am not sure when we stopped calling it the Zvi Plich Hebrew School." Email to author, June 5, 2020.

28 "Rimon Religious School," Beth Israel, https://www.bethisraelworc.org/rimon-religious-school.html, accessed June 17, 2020.

29 This school survives on the internet only in an out-of-date business directory. "Solomon Schechter Day School," Localbiziness.com, http://localbiziness.com/biz/solomon-schechter-day-school-32ba664d0, accessed June 17, 2020.

30 This school survives on the internet only in an out-of-date school directory. "Worcester, MA," K12academics.com, https://www.k12academics.com/national-directories/jewish-school/Massachusetts/Worcester, accessed June 17, 2020.

31 "Yeshiva Academy," Central Mass Chabad, https://www.centralmasschabad.com/templates/articlecco_cdo/aid/2257729/jewish/Yeshiva-Academy.htm, accessed June 17, 2020.

Figure 1. Dedication page of book prize given to the author at Camp Yavneh, 17 Av 5725 [August 15, 1965]. The author is in the exact center of the group in the photograph

CHAPTER 4

Israel Studies and the Hebrew (Teachers) College: A Memoir

Ilan Troen

I did not attend Hebrew Teachers College to become a Hebrew teacher. While the rabbinate was a bit more than a fleeting thought, that was also not my destination. Nor for that matter was Jewish scholarship at that time. Like many other HTC students who went into business or other professions, I expected that what we learned in the classroom and through the associations outside of it was relevant to sustaining and furthering our identity as Jews. In other words, I did not intend to become a scholar and to contribute to shaping a new field of Israel studies.

Nevertheless, I spent eight years, 1954–1962, commuting to Hawes Street five days each week through Prozdor and the College in parallel with Boston Latin and Brandeis. In this choice, I was far from alone. Although there was significant attrition over this time, about twenty-five of us from across the Boston region remained to graduate with a Bachelor's in Jewish Education or Hebrew Literature in addition to our "regular" studies at one of the area's universities.

In the course of time two consequences followed from my Hebrew College experience that included a year of study in Israel. I decided to make *aliyah*. I also became a specialist in the field now termed "Israel studies" and contributed to shaping it both in Israel and abroad. Only in retrospect have I recognized that the Hebrew College was the key to the course my life has taken; only in retrospect does the connection between the present and the past appear linear.

The essay I would like to have written is about the appearance and cultivation of Israel studies in America long before it formally entered the American academy. Its beginnings were located in the Hebrew colleges of some major American cities, with perhaps Boston's HTC having a singular prominence due to several aspects: its teachers, the range of subject matter, and the commitment to providing opportunities for using Hebrew outside of the classroom, largely through study in Israel and through Yavneh, its Hebrew-language summer camp.

I would have liked to retrieve information on my teachers and most importantly, on the curricula they offered. I can nevertheless point out that they were of three types. First there were those from Europe and, I imagine, a *tarbut* or similar background where acquisition and transmission of Jewish culture in Hebrew was central. This aspect was crucial for it reflected the reality of the institution and the student body they taught. That is, in the richly Jewish neighborhood of Roxbury/Dorchester, where an early iteration of the HTC was located on Crawford Street, there was a diversity of Jews. While most students were first generation American, we came from distinctly different households where religious and secular Jewish cultures were practiced in different ways. The key bond, as far as I could then determine, was an identity that incorporated learning the Hebrew language and its texts, sacred, ancient and modern. That was perhaps even more true after the College moved to Hawes Street in Brookline and drew upon the more diverse population that was increasingly dispersed in the Boston metropolitan area.

The Hebrew College grew out of the *'ivrit b-'ivrit* emphasis found in the communal tradition of Hebrew education espoused and disseminated by Samson Benderly and his followers after World War I, in contrast to congregational affiliation that became the norm after World War II. It was therefore not devoted to preparing functional adherents to the various streams of Orthodoxy, Conservative, or Reform Judaism. For those of us who also graduated the College and engaged in Hebrew teaching, if only on a partial and short-term basis as we continued our regular university education, there was the necessary interview with Benjamin Shevach, the long-term head of Boston's Board of Jewish Education who was firmly in the Benderly tradition. The board he headed as well as the system of Hebrew schools he supervised and that served as feeders for the College have been superseded. In their passing, so did the kind of education the College offered.

Many of our teachers had come from Europe. The curriculum I encountered in studying with them reflected diverse approaches to Jewish identity and practice, yet emphasized their common commitment to instilling Jewish culture as found in Hebrew texts. We thus studied Bible, Talmud, and even the siddur as well as other topics such as literature, Hebrew grammar, and Jewish history. That was appropriate for a faculty and student body that included a range from the observant to non-observant. Thus, some of my fellow students became rabbis or educators in the various denominations, while others became Jewishly educated and active members of their communities without regard to religious affiliation.

Our different affiliations were never a barrier. We studied and played together and developed deep and lasting friendships. This experience inevitably nurtured a broader and more inclusive appreciation for and understanding of Jewish community.

But we were also exposed to younger teachers. Some were Israelis engaged in doctoral or postdoctoral studies primarily at Harvard, who generally returned home to take up posts at Israeli universities. In addition, we were taught by a generation of young Americans, most of them Bostonians, who were studying at local universities or had just begun their academic careers and came from the same neighborhoods as the students. Four who I remember as particularly influential pioneers and models in blending American and Jewish/Hebrew culture were Walter "Ackie" Ackerman, Arnie Band, Yitzhak Twersky, and "Doch" Weinstein. They were very important to those of us who were trying to figure out how and what kind of Jewishness could coexist with the American culture into which we were propelled and anxious to acquire while, at the same time, developing a strong Jewish identity.

I regret that I cannot provide details of the subject matter we learned. I now realize that many of the books we read in Boston were imports from Israel. While I do not remember the names, I can recall, for example, that the history texts were paperbound, printed on paper that readily dried and cracked, whose pages sometimes needed to be cut, and were bound in ways that readily succumbed to separation. Still, the content was in Hebrew and what our peers in Israel were reading. The courses in Hebrew literature also necessarily connected us with an appreciation for the canon that was studied in Israel. It was surely not nearly as extensive, but it did engender a sense for the issues that were challenging and engaging many contemporary Jews, and particularly those who were Zionists. This study was unlike the acquisition of other literatures and history, ancient and modern, which were part of my education. It was deeply personal, and I believe had a major impact on the way we formed our Jewish selves.

For example, a few days ago I corresponded with a colleague on an essay he was writing on choices that early twentieth century Jews confronted. I suggested he reread Feierberg's 1899 classic novella "Whither?" (?לאן) about the conflict between the traditional and the modern world. I had read it as a teenager in Boston. It resonated within me and became an item of knowledge and reflection that clearly has stayed with me. Other friends in my neighborhood were also asking questions of identity, as appropriate to adolescence. However, my search was in large measure structured and informed by my exposure to Hebrew texts and Jewish learning at the College. My colleague pointed out how significant that text was for earlier generations of *haluẓim,* something I did not know. Thus,

I spent my mornings at Boston Latin School whose auditorium featured on the frieze the names of its earlier graduates: Franklin, Hancock, Revere, Adams, Emerson, and Santayana. But I spent my afternoons and evenings in the company of Bialik and Tchernichovsky and with classical Hebrew texts that were outside the curriculum of the classical and secular education provided by the Latin School.

This parallel experience provided for diverse and yet complementary influences that animated me during those formative years. My class met with Ben-Gurion and were thrilled to have contact, however brief, with the prophet-like leader of the newly established sovereign, Jewish state. At the same time, it was a privilege to have contact, however removed, from those who founded and shaped America. It is not accidental that in later life I came to hold academic chairs both in American history and in Israel studies and to serve on the faculties of an Israeli and American universities. My scholarship began in American urban history but, after making *aliyah*, readily moved into writing about Tel Aviv and Zionism's urban aspect.

As I mentioned at the outset, the College also provided opportunities to experience life in Hebrew. For summers it was Yavneh and similar camps where the names of bunks resonated with Israeli place names, where we learned as well as spoke Hebrew, played games, and sang new and old Israeli songs. In addition, for students of the College, there was the extraordinary opportunity of spending the junior year in Israel. At a time when the possibility of taking a gap year or a year of study abroad was not the norm, HTC made it possible for students, including myself, to spend a year totally devoted to experiencing the new state in its Hebrew culture and language, undistracted by the other half of the double life we were leading as Americans. I had been attending Latin School and subsequently Brandeis during the day and studying at the College at night. The year I spent in Israel was decisive and formative, and when I left, I made a vow to go back.

I was fortunate in being able to make and fulfill this vow, and to return to Israel, this time as an *oleh*, in 1975. I had never intended or imagined this as a possibility prior to that most impressionable year spent in Jerusalem at Machon Greenberg—the institution established for students at similar institutions in North and South America—and at the Hebrew University. That year I was privileged to study with Haim Gouri, Yehuda Amichai, Nehama Leibowitz, and to meet S. Y. Agnon at the Machon as well as taking courses with such giants of the Hebrew University as Scholem, Halkin, Stern, Ettinger, Flusser, and Davis. When not in class—which was most of the time—I explored the country, engaging extensively in *yedi'at ha-areẓ* on a Vespa motor scooter. I encountered and learned from Jews from Europe, the Middle East and North Africa who were becoming Israelis and engaged in building their lives and the country. I volunteered in an archaeological dig in Jerusalem, a religious kibbutz in Beit She'an and a Hashomer Hatzair kibbutz in the Negev. That year I also attended the Eichmann trial by posing as a reporter for the Brandeis *Justice*. It was a powerful and chilling experience to hear a first-hand narration of the most tragic and terrible trauma of contemporary Jewish history. HTC had prepared me well to take full advantage of both a rich course of study and independent exploration (despite the fact that I amused the waiter at a Tel-Aviv restaurant when I asked for an *umẓa*, the Aramaic term I encountered on Hawes Street to designate "steak"—the term used in modern, Israeli Hebrew). It was that crucial third-year Hebrew College-sponsored experience that provided depth and breadth to what I had acquired back in Boston.

I only now realize how fortunate I was to have experienced the College at a particular moment in its evolution. I discovered relatively recently that it has changed remarkably. At a 2012 reunion with fellow classmates on the fiftieth anniversary of our graduation I was saddened to discover that our suggestion for a class gift for outstanding achievement in Hebrew language acquisition to honor a renowned and beloved teacher was politely refused by the College administration. It was explained that Hebrew was no longer taught with the same intensity since Prozdor and College students no longer attended for up to four hours a day, five days a week for study in Hebrew. College students can take courses in Jewish studies at many universities and participate in study programs that take them to Israel; surely this is one reason for such a change. Although the intensity that so distinguished the Hebrew College experience has passed, the College has retained its important communal orientation through its rededication to preparing non-denominational rabbis and leadership for the community.

Serious study of Jewish culture in its many facets has migrated to other venues and College graduates have participated in this development. Charlie Berlin, who preceded me by several years at HTC and has been the leading force in developing the Judaica Division of the Harvard Library, has had an important career in making Jewish studies an integral part of that institution across the Charles and in creating a library and archive on Israel that is unsurpassed, and contains treasures that do not exist or are not as easily accessible in Israel itself. It is Harvard and Brandeis, which established the first, largest and arguably the most significant Center for Israel studies outside Israel, that are magnets for Boston area residents anxious to acquire knowledge of Israel. It is not surprising that two of the first three directors of the Center at Brandeis (Jonathan Sarna and myself) attended Hebrew College. Israel studies courses, programs, and centers have spread to numerous other university venues across the states and

Canada that offer opportunities for those interested in Jewish culture and Israel, although the kind of immersion experience that was available to my class is now largely undertaken only in Israel.

Members of my generation have left a large imprint in the Jewish community of the United States as surely the many entries and essays in this volume testify. They have also contributed in many ways to Israel. My teacher and later colleague and friend, Walter Ackerman, and I were the founding deans of the Faculty of Humanities and Social Sciences at Ben-Gurion University of the Negev. Former Hebrew College graduates can be found in numerous fields throughout the country and across the Israeli academy.

The commitment we made as students at Hebrew College to live a double existence while growing up in America reflects our search for something beyond the quest of most other friends. We knew what we were doing was unusual and demanding, but were fortified by our parents, many of whom were immigrants, and fellow students who shared similar values and ambitions. To be sure, most of us likely invested more time preparing for our "day" classes but we nevertheless extended ourselves and made the effort our double life required. In different ways we probably cannot fully articulate, our HTC education informed and enriched our identities, what we became, and how and where we contributed to Jewish continuity and community, even if most of us did not become Hebrew teachers. That is a significant achievement for any institution.

CHAPTER 5

What They Celebrated, He Mourned: Arnold Wieder's *The Early Jewish Community of Boston's North End* (1962)

Jonathan D. Sarna

Generations of Hebrew (Teachers) College students studied with Dr. Arnold A. Wieder (1921–2013), beloved teacher of Bible and Rabbinic Literature, who served on the faculty from 1958 to 1991. Alone among the full-time Hebrew College faculty of his day, he was often known by his rabbinic title ("Rabbi Wieder") for he was an ordained Orthodox rabbi who had previously served such Boston-area congregations as Linas Hazedek of Dorchester, Young Israel of Brookline, and Chai Odom in Brighton. He was also the community *mohel*: he had ritually circumcised many of the male students whom he later taught. Like several other Hebrew College faculty members, he was a "brand plucked from the fires of the Holocaust." Born in Sighet, Hungary (today Sighetu Marmatiei), down the block from Elie Wiesel, he was the son of Rabbi Shlomo Dov (Salamon) Wieder, an ordinee of the famed Pressburg yeshiva, and also the nephew of Professor Naphtali Wieder, pioneering scholar of Jewish liturgy at Jews College, London and later London University. With the Nazi invasion of Hungary, in 1944, Arnold Wieder went into hiding and then survived a concentration camp. Following the war, he spent two years, along with his father, working to reestablish Orthodox Jewish life among "Displaced Persons" in Windsheim, Germany, and then immigrated to the United States in 1947. He studied at Yeshiva University and subsequently studied at Brandeis University, where he received an MA in Near Eastern and Judaic studies in 1956. In 1951, he married Sabina (Sheva) Zeigersohn (1930–2020), a Holocaust refugee from Poland.[1]

Nothing in Arnold Wieder's biography explains why, in 1962, he produced a book entitled *The Early Jewish Community of Boston's North End.* He never studied American Jewish history and never lived in Boston's North End. His doctoral dissertation, completed in 1962 under the guidance of Nahum N. Glatzer at Brandeis was entitled "Jeremiah in Aggadic Literature."[2] Wieder's subsequent scholarship dealt with biblical and midrashic themes.[3] He never, to my knowledge, spoke about Boston Jewish history in his classroom, and never returned to the subject in any publication. Nevertheless, a significant story and message underlie *The Early Jewish Community of Boston's North End.* The book that Wieder wrote and Brandeis published under its imprimatur could scarcely have been more different from what the book's sponsors anticipated.

The project to produce a history of the Jews of Boston's North End began in earnest 1950 and had nothing whatsoever to do with Wieder. It was the product of two eminent Jewish sons of the North End: Aaron Pinkney (1873–1951), a retired printer, merchant, and antiquarian, who recalled the community's earliest stirrings, having arrived there as a young child in 1874,[4] and Dr. Joseph I. Gorfinkle (1880–1950), a Reform rabbi, camp director, and scholar, whose parents had likewise come to the North End in the 1870s, and who remained close to his Boston roots (and siblings), though he served a pulpit in Mt. Vernon, NY.[5] Both men wrote columns entitled "Tales of the North End" for Boston's *Jewish*

---

1 I have pieced together this information from Arnold J. Wieder, *The Early Jewish Community of Boston's North End* (Waltham, MA: Brandeis University, 1962), 11; Salomon Wieder to Joint Distribution Committee, June 25, 1951, New York Collection, European Shas VI–VII 1951, JDC Papers, New York; Helen Alper to William Males, September 10, 1952, re: Mrs. Weider, Boston HIAS Papers, Wyner Jewish Heritage Center, Boston; *Jewish Advocate*, November 10, 1988, 25; ibid., December 13, 2013, 17; and other mentions of Wieder in the online *Jewish Advocate*; and an interview with his relative, Mrs. Dvorah Weiss, January 27, 2020.

2 Arnold Aaron Wieder, *Jeremiah in Aggadic Literature* (PhD diss., Brandeis University, Waltham, MA, 1962).

3 Arnold A. Wieder, "Ugaritic-Hebrew Lexicographical Notes," *Journal of Biblical Literature* 84 (June 1965): 160–164; Arnold A. Wieder, "Ben Sira and Praises of Wine," *Jewish Quarterly Review* 61 (October 1970): 155–166; Arnold A. Wieder, "Josiah and Jeremiah: Their Relationship According to Aggadic Sources," in *Texts and Responses: Studies Presented to Nahum N. Glatzer on the Occasion of His 70th Birthday,* eds. Michael A. Fishbane and Paul R. Flohr (Leiden: Brill, 1975).

4 On Pinkney, see *Jewish Advocate,* March 29, 1951, 4, 24; ibid., April 19, 1951, 2A.

5 On Joseph Gorfinkle, see *Jewish Advocate,* March 28, 1950, 10; *New York Times,* December 25, 1950, 19:3.

Advocate.[6] Together, in 1950, they formed a committee ("Descendants of North End Jewish Immigrants") with multiple male officers as well as a "Women's Division," and announced plans "to cast into permanent form the story of 'The Jewish Pioneers of the North End of Boston *and their Descendants*.'" Filiopietism stood at the center of this project. "Our parents and grandparents," Pinkney and Gorfinkle proclaimed with some hyperbole, "braved the stormy Atlantic, coming here with only their bare hands and ten fingers, yet see what they and their children have accomplished in a very, very short time! The success story of the Jewish immigrants is truly amazing." They promised that their book would "perpetuate the deeds of the past which will be an inspiration and an incentive to our contemporaries and our children to continue on the same high plane of civic, cultural, religious and philanthropic endeavor, so that their descendants may rise up in turn and call them blessed."[7]

Another article by Pinkney recounted the achievements of North End Jews and their descendants. It set forth a long list of leaders of Temples and Congregations, heads of hospitals and charitable institutions, authors, veterans, politicians, merchants, cultural figures, and other notables, all of whom traced their roots back to the narrow triangle of streets, not more than a quarter-mile in each direction, that made up the Old North End. The Descendants of North End Jewish Immigrants project aimed to uncover more of these heroic stories, to recall for posterity how these "pioneers," their children, and their children's children built successful lives for themselves in Boston, New England, and beyond.[8]

That goal, of course, was not unique to Pinkney and Gorfinkle. Descendants of Central European Jews in the United States, and, for that matter, descendants of numerous non-Jewish immigrant groups, produced similar volumes in abundance, dating back in the Jewish case to the nineteenth century. Isaac Markens, *The Hebrews in America* (1888), for example, aimed to display the "prominence and influence attained by the Hebrews of the United States." Its triumphalistic opening sentences bespoke the book's central message:

> Marvelous prosperity and steady progress mark the history of the Hebrews in the United States. In every department of commercial and intellectual activity they are continually making

6 See, for example, *Jewish Advocate*, April 14, 1949, 9B; ibid., May 25, 1950, 19; ibid., June 15, 1950, 13; ibid., July 20, 1950, 3.

7 *Jewish Advocate*, March 30, 1950, reprinted in Wieder, *Early Jewish Community of Boston's North End*, 89–94.

8 *Jewish Advocate*, September 22, 1949, reprinted in Wieder, *Early Jewish Community of Boston's North End*, 95–100.

> headway. Subjected to no restrictions and accorded the privilege enjoyed by all citizens of the Republic, they are enjoying unexampled prosperity.[9]

The American Jewish Historical Society, established in 1892, reflected, in the words of historian Beth Wenger, "an attempt by a group of Jewish elites to champion the pivotal role of Jews in American History and to rebut defamatory claims about American Jews." Like so many other ethnic historical societies established around that time, it "sponsored historical studies that cast its own people in the best possible light."[10] A communal history produced by an Orthodox rabbi, Rabbi Simon Glazer's *The Jews of Iowa* (1905)—prior to Wieder, one of few by an Orthodox rabbi—carried similar aims. It underscored Jews' "triumph in every walk of human effort" and looked to prove "that Israel, if only let alone, is capable of contributing everything good to the common cause of mankind."[11]

The major difference in the case of the Descendants of North End Jewish Immigrants lay in the home country of their ancestral heroes. Whereas earlier volumes generally highlighted the "contributions" of German-speaking Jews, the goal here was to show how later-arriving Yiddish speakers, almost all of them from the Russian Empire, likewise attained the pinnacles of success. The destruction of so many of these Jews' communities of origin in the two world wars; the antisemitism that Boston Jews experienced during the inter-war years; the nativism that characterized the early post-war years resulting in the Immigration and Nationality (McCarran-Walter) Act of 1952 that reinforced immigration-limiting quotas; and the inevitable aging of the generation that grew up in the Old North End—all contributed to a sense of urgency on the part of the Descendants of North End Jewish Immigrants. They wanted their stories told while they yet lived.[12]

Sadly, the two men who spearheaded the descendants' project, Aaron Pinkney and Joseph Gorfinkle, died within a year of announcing their plan. In their place, Gorfinkle's younger brother, Colonel Bernard L. Gorfinkle (1889–1974),[13] a

---

9 Isaac Markens, *The Hebrew in America* (New York: Markens, 1888), v, 1.

10 Beth S. Wenger, *History Lessons: The Creation of American Jewish Heritage* (Princeton: Princeton University Press, 2010), 17; John J. Appel, *Immigrant Historical Societies in the United States, 1880–1950* (New York: Arno, 1980).

11 Simon Glazer, *The Jews of Iowa* (Des Moines, IA: Koch Brother Printing, 1904), vii–x.

12 "The Report of the Second Meeting of the Jewish Pioneers of the North End and Their Descendants," April 30, 1950, Gorfinkle Papers, Wyner Jewish Heritage Center, Boston.

13 On Bernard Gorfinkle, see *New York Times*, February 16, 1974 and the biographical note in the *Guide to the Papers of Col. Bernard L. Gorfinkle (1899–1973)*, *P-664, Wyner Jewish Heritage Center, Boston, MA.

lawyer, civic leader, decorated war veteran, and bodyguard for Woodrow Wilson at the signing of the Versailles Peace Treaty, took it upon himself to keep the project alive. Since he was not himself a writer or historian, he conceived the idea of partnering with the then still young Brandeis University, headed by historian Abram L. Sachar, so as to bring the project to fruition.

Sachar understood the perils of associating the university with celebratory history. He underscored, in a letter to Gorfinkle, Brandeis's "wish that the project be completed at the highest level of academic integrity."[14] But as a savvy fundraiser, he also understood that Gorfinkle had friends in high places in Boston who might help the young university financially. So it was that the Ethel Bresloff Fund, of which Col. Gorfinkle was fortuitously the executor, transferred money to Brandeis with a carefully worded purpose: "to be used primarily for research in developing a history of the early Jewish settlers in the North End of Boston."[15] Sachar turned this project over to the chair of the Department of Near Eastern and Judaic Studies, Prof. Simon Rawidowicz, and it was agreed, in November 1956, "to appoint one of our teaching fellows to this project immediately after the beginning of the second semester."[16]

On April 3, 1957, Sachar reported to Gorfinkle that the project was underway. Brandeis awarded Arnold Wieder, who had received his MA in 1956 and was continuing his studies toward a PhD, a fellowship of $2,000 "to get him started." Sachar assigned a recently appointed Assistant Professor of Sociology named Jerome Himelhoch (1916–2001), editor of the journal *Social Problems*, "to offer assistance by way of counsel."[17] This explains how Wieder became involved in the "North End Project." His modest fellowship—about $18,500 in contemporary dollars—was contingent on his assuming the task. For Wieder, who had to support himself and his wife while he studied, the extra income, if not the accompanying assignment, was most likely welcome.

Gorfinkle pronounced himself "pleased" with Wieder and Himelhoch. He sent along two articles from the *Jewish Advocate* (likely the ones authored by

---

14 Saul S. Elgart to Bernard L. Gorfinkle, November 30, 1956, Sachar Papers, Brandeis University.

15 *Brandeis University General Catalogue, 1958–1959*, 24, http://www.ebooksread.com/authors-eng/brandeis-university/general-catalog-volume-1958-1959-nar/page-24-general-catalog-volume-1958-1959-nar.shtml, accessed June 22, 2020.

16 Saul S. Elgart to Bernard L. Gorfinkle, November 30, 1956, Gorfinkle file, Abram Sachar Papers, Brandeis University.

17 A. L. Sachar to Bernard L. Gorfinkle, April 3, 1957, Gorfinkle file, Sachar Papers, Brandeis University. By coincidence, on that very day Himelhoch was introducing Martin Luther King when he spoke at Brandeis; see Julian Cardillo, "When Martin Luther King Jr. Visited Brandeis," January 11, 2021, Brandeis.edu, https://www.brandeis.edu/now/2020/january/martin-luther-king-legacy.html.

his brother and Aaron Pinkney) as proof "that there will be sufficient romance to additionally reward their activities."[18] But "romance" hardly comported with the "highest level of academic integrity" that the university insisted upon. Hoping to move in a new direction, Himelhoch and Wieder paid a visit to Harvard's Pulitzer-Prize winning American historian, Oscar Handlin (1915–2011), an expert in US history, Boston immigrant history, and American Jewish history, and one of Boston's most respected Jewish citizens. Handlin's recommendation, which they took as a command, was to refocus the study so as to examine "the social history of the Jewish immigrants of 'Old Boston' for the period approximately from 1880 to about World War I." Handlin believed that a book on the Jews of the North End would be far too limited in scope. He urged that adjacent Jewish areas such as the West End be included in the study as well. Other historians that the pair consulted agreed: "the Jewish Community of the North End," Himelhoch and Wieder concluded, "could best be studied within the framework of a more general research in the early history of Boston Jewry."[19]

Gorfinkle, however, would have none of it. "The history of the Jewish Pioneers of the Old North End of Boston would most clearly evaluate [sic] an excellent illustration of the role which the Jew has played in the American scene," he opined in an undated letter.[20] He also knew that his uncle, Maurice (Millionthaler) Milontaler, scion of another North End Jewish family dating back to the 1870s, had been working off and on for many years on a manuscript dealing just with the Jews of the North End. While he refused to share it with Wieder and it never found a publisher, it survives in typescript. Milontaler entitled it "The North End of Boston: Gateway to the Goldener Land," and it recounts stories of some of the North End's most distinguished Jewish sons and daughters, and their descendants, including several who intermarried into notable Protestant families.[21] So Gorfinkle concluded that the academics too needed to focus sharply on the North End. He reminded them, in a lawyerly way, that "the grant under

---

18 Bernard L. Gorfinkle to Abram L. Sachar, April 10, 1957, Gorfinkle file, Sachar Papers, Brandeis University.

19 "Project Report on North End Research Project," n. d., 1958?, Gorfinkle file, Sachar Papers, Brandeis University.

20 Undated manuscript letter to Henry Penn, Gorfinkle Papers, Wyner Jewish Heritage Center, Boston, MA.

21 Maurice Milontaler, "The North End of Boston: Gateway to the Goldener Land," copy in the Milontaler Papers, Wyner Jewish Heritage Center, Boston, MA. Many thanks to Stephanie Call for scanning this for me. Another copy is found in the Harvard University Library. See Milontaler ("Uncle Moe") to Gorfinkle, November 23, 1957, Gorfinkle Papers, Wyner Jewish Heritage Center, Boston, MA, for his refusal to share the manuscript with Rabbi Wieder.

which the project was conducted specified the North End as the community to be under scrutiny."[22]

Himelhoch, who was more interested in sociology than history, devised a solution: "to conduct a study based both on interviews with elderly former residents of the area and on available documentary material. Interviews would furnish information on the basis of the interviewees' own childhood experiences and of what they heard from their elders." So, armed with a bulky 1950s tape recorder, Wieder set out to record interviews with selected old-timers with roots in the North End. His personal roots in a small European Jewish community, the fact that he knew from experience what it meant to be an immigrant, and, most significantly, his facility with Yiddish aided him in his work. The use of Yiddish, Himelhoch perceptively noticed, "stimulated some interviewees to revert more deeply into their past and to bring up some characteristic material."[23] In the end, twenty old-timers agreed to be interviewed at length, an average interview taking eighty minutes. "Shorter less formal interviews" with other old-timers yielded additional information.

By no means did these interviewees represent a cross-section of the Jewish North End. Wieder himself later conceded that "most of our interviewees were among the most successful former North Enders." His senior-citizen interviewees, he noted, also suffered from "forgetfulness," "involuntary retrospective distortion," and personal biases.[24] The field of oral history, spurred by the commercialization of the tape recorder, would eventually recognize these kinds of difficulties and discuss means of compensating for them through other kinds of research. Wieder and Himelhoch, writing before "oral history" emerged as a field, sensed these methodological problems too, but they were eager to finish their project and move on.

In the fall of 1958, Wieder began teaching Bible at Hebrew Teachers College. He needed time to devote to his PhD and looked to divest himself of other distractions. So he decided to write a scholarly article for a journal like *Jewish Social Studies* based on his interviews, and then to put the project behind him. Obligingly, Himelhoch wrote a thank-you letter to Gorfinkle that declared the project "a valuable learning experience for Rabbi Wieder" making possible "a small but significant research study." He dispatched copies to Sachar and other members of the Brandeis administration, and declared the work complete.[25]

---

22 "Project Report on North End Research Project."

23 Ibid.

24 Wieder, *Early Jewish Community of Boston's North End,* 13–15.

25 Himelhoch to Gorfinkle, November 7, 1958, Gorfinkle file, Sachar Papers, Brandeis University.

No response to that letter survives. Based upon the book that was published in 1962, however, it is clear that Gorfinkle demanded a much more grandiose final product. The laconic acknowledgment Gorfinke ultimately received—"he followed the project with close attention throughout"[26]—speaks volumes. Gorfinkle even hired the retired Curator of Judaica at the Boston Public Library, Fanny Goldstein (herself originally from the North End), to locate rare old photographs to accompany Wieder's prose. The resulting 100-page volume, "published by Brandeis University under provisions of the Ethel Bresloff Fund" and handsomely bound and printed, shows that Gorfinkle's vision eventually won the day.[27]

The content of the book, however, diverged markedly from anything that Gorfinkle could have anticipated. Gone was the "pride," the success stories, and the focus on "the influence of the pioneer Jews," their "national and even international importance."[28] Wieder highlighted instead the "negative results" of immigration. He reported, for example, that In the North End, "fathers saw their children only on the Sabbath." They devoted far less time "to the education of the young, to charity, and to synagogue activities" than did fathers in Europe. "Parents were tolerant towards the deviation from religious practice displayed by their growing children." This resulted, Wieder concluded, in a "rather quick breakdown in observance by the second generation, demonstrated by a rapid spread of Sabbath-desecration and an extensive neglect of worship."[29]

Himelhoch, who by then had departed Brandeis for Goddard College in Vermont, explained in his introduction that Wieder's findings challenged social scientists' prior assumptions concerning immigrants and their children. The traditional view held that immigrant parents clung "tenaciously to the Old World culture," while their American-born children—the so-called "second generation"—stubbornly rebelled. Wieder showed that in their rebelliousness, members of the second generation actually continued on the path

---

26 Wieder, *Early Jewish Community of Boston's North End*, 6.

27 Ibid., 5–6; Bernard Gorfinkle to Fanny Goldstein, March 6, 1961, Fanny Goldstein Papers, box 2, file 9, American Jewish Archives. On Fanny Goldstein, see Jonathan D. Sarna and Ellen Smith, eds., *The Jews of Boston* (Boston, MA: Combined Jewish Philanthropies, 1995), 338; Ellen Smith, "Fanny Goldstein," in *The Encyclopedia of Jewish Women*, https://jwa.org/encyclopedia/article/goldstein-fanny; and Silvia P. Glick, *With All Due Modesty: The Selected Letters of Fanny Goldstein* (PhD diss., Boston University, Boston, MA, 2018), https://open.bu.edu/handle/2144/33238.

28 Aaron Pinkney and Joseph I. Gorfinkle, "Why a History of the North End?" (March 30, 1950) reprinted in Wieder, *Early Jewish Community of Boston's North End*, 89–91.

29 Wieder, *Early Jewish Community of Boston's North End*, 33, 34, 63.

marked out for them by their fathers. Himelhoch explained the significance of this insight:

> The "revolt" of the second generation was only an overt manifestation of the unacknowledged wishes of the first. Behind their external traditionalism the parents often condoned and perhaps subtly encouraged their children's lapses from orthodoxy. (Conforming parents, according to some psychologists, sometimes unwittingly encourage their children to act out the parents' own non-conformist phantasies.) Inasmuch as many of the parents felt that a synthesis of Judaism and Americanism was impossible, they decided on the former for themselves and on the latter for their children.[30]

Beyond this contribution to sociological theory lay a sharp critique of the basic worldview of the North End's early Jews. What they celebrated as success, Wieder as an Orthodox rabbi read as abject failure. They defined success in secular terms based on achievements recognized within the general community. "In the arts and sciences, in literature and the professions, in drama, music and commercial enterprises, they [Jews with roots in the North End] have made outstanding contributions and achieved great successes," Gorfinkle and Pinkney had boasted. "They are among [the] leaders in all communal endeavors and their names and careers are recorded in many 'Who's Who' publications." Wieder, by contrast, pointed to the religious consequences of these contributions and successes. "The Jewish educational facilities available at the time were inadequate, old fashioned and totally unsuited... . The Jewish knowledge the first generation managed to impart to the second was consequently sketchy and superficial... . The parents were tolerant towards the deviation from religious practice displayed by their growing children."[31]

To drive the point home, Wieder unfavorably contrasted the North End Jews of the late nineteenth century with those (like himself) who immigrated in the wake of World War II. While he found the newer immigrants' orthodoxy "comparable to that of the immigrants of the eighties and nineties," they, unlike their predecessors, "send their children today (with very few exceptions) to Hebrew-English all day schools." In these Jewish day schools, he noted approvingly, "all

30 Ibid., 9–10, 68.
31 Ibid., 62–63, 94.

English subjects are taught in a Jewish environment, thus giving an opportunity 'for cultural integration without ethnic disintegration.'"[32]

Building on this critique, Wieder, far from celebrating the early Jews of Boston's North End, concluded his monograph on a mixed note, noticing "what was good" and "what was bad," "what they did," and "what they failed to do." The book's appendices subtly underscored the point. One reproduced in Hebrew and then translated the 1882 preamble to the by-laws of Chevra Shas, established by pious North End Jews, alarmed at "the ruined condition of Judaism in the United States," who pledged to meet and study Talmud and commentaries every day for one hour. That, for most Jews from the Old North End, was the path *not* taken, and explained, Wieder hinted, why their Orthodoxy attenuated. The other appendices consisted of the two celebratory articles by Pinkney and Gorfinkle in the *Jewish Advocate* that helped to initiate the whole project. Wieder warned readers to evaluate those articles "with an understanding of the underlying attitudinal factors." The appendices' conflicting messages—the one focused on "the privilege to study Torah amidst prosperity and happiness" and the others on "the success story of the Jewish immigrants"—highlighted the gap between Wieder's worldview and that of the "pioneer Jews of the North End of Boston and their descendants." Much of what they celebrated, he mourned.

The Early Jewish Community of Boston's North End, when it appeared in 1962, attracted little in the way of either popular or scholarly attention. The *New York Times* and the *Boston Globe* ignored it. The *Jewish Advocate* devoted an article to the book, but published no review.[33] The only substantive evaluation of the book appeared in *American Jewish Historical Quarterly.* Authored by the then thirty-year-old Judaica scholar, Jacob Neusner, it did not mince words. Neusner (1932–2016), later the best known and most controversial Jewish Studies scholar of his time, was renowned, in part, for his "irascible, sometimes quite nasty, and often pugnacious personality [and] his famous excoriating reviews."[34] He had written his senior thesis at Harvard on "The Rise of the Jewish Community of Boston, 1880–1914," and was familiar with the relevant primary and secondary literature on American Jewry. Completely overlooking the deeper message of Wieder's book, he reported that it exhibited "deficiencies both in method and in treatment of the subject" and that it made "no substantial contribution to our

---

32 Ibid., 59.

33 *Jewish Advocate,* October 18, 1962, 1, 15.

34 Shaul Magid, "Is it Time to Take the Most Published Man in Human History Seriously?," *Tablet Magazine,* August 23, 2016, https://www.tabletmag.com/sections/arts-letters/articles/take-jacob-neusner-seriously; Aaron W. Hughes, *Jacob Neusner: An American Jewish Iconoclast* (New York: New York University Press, 2016).

understanding of Boston Jewry." He criticized its interviews, arguing that the questions posed "could have been answered more accurately through conventional methods of historical inquiry," and he criticized its conclusions for being either overly general or insufficiently proven. He dismissed the book entirely, in his final sentence, as "an amateurish mélange of nostalgic antiquarianism, undigested facts, and inadequate method."[35]

Looking back, and rereading the book within the context of the project that spawned it, Wieder's contribution takes on much greater significance than Neusner imagined. It bravely dissented from the filiopietism of an earlier generation that narrowly defined success on the basis of those listed in "Who's Who," and it questioned, from a religious perspective, whether immigrants' success had been purchased at too steep a price. Respectfully, it asked whether the pioneers had been correct in the compromises they made and the lessons they imparted to their offspring. In tune with the post-war religious revival, the emerging embrace of ethnic and religious pluralism, and the ideology of Wieder's own Modern Orthodoxy, it suggested a different path for immigrants and their descendants, one that emphasized Jewish education. Wieder, through his teaching at Hebrew College and other activities, dedicated the remainder of his own life to that effort.[36]

35 Jacob Neusner, review of *The Early Jewish Community of Boston's North End,* by Arnold Wieder, *American Jewish Historical Quarterly* 52 (September 1962): 341–344.

36 Many thanks to Chloe Gerson, Robert D. Farber Archive, Brandeis University; Stephanie Call, Wyner Jewish Heritage Center, Boston, MA; and to Dana Herman, American Jewish Archives, Cincinnati for making documents available to me; also to Nehemia Polen and Larry Brown for reminiscences concerning Arnold Wieder.

CHAPTER 6

Searching for Treasure: A Journey Back to Hebrew College

Daniel Klein

Reb Simḥah Bunem of Pshiskhe used to tell a story to new visitors about Isaac of Krakow and his recurring dream. Isaac was a very poor person who kept dreaming about a treasure buried under a bridge in Prague. Finally, when he could resist no longer, Isaac traveled to Prague to search for the treasure, only to discover that the bridge was near the royal palace and heavily guarded. Isaac watched the bridge for days, trying to figure out a way past the guards, but to no avail.

One day, a guard approached him and asked him what he was doing, day after day, watching the bridge. When Isaac told him, the guard laughed dismissively and told him of his own dream about a treasure under a stove in Krakow in the home of some man named Isaac. "Do you think I am going to run to Krakow to search for this treasure because of a silly dream?!" said the guard. Isaac immediately headed home and found the treasure under his stove.

I have had a recurring dream of finding a buried treasure since I was a teenager. The treasure is for my life to matter, to be meaningful, to be well lived. Since I dreamed this dream, I have gone on journeys to find it, encountered obstacles where I thought it would be and ultimately have found myself a mile from where I grew up, blessed with personal and professional abundance my dreams only gestured at.

This dream and discovery were only possible because Hebrew College.

From my youth, as a student at Prozdor in the mid-1990s and camper and counselor at Camp Yavneh at the same time, through my education and ordination in 2010 as a rabbi at the Rabbinical School of Hebrew College, to now, in my tenth year as a faculty member of Hebrew College's ordination programs,

Hebrew College has been instrumental in shaping my understanding of the treasure I am seeking and helping me find it. In many ways, Hebrew College is, or at least is part of, the treasure that has been under my stove the whole time.

Dreaming of Treasures: Prozdor and Camp Yavneh

I like to joke that what I learned at Prozdor is how to skip class.

This is, of course, a myth that does not reflect the fullness of my Prozdor experience. I went to class a lot more than I missed it and learned much about Jewish history, culture and tradition as well as Hebrew. In other words, the opposite of my rebellious myth—virtues of dedication, perseverance, and service—were probably as true to my experience. However, what I remember most vividly about Prozdor is feeling a sense of transgressive freedom despite or within the obligation. My older brother initiated me into this. Every Tuesday, we would take the T from Newton to Brookline and walk from the Longwood stop up the hill to the Hawes Street Hebrew College mansion. That journey alone nurtured a sense of independence, but was then comically enhanced by our attempts to elude the watchful eye of the train conductor. Though we came from a home in which we were not wealthy but never lacked for anything and certainly had plenty of money to pay for the T on a weekly basis, we often did not bring enough change to pay full fare. Maybe it was an oversight at times, but more likely it was a conscious act of rebellion that always scared and excited me—to see how little we could pay, while still making it look like we had paid the full fare, so we would not get caught.

The minor transgressions continued at Prozdor with what we thought of as well-timed, judiciously deployed trips to Dunkin Donuts instead of class. It was almost always with a friend, probably to avoid a quiz or just some class that we thought was less important or pressing than a donut and a conversation. We were hardly delinquents. We attended class regularly, participated, even enjoyed ourselves now and again, but we also experimented with the boundaries of engagement and rejection, of reverence and irreverence.

This was behavior, at least for me, that was barely thinkable at "real" school. I was an overachieving student who bought into my suburban educational experience of learning for the sake of grades, and to get into a good college. These are of course worthy goals, but for me, they were too energized by fear: of failure, of disappointing others, ultimately of my own inner hollowness. I always knew that something was off in my fidelity to these ambitions. This dissonance came out in a love of Jack Kerouac, Beat poetry, and the *Grateful Dead*. And it came out in my mildly norm-defying behavior at Prozdor. Though the experience was as much about participating in and going along with the given parameters presented to me, Prozdor was also about breaking free and trying to center life around things that really mattered. And crucially, I think I sensed in Prozdor and by extension in Jewish life, a little more pliability, openness, and genuineness. A willingness to tolerate and maybe even desire and invite some irreverence, particularly from those who were also reverent. It was as if Prozdor and Jewish tradition were winking at me, subtly, slyly calling to a deeper, more essential part of me, even challenging me not just to be a passive receiver of the experience, Jewish tradition, and my life.

****

My Prozdor transcript will show that, technically speaking, Camp Yavneh was in service of Prozdor. Were it not for the credits I earned from classes I took at Yavneh each summer (in addition to the immense generosity of the Director, Mike Libenson, in giving me a credit for working the spotlight at the Prozdor play my senior year that earned me the final credit I needed), I would not have been able to graduate Prozdor.

However, anyone who experienced both, really lived deeply in Prozdor and Yavneh, knows the absurdity of that technicality. Without Yavneh, there was no Prozdor. In fact, without Yavneh, life itself was hard to imagine. As Abraham Joshua Heschel teaches about the work week in relation to Shabbat, Prozdor, and life the other ten months of the year, were only possible and made any sense in relation to and in service of what happened, what we experienced and discovered at Yavneh. If Prozdor was a subtle teacher of the art of living, it got much of its power to offer that to me from life itself, in the form of my summers at Camp Yavneh.

I am immensely blessed to have grown up in a home and family in which Jewish identity and tradition were a seamless and beloved part of our life and identities. It was Camp Yavneh that helped me appreciate that the love and intimacy I experienced in my home and the mingling of life and Jewish tradition it contained could happen on a communal level. Reduced to its essence, I learned through direct, sustained, and ongoing life-giving experience that honest, vulnerable friendship—sharing, honoring, and protecting each of our inner lives in its revealed fullness—was possible, and was the standard for meaningful relationship. This happened within a context of serious Jewish living, in which we lived on Jewish time and with the rituals, myths, stories, and history of our people woven into our days.

For me, the context exponentially increased my Jewish knowledge, as I was socialized into forms and myths I was otherwise only somewhat aware of. I learned to wear *tefillin*, say *birkat ha-mazon*, and lead *shaḥarit* and *qabblat Shabbat*. I learned about the "three weeks," the 9th of Av, and about Yoḥanan Ben Zakkai. I studied Mishna and kept Shabbat in a fairly "traditional" fashion. I had little idea what it all meant. It was what we did because that is what Jews did, at least at Yavneh. Often, I sensed the emptiness of the acts I performed: the words and rituals a shell, a box to check, because that is what we had to do, as Jews, and to avoid an unpleasant interaction with an adult and punishment. But enough of the time, at camp, the communal bonds, sense of tradition and youthful energy could imbue or maybe unlock some secret transcendent power hidden within the strange liturgies and rites of Jewish tradition, even if the words we said were little more than propulsive expulsions of air, shaped into intentional but meaningless words by our lips.

Saturday night is my favorite example. After a beautiful and moving *havdalah*, the camp resolved into a raucous Israeli dance party. At some point, we would sing/scream and jump wildly to an energetic version of:

> אֲנִי מַאֲמִין בֶּאֱמוּנָה שְׁלֵמָה בְּבִיאַת הַמָּשִׁיחַ, וְאַף עַל פִּי שֶׁיִּתְמַהְמֵהַּ, עִם כָּל זֶה אֲחַכֶּה לּוֹ בְּכָל יוֹם שֶׁיָּבוֹא.
>
> I believe with perfect faith in the coming of the Messiah, and, though the Messiah may tarry, I will wait daily for the coming.

If a non-initiate had witnessed the outburst, they would have been forgiven for thinking they were watching religious fanatics, in the throes of messianism. Had I understood the meaning then, I would likely have thought it was absurd, more strange Jewish words with either no meaning or delusional expressions of a world that could not and did not exist; but I would have kept on dancing and singing, the cognitive dissonance no match for the sense of belonging and aliveness we felt.

And yet, ironically, I now see that there actually was no cognitive dissonance. That we were religious fanatics in the throes of messianic fervor—one that I can still affirm. I can hardly think of a fuller expression of a vision of messianic consciousness than a community in which when it worked, and by and large it did work, each person played critical role, was needed and valued, and all feeling and knowing themselves to be a part of something larger, wonderful and cosmically significant.

This feeling of interconnection as part of a sacred community dramatically shaped my vision of what it meant to live a meaningful life. And the experience highlighted the possible role Jewish life could play in finding that treasure.

Searching for Treasures in Haight-Ashbury

In my high school and college brain, Kerouac, the *Dead*, Prozdor, and Camp Yavneh got jumbled together and emerged as a dream of a treasure at the corner of Haight-Ashbury, and the Beat section of City Lights Books.

Like many before me, I moved to the Bay Area after college, with close friends from Prozdor and Yavneh, fueled by romantic notions that life would be transformed and enlivened by living in the sacred place of these creative giants. Once there and settled into an expensive apartment in a strange part of town south of the Mission in the middle of the early 2000s tech boom, it became clear, as was predictable, that we were just there, in a place called San Francisco. There was no automatic magical, life affirming and enlivening experience, even when visiting the Haight or browsing through City Light Books.

And so began the process figuring out what it might mean to take responsibility for constructing a life oriented towards meaning. Professionally, I was in search of work that was in service to human flourishing in some way. But I also knew that spiritual practice that supported this vision would be critical for me. I spent some time at a Shambhala center in the Mission, and am eternally grateful for the enduring mindfulness practices the teachers there introduced me to; but I also sensed that I needed at least to investigate what Judaism might offer me. I had read Heschel's *The Sabbath* in college and was taken with his notion of Shabbat as a restorative center to reconnect with how we want and need to live. It was my evidence that Jewish tradition had something for seekers and was worth exploring to see if the tradition I had inherited could be an orienting force for meaning in my adult life and not an honored but vestigial appendage from my youth.

Enter Rabbi Arthur Green. I had discovered the Jewish Renewal Movement in my San Francisco wanderings, as it happens a fantastic place to explore mystically infused Judaism, and somehow I came into possession of a copy of *Seek My Face, Speak My Name*, one of Rabbi Green's books of theology.

The book transformed my life.

Rabbi Green (now amazingly just Art, my teacher, colleague, mentor, and friend) understands the relationship between God, Torah and human beings as one in which Torah, which is to say all Jewish forms of myth and practice, are meant as a conduit to a relationship with a transcendent and imminent God, a response to and a path back to the Oneness. And this unitary reality that is beyond our regular consciousness of distinctive beings, but also a deeper state of things, makes a claim on us. It demands, obligates, expects, and invites us into a more loving orientation towards and relationship with other human beings. Art's theology reached inside me and simultaneously reflected a truth I already knew and shaped it into a guiding vision more brilliantly, beautifully, and clearly than I could ever hope to. Art created the context for Judaism to be my spiritual home; and, as I explored *tefillah* and Jewish holidays with my eyes clearly fixed on their spiritual possibilities, I began to discover the riches of a life lived through Jewish rituals and time. Increasingly, 3,000 miles from home, largely inspired by a person who lived in my hometown, Torah was becoming the language of my soul, a treasure of meaning already in my house, waiting to be discovered.

Finding the Treasure with Hebrew College

Kafka writes, in his six-sentence short story "The Watchman":

> I ran past the first watchman. Then I was horrified, ran back and said to the watchman: "I ran through here while you were looking the other way." The watchman gazed ahead of him and said nothing. "I suppose I really oughtn't to have done it," I said. The watchman still said nothing. "Does your silence indicate permission to pass?"[1]

I decided to become a rabbi so I could combine my personal and professional aspirations. I sensed that the rabbinate was a way to be involved in people's lives and help them in their most vulnerable and mundane realities and that professional obligation and expectation would be useful for me both in opening doors to do this work and in disciplining me in Jewish spiritual practice. I came to Hebrew College because I needed help getting myself past the watchman.

Even though I knew Jewish forms offered a path to meaning, I still had guards keeping me from the treasure. In my case, the most significant one, more than my own lack of knowledge and rudimentary spiritual practice, was fear. My fear took the form, essentially, of a little *frum* man sitting on my shoulder, whispering in my ear that if I wanted to be a "real" Jew, if I wanted to be taken seriously and prove my piety and thus worthiness as a Jew and rabbi, I had to have encyclopedic knowledge of Jewish tradition and had to practice in a "traditional" way. It was another manifestation, in other words, of the fear of my own inadequacy that had led me in high school to cling to external definitions of meaning and worth and that had fueled dreams of a different, more meaningful way of living.

---

1 Franz Kafka, "The Watchman," in *Collected Stories*, ed. Gabriel Josipovici (New York: Alfred A. Knopf, Inc., 1993), 396.

It was from this fear, I think, that I started my rabbinical education at a movement affiliated school. It seemed safer professionally and because I thought it would confer the external stamp of approval that I longed for internally. However, I discovered that I had given the *frum* watchman on my shoulder a bullhorn. I did not fit in a denominational box. I needed more space to explore what Jewish forms could be, and being in a more homogenized place with clear definitions of how to do Judaism only reinforced the wrong tendencies. I came to Hebrew College's nascent rabbinical program in 2006, the third year of its existence, when I realized I could either go to Hebrew College—and hopefully find a better place to continue my pursuit of the rabbinate—or abandon the rabbinic path.

The gift of Hebrew College for me, the reason it became, as an adult, a place that could nurture my Jewish life and help me into meaningful relationship with God and Torah beyond my own internal obstacles, was most clearly articulated a few years after I graduated. I was already working on faculty overseeing admissions for the Rabbinical School, which I did from 2011 to 2020. One aspect of the work that I treasured was the final moments of applicant interviews, when applicants would ask the panel of faculty interviewers a question or two to help the applicant get to know Hebrew College. In many of the interviews, the applicants gave us the gift of asking why we worked at Hebrew College or what was special about Hebrew College. It was a gift because as much as I sense as a faculty, we are aware of how special the rabbinical school project is and how blessed we are to be working together on this project, the question and setting gave us an organic opportunity to reflect on and reconnect to our own vision of the work.

In one of the early years of working in admissions, I heard the then dean of the Rabbinical School, now president of Hebrew College, Rabbi Sharon Cohen Anisfeld, respond to this question in a way that illuminated the whole project and my aspirations for my life. She said, essentially, that she was drawn to Hebrew College because she sensed it was a place in which people were willing to take the risk of being honest. Like Art's theological writing, Sharon's words, which reflected a whole way of being that she and, I believe, Hebrew College embody, reached inside me and reflected and shaped my soul's longing better than I ever could have. I understood then a new level of truth about a life well-lived through Torah, of finding the treasure under the stove. It could not be found and done passively, simply receiving the wisdom of Jewish tradition like a cistern receives water. It also could not be found and done on one's own, just looking within and finding truth. It requires honest relationship, opening oneself to the wisdom of received tradition while also believing and trusting that the tradition wants and needs our honest response.

According to the *Sefat Emet*, each person has a particular way or path in Torah and Jewish tradition. We find this path through intimacy and vulnerability. "As the inner person is revealed to Torah, so is each person's inward portion in Torah revealed to us."[2] The only way to find this path is by taking the risk to be honest with Torah as part of a committed, ongoing relationship. That is how we participate in the evolving millennial Jewish conversation about God and meaning that we call Torah.

I knew, when Sharon said these words, that I was in the right place, that this was my soul's longing, that I was home and had found the treasure I was seeking.

In my time as a rabbinical student and faculty member of Hebrew College, I have found the fullness of possibility that I began to discover as a youth at Prozdor and Camp Yavneh. I found a way of life within Jewish living that is dedicated to sacred living and a life well-lived. But more than that, I found a project, an institution, and a community that is also dedicated to this vision, of nurturing Jewish souls who are themselves rooted in an honest, passionate, and committed relationship with Jewish tradition to be guides and companions for others as spiritual leaders. I found a role in which I can contribute to this project among inspiring, dedicated colleagues who are my teachers, mentors, and friends.

After wandering across the country and back, I found this treasure all literally within walking distance of where I grew up, and where I now again live: right there under my stove.

---

2 *The Language of Truth: The Torah Commentary of the Sefat Emet: Rabbi Yehudah Leib Alter of Ger*, trans. and interpr. Arthur Green (Philadelphia: JPS, 1998), 402.

CHAPTER 7

Across Five Pesaḥs

Shayna Rhodes

'Erev Pesaḥ 5763 (2003 CE): cleaning, cooking, preparing for the seder. *Kol ḥamira ve-ḥami'a de-ika ve-rshuti,* all the *ḥameẓ* in my possession, may it be considered as the dust of the earth. My brother and his wife arrive from Silver Spring bearing a concordance, a present, for the new rabbinical student. "We know you'll get in." Waiting for the letter to arrive, I am not as confident. My mind goes back several months to a walk to shul with my friend Judi. "They are opening up a rabbinical school at Hebrew College," she said. "I'm applying. You should too." I am astounded at the thought. You can be a wife and mother in Newton, Massachusetts, and go to rabbinical school at the same time? How is that possible? Thoughts of family members in black hats, black suits, white shirts, rows upon rows of *shtenders* with *gemaras* flash through my mind. This would have to be a rabbinical school of a different color, a rabbinical school in color, definitely not black and white. It seemed like a dream.

Twenty years prior I had met with the Bostoner Rebbe. He told me the story of a woman who had many children and then went on to become the head nurse at a hospital. Had she achieved her professional goals first, she never would have had the same family. What a blessing. I understood his message. There is a time for everything. With an undergraduate degree in European history and a master's in computer science, I spent most of my time home with my five children, and I loved it. It seemed ironic to me that the feminist college that I had attended valued everything a woman could do except what I was choosing to do, raise a family. Even my Bais Yaakov teachers and friends sent me the message. "We expected more of you." Again, ironic. I felt it was holy work I was doing. But now that most of the kids were grown and leaving home, it was time to go from *qodesh* to *qodesh.* I had always known that something that suited me would come my way, something exciting, limitless, something that was meant for me to do.

It took a little work convincing myself that I deserved this opportunity. Shouldn't I go back to computer science, earn a nice living? Did I deserve five years of study? In the world I came from women didn't really "study." They didn't deserve five years of expenses. They didn't deserve much of anything except pleasing and taking care of others. But the light of rabbinical school shone too brightly. "Yes, I deserve it." To some this might seem like a given. To me, it was a revelation.

Application: recommendation needed from three rabbis. Three rabbis?! I knew dozens of rabbis, most of whom were related to me, but would they write me a recommendation to "rabbinical school"? I didn't think so. What to do? Did I know *any* rabbis who would write me a recommendation? I did not know Conservative or Reform rabbis. Would three Orthodox rabbis write a recommendation for a woman to attend rabbinical school? Perhaps the head of "New Jew" (that is, Boston's New Jewish High School)? That seemed fitting. One. A lovely, retired, older gentleman that I knew in Newton—that would be two. For the third I went to the rabbi of an Orthodox synagogue I had attended. He would not use the form from Hebrew College. He would not consider it a recommendation to rabbinical school. He would write a letter, put it in an envelope, and seal it. What I did with it was up to me. Three. That was the most difficult part of the application process.

The interview: nine on one. A little daunting. I had never experienced that before. I asked a friend, who was a very successful businessperson, how to handle that. "Stay calm," he said. "When someone asks you a question, begin your answer by looking at him or her. Then look, in turn, at everyone else in the room. Finish your answer by looking at the person who first asked the question." "Good advice," I thought. "I can do that." The first question: "How would you feel about learning Torah with Reform Jews?" I didn't see a problem there. I was ready to learn with anyone. Second question: "How would you feel about learning Torah with Reform Jews?" When they asked me the same question in various words for the fifth time, I didn't know what to say or whom to look at. "Is there something wrong with Reform Jews?" I finally asked. "If so, please just tell me, and we can discuss it."

The interview went from there to questions of theology. I was not used to discussing theology. G-d was everywhere. In my head I talked to G-d often, at times during *davening*, at times not. What was there to discuss? My answers were no longer coherent. "Oh no!" I thought. "I am blowing this." The following day I went to my Tanakh class. The teacher was a wonderful scholar and friend who happened to have been one of the nine at my interview. "I want to tell you," she said, "how impressed we were with your interview, yesterday." "Were you at the same interview I was at?" I asked. "Stop worrying," she said. Indeed, I should have stopped worrying but I could not ... until the letter finally arrived in the mail, *'erev Pesaḥ* 5763.

Kol ḥamira ve-ḥami'a de-ika ve-rshuti, all the *ḥameẓ* in my possession, may it be considered as the dust of the earth. Help me let go of anything that will be an obstacle, that will get in the way of positive learning. I realize that in this stage I am about to encounter, many things will be approached in new and different ways than I'm used to. What exactly they will be, I do not know.

Bereshit

The beginning of—the beginning of—Rashi suggests that, perhaps, there is a word missing from that first verse in the Torah. We have to read it in. In the beginning of ... What *was* I beginning?

> אָכֵן יֵשׁ ה' בַּמָּקוֹם הַזֶּה וְאָנֹכִי לֹא יָדָעְתִּי
> G-d is in this place and I didn't know. (Gen. 28:16)

I walk into the *beit midrash* and immediately, I am at home. I am at home in a place I have never been before. I know instantly that this is where I belong, and that I never want to leave. My classmates value the preciousness of this place, but they know they will be moving on. I will not be moving on. I am staying. Whatever it takes. מוֹדֶה אֲנִי לְפָנֶיךָ ה׳ אֱלֹהַי שֶׁשַּׂמְתָּ חֶלְקִי מִיּוֹשְׁבֵי בֵּית הַמִּדְרָשׁ. "I give thanks before You, Lord my God, that You have placed my lot among those who sit in the *beit midrash*" (B. Berakhot 28b). I am the first woman to study *gemara* in a family of scholars that traces back over four centuries—the first, but, G-d willing, not the last.

> מַה נּוֹרָא הַמָּקוֹם הַזֶּה
> How awesome is this place! (Gen. 28:17)

> וַיֹּאמֶר ה' אֶל אַבְרָם לֶךְ לְךָ מֵאַרְצְךָ וּמִמּוֹלַדְתְּךָ וּמִבֵּית אָבִיךָ אֶל־הָאָרֶץ אֲשֶׁר
> אַרְאֶךָּ: רַבִּי יִצְחָק פָּתַח: שִׁמְעִי בַת וּרְאִי וְהַטִּי אָזְנֵךְ וְשִׁכְחִי עַמֵּךְ וּבֵית אָבִיךְ

G-d said to Abram, "Go forth from your land and from your birthplace and from your father's house to the land that I will show you" (Gen. 12:1). Rabbi Yiẓḥaq opened: "Listen, daughter, look, and incline your ear, and forget your people and your father's house" (Ps. 45:11). (*Bereshit Rabbah* 39:1)

That first year was one of leaving and looking back, of packing and unpacking. It was filled with both light and *tohu va-vohu*, confusion. What to leave behind? What to take with me? Rashi states that G-d did not tell Abram exactly where he was going to make the destination more precious in his eyes. Perhaps it is impossible to tell someone exactly where their promised land is or what it will look like.

Learning Tanakh with Judith Kates was a gift. She took me by the hand and brought me into a new world of understanding. "Listen, daughter, leave behind a world where Tanakh is studied with a closed mind, where it is populated by perfect people, where only certain questions are permitted. Look, and you will find commentary everywhere." What can one learn about the binding of Isaac from a painting by Caravaggio? What can one learn about Adam and Eve from modern feminist scholarship? How do we read between the lines to hear the voices of women in Tanakh? What was Lot's wife's name before she looked back and became a pillar of salt? Who was Rebecca running to after receiving gifts from the stranger? What was her mother's name? Who was that woman who asked for her daughter to stay just a while longer before leaving home forever? What did Rebecca take and what did she leave behind? לכי לך: "Go to yourself. Go for yourself." It was not just Abram who left his father's house to go to a strange land. There are many of us.

Talmud was a world unto itself. It was a revelation, an ocean of text that I could swim in forever. I had grown up surrounded by the lilt of the give and take and yet had not been allowed to study, something akin to watching the dancing on *Simḥas Torah* from behind a fence. At last I was going to be a part of it, to have a seat at the table. It is hard to describe how Talmud spoke to me. Working with the letters on the *daf*, seeing the words that were there and the words that were not there, pointing, punctuating, translating—it was all a joy to me. Jonah Steinberg taught me the mechanics of making sense of the text. Ebn Leader taught me to see beyond the words, to look for the fault lines and uncover what the rabbis were really arguing about.

א"ר אין אדם לומד תורה אלא ממקום שלבו חפץ שנאמר (תהלים א, ב) כי אם בתורת ה' חפצו
Rabbi Yehuda ha-Nasi says: "A person can learn Torah only from a place that his heart desires, as it is stated: But his delight is in the Torah of G-d" (Ps. 1:2). (B. Avodah Zarah 19a)

You have to learn what you love. Art Green once asked me why I love Talmud so much. I didn't have the words.

Shemot

Names. My names have always been Janet and Shayna. From kindergarten through twelfth grade at Bais Yaakov, an ultra-orthodox day school, I was Shayna all morning during religious studies and Janet all afternoon during secular studies. Now that I was going to become a rabbi, which name should come to the foreground and which to the background? Rabbi Janet did not sound right. Rabbi Shayna? That was better, but would it ever ring true? Authenticity in new approaches, new ideas, new concepts—how was it to be found? As a woman rabbi, I myself was an innovation. Would I ever really feel authentic? My mind accepted it ... theoretically ... almost immediately. My heart and soul took longer.

The question of authenticity has no easy solution. A few days ago, my daughter, Yael, asked me to create a ritual that would welcome a baby girl into the Jewish community in a way that would be as meaningful as a bris. She and her wife, Anna, had noticed that somehow the energy, the experience of welcoming baby girls, did not have the same power as that of welcoming baby boys. Of all the *shalom bat* ceremonies they had been to, none moved those present in the way that *brit milah*, a ceremony thousands of years old, did. Perhaps that elusive authenticity is the price one pays for pioneering new ground. And when one starts moving away from tradition, for even the most compelling reasons, where does one stop? How does one blend tradition and innovation?

Can, for example, a woman perform a circumcision? The first time I saw a *mohelet*, that question popped, unbidden, to my mind. Ẓipporah, of course, performed a circumcision. Or did she? We read in the book of Shemot that as Ẓipporah and Moshe made their way to Egypt, Moshe is suddenly attacked by G-d. Ẓipporah takes a flint, cuts off her son's foreskin, and touches his legs with it, saying, "You are truly a bridegroom of blood to me!" The Gemara states:

> And is there anyone who says that a woman may not perform circumcision? But is it not written: "Then Ẓipporah took a flint and cut off the foreskin of her son" (Ex. 4:25)? This verse explicitly states that a circumcision was performed by a woman! One should read into the verse: And she caused to be taken, that is, she did not take a flint herself. But is it not written: "And she cut off"? Read into the verse: And she caused to be cut off, as she told another person to take a flint and cut off her son's foreskin, and he did so. (B. Avodah Zarah 27a)

The scene in Exodus is shrouded in mystery. What is happening? Why is G-d attacking Moshe? How does Ẓipporah know what to do? Whose legs does she touch and what do her mysterious words mean? There are so many unknowns. What is absolutely clear is that Ẓipporah is doing the circumcising. Despite this, in a tradition that frequently disempowers women, the flint is taken from Ẓipporah's hand and put into the hand of a heretofore unmentioned, unknown, male person.

I watched the *mohelet,* a practicing surgeon, pick up the blade and without hesitation perform a flawless circumcision. "May I take photographs," someone had asked "or will that distract you?" "When I am holding a knife," she answered quite calmly, "nothing distracts me." Upon completion of her task, she picked up the baby and showed the beautiful boy to everyone in the room. "Yes," my mind answered, "a woman may perform a circumcision."

Learning with my *ḥevruta* Judi Ehrlich continued to be a joy. We would pack our backpacks and lunches, and she would walk past my house in the morning and pick me up. "How are you today?" she would ask. "So good!" I would answer as we climbed the hill to Hebrew College. There was no question these were magical years. Learning Heschel with Art Green, Rav Kook with Ebn Leader, and Aramaic with Harvey Bock were all incredible gifts for which I will never be able to fully express my appreciation.

Vayikra

Nehemia Polen is the one person who has shown me the unique beauty in the third book of the Torah, the peak, as he sees it. And the Torah has middled. It is not a *sefer* I feel fully able to teach because it does not speak to me in the way it speaks to him. Nevertheless, I have come to appreciate it more and more over the years.

וַיִּקְרָא אֶל־מֹשֶׁה: "G-d called to Moshe" (Lev. 1:1): one of the few places in the Torah with that wording, instead of the usual וידבר ה' אל משה לאמור, "G-d spoke to Moshe, saying… ." ויקרא—a calling. In the third year of rabbinical school I began working in a temple. The congregants called me rabbi, despite the fact that I was not yet a rabbi and did not feel like a rabbi. They wanted/needed me to be a rabbi. As a rabbi, what was my role in the community? How would I personally function? What could I bring to a community that would be the most helpful, do the most good? I watched as the rabbi in the congregation worked with his congregants. He was so comfortable with them, either up there on the *bima,* or greeting each one by name with a smile and a handshake after services. One could see him come alive as he spoke to them. It was clear—he was born to do this work.

My love was study. The *beit midrash* was my home and my life as a rabbi would have to be in the books. How could I convey the joy that I felt to others? How could I help others find their place in a tradition that might not yet feel like home? How could I help them claim their rightful legacy? I have worked with students from elementary school, through rabbinical school through assisted living for the elderly. My calling, as I began to see it, was to help all of them find their voice in Jewish text, to pull up a chair, have a seat at the table and speak up. Talmud, I always tell my students, is not a spectator sport.

Bemidbar

In the desert—or as Avivah Zornberg points out in the classic midrash, אין מדבר אלא דיבור, "wilderness is nothing but speech" (*Bemidbar Rabbah* 2:4). That fourth year I journeyed to Israel with my youngest daughter, Yael. For seven months we lived together in a tiny apartment not far from Emek Refaim. Every Thursday my *ḥevruta*, Judi, and I would meet at Pardes. We spent the morning and most of the afternoon studying the words of Tanakh, midrash, and commentary that Avivah had assigned. Then as the sun began to drop in the sky we would listen as she spun an intricate gossamer web that brought the words of the wilderness into our very classroom. כֵּן בְּנוֹת צְלָפְחָד דֹּבְרֹת (Num. 27:7): "Yes, right are the words of the daughters of Ẓelafḥad" as they make their plea for a share in their father's name. They speak *ken*, justly. Rashi describes their words as יאות and יפות, fitting and beautiful. As Avivah told us of the beauty of their words, I could not help but think that she was unknowingly describing her own.

Midrash *Tanḥuma* (*Pinḥas* 9) tells us that the eyes of the daughters of Ẓelafḥad saw what Moshe's eyes did not. Avivah Zornberg, Judith Kates, Sharon Cohen-Anisfeld, Tamar Biale, and Yochi Brandes are just a few of the modern scholars who empower us to talk of women in Tanakh who see what the men do not. Tamar saw what Judah did not. Rebecca saw what Isaac did not. Sarah saw what Abraham did not. Miriam, Huldah, Esther, Beruriah— the list goes on and on in each generation, whether we know their names or not. ויבן ה' את הצלע מלמד שנתן הקב"ה בינה יתירה באשה יותר מבאיש (B. Niddah 45b). "'And G-d built [from the root *b.n.y.*] the rib [into the woman]' (Gen. 2:22). This teaches that the Holy Blessed One granted women greater understanding [בינה, from a similar root, *b.y.n.*] than that of men."

In Israel that year I learned the true meaning of pluralism. One day a week I went to HUC, the Reform Rabbinical School, to study with Chana Safrai, a gifted Mishnah scholar, may she rest in peace. Several days were spent with Reb Shmuel Lewis of the Conservative Yeshiva. One evening a week was spent at the Shalom Hartman Institute. One day a week I went to Givat Ram to study with Reb Dovid Weiss Halivni, where I was the only woman in a group of formidable scholars, each with his own specialty. And one day a week—with Avivah Zornberg at Pardes. It was all a gift for which I am incredibly grateful.

Devarim

Words. "These are the words" with which I will leave you. The power of words in our tradition is limitless. ברוך שאמר והיה העולם. "Blessed is the One who spoke, and the world was."

Words of Prayer

Of all the challenges I encountered in rabbinical school, *tefillah* was the most difficult and the most rewarding. This was true from the very beginning. That first day, I walked into *tefillah*, saw several people in *tallis* and *tefillin* and turned around. I was almost at the door when I realized that I had not accidentally walked into the men's section. This was where I belonged. I smiled and turned back into the room. At the time, I did not own a *tallis* or *tefillin*. The former seemed like a beautiful concept—to wrap oneself in a garment that would take you straight into a place of prayer. What a wonderful idea! The latter took much longer. It was so clearly "for men only." So much in my past had been for men only. I remember a sign for a Talmud class on a store window in Woodridge, NY. "Everyone Welcome," it said, and directly below, "Men Only." The head of the Hebrew school where I interned my third year asked in an offhand manner if I would help the seventh graders learn how to put on *tefillin*. "Sure," I said, quaking inside. *Tefillin* seemed absolutely taboo, absolutely for men only. I went to my teacher, Ebn, and asked him to "show" me how to put on *tefillin*. I was not taking on the mitzvah. I was just learning so I could teach others. My immediate reaction was civil war. "What on earth do you think you are doing?" half of me asked as I put them on. "What took you so long?" my other half asked. The war lasted one day. I spent that day staring at the disappearing strap marks on my right arm. By nightfall, the war was over.

Tefillah was difficult. I was used to the same words said in Hebrew without interruption. At the rabbinical school the range of prayer services was infinite—from a straightforward traditional *tefillah* to sitting in a spiral-nebulae where signals from outer space that have been converted to audible sound fill the room with *nigun*, wordless melody. Contemplative silence instead of a murmuring hum, English instead of Hebrew, repetitive chanting, readings of varying types were all challenging at first. It took years to adjust and to begin to enjoy it, and while I did give *davening* in English a try, I have since given that up completely. The words of *tefillah* in Hebrew take me places that English never will. The most powerful aspect of prayer at Hebrew College is the music that accompanies it. Words put to song, *nigunim*, guitar, drum—I love it all.

Words of Text

That fifth year we studied Ta'anit with Jane Kanarek, an amazing experience. Ta'anit has become my favorite tractate. Its central theme of a life and death connection to G-d through rain is hauntingly beautiful. Yet, it is its subversive qualities that stand much of the rest of Talmud on its head, that speak to me directly. מאן יחידים, it asks. "Who are the individuals" that should fast at first signs of a rupture in the human-Divine relationship? Who are the first responders who rush in to repair the rift? The rabbis, of course, is the immediate answer, but in subsequent chapters it is not as clear. Great sages fail in their attempts to heal the breach, while seemingly undistinguished persons, housewives, *ḥeder* teachers, and businessmen save the day. Ta'anit is an invitation to all to come and have a seat at the table. It is an invitation I do my best to extend to others.

Words of Gratitude

As we come to the end of my words, I must express my thanks to many people. My children, Moshe, David, Tzippy, Chavi, and Yael were my biggest cheerleaders during the application process. They encouraged me every step of the way. Jonathan, my husband, has been a steadfast עזר כנגדי throughout, knowing when to be supportive and encouraging and when to confront. He has put up with so much and come through it all smiling and dancing. After twenty-five years of marriage, I announced on the eve of first year that I would no longer be cooking dinner every night. It was going to become a communal effort. He took it with a smile and a nod. "No problem." Indeed, the only issue that upset him was when

I took our youngest daughter, the only child still at home, and went to Israel to study. Home alone was not something he had ever experienced or desired. He did come to visit us twice, and when I returned home, there were diamonds on my pillow. He had missed me.

To my teachers and colleagues, thank you for all the learning and support, both in the classroom and out. We were the pioneering class, which by definition includes joy and pain. It was an incredible experience, which I would do all over again, now that I know how to study and what to ask.

Words of Torah/Words of *Tefillah*

My goal when starting rabbinical school was to be able to *daven* like a Hasid and learn like a Litvak. Since then, my goals have shifted. As a faculty member here at the rabbinical school, I created the Talmud Torah Tefillah group where those two paradigms actually merge. The distinction is blurred. Learning becomes prayer, and prayer learning. Litvak and Hasid are one. G-d is in the mix.

I have become co-director of the *beit midrash*, working with Allan Lehmann, learning from his incredible breadth of knowledge, his many years in the rabbinate, and his love of Torah and Israel. The *beit midrash* is and always will be my home. מודה אני. I am so grateful. Thank you, G-d, for giving me life, sustaining me, and bringing me to this day (B. Berakhot 54a).

Section II

STUDIES IN JEWISH THOUGHT, HISTORY, AND LITERATURE

CHAPTER 8

The Fate of the First Clothing[1]

Rachel Adelman

> Thus, there is much to support the view that it is clothes that wear us and not we them; we may make them take the mould of arm or breast, but they mould our hearts, our brains, our tongues to their liking.
>
> —Virginia Woolf, *Orlando*[2]

Introduction

Before banishing Adam and Eve from Eden, God first clothes them with tunics of skin [*kotnot 'or*] (Gen. 3:21). This gesture is understood by rabbinic tradition to model the principle of loving-kindness [*gemilut ḥasadim*]; humans should likewise emulate the divine in clothing the poor, visiting the sick, and consoling the mourner (B. Sotah 14a). Yet one midrashic tradition suggests that the original clothing was made from the skin ['*or*] the Serpent had sloughed off when it was condemned to slither on the ground, eat dust of the earth, and bruise the heel of humankind (*Pirqei de-Rabbi Eli'ezer* 20, from here on PRE).

What an odd gift! Is this garment meant to imbue Adam and Eve with the Serpent's primeval power? Or signal the fallen state they are in? The midrash (PRE 24) extends the life of these skins: they were passed from Adam to Noah, and then worn by the mighty hunter, Nimrod. Coveting the clothing, Esau slayed the hunter in order to usurp the tunics of snakeskin, and Jacob donned this cloak as he stood in guile before his blind father to receive the blessing. In this essay, I

1 An earlier version of this paper was written as part of my doctoral dissertation, Rachel Adelman, *The Poetics of Time and Space in the Midrashic Narrative—The Case of Pirkei deRabbi Eliezer* (PhD diss., Hebrew University, Jerusalem, 2008). It was then reworked as "Primeval Coats," TheTorah.com (2015), https://thetorah.com/article/primeval-coats.

2 Virginia Woolf, *Orlando* (Oxford: Blackwell Publishers Ltd., 1998), 108.

venture into unchartered midrashic territory and speculate that this was the same so-called "Amazing Technicolor Dreamcoat"[3] that Jacob bequeathed to Joseph. The garments of skin from the Garden of Eden (called *kotnot 'or*) were disinterred or foraged from the patriarch's attic to become the tunic that the patriarch gifted to his beloved son (also called a *ketonet* in Gen. 37:3). This distinguishes Joseph as the favored one, but also condemns him to become the object of his brothers' violent jealousy, and the source of their undoing. What light does the fate of this garment shed on its dubious origins? How, in turn, does this mythic origin story enhance our understanding of the role of clothing in the Jacob and Joseph saga?

Joseph's Ornamented Tunic

Clothing functions as a central motif in the story of Joseph and his Brothers (Gen. 37–50), both as a marker of distinction and as a prompt for jealous ire and deception.[4] *Parashat Va-Yeshev* opens with Jacob's inauspicious act of favoritism towards the firstborn of his beloved wife Rachel:

> Now Israel loved Joseph best of all his sons, for he was the child of his old age; and he made him an ornamented tunic [*ketonet pasim*].[5] ... And his brothers saw that it was he their father loved more than any of his brothers, and they hated him and could not speak peaceably [*shalom*] to him. (Gen. 37:3–4)[6]

---

3 The name given to the garment in the Tim Rice and Andrew Lloyd Webber 1968 musical by the same name.

4 On the motif of clothing in the Joseph story, see Victor H. Matthews, "The Anthropology of Clothing in the Joseph Narrative," *JSOT* 65 (1995): 25–36; John R. Huddlestun, "Divestiture, Deception, and Demotion: The Garment Motif in Genesis 37–39," *JSOT* 98 (2002): 47–62; Franziska Ede, "The Garment Motif in Gen. 37–39," in *Clothing and Nudity in the Hebrew Bible*, ed. Christoph Berner, Manuel Schäfer, Martin Schott, Sarah Schulz, and Martina Weingärtner (London: T&T Clark, 2019), 389–402; Avigdor Shinan, "Clothes and Garments in the Rabbinic Midrashim on the Joseph Stories" [Heb.], *Dappim: Research in Literature* 17/16 (2007): 74–89.

5 Scholars debate whether the tunic [*ketonet*] of *pasim* was simply adorned, perhaps with stripes [*pasim*] (Radak), or whether it should be understood as a tunic or cloak with long sleeves reaching to the ankle and wrist (Josephus, *Ant.* 2.2.1), since *pas* may refer to the edge or extremity of the hand. The Septuagint renders it as "coat of many colors [*chitona poikilon*]" and the Vulgate follows. See a review of the commentaries in Nahum Sarna, *The JPS Torah Commentary: Genesis* (Philadelphia: JPS, 1989), 237. Thomas Mann, in his opus *Joseph and His Brothers*, suggests that this was a gift given to Rachel, as the bridal veil in the House of Laban; it was a many-colored garment of splendor, richly embroidered with the figures of "stars, doves, trees, gods, angels, human beings, and animals set in the bluish haze of the fabric" (*Young Joseph*, trans. John E. Woods [New York: Knopf, 2005], 390). See the article by Clayton Koelb, "Thomas Mann's 'Coat of Many Colors,'" *The German Quarterly* 49, no. 4 (1976): 472–484.

6 All translations of the primary texts are the author's unless otherwise indicated.

The gift of the tunic provokes hatred [*s.n.'.*] on the part of his brothers. This emotion is exacerbated by the telling of his first dream of grandeur—the eleven sheaves of wheat bowing down to his sheaf—"and they hated him all the more for his dreams and for his words" (v. 8; cf. v. 5). Jacob, who himself had been an object of his brother's fury after stealing the blessing (Gen. 27:41), sets Joseph up for a similar fraternal enmity. Measure for measure, the patriarch, who had donned goatskins and Esau's clothing to deceive his own father, is later deceived by his sons who present him with Joseph's torn cloak, dipped in a goat's blood.

When Joseph sets off to find his brothers, they see him first from afar—the tunic, like a bull's-eye, becomes the focal point of their sight. When he arrives, it is the tunic they first set upon: "They stripped Joseph of his tunic [*kutanto*], the ornamented tunic [*ketonet ha-pasim*] that he was wearing" (Gen. 37:23). The repetition of the object—"***et** Yosef, **et** kutanto, **et** ketonet ha-pasim*"—concatenates cumulatively as their fury explodes. Joseph is wholly identified with the tunic. When they tear at this garment, the brothers become the figurative "wild beast" (v. 20), whom Jacob later (falsely) names as having "surely torn Joseph apart [*tarof toraf Yosef*]" (v. 33).

The identifying marker "ornamented tunic [*ketonet ha-pasim*]" is repeated here (as it was first introduced in 37:3), to emphasize how it once granted Joseph distinction and to anticipate the contrasting shame to which he will be reduced. The only other time this collocation appears in Tanakh is in the story of Tamar, the daughter of King David, who is distinguished as a princess because she wears an "ornamented tunic [*ketonet pasim*]" (2 Sam. 13:18).[7] Tamar tears her beautiful cloak in despair after her half-brother, Amnon, rapes her and has her thrown out of his chamber despite her pleas. By contrast, Joseph's coat is torn off him at the scene of the pit (Gen. 37:23), and then stained with goat's blood (v. 31). Yet like Tamar, Joseph is violated by his half-brothers.[8] Royalty and shame; glory and perdition—the dual destiny these privileged children meet; the garment becomes emblematic of both extremes!

In the end, the brothers do not kill Joseph but "cast him into the pit [*ha-borah*]; The pit [*ha-bor*] was empty; there was no water in it" (Gen. 37:24). Initially, the plan is to abandon him in the pit—a cistern used to store water, too deep to climb

---

7 "She was wearing an ornamented tunic, for maiden princesses were customarily dressed in such garments" (2 Sam. 13:18, NJPS). The translations vary as for Joseph's tunic (see footnote 5): "variegated robe/reaching to wrist" [χιτὼν καρπωτὸς] (LXX; note this differs from Gen. 37:3); "a garment of divers colours" (KJV); "long robe with sleeves" (RSV, NRSV); "striped robe [כיתונתא פסי]" (Tg. Onq.).

8 See the discussion in Adrien Janis Bledstein, "Tamar and the 'Coat of Many Colors,'" in *Samuel and Kings: A Feminist Companion to the Bible*, ed. Athalya Brenner (Sheffield: Sheffield Academic Press, 2000), 65–83.

out of—and leave him there to die of thirst. The narrative informs us, *sotto voce,* that Reuben intends to circle back to retrieve him (Gen. 37:22, 29–30). Instead, they sell him into slavery for twenty pieces of silver at Judah's suggestion.[9] This pit foreshadows the second pit [*bor*] into which Joseph is cast,[10] the dungeon where the king's prisoners were confined, as Joseph tells the cupbearer: "For indeed, I was stolen from the land of the Hebrews; nor have I done anything here that they should have put me in the pit/dungeon [*ba-bor*]" (Gen. 40:15). In the house of Potiphar, Joseph had again been stripped of his clothing, left behind in the lascivious grasp of his master's wife when he tried to escape her sexual advances. Potiphar's wife, using the garment as evidence, vindictively framed the Hebrew slave for attempted rape, Joseph betrayed again by an item of clothing (called *begged* here, a play on the word betrayal, *biggud,* 39:12–18). While the garment imbues Joseph with status, when torn from him it leaves him bare and vulnerable.

Further, clothing bestows honor and privilege upon the beloved son, yet when the garment is stripped from him, it becomes a prop for deception. As in the garment left in Mrs. Potiphar's hands, the torn and blood-stained tunic acts as a false alibi. It facilitates a *mis*-recognition, a cover story for Joseph's sale into slavery:

> Then they took Joseph's tunic, slaughtered a kid, and dipped the tunic in the blood. They had the ornamented tunic taken to their father, and they said, "We found this. Please recognize it [*haker na*]; is it your son's tunic or not?" He recognized it [*va-yakirah*], and said, "My son's tunic! A wild beast devoured him! Joseph is surely torn, torn apart!" (Gen. 37:32–33)

The blood-soaked tunic accounts for Joseph's absence and conjectured death, yet diverts the grieving father away from the truth about his son's fate—sold ignominiously as a slave. It is Jacob who comes to this false conclusion, using the very

---

9 Medieval exegetes (such as Rashbam) and modern scholars note the ambiguity in Gen. 37:28 (cf. vv. 36 and 39:1): Was it the Ishmaelite traders that drew him out of the pit and sold Joseph to the Midianites or the brothers? See Edward L. Greenstein, "An Equivocal Reading of the Sale of Joseph," in *Literary Interpretations of Biblical Narratives, vol. 2,* ed. Kenneth R. R. Gros Louis, James S. Ackerman, and Thayer Warshaw (Nashville: Abingdon, 1982), 114–125, 306–310.

10 This pit also prefigures Egypt, the land emblematic of the burial of the dead, that "undiscover'd country, from whose bourn no traveler returns" (William Shakespeare, *Hamlet,* act 3, sc. 1, lines 1772–1773). The "abode of the dead" is referred to in Akkadian Ancient Near-Eastern Sources as "the land of no return" (māt la târi), see Theodore J. Lewis, "The Abode of the Dead," in *The Anchor Bible Dictionary,* vol. 2, ed. D. N. Freedman (New York: Doubleday, 1992), 102.

words of the brothers' original plan, "and we will say a wild beast has devoured him" (v. 20). The motif of clothing underscores the workings of poetic justice. Jacob too had used Esau's coveted garments [*bigdei 'Esav ... ha-ḥamudot*] (Gen. 27:15) and goatskins (v. 16) to deceive his blind father in stealing the patriarch's blessing and "he [Isaac] did not recognize him [*lo hikiro,* i.e., Jacob]" (v. 23). Where clothing and slaughtered goats initially led to *mis*-recognition [*lo hikiro*], here Jacob recognizes the cloak soaked in goat's blood [*va-yakirah*] but falls for a cover story.

Just as Iago uses Desdemona's handkerchief, in Shakespeare's *Othello,* to rouse the Moor's jealousy, the "green-eyed monster which doth mock the meat it feeds on" (act 3, sc. 3), which then instigates Othello's tragic murder of his wife, the Joseph story deploys the motif of clothing to highlight *mis*-recognition. Two acts of misconstrual hinge on the display of a garment—the blood-stained tunic presented to Jacob and Joseph's clothing left behind in Potiphar's house. One covers for the brothers' sale of Joseph into slavery; the other bolsters the false allegation of attempted rape. In this way, clothing represents the bestowal of honor that is later betrayed, leading to the hero's shame and near ruin.

The First Clothing

The story of the Garden of Eden, with its emphasis on nakedness and covering up, similarly oscillates between the two poles of honor and shame. The narrative opens with a description of Adam and Eve as naked (*'arumim*), and in the very next verse, the same word *'arum*—really a homonym—is used to describe the Serpent's cunning:[11]

> And they were both naked [*'arumim*], the man and his wife, but they were not ashamed (Gen. 2:25). The Serpent was more cunning [*'arum*] than all the beasts of the field. . . . (Gen. 3:1)

---

11 These are essentially homonyms, the first *'erom* (sg.) / *'arumim* (pl.) [ערום] is related to the root *'.r.h.* [ע.ר.ה.], "to be naked or bare" (BDB, p. 788, entries 6168 and 6172). The second term *'arum* [ערום], meaning "cunning," is derived from the root *'.r.m.* [ע.ר.מ.], "to be shrewd or crafty" (BDB, p. 791, entries 6191 and 6175). Robert Alter (*Genesis* [New York: Norton, 1996], 11) and Harold Bloom / David Rosenberg make a note of the pun. Rosenberg renders *'arom* "smooth [naked]" and *'arum* as "smooth-tongued [the snake's cunning]" (*The Book of J* [New York: Grove Weidenfeld, 1990], 62–63).

Even before Adam and Eve's eyes were "opened" with the "knowledge of good and evil," the primordial Serpent seems to have knowledge—or cunning—and expresses it through the manipulation of language, distorting God's command: "Didn't God say you shall not eat of *all* the trees of the garden?" (Gen. 3:1).[12]

Where does the Serpent's nakedness/cunning come from? The *Ḥizkuni* (commentary of thirteenth-century French exegete R. Ḥezekiah ben Manoaḥ) suggests that the Snake had already eaten of the tree, and thus *knew* that he was naked, had gained "cunning/nakedness" and seduced Eve into eating of the fruit for want of company.[13] Knowing good and evil is accompanied by the consciousness of one's nakedness, the awareness of being boundaried creatures with skin with an inner and outer self. After eating of the tree, Adam and Eve express their bad conscience by hiding and sewing loincloths from fig leaves (v. 7). But the Snake is the first being to be aware of its own nudity, the first to "cover up" through the manipulation of language, and the first to be physically stripped of its outer layer.

As a consequence of the Serpent's deception of Eve through the manipulation of language, it is stripped of its limbs and never speaks again.[14] Similarly, in the Epic of Gilgamesh (Sumer, *circa* eighteenth century BCE), when a snake snatches away the plant that promises immortality before the hero can grasp it, the snake sloughs off its skin.[15] This molting intimates that the snake can now renew its youth (having ingested the elixir of life). In contrast to the Ancient Near Eastern text, the midrashic tradition depicts the stripping of the Serpent as an extension of the divine imprecation, rather than a manifestation of immortality usurped. According to PRE 14, God descends and subjects Adam, Eve, and the Serpent each to nine curses and death. The Serpent, once

---

12 For an elaborate discussion of this scene, see my essay "Re-creating Eve," *Le'ela* 52 (2001): 19–24, reprinted in *Traditions and Celebrations for the Bat Mitzvah*, ed. Ora Wiskind-Elper (Jerusalem: Urim, 2002), 161–172.

13 חזקוני אל בראשית ג:א "והנחש היה ערום"—צריך לומר שע"י מקרה קודם לכן אכל מעץ הדעת שהרי האזהרה לא היתה רק לאדם.

14 In *Bereshit Rabbah* 20:2, the Serpent is called the "Master of Answers [*ba'al teshuvot*]," and is never allowed to respond to God's questions as Adam and Eve do (Gen. 3:11–13). In *Bereshit Rabbah* 20:5 (on Gen. 3:14), the ministering angels descend and lop off the Serpent's hands and legs, releasing a voice that travels from one end of the earth to the other.

15 *Gilgamesh* XI:258–300; *ANET* 96–97. This might be considered a just-so-story for "why the snake sheds its skin" and regains its youth. See Ronald A. Veenker, "Gilgamesh and the Magic Plant," *The Biblical Archaeologist* 44, no. 4 (1981): 199–205. He cites the parallel Greek legend, "The Resurrection of Glaucos" (recounted in J. G. Frazer, *Apollodorus* [Cambridge: Harvard University Press, 1921], vol. 1, 301–313).

the most cunning of all the beasts of the field (Gen. 3:1), becomes the most cursed (v. 14).

> *Pirqei de-Rabbi Eli'ezer* 14 (1st ed.)[16]
> He [God] cut off the legs of the Serpent and made it the most cursed of all the wild animals and beasts. And He cursed it that it should slough off its skin, once every seven years, in great pain, and cursed it that it should crawl on its belly upon the earth, and its food should turn to dust, within its innards, the venom of vipers and death in its mouth. And He placed enmity between it and the woman, that they should crush its head. And after all these [curses]—death.

Condemned to crawl on its belly as the agent who brought death to the world, the Serpent is now forced to swallow its own medicine (so to speak), eating the dust to which humans have been reduced: "for dust you are and to dust shall you return" (Gen. 3:19).[17] "The venom of vipers and death in its mouth" serve as just deserts for its poisonous use of speech. All snakes will live out the condemnation of the Primordial Serpent, molting every seven years with great pain in a reenactment of the lopping off of its limbs. Further, enmity (instead of seduction) would be the fate of the relationship between the woman and the Snake. Yet the sloughed-off snakeskin is not left to disintegrate in the Garden.

Following their consciousness of nakedness and shame, the story concludes with God clothing the first humans: "The LORD God made tunics of skins [*kotnot 'or*] for Adam and his woman and he clothed them" (Gen. 3:21). Presumably, these skins replace the loincloth of fig leaves, which Adam and Eve had made for themselves (v. 7). But from where did God get these skins?[18] There had, as yet, been no death. According to a later chapter in *Pirqei de-Rabbi Eli'ezer* (PRE 20), concerned with the banishment of Adam and Eve

---

16 See the parallel version of this midrash in *Avot de-Rabbi Natan* (version B) 42. This edition (Constantinople, 1514) has been checked against Dagmar Börner-Klein, *Pirke de-Rabbi Elieser: Nach der Edition Venedig 1544, unter Berücksichtigung der Edition Warschau 1852* (Berlin: Walter de Gruyter, 2004), 145.

17 See B. Bekhorot 8a, *Bereshit Rabbah* 20:5, T. Sotah 4:17, 18.

18 Ḥizkuni on Gen. 3:21 suggests that the skins may have come from the Leviathan, one of the sea monsters, [*taninim*] (of Gen. 1:21), who God feared would procreate exceedingly and destroy the world (cf. B. Bava Batra 75a). Louis Ginzberg drew attention to this "unknown midrash" in *Legends of the Jews* (Philadelphia: JPS, 1938), vol. 5, 103, n. 93.

from the Garden, God sewed the clothes from the skin that the Serpent had sloughed off:[19]

> *Pirqei de-Rabbi Eli'ezer* 20 (1st ed.)[20]
> Rabbi Eli'ezer says: From the skin that the Serpent sloughed off The Holy One, blessed be He, made garments of glory (or honor, *kavod*)[21] for Adam and his helpmate, as it says, "The LORD God made tunics of skins [*kotnot 'or*] for Adam and his woman and he clothed them" (Gen. 3:21).

The skins replace the rough fig leaves that Adam and Eve had used to cover their shame when they became conscious of their nakedness. Yet these skins, in covering their shame and lending them dignity—as garments of glory or honor—also symbolize the post-lapsarian sense of *living-unto-death*, the awareness of mortality and the consciousness of the dissonance between the inner and outer being.

Why are *these* trappings used to clothe the newly banished man and his wife? Avivah Zornberg comments: "The serpent—all deception, representation, plausible language, verbal display is constructed into an attribute of human dignity!"[22] Irony abounds. According to midrashic tradition, Adam and his wife were originally covered with light (*Bereshit Rabbah* 20:2), or a shimmering gown of scales and the Clouds of Glory hovering over them (PRE 14), yet lost this covering upon transgressing.[23] The second set of clothing was granted as a gift

---

19 See also the Targ. Ps.-Jon. on Gen. 3:21.

20 Checked against Börner-Klein, *Pirke de-Rabbi Elieser*, 213. For a semi-critical version of the full chapter PRE 20, along with an English translation, see Appendix A of chapter 4, of my doctoral dissertation, "The Poetics of Time and Space," 294–298.

21 Alternative manuscripts read "tunics of skin [*kotnot 'or*]" (Enelow 866); Venice, 1544 (2nd ed.) renders it in the singular: *ketonet* [כתונת]. These "garments of glory [*kotnot kavod*]" replace the original garments of Primordial man, described as "skins of scales [or fingernails] and the cloud of glory [עור של צפורן וענן כבוד]" (PRE 14).

22 Avivah Zornberg, *The Particulars of Rapture* (New York: Random House Inc., 2001), 374.

23 According to PRE 14, Adam and Eve were originally covered with scales or fingernails [*tziporen*] and the Cloud of Glory hovered over them. In one opinion in *Bereshit Rabbah* 20:12, Adam and Eve were originally clothed with light, not skins (*or*, with an *aleph*, not *'or* with an *'ayin*), based on an alternative "Torah" of Rabbi Meir. According to this reading, the verse in Gen. 3:21 should be relocated to the end of chapter 2 when Adam and Eve's nakedness is first introduced. See Gary Anderson, "The Garments of Skin in Apocryphal Narrative and Biblical Commentary," in *Studies in Ancient Midrash*, ed. James Kugel (Cambridge, MA: Harvard University Press, 2001), 101–143; Stephen N. Lambden, "From Fig Leaves to Fingernails: Some Notes on the Garments of Adam and Eve in the Hebrew Bible and Select Early Post-Biblical Jewish Writings," in *A Walk in the Garden: Biblical, Iconographical and Literary Images of Eden*, ed. P. Morris and D. Sawyer (Sheffield: JSOT Press, 1992), 74–90; and Adelman, "Poetics of Time and Place," 124–138.

from God to cover their shame. Clothing makes us, yet testifies to our undoing. It lends us dignity, yet symbolizes the impossibility of total integration between our internal and external selves. Banished from the Garden of Eden, the unaccommodated human is but a "bare forked animal,"[24] self-conscious, sighing in the gap between ideal self and mortal skin. It is this gap that clothing covers over, in leather, velvet, silk or other trim.

The Fate of the First Clothing: From Adam to Jacob

A later passage in *Pirqei de-Rabbi Eli'ezer* (PRE 24) goes on to link this snakeskin tunic to the Jacob drama, via Nimrod, the founder of the Ancient Babylonian Empire, called "a mighty hunter [*gibor ẓayid*] before the Lord" (Gen. 10:8–10):

> *Pirqei de-Rabbi Eli'ezer* 24 (1st ed.)[25]
> ... Rabbi Yehuda said: The garment, which the Holy One, blessed be He, made for Adam and his wife, was with Noah in the ark, and when they went forth from the ark, Ham, the son of Noah, brought it forth with him, and gave it as an inheritance to Nimrod. When he put it on, all beasts, animals, and birds came and prostrated themselves before him. The sons of men thought that this (was due) to the power of his might; therefore they made him king over themselves, as it is said: "... therefore it is said, 'Like Nimrod a mighty hunter before the Lord'" (Gen. 10:9).

The "cloaks of skin [*kotnot 'or*]," are now presented in the singular, "*kutonet*," as they fall into the hands of Nimrod, granting him a mesmerizing power over the animals. Their prostration before him resonates with the animals' original reaction to Adam, when he was first created:

> *Pirqei de-Rabbi Eli'ezer* 11 (1st ed)[26]
> He stood on his legs and was in appearance like that of God. When the creatures saw him, they became afraid of him, thinking that he was their creator, and they came to prostrate themselves before him.

---

24 William Shakespeare, *King Lear*, act 3, sc. 4, lines 113–115.
25 Checked against Börner-Klein, *Pirke de-Rabbi Elieser*, 261.
26 Checked against Börner-Klein, *Pirke de-Rabbi Elieser*, 113–114.

Likewise, the Serpent's skin, when worn by Nimrod, grants the illusion of omnipotence. In response to the animal's reaction, the humans make him king—the second worldwide emperor (following Adam), who would rule from one end of the Earth to the other (PRE 11). Here the snakeskin, when worn by mortal man, is not related to the wily use of language; rather it bestows regal stature based on the illusion of absolute power.

The midrash then collapses time and space, anachronistically leaping generations forward from the Valley of Shinar to the Land of Canaan. Here, the snakeskin cloak becomes Esau's precious clothing (Gen. 27:15), the very same clothing that Jacob dons when he stands before his blind father:

> *Pirqei de-Rabbi Eli'ezer* 24 (1st ed.)[27]
> ... Rabbi [Meir][28] said: Esau, the brother of Jacob, saw the coats of Nimrod, and in his heart he coveted [*ḥamad*] them, and he slew him, and took them for himself. How (do we know) that they were desirable in his sight? Because it is said, "And Rebecca took the *coveted* clothing of Esau her elder son [*bigdei 'Esav ... ha-ḥamudot*]" (Gen. 27:15).

The cloak engenders greed or covetousness [*ḥamdanut*] in the eyes of the beholder—a defiance of the last of the so-called Ten Commandments: "Thou shalt not covet [*lo taḥmod*] (Exod. 20:14; Deut. 5:17). In this case, Esau covets [*ḥamad*] the clothing and murders Nimrod in order to possess it, hence the term "the best [lit. coveted] clothes of her older son Esau [*bigdei 'Esav ... haḥamudot*]" (Gen. 27:15).

For Esau, covetousness arouses the impulse to murder. When worn by the Snake, originally, it had inspired lust for Adam's wife.[29] Absorbing that desire, Eve then saw that the tree "was delectable to the eyes and that the tree was *coveted* [*neḥmad*] to make one wise" (Gen. 3:6). That is, the cloaks induce desire, even lust, for that which does not rightfully belong to oneself—women, trees, power, the tunics themselves, even blessings.

---

27 Checked against Börner-Klein, *Pirke de-Rabbi Elieser*, 267.

28 Correction based on the 2nd ed. (Venice, 1544).

29 In the case of the Serpent, the covetousness resulted in the seduction of Eve, not murder. See *Bereshit Rabbah* 18:6. According to PRE 14, Cain is conceived of the sexual union between Eve and the Serpent. See the discussion in Rachel Adelman, *The Return of the Repressed: Pirqe de-Rabbi Eliezer and the Pseudepigrapha* (Leiden: Brill, 2009), 98–103.

Both Nimrod and Esau are great hunters (Gen. 10:9 and 25:27). Both gain their predator status from the cloak of the original hunter, the Primordial Serpent, who had entrapped Eve with the fruit of the Tree.

> *Pirqei de-Rabbi Eli'ezer* 24 (1st ed.)[30]
> When he [=Jacob] put them on he also became a mighty hero, as it is said, "And Esau was a cunning hunter" (Gen. 25:27). And when Jacob left[31] the presence of Isaac, his father, he said: "Esau, the wicked one, is not worthy to wear these coats." What did he do? He dug in the earth and hid them there as it is said, "The rope for him lies hidden in the ground" (Job 18:10).

When Jacob dresses up in the cloak at his mother's behest, he retroactively becomes aware of its power and buries it, but not before taking advantage of the metamorphosis—the cold-blooded, reptilian transformation the cloak engenders.

Like the snake, Jacob covets and lays claim to what is not rightfully his in stealing the blessing. However, Jacob differs from Nimrod, Esau, and even from the original Serpent, in that he recognizes the danger that the snakeskin embodies, and hides it: "The rope for him lies hidden in the ground ..." (Job 8:10), a noose with which man would hang himself. The clothing, like the precious ring in Tolkien's trilogy, is *too* powerful for any good humans may make of it. So, according to PRE, Jacob never bequeaths these treacherous garments to his son, though one might imagine an alternative ending to the story, where the patriarch might unearth the buried garments and bestows them upon Joseph. The cycle of treachery, of covetousness and jealousy aroused yet again.

The Clothing of the High Priest

In yet another midrashic tradition, the original clothing granted to Adam upon his banishment from Eden is linked to firstborn status and the honors of the priesthood. In a chain of inheritance similar to the links in PRE 24, the tunics, "the garments of the high priesthood," were passed from Adam to Noah to Shem to Abraham, and then to Isaac, and from Isaac to Esau, from

---

30 Checked against Börner-Klein, *Pirke de-Rabbi Elieser*, 267.

31 Or "come before his father" (according to the 2nd and 3rd printed editions): that is, Jacob realizes the garment's power *as he stands* before Isaac to be blessed.

father to firstborn son, for it was the firstborn who performed the priestly sacrificial duties.[32] In the homiletical Midrash *Tanḥuma* (*Toledot* 12, ed. Buber, circa seventh to ninth century CE),[33] Jacob then takes the clothing from Esau, having purchased the birthright (the status of firstborn) in exchange for a bowl of stew (Gen. 25:29–34).

In contrast to PRE, this midrash conveys a positive attitude towards this cloak, and overtly states that the garments of skin inspired Isaac's blessing, their odor evoking associations with Eden, as the patriarch intones, "Ah, the smell of my son is like the smell of the field the LORD has blessed. May God give you of the dew of Heaven and of the fat of the earth ..." (Gen. 27:27–28).[34]

Transferred into the hands of the High Priest, the clothing of the Priest (also called a *ketonet*)[35] then functions as symbol of atonement [*kaparah*]—an appropriate gift following the so-called Fall of man from his pristine state. Midrash *Tanḥuma* never makes the explicit connection between this cloak and the Joseph story, but according to an obscure *piyyut* (liturgical poem) dating to the eleventh century, Rabbi Yosef ha-Levi suggests that Jacob indeed gave the garments of glory to Joseph, as the famous "ornamented tunic [*ketonet pasim*]." Thus, Jacob bestows upon Joseph the status of firstborn and High Priest of Israel before there ever was a Tabernacle or Temple.[36] Yet, those beautiful robes were torn from Joseph at the pit, and stained with goat's blood and presented to his father as false evidence of being "surely torn apart" by a wild animal. I imagine an alternative sequel, where the original snakeskin garment was dug up, dry-cleaned, and mended, and given to Joseph—either to glorify him with the priestly status or to lead, inadvertently, to his perdition. Inspired, I wrote my own sequel to the

---

32 M. Zevaḥim 14:4, cf. *Bereshit Rabbah* 66:1, and various parallels.

33 The *Tanḥuma* (ed. Buber, *Toledot* 12, cf. *Bemidbar Rabbah* 4:8). Lambden suggests that this origin of the priestly garment is consistent with the Targum's reading of Gen. 3:21 as "garments of honor/glory" (Targ. Onq, 1 Targ. Jon.; 2 Targ. Jon.; and Targ. Neof.), "From Fig Leaves to Fingernails," 80. There is also a hint of this tradition in *Bereshit Rabbah* 20:12 (ed. Theodor-Albeck, 197) an opinion given in the name of Resh Laqish on Gen. 3:21: "They were milky-white [in color] and in them the firstborn sons [prior to Sinai] served [as priests]." See Anderson's discussion, "The Garments of Skin," 123 (he quotes Midrash *Abkir*, cited in Theodor-Albeck, *Bereshit Rabbah* 168, cf. *Yalqut Shimoni* 34), and 116–117, esp. n. 35.

34 See also *Bereshit Rabbah* 97:6, where Jacob's gift of Shechem to Joseph in Gen. 48:22 (which is understood as "portion" by Rabbi Yehuda) is identified as the clothing of primordial man. See also Midrash *Abkir* (cited in Theodor-Albeck, *Bereshit Rabbah*, 168; *Yalqut Shimoni* 34). See the discussion in Lambden, "From Fig Leaves to Fingernails," 80–82; and Anderson, "Garments of Skin," 123.

35 See Ex. 28:4, 39 and 29:5, and Lev. 8:7, 16:4, though it seems to be a garment worn under the cloak [*me'il*].

36 *Piyyut* of Rabbi Yosef ha-Levi on *va-yeshev Ya'aqov*, line 13 (Shulamith Elitzur, *She'erit Yosef* [Jerusalem: Magnes Press, 1992], 53).

midrashic tradition but left the fate of the first clothing open-ended (see the Appendix to this essay).

Conclusion

The rabbis seem ambivalent about whether the tunic carries a negative force field, like lust for power (PRE), or whether it bestows glory, like the High Priest's garments, with their power to effect atonement (*Tanḥuma*). In PRE's account, the first humans acquire the skins from the primordial Serpent and don its covetous desire and guile. Nimrod embodies world dominion, donning the cloak to establish his power over all creatures. Esau covets the coat and kills Nimrod to acquire it. Jacob makes use of the coat to steal Esau's blessing and then hides it. In this midrashic account, the patriarch never bequeaths the skins to Joseph, his favorite son, perhaps because he senses the danger they bear. The *Tanḥuma* tells a very different tale, in which the cloak, as the primordial priestly garment, grants the one who wears it an intimate relationship with God. It is passed down, father to son, from Adam, to Noah, to Shem, to Abraham, to Isaac and eventually, after Esau, to Jacob, and becomes the tunic of the High Priest of Israel. Unlike the covetous primordial Serpent who desires that which does not belong to him, in guile enhancing the gap between inner self and outer being, the priest atones for the sins of Israel by emptying himself out, collapsing the gap between outer and inner being as he becomes one with his role as *cohen*.

Both the qualities of envy and honor, reified in Adam's original tunic, inhere in Joseph's cloak, though neither midrashic tradition makes the gift of the first clothing to Joseph explicit. After all, Jacob "makes" the ornamented tunic (anew?) for Joseph "*ve-'asah lo ketonet ha-pasim*" (Gen. 37:3). In linking Joseph's cloak to the tunics of skin granted to the first man and his wife, one intimates the potential for either a positive or negative fate or purpose in the gift. Whether the donning of this special cloak serves as a source of atonement for transgression or as a temptation to transgress, especially the tenth commandment—"thou shalt not covet"—depends on the integrity of the one who wears it. As Virginia Woolf so eloquently penned, "there is much to support the view that it is clothes that wear us and not we, them ..." for they bear the power to "mold our hearts, our brains, our tongues to their liking."[37]

---

37 Woolf, *Orlando*, 108.

Appendix

Jacob's Gift

Rachel Adelman

I stand over the pit where I had buried the coveted cloak and dig,
brush off the dirt and lift it up: sheen of snakeskin,
fragile yet not worn thin by time, embroidered with crimson thread—

torso of Behemoth, winged beasts, and tail of Leviathan.
It shimmers, weightless, a sequin gown
made of fingernails that mirror moonlight.

I wore this robe when I stood before my father:
See the smell, my son,
is like the smell of the field that Yaweh blessed.

Whiff of Eden—this is the cloak
that the Primordial Serpent sloughed off
with a cry that traveled from one end of the Earth to the other.

And God wove the snakeskin into two robes—
one for her and one for him.

All the beasts of the field crowded round,
birds of the air swooped down, sea creatures
swarmed to the waters' edge to bask in the shimmer.

They all declared Adam and Eve king and queen of the Earth.
And Adam passed the cloaks on to Seth, and Seth to Noah,
and Noah passed them to Shem.

Adam's cloak rests with Melchitzedek, High Priest of El Elyon.
But Eve's cloak was passed on to Ham.
And Nimrod inherited her gown of snakeskin.

When the Mighty Warrior wore the cloak,
Esau, my brother, saw how all the beasts of the field came
to bow down, from the gazelle to the turtle dove.

Even the lion crouched at his feet purring like a Persian house cat.
What power! Esau took his bow and arrow and hunted
Nimrod down so that he might don its magic.

I now hold Eve's shimmering cloak in my arms,
designer cloak of desire, that my mother foraged from Esau's wardrobe.
It smells of pungent jasmine and fresh blood.

I had slipped into the cloak like a seal into water.
My mother then overlaid the goat's hair-skin on my neck and arms
should the old man grope through blindness to skin.

When Esau heard, and pleaded: "Bless me too, father!"
He let out a cry that traveled from one end of the Earth to the other,
tore a gash in the clouds, rent the firmament.

I could not return it, even furtively, to his wardrobe
for he'd hunt me down as he had the Warrior.
Its smell made me nauseous. I buried it.

Now Joseph is seventeen. I hold the cloak in my arms,
dazzled by its beauty, its vertiginous power. I will give it to him,
as beautiful as his mother, for only he is worthy of its shimmer.

CHAPTER 9

Seeking Sarah

Anne Lapidus Lerner

Foreword

On my way to the *'aqedah,* the Binding of Isaac, I was sidetracked by Sarah. Let me explain. The *'aqedah* has both fascinated and terrified me for decades. The God who had ordered the sacrifice only to rescind the order when the knife was raised to slaughter Isaac bothered me deeply. I had to understand it better. I was not going to write about Sarah, as suggested by readers of my book on Eve. I did not want to understand only the women of the Tanakh, the Hebrew Bible. However, as I studied the *'aqedah* I became obsessed with Sarah.

The troubling and troubled figure of Sarah is familiar; many of us were told about her at an age when we were deemed too young to understand much of it—and probably were. Like many other biblical characters, Sarah is complex and nuanced, not hagiographic and one-dimensional. Genesis is peopled with such characters—some, of course, more flawed than others. It tells the story of four generations of the Israelite "founding family," but it also tells the story of imperfect individuals who make mistakes and of the connections of some of them with God.

From her first appearance in the text at the end of Genesis 11 to her burial near the close of Genesis 23 Sarai/Sarah is labeled with two names and with more than a half-dozen epithets that complicate her roles in the family saga. Those labels make her a paragon of intersectionality and define her relationships with her husband, sons, maid/slave, and God.

The biblical text, particularly in the narratives in Genesis, is somewhat laconic, allowing plenty of room for commentators and those who want to add new meanings and depth to the story or reduce the ambiguities in the text. Recasting scripture is not a new phenomenon; it has been going on for millennia. While writers of traditional rabbinic midrash may have been certain that they were simply shedding light on the unambiguous text, in practice they also explored ambiguities, often adding to the text or changing its meaning. But this process continues into the modern and contemporary periods where we find that modern midrash, often in the form of poetry, often consciously attempts both to supply additional elements to the text and to reconceive its thrust and message.

Before entering the realm of midrash, we will come to understand better, and perhaps differently, the text of relevant portions of Genesis itself. To explore these midrashic rethinkings of the text, I have chosen to use *Bereshit Rabbah* and *Pirqei de-Rabbi Eli'ezer,* two collections of *midrashim* (plural of midrash) that differ somewhat in form and provenance: the former proceeds through the biblical text providing specific comments and additions; the latter retells the story as a whole. My choices of modern poetry try to illuminate and add to the biblical text with insights or narrative that seems missing. Rereading Genesis with these later texts in mind helps us better to understand the original.

* * * * * *

Sarai, as Sarah is called before God changes her name (Gen. 17:15) is introduced at the end of the genealogy (Gen. 11:10–26) that covers the ten generations from Noah's son Shem to Avram, as Abraham is called before his name change (Gen. 17:5). Although there is no individual woman mentioned in these seventeen verses, often referred to as the Table of Nations, it is clear that, while the named men were begetting "sons and daughters," there must be women bearing them. Unmentioned, unnamed, they are invisible.

The formulaic nature of this Table of Nations or ten-generation genealogy is broken by the introduction of the line of Teraḥ (Gen. 11:27). Only three generations of Teraḥ's line are included in this truncated genealogy, which also does not follow the previous formula. Instead, it names three sons of Teraḥ, leaving us to ponder whether these were his only children. Avram is introduced first, but without indication of birth order. The third listed, Ḥaran, predeceases their father. Curiously, Ḥaran's wife is not named; his son, Lot, who plays an ongoing role in the narrative, is (Gen. 11:27–28).

The text proceeds to state that both Teraḥ's surviving sons, Avram and Naḥor, take wives. Sarai is Avram's wife; Milkah bat-Ḥaran is Naḥor's. Milkah's identity as Ḥaran's daughter is emphasized by immediately telling the reader that Ḥaran is the father of both Milkah and Iskah. In other words, Milkah's uncle marries her. Thus, three women are mentioned here: Sarai and Ḥaran's two daughters, the sisters Iskah and Milkah. Milkah become Naḥor's wife; Iskah disappears from the narrative. Avram marries Sarai, who enters the text without lineage.

Instead of the name of her father we are given a cryptic descriptor: "But Sarai is barren [*ʿaqarah*] and has no child" (Gen. 11:30). This verse (*ve-Sarai ʿaqarah: ein lah velad*) is but six words in the Hebrew and apparently a tautology. Sarai is both parentless and childless. Since the reader has been following a genealogy, this information comes as a shock. Its repetition may have been emphatic, but it may indicate that, as suggested in the Talmud, there are two distinct aspects to Sarai's infertility: she is both lacking reproductive organs and has no child, or perhaps no womb, with the word *velad* substituting for *beit velad* or place, literally home, for a child (B. Yevamot 64b). The prospects for Sarai and Avram having progeny seem bleak as this genealogy draws to its close.

This turn of events, following closely after the conclusion of the Table of Nations genealogy, raises many questions. Prominent among them is why Avram married Sarai if she is known as an *ʿaqarah*. While Sarai's paternity is not important enough to be included here, her status as a potential mother is emphasized and found wanting.

Sarai, destined to become the first matriarch, is barren; she will be followed by three more matriarchs, all of whom also have fertility issues. Rebecca and Rachel are known to be barren. Leah starts out barren, but God takes pity on her because she is hated and "opened her womb but Rachel was an *ʿaqarah* [barren]" (Gen. 29:31). Genesis provides no explanation for the infertility of the matriarchs. Why would God, who is clearly in charge of these matters, cause or even allow this problem to plague all three generations of matriarchs? That is a question raised in rabbinic literature. A discussion recorded in *Bereshit Rabbah* suggests that God wanted to hear their prayers. Another suggestion is so that they would have to depend on their husbands for prayer, despite their beauty. Yet another suggestion is so that they could pass most of their lives unburdened. Yet another is so that their husbands can take pleasure in them, since a pregnant woman is ugly and graceless. Sarah is the one specifically mentioned because for her first ninety years she continued to look like a bride at her wedding (*Bereshit Rabbah* 45:4). For God and their husbands, as even their being unburdened was a benefit to their husbands, it was deemed acceptable to cause these four women, as well as many others, potential incredible pain. There appears to be no concern for the women themselves.

One might have anticipated that the significant information that Sarai is barren would be central to the unfolding narrative, but that is not the case. Instead, we are informed that Teraḥ set out for Canaan, taking some of his family with him: "Avram, his son; Lot, son of his son Ḥaran; and Sarai, his daughter-in-law, wife of his son Avram." Each of the three accompanying family members is defined by his or her relationship to Teraḥ, who is clearly in charge of this uprooting of his family. No reason is given for the trip, nor do we know how the others received the news.

It is in Ḥaran, where Teraḥ settles, that God enters this family saga, ordering Avram to leave all that he has known—the land of his birth and his father's house—and go to the place God will show him. In return for Avram's fealty, God offers him multiple blessings (Gen. 12:1–3). The first is the most striking because it promises that Avram will be made into a great nation (*goy gadol*). Whether *gadol* here means great in number or great in power, this seems improbable for a man who has but one wife and she is barren. Avram neither challenges God nor asks questions but sets out with his wife Sarai, his nephew Lot, and his considerable property for the place God will show him. It would be a stretch to claim that these promises are implicitly a way of highlighting Sarai's infertility. In fact, although God continues to pronounce vague benefits to Avram and his progeny, Avram raises this issue as a challenge to God only much later in the story.

The journey is so unremarkable as to merit no description. The text, seven words in the Hebrew, simply tell us "And they went out to go to the land of Canaan and they entered the land of Canaan" (Gen. 12:5). This journey is not memorable for challenges and adventures but only for its destination. In fact, as they are moving around Canaan, God appears again to Avram to repeat the promise of land to be given to his descendants (Gen. 12:7). Once again Avram does not question God regarding the implicit promise of children, but instead builds an altar to God.

When famine in Canaan drives Avram and his family group to travel to Egypt in search of food it is Sarai's turn to remain silent. Avram does not consult God regarding this change in plans, nor does he appear to take counsel with Sarai. Avram entreats her to say that she is his sister rather than his wife, lest her beauty, of which he seems suddenly aware, cause the Egyptians to kill him and keep her alive. As her brother he will benefit, and things will go well for him (Gen. 12:13–14). Embedded in rabbinic midrash is the suggestion that Avram notices her beauty and its consequences at this point because travelers usually become disgusted with themselves and less beautiful, but Sarai retains her beauty (*Bereshit Rabbah* 40:4). Avram neglects to mention what he thinks would happen to her if she were his beautiful sister; Sarai is silent. Why would he endanger the woman who is apparently to join him in producing a great nation?

But Sarai ends up in Pharaoh's home or harem, while Avram gets gifts of livestock and many slaves "on account of Sarai" (Gen. 12:15–16). When members of Pharaoh's household are afflicted, God intervenes, revealing Sarai's true identity; Pharaoh returns her to Avram and has him and his entourage summarily escorted back to Canaan. Even if, as the text claims, divine intervention prevents Sarai from being violated, this is a traumatic experience for Sarai. From our twenty-first-century point of view, she is commodified, passed from one man to another along with an exchange of property given to Avram on her (Sarai's) account. Although Avram does not ask a price for his wife, he must have expected that he would be rewarded as he asks Sarai to lie so that things will go well for him. Further, he does not reject the gifts, which are clearly a quid pro quo. Taking stock of the Egyptian sojourn, Avram has been enriched but Sarai has suffered. Lacking agency, Sarai literally goes along with his plan.

Rabbinic midrash, however, in at least two passages, restores to Sarai both voice and agency. R. Berakhyah portrays her spending the night in Pharaoh's house, lying on her face and saying, "Lord of the Universe, Abraham went out [of his homeland] with a [divine] promise; I went out with trust in him. Abraham is outside this cage; I am [locked] inside." God, who is elsewhere reported not to speak to women, responds to her plea and accepts her claim of unfairness, saying that all that God does is done for her sake. The text goes on to cite R. Levi's description of that night: an angel with a whip is in the room with Sarai and Pharaoh. When Sarai asks the angel to beat Pharaoh, he beats him; when she asks him to lay off, he does so. Even after she tells Pharaoh that she is married, he continues trying to touch her (*Bereshit Rabbah* 41:2). These are striking depictions of female power through which the rabbis grant Sarai some of the power she is missing in the biblical text.

After this wife-sister episode in Egypt, one might have assumed that Avram would be satisfied to have escaped Pharaoh's wrath with his life, wife, and property intact. That is not the case. Although it breaks the order of the text, we will move ahead from this first incident to the second in which Sarah, no longer Sarai, is set up by Abraham, no longer Avram, to be tempting to a ruler.

The story of the couple's encounter in Gerar, recorded in Genesis 20, is close to a repetition of what had transpired in Egypt. Had Abraham not learned a lesson? He may have learned the wrong lesson. Incidentally, modern scholars generally agree that this incident is dependent on the previous one, rather than the product of a different tradition.

Although Abraham's descent to Egypt had been propelled by famine, there is no reason given for his decision to settle in Gerar. Further, he does not seem to ask Sarah to pretend to be his sister. There is some confusion about that because there is an unexplained ellipsis in the verse where the ploy is mentioned. Although most translations seem to ignore it, the verse actually says: "And Abraham says to Sarah his wife 'She is my sister,' and Abimelekh, the king of Gerar, sent [for her] and took Sarah" (Gen. 20:3). As it stands the text makes no sense, even allowing for its terse nature, because what Abraham said to Sarah could not be "She is my sister." Some words are missing. The bottom line, however, is clear: Sarah has once more been taken. When men take women, it is almost invariably for a sexual relationship, within or without marriage.

God comes to Abimelekh in a dream to tell him that he will die because the woman he has taken is a married woman (Gen. 20:3). Abimelekh protests, telling God that he did not touch her, that Abraham told him that she was his sister, and further Sarah herself said, "He is my brother" (Gen. 20:5). God relents, offering to have Abraham pray on Abimelekh's behalf, and rescinding the death penalty. Confronted by a furious Abimelekh, Abraham claims that he and Sarah are half-siblings with a common father, something that is neither recorded in the genealogy nor mentioned in Egypt. While that claim, if it were true, would clear him of lying, he would still be guilty of passing his wife to another man. Abraham further explains that he had thought that there was no fear of God in Gerar and that the Gerarites would kill him for his wife (Gen. 20:11). That seems unlikely to make him beloved in Gerar. It is striking that here Abraham does respond to a ruler much more articulate than Pharaoh (Gen. 20:12); he does not say a word to Pharaoh. His response is a web of lies. He implicates God in his deception because God had made him wander from his father's house. That wandering, in turn, led Abraham to ask Sarah when they left his father's house: "Do this kindness for me—wherever we go, say of me, 'He is my brother'" (Gen. 20:13). Again, this is different in both timing and contents from the narrative here. The first mention of Sarah's being presented as Abraham's sister is as they approach Egypt; the second is as they come into Gerar. In neither case does Sarah respond. Abimelekh quotes Sarah saying just that, but we do not hear it directly from her. *Bereshit Rabbah* fills in her experience with exactly the same words that we read concerning her night crying in Pharaoh's house.

Once more, Abraham seems to have come out ahead, despite having so grievously tricked Abimelekh and endangered his own wife, who, as he has been informed in the interim, will bear his child and heir. Once more Abraham's chicanery has proved profitable—animals and slaves and his choice of land in Gerar. But there is more: Abimelekh tells Sarah that he has given a thousand pieces of silver to her brother—a term he must be using sarcastically—so that it can serve to cover her eyes—or perhaps so that her brother will serve as her eye covering. Only after he receives the gifts does Abraham successfully entreat God to open all the wombs in the household of Abimelekh that had been closed at Sarah's request. Despite Abraham's apparent success as a woman trafficker, he does not make a third recorded attempt.

But let us return to the point where Abraham has just left Egypt. After their return to Canaan Lot separates from Avram. God tells Avram to look in all four directions and survey the land because it will be given to his descendants, who will be as difficult to count as the dust of the earth (Gen. 13:16–17). Avram settles near Hebron and builds another altar to God without questioning or challenging God.

Although I am fully aware that the Torah takes little interest in recording personal emotions, there is another silence here—the absence of any reference at all to the issue that continues to disrupt genealogy. It is hard to imagine what role Sarai's apparent infertility, the only aspect of her that is introduced when she is first mentioned, may have played in shaping the relations among the actants in this narrative, human and divine. At this distance of millennia, we do not know the degree to which the inability to conceive overshadows other concerns, but we do know that today it is often all-consuming. Why is it not mentioned after Sarah's introduction?

The Hebrew poet Amir Gilboa (1917–1984) in a prose poem entitled "Sarai," describes the hardships of Sarai's journey, walking endlessly over mountains and valleys, crouching down as her legs give out, as did her spirit. In her mind she conceived generations of great-grandchildren, grandchildren, fathers, and grandfathers but they all disappeared; she never had a child to hold. The poem concludes with her crouching to give birth and then holding her son, who looks ready to cry. But Isaac (*Yiẓḥaq*), true to his name, will laugh. Interweaving the salient elements of Sarai's story, as well as some midrashic references, Gilboa mentions Avram only once, when he states that there were those who wanted to buy her from Avram's hands for love, as she was beautiful to look at. Gilboa, through what he includes and excludes, fills in gaps in the biblical story; his interpretation is all about Sarai.

Some time later God appears to Avram in a vision, telling him to have no fear. God will protect him and grant him a very large reward. Finally, Avram, addressing God for the first time, speaks up politely to ask God: "... What can you give me when I go on childless and my household servant is Dammesek Eliezer?" It is striking that in his first communication to God Avram uses the formal, weightier word for I—*anokhi*, responding to God with the same form God had used for "I" in speaking to him. After this somewhat, cryptic opening, there is a pause, indicating perhaps that Avram is collecting his thoughts. The text reports again that Avram spoke; this time he is clearer: "Since you have given me no offspring my household servant will be my heir." God promises that Avram's heir will be the product of his body and shows him the countless stars, indicating that his descendants, too, will be countless (Gen. 15:1–6). Avram asks God for a sign as proof that the divine promise will be carried out; God complies. In both iterations, Avram puts himself first. Neither God nor Avram mentions the apparent cause of Avram's childlessness—Sarai's infertility. In fact, Sarai's absence here cries out for an explanation, but Avram, who had urged her to pretend to be his sister at Pharaoh's court with scant reference to the impact that might have on her, considers childlessness, too, to be all about him.

If Avram confides his concerns for an heir or God's promises to Sarai, it is not recorded. In fact, there is no record of dialogue between the couple. Apparently Avram relies on the promises God has made to him and does nothing to advance the solution to his and Sarai's childlessness. At this point the narrator tells the reader that Sarai had not borne a child—a fact of which the reader is painfully aware—and that she has an Egyptian slave named Hagar (Gen. 16:1). The transition from Avram to Sarai as the main actant is abrupt; Sarai takes a commanding role as she speaks and acts to remedy the situation. The focus on Sarai who discovers her voice and agency here is clarified through a close examination of the opening six verses of Genesis 16. Even in the first verse, where the narrator sets the scene, the words are carefully chosen: "But Sarai, Avram's wife, had not given birth for him but to her there was [she did have] an Egyptian slavegirl whose name was Hagar."[1] There are three characters forming two dyads in this verse, Sarai and Avram and Sarai and Hagar. Sarai is in tension between her relationship with Avram and her relationship with Hagar. The Hebrew words "*lo* [for/to him] *ve-lah* [and/but for/to her]," are right in the middle of the verse, visibly pulling at their relationship. Further, the verse opens with Sarai but concludes with Hagar, again symbolizing the way that the focus and power shifts from one to the other.

Sarai breaks her silence to unveil her plan: "Here, please [*hineih-na*], God has held me back from birthing. Come, please, into my slavegirl [have intercourse with her], perhaps I will be built up through her. And Avram listened to Sarai's voice" (Gen. 16:2). The twelve succinct words Sarai uses to set this up are, unlike Avram's passing her off as his sister, all factually true. Intertexts link this incident of woman trafficking with the other two that involve Sarai. The very first words Sarai uses are identical with those that Avram used when asking her to play the role of his sister in Egypt. Sarai's proposition is her belated response to Avram's previous proposition to her. The word Sarai uses for holding back, *'aẓar,* foreshadows the word that describes the affliction that had been visited

1 My translation of these verses follows the Hebrew word order so as to more clearly reflect the structure of the Hebrew. Here and elsewhere I have, when applicable, translated *'ishah* as "wife," rather than its basic meaning "woman," to reflect the understanding of the text.

on Gerar— God had held back (*'aẓar*) all the wombs in the king Abimelekh's household—when Abraham again has Sarah masquerade as his sister (Gen. 20:18). As was the case in Egypt, there is no verbal response. In Egypt Sarai had learned that whoever has power over a woman can control her. There she was the trafficked; here, from our perspective, although her actions may have been deemed appropriate at the time, she is the trafficker.

There are two more linguistic points to consider. The somewhat explicit language used here to indicate sexual intercourse is an idiom that also appears in other places in the Bible. It most often indicates a class or power differential in which the male is the superior. The word *ibbaneh* that Sarai uses to indicate her interest in providing Hagar to Avram means "to be built up," but here it has the additional meaning of "sonned," due to the appearance of *ben* (son) at its core. Just as Avram was looking out for his interests, not Sarai's, when he set up a way to stay alive in Egypt that involved Sarai's being taken as a sex slave, so does Sarai consider only herself when she sets up this surrogacy plan. Neither Avram nor Sarai demonstrates concern for the other.

Sarai's plan has met no verbal opposition here, but the action is slowed by the next verse, which interpolates information the reader just read. "And Sarai, Avram's wife, took the Egyptian Hagar, her slavegirl, at the end of ten years of Avram's dwelling in the land of Canaan and gave her to Avram, her husband, as a wife for him" (Gen. 16:3). So much repetitive, extraneous detail weighs down the sentence that concludes with the echoing of "*le-Avram ishah* [to Avram her husband] *lo le-ishah* [to him as a wife]" (Gen. 16:3). Did Sarai expect Avram would raise an objection? Marek Halter, in his *Sarah: A Novel*, has Avram counsel Sarai not to go ahead with this plan, sensitively using the "be careful what you wish for" approach. A midrash claims that Hagar was reluctant to be with this old man. Sarai had to persuade her that she was lucky to "be united with this holy body" (*Bereshit Rabbah* 45:3). The narrator gives us an additional reason to consider that Sarai's plan may be flawed: the last man who listened to his wife's voice (*le-qol ishtekha*) was Adam who was punished for listening to his wife's voice and eating the forbidden fruit (Gen. 3:17).

One of the most eloquent conceptions of Sarah's handing Hagar over to Abraham is a painting by Mathias Strom painted in about 1638. It depicts the formation of this *ménage à trois*, which does not appear to be headed for success. Abraham, emaciated and scantily clad, is on the right side of the painting, seated, leaning on his left elbow. He appears to be looking at Sarah, who stands with Hagar on her right arm. Sarai, elegantly dressed, like an observant Jewish woman, complete with head-covering, looks into space. Hagar, looking at Avram, uses her right hand to draw her red dress over her right side, but it stops short of her full left breast, which clearly signals youth and fertility. No words are needed to understand Strom's perspective. None of the participants is happy with this development.

Avram sets directly to work and impregnates Hagar. Particularly in contrast to the slow pace of the preceding verse, here half of the ten words are verbs.

When Hagar realizes that she is pregnant, her mistress becomes light in her eyes. As Hagar gains weight, she also gains status (Gen. 16:4). Note that the text juxtaposes Hagar's legal standing as the property of her mistress with her perspective on the balance of power between her and Sarai. Sarai had probably expected to adopt Hagar's child, hopefully a son, as her own, making him Avram's heir and therefore responsible for her support should Avram predecease her. Hagar is both her property and Avram's wife—a clear case of role confusion: she is both Sarai's property and her co-wife, as Sarah is both Hagar's mistress and her co-wife.

Perhaps already unhappy with Avram's silent acquiescence to her plan, Sarai says to him, *ḥamasi 'alekha,* literally "my wrong is upon you," or, "the wrong done to me is your fault." Sarai uses the strong term *ḥamas,* which also connotes violence. It is the powerful noun used to justify the Flood: "*va-timalei ha-areẓ ḥamas* [and the land was filled with *ḥamas*]" (Gen. 6:11). Sarai calls on God to judge between her and Avram (Gen. 16:5). Although Sarai presents this plan as a way of enhancing her status, she may also have hoped that Hagar would not conceive, rendering Avram responsible for their childlessness. Avram simply returns Hagar to Sarai: "Here is your slavegirl in your hand. Do with her what is good in your eyes. But Sarai afflicts her and she flees from her presence [from before her face]" (Gen. 16:6).

Avram, perhaps wisely, refuses to get drawn into the conflict between his wives. After all. Sarai herself, using the more formal form of I, *anokhi,* says to Avram, "I had placed my slavegirl in your bosom but when she saw that she had conceived, I became light in her eyes" (Gen. 16:5). By using the verb for seeing and the eyes metaphor, the text emphasizes that these two women see things differently: they literally have different perspectives on the situation.

Sarai invokes God each time that she speaks. Both here and elsewhere in the Hebrew Bible it is clear that God is in charge of fertility, particularly of human fertility. God has the power to open wombs and to close them. Like Avram, God, too, sit this one out. Nonetheless, this passage does indicate that Sarai, with whom God had not yet communicated, has developed a relationship with God independent of her husband's. In these six verses she really comes into her own as a person with power, voice, and agency.

The missing details of how these two women tortured each other are provided by both medieval and modern rewriters who fill the silence of the biblical texts.

Often these texts put words into the mouths of Sarah and Hagar. "When ladies would come to ask Sarai about her welfare, she would respond: 'Go and inquire after the welfare of that poor woman.' But Hagar would say to them: 'Sarai my mistress is not the same on the inside as on the outside. She appears to be righteous, but she is not righteous; for were she righteous, look how many years she did not conceive but I conceived in one night'" (*Bereshit Rabbah* 45:4). Although this rabbinic source suggests that Hagar was at fault, it also portrays Sarah as haughty. A contemporary Israeli poet, Edna Afek, suggests that the jealousy that Sarai exhibited comes from her dwelling on the way that Avram was spending all his time with Hagar. Only Sarah's giving birth to her own son could assuage her pain.

Although God, when called upon by Sarai, does not judge between her and Avram, when Hagar flees to the desert God sends a messenger or an angel, or perhaps makes a personal appearance, to reason with Hagar. First, she is ordered to return to her tortured life "under Sarai's hand." Before they part, however, the angel gives her a blessing and the promise of a son who is to be named "Ishmael [literally 'God will listen'] for God has heard your affliction" (Gen. 16:11). Because God cares for Hagar, her progeny will be countless. To the extent that this is a woman-trafficking story, Hagar is the powerless, uprooted woman who suffers at the hands of her owner. But when we read this as part of the infertility saga, Hagar has the upper hand because she is carrying in her womb the heir to the divine promises made both to her and to Avram. When her son is born, Abraham names him Ishmael as God had prescribed.

Thirteen years pass from the birth of Ishmael to God's appearing in a vision to confer covenantal blessings of progeny and land upon Avram and add a letter *heh* to his name, making it Abraham. God further blesses Sarai and changes her name, replacing the final letter, *yod,* with a *heh.* She, too, is blessed, but in absentia, with multitudes of progeny. She will bear Abraham a son who will in turn produce many kings (Gen. 17:16). Reasonably enough Abraham finds this so ridiculous that he falls on his face and he laughs to himself (*va-yiẓḥaq*). The narrator explains that Abraham thought that he at a hundred and Sarah at ninety were too old to have a child (Gen. 17:17). When he recovers his composure Abraham, fearing for the future of his beloved Ishmael interrupts God to plead: "... 'Would that Ishmael would live before You'" (Gen. 17:18). God reassures him that Ishmael will have his own covenant and produce twelve chieftains but makes clear in no uncertain terms that it is Sarah's son who will carry God's special covenant. Isaac [*yiẓḥaq*], as God wants him named, will be born the following year at the same time.

Seeking Sarah, we see her, but do not hear much from her, when three mysterious guests appear at Abraham's tent at Mamre. Sarah is marginal to Abraham's discussion with the angels, which includes the annunciation of the birth of a son to her, but she, standing behind Abraham at the door of the tent, hears it. She reacts silently not with joy or relief, but with laughter, saying, "Now that I am withered am I to have pleasure with my husband who is so old?" (Gen. 18:12). Strangely, God, Who had not chided Abraham when he fell on his face laughing, asks Abraham, not Sarah, why she was laughing because she thought she was too old to bear a child. Receiving no answer from Abraham, God responds, "Is there anything too wondrous for God? I will return next year in this season and Sarah will have a son" (Gen. 18:14). Hearing this, Sarah, frightened, denies her laughter, saying "I did not laugh," to which God responds "Yes, you did." This seems like a childish exchange, but it does present God as responding to a woman, something that the tradition views as Sarah's unique privilege (*Bereshit Rabbah* 45:10). Despite textual examples of other women to whom God spoke, the traditional view often argues that God spoke to women through an angel or messenger (*Bereshit Rabbah* 18:12).

God does open Sarah's womb as promised. Sarah's longest speech follows the birth of her son Isaac. She speaks both prose and poetry, saying: "God has brought me laughter; everyone who hears will laugh with me. And she said, "Who would have said to Abraham/ That Sarah would suckle children!/ Yet I have borne a son in his old age" (Gen. 21:6–7). It is the high point of Sarah's verbal expression.

At this point things might seem to be going well in Abraham's household. He has two wives, each of whom has borne him a son. But the wives are not of equal status, and neither are their sons. The final episode in the trafficking scenario occurs when Sarah sees Ishmael doing something inappropriate with Isaac. What he does and whether or not it is appropriate is less germane here than Sarah's reaction. When she accosts Abraham with the need to banish Ishmael and Hagar, she claims that her goal is to prevent Ishmael from sharing the inheritance with Isaac, whom she refers to as "my son" (Gen. 21:10). As firstborn son, Ishmael would be entitled to a double portion from the inheritance. Sarah might have been looking for an excuse to banish him. When she confronts Abraham, she says nothing about what may have happened between his two sons. Instead, she says, "*Gareish ha-amah ha-zot ve-et benah ki lo yirash ben ha-amah ha-zot ʻim bni ʻim Yiẓḥaq* [Drive out this slavegirl and her son because the son of this slavegirl is not going to inherit with my son, with Isaac]" (Gen. 21:10). Note that Sarah never refers to either Hagar or Ishmael by name. Only her son, Isaac, has a true face and full personhood. The trafficker, no longer in need of the surrogate, wants to remove her. She may be motivated by self-interest. If Abraham dies Isaac will be responsible for her welfare; she wants to be sure that he has substantial means. Abraham is, not unreasonably, concerned for his son. "But the matter was very bad in Abraham's eyes regarding his son" (Gen. 21:11). After all, Ishmael was his only son for thirteen years. Nonetheless Abraham does not say a word. He is very much *his* son, not Sarah's. Her surrogacy plan did not lead to her developing a relationship with Ishmael. But God, uninvited, intervenes not merely to approve the banishment, but also to make the blanket statement: "*Kol asher tomar eilekha Sarah, shema be-qolah* [Whatever Sarah tells you, obey her (literally, hear her voice)]" (Gen. 21:12). This is truly a remarkable statement for God to make, particularly in a time we usually associate with regnant patriarchy. It certainly seems to give Sarah unlimited power and, perhaps, that is the reason for Sarah's disappearance from the text. She is not reported to have said another word.

But *de jure* power does not necessarily lead to *de facto* power. Thus, Sarah's last recorded speech results in the banishment of Hagar, her slavegirl and co-wife, as well as her rival and the mother of her son's rival, along with her son's rival himself. The mistreatment of the trafficked woman and her child is ultimately rectified by God's emissary, but Sarah, too, is gone, perhaps because she had been granted too much power.

Sarah's absence, like her earlier presence, is palpable. It provides an open invitation to imagine what her next steps might have been, as well as how she might have reacted in Abraham's place. As we look to the *'aqedah,* the last significant chapter in Abraham's life, referred to as his last, tenth trial or test by rabbinic traditions, Sarah's absence cries out silently. In fact, rewriters often provide her a voice. *Pirqei de-Rabbi Eli'ezer* proposes that when Samael, the force of evil, heard that Abraham was returning home from the Binding of Isaac, or his near-sacrifice, Samael ran ahead to tell Sarah that her elderly husband had sacrificed their son. She was so upset that she started to sob and weep. The text further connects the pattern of her weeping with the pattern of blasts on the ram's horn sounded on the High Holydays (*Pirqei de-Rabbi Eli'ezer* 32).

Modern writers also reimagine the *'aqedah* to include Sarah and to give her words. It is often transposed to modern situations as a way to wrestle with the reality that Israeli parents have to prepare themselves and their children for the army and, if necessary, for war. While the poems often differ in their details a number of them have God command Sarah, rather than Abraham, to sacrifice Isaac. Unlike Abraham, Sarah challenges God's command. Thus, for example, Raya Harnik (1933–) has the first-person narrator of her poem refuse outright sacrificing her firstborn. Nights, she and God settle accounts. The poem, one of Harnik's poems to her son Guni, is terse—only twenty-five words long—and quite clear; the speaker is adamant. The first-person speaker and God are presented as equals. By writing the *'aqedah* onto the current situation of Israeli parents, Harnik puts it into the echo-box of Jewish history and leaves us wondering again at Abraham's silence.

In her poem "Sarah Talks to God" the American poet Lillian Elkin (1917–1999) poignantly challenges God to justify the death of young children. Using the *'aqedah* as a matrix, Elkin opens not with God's command, but with a first-person mother's voice asking the eternal question: "Why?" She provides no clues or information as to the cause of the death of the child other than Abraham's relaying—accurately or not—a divine command. The narrator describes the child's merits and questions God's needing him. Unlike many poetic *'aqedah* rewriters, Elkin chooses to furnish the reader some insights into Sarah as daughter, wife, and mother. Opening with a call to "Oh King, my God," the speaker appears to have a personal relationship with God. By the end of this poem, Elkin has received no response; the narrator closes with the speaker's bitter "doubts."

Although Sarah is the first matriarch, we do not see her interact with Isaac, except around nursing and that only after he is weaned. I have chosen two additional poems that, while approaching the relationship between Sarah and Isaac in very different ways, create a sense of a mother-son bond.

The Yiddish poet Itzik Manger (1901–1969) fills this gap in the narrative by providing a mother's lullaby to soothe Isaac to sleep. Sarah's Yiddish lullaby is one of a series of *Ḥumesh-lider* (*Songs on the Pentateuch*) that essentially transplants many of the events recorded as sacred history to an environment more familiar to his mid-twentieth-century readers—a slightly earlier Eastern European Jewish world of his imagination.

While recreating for the reader the outlines of a *shtetl,* a small Jewish village in Eastern Europe, the poem actually provides insight into motherhood itself through its depiction of the relationship between Sarah and Isaac. This fanciful, child-oriented poem is rooted in its *shtetl* setting, which Manger brings to life, conveying the words, sounds, and people. Sarah implicitly teaches Isaac about life by introducing him to some iconic occupations: shepherd, shopkeeper, blacksmith, cantor, tailor. The only one of these mentioned in the biblical text is shepherd. Manger's retelling the story in the *shtetl* context follows the rabbinic tradition of placing the biblical patriarchs in their own context. Strikingly, the only female human in the poem is Sarah herself, singing her tender, imaginative lullaby.

In her poem "Sarah's Choice," the Jewish American poet Eleanor Wilner (1937–) brings Sarah into the *'aqedah* to provide Isaac a lesson in moral and ethical behavior. Wilner's Sarah stands as a model of an outspoken, self-sufficient, powerful woman, while engaging both chosenness and Muslim-Jewish détente from her own progressive perspective. God, often referred to here as "the Voice," orders Sarah to take her only, beloved son and sacrifice him. Sarah responds by refusing to obey the Voice, understanding it as a sign of being chosen. Logically she reminds the Voice that her son is the promised heir to Abraham, without him that promise is worthless. If the Voice's real intention is not to take the life of her only son, it is just a trick. In either case she will have no part of it. Sarah will choose her son rather than secure herself a place in "History." She approaches Isaac, telling him that, now that he is on the cusp of manhood, he has to decide whether to be chosen or to choose. Isaac fears that if he were not chosen, he would be nothing. His mother laughs at him, reminding the reader of the biblical Sarah's laughter when she overhears that she will bear a son (Gen. 18:12). She tells him that she is leaving to go to Hagar and Ishmael, whom she, with God's approval, had banished from their midst. Isaac is afraid of meeting Ishmael again. Sarah's response is that if he greets Ishmael as an equal, they will not have to fight forever. Packing up her stylus and some provisions, Sarah once more reaches out to Isaac, hoping he will come along. When he voices his concern about what will happen if they go, Sarah responds that she does not know what will happen if they set out, but that what will happen if he stays behind is already recorded. The poem ends without resolution, perhaps a reference to Wilner's description of Sarah as shaped like a question mark. As readers we are also left with a question, only deepened by the fact that in the margin, near the end of the poem, one reads "The unbinding of Isaac." Is Isaac really unbound, having chosen to follow his mother and be bound for his meeting with Ishmael despite God's command? Does he, as Genesis tells us, follow his father and lie bound on the altar to be released only as the slaughtering knife is about to come down to kill him?

The biblical text never again depicts interaction between Sarah and either Abraham or Isaac. When Sarah is next mentioned, she has died. Reporting Sarah's death the text provides us with some repetitive language that serves as a counterpoint to the double language we saw when Sarah/Sarai is first introduced into the text. A literal translation of the verse allows us to appreciate the doubling, which is usually eliminated in translations: "And the life of Sarah was a hundred years and twenty years, and seven years—the years of the life of Sarah" (Gen. 23:1). Abraham, who was last known to be in Beersheba, makes the trip to Hebron, where Sarah died, to mourn her and bury her. Sarah is the only matriarch whose age at death is recorded. She is also the first Israelite to die, as well as to be mourned and buried. In fact, she is the only woman who is recorded as having been mourned using the verb *s.p.d*; she and the patriarch Jacob are the only persons for whose mourning that verbal root is used (Gen. 50:10).

Even in death Sarah maintains her complexity. As Abraham and the elders of Hebron negotiate a proper burial place for Sarah, she is referred to both as Sarah and as *meit,* a dead person or corpse (Gen. 23:2–19). Curiously, only the narrator uses her God-given name and does so twice in the opening verse and once in closing verse of this section (Gen. 23:2, 19). These appearances of "Sarah" form a bracket or *inclusio* that sets apart the passage relating to the purchase of the Cave of Machpelah, its surroundings, and the trees on it. Further, only in the narration is Sarah additionally identified as "his wife" (Gen. 23:3). Abraham and the Hittites, including most prominently Ephron, with whom he is negotiating refer to Sarah as *meit* with the addition of a first- or second-person singular possessive. Abraham is the first to use the term *meit.* In the entire Hebrew Bible only in this passage does that noun appear in the singular with possessive endings. One might read this as an insulting way for Abraham to refer to his wife of so many years, particularly because Abraham, from the first time he uses it, speaks of burying "my dead from before my face" (Gen. 23:4). It almost seems as though he wants to be rid of her, not to have to deal with her anymore. On the other hand, one may consider it a term that preserves her essence, as represented in "Sarah" as he speaks to the Hittites who never knew her as Sarah. This is a clear example of biblical ambiguity.

Once Sarah is not only dead, but even buried, she might be expected to slip from the narrative as she had entered it, without fanfare or family. That is not the case for Sarah, who, unlike Hagar who saves Ishmael's life and finds him a wife, has done little for her son except banish Hagar and Ishmael to assure Isaac a double portion of his father's inheritance. Before she disappears, Sarah gives Isaac a final, posthumous gift. Isaac, who, strangely, seems to have no part in the mourning or burial of his mother, is apparently inconsolable after her death. Abraham, who never speaks with Isaac after the *'aqedah,* sends his trusted servant off to find a wife for Isaac. When he returns with Rebekah, Isaac "brings her into the tent of Sarah his mother and takes Rebekah to be his wife and loves her and is comforted after his mother's death" (Gen. 24:67). What a touching coda to Sarah's story!

Afterword

In truth, there are many approaches we can use to give coherence to the narrative of Sarah's life. Is Sarah so traumatized both by her status as an *'aqarah,* a barren woman, and by her experiences as a trafficked wife that she has no compassion for Ishmael or Hagar? But is it not also the tale of a dysfunctional, blended family, a *ménage à trois*? Perhaps the tale of a woman who takes a leap of faith to accompany her husband on many journeys and adventures before finally producing the hoped-for and divinely promised heir to his legacy?

Sarah has but one son; Abraham has two. By the time Isaac is born Abraham and his son have bonded; there is really no room for Isaac. Ishmael, as Abraham's firstborn, is his favorite son. In fact, when God tells Abraham that he will have a son together with Sarah, he interrupts God to plead for Ishmael's life. When Sarah, on the other hand, finds an opportunity to argue for Ishmael's banishment, Abraham does not respond at all. We can only conjecture what the reasons for his silence are. Does he realize, finally, that God was serious when assigning different levels of importance for each of Abraham's sons? Isaac would be heir to Abraham's legacy and the father of many generations that will carry on the tradition. Ishmael will also receive special status, but not the covenantal closeness that is reserved for Isaac. Does Abraham feel that he must "pick his battles" with God? Is Abraham simply worn down by the disagreements between his wives? It seems likely that it is a silence of recognition, rather than a silence of resignation. God, who is in control, intervenes quickly, too quickly, perhaps, for Abraham to counter Sarah's self-serving argument.

The tension between Abraham and Sarah plays out in two ways. Abraham and Sarah act separately guided by self-interest without consideration for the effect their actions might have on each other. But, as parents, they also use their children as weapons in the battles between them. Sarah tries to get rid of Ishmael initially when he is still *in utero*. She mistreats Hagar to the point where Hagar feels she has to flee. God intervenes to send her back to Sarah. After the birth of Sarah's son Isaac, Sarah tries, once more, to eliminate Abraham's favorite and favored son Ishmael. With God's approval, this time she is successful; Abraham sends Hagar and Ishmael off with a skin of water and some bread. When their water runs out Ishmael seems close to dying. Again, God intervenes to save him (Gen. 21:14–21).

Ultimately, the biblical Sarah has the power to speak, as well as to act, both persuasively and emotionally. Her use of words is skilled. When she is powerless, as she is as a trafficked woman and when Abraham, probably without her knowledge, sets off to sacrifice their son, she is also speechless. When she is most powerful, as she is at Isaac's birth, she is most eloquent. When she is angry, her emotions drive her words as they do when she confronts Abraham about Hagar and about Ishmael. Even frightened, when God challenges her, she blurts out a two-word lie: "*Lo ẓaḥaqti* [I did not laugh]" (Gen. 18:15) to defend herself. She is a complex character who propels much of the action in the story of the first generation of matriarchs and patriarchs, who seems to have her own relationship with God, and in whose speech—and especially in whose silence—we can find new possibilities of interpretation.

CHAPTER 10

Jacob and Esau: Twinship and Identity Confusion

George Savran

The biblical account of Jacob in Genesis 25–35 relates a complex story—the development of the personal boundaries of the eponymous ancestor as well as the beginnings of an evolving national identity. As is well known, this emergence is reflected most famously in the name change encapsulated in that single climactic moment in Gen. 32:29—"Your name shall no longer be Jacob, but Israel." But it is also reflected in the narrative that precedes the name change, and carried further in the chapters that follow it. Unlike Abraham, whom we meet in his adulthood, and who from the beginning has a well-developed understanding of himself as well as clarity of vision about the focus of his life, we first encounter Jacob in the womb and in his childhood, where his sense of self is less well-formed, to say the least. What I wish to examine here are these earlier stages of the confusion of Jacob's personal identity as reflected in Genesis 25–28, centered around his difficulty in coming to terms with being a twin. This is, of course, followed by the gradual emergence of a clearer awareness of his personal identity in his struggle with Laban in chapters 30–31, and in the crowning event of his renaming mentioned above. This intricate process of identity formation involves all those who come in contact with Jacob: his parents, his brother Esau, his wives Rachel and Leah, and his father-in-law Laban.[1] While this emergent character

---

1 Among the recent studies of the Jacob cycle, which have added to our understanding of the entire narrative, are the following: Michael Fishbane, "Composition and Structure in the Jacob Cycle (Gen. 25:19–35:22)," *JSS* 26 (1975): 15–38; Ronald S. Hendel, *The Epic of the Patriarch* (Atlanta: Scholars Press, 1987); Jonathan Grossman, *Jacob: The Story of a Family* [Heb.] (Rishon LeZion: Yedi'ot Aḥronot, 2019); Zeev Weisman, *From Jacob to Israel* [Heb.] (Jerusalem: Magnes. 1986); Paul Vrolijk, *Jacob's Wealth: An Examination into the Nature and Role of Material Possessions in the Jacob-Cycle* (Leiden: Brill, 2011); Jan P. Fokkelman, *Narrative*

also creates national and religious boundaries for Jacob/Israel, the present article will restrict itself to exploring aspects of Jacob's identity confusion that are connected to his twin relationship with Esau. A subsequent study will address the way in which the concomitant development of a national idea is developed in the second half of the Jacob narrative.

Jacob's struggle to establish his own well-defined identity begins with the unique dynamics of twinship.[2] It is well known that twins—particularly those of the same sex—have particular difficulty establishing their individuality from one another.[3] While this may be more pronounced with identical twins, research has shown that fraternal twins also experience unusual complications in separating from one another and in developing a unique sense of self outside of the twin relationship. Because of the unique characteristics of twinship there is no Biblical kinship relationship quite like that of Jacob and Esau. Although brothers in Genesis are notoriously in conflict with one another, these fraternal twins are unique in the difficulties they have in separating from one another. This enmeshed relationship is impressed upon the reader even before their birth. The exceptional turmoil in Rebecca's womb demands explanation—the narrator describes it with a verb *va-yitroẓeẓu* that can be understood variously as denoting vigorous movement or even violent struggle between the sons.[4] Rebecca seems unaware that she is carrying twins, but even if she suspects this, a multiple birth in the ancient world was regarded as ominous, as illustrated in

---

Art in Genesis, 2nd ed. (Eugene, OR: Wipf & Stock); Claus Westermann, *Genesis 12–36* (Minneapolis: Fortress Press, 1995), 405–557; R. Christopher Heard, *Dynamics of Diselection* (Atlanta: Scholars Press, 2001); Yair Zakovitch, *Jacob: Unexpected Patriarch* (New Haven: Yale University Press, 2012); John E. Anderson, *Jacob and the Divine Trickster* (Winona Lake, IN: Eisenbrauns, 2011); Bradford A. Anderson, *Brotherhood and Inheritance* (New York: Bloomsbury, 2011); Elie Assis, *Identity in Conflict* (Winona Lake, IN: Eisenbrauns, 2016; Dalit Rom-Shiloni, "When an Explicit Polemic Initiates a Hidden One: Jacob's Aramean Identity," in *Words, Ideas, Worlds: Biblical Essays in Honor of Yairah Amit*, ed. A. Brenner and F.H. Polak (Sheffield: Sheffield Phoenix Press, 2012), 206–235; J.-D. Macchi and T. Römer, eds., *Jacob: Commentaire a plusieurs voix de Gen. 25–36* (Geneva: Labor et Fides, 2001); Erhard Blum, "The Jacob Tradition," in *The Book of Genesis: Composition, Reception and Interpretation*, ed. C. R. Evans, J. N. Lohr, and D. L. Petersen (Leiden: Brill, 2012), 181–211; Gordon J. Wenham, *Genesis 16–50* (Dallas: Word, 1994).

2 On twins and mythology see Elizabeth A. Stewart, *Exploring Twins*, (New York: St. Martin's, 2000), 3–11; Raymond Kuntzmann, *Le Symbolisme des jumeaux au Proche-Orient Ancien* (Paris: Beauchesne, 1983), 39–160; Joseph Campbell, *The Masks of God: Oriental Mythology* (New York: Penguin, 1962).

3 See Ricardo Ainslie, *The Psychology of Twinship* (London: Jason Aronson, 1997), 1–54; Stewart, *Exploring Twins*, 63–76; 101–104; 166–67; B. Schave and J. Ciriello, *Identity and Intimacy in Twins* (New York: Praeger, 1983); M. C. Winestein, "Twinship and Psychological Differentiation," *Journal of the American Academy of Child Psychiatry* 8 (1969): 438–440.

4 The verb can be understood as a form of *r.w.ẓ* (to run) or of *r.ẓ.ẓ.* (to crush); See Anderson, *Brotherhood*, 22.

the discussion of twin births in the Akkadian omen series *Šumma Izbu*. Indeed, this is the only case of a tumultuous birth in the Bible, and that alone is reason enough for her to seek understanding in the form of a divine oracle.[5]

In the message she receives the birth of twins is forecast with the ambiguous expression *ve-rav ya'avod ẓa'ir*—which can be understood as the older serving the younger, or the younger serving the older, since there is no clear indication which noun is the subject and which is the object.[6] While there may be agreement that the plain sense of the text is that the elder will serve the younger (there would be little point in stating the obvious claim of the elder over the younger), the deliberate ambiguity built into the poetic parallelism hints at the narrator's subtext—the entangled nature of the twins. On the one hand it would seem that by distinguishing between the two with the terms *rav* and *ẓa'ir* their difference has been clarified. But the distinction between the terms is less clear than one might expect. The term *rav* is not used for age designation in the Hebrew Bible, and the preferred term for younger is *qatan*, not *ẓa'ir*.[7] While Jacob is technically the younger, Anderson has pointed to the similarity in sound between *ẓa'ir* (apparently Jacob) and *sa'ir* (apparently Esau), hinting at a link between the two.[8] Speiser notes the parallelism between the Akkadian equivalents *rabū* and *ṣeḫru* as elder and younger, but he also mentions the transferability of birthright in Hurrian law; the *māru ṣeḫru* and the *māru rabū*, the younger and the elder sons, can effectively change positions—either can receive the inheritance of the birthright.[9]

When we examine the entire oracle, we see a striking emphasis on the similarity of the twins.

1. Two nations are in your womb,
2. Two peoples from within you shall be separated.

---

5 See the discussion of exceptional births in Erle Leichty, *The Omen Series Šumma Izbu* (Locust Valley, NJ: J. J. Augustin, 1970); Esther Hamori, "Heavenly Bodies: Pregnancy and Birth Omens in Israel," *Hebrew Bible and Ancient Israel* 2 (2013): 479–499; idem, *Women's Divination in Biblical Literature* (New Haven: Yale University Press, 2015), 43–60.

6 Zakovitch, *Jacob*, 16; Anderson, *Brotherhood*, 26; Anderson, *Trickster*, 63;

7 In Rebecca's eyes they are *qatan* and *gadol* (Gen. 27:15), and in Gen. 42:13, 15, 20, and so forth, Benjamin is consistently called *ha-qatan*; cf. further Anderson, *Trickster*, 6–63. It is how striking how rarely *rav* refers to age—perhaps only in Job 32:9. Elsewhere the meaning is often quantitative but not with regard to the age of a person.

8 Anderson, *Brotherhood*, 25; Wenham, *Genesis 16–50*, 176; Anderson, *Trickster*, 66. We should also note the assonance between *ẓa'ir* and *ẓayid* (hunt) as an attribute of Esau.

9 Ephraim A. Speiser, *Genesis* (Garden City, NJ: Doubleday, 1964), 194–195. Anderson, *Trickster*, 61 n. 46, suggests that the rarity of an age-related sense of *rav* increases the ambiguity implied in oracle. Cf. also Johannes Taschner, *Verheissung und Erfüllung in der Jakoberzählung* (Freiburg: Herder, 2000), 325.

3. One people shall be mightier than the other
4. *Ve-rav ya'avod ẓa'ir.*

Lines 1 and 2 of the oracle deploy a combination of identical and synonymous language to describe what will emerge from Rebecca's womb—two boys who will become two nations/peoples, *without identifying either one*. By using the same word—*shnei*—twice, the oracle indicates their essential likeness. Only the final word in line 2—*yipareidu*—indicates their separation, but here it refers both to separation from the womb (the two of them together) as well as subsequent separation from one another (each will go his own way).[10] Thus even the final word in the stych moves between similarity and difference, depending on when the separation is to occur, and who will be separated from whom. Line 3 also repeats the same word twice—*le'om*—without specifying which people will dominate the other. We wait impatiently for the fourth stych, where we expect that the essence of the oracle will be clarified. But the reversible syntax of line 4 frustrates the reader even further. Adding to this ambiguity is the conjunctive *waw* at the beginning of the line: If it is understood as "and," it would be a continuation of the similarities we have discussed: as we have two entities that are indistinguishable in lines 1–3, so line 4 continues this uncertainty by implying that either one may serve the other. If, on the other hand, we understand the conjunctive *waw* as "but," it would stand in opposition to what has come before: despite the apparent similarity or identity of the two, one would be subservient to the other. But which of the two is "greater"—the younger or the elder?[11] Does the order of their emergence from the womb have significance? As we will see, the answer is both yes and no.

A further point of identity slippage is supplied by the names of the twins. On the one hand their physical descriptions point to significant differences between them —Esau is reddish and hairy while Jacob is smooth-skinned (as we learn later in Gen. 27:11). At this point Jacob's name is tied to the iconic picture of him grasping the heel (*'eqev*) of his brother, presumably while coming out

10 See K. Vermeulen, "Two of a Kind: Twin Language in the Hebrew Bible," *JSOT* 37 (2012): 135–150, who notes the language of *shnei*—either as "two" or as "scarlet"—which occurs consistently with twin language for purposes of paronomasia.

11 Anderson, *Brotherhood*, 26, citing Heard, *Dynamics*, 100. In Gen. 27:15, 42 the narrator refers to Jacob and Esau with the usual terms for younger and elder, *ha-qatan* and *ha-gadol*. Leah is likewise referred to as *ha-gdola* in Gen. 29:16, and Benjamin is *ha-qatan* in Gen. 42:14, 20, 32, 34. The choice of the less common terms *rav* and *ẓa'ir* in Gen. 25 thus invites a more nuanced reading. Anderson, *Trickster*, 60–63 reads this as intentional ambiguity, part of the "trickster" identity of both God and Jacob; I prefer to see this as indicative of identity confusion between the two twins.

of the womb. What is the nature of this grasping—is it his effort to supplant Esau and to emerge before his brother? This interpretation of his seizing the heel is based upon the twin narrative in Genesis 38:20–27, where Perez and Zerah physically contest with one another who will be born first. The struggle over who will obtain the blessing from the father or from God is common in Genesis, albeit elsewhere outside the womb—so with Cain and Abel, Isaac and Ishmael. This interpretation is backed up by the description of Jacob struggling with his brother in the womb in Hos. 12:4, where the expression *ba-beten ʿaqav et aḥiv* is translated "In the womb he supplanted his brother."[12] But in Gen. 25 the verb *aḥaz* is used to describe Jacob's action, a verb that often indicates grasping with the intent to keep hold, seizing something with no intention of letting go. Adonijah grasps the horns of the altar in 1 Kg. 1:51 in order to protect himself from his brother Solomon and must be persuaded to release his hold. In Ps. 73:23 the psalmist seeks ongoing divine support, and in Ps. 139:10, God clasps the hand of the psalmist. The woman in Song 3:4 grasps and keeps hold of her lover; Eccl. 7:8 advises holding on to both alternatives without releasing either one. It is with this intent that Jacob grasps his brother's heel—in the womb they are two-as-one, and he refuses to be left behind. Wherever Esau intends to go Jacob will remain right there with him. At this point in the narrative there is no separating the brothers; they are bound to one another despite the differences that will develop between them. Esau may be technically the firstborn, the first out of the womb, but it is only a matter of minutes till Jacob catches up with him, effectively challenging the claim of Esau's firstborn status. What the text seeks to suggest by Jacob's holding on is that, on a conceptual level, the twins have been born simultaneously.

Jacob's name in Gen. 25:26 is tied to his heel-holding, but his name is given another twist by Esau in 27:36. Punning on the name *yaʿaqov* with the verb *va-yaʿekveni,* he reinterprets the name to mean one who grabs hold but also deceives and supplants. Everett Fox has translated the name as "heel-holder" in Gen. 25:26 but "heel-sneak" in 27:26.[13] Given this clever wordplay about Jacob's name we should expect some interpretation of Esau's name as well, beyond the

---

12 On the treatment of Jacob in Hos. 12 see Steven L. McKenzie, "The Jacob Tradition in Hosea 12:4–5," *VT* 36 (1986): 311–322; William D. Whitt, "The Jacob Traditions in Hosea and their Relation to Genesis," *ZAW* 103 (1991): 18–43. Yair Zakovitch claims that the account of the struggle between Peretz and Zerah originally was the story of the *in utero* struggle between Jacob and Esau. See Zakovitch, *Jacob,* 18–20; idem, "ʿAqevat Yaʿaqov" [Heb.], in *Sefer Baruḥ Ben Yehudah,* ed. Ben Zion Luria (Tel Aviv: Society for Biblical Research in Israel, 1991), 126; Whitt, "Jacob Traditions," 29.

13 Everett Fox, *The Five Books of Moses* (New York: Schocken, 1995), 115, 127.

mention of Edom and Seir. Most suggestions for understanding Esau's name fail to convince, as the name Esau has little to do with his hirsute body or his reddish complexion; only later will he be dubbed Edom.[14] Esther Hamori, however, has suggested taking Esau's name from the unusual *pi'el* form of the verb *'asah*, meaning "to press" or "to squeeze," as found in Ezek. 23:3, 8, and 21.[15] This is in keeping with the verb describing their action *in utero*—*va-yitroẓeẓu*. "The twins 'crushed one another' in Rebecca's womb ... she [Rebecca] essentially names the first 'Presser' and the second 'Grabber.'"[16] Since the twins have been tussling with one another in the womb, she proposes a synonymous relation between the names, as we might expect for twins.[17] Hamori's interpretation explains both names as reflecting their behavior within the womb, rather than in reaction to their appearance outside of it. The twins are named for their tactics in the struggle with one another—one presses or squeezes his opponent while the other grabs at and seizes his challenger. From Rebecca's perspective, at this point there isn't much distinction between the two.[18] These differences begin to emerge only once they have been born.

The next four verses describe these differences in detail:

	Esau	Jacob
appearance (25:25)	hairy	smooth (Jacob's smoothness is mentioned later in 27:12)
profession (25:27)	hunter	herdsman
favorite parent (25:28)	Isaac	Rebecca

14 Some commentators have suggested a connection between *'Esav* and *sa'ir* since they share two consonants, but this is unconvincing. Others (Schwartz, *Isaac*, 78; Rashi ad loc; Rashbam ad loc) see a connection with verb *'asah* in the *qal*, Esau as doer, but this verb is not associated with his actions in a significant way. An older interpretation tried to develop a connection with a founding pair of Phoenician brothers, one of whom is a hunter named Ousoos—cf. Joseph Blenkinsopp, *Creation, Uncreation, Recreation: A Discursive Commentary on Genesis 1–11* (London: T & T Clark, 2011), 90; T.K. Cheyne, "The Connection of Esau and Usoos," *ZAW* 17 (1897): 97; Westermann, *Genesis 16–50*, 414. This too has proved unlikely.

15 The verb is used only here in reference to pressing the breasts of a young woman. Hamori ("Heavenly Bodies," 489 n. 30) cites an Arabic verb *ġašiya*, which occurs in military contexts, more appropriate to this setting.

16 Hamori, "Heavenly Bodies," 489.

17 Pairs of twins with synonymous or similar-sounding names include Hypnos and Thanatos, Yama and Yami, Romulus and Remus; see T. P. Wiseman, *Remus: A Roman Myth* (Cambridge: Cambridge University Press, 1995), 18–25 and 110–111.

18 The names *Pereẓ* and *Zeraḥ* in Gen. 38 also have a certain synonymity—breaking out in the case of the former, and arising in the latter (in the sense of leprosy appearing in 2 Chron. 26:19).

The oppositions are placed one after the other to heighten the contrast between the twins. We have been told that Esau, the hairy man, is a hunter, and in this he is perforce a planner, one who sets traps and, as we learn in Gen. 27:3, a master of the instruments of the hunt—his bow and arrows. As such he seems to be the dominant brother—first out of the womb, beloved of his father, whose hairiness is a sign of powerful masculinity.[19] His father's attachment to him is tied to his ability to hunt and bring home game, and to his connection to the outdoors. He has been compared to Enkidu as a man of the wild.[20] The contrasting descriptions—*ish sadeh* for Esau and *ish tam* for Jacob—are interesting for what they hint at as well. The man of the field is a man of the outside world, if not sophisticated than highly aware of his surroundings. The description of Jacob as *tam* may indicate his simplicity, his quietness, his innocence, his uprightness, his mild personality—such is the variety of translations that have been suggested.[21]

But no sooner do we hear of these differences than they are turned around in the narrative of the sale of the birthright (Gen. 25:29–34). As the story develops, we see the same technique of contrasting portraits, but their personalities are reversed. Esau has failed at the hunt and comes begging for food. He returns home exhausted—*'ayef*—with nothing to show for his efforts.[22] Rather than being the model of success he finds himself at his brother's mercy. He describes himself as if on the brink of death; this may be a hysterical overstatement or an accurate description of his failure to succeed at the hunt. In either case he is not the dominant figure we have assumed him to be. The reversal goes for Jacob as well; the "quiet," "mild," "innocent" brother has now become the schemer for whom brotherly loyalty comes with a price tag. He is described as the provider of food in a domestic sense, the planner and the preparer. While Esau may be named Edom for the red-colored food, which he craves, it is Jacob who actually cooks *ha-adom*

19 Susan Niditch, *"My Brother Esau is a Hairy Man": Hair and Identity in Ancient Israel* (New York: Oxford University Press, 2008), 114–118. Note that he is named first in each of these contrasting verses.

20 While they are not twins, Enkidu is described as Gilgamesh's double (*zikru*). They have a number of oppositions in common with Jacob and Esau—cultured man vs. man of the field, fair-skinned vs. hairy, and so forth. Cf. Esther Hamori, "Echoes of Gilgamesh in the Jacob Story," *JBL* 130, no. 4 (2011): 633–634; Brian R. Doak, *Heroic Bodies in Ancient Israel* (New York: Oxford University Press, 2019), 47–49. There are, however, significant differences—Esau is a hunter of animals while Enkidu protects the beasts of the field; Enkidu and Gilgamesh begin their relationship in conflict but they quickly become the best of friends.

21 Westermann: "quiet"; Zakovitch: "blameless and upright"; NJPS Tanakh: "mild"; KJV: "plain." See the discussion of the word in Anderson, *Trickster*, 69–71.

22 Anderson, *Brotherhood*, 42. The term *'ayef* is used twice to describe Esau, both by the narrator and by the character himself; in addition to exhaustion, the term can also connote failure or defeat—cf. Jud. 4:21; Is. 5:27; 2 Sam. 17:29.

ha-adom ha-zeh, presumably for himself as well as for his brother. It is he who is at home in the world of cooking as well as in the art of bartering to his own advantage. And here he is sharply contrasted with Esau, who is the very opposite of the planner, who can't imagine what value this birthright can have when he feels himself to be at death's door. Much has been made of Esau's spurning the birthright as a sign of his unfitness for the blessing, including the narrator's explicit negative comment at the end of the story.[23] But the explicit contrast between the highly emotional speech of Esau and the cold, even calculating, demands of Jacob (especially Jacob's insistence upon an oath to seal the bargain) gives the lie to the earlier descriptions of the twins. Has Jacob become Esau while Esau has turned into Jacob? The lines of definition between the brothers are blurred.

As to the *mise-en-scène* of this act, this is not an actual legal transaction, but a situation of serious play between two competitive brothers. What we have here isn't an authentic sale of a birthright but an aggressive contest between the two. It has no real bearing upon the outcome of the blessing in Gen. 27, where Esau is still referred to as the firstborn (27:19, 32) and where neither parent mentions this transaction; it is doubtful that they even know about it. Jacob and Esau are relatively young in this scene—I imagine them to be perhaps around twelve years old—boys on their own but children nonetheless.[24] They are acting out an essential drama of their twinship, but as children they don't have the power to enforce anything other than temporary gratification. Each makes his demand upon the other, and both receive what they ask for—Esau his portion of stew and Jacob the promise of the birthright. But make no mistake: they are dead serious about their intentions, and the narrator uses this to reveal a great deal about who they are. Esau is convinced he will die if he doesn't get some of Jacob's food, and Jacob wants desperately to defeat Esau by getting firstborn status. He cannot deny his brother food, but neither can he give it away. That he makes his brother swear as to his intentions (and that Esau agrees) underlines the urgency of both boys. The function of the episode is not to establish Jacob's purported

---

23 The term *va-yivez* stands out here as the narrator tends to refrain from explicit condemnation of his characters. Robert Alter (*The Art of Biblical Narrative* [New York: Basic Books, 1981], 42–45) uses this as a paradigmatic example of the narrator's art in the characterization of Esau. But at the same time we note the narrator's pointed portrayal of Jacob as anything but "innocent" here.

24 According to rabbinic tradition, Jacob and Esau were fifteen years old at this time, which occurred on the day of Abraham's death (B. Bava Batra 7b; *Bereshit Rabbah* 63—Abraham died at age 175 when Isaac was 75; Isaac was 60 when the twins were born, making them 15 at the time of the sale of the birthright). But their behavior in the biblical text suggests younger adolescents, boys on the way to adulthood with their professions but still under the control of their parents.

primacy but to set up the drama of Genesis 27, showing the reader how Esau can be reckless and deceived, and how Jacob can devise and carry out a plan ruthlessly. There is a certain naiveté about Esau, for he can see only what is right before him; Jacob, for his part, looks ahead and plots his future (though he never actually becomes the *bekhor*) with a cold determination, which will reappear in chapter 27. The story says much about the character of the twins but very little about the possession of the birthright, for apparently this is not in their control. In both Hurrian texts and the Bible it is the testator who determines the status of the firstborn "contrary to the actual order of birth."[25]

Despite the many points of contrast between the brothers it appears that the boundaries of self-definition between the twins are surprisingly permeable, as they shift back and forth in Genesis 25. This becomes even more complex in the theft of the blessing in Genesis 27, for here Jacob tries to become Esau, while Esau wants to rid himself of his twin brother. As the two opposing sides line up in the chapter the strained balance in the family dynamic is obvious. The parents are divided over who deserves the parental blessing, each favoring one twin over the other. Yet the language of the interactions between the characters is remarkably similar—Isaac commands Esau to prepare his favorite meal in Gen. 27:2–3 and Rebecca repeats this to Isaac in 27:6–7.[26] Each son does as he is bidden by his favorite parent, and the central scenes of Isaac and Jacob (27:18–29) and Isaac and Esau (27:30–40) parallel one another and form the center of the narrative. These scenes are similar in their question and answer format, in their request for a blessing, and in certain aspects of the language of that blessing. The episode concludes with the parents' concern for finding a proper wife for each son.

But this symmetrical configuration breaks down when Jacob covers himself with goatskins to play the role of Esau. Instead of parallel situations or contrasting descriptions, by this act Jacob actually tries to become Esau in a way that is far more significant than the purchase of the birthright in Genesis 25. Jacob makes every effort to mimic his brother as fully as possible: not only the feel of his hairy skin, but also his bodily smell as transmitted by the goatskins and his brother's clothing; not only his touch but the very *mata'amim* (delicacies), which he prepares for his father. All these things attest to a Jacob who not only wants to be like his brother, but who would literally step into Esau's shoes.[27] While to his

---

25 Speiser, *Genesis*, 195; Nahum M. Sarna, *Understanding Genesis* (New York: Schocken, 1970), 185–187. Note Jacob's promotion of his grandsons and demotion of his sons in Gen. 48 and 49.

26 On the use of quotation here see George Savran, *Telling and Retelling* (Bloomington: Indiana University Press, 1988), 41–42.

27 A gendered reading of this episode portrays Jacob as a feminized character who is "passing as a man" (Lori Lefkowitz, *In Scripture: The First Stories of Jewish Sexual Identity* [New York:

mother he is Jacob, to his father he declares himself to be *'Esav bekhorekha,* Esau your firstborn (Gen. 27:19). In the same verse he introduces himself to Isaac by recycling Isaac's original request to Esau (as well as Rebecca's command to him in 27:10). One thing he cannot disguise, however, is his voice, and the best description of the fluidity of Jacob's identity is found in 27:22—*ha-qol qol Ya'aqov ve-hayadayim yedei 'Esav* (the voice—it is the voice of Jacob; but the hands are of Esau). When Isaac asks once again for clarification—"Are you really my son Esau?" Jacob's reply is simply *ani*—it is I.[28] What better indication could there be that Jacob sees himself as Jacob-Esau, a hybrid twin identity? Jacob's sense of self here is elastic, pulled in different directions by mother, father and brother.

And what of Esau and his twin identity? The reversal of roles noted above continues with Esau's complete trust that he will receive his father's blessing; he is more like an *ish tam,* an innocent or unsuspecting man, than Jacob ever was. To be sure, he is furious about Jacob's theft of his blessing, but he displays his vulnerability openly (in a way that Jacob is unable to do until much later),[29] begging Isaac no less than four times to bless him as well.[30] His first request in Gen. 27:34 shows him willing to accept his own blessing even if it has been delayed by Jacob's untimely intrusion—"Bless me also, Father" is not a plea for power or authority over his brother but for parity. This begins to change in v. 36, where he shows both bitterness and resentment in his realization of Jacob's double deception of him. In v. 37 he begins to understand that he cannot have the same blessing as his brother. This is reflected in his use of the verb *aẓalta* in his plea for a blessing: Has Isaac not reserved a special blessing for him? Indeed,

---

Rowman and Littlefield, 2011], 47–63). While masculinity does play a certain role in Jacob's behavior here, his position as Esau's competitive twin is more central to his identity.

28 Gen. 27:24. Isaac is hesitant, which leads to the detailed interrogation at the center of this scene. A further indication of this doubt is the narrator's double use of *ve-yivarkhehu,* first in v. 23, followed by more questions and again in v. 27, followed finally by the blessing. In the end it would seem that Jacob is persuaded by his sensory impressions (the food and the smell); he is almost ready to bless Jacob in v. 23, but he suddenly pulls back and seeks further verification by means of his senses. Cf. Grossman, *Jacob,* 147–148.

29 See Jacob's speech to Laban in Gen. 31:36–42.

30 Alter, *Biblical Narrative,* 115–118, does a masterful job of showing the contrast between outside views (of David) and inside views (of Saul) as a narrative technique to gain the reader's sympathy for David and arouse mistrust of Saul. In our case the narrator has done the reverse: the absence of inside views of Jacob make him unsympathetic to the reader, while the resonant description of Esau's pain draws the reader to his side. At the very least the reader is able to understand the emotion behind Esau's desire to kill Jacob even if she doesn't agree with it. Esau conditions this fratricidal desire by waiting until "after the mourning period for my father," balancing his anger at his brother with his love of his father. In this way Esau becomes a very real character in this section, a perception that will be useful later in the narrative when the brothers meet again (Gen. 33).

has Isaac not set aside blessings for both sons? Doesn't twinship mean that both sons have blessings intended for them? After Isaac's statement of helplessness in Gen. 27:37 ("What can I do, my son?") Esau pushes his father still further in v. 38, repeating the words of his request from v. 34 in a more desperate tone; he cannot bring himself to believe that there is only one blessing. At this point his tears turn the tide, and Isaac finally responds with a blessing. This, or course, is both a relief and a profound disappointment for Esau. Like his brother now he too has a blessing, and up to this point we have had no indication that Esau has been dissatisfied with his twin identity—as long as he gets his share of the blessing. The shift in Esau's attitude comes after Isaac blesses him with a diminished portion of the blessing he gave to Jacob, explicitly marking his inferiority to his brother. Isaac concludes the blessing with a prediction of violence—"you shall live by the sword"—as well as the possibility of casting off his brother's yoke, implicitly linking the two. This is the breaking point for Esau, whose anger now turns into hatred (Gen. 27:41a), which in turn is articulated in his plan to be rid of Jacob for once and for all in v. 41b. Killing Jacob will end the twin relationship that has caused him such great pain. This image of Esau as potential murderer comes as a shock to the reader, reinforcing the realization that the situation cannot be reversed; this is much more serious than the contest over the birthright. From this point on Esau wants nothing more to do with his brother, nothing more to do with being a twin. The irony of this resolve to kill his brother is that it may well be an extension of his father's words of blessing. Isaac has said "when you grow restive you shall break his yoke from your neck' in Gen. 27:40; Esau interprets this as "I must rid myself of my brother once and for all."

This dramatic conclusion marks the end of the twin relationship for the time being. The brothers do not meet or even speak with one another for twenty years. Their relationship will be revisited after this long absence, but they will encounter each other in Gen. 33 under very different circumstances.[31] By then each will have assumed a national identity as well, Esau as Edom and Jacob as Israel. Esau's history and genealogy as Edom is described in great detail in Gen. 36; Jacob's distinctiveness as Israel is implied first by the birth of his sons and then concretized in his covenant with Laban in 31:44–54 and in his name change in 32:28.[32] Jacob's return to the land in Genesis 35 is both the conclusion

---

31 See my discussion of this encounter in "Twinship, Identity and Failed Friendship," in *Friendship in Jewish Culture, History and Religion*, ed. Lawrence Fine (University Park: Pennsylvania State University Press, forthcoming).

32 The emergence of national themes in Jacob's covenant with Laban is described in Rom-Shiloni, "Jacob's Aramean Identity," 210–213.

of his personal *nostos*, his homecoming, as well as the emergence of the sons of Jacob/Israel in the land. The repetition of the Abrahamic blessing in Gen. 35:11 highlights the national element as well—"A nation, yea an assembly of nations shall descend from you; kings shall issue from your loins." To a certain degree this new national identity resolves the problematic aspects of Jacob's personal boundaries, for nations have physical borders as well as other defining characteristics. For both Jacob and Esau, the national identity subsumes the personal and recasts the complex and conflicted sense of self, which we saw above. The cost of this refocusing of identity is that Jacob and Esau can never be twins again, nor even brothers—at best they will be neighbors, dwelling side by side in an uneasy relationship. At times Edom will be ruled by Judah, at other times Edom rebels and breaks away from Judean control. And still further along the Edomites participate in the destruction of the Jerusalem temple in 586, and make incursions into Judean territory in the Negev later in the sixth century.[33] Personal identity and national affinity are deeply interconnected in this saga, but the details of that relationship will begin to work themselves out only in the continuation of the story, whose developments will be discussed elsewhere.[34]

---

33 On the history of relations between Israel and Edom see Anderson, *Brotherhood*, 157–230; Assis, *Identity*, 74–91; John R. Bartlett, *Edom and the Edomites* (Sheffield: Sheffield Academic Press, 1989), 175–186.

34 A fuller study of the Jacob narrative will address the continuation of Jacob's identity formation in Gen. 31–35 as well as the figure of Jacob in the Joseph story. It is tentatively entitled: "Jacob and his Identities: From Conflicted Twin to Beleaguered Patriarch."

CHAPTER 11

The Book of Judith: A Literary Appreciation[1]

Judith A. Kates

My official title at Hebrew College has been professor of Jewish women's studies. In practice this has meant a pervasive concern with what I have called "women-centered" questions and perspectives in the process of drawing students into the Jewish conversation around Torah in the broadest sense. Together with students, I have worked toward understanding classical Jewish texts (Tanakh, midrash, medieval and modern biblical commentaries of all kinds), as much as possible in their own terms, as well as self-consciously thinking through contemporary and personal interpretive possibilities.

My feminist concern deepened as I began teaching rabbinical students beginning with the founding of the Rabbinical School of Hebrew College in 2003, both because of the rabbinical students' own questions and challenges to conventional readings of Torah, and because of our shared awareness of the frequent resistances and even alienation from an androcentric Torah within Jewish communities. While committed to our school's goal of transmitting versions of Judaism fully grounded in our past textual traditions and history, I have also been in search of a "usable" past, meaning for me, a past where women can be seen and their voices heard.

The feminist literary scholar Ilana Pardes speaks for me when, quoting Thomas Mann in his great midrashic novel, *Joseph and His Brothers,* she meditates on his image of probing "the well of the past," which promises "significance to all our striving." Yet, she says in relation to efforts to "retrieve the biblical past," it is a quest that is especially "frustrating, when the voices we wish to draw up

1 An earlier version of this essay was published in *A Different Light: The Hanukkah Book of Celebration,* ed. Noam Zion and Barbara Spectre (Jerusalem: Devora, 2000).

from the past are voices of women whose words were only rarely recorded" or, I would add, imagined by ancient authors. Nevertheless, like Pardes and other feminist scholars and teachers, I have been fascinated by what she calls "countertraditions" in our ancient texts. Emphasizing the multivocality of the Hebrew Bible, Pardes explores "anti-patriarchal perspectives [that] have been partially preserved, against all odds, in the canon."[2]

Another important scholarly voice for me is that of Tikvah Frymer-Kensky, a scholar of Hebrew Bible within the ancient Near East. Frymer-Kensky also asks the fundamental question posed by women's studies: "Where are the women?" But she chooses to emphasize the surprising multiplicity of narratives where women figure significantly.

> The Bible, a product of ... patriarchal society, is shaped by the concerns of the men of Israel who were involved in public life. As such it's a public book, concerned with matters of government, law, ritual, and social behavior. But why, then does this clearly androcentric text from a patriarchal society have so many stories that revolve around women? ...Why were they written? Why were they included in this compact text?"[3]

I have differed from many feminist scholars of Hebrew Bible by setting biblical text within the Jewish interpretive conversation, widening the scope of my search for past imaginings of women's voices. In teaching and writing about biblical text, I align myself with Torah scholar Avivah Gottlieb Zornberg, who explains that she has adopted an approach in which "the biblical text is not allowed to stand alone, but has its boundaries blurred by later commentaries and by a persistent intertextuality."[4]

In this essay, however, I have pushed open the boundaries by exploring a text that, from the perspective of Jewish traditions, exists on the margins of the biblical canon. Positioned as it is outside the lines drawn by rabbinic tradition, the Book of Judith could be understood as an anti-patriarchal "countertradition," too radical in its celebration of an autonomous female as leader and defender of the community to be included as an authoritative work "spoken by means of the

---

2 Ilana Pardes, *Countertraditions in the Bible: A Feminist Approach* (Cambridge, MA: Harvard University Press, 1992), 2–3.

3 Tikvah Frymer-Kensky, *Reading the Women of the Bible: A New Interpretation of Their Stories* (New York: Schocken Books, 2002), xv.

4 Avivah Gottlieb Zornberg, *The Particulars of Rapture: Reflections on Exodus* (New York: Doubleday, 2001), 2.

holy spirit."[5] But, in distinction from some feminist readings that champion the book as an adversary to the depiction of women in canonical narratives,[6] I see a text that insists, through its texture of verbal and narrative allusions to language, stories and motifs of the Hebrew Bible, on establishing itself as "inside" biblical traditions. I find it more useful to think of it as—to use Judy Klitsner's resonant term—a "subversive sequel" to biblical narratives of women and national leaders, offering "alternative possibilities" that both "mine and undermine" stories of rescue and triumph over apparent impossibilities.[7] Through a literary exploration of the book both as narrative and as "reworking"[8] of biblical sources, I propose a subversive "reinscription" of Judith in a newly defined canon.

The Book of Judith, preserved in its most ancient form in the Septuagint, the Greek translation of the Hebrew Bible dating from the Second Temple period, is a literary masterpiece.[9] Best described as historical fiction, it was composed, most scholars think, in the Hasmonean period as a Hebrew text that has not survived.[10] Although it remained outside the rabbinic canonization of the Hebrew Bible, it has come down to us as part of the Jewish Apocrypha (*sefarim ḥiẓonim*, "outside" books). Later Jewish traditions in the form of medieval midrashim and

---

5 This is argued by Toni Craven in *Artistry and Faith in the Book of Judith* (Atlanta, GA: Scholars' Press, 1983). Judith, despite its full rhetoric of devotion to God and explicit description of its protagonist's pious practices, differs in this respect from Esther, which is the subject of rabbinic debate, but accepted. See B. Megillah 7a. On the complex issue of Judith's status within the biblical canon, considered non-canonical in Jewish and Protestant bibles, but canonical in Roman Catholic and Eastern Orthodox bibles, see Carey A. Moore, *Judith* (New York: Anchor and Doubleday, 1985), 86–90.

6 See for example, Margarita Stocker, *Judith, Sexual Warrior: Women and Power in Western Culture* (New Haven: Yale University Press, 1984), 12, who describes the book as an "implicitly feminist, iconoclastic and (in its homicide) amoral counter-cultural myth." In contrast, Amy-Jill Levine offers a more complex view. Judith, whose name signifies her identity as "a representation of or a metaphor for the community of faith" and whose "widowhood, chastity, beauty and righteousness suggest the traditional representation of Israel," also, "through the text's association of those traits with an independent woman and with sexuality, subverts the metaphoric connection between character and androcentrically determined community." For Levine, the book both "sustains and threatens" the male-centered and male- dominated text, and, in the end, averts the threat through Judith's "reinscription into Israelite society." Amy-Jill Levine, "Sacrifice and Salvation: Otherness and Domestication in the Book of Judith," in *A Feminist Companion to Esther, Judith and Susanna*, ed. Athalya Brenner (Sheffield: Sheffield Academic Press, 1995), 208.

7 Judy Klitsner, *Subversive Sequels in the Bible: How Biblical Stories Mine and Undermine Each Other* (Philadelphia: JPS, 2009), xvi.

8 Klitsner's term.

9 Quotations from Judith are based on *The New English Bible with the Apocrypha* (Oxford: Oxford University Press, 1971). Quotations from the Hebrew Bible are from *JPS Hebrew-English Tanakh* (Philadelphia: JPS, 1999).

10 Moore, *Judith*, 66–70.

translations into Hebrew of versions of the story brought it "inside," especially in relation to the story of Ḥanukkah.[11]

The Book of Judith presents us with a stark yet stirring image of the land and people of Israel under threat. At its narrative core, an enormous battering ram of an invading army, significantly numbered as 120,000 infantry and 12,000 cavalry, is arrayed against the mere "12"—the symbolic total of the tribes of Israel, reduced further in this story to two individuals—and women at that! With this vast force poised to invade the literal and figurative central space of the Jewish people, the text draws our attention to Jerusalem and the Temple at its center. "When the Israelites who lived in Judea heard of all that had been done to the nations by Holofernes ... and how he had plundered and totally destroyed all their temples, they were terrified at his approach. They were in great alarm for Jerusalem and for the Temple of the Lord their God." The imagined geographical setting of the story, the historically unknown town of Bethulia, is chosen because its inhabitants "can occupy the passes into the hill-country, because they controlled access to Judea, and it was easy to hold up an advancing army, for the approach was only wide enough for two men" (Jud. 4). The "high priest in Jerusalem at that time" looks to the men to hold tight, like the Greek heroes at Thermopylae, to this narrow entrance to the open, vulnerable, and infinitely precious space occupied by the Temple.

Throughout the narrative, we are reminded of this sacred enclosure as the symbolic goal and motivation for action. The heroine and chief actor in the story initiates her action with prayer, "at the time when the evening incense was being offered in the Temple in Jerusalem" (Jud. 5), and as her final deed, leads her people to Jerusalem where they engage in the quintessential rituals of Temple worship: "As soon as the people were purified, they offered their burnt-offerings, freewill offerings and gifts." Judith herself dedicates to God "all Holofernes's possessions" including the bed net, a symbol of the sexually charged strategy of her triumph, which she transforms into "a votive offering" (Jud. 16).

The Temple, or *beit ha-miqdash* (literally "house" or "home of the holy place"), figures as both symbol and microcosm of the homeland, the household of the people. It creates a tangible place where human connection to God, the source of physical and spiritual life, is made manifest and secured. Its spatial configuration draws our awareness inward toward increasingly private spaces of intensifying divine energy and presence, spaces both precious and dangerous. In the symbolic field of the Temple, moving inside means going both higher and deeper, closer

---

11 See B. Shabbat 23a. Rashi's comment ad loc. on "they [women] were in that miracle" alludes to one midrashic version.

to the divine and to the source of all energy, all life. Penetration of this sacred enclosure requires awe, careful preparation, respect for boundaries, and is limited to legitimate "members of the household." Priestly biblical sources describe an outer courtyard open to all ritually pure worshippers, but inner courts where only priests can enter to perform sacrificial offerings and rituals. The most intensely guarded enclosure is the structure's innermost point, the *qodesh qodashim,* "Holy of Holies," which can be entered only by the *kohen gadol,* the "high priest" on only one holy day in the year, Yom Kippur. Yet this very space, in the *Book of Judith,* is the goal of an invading force, which has already violated the outer circle surrounding it, the homeland, *Ereẓ Yisra'el.* In telling its story of an "Assyrian" general who seeks to destroy the Temple and to require that "Nebuchadnezzar alone should be worshipped by every nation" (Jud. 3), this text, like the more familiar narrative of 1 Maccabees, exposes the trauma of the invaded sacred enclosure and, by implication, the larger *bayit* (home): the land itself.[12]

The language of the Book of Judith invites us to perceive this sacred inner space not only as geographical location, but also as the human core of the Jewish people. As in later rabbinic texts in which the word *bayit* (house or home) is understood to signify the woman whose place it is, here the *bayit* of the Jewish people is personified as a virgin threatened with violent penetration.

> Fervently every man of Israel sent up a cry to God and humbled themselves before him. They put on sackcloth—they themselves, their wives, their children, their livestock, and every resident foreigner, hired laborer, and slave—and all the inhabitants of Jerusalem, men women and children, prostrated themselves in front of the sanctuary, and, with ashes on their heads, spread out their sackcloth before the Lord... .with one voice, they earnestly implored the God of Israel not to allow their children to be captured or their wives raped, their ancestral cities destroyed and the temple profaned and dishonored. (Jud. 4:9–12)

Invasion of the land, destruction of the Temple, is a rape. The town on the hill passes, chosen to defend the narrow, tightly closed access to that vulnerable inner space, is suggestively named Bethulia, which resonates with the Hebrew

---

12 My thinking on the Temple as inner space analogous to the female body has been influenced by Bonna Devora Haberman, "The Yom Kippur Avoda within the Female Enclosure," in *Beginning Anew: A Woman's Companion to the High Holy Days,* ed. Gail Twersky Reimer and Judith A. Kates (New York: Simon and Schuster, 1997).

betulah—virgin. In my reading, this invites us to understand the land overrun by a huge invading army; the besieged town whose people are so tormented that they are on the verge of opening their gates to penetration; and most especially the Temple, a place whose innermost space is its most lifegiving, as the precious and beautiful woman, the "enclosed garden" (Song 4:12), violated. Land, people, and Temple, the heart of both, figure here as the infinitely vulnerable, virginal female body, with its fragile, narrow opening guarded by increasingly feeble defenses against the overwhelming thrust of the aggressor.

What astonishes us in Judith is the persona of the rescuer. Salvation for the threatened virgin in this narrative comes not from a *gibor*, a warrior-hero, but through a woman. Even more surprisingly, her tools of rescue are not only her faith, brilliant intellect, and eloquent speech, but also the femaleness of her body, that very sexuality apparently mobilized in the text to represent vulnerability and victimization. The text, with consummate literary artistry, weaves a tapestry out of allusions to earlier narratives found in the Hebrew Bible, to create a character who will both echo and transform representations of women as saviors of the Jewish people.

Her name itself, Judith, as many scholars have suggested, seems designed to point to her role as epitome of the nation—*yehudit* in Hebrew and *ioudeit* in Greek—meaning "the Jewish woman."[13] But this representative function is complicated by apparent contradictions from our first introduction to her. Later biblical, as well as much Second Temple period literature, frequently personifies the community, *kenesset Yisra'el*, as a woman: either as powerless, suffering victim in need of protection and rescue, or as faithless wife, straying after other loves. Conventional connotations would suggest that Judith, who is not only woman, but widow, constantly in mourning, represents the community through the figure commonly invoked in the Torah for the most vulnerable and needy of humans. In the context of this narrative, we might perceive widowhood at its most extreme, the woman/community bereft and abandoned, about to fall before a ruthless predator.

But this widow is given an enormously long genealogy, connecting her back through names associated with the tribe of Shimon (Salamiel-Shelumi'el, Sarasadae, Ẓurishaddai) all the way back to Israel-Jacob. She is described as wealthy, beautiful (using the same Greek phrases that are used for the beauty of Rachel and Esther in the Septuagint),[14] extraordinarily pious, and respected. She is introduced at a moment of communal crisis, when the town has been under siege for thirty-four days and its leaders have given God five more days

---

13 See Levine, "Sacrifice and Salvation," 210; Moore, *Judith*, 179, n. 1.

14 Moore, *Judith*, 181, n.7.

to "show his mercy" before surrendering on what would be the fortieth day of the siege. She herself has lived secluded as a widow for three years and four months—that is, for forty months, the confluence of communal and personal units of forty suggesting the significant spans of time in which crucial leaders have transformed the history of the people of Israel (Moses, Joshua, Deborah).[15] We see her summoning the leaders of Bethulia (including the chief magistrate, also from the tribe of Shimon but the antithesis of his ancestor in activism) to teach them the deficiencies in their theology, and to reinterpret the meaning of this historical crisis. Most crucially, she declares that her action on behalf of the community will not simply be prayer, as conventional expectations and the voice of the male leader suggest, but that she herself will take on the role of protector-rescuer and "go out" to save the people.

> Hear what I have to say.... I am going to do a deed which will be remembered among our people for all generations. Be at the gate tonight yourselves and I will go out with my maid. Before the day on which you have promised to surrender the town to our enemies, the Lord will deliver Israel by my hand (Jud. 8:32–33).

The constant reiteration of Judith (and her female servant) going out (from Bethulia and then back and forth from the enemy camp), highlights the pattern of reversals through the entire second half of the book. In Tanakh this phrase is used to designate a military leader, the one who "goes out before the people."[16] Here male warriors wait helplessly inside the walls, while a woman goes outside the walls to the open space of danger. The enemy "lord" who expects to "achieve his ends" is defeated by another "lord," the God he has held in contempt (Jud. 11:6). The "head" of the vast army literally and figuratively loses his head to a mere woman. Judith may, like Yael (Judg. 4–5) kill the enemy general in a tent, but in this story it is his tent, his "inside," while she comes from "outside." She invades the space of the invaders.

The leitmotif of "going out" not only initiates a narrative pattern of ironic reversals that recalls the similar structures of reversal in the Book of Esther.[17]

---

15 Moses spends forty days and forty nights receiving the Torah (Deut. 9:9) and leads Israel for forty years from Egypt to the border of Canaan (Deut. 1:3). Joshua succeeds Moses in the fortieth year after the exodus (Deut. 34:9). Deborah achieves forty years of tranquility for the land (Judg. 5:31).

16 See, for example: Ex. 17:9, Judg. 3:10, 1 Sam. 8:20.

17 See Esth. 2:20 reversed in Esth. 4:17, Esth. 7:10 ("they impaled Haman on the stake which he had put up for Mordechai"), Esth. 9:1 (*v-nahafokh hu*, "the opposite happened"—literally "it was overturned, reversed").

It also deliberately evokes a narrative that occupies the background of our consciousness as soon as we hear the name Shimon, and is explicitly brought into the foreground in Judith's prayer:

> O Lord, the God of my ancestor Shimon! You took in hand a sword to take vengeance on those foreigners who had stripped off a virgin's veil to defile her, uncovered her thighs to shame her, and polluted her womb to dishonor her. You said, 'It shall not be done'; yet they did it. So You handed over their rulers to be slain, and their bed, which blushed due to their treachery, to be stained with blood. (Jud. 9:2–3)

Judith evokes the story of Dinah (Gen. 34) who "went out" and was violated by the "foreign" ruler, interpreting the revenge of her ancestor Shimon as, in reality, the instrument of God's vengeance for the pollution of the inner space of the virgin's womb.[18]

But this book stands the Dinah story on its head. The one who goes out may look like the unprotected female about to be raped. She is, in fact, the rescuer and avenger. While the foreign rulers see her as juicy prey for their lust ("Go to the Hebrew woman and persuade her to join us.... It would be a disgrace if we let such a woman go without enjoying her company [literally, 'without having her']") (Jud. 12:12), she uses Holofernes's predatory desires as the fulcrum in her strategy. The image of the bed polluted by Dinah's violated nakedness becomes the focus of Judith's aggression and its coverings the symbol of her victory, turned into a "votive offering" in the pristine, unviolated Temple, protected by "a woman's hand."

Most strikingly, the devastating silence of Dinah's voice in the Genesis narrative is transformed into Judith's masterful action and the rhetorical fullness of her voice:

> O God, you are my God, hear now a widow's prayer ... they have planned to desecrate your sanctuary, to pollute the dwelling-place of your glorious name, and to strike down the horns of your altar with the sword. Mark their arrogance, pour out your wrath on their heads, and give to me, widow as I am, the strength

18 This book radically revises the explicit critique of Shimon in Jacob's "blessing" (Gen. 49:5–7) and, perhaps by implication, in the absence of the tribe of Shimon in Moses's blessing (Deut. 33). See the discussion of Judith's genealogy in Levine, "Sacrifice and Salvation," 214–215.

> to achieve my end. Use the deceit upon my lips to strike them dead ... shatter their pride by a woman's hand. For your might lies not in numbers nor your sovereign power in strong men; but you are the God of the humble, the help of the poor, the support of the weak, the protector of the desperate, the deliverer of the hopeless... . You and You alone are Israel's shield. (Jud. 9)

In her language, Judith fuses the purity of the woman and the sanctuary. To protect it, she designates herself as the new Shimon. (The "deceit upon my lips" alludes to the *mirmah*, or deceit of Dinah's brothers in Gen. 34:13.)

Judith also expresses a prophetic humility, an awareness of human action as mere instrument of the God who protects the desperate, very much in the mode of Zechariah (4:6): "Not by might, nor by power, but by my spirit—said the Lord of Hosts." We may see her as another Esther, taking off her clothes of mourning and dressing "so as to catch the eye of any man who might see her" (Jud. 10:4), just as Esther puts on *malkhut*—royal garments or "royalty" (Esth. 5)—to appeal to Ahasuerus. But Judith is even more like the young David, so boyish and beautiful (feminine) that he arouses the scorn of the enormous enemy, Goliath. Yet he confidently declares himself the instrument of the Lord of Hosts: "For the battle is the Lord's and he will deliver you into our hands" (1 Sam. 17:47).

The ambiguities created by these subversions of conventional gender expectations pervade later midrashim explicitly connected to the story of the Maccabees' struggle, some of which include pieces of the Judith narrative. In one medieval midrashic tradition,[19] the rebellion against the "Greek" oppressors is precipitated by the foreigners' violation of the privacy of Jewish homes and the sexual integrity of Jewish women. They make a decree that anyone who affixes a door bolt to his house will be killed. The ability to close one's door, to make an inviolate private space, becomes a symbol of autonomy, integrity of self and identity. Because of this attempt to destroy Israel's honor (*kavod*) and internal integrity (*tzni'ut*), the Jews get rid of their doors altogether, leaving their houses open and eliminating the space of their eating, drinking, conjugal relations and even sleep, the necessities of daily life. The next decree forbids women to immerse themselves in the ritual bath on pain of death, causing the men to give up sexual relations with their wives.

---

19 My translation/paraphrase of the midrash is based on a text in A. Jellinek, *Beit ha-Midrash* (Leipzig: F. Nies, 1853), vol. 1.

The third and climactic oppression comes in the form of *ius primae noctis* (first night privileges): every young bride must go from her *ḥuppah* to a night of sexual submission to the governor (*hegemon*). The Jews suffered this decree for three years and eight months until Hannah, the daughter of Mattathias the high priest, married a Hasmonean named Elazar. At her wedding feast, she tore her clothing and stood exposed to all. When her father and brothers wanted to kill her for shaming them, she called them to account:

> Do you consider yourselves shamed because I stand naked in front of these righteous ones, but not when you deliver me to the uncircumcised one to violate me? Learn from Shimon and Levi, the brothers of Dinah, who were only two. You are five brothers, besides more than two hundred of the flower of the priesthood.

This, according to the midrash, roused up the men of the Hasmonean family to begin the great rebellion that culminated in the victory we celebrate at Ḥanukkah. In this and similar midrashim, the themes of sexual violation and integrity provide the fundamental imagery for the struggle between Jews and "Greeks." Here too violation of women and invasion of inner space express the emotional, as well as conceptual meanings inherent in pollution of the sacred enclosure of the Temple. The female protagonist, as in Judith, displays more clarity of mind and firmness of purpose than the men of the story, and provides the impetus for courageous action. But the woman remains "inside," while the men, the true activists, "go out" to defend the faith.

What remains unique in the literary masterpiece, the Book of Judith, is the extraordinary transformation of the expectations aroused by conventional notions of gender, as well as by the texture of allusions to biblical narratives. The use of a female character as both symbol and literal embodiment of the community of Israel has a long history in Jewish texts by the time of the Book of Judith. But the transformation of that female body from victim to rescuer suggests a more radical message. The female body, for centuries the symbol of the community as victim of oppression, becomes the means of rescue. Judith prays that God's power (*yad ḥazaqah*—literally, "strong hand") manifest itself through "a woman's hand" (Jud. 9:10). Standing "outside," holding the enemy's head in her distinctively female hand, she symbolizes a human community, which can mold its vulnerability and apparent powerlessness, its "femininity," into resources of strength.

CHAPTER 12

A Woman Walks Into a Bar: Betrothal Stories in Bavli Qiddushin

Jane L. Kanarek

Over the past two decades, feminist study of the Babylonian Talmud (Bavli) has taught us to look for cracks in the dominant patriarchal face of rabbinic Judaism, fissures that enable us to notice voices we might once have overlooked while revealing authority structures as less stable than they might appear. Scholars have excavated the Bavli for women's history, rendering women visible as shapers of rabbinic culture. They have read the Bavli for its construction of gender and the role that gender—male, female, and increasingly the *tumtum* and *androgynous*[1]—has played in the formation of rabbinic culture and its rabbinic elite.[2] As Charlotte Fonrobert has observed, each of these two methodological approaches has its strengths and its weaknesses. In the first, we highlight women's voices but run the risk of making these women tokens within the larger

1 On the *tumtum* and *androgynous*, see Charlotte Elisheva Fonrobert, "Regulating the Human Body: Rabbinic Legal Discourse and the Making of Jewish Gender," in *The Cambridge Companion to the Talmud and Rabbinic Literature*, ed. Charlotte Elisheva Fonrobert and Martin S. Jaffee (New York: Cambridge University Press, 2007), 270–294; Sarra Lev, "How the 'Aylonit' Got Her Sex," *AJS Review* 31, no. 2 (2007); idem, "They Treat Him as a Man and See Him as a Woman: The Tannaitic Understanding of the Congenital Eunuch," *Jewish Studies Quarterly* 17 (2010): 213–243; Max Strassfeld, "Translating the Human: The *Androginos* in Tosefta Bikurim," *Transgender Studies Quarterly* 3, nos. 3–4 (2016): 587–604.

2 For an additional summary of these two approaches, see Charlotte Fonrobert, Jane L. Kanarek, Marjorie Lehman, "Introduction," *Nashim: A Journal of Jewish Women's Studies & Gender Issues* 38 (2015): 5–8. For foundational examples of each approach, on the former see Judith Hauptman, *Rereading the Rabbis: A Woman's Voice* (Boulder, CO: Westview Press, 1997); and on the latter see Charlotte Elisheva Fonrobert, *Menstrual Purity: Rabbinic and Christian Reconstructions of Biblical Gender* (Stanford: Stanford University Press, 2000).

male framework of rabbinic Judaism. In the second, we make these stories about women central to rabbinic discourse as a whole but run the risk of abstraction where individual women are lost as each becomes an exemplar of a particular type of rabbinic discourse rather than an actor in her own right. Fonrobert aptly comments that choosing one approach over the other is not a matter of truth but rather of strategy.[3] In other words, what will be the results of preferring one particular reading methodology over another?

As a talmudist, I draw on both of these methodological approaches in my own work. Increasingly, though, I find myself drawn to another mode of reading, one that is built on the two methodologies I have outlined above but then takes another turn, one that is explicitly directed towards the present while acknowledging that it has stepped outside of academic conventions and limitations.[4] This mode of reading is hopeful, playful, and even humorous: it relies on the imagination, but an imagination that is grounded in theoretically possible—even if unconventional—readings.[5] Much as Tosafist readings can turn the meaning of a phrase or *sugya* on its head, this hermeneutical mode aims to make a sugya mean something quite other than its surface reading might suggest.[6] However, it differs from the reading methodologies of earlier commentators through its consciousness of its reinterpretation as well as its introduction of new voices, and even contemporary concerns, into a chosen sugya. Through play and humor this methodology strives to present readers with an option that represents an alternative to either despair or apologetics as responses to the Talmud's patriarchy.

---

3 Fonrobert, *Menstrual Purity*, 127.

4 This more playful approach grew out of my teaching in the Rabbinical School at Hebrew College. However, this is not an article on pedagogy. I do not present a case-study of my classroom or analyze student data. Nevertheless, I will provide a postscript about teaching at the end of this article.

5 The Israeli author Yochi Brandes excels at these grounded but theoretically possible imaginative re-readings of biblical and talmudic stories. See, in their English versions, Yochi Brandes, *The Orchard*, trans. Daniel Libenson (Jerusalem: Gefen, 2018); idem, *The Secret Book of Kings: A Novel*, trans. Yardenne Greenspan (Jerusalem: Gefen, 2016). See also Tal Ilan's excellent analyses and comparison of the works of Brandes and Maggie Anton, an American author who has written novels about Rav Ḥisda's daughter and Rashi's daughters. Tal Ilan, "Jewish Women Writing Historical Novels Based on Rabbinic Sources," in *Rewriting the Ancient World: Greeks, Romans, Jews, and Christians in Modern Popular Fiction*, ed. Lisa Maurice (Leiden: Brill, 2017), 277–297.

6 For a good and short introductory essay on the Tosafists, the twelfth- and thirteenth-century Franco-German talmudic commentators, see Haym Soloveitchik, "The Printed Page of the Talmud: The Commentaries and Their Authors," in *Printing the Talmud: From Bomberg to Schottenstein*, ed. Sharon Liberman Mintz and Gabriel M. Goldstein (New York: Yeshiva University, 2005), 37–42.

A Woman's Place is in Commerce: B. Qiddushin 8b–9a

B. Qiddushin 8b–9a presents three short amoraic legal narratives about three different nameless, and perhaps imaginary, women who try to acquire, respectively, a necklace, a cup of wine, and two dates and to whom a man presents an offer of betrothal. After each story, an amoraic sage rules that the woman is not betrothed.[7] Excavating this passage for women's voices and women's history, I argue that this sugya can help us to reconsider some of our assumptions about the portrayal of women, betrothal, and commerce within classical rabbinic literature. Reading for the construction of gender and authority, I argue that this sugya can be understood both as inscribing male rabbinic authority over betrothal as well as part of the Bavli's implicit response to M. Qiddushin 1:1 with its comparison of a man's betrothal of a woman to the purchase of a field. Reading through my newer lens, I argue that a playful and imaginative methodology, while perhaps not convincing when working in a more purely academic mode of reading, can nevertheless provide us with more expansive and hopeful readings—and thus relational possibilities to the Bavli.

B. Qiddushin 8b–9a[8]

> *Scenario 1:*
> A certain man was selling glass trinkets [*ḥomrei pitakhyata*].[9]
> A certain woman came and said to him, "Give me one full string."[10]

---

7 On the rabbinic genre of legal narrative see Yonah Fraenkel, *The Aggadic Narrative: Harmony of Form and Content* [Heb.] (Tel Aviv: Ha-Kibbutz ha-Me'uḥad, 2001), 220–235. Fraenkel argues that narrative expresses ideas that cannot be expressed by legal statutes. See also Barry Wimpfheimer's critique of Fraenkel for assuming that these other ideas are extralegal rather than part of the legal nomos itself. Barry Scott Wimpfheimer, *Narrating the Law: A Poetics of Talmudic Legal Stories* (Philadelphia: University of Pennsylvania Press, 2011), 39–40. On the idea of the nomos as consisting of intertwined law and narrative see the now well-known Robert M. Cover, "The Supreme Court, 1982 Term—Foreword: Nomos and Narrative," *Harvard Law Review* 97, no. 1 (1983): 4–68; and the excellent explication of his ideas in Gordon Tucker, "The Sayings of the Wise are Like Goads: An Appreciation of the Works of Robert Cover," *Conservative Judaism* 45 (1993): 17–39.

8 Translation based on the Vilna edition. Manuscript differences are slight.

9 See Jastrow s.v. *pitakhyata* p.1264. MS Vatican adds that the man is selling these trinkets in a store (*be-ḥanuta*). This is likely an addition based on the second story.

10 My translation follows Rashi s.v. *ḥad shoka*. MS Vatican 111, MS Oxford Opp. 248 (347), and MS Munich 95 all read a version of the word *shifa*. See Michael Sokoloff, *A Dictionary of Jewish Babylonian Aramaic of the Talmudic and Geonic Periods* (Ramat Gan: Bar Ilan University Press, 2002), 1138 who states that the meaning of the word is uncertain.

He said to her, "If I give it to you will you be betrothed to me?"
She said to him, "Give it, give it."[11]
Said Rav Hamnuna: Every "give it, give it" is legally meaningless.

Scenario 2
A certain man was drinking wine in a shop.
A certain woman came and said to him, "Give me one cup."
He said to her, "If I give it to you, will you be betrothed to me?"
She said to him, "Give me to drink, give me to drink!"
Said Rav Ḥama: Every "give to drink, give to drink" is legally meaningless.

Scenario 3
A certain man was throwing down dates from a palm tree.
A certain woman came and said to him, "Throw me two."
He said to her, "If I throw to you, will you be betrothed to me?"
She said, "Throw, throw."
Said Rav Zavid: Every, "throw, throw" is legally meaningless.

Rabbinic law requires a series of actions for a betrothal to be legally valid: a man must give an object that is worth at least a *perutah* (the smallest unit of rabbinic currency) to a woman, say a phrase that indicates that the purpose of giving this object is betrothal, and the woman must accept that object.[12] Acceptance of the object is often, but not always, understood as indicating a woman's consent to the betrothal, another element required by the Bavli.[13] In each of the above vignettes, these conditions have technically been met: the man gives an object that is worth at least a *perutah*, he says a phrase that indicates betrothal, and the woman appears to accept the object.[14] These legal ingredients set the stage for

11 One can also translate *ha-va mihava* as "Surely, give it" to reflect the emphatic nature of the infinitive absolute. I have chosen to use the doubled language because it better contrasts with the sugya's conclusion.

12 See M. Qiddushin 1:1 and T. Qiddushin 1:1. I refer here to betrothal (*qiddushin*) that is done through money. On the need for the man to give and speak and a sugya that complicates the Tosefta's simple formulation, see B. Qiddushin 5b and Tosafot s.v. *ha natan hu ve-amera hi.*

13 B. Qiddushin 2b.

14 In more traditionalist communities, this is still how betrothal takes place today. The man says, "Behold you are betrothed to me by the laws of Moses and Israel" and then gives the woman a ring, with the ring serving as the monetary gift. On the prohibition of double ring ceremonies, that is ceremonies where both woman and man give one another rings and speak, see Moshe Feinstein, *Iggrot Moshe Even ha-'Ezer* 3:18. For an appreciation and critique of Feinstein's

the necessity of Rav Ḥama and Rav Zavid to rule that the woman's words do not indicate consent to the betrothal; whatever his words and their actions may have been, she is not betrothed.

In excavating the Bavli for women's voices, the reader will notice that in each of these vignettes, the woman is unnamed.[15] Indeed, these scenes are not intended as historical accounts but are rather exempla that by dint of their inclusion, represent the realm of the possible in the Bavli's textual and cultural universe.[16] Textual excavation asks us to notice that these stories are set in places other than the home and depict women as attempting to purchase commodities in a variety of public settings.[17] These women most certainly speak and are active participants in the marketplace. The storyteller is not surprised by these women's presence at a marketplace stall, in a wine store, or near a date tree; their request to purchase an item is not noteworthy. We might also notice that these women ask for a variety of different items: jewelry, drink, and food.[18] It is possible that these stories represent a small window into women's involvement in commerce in the

---

responsa, see Jane Kanarek, "Remaking Ritual," *Sh'ma: A Journal of Jewish Ideas* (2020): 5–6. For a recent proposal for a two-ring ceremony, see Pamela Barmash, "Egalitarian Kiddushin and Ketubbah," https://www.rabbinicalassembly.org/sites/default/files/2020-03/Egalitarian%20Kiddushin%202020%20final.pdf.

15 Of course, unnamed women are also worthy of attention. Two of the more well-known named women are Yalta and Beruriah. On Yalta, see most recently Marjorie Lehman, "Who Gets a Voice at the Table?: Eating and Blessing With Rav Nahman," forthcoming. See also Rachel Adler, *Engendering Judaism: An Inclusive Theology and Ethics.* (Philadelphia: JPS, 1998), 21–59; Fonrobert, *Menstrual Purity*, 118–127; Tal Ilan, *Mine and Yours Are Hers: Retrieving Women's History from Rabbinic Literature* (Leiden: Brill, 1997), 121–129. On Beruriah, see most recently Moshe Simon-Shoshan, "The Death of Beruriah and Its Afterlife: A Reevaluation of the Provenance and Significance of Ma'aseh De-Beruriah," *Jewish Quarterly Review* 110, no. 3 (2020): 383–411. See also Marjorie Lehman, "Rereading Beruriah through the Lens of Isaac Bashevis Singer's Yentl," *Nashim: A Journal of Jewish Women's Studies & Gender Issues* 31 (2017): 123–145. Both articles contain extensive bibliographies of earlier studies on Beruriah.

16 As Marjorie Lehman points out in the context of B. Berakhot 51b, where an interaction between two rabbis and a woman (Yalta) goes wrong, the sugya aims to examine the extent to which women may be excluded from table ritual. Women in Bavli narratives become a way for rabbis to test the extent of their authority, the nature of the communal framework, and the power of their laws. Lehman, "Who Gets a Voice at the Table," 192 and 192, n. 35.

17 By using the word "public" here I do not intend to set up a dichotomy between "public" and "private" realms. As Cynthia Baker has aptly demonstrated, the dichotomy between public and private is anachronistic when applied to classical rabbinic literature. See Cynthia M. Baker, *Rebuilding the House of Israel: Architectures of Gender in Jewish Antiquity* (Stanford: Stanford University Press, 2002), 116. My use of "public" indicates a space that is not defined by a form of local kinship but rather a place portrayed as belonging to the larger community of Israel.

18 Tosafot, as is expected, do not understand these narratives as giving us a window into women and commerce. Rather, they understand the three scenarios as teaching the legal point that no matter what item is involved in the transaction, be it food, drink, or anything else, the betrothal would be invalid. Tosafot s.v. *kol ashkei ashkoyei khu.*

ancient world.[19] A textual excavator might also notice that these stories depict the potential betrothal as occurring outside of a wider social and familial context: the woman's father—or any other relative—is absent from these scenes. While Adiel Schremer has argued that in the case of Babylonian Jewry, parents largely chose the marital matches for their sons and daughters,[20] that does not appear to be the case in these legal narratives. These stories, then, might nuance our understanding of late-antique rabbinic marriage.

Reading for gender and the construction of rabbinic authority, though, leads the reader to notice other details in these stories. As these women go out into the marketplace and request a necklace, a drink, or two dates, the owner—a man—presents each of them with an offer of betrothal. The women respond to the offer by restating their original request instead of responding directly to the betrothal proposal. While we might assume that these women reject the respective proposals, they do not explicitly say either "yes" or "no." Instead, we are left to infer their intentions from their words. On the one hand, we might assume that when Rav Ḥama and Rav Zavid rule that each woman is not betrothed, they rule in accordance with their desires. On the other hand, we can also notice that since these women do not actually say either "yes" or "no" we have no idea what these women really want. With their legal ruling that these women are not betrothed, the rabbis reinforce their authority over marriage law and their ability to declare betrothed (or not betrothed) regardless of what the parties may desire; the sugya leaves the parties' intentions oblique.[21]

---

19 It is intriguing to observe that this passage does not mention the *shuq*, the open marketplace. While necklace-seller in the first anecdote may be located in the *shuq*, the sugya is indeterminate on that note. Like many passages about women in the *shuq*, these women are similarly sexualized. Nevertheless, the fact of their engagement in commerce is itself not surprising. On women in the *shuq* in Roman Galilee, see Baker, *Rebuilding the House of Israel*, 77–112.

20 Adiel Schremer, *Male and Female He Created Them: Jewish Marriage in the Late Second Temple, Mishnah and Talmud Periods* (Jerusalem: Zalman Shazar Center, 2003), 127–136. For two in-depth reconstructions of a history of rabbinic marriage, see Michael L. Satlow, *Jewish Marriage in Antiquity* (Princeton: Princeton University Press, 2001); Schremer, *Male and Female.*

21 Of course, this declaration of law is stylistically typical of the Bavli. However, noting that something is stylistically typical does not preclude interrogating the effect of that particular literary style. Fonrobert makes a similar claim about our lack of knowledge about what a woman actually desires in her reading of M. Niddah 8:3. When a woman comes to Rabbi 'Akiva to consult him about a bloodstain, the Talmud portrays him as the authority—staging him as a "gynecologist"—over her body regardless of what she may want, something that we never learn from M. Niddah. Fonrobert, *Menstrual Purity*, 113–115.

The conclusion of the sugya reinforces this reading through its posing of another legal question:

> They asked a legal question: [What is the ruling if she says]: "Give," "Drink," "Throw"?
> Ravina said: She is betrothed.
> Rav Sama bar Rikta said: "By the crown of the King![22] She is not betrothed."
> And the law is[23] that she is not betrothed.

In the first three scenarios, when the woman responds to the man she utilizes the infinitive absolute, a doubled and emphatic form of the respective verbs. What happens, though, when the woman only responds with an imperative instead of a more emphatic phrase? Although Ravina and Rav Sama bar Rikta disagree about whether or not the woman would be betrothed, neither of them suggests asking the woman if she consented to the betrothal. And although, as earlier, we might read the Bavli's conclusive ruling—she is not betrothed—as supporting the woman, we might also read it as reinforcing these sages' authority over marriage law and her lack of autonomy to choose.

Shall I Compare Thee to a Field?

M. Qiddushin 1:1–5 moves through a social hierarchy of acquisition. From free Jewish woman to Hebrew slave to Canaanite slave, to animals and then finally to

---

22 Sokoloff: royal crown (*taga*, 1193). As this is the sole appearance of the phrase *taga de-malka* in the Bavli, it is impossible to determine with certainty whether the oath refers to the crown of an earthly or divine ruler, that is the crown of God. I have chosen to translate the phrase as referring to God in recognition of classical rabbinic coronation imagery, one aspect of which includes the crowning of God by Israel at Sinai. On this idea as well as further ancient and medieval Jewish mystical traditions concerning the crown of God, see Arthur Green, *Keter: The Crown of God in Early Jewish Mysticism* (Princeton: Princeton University Press, 1997), specifically 78–87.

23 Benjamin Lewin contends that most of the anonymous legal decisions preceded by *ve-hilkheta* are later additions to the Talmudic text. Benjamin Lewin, *Rabbanan Saborai ve-Talmudam* (Jerusalem: Abiavar, 137), 46–47. See also Jackob S. Spiegel, *Later (Saboraic) Additions in the Babylonian Talmud* [Heb.] (PhD diss.. Tel Aviv University, Tel Aviv, 1975), 163–164; and Richard Kalmin's summary of scholarship on the term *ve-hilkheta* in Richard Kalmin, "Changing Amoraic Attitudes toward the Authority and Statements of Rav and Shmuel: A Study of the Talmud as a Historical Source," *Hebrew Union College Annual* 63 (1992): 87, n.11. Unfortunately, Spiegel does not include this sugya in his list of *sugyot* from B. Qiddushin. That this phrase is a later addition to our sugya is reinforced by the fact that it is followed by three other legal rulings that begin with *ve-hilkheta* and all of which refer to other sugyot: "And the law is that silk does not need estimation; and the law is like R. Eliezer, and the law is like Rava [who said] Rav Nahman said."

property, these *mishnayot* detail the ways in which an item—animate or inanimate—may be acquired by a person.[24] These *mishnayot* overlap in terminology (the use of the verbal root *q.n.y.* to describe acquisition) and methods of acquisition (for example, money and document). Scholars have noted the similarity between the way in which a woman is acquired, or betrothed,[25] by a man and the way in which land may be acquired.[26] Indeed, a woman may be acquired by money, document, or sexual intercourse (M. Qiddushin 1:1), and land may be acquired by money, document, or an act that creates a presumption of ownership (*ḥazaqah*; M. Qiddushin 1:5).[27] As Gail Labovitz writes, "The significance of the opening of m. Kiddushin, then, is to identify marriage as an acquisition and place the acquisition of a woman squarely within the economy of other property transactions."[28] This comparison between woman and land is made more explicit in the Bavli's opening sugya,[29] which proposes two different exegetical derivations of betrothal by money: the first from the patriarch Abraham's purchase of the field of Machpelah in order to bury his wife Sarah (Gen. 23:13,

---

24 Scholars have divided the first chapter of M. Qiddushin into two halves: 1:1–6 known as "the chapter of acquisitions" and 1:7–9, known as "the chapter of obligations." For this terminology see J. N. Epstein, *Introduction to Tannaitic Literature: Mishna, Tosephta and Halakhic Midrashim* [Heb.] (Jerusalem: Magnes, 1957), 52–53. See also Natan Margalit, "Priestly Men and Invisible Women: Male Appropriation of the Feminine and the Exemption of Women From Positive Time-Bound Commandments," *AJS Review* 28, no. 2 (2004): 306–309; Avraham Weiss, "Le-ḥeqer ha-sifruti shel ha-Mishnah," *Hebrew Union College Annual* 16 (1941): 10–11; Noam Zohar, *Be-Sod ha-Yeẓirah shel Sifrut Ḥazal: Ha-Arikhah ke-Mafteaḥ le-Mashma'ut* (Jerusalem: Magnes, 2007), 18–32. Margalit divides the chapter slightly differently, understanding M. Qiddushin 1:6 as the linchpin that bridges the two halves.

25 Rabbinic marriage consists of two stages. In the first, *erusin* or *qiddushin* (betrothal) the woman is forbidden to have sexual relations with all men, including her husband. The marriage portion of the ceremony (*nisuin*) permits the couple, *inter alia*, to have sexual intercourse with one another.

26 See Gail Labovitz, *Marriage and Metaphor: Constructions of Gender in Rabbinic Literature* (Lantham, MD: Lexington Books, 2009), 29–32; Margalit, "Priestly Men and Invisible Women," 306–308; Judith Romney Wegner, *Chattel or Person?: The Status of Women in the Mishnah* (New York: Oxford University Press, 1988), 42–45.

27 A number of scholars have noted the ways in which sexual intercourse is comparable to *ḥazaqah*, an action that creates a presumption of ownership. See, for example, Hauptman, *Rereading the Rabbis*, 68; Labovitz, *Marriage and Metaphor*, 31; Wegner, *Chattel or Person*, 44. See also Labovitz's more extensive list in *Marriage and Metaphor*, 54, n.10.

28 Labovitz, *Marriage and Metaphor*, 30.

29 We can also compare a woman's betrothal to the acquisition of a Canaanite slave or a Hebrew slave. Like land, a Canaanite slave is also acquired through money, document, or possession. Similarly, a Hebrew slave is acquired by money, document, or the boring of his ear. The boring of the ear, as another penetrative action, might be viewed as parallel to sexual intercourse. Nevertheless, the Bavli focuses its comparative energy on the field, likely drawing from the Mishnah's unstated comparison.

25:10) and the second from the prophet Jeremiah's declaration that fields may be purchased by money (Jer. 32:4; B. Qiddushin 2a–b).[30]

This comparison between betrothing a woman and purchasing a field might lead us to understand the woman as having a primarily passive role both in the process of betrothal and in the betrothal ritual itself: she is acquired (*ha-ishah niqneit*) by someone else (a man). He gives the woman money or an item worth money; if the roles were reversed and she were to speak and give the man money, the betrothal would be invalid (T. Qiddushin 1:1). However, as feminist methodology has taught, what might seem like a monolithic patriarchal perspective at first glance is often not quite as monolithic as it might appear. Cracks and fissures in this legal world become apparent once one knows how and begins to look for them.[31] The case of betrothal is no different. The three women depicted in B. Qiddushin 8b–9a undercut a comparison to a passive field: instead of being acquired through money in betrothal, they themselves try to acquire items; they speak and ask for the material items they want; they are unaccompanied in the marketplace. While the amoraic rulings do attempt to reframe these stories within a rabbinic legal discourse where male rabbis legislate for female bodies, the stories themselves may be read as a countertradition[32] to that presented by

---

30 B. Qiddushin 2a–3b was first identified as a saboraic sugya by Sherira Gaon. Building on this identification, scholars have strived to identify other sugyot that might be similarly classified. More recent work attempts to shift from a project of classification and reconstruction of the Bavli's redaction history to utilizing these saboraic sugyot in order to interrogate questions about the Bavli's ideology and its cultural world. For examples of this approach, see Yaakov Elman, "The World of the 'Sabboraim': Cultural Aspects of Post-Redactional Additions to the Bavli," in *Creation and Composition: The Contribution of the Bavli Redactors (Stammaim) to the Aggada*, ed. Jeffrey Rubenstein (Tübingen: Mohr Siebeck, 2005), 383–415; Charlotte Elisheva Fonrobert, "The Place of Shabbat: On the Architecture of the Opening Sugya of Tractate Eruvin (2a–3a)," in *Strength to Strength: Essays in Appreciation of Shaye Cohen*, ed. Michael L. Satlow (Providence, RI: Brown University Press, 2018), 437–454; Jeffrey L. Rubenstein, *Talmudic Stories: Narrative Art, Composition, and Culture* (Baltimore, MD: Johns Hopkins University Press, 1999), 212–242; Mira Beth Wasserman, *Jews, Gentiles, and Other Animals: The Talmud After the Humanities* (Philadelphia: University of Pennsylvania Press, 2017). For a list of saboraic sugyot, see Avraham Weiss, *Ha-yeẓirah shel ha-saboraim (ḥelqam be-yeẓirat ha-Talmud)* (Jerusalem: Magnes, 1953), 11. For a summary of arguments about whether it might be better to term these sugyot "late" see Richard Kalmin, "The Formation and Character of the Babylonian Talmud," in *The Cambridge History of Judaism*, vol. 4: *The Late Roman-Rabbinic Period*, ed. Steven T. Katz (New York: Cambridge University Press, 2006), 842–843.

31 These fissures appear in narrative and legal passages alike. For example, the opening (saboraic) sugya contends that the reason the opening clause of M. Qiddushin 1:1 does not frame the man as subject with an active verb—"the man acquires" (*ha-ish qoneh*)—but rather the woman as the subject with a passive verb—"the woman is acquired" (*ha-ishah niqneit*)—is in order to teach that a woman may only be betrothed with her consent. See B. Qiddushin 2b.

32 Here I am utilizing Ilana Pardes's conception of the countertradition—the desire to grant voice to antipatriarchal elements in the biblical text—and extending it to rabbinic texts. Ilana

the mishnah.[33] Instead of being a passive object of acquisition, these women are purchasers in the marketplace.

Thou Shalt Not Compare Me to a Field

The two reading methodologies illustrated above both surfaced women's voices as well as emphasized the Bavli's attempt to impose rabbinic legal authority upon women's activities in the marketplace. Yet, instead of halting in despair at the all-too-usual imposition of rabbinic authority on women's bodies or continuing with excitement at the ways in which these stories of women challenge the comparison between betrothal and acquisition of a field, this next mode of reading takes an alternative turn towards the present. Building on, but not limited by, these earlier readings, this third way of reading steps into the sugya as if it were a novel or a play. Noticing subtexts left unexpressed, it explores character motivation, tone of voice, and situational context. It recognizes the ways in which the Bavli often leaves intent ambiguous and builds on these ambiguities, introducing contemporary questions into the talmudic discussion. Through humor and playfulness, this mode of reading reframes the sugya's primary concerns as something other than a legal ruling on betrothal, instead addressing issues of deep current concern such as consent, power, and sexuality. In shifting lenses, I offer my readings below not as the definitive meaning of the sugya but rather as suggestive of the many possibilities the stories' hidden drama opens.

As I have mentioned, the Bavli recounts these legal narratives without providing any background information about the characters; these are anonymous women and anonymous men. Although this move is stylistically typical of the Bavli, it also allows me to imagine a variety of different relationships between these men and women. Indeed, we do not know whether these characters meet for the first time in these vignettes or whether they have prior relationships. We can entertain the possibility that they have discussed betrothal

---

Pardes, *Countertraditions in the Bible: A Feminist Approach* (Cambridge, MA: Harvard University Press, 1993), 144.

33 I hypothesize that the opening saboraic sugyot of B. Qiddushin and B. Sotah also function as countertraditions to the *mishnayot* of these two tractates. Among other moves, B. Qiddushin, as I wrote above, reads the grammar of M. Qiddushin 1:1 to indicate the necessity of a woman's consent to her betrothal. In the case of B. Sotah, the opening sugya emphasizes male sexual sin as well as female, shifting emphasis to sin in general and the construction of the ideal rabbinic male. On these ideas, see my forthcoming article: Jane Kanarek, "The Moral Man and the Disappearing Sotah: The Bavli's Response to Mishnah Sotah," forthcoming.

before, and that the man refers to these discussions when he makes his proposal. As the Bavli does mention the case of betrothal discussions prior to actual betrothal, this reading would not be entirely farfetched.[34] If the case is one of prior discussions, when the woman replies, "Give, give!" (or any of the other phrases) she could be exclaiming in an exasperated and angry tone of voice, "Enough about betrothal! Leave me alone and give me what I want!" The woman's answer leaves us to wonder whether a marriage proposal is what happens whenever a woman goes outside into the marketplace—or out to a bar. Alternatively, she might also indicate, again with a bit of exasperation but perhaps in a more encouraging tone in recognition of prior conversations, "Now is not the time to be betrothed!" but another time would be more appropriate. As the Bavli is printed without punctuation to direct us toward a particular intonation, we may take on the role of actors or stage directors in interpreting these characters' words.

Indeed, while my above translations portray the man as asking a question ("He said to her, 'If I give it to you will you be betrothed to me?'"), I might also punctuate the phrase as an imperative, that is, "He said to her, 'If I give it to you be betrothed to me!'" In the first instance, a question, we might imagine the man's tone of voice more flirtatiously and her response equally so. In the second, we would imagine it as an unwelcome intrusion: she simply wants to buy something or to have a drink, and instead is confronted with a marriage proposal.[35] Again, we turn to questions of unwanted attention and the ways in which social context shapes a response. Why are the women in these vignettes unable—or why do they not want—to give a direct response of "yes" or "no"?[36]

We might also read these women's responses in a different vein. When she says, "Give it, give it!" (or "give me to drink, give me to drink" or "throw, throw") she could also be hinting at her complete disinterest in the betrothal proposal. In a more explicitly contemporary vein, we might then propose possible reasons for her disinterest in the proposal. Is she independently wealthy? For example, M. Arakhin 5:1 tells the story of the mother of Yarmatya who journeys with her daughter to Jerusalem and donates her daughter's worth in gold to the Jerusalem Temple—a passage that the Bavli understands as indicating the

---

34 On discussions about betrothal prior to the act itself, see, for example, B. Qiddushin 6a and 13a.

35 Anecdotally, I am confident that many women have had the experience of walking into a bar (and many other places) to have a drink and being confronted by unwanted attention.

36 The same question can be asked about the sugya on B. Qiddushin 8b with its *baraitot* describing a woman giving away the betrothal item (including tossing the object into a fire or the ocean) rather than stating whether she accepts or declines betrothal.

mother's wealth.[37] Alternatively, is she not interested in men? The Bavli does, after all, recognize female homoeroticism, deeming women who rub against one another[38] unfit to marry into the priesthood.[39] The point, though, is not to get at some kernel of historical truth, but rather to recognize that approaching these scenes as if we were reading a novel or play with little added direction enables us to imagine interpretive possibilities that might otherwise be closed; indeed, one might even argue that these readings are latent in the Bavli's laconic narrative.

With its legal rulings, it is clear that the Bavli's main concern is legal status: are these women betrothed or not? Yet, we need not be limited by the Bavli's legal frame. We *can* imagine these women as independent actors out in the marketplace: as accepting or refusing betrothal; as responding flirtatiously or with anger. Paradoxically, the fact that the Bavli leaves open the question of these women's intent and consent enables us to find even further fissures in the Bavli's androcentrism. We need not accept the Mishnah's comparison of betrothal of a woman to the purchase of a field but instead playfully imagine these women as consumers[40] in their own right.

Postscript on Teaching

I began to think about this mode of reading sugyot through teaching Bavli Qiddushin in the Rabbinical School at Hebrew College. In searching for ways to help my students find an alternative to a binary of either despair at rabbinic patriarchy and misogyny or a need to apologize for the ancient rabbis and excuse

---

37 B. 'Arakhin 19a. On this passage and the votive practice of donating a person's worth to the Jerusalem Temple, see Jane Kanarek, "Pilgrimage and Piety: Rabbinic Women and Vows of Valuation: Mishnah 'Arakhin 5:1, Tosefta 'Arakhin 3:1, BT 'Arakhin 19," *Nashim: A Journal of Jewish Women's Studies & Gender Issues* 28 (2015): 61–74.

38 *Nashim he-mesolelot.*

39 B. Yevamot 76a. See also B. Shabbat 65a–b. As Daniel Boyarin writes, "[T]he notion that the Talmud, like Queen Victoria, just did not believe in the possibility of female homoeroticism is not a true assumption. It was understood that females could pleasure each other, but this did not form a single category with male intercourse." Daniel Boyarin, "Are There Any Jews in 'The History of Sexuality'?," *Journal of the History of Sexuality* 5, no. 3 (1995): 340. See also Michael Satlow, *Tasting the Dish: Rabbinic Rhetorics of Sexuality* (Atlanta, GA: Scholars Press, 1995), 188–191. On female homoeroticism in early Christianity, see Bernadette Brooten, *Love Between Women: Early Christian Responses to Female Homoeroticism* (Chicago: University of Chicago Press, 2009).

40 While the word "consumer" can have negative resonances, I do not intend those here. Rather, I mean to refer to the way in which the Bavli portrays these women as able to buy items independently rather than be themselves "acquired."

their behavior, I realized that I wanted to help them build a reading methodology that was simultaneously rigorous and playful. My students, I discovered, needed space for anger and for hope. In helping them to understand that rabbinic patriarchy—or any patriarchy—was not monolithic,[41] they might enter into the cracks and fissures of the Bavli, creating dents in its dominant voice to expose overlooked people, ideas, and tensions. In so doing and then learning to read playfully, my students may come to see themselves as having the ability both to ground themselves in a sugya's past interpretations and then to reshape that sugya's meaning within their contemporary context.[42] Through helping my students read the Bavli sensitively and playfully, I hope that they will also be able to find meaning and joy—even fun—in a continued relationship with this sacred and canonical Jewish text.

---

41 Judith Romney Wegner, for example, sought to understand whether Simone de Beauvoir's claim that patriarchal culture treats women as chattel applies equally to the Mishnah. In answering negatively, Wegner argued that women are treated as chattel only when their sexuality belonged to a man; when it does not, they are treated as persons. In other words, a crucial project is to understand the particular ways in which patriarchy operates in different cultures. Wegner, *Chattel or Person*, vi. See also Ishay Rosen-Zvi who argues that we must understand the ways in which, "the mechanisms of exclusion operate in different spheres and specific texts." Ishay Rosen-Zvi, *The Mishnaic Sotah Ritual: Temple, Gender and Midrash* (Leiden: Brill, 2012), 11.

42 Here I draw on Ronald Dworkin's idea of the judge as legal interpreter writing the next chapter in the chain novel. In writing this next chapter, the judge is tasked with not only interpreting the texts coherently but also interpreting them in the best way possible, one that advances a moral vision of society. Judges are simultaneously constrained by the past and creative in the ways in which they write the continued story. See Ronald Dworkin, *Law's Empire* (Cambridge, MA: Harvard University Press, 1986), 225–275.

CHAPTER 13

What Problem? Medieval and Contemporary Responses to the "Oven of Akhnai" Story

Michael Rosenberg

No passage in the Talmud has received so much scholarly and popular attention as the "oven of Akhnai" story (B. Bava Meẓi'a 59b). I no longer precisely remember the first time I was taught the story, but it was sometime during college, at one or another Hillel program—as is likely the case for many Jews of my generation. In the intervening years, I have learned, taught, and watched others teach this story, in Israel as well as in North America; in synagogues of all denominational stripes; in adult education settings, seminaries, Jewish day schools and supplementary Hebrew schools. The story's appeal to twentieth- and twenty-first-century academics is likewise clear: in the fields of both Jewish studies and legal theory, intellectuals have turned to Akhnai's oven again and again, producing what is surely the longest secondary bibliography of any talmudic passage, a bibliography that grows ever longer with each passing year.[1] No question, the tale has a strong pull on the imaginations of twenty-first-century Jews of all kinds.

---

1 As such, an exhaustive listing of secondary literature on the story is nearly impossible, and I do not attempt one here. For one partial (and now dated) attempt, see Jeffrey Rubenstein, *Talmudic Stories* (Baltimore: Johns Hopkins University Press, 1999), 314–315, nn. 1 and 2; see also some more recent attempts cited in Moshe Simon-Shoshan, "The Oven of Hakhinai: The Yerushalmi's Accounts of the Banning of R. Eliezer," *JJS* 71, no. 1 (2020): 25–52, at 25, n. 1. Additionally, several articles addressing the story have appeared in law journals, and these tend to be excluded from the existing surveys; a full bibliography of scholarship on this story, including scholarship in both Jewish studies and legal studies, is needed, but beyond the scope of what I can do here.

I have long wondered: To what extent is the current near-obsession with the oven of Akhnai tale a modern and (perhaps especially) postmodern phenomenon? That is, to what extent has the rise of ideas such as pluralism, nondeterminism, political democracy, and/or egalitarianism, or a general trend toward anti-authoritarianism, not only made the story so popular, but also highlighted aspects of the tale that may have been underappreciated by readers in previous eras? Has the story always been so disproportionately studied, commented on, and invoked, or is this popularity a relatively new phenomenon? And when premodern readers looked to the story, did the same elements of the tale draw their attention as do modern readers, or were the surprises and turns of the narrative perceived in substantively different ways?

In this essay, I begin to answer some of these questions, though space prevents anything approaching an exhaustive study.[2] Due to space constraints, I limit myself specifically to questions of legal theory and epistemology, that is, medieval and modern attention to the interplay between human decision-making and the divine voice ruling against the majority, even though there are other important points of interaction between medieval and modern treatments.[3] Do medieval and modern authors share the same questions in response to the story? And if so, do they answer them in similar ways, or differently? Though they seem, *prima facie*, to be operating on entirely distinct axes of interest, the confessional works of medieval authors engaging the story and scholarly engagement with it are far more similar in their substance than they initially appear. These similarities are less obvious due to formal differences in how they express their concerns and their responses.

2 In this essay, I juxtapose specifically medieval authors with (post)modern ones. A fuller picture requires attention not only to the medieval reception of the story, but also—and perhaps especially—to early modern readers, who were often living in a time and place where some of the story's central themes—authority, epistemology, the relationship between human and divine law—were in flux. I hope to return to these works in the future.

3 Specifically, the relatively recent literary turn in analysis of the story, largely initiated by Rubenstein's attention to the whole of the story and its context, has some important overlaps with medieval commentary. For example, both Rubenstein (*Talmudic Stories*) and Steinmetz ("Agada Unbound: Inter-Agadic Characterization of Sages in the Bavli and Implications for Reading Agada," in *Creation and Composition: The Contribution of the Bavli Redactors [Stammaim] to the Aggada* [Tübingen: Mohr Siebeck, 2005], 293–338) attempt to rehabilitate Rabbi Eliezer's reputation; he is, in their readings, not (merely) a legal irritant in the rabbinic system, but (also) an aggrieved party beleaguered by overzealous colleagues. Treatments in the Tosafot and some Spanish medieval commentators prefigure some of this; I hope to return to this aspect of the readerly comparison in a later work.

The Story

The story is so popular that it is almost redundant to summarize it here. Nonetheless, so that the most salient elements of the narrative are fresh in the reader's mind as we tour the contemporary and premodern responses that it elicited, I will outline here the story's core elements. Rabbi Eliezer and the sages disagree over a point of impurity law, with the former ruling a certain oven (the "oven of Akhnai") ritually pure, and the sages ruling it impure. Rabbi Eliezer calls upon the physical world to support his position via miracles (such as trees becoming uprooted, rivers running backwards, and so forth) When miracles prove unsuccessful in persuading his colleagues, a divine voice (*bat qol*) appears and endorses Rabbi Eliezer's legal position. Rabbi Joshua rejects the divine endorsement with the words of Deuteronomy 30:12, "It is not in heaven," which the *amora* Rabbi Jeremiah interprets to mean that divine voices are legally insignificant, since the Torah had stated "one should incline after the majority" (Ex. 23:2).[4] The narrator goes on to relate that apparently God smiled at this moment, commenting, "My children have defeated me."[5]

Is There a Problem?

As in so much of the popular teaching of the story, scholarly engagement with Akhnai's oven focuses on the implication, shocking to many readers, that human legal decision-making supersedes divine truth. Several scholars equate this defeated divine truth with objective (or, in a more cautious mode, normative) truth.[6] That is, the story seems to teach—scandalously!—that *despite* the "real"

---

4 The translation is in line with the meaning implied by the story, but not the contextual reading of the words in Exodus; see Daniel Boyarin, *Intertextuality and the Reading of Midrash* (Bloomington: Indiana University Press, 1994), 33–37, regarding the radical reinterpretation the story necessitates.

5 As Rubenstein, Fonrobert, and Steinmetz have all pointed out, the story actually continues well beyond this point, and indeed, cutting it off at this point obscures some of the recurring themes and messages of the story as a whole, as well as its appropriateness in the broader context of the talmudic discussion in which the story is situated (Rubenstein, *Talmudic Stories*; Charlotte Fonrobert, "When the Rabbi Weeps: On Reading Gender in Talmudic Aggadah," *Nashim: A Journal of Jewish Women's Studies and Gender Issues* 4 (2001): 56–83; Steinmetz, "Agada Unbound"). However, the bulk of the scholarly interest in the story's legal aspects attends only to the first half of the story.

6 Menachem Elon, *Jewish Law: History, Sources, Principles*, trans. Bernard Auerbach and Melvin J. Sykes (Philadelphia: JPS, 1994), 261–263; Izhak Englard, "Majority Decision vs. Individual Truth: The Interpretations of the 'Oven of Achnai' Aggadah," *Tradition* 15, nos. 1/2 (1975):

truth, human majoritarian decision-making wins out. David Hartman takes from the story a less pious understanding of the divine voice in the story; its words are not objectively true, but rather represent "the nonrational intrusions of miracles and heavenly voices."[7] Framed this way, the "oven of Akhnai" is differently scandalous; rather than the rejection of Truth in favor of democratic rule, it endorses reason over the "nonrational," but equates the divine with the latter.[8] Such a reading portrays the divine voice as something other than "true." In any event, both perspectives emphasize the conflict between human reason and divine will as the story's motivating tension, and both approaches present the tale's message as surprising.[9]

This prioritization of human decision-making, based on the notion of majority rule, even against the explicit will of God, interests modern and postmodern readers precisely because it upends contemporary readers' preconceived notions of "traditional" legal epistemology. Daniel Boyarin calls the story's invocation of majority rule "surprisingly modern."[10] Suzanne Stone contends that the story represents a fissure in the rabbinic façade of juridical self-confidence, a momentary revelation of legislative honesty; though the story vindicates the sages, it reveals rabbinic anxiety that their legal ruling is not in line with divine will.[11] The story thus appeals to modern readers precisely because on the one hand, it feels unexpectedly contemporary, while on the other, it appears to open up a window into the inner anxieties of authors who lived nearly two millennia ago.

137–152 (originally published as idem, "The 'Oven of Akhnai': Various Interpretations of an Aggadah" [Heb.], *Shenaton ha-Mishpat ha-'Ivri shel ha-Makhon le-Ḥeqer ha-Mishpat ha-'Ivri, ha-Universitah ha-'Ivrit bi-Yerushalayim* 1 [1974]: 45–56), at 142–146; David Kraemer, *The Mind of the Talmud: An Intellectual History of the Bavli* (New York: Oxford University Press, 1990), 122–123.

7 David Hartman, *A Living Covenant: The Innovative Spirit in Traditional Judaism* (New York: Free Press: 1995), 33.

8 These two takes are mirror inverses of each other. For the first school of thought, the story endorses, seemingly irrationally, human, potentially errant wisdom over the divine, "correct" decision, while Hartman's take implies that it is precisely the divine will that is subject to whim and logical inconsistency.

9 One interesting exception to this scholarly tendency is Bernard Jackson's claim that the story is an apt summation of the preexisting tendency in late Second Temple and early Rabbinic Judaism to minimize the role of God in law. See Bernard Jackson, "The Concept of Religious Law in Judaism," in *Aufstieg und Niedergang der Römische Welt: Geschichte und Kultur Roms im Spiegel der Neueren Forschung*, vol. 2, ed. Hildegard Temporini and Wolfgang Haase (Berlin: De Gruyter, 1979), 33–52, at 47.

10 Boyarin, *Intertextuality and the Reading of Midrash*, 35.

11 Suzanne Last Stone, "In Pursuit of the Counter-Text: The Turn to the Jewish Legal Model in Contemporary American Legal Theory," *Harvard Law Review* 106, no. 4 (1993): 813–894, at 854.

Several scholars imply that the author-editors of the story are themselves aware of the counterintuitive nature of the story. Menachem Fisch points to God's laughter as softening the shocking claim that the correct ruling is "not in heaven";[12] if the storytellers need to soften the shock, then it must have been shocking to the storytellers or their intended audience. So too Susan Handelman, who points out the paradox of Akhnai's oven appearing in the same literary corpus as the claim of "All that a faithful disciple will expound in the future in front of his master was already disclosed to Moses at Sinai."[13] The latter claim reflects a rabbinic humility, but also a hope that their insights were in line with the divine will as revealed at Sinai. By contrast, Akhnai's oven makes clear that fealty to what God intends is extraneous to rabbinic decision-making. Akhnai's oven, then, is not only at odds with *our* perception of "traditional" theology, but with other texts from the same rabbinic corpus.

By contrast with modern treatments of the story, Suzanne Stone has described traditional interpreters as taking a relatively "measured approach."[14] This "measured approach" appears to manifest in two ways: the lack of an explicit declaration of a problem, and attempts to minimize or explain away the problems. That is to say, scholars such as Stone and Izhak Englard understand premodern authors as presenting the story in a way that minimizes any implication that might be troubling to a traditionalist piety.[15] Where such an implication is unavoidable, these traditionalist readers work to minimize the apparent gap between a stable legal culture and the potentially destabilizing forces of the story.

This apparent lack of engagement is, however, not nearly as clear-cut as it might first appear. For example, both Rav Nissim Gaon and the *Sefer ha-Ḥinukh* describe the story as surprising and commonly misunderstood. Nissim ben Jacob (known as Rav Nissim Gaon), an eleventh-century North African commentator, introduces his interpretation of the story (which he attributes to the earlier Rav Hai Gaon) by stating that the story is "difficult, and many are confused regarding

---

12 Menachem Fisch, "Deciding by Argument versus Proving by Miracle: The Myth-History of Talmudic Judaism's Coming of Age," *Toronto Journal of Theology*, supplement 1 (2017): 103–127, at 119.

13 Susan Handelman, *The Slayers of Moses: The Emergence of Rabbinic Interpretation in Modern Literary Theory* (Albany, NY: SUNY Press, 1982), 40.

14 Stone, "In Pursuit of the Counter-Text," 861. See also Englard, "Majority Decision," 142.

15 Importantly, however, Stone and Englard disagree in their explanation for this relative reticence. Stone writes that "inherent ambiguities in the *Oven of Akhnai* story" explain it, while Englard claims that "their understanding of the story is directed to avoiding the creation of such a profound normative conflict in the religious sphere."

its interpretation" (*u-mishtabeshin be-feirushah*).[16] He does not explain what these difficulties and confused interpretations were, but presumably he refers to the legal-theological challenges the story poses.[17] Like Rav Nissim Gaon, the *Sefer ha-Ḥinukh,* a thirteenth-century work of debated authorship, but which clearly derives from the school of the Ramban, begins with an explicit acknowledgment that the story is challenging, referring to it as "a certain legend…that shocks all who hear it."[18] It is therefore not the case that medieval authors never express surprise at the story's implications, even if they do so by assigning that surprise to others who "are confused" or are "shocked" by the story.

To be sure, most commentators do not explicitly express any surprise at the theological or legal-theoretical content of the story. A paradigmatic example is the commentary of the Tosafot.[19] As is typical for tosafistic commentary, the problematics of the story are framed not as questions of theology or legal theory, but rather as stemming from a contradiction with another talmudic text. The Tosafot juxtapose our story with another well-studied tale, which appears in B. Yevamot 14a. In the midst of a discussion about whether the Shammaites followed their own view in practice or maintained them only in theory, the Talmud references a third passage (B. ʿEruvin 13b). There, after three years of debate between the houses of Hillel and Shammai, a divine voice—a *bat qol,* as in the oven of Akhnai story—emerges to rule in accordance with the House of Hillel. In Tractate Yevamot, the editorial voice of the Talmud takes for granted that since the *bat qol* declared the Hillelites the legal victors, "the Law" indeed accords with them. The Tosafot contrast Bavli Yevamot with the story of Akhnai's oven: If as Rabbi Joshua put it, *it is not in heaven,* and as Rabbi Jeremiah explicated, "we do not pay heed to a *bat qol,*" then why does the Talmud in Tractate Yevamot take for granted that the divine endorsement given to the Hillelites is legally determinative?

---

16 Rav Nissim Gaon addresses the story, in almost identical terms, in his *derashot* nos. 3, 5, and 7 (unless otherwise noted, all translations of medieval texts are based on the transcriptions found in the Bar-Ilan Responsa Project).

17 Immediately following this introduction, Rav Nissim Gaon goes on to explain the halakhic details relevant to the case of the oven at hand, details that may seem arcane and confusing to many modern readers. Given the prevalence of purity law in rabbinic literature, however, it seems likely that these are not the confusions to which he refers in his opening clause.

18 *Sefer ha-Ḥinukh* 496. (Some editions of the work arrange the commandments differently, such that this passage appears as no. 508).

19 "Tosafot" refers to a school of commentators rather than a specific, single author or work. The tosafistic tradition regarding the oven of Akhnai appears in several recensions; I cite and translate it here based on its appearance in the collection known as *Tosfot ha-Rosh,* on the story at B. Bava Meẓiʿa 59b, s. v. *lo*.

The problem the Tosafot raise is literary, intertextual, technical: The problem is not that Akhnai's oven contains "problematic" content, but rather that its content is at odds with another, equally authoritative text. However, the technical problem they raise is clearly congruent language for a substantive, that is, legal-theological one. Consider the coda to their discussion of the story: They explicitly conclude that Rabbi Jeremiah's explanation ("we do not heed a *bat qol,* for you have already written 'incline after the majority'") implies that the rejection of divine interference in the law is meant to be universal. That is, not only in this debate between Rabbi Eliezer and the sages, but as a general principle, God cannot intervene in legal decision-making. This conclusion heightens the sense that the story of the oven of Akhnai is of broad significance to the entire rabbinic enterprise; it accordingly intimates that, even if they do not express it explicitly, the Tosafot's concerns are about something other than (mere) literary consistency.

Indeed, the very nature of the intertext that the Tosafot invoke draws our attention to the legal-theoretical and epistemological questions that so intrigue moderns. The passage in B. Yevamot raises, and even seems to endorse, the possibility that the principle of majority rule applies only to cases where the two debating sides are "equivalent."[20] The problem the Tosafot raise, then, is on its surface about the internal consistency of rabbinic literature; at a deeper level, however, it is about the competing sources of authority that make claims to truth. The oven of Akhnai pits divine will against democratic decision-making; the invocation of B. Yevamot adds to the mix intellectual firepower (or, in the language of the text, "sharpness"). The Tosafot may frame their concern as one of consistency, but it is also—and indeed, fundamentally—about the ambiguity of truth and its sources.

This different way of framing the problem is unsurprising to anyone who has studied the Tosafot before; pitting two talmudic texts against each other is their standard operating procedure, even when something else is clearly at stake. It also seems, *prima facie,* to be a pious mode of engagement, since it pretends to admit of questions only from within the talmudic corpus. Yet we can also find an instructive cognate for what the Tosafot are doing here in a modern scholarly treatment. In a journal of theology, Menachem Fisch mines meaning from the tale in precisely the same way, pitting the oven of Akhnai against another talmudic text, in this case, the already-mentioned passage from B. Eruvin in which the divine voice makes its appearance in support of the Hillelites. Reading the

---

20 The Talmud there suggests that perhaps "when we follow the majority, [it is only] where they are equal; here, the House of Shammai are sharper."

two tales of divine voices alongside each other, Fisch sees not contradiction but development. The story in B. Eruvin provides a foundational story to endorse a rabbinic vision of intellectual pluralism; the oven of Akhnai reveals the growing rabbinic awareness that this kind of big-tent pluralism cannot work where one of the parties rejects the fundamental terms of debate.[21]

Fisch's article is a fascinating reading of the story, and it emerges precisely from the kind of seemingly pious intertextual reading that I have ascribed to the Tosafot. To be sure, unlike the Tosafot, Fisch lays out his philosophical questions and conclusions alongside his tosafistic juxtaposition, and that difference of genre and style is important. At the same time, Fisch's analysis is an important reminder that intertextual reading can serve not only literary goals, but legal and theological ones as well. The Tosafot's framing of the problem as one of internal consistency does not mean that they were insensitive to the surprising content of the story's legal-theological message; to the contrary, their proposed resolutions to the problem of contradiction suggest that it was a significant concern for them.

Responses to the Problem

Medieval authors, then, like their modern counterparts, were sensitive to the theologically radical nature of the oven of Akhnai story, even as they sometimes framed it in quite different ways. But the claim of Englard and Stone—that the medieval interpreters were restrained in their engagement with Akhnai's oven—reflects not only their acknowledgment (or not) of the theological challenges in the story, but also their responses to it. And indeed, when we analyze medieval commentaries and interpretations, we do find a tendency to minimize the tension between competing sources for authority.

Let's return to the Tosafot, who offer two resolutions to the contradiction between Akhnai's oven tale and the text in B. Yevamot. The first attends to Rabbi Jeremiah's bipartite statement: "We do not pay heed to a *bat qol*," because God has "already written, at Mount Sinai, in the Torah, 'incline after the majority.'" In the story of the oven of Akhnai, we find two competing divine directives, one given in writing—"incline after the majority"—and the other orally ("the law follows Rabbi Eliezer"). In this case, the Tosafot claim, the preexisting written command supersedes the contemporary oral injunction.[22] We do not find in the

21 Fisch, "Deciding by Argument."

22 A similar minimizing of this tension appears in yet another medieval comment, this from Baḥya ben Asher (Rabbeinu Baḥya), a thirteenth- to fourteenth-century biblical interpreter.

oven of Akhnai a rejection of divine truth in favor of human whim, but rather, an authoritative divine voice being overruled by an even more authoritative divine voice. By contrast, in the case of the Hillelites and the Shammaites, the two divine commands are complementary: The principle of majority rule, according to the Talmud, favors the dominant Hillelite party, and the divine voice simply affirms that.

Of course, if that's the case, one might wonder why a divine voice was necessary, for which the Tosafot provide a response as well: "Since the House of Shammai was sharper [*ḥarifei tefei*]," one might have been unsure whether to follow the majority rule injunction; the divine voice therefore confirmed that the law was in accord with the Hillelites. In invoking the idea, already explicit in the B. Yevamot passage, that the principle of majority rule applies only when the two debating sides are intellectually equivalent, the Tosafot also defang, if only partially, the most radical version of majority rule. If the majority will not emerge victorious when confronted with a "sharper" interlocutor, then "truth" remains an important aspect of decision-making—even if the occasional divine voice is still to be rejected.

The Tosafot's second resolution moves in a different direction. Rabbi Joshua and the sages did not reject the divine voice in support of Rabbi Eliezer because it was legally contradictory. Rather, the Tosafot claim, they recognized that the *bat qol* emerged "solely because of Rabbi Eliezer's honor." That is, God, it appears, enters the legal fray not to correct a mistake in legal decision-making, but rather to protect the reputation of a beloved sage. Recognizing that this divine communication had more to do with God's protective instincts for Rabbi Eliezer than with the intricacies of impurity law, the sages rejected its legal relevance.

Englard compares the Tosafot's second resolution—that the divine voice deviated from normative truth in order to defend Rabbi Eliezer's honor—to the commentary of Rav Nissim Gaon.[23] Like the Tosafot, Rav Nissim Gaon provides two routes for understanding for the sages' rejecting the *bat qol*. One contends that the divine voice spoke in this story only "to test the sages, if they would relinquish

---

Discussing Deut. 13:5, which condemns false prophets, he writes: "Even if we hear a *bat qol* from the heavens [that is] opposed to the commandments, we do not listen to the *bat qol* to uproot the commandment, because the commandment comes to us by means of prophecy, which is higher than a *bat qol*." Here again, we find an implicit recognition of the theological challenge presented through the story's rejection of a divine voice, and an attempt to massage that challenge into submission. It is not the sages who reject the divine voice, but rather the divine text, which is categorized as prophecy, apparently unlike the *bat qol*.

23 Englard, "Majority Decision," 144. I cite Rav Nissim Gaon's commentary on the story from his comments at B. Berakhot 19a, though the same ideas are preserved in the *Shitah Mekubetzet* on B. Bava Meẓi'a.

the tradition in their hands and the received learning in their mouths because of a *bat qol*." Like the tosafistic claim that the divine voice deviated from normative law in order to defend Rabbi Eliezer, this understanding likewise asserts that the divine voice departed from ontological truth in order to accomplish some other end, and therefore its rejection should not be so shocking.

Rav Nissim Gaon's other interpretation likewise minimizes the scandalous implication that the Law need not be aligned with Truth. Paying attention to the specific language of the divine voice—"What have you with Rabbi Eliezer, that the law is like him in every case!"—Rav Nissim Gaon suggests a rather implausible interpretation: the law follows him in "in every case other than this one," that is, he is normally correct ("in every [other] case"), but not in *this* particular ruling. The divine voice issues correct legal guidance, but that legal guidance is not at odds with the human majority decision. Again, Rav Nissim Gaon claims that the oven of Akhnai does not endorse human decision-making over and against divine will.

Rav Nissim Gaon also minimizes the gap between human logic and divine ruling in his presentation of the story. The sages reject Rabbi Eliezer's miracles, because "the law stands only according to that which has been made clear via the received tradition of the majority." This represents a significant reframing of the debate, since the talmudic passage implies a scholastic debate ("they surrounded it[24] with words like a snake.... Rabbi Eliezer responded with all of the responses in the world ...") as the immediate precursor to Rabbi Eliezer's miracles. In Rav Nissim Gaon's telling, however, Rabbi Eliezer is rejecting not only—and not even primarily—a ruling endorsed by the majority, but rather, a ruling undergirded by the authority of received tradition.[25]

By presenting the sages as not merely a majority, but a majority defending received tradition, Rav Nissim Gaon minimizes the gap between what we had

---

24 Regarding the ambiguity of whether it was the oven or Rabbi Eliezer himself that was surrounded by the sages' words, see Steinmetz, "Agada Unbound," 315–316.

25 See also *Ḥiddushei ha-Ramban* on the story, which likewise suggest, albeit more hesitantly, that Rabbi Eliezer's refusal to back down is made problematic by the possibility that "they were speaking from received tradition (*mi-pi ha-shemu'ah*), but he was saying 'so it seems in my eyes.'" These depictions of Rabbi Eliezer's interlocutors as the proponents of received tradition, opposed to Rabbi Eliezer's logocentric argumentation, are all the more surprising in light of the common depiction of Rabbi Eliezer, specifically, as a fierce traditionalist and preserver of received wisdom; see, for example, Yehuda Gilat, *R. Eliezer ben Hyrcanus: A Scholar Outcast* (Ramat Gan: Bar-Ilan University Press, 1984), and, more recently, Vered Noam, "Traces of Sectarian Halakhah in the Rabbinic World," in *Rabbinic Perspectives: Rabbinic Literature and the Dead Sea Scrolls: Proceedings of the Eighth International Symposium of the Orion Center for the Study of the Dead Sea Scrolls and Associated Literature, 7–9 January 2003* (Boston: Brill, 2006), 67–85.

previously considered human decision-making processes and divine wisdom. Insofar as tradition, in a traditionalist society, is perceived as having divine origins and reflecting divine truth, the story now reads as a conflict between two sources of divine wisdom, tradition, and revelation, rather than one between human understanding and God's will.[26] In Rav Nissim Gaon, then, we truly have a shared set of concerns and, broadly speaking, a response to those concerns similar to what we find in the Tosafot: the theological and legal question of human decision-making defeating God's will, followed by attempts to minimize the tension between these two potential sources of authority, saving the divine from juridical rejection.

Medieval attempts to subsume the theologically radical claim that human decision-making could trump explicit revelations of the divine will are unsurprising, if we assume—rightly or wrongly—that premodern commentators would display pious tendencies. The opposite tack, then, taken most prominently by another Nissim—this time Nissim Gerondi (the Ran), a fourteenth-century Spanish commentator—is instructive. In three places in his *derashot*, sermons that delve into philosophical and theological matters, he addresses the story in similar terms. He writes that the sages in the story

> were inclined to rule impure; *even though they knew that they were opining the opposite of the truth,* they did not want to rule pure, for they would be transgressing their rule [*datam*] if they ruled pure, since their intellect inclined toward ruling impure. For decision-making was transmitted to the sages of the generations.[27]

Unlike the commentators surveyed above, the Ran emphasizes the tension between the sages' ruling and the truth value of the *bat qol*'s claim. The divine voice was not deviating from the "true" law in order to defend Rabbi Eliezer or test the sages, nor was it making a general claim that was not in fact relevant to the specific case at hand. The Truth was that the oven in question was indeed ritually pure. Nonetheless, because decision-making had been "transmitted to the sages of the generations," to rule against the conclusion that the

---

26 Rav Nissim Gaon does not entirely erase human logic and decision-making from the story; although he portrays the sages as guardians of tradition, he also describes them as attacking Rabbi Eliezer with "clear proofs that cannot be refuted" and "clear attacks that destroy his words." But in this telling, rabbinic logic is in support of Jewish tradition.

27 *Derashot ha-Ran* 3; see also nos. 5 and 7.

sages came to through intellectual investigation would itself be a miscarriage of the law.

Unlike the Tosafot and Rav Nissim Gaon, who sought to smooth over the tension between human decision-making and divinely revealed truth, the Ran ramps up the conflict. Nor is he unique in this move. The *Sefer ha-Ḥinukh* baldly states that "in this debate … the truth was like Rabbi Eliezer and like the words of the *bat qol* that ruled like him … ." Like the Ran, the *Sefer ha-Ḥinukh* explains the rejection of truth by saying that the sages "brought proof from the fixed law in the Torah that commands us always to go after the majority, *whether they speak truth, or even if they err* … ." Though this explanation shares with some of the earlier-cited interpretations the claim that the written revelation supersedes the more recent oral one, the explicit rider that human judges should be victorious "even if they err" widens the gap between human juridical processes and ontological truth. Perhaps in order to help such a bitter pill go down, he contends that the reason the sages rejected the logical basis for Rabbi Eliezer's opinion was that "because of his superior dialectic [*be-yitaron pilpulo 'al ḥaveirav*], they could not understand the depths of this thought." But lest we miss the point that they indeed ruled against the "correct" law, the *Sefer ha-Ḥinukh* concludes this passage saying that "it was necessary to concede in this case to their words, *that the truth should be lacking*, and it was *as if the Master of Truth was defeated*." As with the Ran—and against Tosafot and Rav Nissim Gaon—the *bat qol* reveals the Truth. The sages follow the majority anyway.

Some medieval authors, then, did attempt to gloss over the theological and epistemological tensions in the oven of Akhnai story, but such a depiction does not adequately describe the breadth of medieval engagement with the tale. This diversity, however, is not unique to the medievals. After all, while many modern commentators relish the boldly stark tension set out between human decision and divine will, others, like their premodern forebears, attempt to tame it. David Weiss Halivni, for example, frames the conflict between the majority-rule sages and the divinely supported Rabbi Eliezer as reflecting the difference between practical law and theoretical law, respectively.[28] Surely a plausible reading, this interpretation nonetheless has the effect of flattening what so many others have pointed to as a curiosity. It implies that there is no real conflict between human decisions and divine truth, because each is appropriate for its respective context: majority rule on earth, and divine will in heaven. Likewise, Handelman resolves the apparent contradiction between the oven of Akhnai's radical interpretive

28 David Weiss Halivni, *Peshat and Derash: Plain and Applied Meaning in Rabbinic Exegesis* (New York: Oxford University Press, 1998), 108–109.

openness and the rabbinic commitment to Sinaitic foundations with her conclusion that "while 'all was already given at Sinai,' the revelation was ongoing and mediated by the interpreters."[29]

Medieval commentators, then, much like their twentieth- and twenty-first-century counterparts, were surprised by the implications of Akhnai's oven. Like modern and postmodern readers, they were aware of the counterintuitive claims that human decision-making could supersede divine injunction, that God could be defeated, and that a majority vote could become law irrespective of capital-T Truth. Their responses to the story also parallel that of more recent engagements, with both those who attempt to minimize the gap between the sages' ruling and the divine decree, and those who emphasize it.

One difference does stand out, however, as already noted by Devora Steinmetz. Steinmetz points out that commentators focused on the legal-theoretical questions tend to paint Rabbi Eliezer in a negative light, a phenomenon common to both medieval and modern responses. Their understanding of *how* Rabbi Eliezer erred, however, differs significantly.[30] For example, for the Ramban (thirteenth-century Spain), Rabbi Eliezer failed because he rejected a received tradition in the sages' hands.[31] By contrast, Steinmetz points to critical scholars who assume Rabbi Eliezer's obstinacy resulted precisely from his own overly stubborn commitment to received tradition and his resultant unwillingness to listen to reasoned discourse as a competing mode for determining the truth. Steinmetz writes, "This reversal of assumption ... reflects, it would appear, a shift in contemporary thinking about the value and authority of tradition."[32]

This shift in attitudes toward tradition is a significant difference between some medieval and many modern approaches to the story. Yet for most of the interpretations I have surveyed here, tradition is not a significant factor in the story at all. The most relevant distinctions for most interpreters are those between the human and the divine, the reasoned and the asserted, majority rule and Truth/intellectual acuity. With regard to these divides, medieval exegetes are, like their modern and postmodern descendants, highly attuned to the challenging and sur-

29 Handelman, *The Slayers of Moses*, 41.

30 Steinmetz, "Agada Unbound," 313, n. 40.

31 See above regarding the same phenomenon in Rav Nissim Gaon.

32 Steinmetz, "Agada Unbound," 313, n. 40. Steinmetz does go on to point out that the contemporary scholarly interpretation "is based largely on the association within rabbinic sources of Rabbi Eliezer with received tradition," such that the shift from medieval to modern readings cannot be attributed solely to changing attitudes toward tradition. Nonetheless, she also points out that "this inter-agadic reading is not supported by evidence *internal* to this agada: there is nothing in this agada that suggests that Rabbi Eliezer is working with a received tradition" (emphasis added).

prising implications of the oven of Akhnai. So too, their responses to the story, again as with contemporary treatments, reflect a diversity in which some seek to minimize the apparent conflicts, while others dig into and emphasize them. Even as they typically—though not always—use different genres, forms, and modes of expressing their questions and answers, medieval and modern interpretations of the oven of Akhnai reveal far more similarity than difference. Whether that means the medieval authors were less pious than one might have assumed, or that modern authors are more so, will remain in the eye of the beholder.

CHAPTER 14

Legal Authority, Memory, and Moral Worthiness: Tosefta *Pisḥa* 4.13–14 and Later Rabbinic Traditions

Michael Fishbane

"Turn it, and turn it again."—It is a tried but still valuable truism that well-known and frequently studied passages in rabbinic literature may continue to instruct when held to the light of new scholarly perspectives. Such is the case in the present inquiry, which turns again to the episode of Hillel and the elders of Beteira, but now from the perspective of its tradition- and redaction-history. As we shall consider, a straightforward "legal-historical narrative," concerned with resolving a halakhic conundrum and issues of exegetical authority, unfolds into a drama with a focus on certain religious values and their import for the transmission of tradition. Thus, if the original account of this episode (found in the Tosefta) purports to highlight several historical dimensions of the legal tradition, in the process of its reception and diffusion, the negative effect of certain moral traits is subject to a strong religious-cultural critique. These matters were not initially part of the accounts, but gradually find a significant role in the subsequent redactions. Accordingly, if the inaugural consideration deals with the emergent authority of the hermeneutical tradition, it is hard to ignore another consideration of crucial importance to the developing scholastic culture of the sages. That issue is the emotional sobriety and worthiness of a sage. Taken together, both the authority of the interpretative tradition *and* the emotional virtue required of its teachers interact as crucial factors in the transmission of authoritative rabbinic knowledge.

When considering matters of authority and legitimacy in general, and the sociology of religious culture in particular, the work of Max Weber comes to mind. According to his famous classification, there are three primary types of legitimacy. The first is "traditional," in the sense that *nomos* or accepted practice derives from the hoary past and its unassailable authority; the second is deemed "rational-legal," because the laws and values are subjected to logical inquiry, such that (prior) authority or (present) legitimation is derived from public forms and modes of argumentation; and the third is referred to as "charismatic," because of the belief that the laws and values are derived from certain (holy) persons, who are imbued with a divine spirit of wisdom.[1] It is evident that although this classification is neither exhaustive nor without ambiguity, it touches on three important components. The first deals with inherently self-justifying types of authority derived from the past; the second touches upon modalities of justification subject to public scrutiny and evident in the present cultural domain; and the third concerns special revelations, derived from the transcendent realm and documented for all succeeding generations.

One can readily see the pertinence of this schema to rabbinic concerns with the divinely revealed Written Torah of Moses, the authoritative traditions of the Oral Torah (based on both tradition and reason), and the spiritual and intellectual character of the teachers through whom Written Torah is interpreted. To the degree that this hierarchical sequence is firmly established, and the flow of theological authority unbroken, the charismatic elements are mutually entailing and reinforcing. But other considerations may complicate this internal coherence. These may become evident if and when there are structural or authoritative differences between the way exegetical practices are justified—for example, if they are based on verbal transmission alone or also sometimes on their exegetical construction or reconstruction. Further complicating these issues are the factors of emergent gaps or concrete problems in the application of the tradition, especially where precedents are either unknown or not remembered because of moral failure. These raise considerable problems both for the unassailable continuity and comprehensiveness of the tradition, and with respect to the worthiness of the individuals involved in its transmission. Reflection on these intersecting matters will occupy our attention in what follows. In the ensuing presentation, we shall follow the lead of several sources that place these issues at the center of reflection and evaluation. Through the lens of tradition and redaction-history we can observe diverse treatments of the legal issues in several strata of rabbinic literature, reflecting different times and locales, and the way certain themes assume a distinct moral-cultural valence.

---

1 See Max Weber, *Wirtschaft und Gesellschaft*, 2nd ed. (Tübingen: J. C. B. Mohr, 1925), 16–20.

I.

We shall begin with a famous passage found in Tosefta, *Pisḥa* (chapter 4, *mishnayot* 13–14). I cite the text *in toto,* since it provides the core of the tradition incorporated into the later Talmudic discourses, and inasmuch as its formulations became the basis for ongoing treatments and formulations of the issues.[2]

> 13. Once the 14th [of Nisan] fell on the Sabbath. They asked [*sha'alu*] Hillel the Elder: Does the paschal-offering override the Sabbath? He said to them: Do we have only one paschal-offering a year that over rides the Sabbath?—There are more than 300 paschal-offerings a year that override the Sabbath! The assemblage gathered against him.[3] He [then] said: The *tamid*-offering is a communal sacrifice, and the paschal-offering is a communal sacrifice; just as the *tamid* overrides the Sabbath, so does the paschal.
>
> 14. Another case: Scripture refers to the *tamid*-offering as [occurring] *be-mo'ado* ["at its appointed time"], and similarly regarding the paschal-offering; thus, just as the *tamid*-offering, offered *be-mo'ado,* overrides the Sabbath, so does the paschal-offering. And another [proof, now] *ad minori ad maius* [*qal va-ḥomer*]: If the *tamid*-offering, for which there is no excision [*karet*], overrides the Sabbath, it logically follows that the paschal-offering, which requires excision, overrides the Sabbath [as well]. Moreover: I received from my masters (*mequbalni mei-rabbotai*) [the ruling] that the paschal-offering overrides the Sabbath—and not just the first paschal-offering [in Nisan], but also the second (a month later, if necessary]; and not just the communal paschal-offering but the individual one [as well]. They [then] said: What shall be the case with the people who didn't bring [their] knives and paschal-offerings to the Sanctuary [before the onset of the Sabbath]? He said: Let them be; the "holy spirit" [*ruaḥ ha-qodesh*][4]

---

2 The translation is based on the critical edition of Saul Lieberman, *Tosefta ki-Feshutah,* part 4, *Mo'ed* (New York: The Jewish Theological Seminary of America, 1962), 165ff.

3 *Ḥavru 'alav.* For this meaning of the idiom, see ibid., 566.

4 The translation "holy spirit" is conventional; but I would propose regarding it as referring to the revelatory spirit of God, called *Qodesh,* the "Holy One." On this latter designation, see E. E. Urbach, *Ḥazal. Emunot ve-De'ot* (Jerusalem: Magnes Press, 1969), 63–67.

> is upon them: if they are not prophets [then] they are sons of prophets! What did Israel do at that time? Those whose paschal-offering was a young lamb, stuck [the knife] into its wool; and [those whose offering was] a goat, tied it to its horns—and [they thereby] brought their knives and paschal-offerings to the Sanctuary and slaughtered their paschal-offering.—On that day they appointed Hillel [their] *nasi*, and he instructed [*moreh*] them in the laws of Passover [*be-hilkhot Pesaḥ*].

A number of issues leap to our attention from the outset. First, this episode is reported as an actual case dealing with an otherwise *unknown* ruling. The Mishnah itself (in Pesaḥim 5:1) gives an established list of actions related to the paschal-offering that override the stringencies of prohibited Sabbath labors. But the situation brought before Hillel is not included; and thus the purpose of the question posed is to determine the law in such a circumstance. For if we have an authoritative rule (prohibited Sabbath labors) and assorted addenda (which modify it), the calendrical congruence of the onset of the Sabbath and the Passover presents a complication that must be resolved—a gap that must be filled. We are thus faced with an example of what the legal historian H. L. A. Hart famously described as the need for every viable legal system to have both primary and secondary rules: the first being established or settled laws, the second being means for the establishment of legal derivatives in an efficient and authoritative way.[5] Or, to formulate this in terms of the classification introduced earlier, the received legal tradition is faced with a new situation; and those who seek to enact this tradition turn to an individual whose legal mastery is assumed—though whether this is based on inherited tradition or intellectual capacity is not stated at the outset.[6] In the unfolding give-and-take, these issues come into play. The sequence is not haphazard, and invites closer scrutiny.

In his first answer, Hillel simply gives a clever rhetorical retort—a logical inference, to be sure, but also one without any formal or detailed scriptural proof. That is, he dismissed the entire problem by suggesting that the present case is neither unique nor without precedent, since there is a clear (overall) scriptural warrant for numerous sacrificial offerings on the Sabbath or other holy days falling on the Sabbath, without causing any concern, and one should treat this

---

5 See H. L. A. Hart, *The Concept of Law* (Oxford: The Clarendon Press, 1961), chapter 6.

6 The recognized capacity for authoritative judgment has also been termed "epistemic authority." See Richard De George, *The Nature and Limits of Authority* (Lawrence, KS: The University Press of Kansas, 1985), 34–42.

event in a like manner.[7] But the people demurred (*ḥavru alav*); for such a casual response (thought admittedly derived from Scripture) hardly deals with specifics or loopholes. Presumably, the people wanted more precise proofs that would correlate the paschal with the *tamid*-offerings—proofs that would (1) designate the paschal sacrifice as a communal and not only an individual or family ritual; (2) fix the appointed day of the Passover in no uncertain terms (so that there would be no leeway to defer the paschal-offering); and (3) show that certain ostensible differences between the paschal and *tamid*-offerings do not undermine (but actually reinforce) a Sabbath override. The ensuing (three) formal arguments, each one constructing its proof on the basis of Scripture, deal with these matters: the first, on the basis of a purely formal (verbal) analogy (*heqesh*); the second, on the basis of a combined verbal-formal analogy (*gezerah shavah*); and the third, on the basis of a graded analogy, proceeding from minor to major premises (*qal va-ḥomer*). Each of these separate proofs is logical and formal—a valid hermeneutic procedure in the precise sense—and presumes an inherent precedence *in* the Written Torah for the deductions made *by* the oral tradition. That is, the three logical instruments articulate the unstated (but implicit) tradition on the precise basis of (explicit) Scriptural statements, thereby moving up the chain of authority—from human reason, to inherited tradition, to divine revelation. Underlying all this is the assumption that oral tradition is encoded in written Scripture, and that the intent of rabbinic logic is to demonstrate this. Paradoxically, second-order interpretations (the hermeneutic procedures) participate in the first-order charisma of the Divine word, and even establish the charismatic basis of tradition itself. Reciprocally, the cluster of logical arguments valorizes exegesis as an instrument of received tradition. Taken together, they are mutually entailing.

A fourth consideration follows, and it establishes the independent authority of Tradition—that is, the reception of apodictic traditions from the authoritative bearers of tradition, *without recourse* to its grounding either in Scripture or in legal exegesis. For after offering the just-mentioned formal proofs, Hillel simply invokes received rabbinic authority *as such*—an invocation that serves as a separate proof, and not one that is proposed to overrule the preceding ones. Moreover, even after the string of logical expositions and one traditional

---

7 The reference to 300 offerings is hyperbolic, and is meant to indicate the vast total of possible Sabbath overrides. It includes, for example, the animals offered during the twice daily *tamid*-offering—this itself totaling more than 100 cases; and then there are the additional Sabbath *musaf*-offerings, and all similar offerings for festival days and their intermediate periods, as well as for the new moon, when these occasions fell on the Sabbath.

disposition, there is still no conclusive response from the people. Instead, they ask yet another question, this time dealing with a more specific detail bearing on such putative overrides. The query takes up the situation of people who have not brought their animals or sacrificial knives into the courtyard of the Sanctuary by the onset of the Sabbath, when doing so thereafter would violate Sabbath stringencies regarding prohibited acts of transferring objects between legal domains. Hillel's answer to this halakhic question is remarkable. He states that the pious Israelites enjoy the charismatic authority of the "holy spirit" and will therefore resolve this matter through Divine inspiration—which they do; since in due course they "find" a permitted loophole whereby the animals themselves, with the knives fixed upon them, move across the domains of Jerusalem into the Sanctuary. This hypothetical (or real) predicament takes place on the eve of the 14th of Nisan (with the onset of the Sabbath), and thus appears as a secondary matter inserted to address a subsequent problem—since it interrupts the initial query about the conflict between the Sabbath and the Passover offerings themselves, which took place on the Sabbath day (that is, prior to the onset of the festival) and its institutional consequence, the people's appointment of Hillel as their *nasi* and his engagement in teaching the laws of Passover by the authority they had vested in him. In Weberian terms, this appointment to office is the "routinization of charisma," or the institutional investiture of rabbinic authority.[8] It stands in stark contrast to the people's solution, itself granted and authorized by Hillel himself! The inclusion of this issue thus adds another dimension to the resolution to halakhic issues, even if the presentation legitimates such an *ad hoc* solution by the halakhic decisor.

Let us return to the purported historical events. Several factors stand out. First, in this episode, the locale (Beteira) is not specified, the people are not named, and the basis for Hillel's prestige not indicated. Second, the teachers of Hillel (Shemaiah and Avtalyon, the sources of his oral tradition) are also not mentioned, and there is no indication that he derived his hermeneutics from them or that these proofs are inferior to oral authority.[9] And third, it is only after all these events of justification and explanation that Hillel is appointed to serve as the people's teacher. In reporting this, the emphasis falls on his subsequent role as instructor (the verb being *moreh*), and not his exegetical skill

---

8 See Lieberman, *Tosefta ki-Feshutah, Mo'ed*, 172.

9 That is, Hillel's formulation speaks of receiving the substance of this tradition from his masters, not the prior methods of deduction; and it is offered to supplement the logical proofs and not degrade them. It is hard to ignore the force of the formulation, despite frequent readings to the contrary.

or his role as a key conduit of tradition. All this bears on the various forms of authority that are presented. For it is precisely Hillel's proven abilities of (1) justifying *halakhah,* (2) transmitting received traditions, *and* (3) respecting pious practice that combine to legitimate him in the people's eyes. Put differently: it is his demonstrated competence to establish the charismatic basis of tradition in Scripture, in the sages, and in the people that earns him the role of *nasi*. Thus the Tosefta indicates a three-fold basis for Tradition: (1) Divine Scripture, (2) rabbinic transmission, and (3) popular (inspired) piety. Each stands on its own in this source: tradition does not override reason, nor does either of them eclipse inspired practice. Ultimately, tradition depends on justified law (via exegesis), trust in the sages (as bona fide transmitters of tradition), and a life of piety. Each is worthy in its own right and rightful place—with the worthy teacher able to affirm them all and keep them in legitimate balance.

But this was not how ongoing receptions of the Tosefta account in the two Talmuds (Jerusalem and Babylonian) dealt with these matters; or how they revised the initial report to serve other religious ends. In the process, these revisions open a different perspective on rabbinic tradition and culture. Ostensibly responding to features and lacunae in the narrative, the original tannaitic tradition was supplemented, interpolated and rerouted into new explanations and channels.

II.

These matters come into dramatic view when we examine the reception of the Tosefta materials in the Yerushalmi (Jerusalem Talmud, J. Pesaḥim 6:1; 33a). In this version of the tradition, instead of beginning with the problematic legal episode and the attempt to resolve or determine the law, we first encounter a striking prologue: "This *halakhah* was forgotten [*ne'elmah*] by the elders of Beteira." With this introduction we are led to presume two matters from the outset: first, that the prior citation of the *mishnah,* that paschal "slaughter overrides the Sabbath," was only the tip of a fuller (unstated) tradition dealing with its specific circumstances; and second, that its loss to the elders of Beteira (who are now named) meant that the queries of the elders were not to "find" law (or deduce it), but to "recover" it; that is, not to construct the law, but to reconstruct it (authentically). For this new version, any presumption implied by the Tosefta that there was a gap in the tradition is countered: the oral law was complete and encompassing, and any resultant complication is due to human failure. This important point emerges from the sequel, as well; for even before Hillel is invited on the scene, the elders invoke him as one "who served [*shimmesh*]" the first pair of elders, Shemaiah and Avtalyon, and would thus be presumed to "know" this law—"and if not, perhaps something good can (nevertheless) come from him."[10] That is, even if he doesn't have a true (oral) tradition, he can perhaps help reconstruct that lost tradition (through exegesis).

That this is apparently the elders' purpose is corroborated by the ensuing presentations. They first ask Hillel, "Have you ever heard [*shama'ta*]" an oral tradition on this case? And then he launches into his rhetorical retort about there being numerous cases of Sabbath overrides that are routinely enacted. But significantly, Hillel does not give any authentic derivation here for the tradition, but only provides his personal reaction (to what he takes as an unnecessary problem). Accordingly, the elders (after a brief interpolation, which tries to justify his hyperbolic account) tell him that they had already commented that if this were the case (that is, if he doesn't report the tradition) he could still be of help—and then Hillel proceeds "to expound [*lidrosh*]" Scripture using the three formal proofs already noted. When he finishes his expositions (offering the help of hermeneutics), the people seem satisfied, saying to him: "We had said that help would come" from you. Ostensibly, this is the end of the matter (the case at hand), and we may presume that the Yerushalmi tradition regarded halakhic midrash as a second-best procedure in the absence of the authentic oral tradition. That this is so seems clear from the sequel as well. For immediately after the first expression of "help," a long interpolation is inserted that deftly dismantles the several exegetical proofs, one after the other—on the basis of pure logic as well as the presumptive legitimacy of using certain exegetical instruments (the *gezerah shavah*) on one's personal authority. These rebuttals reopen the issue, and thereby cast doubt on the closure that seemed effected by Hillel's hermeneutical derivations. Hence, although Hillel continued to expound (*doresh*) all day long, the people did not accept (*qibbelu*) any of these expositions *until* he swore (*yavo alay*): "*Just this* [referring to the exegetical solutions] I heard [*kakh shama'ti*] from Shemaiah and Avtalyon!" And with that testimonial regarding the ultimate authority for his exegesis in oral tradition, he was immediately appointed the people's *nasi*.

Clearly, the Yerushalmi has reported a more complicated cultural situation in order to valorize the oral tradition. Building upon the account in the Tosefta, it construes the latter as a gapped narrative whose episodes must be supplemented: beginning with the presenting situation in which the true tradition was forgotten;

---

10 The noun *toḥelet* suggests a positive, hopeful outcome.

continuing with the successive attempts of Hillel to convince his auditors of the validity of his expositions; and culminating with the correlation of his exegetical logic with the received traditions of the masters. That is, the Yerushalmi privileges the oral rabbinic tradition over all hermeneutic proofs, and either explicitly (through interpolations) or implicitly (through narrative comments) deems proofs deficient or inconsequential. It deems them deficient because of the easily assailable logic or exegetical method; and deems them inconsequential, since they are insufficient in their own right. Accordingly, "hearing" (or receiving) the oral law overrides "exposition" (by exegesis). It has unassailable authority through the authoritative chain of transmission by its teachers; whereas, by contrast, mere (exegetical) logic is subject to rebuttals in kind. For this version of our legal case, then, scriptural exposition is minimally a stopgap measure, if it cannot be refuted, and is maximally a logical support, through scriptural evidence of what has come down through oral tradition. It is doubtful that Hillel's concluding oath means that he is justifying his expositions about Sabbath overrides with a tradition from his teachers, and far more likely that it is invoked here to indicate that his arguments (based upon his rational authority) run parallel to the traditions of the elders (based on their chain of personal authority). Hence, in this Yerushalmi version, the "heard tradition" supersedes the authority of the "exegetical teachings," and does not imply that Hillel received these expository methods from his masters. Perhaps, at best, the "help" that the elders of Beteira hoped for was that the midrashic process might temporarily fill-in or remind them of the lost oral tradition—which alone is primary and privileged.

The Yerushalmi adds another consideration, and by so doing inserts a new topic into this cultural tradition. After the matter of authority was resolved, and Hillel was appointed *nasi*, we learn that he began to castigate the people—blaming their need for his help on their not having "served" (that is, received living traditions from) Shemaiah and Avtalyon ("the two great ones of the world," *shenei gedolei 'olam*). And this rebuke resulted in a failure of memory. The talmudic transformation of the earlier report is striking. For whereas the foundational Tosefta version simply added a hypothetical question after Hillel's various proofs (by logic and tradition), his inability to answer the final query about the knives apparently suggested to students of the Yerushalmi that the answer somehow escaped him, and they went on to suggest a reason: because of his intemperate rebuke "the *halakhah* was forgotten [*ne'elmah*]" by this sage. Accordingly, Hillel was punished "measure for measure" for his angry outburst: just as the people had forgotten the law, so did he in turn. Indeed, when the elders ask him about the law should one forget to bring the slaughter knives for the paschal-offering into the Temple before the Sabbath day festival, he reportedly tells them: "I heard [*shama'ti*] this *halakhah* but have forgotten it"—hence they should go and observe what the people do (through inspiration).

The sequel restores the situation. After seeing the people's "deed [*ma'aseh*] he [Hillel] recalls [*nizkar*]" the law, and proclaims that "just so [*kakh*] did I hear [it] from Shemaiah and Avtalyon." Once again, the oral tradition predominates; and if, in its absence, there are grounds for relying on the inspired actions of the faithful, here too we have but a stopgap measure and a potential mnemonic for confirming or reconstructing the authentic oral tradition. Thus, in contrast to the remedy presented in the Tosefta, for the Yerushalmi it is *only* the oral tradition (both heard and received) that is inherently and unassailably authoritative. Accordingly, all rational expositions (via legal midrash) and charismatic praxes (via the holy spirit) are at best subordinate or propaedeutic devices; for if some piece of the tradition has been lost or was otherwise unknown, it is the task of tradition to secure its own repair (through queries of teachers, exposition of texts, or pious practice). But (to repeat) these are only provisional measures in the absence of the authentic tradition, passed on by word of mouth, in faithful transmission, from one sage to another.

*

The treatment of the Tosefta passage in the Bavli (Babylonian Talmud, B. Pesaḥim 66a–b) is more streamlined than in the Yerushalmi, both with respect to the report itself and later exegesis of its topics. And notably like it, the Bavli version is also inflected with a distinct hierarchy of values about tradition and other matters that move beyond halakhic considerations to the topic of the moral worthiness of the tradents. Distinctive in this case is that the elders who have "forgotten" (*ne'elmah*) the *halakhah* seek out Hillel, who has "served" the masters Shemaiah and Avtalyon, and ask him if he "knows" (*yada'ta*) the law (not if he has received it as an oral tradition). Here too the sage chides the people that such a question is unnecessary, and offers simple logic for an answer. But this time the people accept the rules of reason and want him only to back up his assertion (that there are many cases of legal overrides) with explicit biblical support (asking: *minayin lakh*, "from where [in Scripture] do you derive this?"). That is, in this version of the tradition, the people immediately request exegetical proofs, which Hillel provides (using the traditional rabbinic logic of *gezerah shavah* and *qal va-ḥomer*);[11] and then, on this basis, they immediately appoint

11 The logic of *heqesh* is omitted.

him their leader and he proceeds to publically expound the laws of Passover all day long! Hence, in this Bavli account, the issue of exegetical "knowledge" is highly valued and esteemed, and accepted without immediate rebuttal (such instances appearing only at the end of the unit, an addition that seems part of ongoing logical exercises in the academy, presumably for training law students). Moreover, neither Hillel nor the people need the supporting assertion or verification that the rulings agree with the tradition of Shemaiah and Avtalyon. This is a striking difference between the Bavli and Yerushalmi presentations.

Another difference is that Hillel began his full exposition only after demonstrating in two cases that he could derive rulings from Scripture (that is, hereby "exegesis" supersedes "oral tradition"). It is only after this that he chides them for being lazy and not serving the grand masters, thereby requiring his services (which have independent value). The Bavli also sharpens the irony of this rebuke. For when the people now ask for a ruling for a situation where one has forgotten to bring a slaughter knife into the Temple precincts by Sabbath eve (a query asked in more formal terms than in the Yerushalmi),[12] Hillel reportedly says that he had himself "heard" this ruling "from Shemaiah and Avtalion" but subsequently forgot it. This instance of forgetting is now set forth as an ironical contrast to his rebuke of the people, and not as an explicit punishment for it, as in the Yerushalmi.[13]

*

In the main report, then, the Bavli version has tempered the critique of Hillel. But in the subsequent supplements to this tradition, at the end of the pericope, a strong moral judgment is appended. To reinforce the teaching of Rav (third century CE), who had said that "whoever acts haughtily [*mityaher*]" is deprived of his prophecy (if a prophet) and his wisdom (if a sage),[14] Mar applies the second case to Hillel himself and provides the textual logic for this by juxtaposing the phrase "he demeaned them verbally [*qinteram bi-devarim*]" to the subsequent phrase "he forgot [*shakhaḥ*]" the ruling. The emotional logic of punishment found in the

---

12 The Bavli formulation is formal and terse: *shakhaḥ ve-lo heivi sakin me-'erev Shabbat mahu*; it thus contrasts with the more narrative interrogative style of the Yerushalmi).

13 The logic of consequences is stated explicitly in the Yerushalmi: *keivan she-*, "*because he* rebuked them, he forgot" the ruling.

14 The collocation of prophecy with wisdom implies that the latter (*ḥokhmah*) is the traditional knowledge of the sage (*ḥakham*). On the juxtaposition of the two, and the privileging of the sage to the prophet, cf. the famous (and programmatic) epigram "a sage is preferable to a prophecy" in B. Bava Batra 12a.

Yerushalmi thus returns, but now the point is accentuated by a moral coda on the negative effects of pride. At one level, the grounds for this discussion derive from a formal attempt to understand the meaning of the verb *qinteram*. Support for this assumption may be found in a second coda, which uses Moses as an exemplar for (now) how "anger" (*ka'as*) can cause one to forget a halakhic ruling. The case adduced is the biblical episode at the conclusion of the war with Midian, in which it is first reported that Moses became "incensed" (*va-yiqẓof*) upon learning that the army commanders had spared the Midianite women (Num. 31:14), and thereafter that Eleazar (the priest) taught the ritual law of purifying vessels, "that the Lord had enjoined upon Moses" (v. 21). The sages drew a strong moral lesson from this juxtaposition, concluding that Eleazar taught the law that Moses had received from God *because* Moses had forgotten it in his state of anger.

Clearly, the scholars in the academy were interested in more than the external meaning of words (such as *qinter*), and voiced their concern about the deleterious effects of pride and anger on knowledge of the Written and Oral Torah. In a culture of memory, nothing was more dangerous than forgetting. It is thus striking that such a failure is linked to moral or emotional defects, and not merely to the burden of recalling the voluminous tradition.[15] Thus both in their formulation of the case of Hillel, and in subsequent discussions about it, the sages reflected critically upon the relationship between one's personal character and knowledge. The upshot of these deliberations is clear: halakhic mastery and technique is not separate from moral virtue; indeed, the tradition is grounded upon it. Moses and Hillel, masters of the Written and Oral Torah, prove the point. Deliberations on the authority or derivation of tradition (based on oral chains between master and disciple, or on exegetical skill) are thus only part of the story. The proper character of the sage, who transmits the tradition, is the complementary element—itself deemed a core value and a religious ideal of the first rank.

III.

As noted, rabbinic reflection on the relationship between human character and halakhic knowledge is based on their close study of Scripture and its narrative

---

15 For a vigorous and masterful defense of the idea that the oral tradition depended on memory *in toto*, and was without mnemonic notes of any sort, see the monumental study by Ya'aqov Sussman, "Torah she-be'al Peh, Peshutah ke-Mashma'ah: Qotzo shel Yo"d," in *Meḥqerei Talmud*, ed. Ya'aqov Sussman and David Rosenthal, vol. 3, part 1 (Jerusalem: Magnes Press, 2005), 209–384.

gaps or sequences *with this consideration in mind*—for without this prior moral consideration, the textual issues would not have been perceived or discussed in these terms. Such a hermeneutical focus may be traced to the earliest (tannaitic) halakhic *midrashim*—the *Sifra* (or *Torat Kohanim*) on Leviticus, and the *Sifra de-Vai Rav* on Numbers. In the first case (*Shemini* 2.12), where Moses became enraged (*va-yiqẓof*) with the surviving sons of Aaron, Eleazar, and Itamar (after the death of Nadav and Avihu)[16] and rebuked them for not eating the *ḥata'at*-offering at that time (Lev. 10:17), he is said to have ruled "erroneously" (and not taken into consideration their ritual status of *aninut*, when the corpse of a relative was still unburied) "because he reacted impetuously [*haqpadah she-garmah lo ... lit'ot*]."[17] In the second source (*Mattot, piska* 157),[18] we learn that: "Rabbi Eleazar ben Azariah used to say: In three circumstances Moses became completely angry (*ba lekhlal ka'as*) and consequently acted completely erroneously (*ba lekhlal ta'ut*). These include the aforementioned instance of the sons of Aaron, the previously mentioned situation of the army commanders, and the case when Moses struck the rock twice in fury against the "rebels" (Num. 20:11). The tradition is reported laconically here as a cluster of related instances, and thereby bears further witness to an established exegetical theme that was undoubtedly elaborated homiletically.

Our tannaitic sources do not provide a distinct instance of such homilies; but we do have an instance of how a related homily on this topic incorporated our theme into it. As this case provides a fine instance of the expansion of a tannaitic homily by subsequent amoraic tradition, and also shows how other virtues were taught by juxtaposition to the theme of impetuous anger, we shall present it here in full (in the units noted below as A and A^1). In the present case, it brackets off various thematic and exegetical interpolations (collectively designated below as B). We shall highlight these distinct units, to best present the difference between the stylized, literary homily (A and A^1) from the editorial insert (B). I do this for purposes of presentation and distinction only; for in fact, both units (those marked A/A^1 *and* B) are of importance to our theme of the intersection of moral virtues within halakhic episodes. The homiletic source we now adduce is Midrash *Vayiqra Rabbah* 13.1 (*seder Shemini*).[19]

---

16 According to this source (*Shemini* 2.3), Moses was also enraged at Aaron.

17 Rav Yehudah reports this evaluation in the name of Ḥananiah ben Yehudah.

18 See in the edition of H. S. Horovitz, *Siphra de-Bei Rab* (Jerusalem: Wahrmann Books, 1966), 217.

19 See in the edition of Mordecai Margulies, *Vayiqra Rabba* (Jerusalem: Wahrmann Books, 1972), vol. 1, 268–272.

A. Rabbi Pinḥas and Rabbi Yirmiyah [reported] that Rabbi Ḥiyya bar Abba began [his homily with this verse]: "The ear that hears reproof while alive dwells among the wise" (Prov. 15:31).[20] "The ear that hears reproof while alive": This refers to the sons of Aaron,[21] who were included among those deserving death.[22] "Dwells among the wise": Means that they merited [*zakhu*] that the [Divine] Word be revealed to them,[23] their father, and the brother of their father in their lifetime. As Scripture says, "Then Moses inquired [*darosh darash*] [of God] about the goat of the sin-offering" (Lev. 10:16). What is the meaning of *darosh darash*? This refers to two inquiries: [the first,] if you slaughtered [it], why did you not eat [of it]?; and [the second,] if you did not intend to eat it, why did you slaughter it? Whereupon, "He [Moses] became enraged at Eleazar and Itamar, the sons of Aaron" (ibid.); and because he got angry, he forgot the *halakhah*.[24]

B. Rav Huna said: In three instances Moses got angry and forgot the *halakhah*: with regard to the Sabbath, with regard to metal utensils, and with regard to an *onen*.[25] Where do we learn this with respect to the Sabbath? [From the verse] "And some of the men left of it until morning.... Whereupon Moses became angry with them" (Exod. 16:20);[26] and since he became angry, he forgot [*shakhaḥ*] to tell them the law of the Sabbath. What did he say to them?—"Eat it today, for today is a Sabbath of the Lord" (v. 25). Where do we learn this with regard to the metal utensils? [From the verse] "And Moses became enraged at the army commanders" (Num. 31:14); and since he became angry, he forgot [*nit'almah*] the *halakhah*, and forgot [*shakhaḥ*] to tell

---

20 Literally, "The ear that heeds [*shoma'at*] the discipline of life [*tokhaḥat ḥayyim*] dwells among the wise." The translation above anticipates the homiletic construal by R. Ḥiyya.

21 That is, they heard the reproof of Moses (yet remained silent).

22 This clause renders the Hebrew words *be-ẓad ha-mitah*, and refers to the other sons of Aaron (relatives of the dead ones), but saved by the prayer of Moses. See also Margulies, *Vayiqra Rabba, Shemini*, 204, line 3. The editor suggests that in the above text the phrase "seems" supplementary (269, note 1).

23 The text used by Margulies has *dibbur*, but he correctly prefers *dibber*, found in the textual variants.

24 This formulation of action-result (*keivan she-ka'as nit'almah halakhah mimmenu*) follows that found in the Yerushalmi concerning Hillel.

25 That is, one who has the ritual status of *aninut* (see above).

26 The ellipse is missing in the midrash.

them the laws for [purifying defiled] metal utensils; and because he did not speak, Ele'azar spoke in his stead; [as Scripture says] "And Ele'azar the priest said to all the army" (v. 21); that is, he said to them: "[God] spoke to Moses, our master, and did not command me."[27] Where do we [also] learn this with regard to an *onen*? [From the verse] "And [Moses] became enraged at Eleazar and Itamar, the sons of Aaron" (Lev. 10:16); and since he became angry he forgot [*shakhaḥ*] to teach that an *onen* is forbidden to eat from holy things.

A[1] "Who remained, and said: Why did you not eat the sin offering in the sacred area? ..." (vv. 16–17). Rabbi Pinḥas and R. Yehudah bi-Rabbi Simon [explained this passage]. Rabbi Pinḥas taught, He [Moses] said to them, "The good ones died and the bad ones remained"; and Rabbi Yehudah bi-Rabbi Simon taught, He said to them, "Would that even you had not remained."[28] "Then Aaron said to Moses," (v. 19)—in direct response, as it is said, "The man who is lord of the land spoke harshly to us" (Gen. 42:30):[29] "See, this day they brought their sin offering" (ibid.). [That is) He said to him, "[On] this day my sons died [and on] this day I shall offer a sacrifice? [On] this day my sons died [and on] this day I shall consume holy things?!"[30] Then Aaron immediately provided Moses a *qal va-ḥomer* exegesis [*darash*], [saying] "If with respect to tithes, which are of lesser sanctity, a mourner [*onen*] is forbidden to eat, how much the more so should a mourner be forbidden to eat of sin offerings, which are

---

27 This gloss specifies the language of Scripture, wishing to remove any doubt that the original revelation came to Moses alone.

28 Both comments are in Aramaic, and try to specify the angry words that Moses "said" to the "remaining" sons of Aaron. Cf. *Sifra, Shemini* 2.7: *ein dibber ela lashon 'oz* ("the verb *dibber* means/connotes force/brazenness").

29 This interpolation interprets *dibber* in its traditional rabbinic sense of "harsh" or "strong speech," as compared with *amar*, which traditionally denotes a "soft" or "kind" word.

30 That is, Aaron concluded that during *aninut* the sacrifice should be burnt and not eaten. See the related formulation in *Avot de-Rabbi Natan*, ed. Solomon Schechter (Vienna, 1887; corrected edition, New York: Feldheim, 1967), 56a (chapter 37), "See, this day they have sacrificed, and we are *onenim*!" The passage is used to teach the morality of not interrupting (Aaron waited until Moses finished his rebuke). An alternate opinion has Aaron respectfully take Moses aside and provide a *qal va-ḥomer* argument. In our midrash, Aaron gives this argument right after the rhetorical question (which assumes Moses would realize his error). See above.

> of a higher sanctity!"[31] Immediately [thereafter, Scripture adds], "And Moses heard [this, and approved" (v. 20); and sent a proclamation throughout the entire encampment, saying, "I erred [*ta'iti*] regarding the *halakhah*, and my brother Aaron taught me [*limmedani*]." Since Eleazar [also] knew the *halakhah*, but kept silent, and Itamar [also] knew the *halakha* but kept silent, they merited that the Divine Word visit them, their father, and their uncle in their life-times; as it is written, "And the Lord spoke to Moses and Aaron, saying to them" (*leimor aleihem*; Lev. 11:1). (Rabbi Ḥiyya [applied the words] *leimor aleihem* to the sons [of Aaron], Eleazar and Itamar).[32]

*

This is a remarkable (composite) homiletic unit from which we can learn various inner-cultural presumptions about prevailing exegetical traditions, as well as presumptions about the role of moral character in their presentation and dissemination. In addition, we also learn about the perception of (apparent) gaps in the law in both Torah and Tradition, and how these were evaluated and overcome. Indeed, if there is an unstated presumption that the *halakhah* was complete and fully enjoined to Moses, providing the authoritative basis for all (biblical and subsequent) rulings, the sages could not ignore the actual wording of the Torah in specific instances, and drew conclusions based on their underlying value concepts, and presented these cases as ethical paradigms for instruction and reflection. As they make clear again and again, the authority of learning was not infallible, since moral fallibility could cause a crucial gap or rift in the received oral tradition.

The homiletic unit is a valuable instance of these factors. In evaluating it, we return to the observation that the issue of anger with regard to the recall of the tradition first occurs in tannaitic sources from Ereẓ Yisra'el. We noted this regarding such anthologies as the *Sifra-Torat Kohanim*, the *Sifra de-Vei Rav*, and the presentation of the unit about Hillel in the Yerushalmi.[33] We can now add

---

31 This *qal va-ḥomer* argument is presumed in Targ. Yer. 1.

32 That is, he construed the apparent pleonasm to include the sons, for the text could have simply concluded with *leimor*, with the plural imperative *dabberu* in v. 2 following directly. This is also the understanding of the *Sifra* (*parsheta* 2.1), which gives no reasons for this inclusion. The Targum on Lev. 11:1 reflects the reading *lahem*; the entire word is missing in the Septuagint and Vulgate.

33 It was noted that the Tosefta unit is cited in the Talmud as a tannaitic tradition.

that the central sages noted in the halakhic *midrashim* are both *tannaim* from this time and place (Rabbi Eleazar ben Azarya and Ḥananya ben Yehuda are both second-generation *tannaim*). The same holds true in the preceding midrashic homily, which is reported by two late *amoraim* in the name of Rabbi Ḥiyya, who was a fifth-generation *tanna*. The particular thrust of his teaching is to demonstrate the virtue of restraint or self-containment (here, by the sons of Aaron) when faced with an angry (and unjustified) reproof (by Moses), even though they know the correct *halakhah* and their master does not. There is thus a two-fold display of probity and character by the priests Eleazar and Itamar. First, they do not respond to the harsh rebuke of having acted erroneously, voiced by an elder; and second, they do not teach *halakhah* in the presence of their master, even though they have the correct tradition. It is Rabbi Ḥiyya's special sensibility to the virtue of silent restraint that inspires him to develop his homily via the opening (proemial) citation from Proverbs (whose meaning he deftly bends to his rhetorical and ethical purposes). But we should add that if it was his homiletic genius to connect the restraint of the sons of Aaron in Leviticus 10:18–19 to their presumptive reception of Divine revelation in Leviticus 11:1[34]— and to interpret that latter as a reward for the former—Rabbi Ḥiyya was led in this overall direction by the exegetical traditions found in *Sifra-Torat Kohanim*, which he silently sifts and cites in the sequence of explications (from beginning to end).[35] In typical homiletic fashion, the sage first presents the overall conclusion as a prologue based on the verse from Proverbs, and then develops his argument though a series of explications of the Biblical passages involved.

At the point where Rabbi Ḥiyya invokes the relationship between anger and forgetting, later tradents of the homily (Rabbis Pinḥas and Yirmiyah, or some anonymous redactors) inserted an expansion of this topic (in the name of Rav Huna).[36] This interpolation splits a cited verse (v. 16); and after it resumes (picking up with reference to the sons "who remained"), an additional interpolation was inserted, which comments (in Aramaic) about these survivors. Only after this addition does the text resume with the speech of Aaron to Moses (with a brief citation added, to support the tone of the verb *dibber*) and drawing out the final drama of the episode. The final point, regarding the merit of receiving

---

34 This is an instance of exegesis by "proximity of pericopes," or *semikhut parshiyot* (though of course it involves thematic presumptions and interpolations).

35 Not all the features are found there, however; notably absent is the *qal va-ḥomer* argument (on this, see above n. 27).

36 If this is not Rabbi Huna, the fifth-generation *tanna* in Ereẓ Yisra'el (contemporary of Rabbi), it is Rabbi Huna b. Abin, a fourth-generation *amora* in Tiberias. This is a mixed tradition, as it uses both *shakhaḥ* and *nit'almah* to connote the loss or forgetting of traditions.

revelation, was stated at the beginning of the homily by Rabbi Ḥiyya himself. (It is produced again at the conclusion by the later tradents, who now refer to this sage impersonally).

With respect to the overall content and thrust of this homily, it is evident that a major moral virtue is valorized; this being the capacity to respond to impetuosity or anger with restraint, even when this appears unjustified. Since this overall thematic is introduced by an outbreak of Moses's anger, which causes him to forget the law, later tradition supplemented the central virtue of the homily (emotional control) with the issue of volatility and rage. One cannot doubt that here, as well, there is a concern to promote moral values through a dramatic rereading of Biblical episodes, even one involving Moses himself. This said, it is also significant that the tradition is quick to report that, after Aaron taught Moses the correct *halakhah,* Moses publicly acknowledged his error.[37] Here is another instance where a moral lesson and scholarly virtue are imparted through scriptural exegesis. The hortatory voice of midrash is dramatically exemplified here, even if that voice is now a stylized literary entity. These materials provide a significant complement to the Talmudic episodes studied at the outset. Repeatedly, halakhic issues are integrated with moral instruction for inheritors of the tradition—with the virtues assuming a dominant status.

A Concluding Tribute

The preceding exploration of comparative reception-history has obviously much to teach about the development of rabbinic legal and moral traditions, and their presentation of values in diverse settings. I offer it here in grateful tribute to the cultural preeminence of the Hebrew College over the course of a century, and its impact on so many. Generations of students, myself included, were decisively shaped in its classrooms, benefiting from the close study of traditional and secular sources, and the emphasis on their enduring cultural worth. It was in its setting, over six decades ago, when I was just a high school student, that I first witnessed the devotion of scholarly teachers (trained in all the diverse centers of traditional and academic culture in Europe), concerned with the inculcation

37 In *Sifra, Shemini* 2.12, the phrase is *hodah miyad ve-lo biyyesh lomar lo shama'ti,* "he acknowledged [his error] immediately, and was not ashamed to say 'I hadn't heard it'" (meaning that he did not have the true tradition). The use of the term *shama'ti* signals his reception of the oral tradition, and echoes the verb *vayishma'* ("And Moses heard [or received the ruling]") in the scriptural passage. The sages thus understood Scripture to refer to Moses's hearing the oral tradition! For them, rabbinic exegetical terminology is also inscribed in the Written Torah.

of careful study and the transmission of cultural values (Jewish and Zionist). These virtues have remained the legacy of this major cultural institution in its many iterations and transformations. It is a crown jewel of Jewish life in Boston, and through its students has influenced Jewish communities in both America and Israel. Like so many, I began my life journey in Judaic Studies under its formative auspices, and remain permanently indebted to it pedagogic purposes and majestic example. We used to joke about having to carry a "double load" (secular studies and Hebraic studies) while in high school and college. But burdensome or not, we were the products of a strong and integral Hebrew humanism for eight years, and this shaped our personal lives and communal commitments in the most fundamental ways.

CHAPTER 15

Mystical Ethics: Rabbi Moshe Cordovero and *Tomer Devorah* as Commentary on the *Idra Rabbah*

Melila Hellner-Eshed
Translated by Minna Bromberg and Melila Hellner-Eshed

How can we as human beings emulate, aspire to, and embody the elevated teachings of Jewish mysticism in our own lives? This key question is addressed in a most surprising and moving way by Rabbi Moshe Cordovero—one of the most prolific and interesting of the Kabbalists of Safed in the sixteenth century. From his writing emerges a personality of wide scope, spiritual depth and balance—of one who carries within him great love for both divinity and humanity. This essay deals with the relationship between Cordovero and the *Idra Rabba* (the Great Assembly) of the *Zohar*—how he read it, how he chose to interpret it, and especially how he translated the Idraic conception of divinity into human practices—practices he bequeathed to people of flesh, blood, and spirit who were and are his students and readers.

The *Idra Rabba* (Great Assembly) along with the *Idra Zuta* (Lesser Assembly)—a gathering that takes place at the time of the death of Rabbi Shim'on bar Yoḥai—and a few other smaller Idraic sections make up a special strata in Zoharic literature. The *Idra Rabba* is the story of an emergency assembly, which is convened by the *Zohar*'s hero, Rabbi Shim'on bar Yoḥai (or Rashbi). Declaring that it is "time to act for YHVH" (Ps. 119:126), Rashbi gathers his students and charges them with nothing less than the audacious task of realigning and reconfiguring the faces of God in order to bring healing to God, to the Jewish religion, and to the whole world.

This shocking, highly anthropomorphic vision of God's multiple faces is what sets Idraic literature apart from the rest of the *Zohar.* In contrast to the main body of the *Zohar,* which refers to the divine in terms of ten *sefirot*—divine attributes or "symbol clusters" as Art Green refers to them[1]—the *Idra Rabba* speaks of three divine faces or *parẓufim*: *Arikh Anpin,* "Long-faced" "the One with extended breath,"[2] or slow to anger, also referred to as *'Attiqa Qadisha,* the Ancient Holy One; *Ze'eir Anpin,* "Small-faced" or quick tempered, and *Nuqba*—the divine feminine. While the *sefirot* are more abstract and map-like, the *parẓufim* offer a more holistic, integrative conception of the divine.

As the story of the *Idra Rabba* unfolds—in a field of trees in a time beyond time—alongside the mysteries revealed by Rabbi Shim'on himself, each of Rashbi's disciples comes forward to speak of one feature of the divine faces. Through these revelations of sacred mysteries, the disciples join Rashbi in becoming "pillars" that uphold and sustain all of reality. Taken as a whole, a bold myth emerges from the *Idra* in which human beings can encounter the multifaceted divine—through thought, imagination, and experience. In this myth, all of reality is imprinted within the likeness of *adam*—the human. We read in Genesis (1:27) that the *adam* who is created in God's image is both male and female. From this, the kabbalistic tradition interprets divinity as having a human likeness, which contains both the masculine and the feminine.

The Idraic strata of the *Zohar* is unique in its religious, conceptual, linguistic, and literary characteristics. Among the diverse mystical-religious descriptions in the *Zohar,* the language of the *Idrot* probes the human and divine psyches with particular depth. Their sacred status within the *Zohar* has become more exalted still through their reception and canonization over the generations, as they have

---

1 Defining *sefirot* as "symbol clusters" is an innovation first found in Arthur Green, *A Guide to the Zohar* (Stanford: Stanford University Press, 2004), 28–59.

2 The term *appin* or *anpin* is used in the Zohar to mean "face," "spirit," "breath," "nose," and "temperament." "Nose," in Hebrew *af,* is the facial feature associated with temper and temperament. For example, *Arikh Anpin* is the Aramaic and personalized version of the Biblical Hebrew term *erekh appaim,* which is one of God's attributes of mercy and means "slow to anger" or "patient," and also "long-nosed" and "extended breath." *Ze'eir Anpin* means "small-faced" or "young-faced," as well as "short-nosed" and "short-tempered." For a discussion of the face in classical rabbinic literature and Kabbalah, see Moshe Idel, "Panim: On Facial Re-Presentations in Jewish Thought: Some Correlational Instances," in *On Interpretation in the Arts: Interdisciplinary Studies in Honor of Moshe Lazar,* ed. Nurit Yaari (Tel-Aviv: Yolanda and David Katz Faculty of the Arts, Tel Aviv University, 2000), 21–56.

drawn the attention of some of the most creative kabbalistic interpreters and commentators.

The *Idra Rabba* highlights certain problems in Jewish religion that emerge from an overly strong emphasis on law and systems, focusing on a masculine divine who responds with Judgment (*din*) or Love (*ḥesed*) to the actions and intentions of human beings in this world. This emphasis of Judaism on a single, masculine God manifesting as a dualistic consciousness that tends toward wrath and judgment has come at the cost of losing the vital connection with other faces and aspects of divinity. This brings about a reality in which the relationship between humanity and divinity lacks integration and becomes too narrow, standing only on "one pillar," in the language of the *Idra*. This narrowness threatens to lead to the demise of religion itself and it is this threat to which Rashbi and his students respond with bold action.

The *Idra* wishes to repair this problematic situation through a radical expansion of religious language and sacred imagination so that they may contain—alongside the image of divinity as *Ze'eir Anpin* (that is, structure and discernment)—both the aspect of divinity as oneness, as *Arikh Anpin*, with a face radiating unconditional love and patience, as well as the feminine aspect of the divine. The absence of divinity as Oneness—overflowing with *ḥesed*—in Jewish religious reality, is seen in the *Idra Rabba* as endangering the well-being of Judaism itself. The healing and rejuvenation of religion demands the opening of channels that will allow these aspects to be present in the religious and spiritual lives of Jews.

The immediate questions that emerge for us as we read the dramatic opening of the *Idra Rabba*—with its sense of dire emergency—are: How might *we* invoke divinity in its primordial face of Oneness in our religious language? How could it be possible in the realm of liturgy and ritual, with their highly discursive language and dualistic thought, to make present the aspect of God as *Arikh Anpin*, which has not explicitly appeared in Jewish religious language as we have known it up until now?

The *Idra Rabba* itself begins to answer these questions. From beginning to end, it is a great act of manifesting the different faces of divinity in the realm of religious language. The speech of Rabbi Shim'on and his disciples, their *drashot* (homilies), the visual imagery drawn in words by the participants of the *Idra* turn this divinity from abstraction and transcendence, the unknown and the unknowable, into an active and living presence for its participants, its authors and its readers.

Additionally, in a mode of spiritual activism, Rashbi innovates formulas of blessing that relate to *'Attiqa Qadisha*. When his disciples end their *drashot*—

in which they describe different attributes of divinity manifest in the divine faces—he blesses them in a language of blessing that connects them to this face of divinity (*'Attiqa*). For example:

> "Blessed are you my son by the Ancient of Days! You will find favor of the forehead when you have need of it." (3:129a, trans. Matt, vol. 8, 339)
>
> "Blessed are you by the Ancient of Ancients ... blessed are you by the Holy Ancient One. 'How fine! The Ancient of Days will open his eye upon you'" (*Zohar* 3:129b; Matt, vol. 8, 339)
>
> "You are worthy of beholding the glory of the enhancements of the beard and the countenance of the Days of the Ancient of Ancients" (3:132, Matt, vol. 8, 358)

Drawing the elevated and concealed face of divinity as the holy ancient one into the language of blessings of this world is the way in which the theology-theosophy of the *Idra* turns into praxis within the *Idra* itself.

Let us turn now to Rabbi Moshe Cordovero, one of the all-time great lovers of the *Zohar*. Cordovero regarded the *Idrot* with adoration. He saw in the *Idrot* the most highly perfected expression of Rashbi's teachings in the *Zohar*. In his many writings, Cordovero related in various ways to the literature of the *Idrot*. In *Or Yaqar* ("Precious Light"), his monumental commentary on the whole of the *Zohar*, he interpreted the narrative stories of the *Idra Rabba* and the *Idra Zuta* in the respective places in which they appear in the *Zohar*. Yet he chose to comment on the specific content of the mystical-mythical teachings of the *Idrot*, dealing with the divine faces and body, in a different manner.

Cordovero identified a single theological, metaphysical, mystical language in both Idraic stories. Therefore, in contrast to his usual manner in *Or Yaqar*—in which he interprets the *Zohar* in the order in which it is laid out—he chose to take apart the literary wholeness of the *Idrot* and weave their ideas into one systematic essay that relates their content. He named the three volumes that contain this thematic and encyclopedic approach to Idraic literature *Ḥeleq Shi'ur Qomah*[3] ("The Section on the Mystical Form of the Body Divine").

In his introduction to this commentary, Cordovero explains that he chose this path because it is too complicated to explain each Idraic section in and of itself,

---

3 *Ḥeleq Shi'ur Qomah* (hereafter HaSHaQ) is printed in volumes 21–23 of *Or Yaqar* (Jerusalem: Aḥuzat Yisra'el, 1991). It contains also his commentary on *Sifra di-Ẓni'uta* and other Idraic sections of the *Zohar*.

and that the only way to understand them properly is to study them together, as they illuminate one another:

> [the secrets of] *Ḥeleq Shi'ur Qomah* ... could not be comprehended while I was commenting on each and every one in their place, but rather [only when I put them] all together, because of the quality of understanding in comprehending those secrets ... this from this and that from that. (HaSHaQ, introduction, 81)

After the introduction, the sections of *Ḥeleq Shi'ur Qomah* contain thematic chapters each of which deals with a single part of the divine face or body (such as eyes, forehead, nose, beard, and other features) with side-by-side explanations of a given organ according to how each is understood in the *Idra Rabba* and the *Idra Zuta*.[4] In this expansive commentary one can discern the sometimes heavy-handed effort of harmonizing between the two different Idraic sources for the purpose of weaving them into one systematic theosophy.

Other important discussions of the *Idrot* are found in the opening sections of his great opus *Elimah,* which is a theosophic cosmology that is a "book of all realities," a reality map, the full description of the Godhead. This book deals with different realms of reality, beginning with divinity coming forth from its hidden infinity and continuing all the way to the world of human beings.

Cordovero identified that there is something more elevated and complex in the secrets of divinity as disclosed in the *Idrot* that is not contained in the language of *sefirot* or abstract qualities that is found in the rest of the *Zohar.* In a moment of sensitive introspection on his earlier writings, Cordovero testifies to the fact that in his early work *Pardes ha-Rimmonim* he focused on the language of the ten *sefirot,* whereas his understanding of the language of divine faces and divinity in the structure of *adam,* as developed in the *Idrot,* became central in his writing only later in his life:

> The ten *sefirot,* in the mystery of ten levels that flow one from another, do not form together the likeness of *adam.* This is the secret of the study of the *Zohar* as the path that I walked in my first book, the Book of *Pardes Rimmonim,* that is the secret of the ten *sefirot*... and it is very remote to attribute to this image [of

4 HaSHaQ A, third gate, A, 199.

> the ten *sefirot*] the image of the likeness of *adam* ... for the image of *adam* contains all created dimensions ... and there is no image that contains all images, by which all realities will be imprinted with the image of *adam* [!]. Therefore this image of *adam* is rooted in its likeness in the secrets of the arraying of *Arikh Anpin*. (Cordovero, *Or Yaqar*, vol. 23, 3132)

We have here a testimony to Cordovero's deep personal understanding that imagining the divine in the language of face and body provides a more holistic and integrative understanding of divinity that is not found in the *sefirot*. Furthermore, we learn from this passage that there is no image more complex than the human image and that therefore the *Idra* chose to portray even the highest and most concealed aspect of divinity in the likeness of *adam*. In reading *Ḥeleq Shi'ur Qomah*, as we stand facing the huge amount of detailed work that Cordovero put into organizing, classifying and analyzing the various divine organs, we might have thought that Cordovero is taking the *Idra* into a highly theoretical reading, but that is not the case.

A close reading of his study of the *Idrot* shows that Cordovero deeply internalized the insight that the likeness of *adam* is truly the image of all images. It is the imprint found in all dimensions of reality. *Adam*, flesh and blood, living upon the earth is the one who has been given the task, in his life, of connecting and binding together all the images in all parts of reality. *Adam* is, as Cordovero says, "the chain that binds all realities together."[5]

Cordovero listened intently to the anxiety arising from the *Idra Rabba* from the notion that the *Torah dile-'ila* ("celestial Torah"), the Torah of *'Attiqa*, stood to be annulled if the great *tiqqun* ("arraying") of the *Idra Rabba* did not take place. In other words, he understood the warning of the *Idra Rabba* that the great teaching of divinity as Oneness and mercy, might disappear from human consciousness and experience if nothing were done to draw it into our reality. Cordovero's argument is not that *'Attiqa* will disappear ontologically; it will continue existing unto itself in its own unattainable dimension. The anxiety is rather that the axis that connects this divinity to humankind will be closed off, and that this aspect of divinity would therefore not be present and impactful in the realm of human awareness. In the opening of the *Idra Rabba*, Rashbi awakens the sense of danger and emergency and the urgent need to gather forces and act in response to the disastrous possibility that the presence of *Arikh Anpin* will

---

5 Moshe Cordovero, *Elimah, Ma'ayan 'Ein Adam* (Jerusalem: Nezer Shraga, 2013), *tamar* 1, chapter 28, 762.

disappear from religious language and imagination, from human consciousness, and perhaps from reality altogether.

But how does Cordovero address the task of drawing *Arikh Anpin*, the primordial divinity-as-oneness, into the religious life of human beings? This is in no way an easy task. For it is difficult for human consciousness—whose default structure is binary and differentiated, and characterized by organizing reality into dichotomous categories of good/bad, reward/punishment, permitted/prohibited—to make space for the generous, long-breathed, unified face of *'Attiqa Qadisha*.

Tomer Devorah, the Palm of Deborah, Cordovero's last and perhaps most famous work, is the place where we find his most striking, creative response to the challenging call of the *Idra*. *Tomer Devorah* has a clear connection to Cordovero's great opus *Elimah*. The sixth section (*tamar*) in *Ma'ayan 'Ein Adam* in the book of *Elimah* is a draft or first version of *Tomer Devorah*.[6]

Tomer Devorah is the most popular of Cordovero's writings and it is written in beautiful Hebrew. The clear and concise language that Cordovero chose for this work differentiates it from his other lengthy, seemingly unedited works and attests clearly to his goal of transmission.

Though *Tomer Devorah* is written in direct and clear language, let us not be mistaken: this is not a simple work in any way, especially if we observe the demand it makes on us as human beings. In *Tomer Devorah*, Cordovero invites humans to emulate divinity in all aspects of the divine stature in our daily lives, as well as in our observances of holidays and special occasions.[7] In the work's introduction, Cordovero states that the human body and the structure of its organs is divine, for we have been created in the image and likeness of the divine stature, yet this is not enough:

> It is proper for a human being to imitate his\her Creator. Then they shall be in the secret of the supernal form, resembling their Creator both in likeness and image. For if a human resembles

6 The Kabbalists of the sixteenth century already pointed out this connection, and Professor Bracha Sack further researched and illuminated it. See Bracha Sack, *Kabbalah of Rabbi Moshe Cordovero* [Heb.] (Beer Sheva: Ben Gurion University Press, 1995), 214–229; idem, ed., *From the Fountains of Sefer Elimah by Rabbi Moshe Cordovero and Studies in His Kabbalah* [Heb.] (Beer Sheva: Ben Gurion University Press, 2013), 203–213. Professor Sack's scholarship is particularly apt for this volume, as she taught in 1968–1970 at Hebrew College while pursuing her doctorate in Boston.

7 See Patrick B. Koch, *Human Self-Perfection: A Re-Assessment of Kabbalistic Musar-Literature of Sixteenth-Century Safed* (Los Angeles: Cherub Press, 2015), 78–103.

> (the divine) merely in bodily appearance and not in deeds, why then he/she is debasing the divine form.
>
> Of such a person it is said: "A handsome form with ugly deeds," for the essence of the supernal image and likeness is in deeds, therefore what value can there be in one's resemblance to the supernal form in bodily limbs if one's deeds have no resemblance to those of her/his Creator?![8]

But which aspects of divinity should we imitate? In order to answer this, we need to look at the roots of the concept of *imitatio Dei* in Jewish religious literature. The first discussions of the idea of the human emulation of God are found in rabbinic literature:

> Abba Sha'ul says: (Ex. 15:2) "I will liken myself to Him" [*ve-anvehu* = *ani ve-hu*, "I and He"]. Just as He is merciful and gracious, you, too, be merciful and gracious. (*Mekhilta de-Rabbi Yishma'el* 15:2:2)

In the Babylonian Talmud we find a similar formulation in answer to the question of how human beings can possibly "walk after" God when we know that God is a "consuming fire":

> Rather one should follow the attributes of the Blessed Holy One. Just as He clothes the naked, as it is written: "And the Lord God made for Adam and for his wife garments of skin, and clothed them" (Gen. 3:21), so too, should you clothe the naked. Just as the Blessed Holy One visits the sick, as it is written "And the Lord appeared unto him by the terebinths of Mamre," so too, should you visit the sick. (B. Sotah 14a)

And yet, what is this image of the divine that Cordovero wishes us to emulate?

Cordovero's concept of God is very different from that of rabbinic literature. It is shaped by the *Zohar*'s two main modes of describing the divine: the language

---

8 We find two different introductions to the sixth chapter of *Ma'ayan 'Ein Ya'aqov*, both related to *Tomer Devorah*. One introduction was printed in Bracha Sack's edition of the chapter of *Elimah*: "The deeds of a human being and their benefit to the Upper Worlds in light or flow, and how they sway the Upper Worlds, and their being a chariot to the *sefirot*. . . ." The introduction in the JTS manuscript reads "the straight path a human being makes and his contemplation and its aim, and contemplation of his ways." See Sack, *From the Fountains of Sefer Elimah*, 203–214.

of the ten *sefirot* and the complex and dynamic relationships between them, and the language of divine faces found in the *Idrot*. The surprising thing that one finds in reading *Tomer Devorah* again and again is the discovery that the first two chapters, which are the work's longest, call upon the human being to imitate and intensively emulate—as audacious and shocking as this sounds—the face of divinity as Oneness, *Arikh Anpin, 'Attiqa Qadisha.*

Cordovero opens *Tomer Devorah* with the statement that in order for human beings to be in the mystery of the supernal image they must imitate the "acts of the supernal crown"—the *sefirah* of *Keter*:

> For *adam* to resemble his Creator according to the mystery of the supernal crown (*keter*) *adam* must possess, too, many of the active qualities (*gufei pe'ulot*) that are of the essence of leadership. (*Tomer Devorah,* chapter 2)

These "active qualities" are the thirteen Attributes of Mercy hinted at in the verses:

> Who is a God like You, removing iniquity and passing over the transgression of the remnant of His people? He does not retain His wrath forever, for He delights in love. He will return and have compassion upon us; He will subdue our iniquities; and You will cast all their sins into the depths of the sea. You will grant truth to Jacob, love to Abraham, as You swore to our fathers from days of old. (Mic. 7:18–20)[9]

On the face of it, according to Cordovero's formulation, the first chapter of *Tomer Devorah* deals with the "actions" of the *sefirah* of *Keter* and the second with "the body" of the qualities of this *sefirah*. What does Cordovero mean here by "actions" and "the body?" These words are very unclear if we think about them in terms of the *sefirah* of *Keter* by itself. *Keter*, after all, is a pristine and transcendent quality of the divinity and certainly has body or facial features. Yet, as we study the language of these two chapters in greater depth, we find that they are a brilliant reworking of the face of *Arikh Anpin* and his long white beard—as invoked in the first parts of both the *Idra Rabba* and the *Idra Zuta*—into a mystical ethics, a human spiritual praxis.

---

9 A different list of thirteen attributes of mercy—and one that is more well-known to those familiar with Jewish liturgy—appears in Ex. 34:6–7.

The first chapter of *Tomer Devorah* is dedicated to a detailed spiritual practice that Cordovero crafted in order to "translate" the white beard of *'Attiqa Qadisha* with the thirteen rivers of *raḥamim* (mercy) that flow from it into our life as human beings. In this chapter he guides human beings to emulate in their behavior with one another the attributes of mercy that flow from all thirteen parts of the white beard and to learn from them the mystery of the many manifestations of *arikhut af*—patience, spaciousness of spirit, expansiveness of breath—that are learned from the vast graciousness in the face of *Arikh Anpin*.

Corresponding to each of the thirteen aspects of the beard of *Arikh Anpin*, Cordovero constructs a complex lexicon of different understandings of *arikhut af* that a person can cultivate consciously in relationship to other human beings. Unlike many other kabbalistic practices, the practices Cordovero offers are not characterized by the addition of specific kabbalistic *kavanot* (intentions) to existing mitzvot. They are, as Moshe Idel calls them, "anomic," that is, they do not correspond to particular parts of *halakhah* (Jewish law). Rather these thirteen practices are spiritual-ethical innovations designed to cultivate in us love for our fellow humans. We are called upon, for example, to cultivate: the patience to withstand others' inappropriate behavior; the ability to be desirous of lovingkindness, always seeking the well-being of the other; the ability to cultivate a lived experience of ourselves as constituting a single human fabric in which each of our actions influences and is influenced by the reality of those around us, a deep knowing that our fellow human beings carry with them parts of our soul just as we carry parts of theirs.

The demand from us as human beings expressed in this chapter is vast and seems almost impossible. Who would have believed that anyone would venture to turn each one of the thirteen attributes of *Arikh Anpin*'s beard—that ever-flowing river of life, of divinity as Oneness—into an applied practice for human beings of flesh and blood living their finite lives?! Rabbi Isaac Luria did indeed construct whole worlds on each and every part of the face of *Arikh Anpin* in the *Idrot*, yet Cordovero's interpretation is even more astounding, in his insistence that we see the *Idrot* as placing an ethical and behavioral demand on human beings here on earth.

The second chapter of *Tomer Devorah*, dealing with the *sefirah* of *Keter*, presents us with facial features that all come from the face of *Arikh Anpin* in the *Idra Rabba*: forehead, eyes, nose, apples of the cheeks, etc. Each part of the face of *Arikh Anpin* expresses a specific aspect in the divine personhood and for each one of these facial features Cordovero offers a translation to its corresponding feature of the human face. According to the *Idra* "as above, so below": our face is an expression of our entire persona. Let us look at some examples of the manner in which the human face is constructed in relationship to the face of *Arikh Anpin*.

In the *tiqqun* of the forehead of the human being, Cordovero says:

> One's forehead should have no hardness whatsoever but should resemble at all times the forehead of *raẓon* ("appeasement")[10] and he/she should be pleased to accept everyone. Even when he meets with provokers he should appease them and quiet them with good will. For the forehead of *raẓon* constantly accepts and appeases the divine powers and perfects them. So a person, too, should appease those whose anger prevails and lead them on in good will, drawing on great wisdom to weaken their anger that it does not overstep its boundaries and cause harm, God forfend. He should behave as the supernal *raẓon*, which proceeds from the wonderful wisdom in the forehead of the Ancient One and from there appeases all.[11]

The way in which we emulate the forehead of *'Attiqa* is by cultivating our own "forehead"—that is, how we turn toward others—to be soft, radiant and full of good will and appeasement.

Another example is in the *tiqqun* of the eyes:

> His eyes should not gaze at any ugly thing. They should, however, be ever open to notice and show mercy to those who are suffering as much as possible. One should in no way close one's eyes when one sees the sufferings of the poor, but give as much thought to their predicament as lies in one's power and awaken the mercy of Heaven and of humans upon them … just as the supernal eye [of *Arikh Anpin*] is ever open to look immediately at the good.

In order to emulate the eye of *Arikh Anpin*, which the *Idra* describes as being always open and always radiating forth life and forgiveness, we as humans must

---

10 *Raẓon* can mean "will" but in this case it is connected to unconditional acceptance and appeasement as found in the diadem of the High Priest—*le-raẓon* (Ex. 28:36–38)—or in the idea of "a moment of favor," as in *'et raẓon* (Ps. 69:14).

11 Unless otherwise noted, all of the following quotations from the *Tomer Devorah* can be found in chapter 2.

not shut our eyes to the suffering around us. And just as the supernal eye is always open and always seeing the good, so should our eyes always pay attention and be filled with mercy toward the sorrows of the poor and suffering.

Another beautiful example can be found in Cordovero's *tiqqun* of the nose:

> As for his nose there should be no anger in it whatsoever. But there should be at all times vitality, good will and great patience (*arikhut af*) even to the unworthy.

Contrary to Maimonides's choice in the *Guide to the Perplexed*—in which every biblical description of a physical feature of God is read strictly as metaphor and as attesting to the limited nature of language (for example, "God's eyes" for Maimonides means God's providence) the *Idra Rabba* takes an insistent stance against the over-abstraction of religious language. Instead, the *Idra* chooses to hold simultaneously both the mythical, physical, and sensuous aspects of the countenance of the divine, along with their metaphoric and symbolic aspects. The eye of *'Attiqa* is the physical expression of the divine providence of the Ancient One and this providence receives its ultimate form from the white, ever-open, ever-joyous eyes of *'Attiqa*.

Cordovero, following the *Idra*, presents us with a language in which there is an interplay between a metaphoric, symbolic understanding of the parts of the divine face and their existence as an actual divine facial feature. That is, a human being emulates the divine nose in a metaphorical way by having *arikhut af* even toward the unworthy, yet also in a very physical and sensuous way. We can experience breathing out forgiveness and the passing over of transgressions. In Hebrew, the word "forgiveness" (*meḥilah*) and the word "passing over" (*'over*) find their place in an innovative Cordoverian midrash that conflates the sound and the meaning of the words *meḥilah* ("tunnel") and *ma'avar* ("passageway") to the nasal ducts and the channels of the nose as described in the *Idra Rabba* through which the spirit of life and forgiveness is exhaled.

Cordovero's choice to structure his ethical model on the *Idra Rabba* obligates him to remain in relationship with and not to disconnect from the language of faces and all their parts and features. Each part of the beard of *Arikh Anpin* and each aspect of his face turn, under Cordovero's quill, to a model of ethical behavior for those of us who desire to cultivate these qualities in ourselves. This cultivation, remarkably, is intimately related to our own human faces. Cordovero offers us a physical-spiritual practice for shaping how we face the world and face one another: softening our foreheads, attending to the kind of gaze with which we look at one another, being mindful of what comes out of our mouths.

All this very demanding spiritual, psychological cultivation has a theurgic aim. At the end of chapter 1, Cordovero summarizes this goal:

> Until now, we have expounded the thirteen qualities by which a person resembles his Creator. These are the qualities of higher mercy and their special property is that just as a person (*adam*) conducts him/herself here below so will he/she be worthy of opening that higher quality from above. Just as a person behaves [in this world], so will be the affluence from above and he/she will cause that quality to shine upon earth.

After surveying the features of the face of *'Attiqa,* Cordovero summarizes:

> And at any time a person wishes to draw closer to Above to resemble him and opening his (that is, *Arikh Anpin*'s) sources to those below, one must become adept with these two chapters.

This means that in order to draw the divine plenty from the *tiqqunim* of the parts of the face of *'Attiqa* into human reality, there is a need to create in human reality a resemblance to this face, to create a disposition, to prepare vessels and a space into which this divine *shefa'* can flow. This is what Cordovero repeats again and again: there is no possibility of accessing the plenty, the *shefa'*, of *'Attiqa* if there is no preparation—both on the level of consciousness and behavior—of vessels that can properly receive it.

Cordovero's work here is very different from that of, for example, the thirteenth-century Spanish rabbi Joseph Gikatilla, who, in his essay "The Thirteen Fountains of Redemption Emitted by *Keter*," transmits these thirteen secrets emanating from *Keter* as *gnosis,* esoteric knowledge that places in human hands the keys to open up the storehouses of the divine flow. By contrast, according to Cordovero, the ability to channel and to regulate the flow of love and *raḥamim* from the face of *'Attiqa* is dependent upon the existence of a semblance of that face in the body and behavior of a person of this world. Cordovero's project here is also very different from that of the Ari, Rabbi Isaac Luria, who extensively developed the Idraic myth and created, by his apparatus of *kavanot* (intentions), a way for a human being to enter into the realm of divine myth, partake in it, and influence it. For Cordovero, the goal is to draw divinity, even in its highest, most primordial and concealed aspects, into human life, into the interpersonal domain of *ben adam le-ḥavero,* and into everyday conduct in this world.

Structurally, the first and second chapters of *Tomer Devorah* deal with the way a person can resemble the parts of the beard and the parts of the face of *Arikh Anpin* in the *Idra Rabba*. The heading of the chapter—"Interpretations of the Thirteen Attributes of the Name and Human Emulation of Them"—might appear at first to have nothing to do with the language of the *Idrot*. Already beginning of the first chapter, however, we realize that the thirteen attributes mentioned are from the verse in Micah 7:18 that relates to the *tiqqunim* of the beard of *Arikh Anpin* in the *Idrot*. The heading of the second chapter is "the interpretation of the *sefirah* of *Keter* and actions dependent on the head." Here we already find the mixture of the language of *sefirot* (that is, the use of the word *Keter*) with the anthropomorphic image of the divine head that comes from the *Idra Rabba*.

In the next six chapters, Cordovero discusses the various ways that a person can acquire in his behavior qualities of the *sefirot* from *Ḥokhmah* to *Yesod*. While we do not find Idraic terminology (such as *Ze'eir Anpin*, body, arms, genitals, or other terms) in these chapters, they nonetheless retain the Idraic structure of following the discussion of the *tiqqunim* of *Arikh Anpin* with those of *Ze'eir Anpin*. Cordovero makes his method of combining the language of *sefirot* with the language of divine faces explicit in *ma'ayan* 4 of *'Ein Shemesh*, where he writes: "the interpretation of the concatenation of the *sefirot* from *Ḥokhmah* to *Yesod* … are all included in the name *Ze'eir Anpin*."

A careful reading of these chapters (3–8) on the *sefirot* of *Ḥokhmah* to *Yesod* (and *Ze'eir Anpin*) shows that they are not only pointing to the ways in which all these *sefirot* make up the masculine divine body and have their parallels in the human world. Rather they are exploring the cultivation of this masculine body so that it may support, array, soothe, embrace, and come into loving coupling with the *shekhinah* (corresponding to *Nuqba*, the feminine divine body in the *Idra Rabba*). Indeed, the beautiful ninth chapter of *Tomer Devorah* concerns itself entirely with the *shekhinah*—Cordovero's great love—and how a person can emulate her so as to become a chariot for the *shekhinah*: to love her and to invoke the presence of her image in the world.

The last and tenth chapter of *Tomer Devorah* is about general modes of behavior that will retain, in a living way, the consciousness of imitating divinity. The structure and flow of the chapters testifies to the fact that while the paradigm through which Cordovero chose to transmit his teaching about *imitatio dei* has the schema of the ten *sefirot* in the names of the chapters, it is, in fact, actually structured according to the tri-part structure of the faces of divinity in the *Idra Rabba*—*Arikh Anpin*, *Ze'eir Anpin*, and *Nuqba*.

In a paraphrase of the *Idra Zuta* found in the sixth Tamar of *Elimah* that comes under the heading "how can a person influence the *sefirah* of *Keter* by a good deed," Cordovero explains the unique quality of the *sefira* of *Keter*. *Keter* is not activated by the discernment of good or bad deeds, but rather presents endless emanation flowing to all.

What he stresses is the importance of creating vessels to receive that flow unhindered.

Even though he is relating explicitly to the *Idra Zuta*, he does not choose, in what seems to be a conscious choice, to speak in the language of the faces of *Arikh Anpin* but rather in the language of *sefirot*:

> We have an introduction laid out by Rabbi Shimon at the hour of his passing: *Keter* is never activated from any good action or bad one at all, because its radiance is extended to all. However, the intention is that by the good deed the *sefirot* will become primed so that the light of *Keter* will shine in them and there will be no hindrance found that will delay its light and flow. For when the lower *sefirot* are not themselves properly prepared they cause [a situation in which] the light of *Keter* does not shine in them; and when they are prepared, immediately its generous light flows. (*Ma'ayan 'Ein Adam, tamar* 6, chapter 1)[12]

Cordovero chose to develop *Tomer Devorah* into a book in its own right, with both of the first two chapters focusing wholly on the beard and the face of *Arikh Anpin* as laid out in the *Idra Rabba*—the first "translating" the *tiqqunim* of *'Attiqa*'s beard into thirteen different paths of cultivating patience and generosity of spirit (*arikhut ruaḥ*); and the second reworking the parts of the face of *Arikh Anpin* into human ethical practices. This choice testifies to the great importance that Cordovero recognized in the teachings of the *Idra Rabba*, which both critiques Jewish religion and calls for its healing. Cordovero clearly took upon himself the responsibility of responding to this call and actualizing the teachings of the *Idra Rabba* in our human realm. The choice to take this yoke upon himself is an expression of the dynamic quality of Cordovero's religious thinking, which developed throughout the years and came to its fullest fruition in *Tomer Devorah*.

In closing, let us return to the final words of the first chapter of *Tomer Devorah*:

> Therefore, let not these thirteen qualities depart from the eyes of the mind and let not the verse [*mi el kamokha*, "Who is a God

---

12 See Sack, *From the Fountains of Sefer 'Elimah*, 214.

> like you …" (Mic. 7:18)] depart from the mouth, so that it be a permanent reminder. And whenever there is the opportunity of exercising one of these qualities one will remember, saying to oneself: "Behold, this depends on this particular quality. I shall not depart from it, so that the quality may not be hidden and depart from the world."

These final words "that the quality may not be hidden and depart from the world" are a precise expression of Cordovero's internalized identification with the call of the *Idra Rabba* to act against the terrible threat that the supernal Torah of *Arikh Anpin* could be annulled. He constructs his directives to us as human beings so that the *Idra Rabba* will not remain merely a story conveying deep esoteric and theoretical mysteries. He puts in a relentless effort to find a way to draw the Idraic theology of the divine faces into the human realm so that they will not disappear from our world. In doing so, Cordovero bequeaths the *Idra Rabba* to us as a living Torah. The presence of *Arikh Anpin* will not disappear from the religious-spiritual world of human beings so long as we as humans cultivate, in our own flesh-and-blood lives, the qualities of *arikhut ruaḥ* that are the earthly vessels in which the spirit of *Arikh Anpin* can come to dwell.

CHAPTER 16

R. Levi Yiẓḥaq of Zelichow and His Quest for Leadership in the Early Hasidic Movement

Avraham Yiẓḥaq (Arthur) Green

The emergence of the Hasidic movement as a major force in eastern European Jewish life, and in what was to emerge as Jewish modernity altogether, was almost entirely the creation of the circle of disciples around Dov Ber, the Maggid of Mezritch. It was they who turned outward, during their master's lifetime but even more fully after his death, to extend the Hasidic message over broad areas of territory, and to articulate its message. In the years following 1772, that message was made accessible to ordinary Jews, as well as to the sort of learned and enthusiastic devotees to whom the Maggid had originally addressed himself. In the various controversies and debates about Hasidism, lasting until the end of the eighteenth century, it is always the Maggid's disciples who are in the foreground. Almost all of the major schools and dynasties that came to dominate Hasidic life have their ultimate origins in Mezritch.[1]

---

1 Such non-Mezritch-based figures as R. Ya'aqov Yosef of Polonnoe and R. Mikhl of Zlochow are denounced in the *ḥaramim,* to be sure, but their "crimes" are either publication or local activities, not active movement-building. For discussion of the early spread of Hasidism, see Ada Rapoport-Albert, "Hasidism after 1772: Structural Continuity and Change," in her edited volume *Hasidism Reappraised* (London: Littman Library, 1996), 76–140 and Arthur Green, "Around the Maggid's Table," in English in my *The Heart of the Matter* (Philadelphia: JPS, 2015), 119–166 and in Hebrew in *Zion* 78, no. 1 (2013): 73–106. My own views differ slightly from those of Rapoport-Albert. While I agree that there was no center of authority in the spread of Hasidism, I place greater emphasis on the closeness and mutual support of those who saw themselves as disciples of the Maggid, and on their key role in the movement's spread and success. I also see an ongoing rivalry between the Mezritch circle, mostly as a defined group, and other, mostly less intellectual, Hasidic circles. Eventually, that line-up changed,

Writing in the mid-nineteenth century, the Hasidic bibliographer Aaron Walden offers a list of thirty-one figures whom he describes as Dov Ber's disciples, based mostly on quotations from the Maggid as "my teacher" in their writings. We do not know how close the discipleship of each was, nor do we have any idea how frequently each of them visited the Maggid's court, or how long he stayed.[2] Attempts to identify the key figures in this group, as it existed before the Maggid's death, are also problematic. Often they rely either in the success of the disciple's reputation for written texts, collections of sermons published only decades later, or on his role in the later growth and spread of Hasidism, either through disciples or descendants who themselves became *rebbes* in the early nineteenth century.

The Maggid's circle included a wide range of personality types, religious attitudes, and degrees of traditional learning. A few of them were ordained rabbis and served in the professional capacity of city or town rabbinates. In addition to Levi Yiẓḥaq, these included the brothers R. Pinḥas and R. Shmelke Horowitz, who were to leave the Hasidic heartland altogether and serve in the distinguished central European communities of Frankfurt and Nikolsburg.[3] R. Shne'ur Zalman of Liadi, the founder of the Chabad school, clearly had the erudition and reputation to have served as a town rabbi, but chose not to do so, in order to devote himself fully to the spread of Hasidism. Most, however, were learned in the aggadic and mystical traditions, but less so in talmudic law, and thus followed their master's example and served as *maggidim* or communally appointed preachers. These included R. Menaḥem Mendel of Vitebsk, R. Aharon of Karlin, R. Menaḥem Naḥum of Chernobyl, and R. Ze'ev Wolf of Zhitomir. Still others, to whom almost no learned teachings are attributed, were more like folk-figures, known in the Hasidic tales as personal exemplars of great piety, but not as teachers. Best known among these are R. Zusya of Anipol[4] and R. Leib Sarahs. R. Elimelekh of

---

and such Mezritch disciples as Avraham Kalisker and Shlomo Karliner joined with the latter group, which came to be led by Barukh of Miedzybozh.

2 Neither the frequency with which the Maggid is quoted nor the precise way of referring to him ("my teacher," "our master and teacher," and so forth) in their writings is a good indicator. These matters are largely the work of editors, not the original preachers. Regarding one on the list, R. Meshullam Feibush Heller of Zbarash, we know from his testimony that he visited the Maggid's court only once, and was more closely linked to the group around R. Yeḥi'el Mikhl of Zloczow.

3 Others include R. Yissachar Ber of Zloczow, who was close to Levi Yiẓḥaq from their youth, and R. 'Uzi'el Meisels, who served as rabbi of Satanov and authored several halakhic works in addition to his Hasidic *Tiferet 'Uzi'el.*

4 There is no early book of Zusya's teachings, and there are famous Hasidic tales accounting for that. But I note that he was regularly sought out for *haskamot* (unlike R. Leib Sarahs and R. Barukh of Miedzybozh, for example), including by R. Shne'ur Zalman for the *Tanya*. This makes me wonder whether the image of him as unlettered might be exaggerated.

Lizhensk, the brother of R. Zusya, was also one who clearly might have served as a communal *maggid,* but chose, like R. Shne'ur Zalman, to be supported by his disciples, so that he could devote himself entirely to cultivating them as future leaders and to what we moderns would call "building the movement."

Despite our lack of certainty about how central each of these was to the Maggid's court, there is good reason to assume that Levi Yiẓḥaq,[5] thirty-two years old at the Maggid's death, played a pivotal role in this group. There are three reasons for making such a claim.

The first fact to be considered is that Levi Yiẓḥaq is the chief object of attack in the persecutions of early Hasidism, except for those of the Maggid's students who chose to go northward and face the anti-Hasidic bastion of Lithuania, arousing the wrath especially of R. Eliyahu of Vilna. Levi Yiẓḥaq was driven from the rabbinate of Zelichow in central Poland (c. 1771 or 1772) and possibly from Pinsk in Polesia (c. 1784) apparently for the "crime" of using his rabbinic post to spread Hasidic teachings and customs, before accepting the position in Berdichev in 1785. He was also the one who stood up to R. Avraham Katzenellenbogen in the most famous Hasidic/Mitnaggedic debate, held in Warsaw in 1781.[6] He was probably chosen (or "chose" himself) because he was considered the most respectable spokesman that the Hasidic forces could muster.

Second, of all the disciples who remained in Hasidism's expanding heartland, he was the one who held the most prestigious posts, and hence was most publicly noticeable, both by supporters and enemies of Hasidism. Pinsk was a distinguished rabbinic seat, the southernmost extension of what was considered the Lithuanian rabbinate's sphere of influence. Berdichev, in the eighteenth century, was the most prosperous Jewish community in the Ukraine, as has been shown.[7] The fact that the rabbi of these communities preached the new Hasidic doctrine, largely that of the Maggid, had to be noticed.

Third, there is an unusually high degree of overlap of both content and style between teachings attributed to Dov Ber and Levi Yiẓḥaq, master and disciple.[8] The abstract mystical teachings attributed to the Maggid, centered

---

5 He was still referred to as the Zelichower many years after he left that town. Hence the use of that designation in the title of this article.

6 Texts relating to this debate are included in Mordecai Wilensky, *Ḥasidim u-Mitnaggedim* (Jerusalem: Mossad Bialik, 1970), vol. 1, 115–118 and n. 4 there, 122–131.

7 Yohanan Petrovsky-Shtern, "The Drama of Berdichev: Levi Yitshak and his Town," *Polin* 17 (2004): 83–95.

8 I leave aside here the problematics of defining the Maggid's corpus itself, distinguishing it from the larger body of early anonymous Hasidic teachings. I am thus tentatively assuming such works as *Maggid Devaraw le-Ya'aqov* (1781) and *Or Torah* (1804) to belong to "*kitvei ha-maggid.*" See the discussion of sources in Ariel Evan Mayse, *Speaking Infinites: God and*

mostly around the possibility of attaining self-negation (*bittul*) by entering into the divine *'ayin*, are found almost unchanged in the sermons of Levi Yiẓḥaq. This central but highly abstruse part of Dov Ber's oeuvre is not to be found to nearly the same degree in the writings of most other members of the circle.[9] Another key item, both doctrinal and practical, is the role of the *ẓaddiq* and his relationship to the divine will. In this matter, Levi Yiẓḥaq will proceed to expand on his master's teaching, expressing it in even more radical language. But at root his ideas on this subject are very much those of his teacher, and expressed in similar language, more so than is the case with most others.

Since the turn of the twentieth century, it has been claimed that Levi Yiẓḥaq was to some degree the scribe of the Maggid, or at least a key recorder of his teachings. This claim began with the 1899 publication of a work called *Or ha-Emet*, a partially new (though much overlapping with three prior collections) group of teachings belonging to the Maggid or his immediate school. The editor of the volume introduces it with a complicated tale of his grandfather, supposedly a disciple of Levi Yiẓḥaq (though his name is not one we know from elsewhere) who had preserved a precious manuscript, including his own copying from another manuscript, supposedly written by Levi Yiẓḥaq himself, of the Maggid's teachings. Current scholarship has no way of confirming or disestablishing this claim.

Another important document that makes a claim of great importance regarding Levi Yiẓḥaq's early views was published in Warsaw in 1938, on the eve of Polish Jewry's destruction, under the title *Shemu'ah Tovah*, and attributed in its entirety to the Maggid and Levi Yiẓḥaq. It was primarily copied, its editor tells us, from a manuscript that was included in the library of the *ẓaddiqim* of Kozhenits, a collection that was lost during the ensuing catastrophe. The short teachings that comprise the bulk of this volume are parallel versions to texts previously published in collections attributed to the Maggid, under the titles *Kitvei Qodesh* and *Or ha-Emet*. They may or may not have been taken from the same manuscript from which these earlier collections had been copied. In any case, they are another rendition of known teachings, associated with the Maggid. But

---

Language in the Teachings of Rabbi Dov Ber of Mezritsh (Philadelphia: University of Pennsylvania Press, 2021), 235–253. The ideological affinity between Levi Yiẓḥaq and the Maggid will be demonstrated at greater length in my forthcoming book *Defender of the Faithful* (coauthored with Yohanan Petrovsky-Shtern).

9 It is largely absent, for example, from the *Me'or 'Einayim* and the *Or ha-Me'ir*. In the writings of R. Shne'ur Zalman of Liadi, it is indeed present, but significantly reworked. In this matter (though not in some others), Levi Yiẓḥaq is closest to R. Avraham, the Maggid's son, and R. Menaḥem Mendel of Vitebsk.

Shemu'ah Tovah includes two other items, published for the first time. One is a group of longer sermons, each of them dated to 1773 and 1774, the two years following the Maggid's death. It also contains a page of questions and answers, mostly on Kabbalistic subjects. There are each headed: "I asked our lord and master," a typical way of referring to a Hasidic rebbe.[10] In two places, the question-and-answer texts are signed by the initials LY, leaving little reason to doubt their origin.

The sermons cover most of the Torah portions from Numbers and Deuteronomy, tied to passages from *Pirkei Avot,* which means that they were delivered in the summer months of those two years. They are written in a florid and repetitive rabbinic prose, and are marked by lengthy and highly detailed parables. They give the impression, unlike most Hasidic sermons, of having been written out in detail by their creator, perhaps in preparation for their oral delivery. What we seem to have here are sermons by a young rabbi, not yet confident enough to rely on his rhetorical skills, needing to write out every word in advance. These sermons too are quite clearly by Levi Yiẓḥaq, as can be shown by a comparison of both themes and specific biblical and rabbinic quotations repeated in later (and shorter) versions of them to be found in the *Qedushat Levi.* These sermons represent the earliest stages in the development of both his thought and his style of expression.[11]

I shall have occasion elsewhere to deal with the theology of those sermons and their significance in that regard. But here we are interested in proposing historic settings for three particular sermons: one on *parashat Be-Ha'alotekha* in 5533,

---

10 Levi Yiẓḥaq refers to the Maggid in this way in various pages of the *Qedushat Levi* on Hanukkah and Purim, which he published in 1798. See, for example in the edition edited by Michael Aryeh Rand, *Qedushat Levi* (Ashdod: Makhon Hadrat Ḥen, 5765 [2004–2005]), vol. 2, 288, 350, 349, and 366. The Zoharic phrase *buẓina qadisha,* "holy lamp," is often added.

11 The overlap between the *Shemu'ah Tovah* homilies and material found in *Qedushat Levi* is extensive. The *parashat Devarim* sermon in *Shemu'ah Tovah* is found in abbreviated form in *Qedushat Levi, Liqqutim,* vol. 2, 262–263, linked to the same Avot passage. The second sermon on *Va-Etḥanan,* beginning with *atah horeita,* is found in *Qedushat Levi, Ve-Zot ha-Berakhah,* vol. 2, 182, though with a sharper anti-Gentile tone, perhaps caused by Levi Yiẓḥaq's experiences in the course of his career. The lengthy sermon on *yire'ah* in *'Eqev* is repeated in shorter form in *Qedushat Levi, 'Eqev,* vol. 2, 121–125. The theme of giving pleasure to God, strongly stated in connection with the passage from B. Pesaḥim 112a ("More than the cow wants to nurse ...") is a major theme in *Qedushat Levi,* witnessed, for example, in *Va-Yera,* vol. 1, 67; *Re'eh,* vol. 2, 130; *Liqqutim,* vol. 2, 257–258. The intimacy of kissing between friends, described quite passionately in *Shemu'ah Tovah, 'Eqev* 23b, is strongly echoed in *Qedushat Levi,* vol. 2, 418. The second sermon in *Ki Teẓe,* beginning on 35a (linked with the Avot passage in the preceding sermon), is found in shortened form in *Qedushat Levi, Liqqutim,* s.v. *ve-lo kol ha-marbeh.* This is probably the clearest example of the abbreviation of both sermon text and parable. Further parallels are likely to emerge through close comparative study.

May or June of 1773, about five months after the Maggid's death; the second a year later, delivered for *parashat Qoraḥ* in the summer of 1774;[12] and a third (actually the opening text of the collection) on *parashat Massa'ei*, undated, but almost certainly also from summer of 1773. In this period, Levi Yiẓḥaq is rabbi in Zelichow, but there is no indication of where—or whether—these sermons were delivered orally.

In the first of these sermons, he speaks of a matter we know from his later homilies as well, the importance of spreading the Hasidic message to others, rather than devoting oneself to the cultivation of private piety alone:

> Hillel says: "Do not separate yourself from the community, do not believe in yourself until the day you die, and do not judge your fellow until you reach his place. Do not say anything that cannot be heard [in public], for in the end it will be heard ..." (M. Avot 2:5).
>
> In a simple sense, this seems to be a warning for those who seek to partake of God's holiness and to purify themselves, to step up to Torah and God's service. Such a person should not say: "Peace upon you [that is, "Rest easy"], my soul! I read scripture; I study the teachings. These suffice to fulfill my obligation."[13] Such a one does not place it as his goal to turn toward the community of Y-H-W-H, bringing the many back from sin. He declines to teach them the ways of God in which they should walk, to be earnest in His worship, with awe, love, and attachment [*devequt*]. To these, Hillel says: "Such is not the way in which the light of wholeness shines. This is not how you awaken the spirit of holiness and purity upon yourself, as was truly intended."
>
> A person who serves his Creator fully out of love, with no intent of receiving reward, but only to bring pleasure to the Creator, will never stop or rest with his own service alone, but will work constantly toward the goal of "If only all the people of Y-H-W-H were prophets, as He places His spirit upon them!" (Num. 11:29).

---

12 These two sermons, plus one other, are printed near the end of *Shemu'ah Tovah*, 84a–87, not in the order of the others. The reason for this is not indicated. They are not as elaborately written out as are those printed at the head of the volume. My guess is that they were intended for a different audience, preached in a more informal setting.

13 *Shalom 'alayikh nafshi*, in connection with separating from the community's needs, is found in B. Ta'anit 11a.

In this way, the Creator's joy and pleasure will surely be increased and His glory made abundant. This one is acting like a faithful and clever servant of the king. He loves his master so much, with whole heart and longing soul, that he wants all the king's servants to serve him faithfully... .

Scripture addresses such a servant when it says: "If you bring the precious forth from the unseemly" (Jer.15:19).[14] This is what Hillel means by "Do not separate yourself from the community." Do not separate yourself from showing them the way they should walk in serving their Creator. Those are the paths of awe, love, and attachment. He then lays out the reason for this. In addition to this being the proper thing to do out of loving God, it will also bring great benefit to your own self. We know what the sages said: "Whoever brings merit to the public will not be the cause of sin."[15]

But perhaps you will say that you have no need for such benefit, having already attained the highest of rungs, worshipping with a great sense of attachment to God. [You think that] "Your heart has attained the heights in the ways of Y-H-W-H" (2 Chron. 17:16). Your heart is already hollow within you,[16] and no sin will come your way. Hillel (continuing the passage from Avot) tells you that this is not the case. "Do not believe in yourself until your dying day."[17]

---

14 That is, "Work to bring out the best in people."

15 M. Avot 5:21.

16 That is, you are already in a state of deep spiritual devotion; based on Ps. 109:22.

17 *Shemu'ah Tovah*, 87a–b. הלל אומר אל תפרוש מן הצבור ואל תאמין בעצמך וכו׳ [עד יום מותך] ואל תדין את חבירך וכו׳ [עד שתגיע למקומו] ואל תאמר דבר שא״א לשמוע וכו׳ [שסופו להשמע...] ע״ד הפשוט יראה כי בא להזהיר האיש הישראלי הבא להתקדש בקדושתו ית׳ ולהטהר לעמוד על התורה ועל העבודה. לבל יאמר שלום עלי נפשי לדידי קראי לדידי תנאי ודיינו להפקיע א״ע. ולא ישים מגמתו אל עדת ד׳ להשיב רבים מעון. וימנע מלהורותם דרך ד׳ ילכו בה להזדרז בעבודתו ביראה ואהבה ודביקות. ע״ז אמר כי לא זו הוא הדרך ישכון בה אור השלימות ולא זו העיר רוח קדושה וטהרה על עצמו כפי השלימות התכלית האמיתי הנרצה .כי הנה העובד את בוראו מאהבה שלימה שלא ע״מ לקבל פרס. רק לעשות נחת רוח ליוצרו לא ישקוט ולא ינוח לו במעשי עבודתו את הבורא ית׳ לבד. אבל ישים כל מגמתו תמיד לאמר מי יתן והיו כל עם ד׳ נביאים כי יתן ד׳ את רוחו עליהם שבזה יתגדל ויתרבה הנחת והשעשוע להבורא ב״ה ויתעצם כבודו. כעבד מלך הנאמן המשכיל אשר לאהבתו את אדוניו בלב שלם ונפש חפיצה יחפוץ שכך עבדי אדוניו יעבדוהו באמונה. [...] וסיפר הכתוב במעלת העבד הזה. אם תוציא יקר מזולל כפי תהי׳. וז״ש אל תפרוש מן הצבור ר״ל אל תפרוש מהם מלהורותם הדרך ילכו בה בעבודת הבורא ב״ה הם דרכי היראה והאהבה והדביקות וביאר טעם הדבר. כי זולת שהדבר ראוי ונכון מצד האהבה לבורא ית׳ כנ״ל. עוד ימשוך מזה תועלת גדול אל עצמותך. כי נודע מ״ש רז״ל כל המזכה את הרבים אין חטא בא ע״י. ושמא תאמר שאינך צריך לזאת התועלת. כי כבר הגעת אל ראש המעלות הרמות בעבודתו ודביקותו ית׳ וגבה לבך בדרכי ה׳ וכבר לבך חלל בקרבך ולא יאונה לך כל עון אשר חטא. לזה אמר לא כן הדבר שלא תאמין בעצמך וכו׳.

This issue, that of serving as an example and reprover (but always in a positive spirit) for others, was crucial to Hasidism's vision for the transformation of Jewish life. In pre-Hasidic Ashkenazic culture, the *ẓaddiq* was generally understood to seek anonymity. Certainly self-proclamation as a "righteous one" would have violated all the norms of modesty. There was a strong folk-belief in hidden *ẓaddiqim*, sometimes numbered thirty-six, by whose merit the world continued to exist.[18] *Ẓaddiqim* who were already gone from this world could indeed intercede on behalf of the living, and supplication at their graves was an established practice, especially in the post-Safed generations. But living *ẓaddiqim* were not easily to be sought out.

Hasidism represents a transformation of this norm, the call to which is found in the Maggid's own writings and in those of his disciples. This particular text is significant because of its date, indicating that Levi Yiẓḥaq was urging efforts at outreach immediately after the Maggid's death. *The words "to teach them the ways of God in which they should walk, to be earnest in His worship, with awe, love, and attachment" is precisely a call to build the Hasidic movement, to carry its message out to the broader public.* I am suggesting that Levi Yiẓḥaq is addressing himself directly to his colleagues, fellow members of the Maggid's circle, though he never says so explicitly. There were those in the group, including the Maggid's only son, R. Avraham "the Angel," who were inwardly focused. They would have been content to allow Mezritch to remain another *kloiz,* on the earlier proto-Hasidic model—a place where intense piety was cultivated for a small group, but not serving as the font of mass movement. Levi Yiẓḥaq is speaking for the other side of this argument. "We cannot separate ourselves from the broader community of Jews. We need to teach them the ways *of yire'ah, ahavah,* and *devequt*"—which is the essence of the Hasidic revivalist message.

The choice of Numbers 11:29, the verse where Moses reproves Joshua for his concern over the unchecked spread of prophecy (the case of Eldad and Medad) is also quite significant. Levi Yiẓḥaq could easily have chosen a scripture that dealt with the fear of God, or some other more innocent religious emotion. This verse says that the task of the one who takes on this role of leading the community is to encourage religious enthusiasm or "prophecy," precisely of the sort that early Hasidism sought to inspire and also was the source

---

18 See Arthur Green, "The *Zaddiq* as *Axis Mundi* in Later Judaism," included in his *The Heart of the Matter* (Philadelphia: JPS, 2015), 204–226; and Gershom Scholem, "The Tradition of the Thirty-Six Hidden Just Men," in his *The Messianic Idea in Judaism* (New York: Schocken, 1971), 251–256.

of much controversy.[19] The dispute between Moses and Joshua here may be read as saying that we should not hold back, following Moses's view that it is more important to spread this spirit of "prophecy" than it is to restrict it. Note how *devequt*, mystical "attachment" to God, has casually slipped into the well-known pair of *ahavah* and *yire'ah*, love and awe, and that something akin to prophecy is to be spread among the masses as well, "all of God's people."

The final statement in Levi Yiẓḥaq's argument is that your own merit depends on this. This is no time for merely cultivating one's own inner religious life. He uses Hillel's words in a strong and demanding way, claiming that one who does not reach out to others has to worry about the status of his own piety as well.

No less interesting, however, is the central section of this same sermon (partly ellipsed above, for the sake of order). Here Levi Yiẓḥaq takes a stand against competition for piety—a typical problem among younger devotees in enthusiastic religious groups—and also against backbiting, people sniping against one another by saying things they would not dare to express in public:

> If one's companions [fellow-servants of the master mentioned above] are more competent and attentive in their devotion than he is, attaining higher rank and greater glory than his, he should not resent them out of jealousy. He should take great pleasure and joy in the delight that his master has from their service. He should rather reprove his own self at his shortcomings, feeling shame that he has served less well than his fellows. When he sees other servants fall short, he should reprove them directly, showing them the way to get back on track toward more wholehearted service… .
>
> He [Hillel] then goes on to warn the person never to turn away from the fear of God, even for a moment, but rather to practice "I place Y-H-W-H ever before me" (Ps. 16:8), as R. Moshe Isserles says in the *Oraḥ Ḥayyim* (1:1), in the name of Maimonides, as

---

19 The question of "prophesying," without any clear definition, was around even prior to Hasidism, in the circle of R. Naḥman of Kuty. R. Naḥman was capable of prophecy (the term is not clearly defined), but the members of the circle had agreed to avoid it, most likely a reaction to the widespread phenomenon of prophecy in Sabbatian circles, where both the act and the term were welcomed without hesitation. See Abraham J. Heschel, *The Circle of the Baal Shem Tov: Studies in Hasidism*, ed. Samuel H. Dresner (Chicago: University of Chicago Press, 1985), 116. The later conflict between R. Shne'ur Zalman of Liadi and R. Avraham Kalisker, where the latter was accused of have stirred up the first opposition to Hasidism, may also relate to the place of prophet-like forms of extreme behavior.

> is known. On the verse "He tells a person what he speaks" (Am. 4:13), our sages taught: "Even in lighthearted conversation."[20] This is the meaning of [Hillel's] "Do not say anything that cannot be heard, for in the end it will be." Anything you would be embarrassed to say publicly [lit.: "into people's ears"], do not say even in your innermost chamber. Scripture says: "[Even] of the one who lies in your bosom, take care" (Mic. 7:5). The reason is that it will come out in the end. Not only is it the case that you are removing yourself from fear and shame before the One whose "glory fills all the earth" (Is. 6:3), but at the time of judgment you will be told what you have said. Woe for that shame and disgrace! That thing you would not say publicly before those who, like you, dwell in earthly darkness, is now revealed in heaven as your sin. It will be proclaimed before the assembly above and all the righteous! So be careful about everything you say and every move you make. Never turn aside from the awe and shame you feel before your Creator, and it will be well with you.[21]

Of course, it is possible that Levi Yizḥaq is addressing some *other* group in which competition and backbiting are taking place. It is also theoretically possible to say that these admonitions are to be read as nothing more than good moral advice. Indeed, if we were to come across them in such a more general collection as the author's *Qedushat Levi* on the Torah, that is how we might read them. But the *dating* of this sermon suggests otherwise. The Maggid is dead less than half a year, and these are the issues on young Levi Yizḥaq's mind. It seems entirely likely that he is addressing concerns within the circle of disciples (to whom he refers as *ḥaverekha*), struggling among themselves to find leadership

---

20 B. Ḥagigah 5b.

21 *Shemu'ah Tovah*, 84–85. ואם חביריו יעבדו עבודתם בחריצות ושקידה רבה יותר ממנו. אשר בזה יגיעו למעלה רמה ונשגבה יותר ממנו. לא ישנא אותם מקנאתו בהם. אבל יהי' לו זאת לשעשוע ועונג. גדול הנחת אשר אדוניו מקבל מעבודתם. רק שיוכיח את נפשו ויכלמנה על קיצורו בעבודה מחביריו. ולעבדי המלך המקצרים בעבודה. יוכיחם על פניהם ויורם את הדרך אשר בה ישובו להזדרז בעבודה על תכלית השלימות. [...] עוד בא להזהיר את האדם לבל יסור יראת ד' מעל פניו אף רגע אחת אבל יעשה כמש"ה שויתי ה' לנגדי תמיד וכמ"ש הרמ"א ז"ל בא"ח (סי' א') בשם הרמב"ם כנודע. ואמרו רז"ל מגיד לאדם מה שיחו אפי' שיחה קלה וכו' וז"ש ואל תאמר דבר שא"א לשמוע. ר"ל דבר שהיית בוש מלהשמיעו לאזני בני אדם אל תאמרהו אפי' בחדרי חדרים. וכמש"ה משכבת חיקך שמור וכו' וטעם הדבר שסופו להשמע. ר"ל זולת זאת שהוא ית' מלא כל הארץ כבודו ואתה מסלק בזה המורא והבשת מעליך. עוד גם שבשעת הדין יגיעו לך שיחתך זאת ואוי לאותו בושה וכלימה אשר יגיעך אז שהדבר אשר לא היית מדברו בפני בני אדם יושבי חושך כמותך שוכני בתי חומר גלו שמים עוונך ויפרסמוהו לעיניך בפני פמליא של מעלה וכל הצדיקים ולכן תהי' נזהר בכל דבורך ותנועותיך ותמיד על יזוז מורא בוראך ובושתך ממנו מעליך וטוב לך.

and direction in the period following their master's passing, and stumbling into conflict with one another, competition for demonstrations of piety, leading to some shameful secret tale-telling. Some bit of nastiness—the details of which we will never know—has broken out within the group, and Levi Yiẓḥaq is speaking out against it.

We do not know where or whether this sermon was preached orally. It is possible that it was distributed in writing among those to whom its author wanted to deliver the message. But it is clear that pronouncing these words was an act of taking on the mantle and the risk of leadership within the group. Either Levi Yiẓḥaq already had that role of leader in the year following the master's death, or these statements of warning and reproof are evidence of his attempt to assert such a role within the now bereft and leaderless circle.

A year later, in the summer of 1774, he again preached a sermon that most likely had a clear "address" within the emerging Hasidic community. The Torah portion was *Qoraḥ,* where the question of rivalry over leadership is the key theme. As in all these summer season sermons, he begins by quoting from Avot, which is being publicly read on Shabbat afternoons:

> "Be warmed by the fire of the sages, but be careful of their coals, lest you be burned" (M. Avot 2:1).
>
> We should first take note that Moses our Teacher, peace be upon him, said "If they [Qoraḥ and his followers] descend alive into Sheol, [you shall know that these people have rejected Y-H-W-H]" (Num. 16:30)… .[22]
>
> Our sages taught that "Qoraḥ was a clever person. [They asked] what, then, he saw in this folly (of rising up against Moses)? [They replied that] it was his eye that led him astray."
>
> Qoraḥ's controversy with Moses did not come about because he was a fool. He wanted to become high priest in order to bring forth the flow of divine bounty (*shefa'*) instead of Aaron. He too was a great man, but he wanted to bring forth the *shefa'* in a different manner, as has been explained elsewhere. But [if he was] such a great person, one in whom intellect shone, how could he not have understood that he should not sin against Moses and against the blessed Creator?

---

22 Here follows a lengthy digression concerning the judgment of body and soul.

> The fact is that the intellect he possessed was not due to his own self. "He rather saw a great dynasty proceeding from himself."[23] The source from which his soul was drawn was [also] great and powerful. But when a person like this wants to rise up to that source, and is unable to do so, because he does not know the order of such ascents, he is uprooted from the world… .
>
> The sage is called "wood" [lit.: "a tree of the field"] and the holy Torah within him is the fire attached to that wood or coal, of which scripture says: "the Torah is light" [or "fire"].
>
> … In matters of Torah, opposing views are good, when the intent is to come to the true conclusion. The heat [of argument] makes for increased learning. But if the opposition to a sage becomes personal, the one opposing will get burned by the sage's coal. This is the meaning of "Be warmed by the fire [of the sages]." Stand up to the fire within them, their Torah. But of the coal, which is the sage's own person, be wary, lest you be burned… .[24]

Once again, it seems likely that there is a contemporary situation in the background here. Levi Yiẓḥaq is a preacher, not a biblical interpreter; there is a reason why he chooses to read *parashat Qoraḥ* this way. Someone is coming forth to make a rival claim of leadership, and the fight has gotten nastily personal. Levi Yiẓḥaq is speaking out, here perhaps as a defender of the Maggid's school, against someone he sees as a usurper. He is being somewhat nasty himself, saying that the claimant is less great than his illustrious ancestors and that he hopes his offspring might be. While one cannot say for sure toward whom this barb is being turned, I believe there is a most likely candidate. I want to suggest—for that is all one can do—that he is referring to R. Yeḥi'el Mikhl of

---

23 All this, including the word *shalshelet,* is taken directly from Midrash *Tanḥuma, Qoraḥ* 5.

24 *Shemu'ah Tovah,* 85–86. והוי מתחמם נגד אורן של חכמים והוי זהיר בגחלתן וכו׳ [שלא תכוה]. נקדים לשום לב אל מ״ש משה רבע״ה וירדו חיים שאולה [וידעתם כי נאצו האנשים האלה את ה׳ ...] והנה ארז״ל קרח שפקח הי׳ מה ראה לשטות זה. עינו הטעתו וכו׳ כי הנה ענין מחלוקת קרח שחלק על מרע״ה לא שהי׳ שוטה רק שרצה להיות כה״ג שסבור שהוא יוריד השפע הקדוש ויהי׳ במקום אהרן. כי הי׳ ג״כ אדם גדול. רק שהי׳ רוצה להביא השפע באופן אחר כמבואר במקום אחר. אך הנה אדם גדול כזה שהשכל מאיר בו קשה עליו איך לא הבין שלא יחטא נגד משה והבורא ב״ה אך הענין שהשכל שהי׳ לו (בו) לא הי׳ בו מצד עצמיותו רק שראה שלשלת גדולה יוצאה ממנו ומקום מחצב נשמתו הי׳ רב ועצום ואדם כזה כשהוא רוצה לעלות למקום מחצבו ואינו יכול מחמת שאינו יודע סדר העליות הוא נעקר מן העולם. [...] והנה הת״ח נקרא עץ השדה וגחלת והתורה הקדושה שבו הוא האור הנאחז בהעץ הוא הגחלת כמ״ש ותורה אור. [...] בד״ת ההתנגדות הוא טוב כשהכוונה הוא לעמוד על אמיתת הדין שמהחימום ההוא רווחא שמעתתא כנ״ל. אבל אם ההתנגדות הוא לעצמות גופו של הת״ח יכווה המתנגד בגחלתו כנ״ל. וזהו והוי מתחמם כנגד אורן וכו׳ ר״ל הוי מתנגד להאור שבו זו התורה ומהגחלת הוא עצמיותו הזהר שלא תכווה כנ״ל.

Zloczow, a leading figure of Hasidic literature who stood outside the Mezritch circle.

Yeḥi'el Mikhl (1726?–1781), and he alone, fits the description offered here exceptionally well.[25] He was a person of distinguished lineage, the son of the well-known R. Yiẓḥaq of Drohobycz, a contemporary of the Besht involved in the emerging proto-Hasidic circles.[26] Meshullam Feibush Heller refers to his teacher R. Yeḥi'el Mikhl as "a *ẓaddiq* and the son of a *ẓaddiq*, of holy descent."[27] The family was descended from an old Prague-connected clan, one that claimed descent from Rashi, and hence from the Davidic dynasty (as did the family of the Besht). Yeḥi'el Mikhl also had five sons, each of whom became a Hasidic *ẓaddiq*. They were younger contemporaries of Levi Yiẓḥaq,[28] and perhaps were already acting as Hasidic leaders. It is also fair to say that R. Yeḥi'el Mikhl's approach to Hasidism was quite different from that of the Maggid. He was indeed one who might well have sought to become "high priest" in order "to bring forth the *shefa'* "in a different manner." His father was well known as something of a magician, an expert in holy names.[29] The son continued in this path, especially as a miracle worker and as a dispenser of blessings. He was the main font for the sort of Hasidism later identified with R. Barukh of Miedzybozh, who would clash with the Maggid's school in the early years of the nineteenth century.[30] We are told that R. Shlomo of Karlin, the one among the Mezritch disciples who was indeed known as a wonderworker, turned to him following the Maggid's

---

25 On R. Yeḥi'el Mikhl, see Mor Altshuler, *Rabbi Meshulam Feibush Heller and His Place in Early Hasidism* [Heb.] (PhD diss., Hebrew University, Jerusalem, 1994), 30ff. While I do not agree with all of Altshuler's conclusions, there is much to be learned from a careful reading of her work. Without saying so directly, she does seem to point to a rivalry between these two *maggidim* and their followers.

26 On R. Yiẓḥaq, see Heschel, *The Circle of the Baal Shem Tov*, 162–181.

27 *Liqqutim Yeqarim* (Jerusalem, 1974), 110a. Cited by Altshuler, *Meshulam Feibush Heller*, 30.

28 R. Yosef of Yampole was the eldest of the five sons. Yitzhak Alfasi, in *Sefer ha-Admorim* (Tel Aviv: Ariel, 1961), does not list a birth date for him, but does list his brothers Yiẓḥaq of Radziwill as born in 1741 and Mordekhai of Kremnitz in 1746. This contradicts Altshuler's assertion (*Meshulam Feibush Heller*, 41) that R. Yosef was born only in the late 1750s, based on a story in *Shivḥey ha-Besht*. Heschel, however (in *The Circle of the Baal Shem Tov*, 174 n. 83), suggest a date as late as 1734 for the birth of R. Yeḥi'el Mikhl. If that is true, Altshuler's dating for his son's birth would make more sense.

29 Heschel, *The Circle of the Baal Shem Tov*, 170–174. R. David of Makow (*Shever Poshe'im*, 71b, in Wilensky, *Hasidim u-Mitnaggedim*, vol. 2, 170), quotes a Hasidic tradition that R. Mikhl was a reincarnation of the prophet Ḥabbakuk.

30 R. Yosef of Yampole married the daughter of R. Barukh (Altshuler, *Meshulam Feibush Heller*, 58 n. 128). This may confirm the sense of an ongoing non- or anti-Mezritch strain within early Hasidic leadership.

death.[31] These "ways of bringing forth the *shefa*'" were recognizably different from the more intellectualist school of Mezritch, represented by Levi Yiẓḥaq and Shne'ur Zalman of Liadi, among others. For them, the divine presence was to be encountered through the preacher's clever reinterpretations of the Torah text, the Hasidic version of *talmud torah*. Read this way, our text is also the earliest usage of the term *shalshelet* or "dynasty" (although taken from the midrash) to be found in Hasidic sources. In 1774, it is hard to think of any family other than that of the Zlochever to whom it might refer.

Both of these sermons show something of the atmosphere that surrounded the Mezritch circle in the period immediately following the Maggid's death. Not surprisingly, both inner and outer forces threatened the bonds that were beginning to create a sense of shared purpose, the spreading of a doctrine and religious style that was at the earliest fragile stage of becoming a great religious movement. Levi Yiẓḥaq, in callswing for leadership and dedication in spreading the movement's message, in seeking to smooth out inner conflicts, and in protecting the Maggid's circle's turf against a rival claimant, is asserting his own leadership within that circle, announcing himself as a central figure in the spread of Hasidism in its very earliest stage.

Now we turn to a third text, the opening page of *Shemu'ah Tovah*, as mentioned above. This, too, was delivered during the summer months, and it too opens with a passage from *Pirkei Avot*. Here Levi Yiẓḥaq chooses M. Avot 2:4: "An ignoramus cannot fear sin, nor can a peasant (*'am ha-areẓ*) be a *ḥasid*." In 1773, less than a year following the original bans against Hasidism, that was a lively choice for the young preacher, to say the least. The bans had used accusations of ignorance to denounce the nascent movement, which they sometime refer to as one of *mitḥassedim*, "self-proclaimed pietists."[32] They cannot be true *ḥasidim*, so the argument goes, while being ignorant of talmudic knowledge. Levi Yiẓḥaq, whom no one could describe as an *'am ha-areẓ*, takes them on directly. He begins, however, with an equally interesting typologization of the difference between a *ẓaddiq* and a *ḥasid:*

> With regard to the essential meaning of the term *ḥasidut:* The difference between *ẓaddiq* and *ḥasid* lies rooted in the following distinction. A person called a *ẓaddiq* is one who makes a constant effort to justify (*le-haẓdiq*) himself before his blessed Creator.

31 Avraham Abusch Schorr, *Ketavim* (Jerusalem: Makhon Bet Aharon ve-Yisra'el, 2018), especially 437–438, nn. 71–72.

32 Wilensky, *Ḥasidim u-Mitnaggedim*, vol. 1 or 2?, 70–83, 101–121.

> He is careful not to transgress even a single one of the prohibitions or negative commandments, and fulfills the 248 positive commandments in every condition and detail. This is the whole of humanity, to perfect one's soul in every limb and sinew, totaling 613. That is why he is called *ẓaddiq*, because he is justified in arguing [his case] as he stands before the King who loves justice. All his deeds are just and upright, with no admixture of sin. But he does not act with lovingkindness (*lo nitḥassed*) to do things that are beyond the letter of the law. Thus he is to be considered a servant, one who fulfills the command of his Owner.
>
> The title *ḥasid* applies to one who does act with lovingkindness toward his Owner. His goal in all he does is to bring pleasure to his Creator. Taking care to fulfill his Creator's commands does not suffice for him. In everything he attains, [he seeks out] some possible device to draw pleasure to his Creator. He will hold fast to this and not let go of it, even though he hasn't been warned or commanded concerning this matter. This one is to be called a son; he is like a son who loves his father greatly, even wondrously, and tries constantly to seek out ways to bring his father pleasure and happiness.[33]

This typology is entirely pre-Hasidic, based on old rabbinic usages. *Ḥasid* is clearly superior to *ẓaddiq*, which is to say that there is no evidence at all that *ẓaddiq* is to be seen as the leader of Hasidic community, even as one who commands the will of God, as is widespread in Levi Yiẓḥaq's later writings. This old typology exists elsewhere as well in the very earliest of post-Beshtian Hasidic sources.

Then Levi Yiẓḥaq goes on to make his central interpretive point:

> This is the meaning of "an *'am ha-areẓ* is not a *ḥasid*." The rung of *ḥasidut* can only be attained by one who has achieved rule over his worldly desires, separating from them and cleaving to the intellects alone. From there he rises into the secret level of knowing a bit of God's exalted greatness. Then he is lit afire and desires passionately to bring pleasure to his Creator. [Only] then he can reach the rung of *ḥasid* that I have mentioned. This is not true

33 *Shemu'ah Tovah*, 5.

> of one who has not yet detached himself from his material and earthly (*arẓit*) desires. He cannot be a *ḥasid*. This is the meaning of "an *'am ha-areẓ* is not a *ḥasid*": no one who is attached to *arẓiyyut*, earthliness, can be a *ḥasid*.[34]

Here Levi Yiẓḥaq has turned the tables on those who have just denounced the emerging new movement, using the rabbinic canon that he and Hasidism's detractors so clearly share. Being a true *ḥasid* does not depend upon scholarly knowledge, but upon one's ability to become detached from things of this world.

Thus we see Levi Yiẓḥaq acting in every way as a leader within the recently bereft circle of disciples. He seeks to keep peace among them, to fight off rival claims of Hasidic leadership from outside the group, and to respond to the fierce denunciation of Hasidism that has just been issued by the rabbinic courts of Vilna and Brody.

To these three passages in the *Shemu'ah Tovah* sermons, I wish to add a fourth text, attributed to Levi Yiẓḥaq in the early collection *Ge'ulat Yisra'el*. Here the preacher is defending the phenomenon of wandering *ẓaddiqim*, something that was new, certainly with the title *ẓaddiq*, in the years of Hasidism's early spread. *Ge'ulat Yisra'el* was published in Ostrog in 1821, attributed to one Yehoshu'a Avraham ben Yisra'el. It is divided into two sections, one a collection of teachings by various Ukrainian *ẓaddiqim*, but featuring especially the line extending from the Maggid to Levi Yiẓḥaq and on to his most important disciple R. Aharon of Zhitomir. It seems likely that he was working directly from oral or written sources collected within that circle.[35] The second section of the volume contains the earliest printed material from the circle of R. Pinḥas of Korzec. The section of Levi Yiẓḥaq's materials includes this discussion, set into the homiletic context of a dispute between king and prophet:

> "Hezekiah (king of ancient Judea) said: 'Let Isaiah come to me. Even though he is a prophet, I am the king.' Isaiah said: 'Let Hezekiah come to me. He may be king, but I am a prophet.'"[36]
>
> This seems most surprising. How could righteous folk like these be so casual about the issue of [holding onto their] pride, which is really tantamount to idolatry!

---

34 Ibid.

35 The first section of *Ge'ulat Yisra'el* was republished later, anonymously, under the title *Pitgamin Qaddishin* (Warsaw, 1886).

36 B. Berakhot 10a.

The matter is like this. Truly faith and trust in God is the most essential [religious] quality. It sustains life, both physical and spiritual, life of body and soul. Our sages taught that Habakuk reduced all the commandments to one: "The righteous one lives by his faith" (Hab. 2:4).

But if that is the case, how and why do we see great *ẓaddiqim* leaving their homes and travelling about so much? On the face of things, it appears they are doing so for their own needs, in order to earn their livelihood. But could it be said that this is the intent of such righteous ones? Do they not have faith and trust in blessed Y-H-W-H, who can sustain them fully, even as they sit in their own houses? Blessed Y-H-W-H can do anything!

The truth is that these *ẓaddiqim* see the strength of Israel, the holy people, diminished and weakened, due to our many sins. [Israel are unable] to be heroes in the battle of Torah, that of overcoming the evil urge, each in his own way. They require healing of soul through moral teaching and fear of heaven, good counsels in the service of blessed Y-H-W-H. That is why the *ẓaddiqim* of the generation, the eyes of the community, leaders of their people, trouble themselves so greatly to travel the roads, wandering from place to place through the world. [They seek to] bring merit to Israel, the holy people, causing them to return to God in a complete way, through such moral teachings and fear of heaven, goodly counsels that will bring them close to blessed Y-H-W-H, each on one's own level and in one's own way. This is their main intent and purpose. [Fulfillment of] their own needs and livelihood come to them incidentally, from Y-H-W-H, so that they can sustain themselves and their households, as well as perform acts of charity and good deeds.

But if someone should whisper to you: "Couldn't the *ẓaddiqim* arrange that people come to them, so that they wouldn't have to make the effort of travelling around to others?" know that there is [another] deep meaning to this [travel]. They seek to effect powerful and awesome mystical unifications. Masters of secret lore know that when a greater one goes to a lesser one, such an awesome union is performed. This is referred to as the bowing down [of the letter *heh* to the letter *waw*], as is known. That is why great *ẓaddiqim* trouble themselves to travel out to the common folk [scattered] around the world, to bring about many such

> unifications. This is their main task in this world, by means of [teaching] Torah and [fulfilling the] commandments, bringing great pleasure and joy to blessed Y-H-W-H.
>
> This was the intent of those righteous and humble *ẓaddiqim* Hezekiah and Isaiah. Each of them thought of himself as nothing and without value, when compared to the other. Each wanted to bring about divine glory, performing these unifications for God's pleasure and joy. That is why Isaiah said: "Let Hezekiah come to me," for I am less than he… .
>
> All this was to increase and glorify Torah. "May His great name be made great and holy [*yitgadal ve-yitqadash shmei rabba*]. Amen."[37]

This sermon is an important historical document, when viewed in the context of Hasidism's early spread. The wandering *ẓaddiq* is a new phenomenon, something that has to be explained and justified. Here we have Levi Yiẓḥaq describing the situation as it was in the 1770s or '80s, not in the later and more established era of Hasidic dominance. Then the people indeed did

---

37 *Shemu'ah Tovah*, 85b–86b. חזקיהו אמר ליתי ישעיה לגבאי דאע״ג דאיהו נביא אנא מלך וישעיה אמר ליתי חזקיה לגבאי דאע״ג דהוא מלך אנא נביא. הנה לכאורה יפלא. האיך אפשר אשר צדיקים כאלו יתרשלו ידיהם ח״ו במדות הגאות אשר הוא ממש כע״ז. אמנם ביאור הענין כן הוא. כי הנה הן אמת שמדת האמונה והבטחון בהשי״ת הוא ראש לכל המדות והוא המחיה את האדם. הן בגופניות הן ברוחניות. הן בחיות הגוף והן בחיות הנשמה וכאשר חכמים הגידו. בא חבקוק והעמידן על אחת. וצדיק באמונתו יחיה. נמצא א״כ מה זה ועל מה זה שאנו רואים שיש צדיקים גדולים אשר זזים מביתם ונוסעים בדרך. זמן זמנים טובא משמע. ולפום רהיטא נראה שכוונתם עבור צרכיהם ופרנסותיהם. אבל הכי יאומן כי יסופר אשר צדיקים כאלו לזה שמו כוונתם. כי הלא בוודאי מאמינים ובוטחים בהשי״ת באמונה ובטחון באמת שביכולת השי״ת לפרנסם בכל מכל כל אפילו כשישבו בביתם כי הוא יתברך הכל יכול. אמנם אמיתית הענין כן הוא. כי צדיקי הדור רואים אשר מגודל גלות המר בעו״הר נתמעט ומתרושש כח ישראל ע״ק [עמא קדישא] להיות גבורים בעצמם במלחמתה של תורה. ואיזהו גבור הכובש את יצרו כל אחד לפי מדרגתו ובחינתו. וצריכים הם לרפואת הנפש במוס׳ ויראת שמים ועיטין טבין לעבודת השי״ת. ע״כ צדיקי הדור אשר הם עיני העדה רישא דעמא מטריחים עצמן בטירחות יתירות בנסיונות הדרכים ונעים ונדים בעולם כדי לזכות את ישראל ע״ק להחזירם בתשובה שלימה במוסר ויראת שמים ועיטין טבין לקרבם להשי״ת את כל אחד לפי מדרגתו ובחינתו. וזאת היא עיקר כוונתם ומגמתם. אמנם צרכיהם ופרנסותיהם ממילא באה להם מאת ה׳ היתה זאת כדי שיהיה להם במה להתפרנס עצמן וב״ב. ולעשות צדקה ומעשים טובים. ואם לחשך אדם לומר א״כ הלא היו יכולים הצדיקים לפעול שיבואו אנשי העולם לביתם, ולא יצטרכו המה להיות מטריחים עצמן מביתם ולנסוע אל אנשי העולם. אמנם תוכן עומק הדבר הוא כי גם לזאת הוא כונתם הק׳. להיות עושים ופועלים בזה יחודים גדולים נוראים ועצומים כאשר ידוע לי״ח שבהיות הגדול הולך אצל הקטן ממנו אז נעשה יחוד גדול ונורא. כי הוא כריעת וכו׳ כידוע. וע״כ מטריחים עצמן הצדיקים הגדולים בנסיעות אל המון העם אשר בעולם למען רבות יחודים קדושים ונוראים אשר כל זה עיקר עשיתם ופעולתם בזה העולם תורה ומצות למען רבות נחת רוח ותענוג להבורא ב״ה. וזהו היתה כונת הצדיקים הענוים במדת הענוה הקדושה חזקיהו וישעיהו אשר כל אחד ואחד היה בעיני עצמו במה נחשב ובטל וטפל לגבי דחבריי׳. וע״כ כל אחד חפץ למען צדקו שיגדיל ויאדי׳ התיחדו׳ יחודים הק׳ ויתרבה נחת רוח ותענוג להבורא י״ת. וע״כ אמר ישעיהו ליתי חזקיהו לגבאי כי אנא קטן מניה[...] נמצא כל אחד ואחד חפץ למען צדקו שיגדיל תורה ויאדיר ויתגדל ויתקדש שמיה רבא. אמן.

travel to the *ẓaddiqim*. In the early days, before they were established, they did precisely this: wandered from town to town, offering blessings, spreading the message, hoping to be rewarded with both disciples and donations to the cause.[38] "What are these people doing out there on the roads," he asks, going to preach and effect healings among rural Jews in small and remote communities? Wouldn't they be better off staying home, engaging in full-time prayer and Torah study, as *ẓaddiqim* are supposed to do? Surely that is what the famous hidden *ẓaddiqim* of former generations used to do! It must be (as opponents of Hasidism were saying loudly) that they are just some sort of peddlers, out there trying to make a living.[39]

Levi Yiẓḥaq was the right person to reply to this critique. He, after all, was *not* one of those wandering *ẓaddiqim*; he had a most respectable livelihood as rabbi of a major town. His twofold answer is strong and unequivocal, even though typically wrapped in homiletic garb. They are out there not for themselves, but to strengthen the faith of Israel, to bring them closer to God through repentance and good deeds. That reply may readily be translated, from the historian's point of view, into "They are engaged in building the Hasidic movement!" That was precisely how Hasidism saw itself, as the effort of enlightened teachers to transform the religious lives of the masses, bringing them closer to God. But they are also, in the course of humbling themselves before the masses—and the wandering *ẓaddiq* surely did suffer the risk of humiliation, and more—engaging in mystical acts that unify the upper worlds.

What we see here is another example of Levi Yiẓḥaq's assertion of leadership within the emerging movement. As the most securely established figure among the Maggid's disciples, he is spreading his protection over those of his colleagues who are still out "on the roads," doing the precise thing he said they ought to do in the first text quoted above from *Shemu'ah Tovah*.

Perhaps not surprisingly, in a parallel text, also printed in *Ge'ulat Yisra'el*,[40] Levi Yiẓḥaq turns to those wandering preachers themselves, warning them to do their

38 Dov Ber was an exception, having an early established "court" in Mezritch and later in Rovno. This may have been due to a physical disability, which would have made regular travel difficult.

39 Compare this to Menaḥem Naḥum of Chernobyl's comparison of the *ẓaddiq* to a peddler, found in *Siftei Ẓaddiqim*, and translated in my introduction to his *The Light of the Eyes*, 95–96. See also the very interesting parallel defense of the *ẓaddiq*'s travel by the *Degel Maḥaneh Efrayim*, in *Masa'ei*, 463a.

40 *Ge'ulat Yisra'el* #13, 20. In *Pitgamin Qaddishin*, the corresponding text is #12, 20. ומכש"כ מי שזיכהו השי"ת לומר תורה ברבים ולהשיב רבים מעון יהיה כל עיקר כוונתו ומגמתו רק עבור תיקון והשלמת השם הקדוש הנכבד והנורא, ועבור תיקון והשלמת הכסא הקדושה. ולא יהיה ח"ו כוונתו שידבק בידו מאומה מן אחרים השומעים את תורתו בשביל מזונות ופרנסת גופו. וד"ל.

work only for the glory of God, to make whole His broken throne by returning His wayward children to him in repentance, and not to be concerned with seeking out their own livelihood by being on the road. These two sources together attest to Levi Yiẓḥaq's voice as a shaper of the movement's spread, defending the new crop of wandering *maggidim* as they spread the word among small-town and rural Jews, but also trying to exercise influence over their conduct. In a movement characterized by spontaneous growth, having no formal standards of ordination or means of quality control, Levi Yiẓḥaq, perhaps Hasidism's most respectable spokesman, is trying to make sure that the emerging *ẓaddiqim*—including some self-proclaimed as such—would embody the Hasidic message at its best.

CHAPTER 17

"Seek Me and Live": Reflections on the Spiritual Journey

Ariel Evan Mayse

All journeys have secret destinations of which the traveler is unaware.[1]

—Martin Buber

The spiritual journey is a long trip. Moreover, your experience will seem to recycle and you'll feel that you are back to where you started and haven't made any progress at all. Recycling is like climbing a spiritual staircase. You seem to be returning to the point from which you started, but in fact you are at a higher level. An eagle rising toward the sun keeps returning to the same place on the horizontal plane, but to a higher place on the vertical plane.[2]

—Thomas Keating

Introduction

Rabbi Simlai's fanciful description of biblical figures who distilled the 613 commandments to smaller numbers of foundational precepts is surely among the most long-lived Talmudic *aggadot*. Two opinions are given regarding the single

---

1 Martin Buber, *The Legend of the Baal-Shem*, trans. Maurice Friedman (Princeton: Princeton University Press, 2020), 36.

2 Thomas Keating, *Open Mind, Open Heart: The Contemplative Dimension of the Gospel* (New York: Continuum, 2002), 106.

essential mitzvah of the Torah. Of these, the verse from Habakkuk is undoubtedly the more famous: "and the righteous lives through faith" (Hab. 2:4). But the editors of the Talmud suggest another source that encapsulates the entire Hebrew Bible: "Thus says Y-H-V-H to the house of Israel: 'Seek Me and live'" (Amos 5:4). Rather than steadfast dependability for faith, as in Habakkuk, this verse from Amos suggests that the quest for God is the central through line of Torah. A rabbinic interlocutor, however, rejects that this prooftext should be seen as Amos's attempt to condense the message of Scripture. Rather than pruning the Hebrew Bible to a single principle, Amos was lifting up and expanding devotional heart of the Torah: *dirshuni vi-ḥeyu*—the act of seeking God gives life.

The present essay explores the endless search for God as an animating impulse in Jewish theology, and in Hasidism in particular.[3] These mystical sources below portray religious life as an unceasing quest, a never-ending journey that intertwines creative exegesis, self-discovery and sacred community. The Hasidic homilies join biblical and Talmudic themes with Neo-Platonism and the competing impulses of rationalist philosophers and kabbalists, literatures that draw upon a devotional culture shared with medieval mystics both Jewish and Christian. Hasidic teachings on the quest pivot upon two interrelated themes inherited from this theological mélange. The first is the permanent inscrutability of God, a "dazzling" mystery that remains even as the seeker approaches—and moves beyond—the shores of human language and mind.[4] Hasidic teachings affirm the value of this quest not in spite of its interminability, but precisely because of its eternal nature. The second theme is that these Hasidic sermons understand the journey to be personally transformative and cosmically significant. Rather than defining religious meaning exclusively in terms of heightened *devequt*, Hasidic sources emphasize that God is revealed—with potency and majesty—within the quest itself. "Today, in the time of exile," declared one early Hasidic master, "it is easier to attain the Holy Spirit than in the time of the Temple. While one cannot draw close to the king in the palace, anyone who wants to approach him while on the path may do so."[5] This chapter intends to provide a brief overview of such dynamic conceptions of the religious life as a journey.

---

3 Present constraints demand brevity, but I hope to develop this theme on another occasion, where I will also deal more fully with the idea of religious life as a quest in Hasidic stories.

4 See *Moreh Nevukhim* 1:59; and Menachem Lorberbaum, *Dazzled by Beauty: Theology as Poetics in Hispanic Jewish Culture* [Heb.] (Jerusalem: Yad Izhak Ben-Zvi, 2011).

5 See *Maggid Devarav le-Ya'aqov*, ed. Rivka Schatz-Uffenheimer (Jerusalem: Magness, 1976), no. 49, p. 70.

I.

Hasidic reflections on religious life as a quest emerge from biblical literature. They are imaginatively layered upon the physical peregrinations and travels of Scriptural heroes, but the Hasidic sources may be said to build upon an important tension in biblical literature. While the book of Exodus notes that God's face cannot be seen ("no person shall see Me and live," Ex. 33:20),[6] the yearnings of the Psalmist cut in the opposite direction. "Seek My face!" he declares, "O Y-H-V-H, I seek Your face. Do not hide Your face from me" (Ps. 27: 8–9). God's countenance is a symbol of blessing, intimacy and favor,[7] whereas its concealment (*hester panim*) generates feelings of abandonment and seemingly unrequited love and devotion.

Standing in the breach between the yearning to know God and impossibility of attaining that goal is the Song of Songs.[8] The plain-sense meaning of this work highlights a poetic dance of desire filled with verdant, pastoral images, though the lovers' intense quest remains, for the most part, unconsummated. The few moments of intimate embrace are hidden from the reader and couched in the veil of silence.[9] The Canticle offers a textured landscape of erotic language, a vocabulary that rabbinic sources apply to the love of God and Israel.[10]

Rabbinic literature includes some references to personal quests and fantastic journeys,[11] certain sources highlight meetings with curious individuals who present blessings or relate astounding teachings.[12] Most important for the rabbis, however, is the act of Scriptural interpretation—*derashah* or *midrash*[13]—as

---

6 See Rachel Adelman, "From the Cleft of the Rock: The Eclipse of God in the Bible, Midrash, and post-Holocaust Theology," in *Be-Ron Yaḥad: Studies in Jewish Thought and Theology in Honor of Nehemia Polen*, ed. Ariel Evan Mayse and Arthur Green (Boston, MA: Academic Studies Press, 2019), 50–73; and, more broadly, George Savran, "Seeing is Believing: On the Relative Priority of Visual and Verbal Perception of the Divine," *Biblical Interpretation* 17, no. 3 (2009): 320–361.

7 See also Ps. 67:2, building upon Num. 6.

8 Michael Fishbane, *Song of Songs: The Traditional Hebrew Text with the New JPS Translation* (Philadelphia: JPS, 2015).

9 See Song 3:4–5, and Michael Fishbane's commentary ad loc.

10 Reuven Kimelman, "Rabbi Yokhanan and Origen on the Song of Songs: A Third-Century Jewish-Christian Disputation," *The Harvard Theological Review* (1980): 567–595.

11 See B. Bava Meẓi'a 85a; B. Bava Batra 73a–74b; and B. 'Eruvin 54a.

12 The third chapter of B. Ta'anit is filled with such tales.

13 The Psalmists' yearning often invokes words constructed from the synonymic roots *darash* and *baqash*, both of which intertext with other biblical passages and continue to echo in later Jewish literatures. See, inter alia, Deut. 11:12; Lev. 10:16; Ps. 14:2 and 53:3; Isa. 55:6; and Ovid R. Sellers, "Seeking God in the Old Testament." *Journal of Bible and Religion* 21, no. 4 (1953): 234–237.

a doubled quest for God that leads through the heart of Torah. The ancient *hekhalot* and *merkavah* sources, which reflect elements of Greek mystery religions, Gnosticism and the apocalyptic ascent texts of late Antiquity, describe the quest for God in strikingly visual and experiential terms.[14] But in early rabbinic literature God is indeed to be sought in the text, through the act of what Nehemia Polen has called "performative" or "illuminated" exegesis, suggesting that the interpretation of Scripture was understood as an act of communion with the Holy Spirit.[15] The development of these traditions is development in the famed Talmudic narrative about Rabban Yohanan ben Zakkai riding on his donkey, who descends in order to study the "works of the chariot" with his student Rabbi El'azar ben 'Arakh:

> He said: Is it possible that you interpret [*doresh*] the "works of the chariot," that *Shekhinah* is with us and the ministering angels are accompanying us, while I ride upon the donkey? Immediately, Rabbi El'azar ben 'Arakh began to discuss the "works of the chariot." Fire descended from heaven and encircled all the trees in the field, all of which began to sing.[16]

This moment of rapturous exegesis or *derashah,* an experiential vision of the "works of the chariot" studied by a master and disciple traveling, stopping to engage in esoteric Torah study, became a veritable type-scene for later Jewish mystics. And the rabbinic understanding that God, simultaneously hidden and revealed, must be sought through the exhaustible wellspring of the sacred text was a key contribution to all later mystical sources.

---

14 See Gershom Scholem, *Major Trends in Jewish Mysticism* (New York: Schocken, 1995), 40–79; Elliot R. Wolfson, *Through a Speculum That Shines: Vision and Imagination in Medieval Jewish Mysticism* (Princeton: Princeton University Press, 1997), 74–124; Joseph Dan, "The Religious Experience of the *Merkavah,*" in *Jewish Spirituality: From the Bible through the Middle Ages,* ed. Arthur Green (New York: Crossroad, 1986), 289–307; Peter Schäfer, *The Hidden and Manifest God: Some Major Themes in Early Jewish Mysticism,* trans. Aubrey Pomerance (Albany: State University of New York Press, 1992).

15 Nehemia Polen, "Derashah as Performative Exegesis," in *Midrash and the Exegetical Mind,* ed. Lieve Tuegels and Rivka Ulmer (Piscataway, NJ: Gorgias Press, 2010), 123–153; and idem, "The Spirit Among the Sages: *Seder Olam,* the End of Prophecy," in *It's Better to Hear the Rebuke of the Wise than the Song of Fools,* ed. W. David Nelson and Rivka Ulmer (Piscataway, NJ: Gorgias Press, 2015), 83–94. See also T. Ḥagigah 2:3-4; *Shir ha-Shirim Rabbah* on Song 1:2; Y. Ḥagigah 2:1.

16 See B. Ḥagigah 14; and cf. the "Prince of Torah" traditions in David J. Halperin, *Faces of the Chariot: Early Jewish Responses to Ezekiel's Vision* (Tübingen: J. C. B. Mohr-Paul Siebeck, 1988).

Jewish reflections on religious life as a quest changed significantly in the medieval period. This reflects, in part, their growing acquaintance with neo-Platonic and Aristotelian understandings of the soul's yearning for and love for God. Jewish thinkers in Andalusia and the Maghreb began to enter a sustained dialogue with Sufism, a religious tradition in which the idea of the *ṭarīqah*—the journey along the path—is an animating metaphor. This grows from earlier Islamic sources on mystical journeys and ascents, such as Muhammad's night journey from Mecca to Jerusalem and his ride into heaven (*al-'Isrā' wal-Miʿrāj*) and the elaborate hagiography thereupon. Sufi sources depict the path as leading to *fanāʾ* (extinction or annihilation of the self), and in some systems, *baqāʾ* (permanent subsistence) as the ultimate stage of happiness and endurance.

One of the most repercussive meditations on the religious path is the *Conference of the Birds* by the twelfth-century Persian Sufi Farid ud-Din Attar. This enormously influential work describes the journey of a group of birds as an extended metaphor for the interior mystical quest to take flight and become freed from the ego's bonds:

> Whoever can evade the Self transcends
> This world and as a lover he ascends.
> Set free your soul: impatient of delay,
> Step out along our sovereign's royal Way... .[17]

The perceived self, the boundaries of individuation set by the ego, prevent one from standing in true friendship with the One. The Sufi must, therefore, move beyond the confines of the physical body and shirk attachment to the physical world, courageously following the nearly infinite path that leads to soulful extinction and eventually to the dissolution of the self. In sum, the Sufi initiate or worshipper progresses in ritual from *sharia* (law) to *ṭarīqah* (the path), with its many stations of trust, poverty, humility, love of God, and then to *haqiqat* (the ultimate real).[18]

---

17 Farid ud-din Attar, *The Conference of the Birds*, trans. Afkham Darbandi and Dick Davis (London: Penguin Books, 1984), 33.

18 See Annemarie Schimmel, *Mystical Dimensions of Islam* (Chapel Hill: The University of North Carolina Press, 2011), 98–186; Shahzad Bashir, *Sufi Bodies: Religion and Society in Medieval Islam* (New York: Columbia University Press, 2011), 50–77; and Peter Awn, "Classic Sufi Approaches to Scripture," in *Mysticism and Sacred Scripture*, ed. Steven T. Katz (Oxford: Oxford University Press, 2000), 147–150. Key to success along this path is the *sheikh* or spiritual master, a figure who gives spiritual instruction (*tarbiyah*) and shepherds the students along the journey.

The legacy of interiority found in Sufism left a deep impression upon Bahya ibn Pakuda, whose *Ḥovot ha-Levavot* describes religious life as an inner quest to uncouple one's attachments to the physical and to cultivate burning, passionate love (Arab. *ishq*; Heb. *teshuqah*) for God.[19] This project of bringing Sufi modes of devotion into Jewish spirituality continued in the works of Yehudah ha-Levi, who underscored the importance of experiencing God through witnessing (Arab. *mushāhadah*; Heb. *'edut*) and tasting (Arab. *dhawq*; Heb. *ta'am*) rather than logical inference or philosophical proposition.[20] This ethos of the interior quest shimmers throughout Ha-Levi's poems as well:

> Where, Lord, will I find you:
> your place is high and obscured.
> And where
> won't I find you:
> your glory fills the world … .
> I sought your nearness:
> With all my heart I called you.
> And in my going
> Out to meet you,
> I found you coming toward me.[21]

Ha-Levi's poem picks up on the motifs of divine omnipresence in Psalms 139 (as well as Isa. 6), twinning these with the lovers' mutual quest in Song of Songs. Whereas the Psalmist expresses frustration in his inability to flee from God, this speaker is enthralled and animated by the search for God. Such verses are representative of the quest for God as expressed by the religious Hebrew poets of Muslim Spain and Andalusia.

The medieval rationalists saw the religious quest in philosophical terms, describing knowledge of God as an intellectual journey and indeed a religious obligation.[22] This framing of the intellectual journey is perhaps best expressed in

---

19 See Diana Lobel, A *Sufi-Jewish Dialogue: Philosophy and Mysticism in Bahya ibn Paquda's "Duties of the Heart"* (Philadelphia: University of Pennsylvania Press, 2007).

20 Idem, *Between Mysticism and Philosophy: Sufi Language of Religious Experience in Judah Ha-Levi's Kuzari* (Albany, NY: State University of New York Press, 2000), esp. 89–102. Writing in Judeo-Arabic and thus choosing which Arabic words to translate and which to render in Hebrew characters, both ibn Pakuda and ha-Levi—as well as their translators—left a significant impression upon the lexicon of devotion.

21 Peter Cole, *The Dream of the Poem: Hebrew Poetry from Muslim and Christin Spain, 950–1492* (Princeton: Princeton University Press, 2007), 155–156.

22 Herbert Davidson, *Religion in a Religious Age*, ed. Shlomo Dov Goitein (Cambridge, MA: Association for Jewish Studies, 1974), 53–68.

the writings of Maimonides, including his account of Abraham's philosophical quest[23] as well as his stirring reflections—invoking the Canticle—on repentance when undertaken as an expression of love for God.[24] The quest for knowledge also undergirds Maimonides's famous parable about the denizens of a city,[25] of whom only a select few truly seek to deepen their understanding of the king through traveling to the innermost sanctum of the king. While most individuals remain content to stand outside and sate themselves with their ignorance, the true philosophers and prophets attain intimate knowledge of God, and, in doing so, enter into a state of unrivaled private intellective communion.[26] Although the elitist thrust of this kind of search is abundantly clear, we should mention Maimonides's description of human knowledge of God as akin to recognizing a dear friend from behind by means of his structure and mannerisms rather than his face.[27] Moses achieved this in witnessing God's "back" in Exodus 33, but Maimonides's choice to include this description—or exercise—in the opening chapter of *Mishneh Torah* suggests that it may be the goal of all seekers who wish to cultivate knowledge of the Divine.

It is in the writings of the medieval kabbalists that the visions, journeys and quests of the religious life reached some of their fullest and richest expression.[28] Nowhere is this clearer than in the *Zohar*, a work that infuses its theological landscape with new symbolic language, representing a vital outpouring of religious language surrounding the *sefirot*. The *Zohar* is an associative work of biblical exegesis similar in style to that of classical rabbinic midrash, and verses from all over Scripture are cited and interpreted in light of one another. That the Song of Songs, first moved to the heart of the mystical canon by Rabbi Ezra of Gerona, is present on nearly every page suffuses the religious quest with an amorous vitality.[29] The *Zohar* uses interpretive form to elevate

---

23 *Mishneh Torah, Hilkhot 'Avodah Zarah* 1.

24 *Mishneh Torah, Hilkhot Teshuvah* 10. This is, to my knowledge, the first instance of reading Song of Songs as a devotional dialogue between God and the soul attested in Jewish literature.

25 *Moreh Nevukhim* III:51.

26 Peter E. Gordon, "The Erotics of Negative Theology: Maimonides on Apprehension," *Jewish Studies Quarterly* 2, no. 1 (1995): 1–38; and David R. Blumenthal, *Philosophical Mysticism: Studies in Rational Mysticism* (Ramat Gan: Bar-Ilan University Press, 2006).

27 *Mishneh Torah, Hilkhot Yesodei ha-Torah* 1:10. See also Don Seeman, "Reasons for the Commandments as Contemplative Practice in Maimonides," *The Jewish Quarterly Review* 103, no. 3 (2013): 298–327.

28 See, more broadly, Avishai Bar-Asher, *Journeys of the Soul: Concepts and Imageries of Paradise in Medieval Kabbalah* [Heb.] (Jerusalem: Magness, 2019).

29 See Arthur Green, "Intradivine Romance: The Song of Songs in the Zohar," in *Scrolls of Love: Reading Ruth and the Song of Songs*, ed. Peter S. Hawkins and Lesleigh Cushing Stahlberg (New York: Fordham University Press, 2006), 214–223; idem, "The Song of Songs in Early

the symbolic language of earlier Kabbalah to an entirely different level, situating the journey to know God within a quest to push imaginative language to its furthest limits.[30]

The collection of protagonists and fellow travelers at the heart of the *Zohar*—the *ḥevraya*—are seekers of God whose yearning to uncover divinity and Torah spur their travels across the Galilee.[31] These journeys, literary inventions as they are, reflect the *ḥevraya*'s flights of interpretation across the text of Scripture in what Michael Fishbane has called the "exegetical spirituality" of the *Zohar*, a religious ethos in which new discoveries of the self, of God, and of the text woven together in the interpretive quest.[32] The exegetical movement is described as a revelatory experience, and creative exegesis of Scripture is extolled with the highest praises.[33] Much of the *Zohar* unfolds as Rabbi Shim'on bar Yohai and his disciples offer differing interpretations of a single biblical passage, one after another. These assemblies are like mystical jazz sessions, as Melila Hellner-Eshed has put it, in which each kabbalist takes up the exegetical quest through presenting variations on a theme.

The central place of seeking and the religious quest is often highlighted by later commentators on the *Zohar*. Rabbi Shim'on ibn Lavi, for example, does just that in his re-reading of a particularly stirring text. Since God "is hidden, concealed, far beyond," declares the *Zohar*, both humans and angels are locked in an endless quest for a hidden Divine that is revealed neither in transcendent majesty nor in immanent presence. This leaves but one solution: "He is known and grasped to the degree that one opens [*mesha'er*] the gates of imagination!"—the quest to know God leads through the creative portals of mind and heart.[34] Ibn Lavi

---

Jewish Mysticism," *Orim* 2 (1987): 57–58; and Yehuda Liebes, "Zohar and Eros" [Heb.], *Alpayim* 9 (1994): 67–119.

30 Melila Hellner-Eshed, *Seekers of the Face: The Secrets of the Idra Rabba (The Great Assembly) of the Zohar* [Heb.] (Jerusalem: Idra Press, 2017), 13–18, has described the imaginative work of the early kabbalists as a response to the attempt of the rational philosophers to cleanse religious discourse of the dross of the imagination.

31 Hellner-Eshed, *Seekers of the Face*; idem, *A River Flows from Eden: The Language of Mystical Experience in the Zohar*, trans. Nathan Wolski (Stanford: Stanford University Press, 2009), esp. 111–120; and Eitan P. Fishbane, *The Art of Mystical Narrative: A Poetics of the Zohar* (Oxford: Oxford University Press, 2018).

32 Michael Fishbane, "The Book of Zohar and Exegetical Spirituality," in *Mysticism and Sacred Scripture*, ed. Steven T. Katz (Oxford: Oxford University Press, 2000), 101–117.

33 Hellner-Eshed, *A River Flows from Eden, esp.* 352–353; Liebes, "*Zohar* as Renaissance" [Heb.], *Da'at* 46 (2001): 5–11; Wolfson, *Through a Speculum that Shines*, 326–392; Moshe Idel, *Kabbalah: New Perspectives* (New Haven: Yale University Press, 1989), 212–218.

34 *Zohar* 1:103a–b. The text plays on similarity between *lesha'er* ("to imagine") and *sha'ar* ("gate"), building upon Prov. 31:23.

explores the implications of this Zoharic homily, combining late medieval or early modern science with a devotional reading of the text:

> Perhaps ... their quest spurs forward the movement of the heavenly arrays as they cycle around and around. To seek without finding is not accounted as foolishness for them, because, if the only goal of their rotation was to succeed, they would believe that their quest will always be in vain after the first or second failed attempt.
>
> But one who yearns will never allow himself to rest from the search, even if he does not succeed. This is like the desire of the lover for her Beloved, as it says, "I will arise and circle about, in the town, in the markets and the streets. I shall seek the One whom my soul loves; I have searched and not found" (Song. 3:2).[35]

Ibn Lavi deepens the Zoharic exegesis by suggesting that the endless quest for God sustains the universe. This perpetual journey is the vital source of continuous renewal, and therefore it must remain forever unconsummated. *Kol mishtoqeq lo yanuaḥ mi-levaqesh*—one who truly yearns for God cannot ever put down the quest. This emphasis on the interminability of yearning for the Divine, a sentiment that fills medieval Western religion, resonates with the writings of Bernard of Clairvaux (1090–1153). This Cistercian mystic and monk's *Sermones super Cantica Canticorum* present a felicitous vision of spiritual longing for a God that cannot ever be fully known:

> It is a great good to seek God. I think that, among all the blessings of the soul, there is none greater than this.... Is the consummation of the joy the extinction of the desire? It is rather to it as oil poured upon a flame; for desire is, as it were, a flame.... The joy will be fulfilled; but the fulfillment will not be the ending of the desire, nor therefore of the seeking.[36]

For Bernard of Clairvaux the essential crux of religious life is the journey and the seeking. Stepping toward God, he claims, and looking for God can only

35 *Ketem Paz* (Jerusalem, 2014), 240–241.

36 *Life and Works of Saint Bernard, Abbot of Clairvaux*, vol. 4: *Eighty-Six Sermons on the Song of Solomon*, ed. Dom John Mabillon, trans. Samuel J. Eales (London: John Hodges, 1896), 511–512.

further kindle the desires of the heart and spirit. The goal is not to sate this yearning, but about allowing it to flourish. For Bernard of Clairvaux, as for the Jewish seekers detailed both above and below, such fleeting moments of communion are only stages along the way. The touch of the Beloved simply fans the flames of religious passion, demanding that the quest to continue with ever-increasing intensity.

II.

Medieval reflections on the threshold of knowledge, language and experience in the quest for God were amplified and transformed in the movement of mystical renewal that came to be known as Hasidism. Because seeking the divine in Hasidic texts could easily be the subject of its own book, for the purposes of this essay I will restrict myself to a few examples that illustrate broader themes. The first of these, and in some respects the most essential, grows directly out of the medieval sources noted above: God is to be sought even though the quest is never-ending. In lifting up this theme, the Ba'al Shem Tov (or Besht) gives theological meaning to an oft-cited medieval *bon mot* on the nature of knowledge:

> "The ultimate aim of knowledge is unknowing" [*takhlit ha-yedia'h de-lo neda'*].[37] There are, however, are two kinds of not knowing. One is immediate, [exemplified in] one who does not even begin to seek or to know because such knowing is impossible. The second [type] is one who searches out and seeks [*ḥoqer ve-doresh*] until he [too] knows that it is impossible to know.
>
> The difference between them, to what may it be compared? It is like two individuals who wish to know the king. One enters all the king's rooms and takes pleasure in the treasure-troves and palaces, [even though] he still cannot know the king. The second says, "Since it impossible to know the king, I will not go into the king's chambers at all!" He immediately arrives at his unknowing.[38]

37 The various forms of "the ultimate aim of knowledge is unknowing" was inherited from medieval Islamic philosophy, but sourced more deeply in the writings of the Greek ancients. See the sources quoted in Israel Davidson, *Oẓar ha-Meshalim ve-ha-Pitgamim* (Jerusalem: Mossad ha-Rav Kook, 1957).

38 *Ben Porat Yosef* (Korets, 1781), *haqdamah*, interpreting *Eikhah Rabbah*, *petiḥta* no. 2 and Jer. 16:11.

The Besht animates the medieval truism of "the ultimate aim of knowledge is unknowing" in describing the unattainable quest to see the king—or better, King. There are, however, two modes of unknowing. The seeker who gives up immediately upon realizing that the journey is interminable, claims the Besht, has attained only indolent ignorance. One who diligently continues the quest, despite understanding that it cannot ever be completed, has a deep, even intimate kind of incomprehension rather than an unstudied lack of awareness. That which separates between them is the commitment to the transformative power of the process.

This position contrasts with other traditions attributed to the Besht that refer to radical, if temporary, awakening to the fullness of God's immanent presence. The Besht's famed parable about the king who builds an illusory palace, for example, describes the journey of a prince to his father's home. The king's child eventually comes to the realization that "that there is no boundary between him and his father; it was all an illusion."[39] Unlike the highly intellectual journey described in Maimonides's account, the Besht's quester is an industrious seeker who seeks to become awoken to God's immanence but not necessarily a member of the philosophical elite. And this goal seems to be attainable, at least for a fleeting moment.

In the Besht's homily on the ultimate aim of knowing, however, God's hiddenness remains inscrutable even as the worshipper is changed by the journey toward the permanent cloud of "unknowing." Indeed, this notion of a perennial veil—and hence, an everlasting quest—mirrors the initial teaching preserved in the Besht's name published in the first Hasidic book: "If you know that the blessed Holy One is hiding," claims the Besht, "then He is not truly hidden."[40] God's concealment cannot every be fully overcome, yet the religious journey is about opening the eyes and realize that awareness of this fact will itself unmask some measure of divine hiddenness.

Another clear example of this Hasidic emphasis on slow and asymptotic—but steady— spiritual growth[41] appears in the writings of Rabbi Levi Yiẓḥaq of Berditchev. This homily, building upon the dynamic divine name "I am that I

---

39 *Keter Shem Tov ha-Shalem* (Brooklyn: Kehot, 2004), no. 51b, 31, and the parallels listed there. See also Moshe Idel, "The Parable of the Son of the King and the Imaginary Walls in Early Hasidism," in *Judaism—Topics, Fragments, Faces, Identities*, ed. Haviva Pedaya and Ephraim Meir (Beer Sheva: Ben Gurion University of the Negev Press, 2007), 87–116; Immanuel Etkes, *The BeSHT: Magician, Mystic, Leader*, trans. Saadaya Sternberg (Waltham, MA: Brandeis University Press, 2005), 135–137.

40 *Toledot Ya'aqov Yosef* (Korets, 1781), *Bereshit*, 1a; interpreting Deut. 31:18.

41 See also *'Avodat Yisra'el, Shemini*, 114, for a dream in which the Besht explains the necessarily limited speed of spiritual growth.

am" (*Ehyeh asher Ehyeh*, Ex. 6:11), underscores constant seeking as the key to religious attunement:

> The *ẓaddiq*, meaning one who serves God, must know this. Each time some sort of understanding is achieved, there always lies another level of understanding beyond this one… . And as one comes to this [higher] understanding, one must know that there is an even deeper [rung] as well. This idea has no end [*ein lo sof*]… . This is the greatest way of serving God—always knowing that you have not achieved perfection, and therefore longing and desiring to ascend even higher.[42]

The *ẓaddiq*, here defined as one who understands and progresses through the stages of the religious quest, refuses to gather moss in the spiritual journey. Each rung or moment of attainment become a launching pad for further ascent—or depth—in the project of endless growth to the infinite One.

> I have heard in the name of the holy man R. Yeḥi'el Mikhl [of Zloczow] this explanation of the following verse: "One thing I have asked of God, it shall I seek. To gaze upon the pleasantness of God [and to visit His palace]" (Ps. 27:4). I have asked to gaze upon the pleasantness of God—I will seek, eternally, knowing that there are always higher and higher levels … [for] this quest is unending… .[43]

The Psalmist's "one thing" is thus expansively redefined as always searching for the next rung of the religious journey; rather than sinking into complacency, the seeker constantly looks for the "one" next stage. Rabbi Levi Yiẓḥaq continues with a parable inherited from the famed *paterfamilias* of Hasidism:

> Now the Ba'al Shem Tov explained the verse "He leads us onward eternally" (Ps. 48:15) with a parable of a parent who is teaching his small child to walk. Sometimes the child walks two or three paces toward his parent, who then steps back in order to force the child to walk farther. After the child moves closer, the parent moves a bit more.[44]

---

42 *Qedushat Levi*, ed. m. Derbaremdiger (Monsey, 1995), vol. 1, *Shemot*, 163.
43 Ibid.
44 Ibid.

Homiletically linking the Aramaic word "child" (*'alumaya*) to "eternally" (*'almut*), the Besht compares our search for God to the strivings of a youngster learning to walk. This eternal hiddenness, he claims, is why we describe the Divine as "the hidden God" (Isa. 45:15)—like a parent who tenderly leads a child into gradual independence, the concealed Divine guides the seeker along an eternal path that is driven by love.

Such teachings underscore that it is commitment to the quest which propels us along the path. The spiritual realizations and encounters with the divine that transpire along the way, while always complete, are powerful indeed. God's presence in the quest—or at least, our perception of that presence—cannot be assumed. Reflecting this concern, a homily from Rabbi Binyamin of Zalocze transforms a petition for God to answer our prayers into a powerful declaration of yearning:

> In the Seliḥot liturgy we recite, "present us with our request" [*himmaẓei lanu be-vaqashatenu*]. This is related to the verse "And from there you shall seek [the Eternal, your God], and you shall find Him" (Deut. 4:29).... What does "with our request" [*be-vaqashatenu*] mean? It could have said, "Present our request [*baqashatenu*] to us."
>
> The answer is as follows. We are asking that God be present with us in our quest, that our mouths [intoning the prayer] become a sanctum for the source of all Being. This is the meaning of "with our request"—within our request. We are not asking for our entreaty to be answered, but rather that God be made present within the quest....[45]

Rather than beseeching God for a specific result, we are called to pray in order to encounter the divine in the endless quest for meaning, to hear God's voice through the act of worship itself. Prayer is a path in which the goal is not—or not simply—a divine response, but a quest in which the search has become more important than the answer. The liturgical phrase "present us with our request," seemingly goal-oriented and focused upon a clear answer, is thus reinterpreted as a soulful entreaty that God be "present within our request"—we seek the divine, claims Rabbi Binyamin, to become revealed from within the yearnings of the journey itself.

---

45 Binyanim of Zalocze, *Torei Zahav* (Jerusalem, 1989), 250–251.

The second point I wish to draw out from early Hasidic sources is that the religious quest is non-linear in addition to being endless. This insight undergirds countless Hasidic formulations of the maxim that "constant pleasure is not really pleasure" (*ta'anug tamidi eino ta'anug*), reflecting a belief that religious consciousness goes through natural and necessary ebbs and flows.[46] Both heightened and diminished states are necessary, since moments of spiritual contraction along the journey provide stability and prevent the seeker from becoming overwhelmed with yearning. The Besht is remembered as having offered the image of ascending the spiral staircase (*shvindl trepf*) to illustrate this cyclical journey to God.[47] One who traverses its rungs cannot always see the destination, but, rather than signaling that growth has stalled, moments of occlusion—and divine hiddenness—prove that the worshipper is moving in the correct direction.

The swings of the mystical journey are described with great power by the Besht's great-grandson Rabbi Naḥman of Bratslav. His multitudinous teachings are so filled with evocative—and autobiographical—accounts of the perseverations of the quest that they are best left for a separate study.[48] But a similar, if notably less dramatic, portrait of the ascents and descents of spiritual journeying appears Rabbi Menaḥem Naḥum of Chernobyl. His *Me'or 'Einayim* includes a striking number of homilies that directly address the question of why one must descend from their spiritual level in order to move farther along the path:

> The truth is that a person cannot constantly stand on a single rung. "The life-force flows and ebbs" (Ezek.1:14); it comes and then vanishes. When you are attached to blessed Y-H-W-H you feel the pleasure of that surge of energy. Afterwards that disappears and you fall from your rung.
>
> There are secrets of Torah in the reason why you have to undergo such a fall. One is that you [fall] in order to rise up

---

46 See, inter alia, *Me'or 'Einayim*, vol. 1, *Ki Tissa; Qedushat Levi, Teẓave; Toledot Ya'aqov Yosef, Tazria'; Or Torah* on. Deut. 11:22.

47 *Ma'amarei Admor ha-Zaken* 5565 (Brooklyn: Kehot, 1981), vol. 1, 214–215; Elliot R. Wolfson, *Abraham Abulafia—Kabbalist and Prophet: Hermeneutics, Theosophy and Theurgy* (Los Angeles: Cherub Press, 2000), 135.

48 This ethos is found in his homilies as well as his fanciful stories, many of which involve a transformative quest or journey. See, inter alia, Arthur Green, *Tormented Master: A Life of Rabbi Nahman of Bratslav* (Woodstock, VT: Jewish Lights, 1992); Roee Horen, ed, *Ha-Ḥayyim ke-Ga'agu'a: Qeriyot Ḥadashot be-Sippurei Ma'asiyyot shel R. Naḥman mi-Bratslav* (Tel Aviv: Yediot Aḥronot, 2010); and Dov Elbaum, *Masa' ba-Ḥalal ha-Panui: Otobiyografyah Ruḥanit* (Tel Aviv: Am Oved, 2007).

> afterward to a yet higher level... . You must have faith that "The whole earth is filled with God's glory" (Isa. 6:3), and that "there is no place devoid of God."[49] God is present even at your present rung; there is no place from which God is absent. It is just that God is present in much contracted form.[50]

The initial "surge of energy" that accompanies spiritual elation, notes our author, is often followed by an abrupt period of distancing and diminishment. Rather than begetting spiritual fallowness, this is meant to renew one's desire for the quest. But there is more to the story, claims Rabbi Menaḥem Naḥum, because the journey into lower states of consciousness is undertaken to gather up new modes of understanding or experience. Divinity is present in all personal states of being, much as God's glory fills the entire cosmos, and therefore the seeker is tasked with discovering new ways to serve God in even these moments of diminishment. Descent requires care, of course, since going down into the realm of the "husks" (*qellipot*) presents the danger of becoming entrenched. The journey down must, therefore, must always be undertaken in order to rise up once more.[51]

Hasidic teachings on the religious quest often seek to map this metaphor onto the real-life journey or pilgrimage to the *ẓaddiq*,[52] a third dimension of our exploration of this theme.[53] This special turn, particularly characteristic of Hasidic sermons starting from the early and mid-nineteenth century, reflects a growing physical distance between spiritual masters and their disciples.[54] Hasidic

---

49 *Tiqqunei Zohar*, no. 57, 91b.

50 *Me'or 'Einayim*, vol. 1, *Yitro*, 172; based on Arthur Green, *The Light of the Eyes: Homilies on the Torah* (Stanford: Stanford University Press, forthcoming).

51 See his formulation in *Me'or 'Einayim*, vol. 1, *Lekh Lekha*, 40.

52 See David Biale, David Assaf, Benjamin Brown, Uriel Gellman, Samuel Heilman, Moshe Rosman, Gadi Sagiv, and Marcin Wodzinski, eds., *Hasidism: A New History*, afterword Arthur Green (Princeton and Oxford: Princeton University Press, 2018), 228–231; Tsippi Kauffman, "Doctrine of the Distant Tsaddik—Mysticism, Ethics, and Politics," *Shofar* (forthcoming); and Uriel Gellman, "Becoming a Movement: Early Nineteenth-Century Hasidism in the Eyes of R. Kalonymus Kalman Epstein of Kraków," *Modern Judaism-A Journal of Jewish Ideas and Experience* 38, no. 3 (2018): 307–327.

53 Elliot R. Wolfson, "Walking as a Sacred Duty: Theological Transformation of Social Reality in Early Hasidism," in *Hasidism Reappraised*, ed. Ada Rapoport-Albert (London: Vallentine Mitchell, 1996), 180–207.

54 To a certain degree the custom begins with the Maggid, who, unlike legendary image of the Besht, established a center in Mezritch that was visited by those seeking his teachings. This was, at least in part, a departure from the model exhibited by his own teacher. Many legends describe the Besht as a peripatetic spiritual master, though historical records reveal that the he was employed by the community in Miedzybozh. This hagiographical image of the Besht as a wanderer seems to be confirmed by the wide variety of disciples throughout Volhynia whose

texts refer to journeying to the *ẓaddiq* in order to hear teachings directly from his mouth,[55] but many sources highlight the spiritually transformative power of the journey itself. The homilies of Rabbi Kalonymos Kalmish, for example, underscore that neither intellectual revelations nor the *ẓaddiq*'s prayer and miracles should be seen as the aim of pilgrimage. "This is not the essential journey," he writes. Rather, "the purpose of this assembly must be for them to be as one. All must seek a single goal: to find the blessed One.... Every individual must listen to the others ... desiring to learn how to serve God—how to find God—from the others."[56]

Such teachings take the notion of *dibbuq ḥaverim* ("spiritual community"), a value and social practice with very deep roots in early Hasidism, on the road. One is called to visit the *ẓaddiq* primarily because of the opportunity to hear from his fellow-travelers and to learn from their individual modes of service. This may happen in the *rebbe*'s court, but the primary theatre of experience is the physical journey. The ethos of the fellowship along the path was immortalized in by the Yiddish song about traveling to the Kotsker Rebbe:

Keyn Kotsk fort men nisht	To Kotsk, one does not travel by vehicle
Keyn Kotsk geyt men	To Kotsk, one journeys by foot
Vayl Kotsk iz dokh be-moqem ha-miqdosh	Since Kotsk stands in place of the Temple
Keyn Kotsk darf men 'oyle-regl zayn	To Kotsk, one must make a pilgrimage
...	...
Regel, heys dokh a fis	Pilgrimage means going by feet
Keyn Kotsk, geyen khasidim tsu fis	To Kotsk, the *ḥasidim* go by foot
Zingendik, tantsendik,	Singing, dancing,
Veyl khasidim geyen keyn Kotsk, geyen zey mit a tants	For when *ḥasidim* go to Kotsk, they go with a dance

These verses liken the journey to the *ẓaddiq* to the historical pilgrimage to the Jerusalem Temple, noting that such travels much be undertaken by foot. The *ḥasidim*, joining together in song and dance, revel in the journey precisely

---

lives he touched. See Joseph G. Weiss, "The Beginnings of Hasidism" [Heb.], in *Studies in Hasidism*, ed. Avraham Rubinstein (Jerusalem: Zalman Shazar Center, 1977), 179–181; Moshe Rosman, *Founder of Hasidism: A Quest for the Historical Baal Shem Tov*, 2nd rev. ed. (Oxford: Littman Library, 2013), 117–119; Etkes, *The Besht*, 218–223.

55 Ariel Evan Mayse and Daniel Reiser, "Territories and Textures: The Hasidic Sermon as the Crossroads of Language and Culture," *Jewish Social Studies*, n.s. 24, no. 1 (2018): 127–160.

56 *Ma'or va-Shemesh* (Jerusalem, 1992), vol. 1, *Va-Yeḥi*, 139.

because it is long, arduous and filled with obstacles. In tackling such complexities and turning them into opportunities for spiritual growth, one needs friends and fellow-travelers to help one along the path.

Hasidic sources map the pilgrimage to the *rebbe* onto the biblical tales of Israel wandering in the desert and the Exodus, seeing these scriptural narratives as descriptions of the spiritual life as well. "I heard from my sainted grandfather and teacher [the Besht] that all the journeys [of Israel in the desert], which number forty-two, exist with each person from the day he is born until he returns to eternal world."[57] The Hasidic seeker, like the Israelites who went down into Egypt, is compelled to venture into places of darkness and constriction to discover those unexpected sparks of holiness. This process carries important spatial implications as well, since the *ẓaddiq* is drawn to new physical places in order to uplift the sparks. This is extended far beyond the religious elites, as Hasidic sources emphasize that *each person* must physically travel—often to unexpected locations—in order to raise up shards of divinity that are, in fact, parts of the seeker's own fragmented self:

> the sparks belonging to a particular person's soul-root can only be raised up by that person. They are really of that soul. That is why each of us has to journey to some particular place. Our Creator conducts the world based on the knowledge that fragments of sparks belonging to our soul are to be found in some object of business or in food or drink in a particular place. He brings it about that the person travel there, putting a desire into his heart to make it happen, to make that person feel like he needs to travel there. The real point is that he eat, drink, or engage in business there. In this way he will raise up those sparks... .[58]

One must set out along the path, engaging with the physical world and with other people in order to redeem these sacred sparks that have been scattered across the world. Rather than bemoaning such physical perambulations as taking time away from Torah study or other modes of worship, Hasidic sources hold them up as essential components of the religious journey: "Do not be distressed by this, for God needs to be served in all ways, sometimes one and

---

57 *Degel Maḥaneh Efrayim* (Jerusalem; 2013), *Massa'ei*, 200.
58 *Me'or 'Einayim*, 1, *Mattot*, translated in Green, *Light of the Eyes*.

sometimes another. That is why it came about that you needed to travel, in order to serve God in this way."[59]

Hasidic sources thus intertwine biblical narratives of exile and redemption, including the Israelite wanderings in the desert, with the journeys of present-day seekers. Such travels are united by a common set of interrelated goals: the redemption God's sparks through breaking open the *qelippot*, restoring fallen parts of the self.[60] The Hasid travels to the *ẓaddiq* and the court, as well as elsewhere, but the *ẓaddiq* also needs to value being on the road, where the sparks are waiting for him to find them. Both of these are aspects of the quest, and they underscore Hasidic notions that that *ẓaddiq*, too, must view himself as a seeker. Rather than a static being of inherent perfection, many early Hasidic sources describe the *ẓaddiq* as a dynamic individual who rises and falls in search of religious inspiration and in order to shepherd others along the path.[61]

One fifth, and final, point about Hasidic conceptions of the never-ending religious journey bears brief mention. Hasidic sources highlight the communal—and temporal—dimensions of the quest, but they also pay careful attention to the role of the individual spiritual adventure or journey. Though surely present in the earliest Hasidic sources, this impulse toward the personal nature of the religious quest is amplified and brought to the foreground in the well-known Polish Hasidic schools that stem from Pshiskhe and Kotsk. "Each Jew drawing near to God's service," taught Rabbi Simḥah Bunem of Pshiskhe, "must dig [his own] well to connect with the blessed Creator."[62] Inherited modes of worship swiftly lose their luster, no longer serving to open the heart and mind to the Divine.

Of equal importance, however, is the fact that one who accepts such modes of piety cannot actualize his own spiritual potential or accomplish the unique task—and journey—for which he was created. Hasidic sources in this school see the yearning to forge a new religious path as an issue of self-realization, a journey that is driven by love for God rather than self-aggrandizement or hubris. This burning desire leads one beyond religious forms bequeathed by earlier

---

59 *Or ha-Ganuz la-Ẓaddiqim, Massa'ei*, translated in Arthur Green, *Speaking Torah: Spiritual Teachings from around the Maggid's Table*, ed. Ebn Leader, Ariel Evan Mayse, and Or. N. Rose (Woodstock, VT: Jewish Lights, 2013), vol. 2, 75.

60 See *Qedushat Levi, Massa'ei*, translated in Green et al, *Speaking Torah*, vol. 2, 77–78.

61 For one striking formulation of this idea, see Ya'akov Barnai, *Hasidic Letters from Ereẓ Yisra'el* [Heb.] (Jerusalem: Yad Yizhak Ben-Zvi, 1980), no. 58, 222–224. See Nehemia Polen and David Maayan, "Theology, Succession, and Social Structure in the Dispute between Rabbi Abraham Kalisker and Rabbi Shneur Zalman," *Shofar* (forthcoming).

62 *Qol Simḥah* (Piotrkow, 1903), 10a, translated in Ariel Evan Mayse and Sam Berrin Shonkoff, *Hasidism: Writings on Devotion, Community, and Life on the Modern World* (Waltham, MA: Brandeis University Press, 2020), 143–144.

generations, but it also brings the seeker to push beyond the letter of the law.[63] This notion undergirds Rabbi Yehudah Aryeh Leib Alter of Ger's description of Abraham's journey to the land of Israel:

> Now surely [each] person was created for a particular purpose. There must be something that we are to set right. A person who achieves that is called righteous [*ẓaddiq*], walking a straight path of justice.
>
> But Abraham our Father is called a lover of God [*ḥasid*]; he went beyond the line demanded by the law. The one who serves God out of love can arouse a desire within God to let flow the source of his own soul in a way that cannot be comprehended by the human mind.[64]

Returning to the old pre-Hasidic paradigm, where *ḥasid* is on a higher rung than the *ẓaddiq*, Rabbi Alter argues that the seeker must strive to move beyond habituation and beyond even the confines of normative obligation. Such a person must bravely look toward a new spiritual landscape, seeking to unearth the essential task for which he has been sent into this world. Treading this new path requires constant vigilance and attentiveness to the spiritual call of the moment, seeing to it that one's every action is for God's sake alone.[65] This quest for authenticity and worship grounded in personal truth, claims Rabbi Alter, is itself a species of never-ending journey:

> "Righteousness, righteousness shall you pursue [*ẓedeq ẓedeq tirdof*]" (Deut. 16:20). The explanation: if one attains just a bit

---

63 See Haym Soloveitchik, "Three Themes in the *Sefer Hasidim*," *AJS Review* 1 (1976): 312–325; Elliot R. Wolfson, *Venturing Beyond-Law and Morality in Kabbalistic Mysticism* (Oxford University Press, 2006); idem, "Heeding the Law beyond the Law: Transgendering Alterity and the Hypernomian Perimeter of the Ethical," *European Journal of Jewish Studies* 14, no. 2 (2020): 1-49; Shaul Magid, *Hasidism on the Margin: Reconciliation, Antinomianism, and Messianism* (Madison, WI: University of Wisconsin Press, 2004); and Maoz Kahana and Ariel Evan Mayse, "Hasidic *Halakhah*: Reappraising the Interface of Spirit and Law," *AJS Review* 41, no. 2 (2017): 375–408.

64 *Sefat Emet* (Piotrkow, 1905), *Lekh Lekha* 5643 [1882], translated in Arthur Green, *The Language of Truth: The Torah Commentary of the Sefat Emet, Rabbi Yehudah Leib Alter of Ger* (Philadelphia: JPS, 1998), 19.

65 Yeraḥmi'el Yisra'el Yiẓḥaq Danziger, *Yismaḥ Yisra'el* (Jerusalem, 2002), *Va-Yiggash*, fol. 102a–b: "It is as if one is ascending a rope above a stormy sea. One must take care and focus all of his attention not to lean to one side or the other. If one inclines even a hairsbreadth, he will plunge into the sea."

> of truth, one must guard himself against ceasing to pursue the truth. For if, God forbid, one then descends into lies, it is better [to have done so] before attaining the truth.
>
> Therefore, the righteousness that we seek after finding the first righteousness is the search for true righteousness. This formulation appears in the Torah in many places: "If you listen to my voice [*shamo'a tishme'u*]" (Ex. 19:5; Deut. 11:12); "surely keep [*shamor tishmeru*]" (Deut. 6:17, 11:22) ... the repetition (*kefel*) is the essential point.[66]

Constant repetition and commitment, when approached with a sense of mindfulness and purpose, will eventually lead one to new levels of enlightenment. The legendary strength of a samurai sword, for example, is the result of the smith beating out the hot metal and folding it back countless times. This intensive, repetitious forging process removes impurities and grants the blade its resilience and power. So too, in the quest of religious life, revisiting texts or ideas and shedding ulterior motivations and prior assumptions, the seeker's eyes are opened to new modes of ever-deeper illumination.

The search for such radical integrity is extremely difficult and is not without its hazards. Rabbi Menaḥem Mendel of Kotsk's sudden move to twenty years of self-isolation, perhaps following a mental break, has been much noted.[67] Many of the sermons of Rabbi Mordecai Yosef Leiner, an erstwhile disciple who left Kotsk in 1838, may be read as a moderating response to the Kotsker's furious enthusiasm, restraining the latter's paralyzing quest for purity and integrity without compromising the emphasis on the individual's unique spiritual path.[68] Indeed, in one homily Rabbi Leiner notes that an extreme or unfettered quest for truth can be a force of death rather than animating energy.[69] But Rabbi Leiner, too, acknowledges that the individual's road is filled with dead-ends and missteps. In commenting on the verse, "It is eleven days journey from Horev" (Deut. 1:2), He asks why the Israelites were forced to wander in the desert for forty years if the road from revelation was so short. "The words of Torah have

---

66 *Sefat Emet, Shoftim* 5635 [1875]. See also ibid., 5631 [1871]: "one must also delve deeper and deeper, finding the truth of truths."

67 Morris M. Faierstein, "The Friday Night Incident in Kotsk: History of a Legend," *Journal of Jewish Studies* 34, no. 2 (1983): 137–156.

68 See, for example; *Mei ha-Shiloaḥ* (Brooklyn, 1973), vol. 1, *Shemot*, 20a–b.

69 *Mei ha-Shiloaḥ*, vol. 1, *Shemot*, 19a; ibid, *Va-Yeshev*, 15b–16a. My thanks to David Maayan for helping me see the significance of these sources.

not been established in your hearts until [you have lived through] forty years of stumblings and tests," writes Rabbi Leiner. "Your hearts were purified through this, since 'one cannot truly understand words of Torah until he stumbles in them.'"[70] Taking the shortcut, or even walking along direct route, curtails spiritual growth. True religious attainments, claims Rabbi Leiner, become etched in the self only through struggle—and failure—along the path.

Concluding Remarks

A parable is often told in the name of the late Rabbi Shlomo Twerski of Denver. Between every person and God, said Rabbi Twerski, there is a baffling maze. Our job in this world is to strive forward with bravery and, over the course of our lifetime, make progress along this path to the best of our ability. The spiritual teacher, he notes, has an additional responsibility. The *tzaddiq* must be a seeker, but a teacher must also tell others about the dead ends found along her or his own path. Rather than serving as superheroes or perfect conduits for divine instruction, our leaders are also walking along the never-ending path together with us. They are the ones, however, who have mustered the courage to share their journey with others.[71]

The quest to discover ever-deeper dimensions of Torah, to draw near to God, to gather up and uncover parts of the self is difficult indeed. It does not, and cannot come easily, and it includes educative experiences of failure and stumbling together with moments of uplift. The texts above offer a vocabulary for committing to this process despite—or because of—the challenges it affords. These Hasidic sources portray religious life as an intense and endless journey rather than a goal-oriented or linear process, weaving together complementary impulses of communal vision, individual inspiration and devotional yearning into a powerful vision of what it can mean to seek and stand in relationship with God.

---

70 *Mei ha-Shiloaḥ*, vol. 1, *Devarim*, 56a–b, quoting B. Gittin 43a.

71 See also S. Y. Agnon, ed., *Days of Awe: A Treasury of Jewish Wisdom for Reflection, Repentance, and Renewal on the High Holy Days* (New York: Schocken, 1995), 22–24; and Ariel Evan Mayse, "Neo-Hasidism and *Halakhah*: The Duties of Intimacy and the Law of the Heart," in *A New Hasidism: Branches*, ed. Arthur Green and Ariel Evan Mayse (Philadelphia: JPS and University of Nebraska Press, 2019), 155–222.

CHAPTER 18

Rabbi Elimelekh Shapiro of Grodzisk: Sketching a Nineteenth-Century Hasidic Leader

Nehemia Polen

Not long ago, the conventional wisdom among scholars of Hasidism was that by 1815, the Hasidic movement had reached maturity and that the spiritual boldness, religious vitality, and innovative thinking that characterized the early years, the time of the Ba'al Shem Tov (d. 1760), and the Great Maggid of Mezritch (d. 1772) and his disciples, had largely abated.[1] In recent decades there has been a correction to this earlier approach, with a wave of studies on creative developments in the nineteenth century, focusing largely on Hasidism in Poland. Here, too, another categorization arose that distinguished two trends in Polish

1 Simon Dubnov points to 1815 as a watershed, in part due to a striking pattern, the deaths of a large number of prominent early leaders, most of them disciples of the Great Maggid of Mezritch, during or shortly before this year. Rabbi Ya'akov Yiẓḥaq Rabinowitz (the "Holy Jew" of Pshiskhe) died in 1814; Rabbi Menaḥem Mendel of Rimanov, 1815; Rabbi Ya'akov Yitzhaq Horowitz (the "Seer" of Lublin), 1815; Rabbi Yisra'el the Maggid of Kozienice, 1815. We might add that Rabbi Levi Yiẓḥaq of Berditchev died in 1809; Rabbi Naḥman of Bratslav, in 1810; Rabbi Shne'ur Zalman of Liadi, 1812. There appeared to be a generational transition, a handover from the incandescent spirits who knew the founders directly, to successors who might be perceived as latecomers, epigoni who, some thought, could preserve and transmit but not create. See Simon Dubnov, *History of Hasidism* [Heb.] (Tel Aviv: Dvir, 1960), 332. See also Benjamin Brown, "Substitutes for Mysticism: A General Model for the Theological Development of Hasidism in the Nineteenth Century," *History of Religions* (2017): 248, n. 4. In addition to the remarkable cluster of deaths around 1815, Brown points to the Congress of Vienna in 1815, which established a semi-autonomous Polish state ("Congress Poland") under the control of Russia, impacting the further development of Hasidism in that region.

Hasidism. The first, so the narrative goes, was a popular school, derived from the *Ḥozeh* ("seer," "clairvoyant") of Lublin, that believed in the paranormal powers of the *ẓaddiq* ("saint," "righteous one") and that appealed to the masses on the basis of miracle-working and required little more of followers than devoted attachment to the *ẓaddiq* and his court. The second trend began with Rabbi Ya'aqov Yiẓḥaq of Pshiskhe, known as the Yehudi, the *Yid ha-Qadosh* ("the holy Jew"), characterized by intellectual acuity, excellence in talmudic studies, and responsibility for one's own spiritual growth rather than relying on attachment to the *ẓaddiq*. In this school the yearning for miracles was contemptuously rejected as a weakness of spirit and a religious embarrassment. When the Holy Jew passed away in 1814, many prominent devotees chose as his successor not his son Rabbi Yeraḥmiel, but one of the disciples, Rabbi Simḥah Bunem, a master of talmudic literature who was also knowledgeable in secular sciences and a licensed pharmacist. When Rabbi Simḥah Bunem passed away in 1827, some *ḥasidim* looked to his son as successor, but the most outstanding *ḥasidim* gravitated to the brilliant and penetrating personality of Rabbi Menaḥem Mendel Morgenstern of Tomashov, later of Kotsk.

Studies of Polish Hasidism have tended to focus on the Pshiskhe-Kotsk school, to the relative neglect of other lineages. This preference is evident in recent surveys of Hasidism. For example, the section under "Congress [central] Poland" in the article on Hasidism in the *YIVO Encyclopedia of Jews in Eastern Europe* (2008) begins with the statement that "After 1815 the dynamic center of Polish Hasidism shifted from Lublin to Pshiskhe and its environs." The entry covers Rabbi Simḥah Bunem, the Kotsker, and subsequent Hasidic trends that were influenced by or formed in reaction to these luminaries. Toward the end of this sizeable section, mention is made of another school that, it is claimed, "placed emphasis on material well-being as a basis for religious life." In this school, it is asserted, the *ẓaddiq* was a major channel of reception of divine abundance, and miracles are foregrounded. One sentence is devoted to the descendants of Rabbi Yisra'el the Maggid of Kozienice, including the leaders of the courts of Mogielnica and Grodzisk, who, we are told, "rejected the doctrines of Pshiskhe." This treatment appears to cast all non-Pshiskhe trends in Polish Hasidism as recalcitrant loyalists, holdovers from an outdated past.

That is not whole story, however. Another landmark reference work, *Hasidism: A New History* (2018) notes that the various branches of the Kozienice lineage stemming from Rabbi Yisrael the Maggid of Kozienice (d. 1814) left voluminous works that have been almost totally neglected by scholars, and that Rabbi Elimelekh of Grodzisk, great-grandson of the Kozienicer Maggid, was "one of the most famous nineteenth-century tsaddikim,"[2] thus suggesting that a study of the Kozienice lineage is a scholarly desideratum.

Rabbi Yisra'el ben Sabbatai Hapstein (c. 1737–1814), known as the Maggid (preacher) of Kozienice, a founder of Polish Hasidism, was an erudite talmudic scholar and halakhist, prolific author, and publisher of rare kabbalistic manuscripts. Famed for ecstatic prayer, reputed paranormal powers, efficacious blessings, and mentoring of disciples, he also was esteemed in Polish aristocratic circles. His descendants established marital alliances and close affiliations with many of the major families of the Hasidic world, including lineages from Lublin, Krakow, Chernobyl (Ukraine), Karlin-Stolin (Belarus), and Ruzhin-Sadigura (Austria). This essay focuses on one scion of this family, Rabbi Elimelekh Shapiro of Grodzisk.

Rabbi Elimelekh of Grodzisk (we will call him "the Grodzisker") was a great-grandson of both the Kozienicer Maggid and Rabbi Elimelekh of Lizhensk (d. 1786), after whom he was named. While we know that he died in 1892, the year of his birth is given variously, ranging from 1816 to 1824.[3] The early date would have made him seventy-six at the time of his death. Towards the final decade of the nineteenth century he was revered as a surviving elder among Hasidic masters of his day, a remnant of the last echoes of Hasidism's early period. His life was a bridge arching over Hasidism's stage of expansion and consolidation, and he could legitimately lay claim to traditions stemming from famed disciples of the Great Maggid of Mezritch such as the aforementioned Rabbi Elimelekh of Lizhensk and Rabbi Yisra'el the Maggid of Kozienice. His ancestry also included the *Ḥozeh* ("seer") of Lublin (d. 1815), famed for clairvoyance and powers of blessing, and Rabbi Kalonymos Kalmish Epstein of Krakow (d. 1823), author of the classic Hasidic work *Ma'or va-Shemesh*. In addition to this deep embedding in the family trees of early Polish Hasidic luminaries, the Grodzisker considered himself a *ḥasid* of Rabbi Yisra'el of Ruzhin (1796–1850), great-grandson of the Maggid of Mezritch, and he frequently transmitted teachings and stories from this celebrated master, about whom we will say more shortly. These threads of association place the Grodzisker at the heart of Hasidism's spiritual aristocracy, though not of the Pshiskhe-Kotsk school.

---

2 David Biale, David Assaf, Benjamin Brown, Uriel Gellman, Samuel Heilman, Moshe Rosman, Gadi Sagiv, and Marcin Wodzinski, eds., *Hasidism: A New History*, afterword Arthur Green (Princeton and Oxford: Princeton University Press, 2018), 334.

3 Ya'aqov Yisra'eli (Kula), *Bet Karlin-Stolin* (Tel Aviv: Keren Ya'aqov ve-Raḥel, 1981), 251, states that Rabbi Elimelekh was born in 1816; Yitzhak Alfasi, *Encyclopedia of Hasidism* (Jerusalem: Mossad ha-Rav Kook, 1986), vol. 1, 243 gives 1824 as the year of his birth.

Rabbi Elimelekh's first marriage was to a daughter of Rabbi Yeraḥmiel, son of the "Holy Jew" of Pshiskhe.[4] The Grodzisker's son from this first marriage, Rabbi Ḥayyim Me'ir Yeḥi'el, had passed away in his lifetime[5] and when his wife died, Rabbi Elimelekh decided to marry again.

An interesting document provides further information on the circumstances surrounding his second marriage late in life. This is a responsum of Rabbi Ḥayyim Ele'azar Wachs (1822–1889), Rabbi of Piotrkow, dated 5 Tammuz 5648 (1888) and addressed to Rabbi Elimelekh of Grodzisk.[6] Rabbi Wachs, a noted halakhic authority whose responsa are collected in *Shem u-She'erit le-Nefesh Ḥayyah,* addresses R. Elimelekh of Grodzisk with effusive honorifics including "Light of the World, the glory of Israel, master like an angel of the Godly host." Even allowing for the extravagant encomia customary in rabbinic epistolary etiquette, this is high praise and indicative of the esteem in which he was held and his stature in the constellation of Hasidic masters of the day.

While Rabbi Elimelekh's letter has not been preserved, the nature of his query is clear from Rabbi Wachs's response. The question concerned a holy man whose wife had recently died and who wanted to marry again in order to be able to pray for all Israel in the upcoming High Holidays. Like the high priest on Yom Kippur, a prayer leader of this stature must have a wife in order not to be "half a body."[7] Mention is made of the questioner's tragic loss of male progeny and his desire to have sons in his old age. Rabbi Wachs rules that the requisite period of waiting after the death of a spouse can be waived so that on the Days of Awe the saintly man could "atone for his household and for all Israel" (see Lev. 16:11, 17).[8] While the responsum does not make this fully explicit, there is no doubt

---

4 This does not locate him in the Psyshkhe-Kotsk school, since, as noted above, the elite members of the circle of the "Holy Jew" gravitated to the latter's formidable disciple Rabbi Simḥah Bunem of Pshiskhe, rather than his son Rabbi Yeraḥmiel. The charismatic Rabbi Simḥah Bunem, with his penetrating intellect, scintillating wit, and gift for wisdom parables, was widely considered to be the spiritual successor of the "Holy Jew." See Michael Rosen, *The Quest for Authenticity: The Thought of Reb Simhah Bunim* (Jerusalem and New York: Urim, 2008).

5 The Grodzisker mentions him in his first published work, *Imrei Elimelekh* (Warsaw: Hayyim Kelter, 1876), 66 [33d in the Hebrew pagination, *parashat Va-Yeshev*]. After mentioning his son's name, the Grodzisker appends "his memory be a blessing." Since *Imrei Elimelekh* was published in 1876, his son passed away before that time. But the name "Ḥayyim Me'ir Yeḥi'el" is that of the Grodzisker's father, who died in 1849. Since Ashkenazim do not name after living relatives, this means that the son was born 1849 or later, and he would have been in his mid-twenties or younger when he died.

6 Ḥayyim Ele'azar Wachs, *Shem u-She'erit le-Nefesh Ḥayyah; Kolel She'elot u-Teshuvot Ḥiddushei Torah u-Derashot* (Jerusalem: Horeb, 1961), 28.

7 See *Zohar* 3:296a.

8 See B. Mo'ed Qatan 23a: "A man who lost his wife must wait for three pilgrimage festivals to pass before marrying again. Rabbi Yehuda says: Until the first and second Festivals have

that the question related to Rabbi Elimelekh of Grodzisk himself; the *ẓaddiq* was asking to remarry in time for upcoming High Holidays in fall 1888, which he indeed proceeded to do. It was evidently Rabbi Elimelekh's practice to serve as prayer leader for the most sacred segments of the services, such as the closing *ne'ilah* service on Yom Kippur. His second wife, whose name was Ḥannah Berakhah, bore Rabbi Elimelekh two sons—Kalonymos Kalmish (1889–1943),[9] and Yeshayah (1891–1945).[10] Shortly after the birth of his younger son, Rabbi Elimelekh of Grodzisk died, in 1892.

Another important document that sheds light on the character of Rabbi Elimelekh is a letter, written in 1869, from Rabbi Elimelekh of Grodzisk to Rabbi Ḥayyim Halberstam of Sandz, relating to Rabbi Yisra'el of Ruzhin (1796–1850; "the Ruzhiner"), a great-grandson of the Maggid of Mezritch. The Ruzhiner was revered as a true *ẓaddiq*, an angel of God on earth and noble inheritor of the saintly traditions of his illustrious ancestors. At the same time, he was a

---

passed, he is prohibited from marrying; before the third Festival, however, he is permitted to do so." For discussion and halakhic codification, see *Bet Yosef* on *Tur Yoreh De'ah* 392 and *Shulḥan Arukh* ibid.

9 Rabbi Kalonymos Kalmish Shapiro (1889–1943), known as the Piaseczner Rebbe, was a twentieth-century Hasidic leader who lived and taught in Warsaw and the nearby town of Piaseczna. He preached and wrote profound theological reflections in the Warsaw Ghetto during the Holocaust, and was prominent before the war as a Hasidic educational theorist and head of a major yeshiva. His prescient pedagogical methodology, his deep awareness of contemporary sensibilities, his psychological astuteness, personal warmth and caring heart, as well as his spiritual heroism and astounding theological writings from the Holocaust period, have combined to make him a figure of great scholarly interest and an inspiring personal model. See Nehemia Polen, *Holy Fire* (Lanham, MD: Jason Aronson, 1999); Daniel Reiser, *Rabbi Kalonymus Kalman Shapira: Sermons from the Years of Rage*, 2 vols. (Jerusalem: Herzog Academic College Research Authority, World Union of Jewish Studies, and Yad Vashem, 2017).

10 As a youth, Yeshayah Shapiro expressed a passionate yearning for the agrarian life and settlement in the Holy Land, sentiments that were considered quite unusual at the time for the scion of a noted Hasidic master. He indeed left his home for *Ereẓ Yisra'el* in 1914, eventually becoming a leader in the Religious Zionist movement. *Encyclopaedia Hebraica* (Jerusalem: Pelli, 1988), vol. 32, col. 298 states that during a temporary return to Poland he "persuaded two young rebbes, one from the Yablona lineage and one from Kozienice, to emigrate to the Holy Land with their *ḥasidim*," leading to the founding of Kfar Ḥasidim. S. Don-Yahiya, *Admor Ḥaluẓ* (Tel Aviv: Moreshet, 1961), 10–17 provides a vivid description of young Shapiro's determination to make *'aliyah* despite fierce opposition from within his family. According to Don-Yahiya, Yeshayah sold silver cups and other wedding gifts in order to fund his journey, and on the eve of his departure from Poland for the Holy Land he did not say goodbye to his mother or grandfather for fear that they would make a final effort to dissuade him. A memoir of his son Shmuel confirms these details; see Yitzhak Recanati, *And the Work Is Ours to Complete: Teachings and Stories of R. Yeshaya Shapiro ... with Biographical Vignettes* (Bet-El: Sifriyat Bet-El, 1992), 16. This work, published to commemorate the centenary of Yeshayah's birth, describes him as having "absconded" when he first left home for *Ereẓ* Yisra'el in 1914. See also Pini Donner, "The Amazing Return of the Yabloner Rebbe," *Tablet*, September 17, 2018.

controversial figure sharply criticized for his opulence that in some eyes mirrored the lifestyle of a decadent aristocracy. Rabbi Ḥayyim Halberstam of Sandz (Galicia; 1793–1876), a leading halakhic authority and Hasidic master noted for piety and charitable works, bitterly opposed the ways of the Ruzhiner. It is significant that Rabbi Elimelekh of Grodzisk had the boldness to intervene in a protracted and rancorous clash between two differing approaches to Hasidic leadership and life. The Grodzisker's letter is a full-throated and vigorous defense of the Ruzhiner and his family against the critiques leveled at them by their detractors.[11] In this letter, the Grodzisker transmits statements by earlier *ẓaddiqim* that exalt the Ruzhiner. In particular, he cites Rabbi Avraham Yehoshu'a Heschel of Apta (whom he refers to as "the holy *ga'on* of Miedzybozh"; d. 1825) that the Ruzhiner does not need to learn Torah because the angel of forgetting "did not dare to slap such a holy mouth" at the moment of his birth, so he never forgot what he learned in his mother's womb. The letter relates that once, when the Apter Rav and other *ẓaddiqim* including Rabbi Naftali of Ropshitz visited the Ruzhiner, they rose in his presence and remained standing until he instructed them to sit, even though Rabbi Yisra'el was still a youngster and the Apter was an old man. The Grodzisker concludes this vignette by saying, "From this you may guess the magnitude of his holiness."

The Ruzhiner's son Dov Ber of Leova, who was reported to have abandoned religious observance,[12] is alluded to cautiously and with circumspection, but the other sons of the Ruzhiner are said to be manifestly of great holiness: "The fear of the Lord shines distinctly on their faces.... Their bodies are on this physical earth, but their spirits and thoughts are with holy angelic beings. They do not partake of worldly pleasures, their hearts are broken in utter humility. I saw all this with my own eyes when I visited their residence. I may not be a great person, but I do have the capacity of discernment, thank God."[13]

In addition to traditions from the Apter, Rabbi Elimelekh in this letter quotes his own father, Rabbi Ḥayyim Me'ir Yeḥiel of Mogielnica (d. 1849), grandson of the Kozienicer Maggid, that the Ruzhiner was "as great as the *rishonim* [early medieval Rabbinic authorities of undisputed eminence]." Rabbi Elimelekh indicates that his father bestowed even more fulsome praises on the Ruzhiner

---

11 The letter was published by Meir Wunder in *Sinai* 81 (1977) and cited by David Assaf in his authoritative biography of the Ruzhiner. *Derekh ha-Malkhut: R. Yisra'el me-Ruzhin u-Meqomo be-Toledot ha-Ḥasidut* (Jerusalem: Zalman Shazar Center, 1997). English translation: David Assaf, *The Regal Way: The Life and Times of R. Israel of Ruzhin*, transl. David Louvish (Stanford: Stanford University Press, 2002).

12 See Assaf, *Regal Way*, 13 and throughout.

13 That is, "I know a real saint when I see one!"

but Rabbi Elimelekh hesitated to convey them because he was "afraid to say more."

In this letter, Rabbi Elimelekh emerges as a person of extreme piety and guileless faith in *ẓaddiqim* in general and the Ruzhiner in particular. He affirmed the Ruzhiner's exalted status without a trace of distance, hesitation, or critical skepticism. Indeed, there is a sense of artless innocence in these statements from the Grodzisker. Having grown up in the household of a *ẓaddiq* with direct knowledge of how such households functioned—economically as well as spiritually—one cannot accuse the Grodzisker of blind naïve acceptance of the mythos surrounding the Ruzhiner and his children. An insider himself, he would certainly have been able to detect dissimulation and pretense, and his utter faith in and subordination to the Ruzhiner—whom he related to as devoted disciple to saintly master—say much about both personalities.

After his death, an obituary of Rabbi Elimelekh of Grodzisk appeared in *He-'Asif*,[14] a Hebrew-language journal edited by Naḥum Sokolow. I present it here in translation:

> One of the most eminent *ẓaddiqim* of this generation. A descendant of the *ẓaddiq* R. Yisra'el the Maggid of Kozienice. Passed away Tuesday evening *Rosh Ḥodesh Nisan* 5652 (1892).
>
> Revered and acclaimed as a holy man amongst his many *ḥasidim*, he was also greatly respected in the eyes of the *maskilim* ["enlightened" Western-oriented Jews], and *mitnaggedim* [opponents of Hasidism] for he was a true *ẓaddiq*, completely immersed in Torah at all times, as well as a master of the world of Kabbalah.
>
> All the monies, which his *ḥasidim* gave to him, he gave to the poor, so he left no material wealth behind.
>
> Rabbi Elimelekh was sixty-eight when he died. He was Rabbi of Grodzisk for forty-three years. His many discourses are printed in his two books, which he published during his lifetime. They are *Imrei Elimelekh* published fifteen years ago, and *Divrei Elimelekh* published in 5651 [1890/1891].

This glowing posthumous tribute by Naḥum Sokolow, himself a *maskil* Hebraist, multilingual journalist, leading activist for the Zionist cause, and author of a biography of Benedict Spinoza among other works, is indeed

14 *He-'Asif* 6 (1893): 150.

testament to Rabbi Elimelekh of Grodzisk's reputation for virtue and selfless piety beyond insular Hasidic circles.

There is another kind of evidence that sheds light on Rabbi Elimelekh of Grodzisk and his family, namely portraits from a wedding that took place in 1883. Shortly before the High Holidays that year, Rabbi Elimelekh's grandson Yisra'el married Berakhah Sheindel, the granddaughter of Rabbi Yoḥanan Twersky (1816–1895; Chernobyl lineage), in Rachmastrivka (Rotmistrivka, Ukraine). The tightly woven fabric of Hasidic endogamy brought together notables from Belarus, Ukraine, and Poland, representing the Chernobyl, Karlin-Stolin, and Kozienice dynasties. The grand occasion was commemorated in two paintings, depicting two stages of the wedding celebration. The first is a portrait of the groom's evening, a tradition going back to the founders of the Twersky/Chernobyl lineage. The evening before the wedding, the bride's and groom's families gather for a festive celebration, whose highpoint is the dance of the bride and groom, accompanied by music and joyous applause. (The custom was controversial and was opposed in some Hasidic circles as being "against *halakhah*" but was vigorously upheld in Chernobyl as having been instituted by the revered founders of the dynasty.) Judging by the level of detail and sophistication of the portrait, it is evidently the work of a professional artist, expressly commissioned to capture the occasion. The most prominent figure on the canvas is the bride Berakhah Sheindel, radiant in a soft pink floor-length gown with matching bonnet, her face unveiled. Her mother stands at her side and her grandmother is seated nearby. Behind her is a group of young women, identified as sisters of the groom. To the bride's left is a klezmer band, including two fiddlers, a cymbalist, and a double bass.

About eight feet away we see the groom Yisra'el wearing a Hasidic youngster's cap (similar to the kind later to be memorialized in the photographs of Roman Vishniac). He is very young, the only male in the portrait without a beard. (Born in 1868, he would have been fifteen at the time of his wedding.)[15] Standing at his side is his mother, Sarah Devorah Shapiro-Perlow (1844–1921), resplendent in a green gown with chiffon overlay and gold trim. With her right hand she firmly grasps her son's right hand (not, as might seem more natural, his left hand; this requires her to reach over his chest), and gestures with her left hand toward the bride, who looks expectantly in his direction, leaning toward the open space on

---

15 For more on Rabbi Yisra'el Perlow of Stolin, known as the *Yenuqa* ("child prodigy"), see Nehemia Polen, "Rebbetzins, Wonder-Children and the Emergence of the Dynastic Principle in Hasidism," in *Shtetl: New Evaluations*, ed. Steven T. Katz (New York and London: New York University Press, 2006), 53–84.

the parquet floor. The bride lifts the taffeta outer layer of her gown demurely off the floor with both hands. Her face reflecting self-possession and maturity, she is obviously beckoning her groom to dance with her. But he does not respond to his bride's gesture, nor to his mother's efforts to move him toward his bride. Young Yisra'el's eyes are trained forward, avoiding the gaze of his betrothed. The artist has captured the poignancy of this moment, when a young Hasidic lad, raised in strict piety and without contact with young women other than siblings, is now expected to pivot completely, preparing to relate in loving intimacy with his life partner.

The second painting depicts the following day, the day of the wedding. The scene is the *ḥosens tish,* the groom's table just before the actual ceremony. The young groom is no longer wearing a cap but a *shtreimel,* signaling his new status as an ostensibly mature, about-to-be married man. At his left sits his grandfather, Rabbi Elimelekh of Grodzisk, in the very center of the portrait, his face illumined by an oil lamp hanging above him, two tall candlesticks at his right. His beard is very full, very long, grey with reddish streaks. Although there is a bit of food on the table, no more than some sliced bread or cake, no one is eating. There is a wine or liquor decanter and glasses, but they appear empty and unused. Rabbi Elimelekh is the only person facing directly forward. His eyes do not seem focused on any nearby object; they gaze far away, perhaps beyond this world. His hands and forearms are not visible, positioned straight down and hidden under the table and tablecloth. He is deep in contemplation. He is not smiling. The groom sits to his right, his eyes nearly closed, directed downward toward the table. He seems overwhelmed and filled with trepidation. Fiddlers are playing and some *ḥasidim* in the background are dancing spiritedly in a circle, but everyone seated at the table has a plaintive look, overtaken by holy solemnity. Our attention is drawn to Rabbi Elimelekh and his face, bespeaking neither joy nor sadness, neither confidence nor fear, fixed in an otherworldly reverie of mystical abduction.

This portrait of Rabbi Elimelekh has previously appeared in print, in low quality black-and-white reproductions. Grainy and cropped, it revealed very little about his personality. But Avraham Avish Shor, librarian and archivist of the Karlin-Stolin lineage, has recently collected the fruits of his decades-long researches into the history of his group and of early Hasidism in general.[16] In

16 Academy-based scholars have greatly benefitted from Avraham Avish Shor's enthusiastic participation in conferences; he has appeared on panels of the World Congress of Jewish Studies in Jerusalem and the Association of Jewish Studies. I thank him for his gracious sharing of insider's knowledge and rare documents.

a volume called *Ketavim: Pirkei Toladah ve-'Iyyun be-Mishnat Karlin-Stolin* (Writings: On the History and Teachings of Karlin-Stolin Hasidism), Shor has made available high-quality full-color reproductions of the painting (Fig. 2 below), together with notes, commentary and documents relating the wedding and its background.[17] Furthermore, Shor has reproduced the companion portrait of the groom's evening, capturing the evocative scene of the poised and confident bride, the shy reluctant groom, and his mother's firm gesture pulling him in the direction of his betrothed (Fig. 1 below). The two paintings on facing pages together reveal complementary aspects of the culture of these Hasidic families. In the contemporary Hasidic world, separation between the sexes at weddings often approaches a peak of rigid compartmentalization, and authorized photographs may crop out women altogether, sometimes even the bride. By contrast, the 1883 painting depicts a very different culture. There are about as many women in the scene as men, there is no physical separation between them (the women are clustered in the center of the room, surrounded by men on either side of them), and a matriarch of the family—the groom's mother, Sarah Devorah Shapiro-Perlow, who is Rabbi Elimelekh Shapiro's daughter—is in control, directing her son. In the companion painting of the groom's table or *ḥosens tish*, the anchor is Sarah Devorah's father Rabbi Elimelekh, and the dominant mood is not a celebration of romantic bonding and familial domesticity but sublime otherworldly reverence. The two portraits capture two stages of the wedding and complement each other. The paintings were no doubt commissioned expressly for the occasion, by someone who possessed a clear sense of the aristocratic lineage of the families and the couple's nobility, and who wished to commemorate the scope and significance of the events that surrounded their wedding. I suspect it was Sarah Devorah, daughter of Rabbi Elimelekh and mother of the groom. Like all portraits of aristocracy, these paintings navigate between the realistic and the idealized. Intended to accurately capture a historical moment, they also reveal how the families saw themselves and how they wanted to be represented. Precisely for this reason, they give a rare and precious glimpse into the familial and religious ideals of the families of these *ẓaddiqim*, in particular Rabbi Elimelekh of Grodzisk, who is at the center of one painting, and whose daughter and grandson have pivotal roles in the companion

---

17 Avraham Avish Shor, *Ketavim: Pirkei Toladah ve-'Iyyun be-Mishnat Karlin-Stolin* (Modi'in Ilit: Makhon Bet Aharon ve-Yisra'el and 'Ad Ḥenah, 2018). This work anthologizes Rabbi Shor's essays that appeared over decades in the journal *Qoveẓ Bet Aharon ve-Yisra'el* published by the Karlin-Stolin *ḥasidim*. The paintings appear on unnumbered glossy pages at the back of the book. The wedding and related documents are discussed ibid., 1041–1044.

painting. Taken together, they reveal a navigation between the aesthetic and the ascetic, between sophisticated elegance, familial warmth and romantic affections on the one hand, and ethereal detachment from worldly entanglements on the other. My contention is that this congenial cooperative arrangement between religiosity and modish refinement, between mystic reverie and familial intimacy, represents the spirit of Polish Hasidic culture very differently than the convention-flouting, at times deliberately anti-social tendencies of the Pshiskhe-Kotsk school. In the school of Pshiskhe-Kotsk, the cultivation of elite young scholars and the quest for personal integrity, nonconformity and independence of spirit led at times to an eagerness to break with conventional ideas of propriety to the point of provocative actions that upset traditional ideas of order.

By contrast, the family traditions of Rabbi Elimelekh of Grodzisk deliberately held the religious and cultural center, a place of balance and grace. This was surely due in large measure to personal disposition and the example of saintly ancestors such as the Maggid of Kozienice, but the ideals and aspirational vision of women in the family, in particular the Grodisker's daughter Sarah Devorah, were very influential.

As depicted in a memoir by her granddaughter Malkah Shapiro, Sarah Devorah Shapiro-Perlow (1844–1921) was a strong and assertive woman, confident in her elegance and cultural refinement.[18] Speaking Polish, Russian, and German along with her native Yiddish, she maintained excellent relationships with local families of the landed aristocracy, who respected her wisdom, family heritage, and sophistication. Devoutly pious, her blessings were sought by non-Jews as well as by *ḥasidim*. She managed the *ẓaddiq*'s material affairs and made all major decisions, overseeing a large household comprising immediate and extended family, resident *ḥasidim*, kitchen staff, children's nannies and tutors, artisans and craftspeople, and the Rebbe's personal and administrative helpers. She also supervised hospitality for a constant stream of visitors and directed assistance to orphans, widows and others in need.

Sarah Devorah assumed responsibility for the continuity of her lineage and its dynastic vision. As a child she had apparently enjoyed unfettered access to her

---

18 Malkah Shapiro's memoir, written in Hebrew, is called *Mi-Din le-Raḥamim* (Jerusalem: Mossad ha-Rav Kook, 1969). For an English translation with introduction and annotations, see Nehemia Polen, *The Rebbe's Daughter* (Philadelphia: JPS, 2002). Sarah Devorah Shapiro plays a central role in the memoir. See also Nehemia Polen, "Coming of Age in Kozienice: Malkah Shapiro's Memoir of Youth in the Sacred Space of a Hasidic Zaddik," in *Celebrating Elie Wiesel: Stories, Essays, Reflections*, ed. Alan Rosen (Notre Dame: University of Notre Dame Press, 1998), 123–140. See also Benjamin Brown, *"Like a Ship on a Stormy Sea": The Story of Karlin Hasidism* (Jerusalem: Zalman Shazar Center, 2018), 81–84.

father Rabbi Elimelekh's inner office. Her presence in private meetings between her father and *ḥasidim* could be nearly invisible. Dismissed as an adorable youngster at play, she actually gained familiarity with what a *ẓaddiq* does, how audiences are conducted, how blessings are bestowed, how advice is given. Her father transmitted to her, both directly and tacitly, traditions from his ancestors and teachers, knowledge from the first decades of the nineteenth century and even earlier. Having intimate awareness of her family's Hasidic legacy, she was the repositor of the dynastic vision of the founding lineages of Polish *ḥasidim*, especially the Shapiro branch stemming from Rabbi Israel the Maggid of Kozienice. With her second marriage to Rabbi Asher Perlow II of Stolin (1827–1873) she also became a central figure in the house of Karlin-Stolin, mother of the young dauphin Israel Perlow, who, at her direction, became the Stoliner Rebbe at a very young age.[19] This aligns perfectly with the way she is portrayed in the painting of the groom's evening, firmly grasping her son's right hand in hers and gently insisting that he approach his bride, in a union that would enhance her son's noble status, linking it with the storied house of Chernobyl.

There was a complementarity between Sarah Devorah Shapiro's elegance, self-possessed confidence, and wise governance, and her father Rabbi Elimelekh's sanctity and otherworldly reveries. In this version of Polish Hasidism, ideals of beauty, well-ordered material existence and domesticity were no contradiction to a life of spirit and surrender to the will of God. As we now turn to Rabbi Elimelekh's published discourses, we will see a similar holding fast to two aspects of a sublime religious ideal.

Rabbi Elimelekh's two published works, *Imrei Elimelekh* (1876) and *Divrei Elimelekh* (1890) were brought to press in his lifetime. The author's preface to *Imrei Elimelekh* informs us that the manuscript of the *derashot* (discourses) is not from Rabbi Elimelekh's own hand, but recorded and assembled by followers, in particular a certain R. Berel of Grodzisk, with Rabbi Elimelekh's consent, and presumably under his supervision. Taken together, the two works comprise an extensive body of writing, over eight hundred double-column pages of small print. So far as I know, the books have never been republished (other than photographic reproductions of the original editions), but if they were to be reissued in a modern edition in large format with more readable layout, clearer font, notes, references and the like, they would certainly comprise a substantial multi-volume set.

The basic theme undergirding the entire corpus is *yire'ah* (fear), as Rabbi Elimelekh announces in his preface. *Yire'ah,* according to him, is the foundation

---

19 I discuss this episode in Polen, "Rebbetzins, Wonder-Children and the Emergence of the Dynastic Principle in Hasidism."

of all meaningful religious life. *Yire'ah* progresses from lower to higher modalities, but not quite in the way that we may have come to expect—from fear to reverence and awe. Rather, as one moves to ever-higher states of *yire'ah,* the fear returns, but with its nature and direction having shifted. Lower fear is really fear for oneself, fear of the disastrous consequences to the self of distancing oneself from God.[20] There is nothing wrong with this fear; indeed, it is entirely appropriate, a sober realization that one's personal destiny is dependent on right action and alignment with God's call, as specified in the Torah and commandments.

As one moves to higher levels, *yire'ah* becomes concern for the destiny of the world and the fate of divinity within it, for the actualization of the divine will in creation. Closely associated with this is a rapturous, intense love that the servant of God experiences, called *ahavah be-ta'anugim,* "ardor of delights." This refers to the soul's ecstatic bliss that is the spiritual analog of the pleasure of physical eros, the result of intimate contact with one's divine beloved. As exalted as these experiences are, their locus remains in the individuated personality of the devotee.

There is yet a further stage, involving surrender of all concern for one's own fate and destiny, entering the divine realm with ego-transparency, undergoing self-annihilation that is simultaneously an apotheosis. *Yire'ah* at this sublime level might once again be called "fear," but the fear is awareness of the fragility of being and one's position in the cosmos balanced ever so delicately between divergent forces and in need of unification.[21] Nothing more sharply concentrates the mind than seeing creation from the divine perspective. The move is one of transition from self-centered fear—awareness of danger to the self—to ever-higher states of alertness, awareness of one's position at an ever-more sensitive cusp, at the tipping-point of the cosmos. The path of *yire'ah,* then, is a journey to ever more sharply focused levels of awareness and presence. Higher *yire'ah* is an intense focusing that does not cause the person to freeze or recoil but propels one's being forward in ever more self-forgetting, self-effacing agency.

Movement to higher states involves total negation of ego. One must surrender one's sense of having made right choices on the path to God. Rabbi Elimelekh frequently quotes the teaching of his ancestor the Kozienicer Maggid that all wise decisions come from God, and that after a religious achievement one must consider that one has "done nothing." If one takes credit for spiritual

---

20 This theme is treated in the very first piece in *Divrei Elimelekh, parashat Bereshit,* folio 2a/page 3 and throughout the book.

21 This is referred to a *yire'ah me-ahavah,* "fear arising out of love," or *hitkallelut yire'ah be-ahavah,* "the inclusion of fear within love." *Divrei Elimelekh,* 3 and throughout.

attainment—even silently, in the recesses of one's heart—then the attainments collapse and one has entered the domain of idolatry.[22]

But even this is not the end. After reaching the state of self-annihilation, one must return to earthly existence to continue the work of elevation of the human condition and the cosmos. The Grodzisker asserts that the sin of Adam in the Garden of Eden was stopping too soon, eating of the Tree of Knowledge without eating from the Tree of Life. The Tree of Knowledge represents self-awareness and agency, the confidence to act in the world as a force for good, with boldness. One must be able to fulfill the verse "And his heart was lifted up in the ways of the Lord" (2 Chron. 17:6). But at the same time one must hold fast to the Tree of Life, considering oneself as nothing, in utter humility and self-abnegation, surrendering to the Absolute. When maintaining both modalities of awareness simultaneously, the person unites the two Trees, being completely transparent to Divinity while "acting confidently in the ways of the Lord, advancing the view that one is indeed a unique being, a person of significance."[23]

Rabbi Elimelekh engages with radical theological motifs such as *'averah lishmah,* sin for the sake of heaven. He avers that this mode of action is available only for those who are acting on the level of complete *bittul*—self-abnegation. If one is completely without self-interest, even spiritual self-interest, then *'averah lishmah* may be a permissible option.[24]

There is in general no suggestion that radical theological postures are limited to a select class of spiritual virtuosi, the *ẓaddiqim.* If one is on the level of transparency and self-annihilation, then one may intuit the divine will without being commanded, without an utterance from God. This level is clearly difficult to achieve, but there is no *a priori* barrier. We see here a remarkable feature of Rabbi Elimelekh's corpus, radical teachings in line with what we have come to expect from the more elite schools of Polish Hasidism, but with an invitational spirit that seems to open the pathway to advancement for all to the highest levels. This seems to me to erode the shopworn distinction between "popular" Hasidism and "elite" Hasidism. Rabbi Elimelekh's corpus is striking for its theological boldness that yet preserves a welcoming, beckoning quality, with no *a priori* bars to entry.

In the section on *parashat Niẓavim,* Rabbi Elimelekh explains that the curses near the end of Deuteronomy can be transformed into blessings. This alone is not so remarkable, as it picks up on a motif from early Hasidism, as far back as

---

22 *Divrei Elimelekh, parashat Bereshit,* folio 4a/page 7 and throughout.

23 *Divrei Elimelekh, parashat Be-Shlaḥ,* s.v. *mi kamokhah ba-elim Hashem …* , folio 79b/page 158.

24 *Divrei Elimelekh, parashat Bereshit,* s.v. *be-Midrash Rabbah parashah bet,* folio 5a/page 9.

the Ba'al Shem Tov. Yet *Divrei Elimelekh* pursues the theme with sedulous determination throughout the *parashah*, culminating in the words *u-makhah Hashem et shemo*—"and God will erase his name" (Deut. 29:19)—which are understood to mean that the individual, like Moses, reaches the state of complete self-nullification and absorption into the divine Nothing. This state is not limited to Moses but is apparently open at least in principle to everyone; it is a state that everyone can and should aspire to.[25] Indeed, at the beginning of *parashat Niẓavim*, on Deut. 29:9, Rabbi Elimelekh focuses on the words *kol ish Yisra'el*—"every Israelite person," which he understands to mean that each and every Israelite without exception should feel themselves invited to realize their divine stature embracing all the worlds, including the highest.

In *parashat Shemini* Rabbi Elimelekh takes up the episode of Nadav and Avihu (Lev. 10). While many interpreters search for the sin these two sons of Aaron committed that warranted the punishment of their deaths, there is another interpretive tradition that mitigates the sin or denies that it was a sin altogether; the two brothers died in a rapturous approach to the divine light.[26] Rabbi Elimelekh avers that the aim of Nadav and Avihu was entirely admirable, the mystical goal of absorption in the divine light. But their sin was to attain a level for which the rest of the people of Israel was not ready: "They pushed themselves to rise to a sublime state of sacred service that was incompatible with the level of the people Israel as a whole."[27] The overreach of Nadav and Avihu was the attempt to reach an exalted state without bringing along all of Israel. This may be an oblique critique of elite Hasidic schools that do not make room for common people in their aspirations.

Imrei Elimelekh and *Divrei Elimelekh* are important sources for stories and otherwise unrecorded traditions about the early leaders of Hasidism, including the Great Maggid of Mezritch, Rabbi Menaḥem Mendel of Vitebsk, Rabbi Elimelekh of Lizhensk, and Rabbi Zusya of Anipol, as well as the Ruzhiner. The stories are not treated as a separate genre but are embedded in and serve to illustrate the theoretical discourses. For example, Rabbi Elimelekh relates a story, which he heard from his father Rabbi Ḥayyim Me'ir Yeḥi'el of Mogielnica and which his father heard from the Ruzhiner. The central figure in the story is

---

25 *Divrei Elimelekh, parashat Niẓavim* s.v. *ve-'al pi zeh yevo'ar kan*, folio 233b/page 466; see *Imrei Elimelekh, parashat Teẓaveh*, folio 73b/page 146.

26 See *Or ha-Ḥayyim* on Lev. 16:1. For a comprehensive study, see Ariel Evan Mayse, "'Like a Moth to the Flame': The Death of Nadav and Avihu in Hasidic Literature," in *Be-Ron Yaḥad: Studies in Jewish Thought and Theology in Honor of Nehemia Polen*, ed. Ariel Evan Mayse and Arthur Green (Boston, MA: Academic Studies Press, 2019), 364–406.

27 *Divrei Elimelekh, parashat Shemini*, s.v. *uva-Zeh yesh lomar*, folio 134b/page 268.

Rabbi Menaḥem Mendel of Vitebsk (c. 1730–1788), one of the foremost disciples of the Maggid of Mezritch, who, in 1777, along with fellow disciple Rabbi Abraham Kalisker, emigrated to the Holy Land and settled in Tiberias on the Sea of Galilee, where they established a small, intense community of Hasidic devotees. The story, as presented in *Divrei Elimelekh, parashat Qoraḥ*:[28]

> The holy Rabbi the *ẓaddiq* Rabbi [Menaḥem] Mendel of Vitebsk of blessed memory was once in Jerusalem. A foolish and unstable individual climbed the Mount of Olives and began sounding the shofar, managing to stay out of sight. [The shofar blasts appeared to be emanating eerily from the Mount without human agency.] The general Jewish populace began to assume that this sounding of the shofar was the harbinger of the messianic redemption. When news of this matter reached the *ẓaddiq* [Rabbi Menaḥem Mendel], he opened the window and peered out into the air. Immediately he said, "Nothing is new; nothing has changed." Had there been a genuine harbinger of redemption, it would have been noticeable in the atmosphere.

The story clearly stands as a caution against false messianism and premature eschatological hopes. But the tale is embedded in a lengthy discourse on the Qoraḥ rebellion (Num. 16–18), its theological underpinnings and denouement. As explained at length by the Grodzisker, Qoraḥ was arguing for the universal priesthood of all Israel, with no need for specially designated Aaronide priests. This was akin to the original situation before the sin of the Golden Calf. At that time every Israelite could offer sacrifices to God without the mediation of the Levites. The Sinai revelation had brought all Israelites to the level of *'Aẓilut*, transparent absorption into the realm of divine Thought, dissolving all sense of personal agency and expectations of reward for good actions. Qoraḥ's view was that the time was ripe for return to that state. Moses, for his part, was alert to the danger of premature eschatological realization, knowing that this had been the mistake of Nadav and Avihu, who offered incense and, with all their virtuous intent, were struck by divine fire. Despite this fear, Moses recognized Qoraḥ's position as having spiritual integrity and wanted to give Qoraḥ every chance to succeed. Moses's falling on his face (Num. 16:4) was a performative enactment of raising up fallen sparks of holiness, an effort to assist the Qoraḥites at bringing

---

28 *Divrey Elimelekh, parashat Qoraḥ,* folio 177a/page 353.

the "complete rectification," the eschatological fulfilment. But the time was not ripe, Qoraḥ had misjudged his own stature and historical role, and his project failed.

In the Grodzisker's framing of the Moses-Qoraḥ episode, this was not a conflict between right versus wrong, good versus evil. Moses and Qoraḥ held different views of the religious landscape that lay ahead and how to move forward to a higher state of realization.[29] Qoraḥ's view had its own integrity and, though dangerous and ill-advised, it was not outside the realm of possibility that it might succeed, so Moses actually assisted Qoraḥ in his efforts. If Qoraḥ's incense offering had been accepted, it would have been the last sacrificial offering ever needed. But in that case the new dispensation would be immediately noticeable to all Israel. As the Grodzisker puts it, "All Israel would immediately sense the aura of redemption and rectification." At that point in his exposition, the Grodzisker tells the story of Rabbi Menaḥem Mendel of Vitebsk, his opening the window and gazing at the atmosphere for evidence of genuine change. The point of story is that claims of redemption are not ruled out *a priori*, but must be tested empirically. When the eschaton really arrives, there will be no mistaking it; it will be evident to all, in the air itself. Until that time, claims and claimants must be treated with great caution. The Vitebsker story is a sidebar to the biblical exegesis, meant to illustrate and support it. The entire exposition of the Qoraḥ episode in *Divrei Elimelekh* is a reading against the grain, a bold reframing of a familiar biblical story cast in a fresh light. The Grodzisker displays surprising sympathy with Qoraḥ and the idea of universal Israelite priesthood, consistent with his invitational posture on religious growth, not reserving the highest states for one individual endowed with superhuman gifts through whom all beneficence, spiritual as well as material, are channeled. Genuine religious attainment is difficult, very difficult, always freighted with false starts, missteps, obstacles, dangers. But there is no inherent bar to advancement, and all persons are invited to move forward on the path as far as they can reach.

Another discourse transmits an illuminating remark of the Grodzisker's great-grandfather, the Kozienicer Maggid, as conveyed to him by his father Rabbi Ḥayyim Me'ir Yeḥi'el. The Kozienicer is quoted as saying, "I stand ready before God as a messenger-boy [*na'ar meshulaḥ*]." Rabbi Ḥayyim Meir Yeḥi'el explained his grandfather's words as follows: "When a person reaches the state of self-abnegation [*bittul*] and the divine Nothing [*Ayin*], then the person is able

29 See Arthur Green's reading of a Levi Yiẓḥaq sermon on Qoraḥ elsewhere in this volume, where he suggests that Moses and Qoraḥ are the two *maggidim*, Dov Ber of Mezritch and Yeḥi'el Mikhl of Zlochov, precisely with different views of how to shape the emerging movement.

to encompass more than their receptive capacity [*kelim*] would seem to allow." Rabbi Elimelekh elaborates:

> Each *ẓaddiq* has a particular mode of sacred service—Love, Fear, and the like. But when *ẓaddiqim* gaze at their root in the divine Nothing, then they are able to serve God in all modalities, on all levels.
>
> This is what my great-grandfather meant when he said that "I stand ready before God as a messenger-boy"—he had reached the state of self-abnegation and *Ayin,* to the point where he no longer had a preferred way of being in the world; rather he stood ready for any and every disposition and emotive state, as God would show him.[30]

Moshe Idel cites this teaching in his *Hasidism: Between Ecstasy and Magic,* explaining that in the state of annihilation "one expands his capacity to receive the influx even more than before he 'annihilates himself.'"[31] Annihilation is not self-erasure; it actually leads to "a positive expansion of consciousness."[32] In other words, self-annihilation leads to a newly reborn, higher self that contains multitudes, an expanded self that transcends the limitations of one's former personality and temperament.

In this passage and many similar ones throughout *Imrei Elimelekh* and *Divrei Elimelekh,* there is no disclaimer that such lofty states are no longer accessible. To the contrary, as noted above, there is a beckoning, invitational quality to the writing. Rabbi Elimelekh apparently felt that with all the dangers of spiritual ascent, his auditors and readers could be trusted to know their limits and act responsibly. There is no retreat from the intense mystical vision of the founders of Hasidism, including his own illustrious ancestors.

Imrei Elimelekh and *Divrei Elimelekh* are laden with exegetical gems, mystical insights, and accounts of prior generations of Hasidic greats, and it is my hope that this brief highlighting of some salient themes will spark further interest in these important but thus far largely neglected volumes.

---

30 *Imrei Elimelekh, parashat Lekh Lekha,* folio 6b/page 12.

31 Moshe Idel, *Hasidism: Between Ecstasy and Magic* (Albany: State University of New York Press, 1995), n. 106 to chapter 3, 316–317. The page reference to *Imrey Elimelekh* needs correction; it should read "6b" rather than "63."

32 Ibid., n. 48 to chapter 3, 311.

We know from other sources that Rabbi Elimelekh of Grodzisk received supplicants on matters relating to family, health and livelihood—in Hasidic terminology, the triad of *banei, ḥayyei, mezonei,* and was reputed to have powers of clairvoyance and efficacious blessing.[33] He accepted *qvittlakh* [petitions containing the *ḥasid*'s name and mother's name, sometimes followed by a brief description of the concern and the requested intercession]. According to one source, he was authorized and encouraged to receive *qvittlakh* by the Ruzhiner Rebbe.[34] There were those in the Hasidic world who viewed such engagement as unworthy of the attention of genuine religious leaders, and academic scholars on Hasidism have often fallen in line with this attitude, focusing their attention on personalities perceived as strongly intellectual.[35] While such virtuosi are indisputably worthy of the interest they have received, we must resist the notion that *ẓaddiqim* whose courts were more open, who gave advice and blessings in response to requests on personal matters, were on a lesser rung. This is especially so since until very recently, the pursuit of intellectual and mystical excellence meant the near-total exclusion of women, while family health and happiness were the primary foci of wives and mothers. Following in the footsteps of his noble ancestors going back to the Maggid of Kozienice and Rabbi Elimelekh of Lizhensk, the Grodzisker saw no conflict between attending to his community's acutely pressing material needs on the one hand, and intensely mystical teachings on the other.[36]

---

33 See the material collected in Ele'azar Dov ben Aaron of Kozienice, *Safran shel Ẓaddiqim* (Bnei Brak: Mitzvah Institute, 5758/1998), 26–27; idem, *Gan Hadasim* (Bnei Brak: Mitzvah Institute, 5758/1998), 6–7.

34 *Oholei Ya'aqov*, cited in Chaim Dov Stern, *Ner Yisra'el* (Bnei Brak: Bregman, 1990), vol. 4, 203.

35 I have discussed this in an essay entitled "Inconvenient Wonders: Ambivalence in Hasidism about the Miraculous Powers of the Tsaddik," forthcoming in a series from Drake University Comparison Project (Comparative Philosophy of Religion), published by Springer.

36 Ebn Leader has recently characterized the leadership style of Rabbi Elimelekh of Lizhensk as follows: "[R]ecreating an environment of love and shared purpose for a large community meant training *tzaddiqim* who were first and foremost teachers who share the same journey with their followers, accepting that each person is on a different stage of the path." See Ebn Leader, "Leadership as Individual Relationship: A Close Study of the *No'am Elimelekh,*" in *Be-Ron Yaḥad: Studies in Jewish Thought and Theology in Honor of Nehemia Polen,* ed. Ariel Evan Mayse and Arthur Green (Boston, MA: Academic Studies Press, 2019), 177–202. Leader's essay clarifies that Rabbi Elimelekh of Lizhensk was not at all the caricature of a popular *ẓaddiq* who demanded simple faith without personal effort; to the contrary, only intense effort on the part of the individual could put them on the path of genuine and lasting spiritual advancement. The leader can assist and inspire, but the work must be done by the individual. Furthermore, the leader himself is imperfect, aware of his shortcomings, in process, and thereby connects with disciples in a truly meaningful way. This description of the leadership style of Rabbi Elimelekh of Lizhensk is suggestive for his descendants, especially Rabbi Elimelekh of Grodzisk, and his son Rabbi Kalonymus Kalmish Shapiro.

As noted above, the Pshiskhe-Kotsk school was not noted for promoting family life. An essay on Hasidism in the *Encyclopaedia Hebraica* has this to say this about Rabbi Simḥah Bunem: "He gathered a group of sharp-witted young men, exceptional Torah scholars, who abandoned their families for extended periods, engaged in Torah study and Hasidism, and mocked 'practical' [popular] Hasidism."[37]

The stream of Polish Hasidism exemplified by Rabbi Yisra'el the Maggid of Kozienice displays a deep appreciation for familial feeling and spousal tenderness. While erotic imagery is a staple of many kabbalistic and Hasidic texts, the writings of the Maggid of Kozienice reveal a prizing of domesticity and romantic affection evidently based on personal experience and disposition. Take, for example, a passage in his work *'Avodat Yisra'el* where he speaks of groom and bride in their private *yiḥud* ["union"] room just after the wedding ceremony: "It is the way of the bride to bless the groom and to say, 'May you merit long life and to unite [with me] in love from now and forever.' And if the bride does not think to do this, it is the way of the groom to instruct her in giving the blessing, saying, 'Bless me that I should merit to live with you forever.'"[38] The Kozienicer Maggid applies the simile to a verse in Psalms, understood as the intimate conversation between God and Israel. The tenderness and warmly romantic spirit are the signature of the Kozienicer Maggid, and convey not only the emotional warmth of his love of God but, likely, the texture of feeling in his own family life.

Rabbi Yiẓḥaq Eiziq Yehoshu'a Yeḥi'el Safrin of Komarno (1806–1874), in his *Noẓer Ḥesed,* reports that the Maggid of Kozienice, as well as other Polish masters including Rabbi Ya'aqov Yiẓḥaq (the Seer of Lublin) and Rabbi Naftali of Ropshitz, remarried in their old age "even though sexual desire and capacity had ceased entirely for them, and they were not able to perform this great and holy mitzvah [of sexual intercourse]. Nevertheless they married, and their *yiḥudim* [unions] took the form of words of love, tender affection, and closeness of hearts."[39] I assume that this culture of domesticity and spousal affection continued throughout the generations, and may shed additional light on why

---

37 *Encyclopaedia Hebraica,* vol. 17, cols. 756–821; quote in column 762. This essay—a virtual monograph—is a classic effort at summing up the entire sweep of the Hasidic movement: origins, development, personalities, social structure, theology, cultural features. While aspects of the article have been overtaken by recent scholarship, it still stands as a comprehensive portrait of the field by an eminent team of researchers.

38 *'Avodat Yisra'el* (Bnei Brak: Zvi Halberstam, 5733/1973), *Liqqutim,* s.v. *hineh anu omrim be-Qedusha de-Amidah,* folio 3a.

39 Yiẓḥaq Eiziq Yehoshu'a Yeḥi'el Safrin of Komarna, *Noẓer Ḥesed 'al Massekhet Avot* (Jerusalem: Avraham Mordecai Safrin, 1982), 26 [chapter 3, mishnah 4: *Ha-Ne'or ba-Laylah*].

Rabbi Elimelekh of Grodzisk wanted to remarry late in life after the death of his first wife, as discussed above. In the event, the Grodzisker did have two children with his second wife Ḥannah Berakhah: Kalonymos Kalmish and Yeshayah. Kalonymos Kalmish in particular has been the focus of much study due to his extraordinary Holocaust-period discourses, his path-breaking manuals on Hasidic education,[40] and his profound interwar sermons, published under the title *Derekh ha-Melekh*. We can be thankful that the Warsaw Ghetto writings of Rabbi Kalonymos Shapiro, son of Rabbi Elimelekh of Grodzisk, survived the catastrophe, were discovered in the rubble of postwar Warsaw, and are now the focus of intense analysis, assisted by a spectacular new critical edition based on the rabbi's autograph manuscript. That said, our understanding of the Piaseczner will be greatly enhanced when we become more familiar with the writings of his father, Rabbi Elimelekh of Grodzisk. The generational shift between father and son is very clear. The works of the Grodzisker do not have the pedagogic sophistication, phenomenological meticulousness or literary expressiveness of the Piaseczner. This is not to make an unfair comparison, only to point out the obvious, that while the son is manifestly a person of the twentieth century, the father is firmly positioned in the nineteenth.

Yet the commonalities and continuities between father and son are also very strong. For example, they both emphasize surrender of one's religious achievements back to God. They both aim for peaks of mystical intensity while remaining deeply bonded to one's social and familial world. Both are evidently overwhelmed by the reality of God, the most palpable presence in their lives. The immensity of the divine did not divert their gaze from the human; it fostered an intense love of people in general and their own family members in particular. In line with the Kozienice tradition, domesticity was a positive value, sought after and cherished.[41] When we gain a clearer grasp of the voices of both the Grodzisker and the Piaseczner, we will have attained a deeper understanding of intergenerational transmission, as well as the innovative creativity that each new era is called upon to realize.

---

40 For an exploration of Kalonymos Kalmish's work on spiritual pedagogy, see Michael Shire's essay elsewhere in this volume.

41 On the Piaseczner Rebbe's esteem for his wife Raḥel Ḥayyah Miriam, see Nehemia Polen, "Miriam, Moses, and the Divinity of Children," in *Hasidism, Suffering and Renewal: The Prewar and Holocaust Legacy of Kalonymus Kalman Shapira*, ed. Don Seeman, Daniel Reiser, and Ariel Evan Mayse (Albany: State University of New York Press, 2021), 213–234; Polen, "Miriam's Dance: Radical Egalitarianism in Hasidic Thought," *Modern Judaism* 12 (1992): 1–21.

Figures 1 and 2. Two scenes from wedding celebration of Bracha Sheindel Twersky (Chernobyl lineage), in Rachmastrivka (Rotmistrivka, Ukraine), 1883, to Yisrael Shapiro Perlow (Karlin-Stolin and Kozienice lineages)

CHAPTER 19

The Lives of Berish *Ba'al Teshuvah*[1]

Avinoam J. Stillman

> I do not know if it is true or not. I only know that the stories of the righteous contain a power through which one can do anything that one desires.
>
> —R. Ḥayyim Halberstam of Sandz[2]

I.

In Kazimierz, Krakow's Jewish quarter, two Jewish cemeteries survive. The older one, on Szeroka Square, contains the monuments of many eminent early modern rabbis. Nearby, on Miodowa Street, is the "new cemetery," opened in 1800. There, in June 2016, I found a tombstone nestled by the northern wall, remarkably clean of vines and dirt, and easily legible:

> A righteous and honest man, God-fearing and avoiding evil, who
> All his days behaved with holiness and with exceeding abnegation
> He illumined the night like the day as he studied Torah
> All his days he spent in fasting, wrapped in his *tallit* and in his *tefillin*
> In holiness and purity, my own teacher and ours, the light of our eyes

1 This essay originated in my undergraduate thesis at Columbia College, completed under the gracious guidance of Clémence Boulouque and Agi Legutko. Special thanks to my grandfather, Professor Menahem Schmelzer, for sharing of his knowledge of Central European Jewish history. I offer this portrait of a unique and complex Jewish life in appreciation for Hebrew College and its role in many other such lives.

2 Quoted by Raphael Mahler, Sefer Sants (Tel-Aviv: Yisro'el-bukh, 1970), 247.

Rabbi Yissakhar Dov Ber son of R. 'Akiva
Known among his people by the name
Rebbe Reb Berish'l *Ba'al Teshuvah*
From the great Levite lineage called **Horowitz**
Descendent of the holy genius the author of the *Shla"h* [Yeshayahu Horowitz]
Who departed from this life on the 10th of the consoling month of Av 5691
The sixty-first year of his life's days, may his soul be bound up in life
May his dormant lips be given voice, and may he be remembered unto the last generation
Every passerby from his peers shall cry and lift his voice in wailing, tears
At the death of the righteous man, shield and defense of his generation[3]
By his righteousness, holiness, abnegation, and piety dispelling our accusers
His awesome devotion, including fasts from Shabbat to Shabbat and many mortifications
His rolling in the snow and immersions for purity in cold running waters
His majestic reverence, his cleaving to God, and his intense supplications
His dwelling, day and night, on both the secret and Talmudic traditions
His abstention from all pleasures and from all of the world's gratifications
His heartfulness and joy as he exerted himself to fulfill each divine commandment
His righteous generosity in offering vital support, uplifting the spirits of the forsaken
May these merits protect us forever!

The epitaph describes a learned and charitable ascetic with a fine rabbinic pedigree. I wondered at the exceptional appellation *ba'al teshuvah*—literally a "master of return," rabbinic parlance for a penitent. This honorific hinted at a

---

3 Meaning of Hebrew uncertain.

complex past, perhaps an impious one. This portrait in stone marked the edge of a darkness, a gap between past and present, which kept following me. Already in 1924, the German Jewish writer Alfred Döblin had wondered about Jewish Krakow:

> Is it a dead world and a new world? The old one isn't dead. I feel intimately and violently attracted to it. And I know that my compass is reliable. It never points to anything aesthetic, it always points to living, urgent things.[4]

In my moment, I wondered whether a dead world, a memorial, could learn to speak. As I sought out traces of Berish's life, of his struggles and his piety, he led me through the tangles of Döblin's opaque and piercing question.[5] I found that Berish's story, told and retold over many decades, undermined the condescending and romanticizing narratives about East Central European Jewry that often inform both scholarship and collective memory.[6]

II.

Most of the information about Berish's early years comes from two accounts published in his lifetime. In 1927, the journalist Ẓvi Rumeld published a serialized narrative about Berish in *Ha-Ẓfirah*, a popular Hebrew periodical.[7] Rumeld himself was based in Zakopane, and wrote numerous articles about the Jews of the Tatra Mountains. In 1931, the prominent Jewish historian Majer Bałaban drew on Rumeld's earlier account and published a shorter article about Berish in the popular Warsaw Yiddish daily *Unzer Express*.[8] By both accounts, Berish

---

4 Alfred Döblin, *Journey to Poland*, trans. Joachim Neugroschel (New York: Paragon, 1991), 187.

5 I found many sources thanks to a post on an internet forum by Yatziv Pitgam, "Rebi Berish'l Ba'al-Tshuve mi-Krakow ztz"l" [Yiddish], Yiddishe Velt Forums, accessed April 12, 2021, http://www.ivelt.com/forum/viewtopic.php?t=25583.

6 Glenn Dynner, "Jewish Traditionalism in Eastern Europe: The Historiographical Gadfly," *Polin* 29 (2017): 287.

7 Ẓvi Rumeld, "Ba'al Teshuvah" [Heb.], part 1, *Ha-Ẓfirah*, February 11, 1927; idem, "Ba'al Teshuvah" [Heb.], part 2, *Ha-Ẓfirah*, February 14, 1927; idem, "Ba'al Teshuvah" [Heb.], part 3, *Ha-Ẓfirah*, February 15, 1927.

8 Meir Bałaban, "Der Rebbe R' Berish Ba'al-Tshuve fun Krakow," *Unzer Express*, February 6, 1931. For a transcription and my translation, see idem, "The *Rebbe* R. Berish Bal-tshuve of Krakow," trans. Avinoam J. Stillman, *In geveb* (February 2019), https://ingeveb.org/texts-and-translations/bal-tshuve-of-krakow.

was born in 1870 in or around Hunsdorf, a village in the Podhale region of the Tatra mountains, then part of the Austro-Hungarian Empire, but near the Polish border. Hunsdorf was mainly populated by ethnic Gorales, who often worked as mountain shepherds. Rumeld relates that the Jews of Hunsdorf lived in peace with their neighbors, notwithstanding his description of antisemitic incitement by a local priest. Bałaban also exhibits this sort of idealization when he refers to the Jews of Hunsdorf as "Jewish Gorales," and Berish's friendships with the Gorales are described at length in both accounts. Rumeld notes sarcastically that

> [S]trong hatred of Israel, which the noble lords, those with "high culture," as it were, transported from Posen, from Warsaw, from Lvov, and from Krakow, and even to Zakopane and its daughters and to Poronin and its environs, still has not reached here. Since Hunsdorf is far from the mountain forests and the railway station ... this place has not yet merited to the visit of summer tourists. Thus, there is no one to bring "high culture" there.[9]

By the end of the nineteenth century, the Gorales and the Tatras had become tourist attractions and symbols of rugged simplicity and purity for Polish nationalists.[10] Rumeld claims that Hunsdorf was free of tourists and nationalist sentiments, yet he himself romanticizes the tranquil coexistence of Jews and Gorals in an idyllic mountain landscape. Thus, Rumeld describes the Jews of Hunsdorf as having a "patriarchal charm"; the forefather of the Jews of Hunsdorf was, ostensibly, Berish's namesake, one Dov Ber Hartzblut.[11]

Bałaban and Rumeld place the young Berish in the hagiographic lineage of earlier Jewish holy men.[12] The story is told that, as an infant, Berish only cried once, when his mother left him alone in a room with a printed Hebrew Bible on the table. In her absence, he grabbed the book; when she returned, she took it away from him, and the precocious child burst into tears. Berish is imagined as a shepherd of his father's sheep in the mountains, recalling the biblical stories of

9 Rumeld, "Ba'al Teshuvah," part 1.

10 Anna Brzyski, "The Paradox of the Ethnographic Superaltern: Ethnonationalism and Tourism in the Polish Tatra Mountains at the Turn of the Nineteenth Century," *RES: Anthropology and Aesthetics* 53/54 (2008): 282–292.

11 I have been unable to identify other Jews from the region with the surname Hartzblut. Berish's epitaph gives his surname as Horowitz.

12 Susanne Galley, "Holy Men in Their Infancy: The Childhood of Tsadikim in Hasidic Legends," *Polin* 15 (2002): 169–186.

Jacob, Moses, and David and the rabbinic story of 'Aqiva. Rumeld's descriptions of Berish's wanderings in the mountains also owes much to the aesthetics of the Hasidic tale:

> Berish'l was roused from the ecstasy, which he was entirely given over to, and felt that he had to do something to participate himself in the rejoicing of the evening that the entire world celebrates. He got up and took his "alpha beta" out of his pocket and began to read out loud and with great fervor: *alef, bet, gimel, daled, heh, waw, zayin* . . . .[13]

The story of Berish ecstatically reciting the Hebrew letters in prayer draws on one of the most famous of Jewish folktales, that of the pious yet simple shepherd, which has its roots in the medieval Ashkenazi pietistic work *Sefer Ḥasidim*. Several Eastern European Hasidic stories popular in the nineteenth century also describe young children or simple people who pray by reciting the aleph-bet and asking God to combine the letters into words for him. These Jewish folkloric motifs prime the reader to expect that Berish might become a holy man.

The depiction of pious young Berish frolicking in a pastoral landscape belies the political and religious upheaval in the Jewish community at the time.[14] The dual monarchy of Austria and Hungary was established in 1867, and the emancipation of the Jews followed shortly thereafter. In anticipation, Jewish communal leaders in Pest proposed the establishment of a centralized national assembly of Jewish leaders. When this proposal was circulated in Hungary, it met with sharp criticism from the Pressburg community, which, under the rabbinate of R. Moses Sofer, the *Ḥatam Sofer*, was a bastion of conservatism. There began a protracted and fierce debate over the official status of the Jewish community, which eventually resulted in an institutional split between the Orthodox and liberal Neolog denominations. For their part, the Jewish leaders in Hunsdorf sided with the Pressburg faction; they agreed to an assembly on condition that only administrative, and no religious, topics were raised. Furthermore, they categorically opposed a centralized religious institution, "for, in light of the difference in religious views, the conscience of many is likely to be troubled."[15] Rather

---

13 Rumeld, "Ba'al Teshuvah," part 1.

14 Jacob Katz, *A House Divided: Orthodoxy and Schism in Nineteenth-Century Central European Jewry* (Waltham, MA: Brandeis University Press, 1998).

15 Ibid., 95.

than a peaceful town of "Jewish Gorales," Hunsdorf was an active part of Austro-Hungarian Jewish communal politics.

Not only was Hunsdorf's aligned with Orthodoxy comes; three *yeshivot* were active there in the early nineteenth century. However, by the time Berish was born, the community was dwindling, affected by the freedom of movement and opportunity that came with emancipation.[16] The town had a population of 939 Jews in 1828, yet had shrunk to 364 by 1880.[17] By the end of the century, Hunsdorf's yeshivas closed, and its Jewish primary school taught both Judaic and secular studies in German.[18] Rumeld is effusive in praising the teachers at the school, who came from Hungarian seminaries. By his account, they taught Torah with Rashi's commentary, but also German language and grammar; they made particular use of Moses Mendelssohn's Bible translation.[19] Rumeld paints Berish as a savant, an *'ilui*, who quickly outstripped his teachers. After four years in primary school, Berish had to leave to get a secondary education. Rumeld reports that the Judaics teacher wanted Berish to go to a Hungarian yeshiva, much to the dismay of "his relatively progressive mother, who read the novels of Moritz Jakai with great dedication," and who did not want Berish to become "a zealous rabbi." On the other hand, his secular teachers suggested that he be sent to a city for continued secular education. This upset his father, who wanted Berish to continue shepherding and opposed the impiety and the expense of secular education. Berish's family drama thus recapitulates in miniature the controversies that beset Central European Jews in the late nineteenth century.

III.

In the end, Rumeld writes, a balance was struck. Berish was sent to a liberal Jewish school—a gymnasium—in the Hungarian village of Tertze (Tarcal), approximately 170 kilometers to the south-east, to become a *Doctor-Rabbiner*. As in Hunsdorf, the Jews of Tertze were officially aligned with Orthodoxy, but many were also more liberal.[20] Adolescence and the move away from Hunsdorf transformed Berish's life. According to Rumeld, the year was 1886, and Berish

16 Ibid., 34.

17 *Encyclopedia Judaica*, 2nd ed. (Detroit, MI: Macmillan Reference USA, 2007), s.v. "Huncovce." See also *Pinqas ha-Qehillot: Slovakia* [Heb.] (Jerusalem: Yad Vashem, 2003), 161–163.

18 Katz, *A House Divided*, 37.

19 Rumeld, "Ba'al Teshuvah," part 2.

20 *Pinqas ha-Qehillot: Hungary* [Heb.] (Jerusalem: Yad Vashem, 1976), 305–306.

was sixteen, already in the eleventh grade, when he went to hear a Hasidic rabbi in Tertze:

> When the boy's footsteps rested on the threshold of the room the *ẓaddiq* lifted his large, thick eyebrows and set his eyes on him.... Suddenly from the lips of the boy escaped a fearful voice, and afterwards he broke out in great and bitter crying. Then the *ẓaddiq* stretched out his "right hand that draws close," and was alone with him in a special room.... What was done and spoken there, in the inner sanctum, no man knows until today. But this is known to everyone: When the *ẓaddiq* left the place, he took Berish'l with him.[21]

Bałaban's account is slightly different; Berish excelled as a student in Tertze, and a local Neolog Jew convinced him to pursue more advanced study. Berish ran away to Budapest, where he studied at the expense of the Neolog community for two years until he matriculated, and began to study philosophy at the university. One day, Berish was walking down Sip Utca in Budapest's Jewish quarter, the center of the Neolog movement. He overheard beautiful singing from a house. Upon entering, Berish encountered R. Hertzka Ratzferter, also known as R. Naftali Hertkza Zilberman (d. 1897), the rabbi of the Orthodox Hungarian town of Ratzfert—modern day Újfehértó. Zilberman preached about ethics (*mussar*) to his audience, as he was accustomed to do across Hungary, and Berish was inspired. He joined the *rebbe*'s retinue, and left his student life behind.

Regardless of the chronological differences between the accounts, the real drama of these scenes is internal. Taken from his mountain village to an urban center, the deep religious feelings that characterized Berish as a young shepherd are catalyzed again when he encounters a *rebbe*. Berish followed Zilberman to Ratzfert, and presumably stayed there until Zilberman's death approximately a decade later. As Bałaban notes, Zilberman was a student of the prominent R. Ḥayyim Halberstam of Sandz (1797–1876); indeed, R. Ḥayyim's son R. Sholom Eli'ezer Halberstam established his own Hasidic court in Ratzfert after Zilberman's death.[22] Halberstam had died by the time Berish "repented," but Sandz (Nowy Sącz), is approximately eighty kilometers from Hunsdorf, and

---

21 Rumeld, "Ba'al Teshuvah," part 2. For another mention of Zilberman's long eyebrows, see *Zikhron Naftali*, ed. Shalom Segal Beilush, 2nd ed., vol. 1 (Brooklyn: C. M. Weissman, 1980), 8.

22 *Pinqas ha-Qehillot: Hungary*, 138.

Berish must have heard of him earlier.[23] Halberstam was influential, and no stranger to politics; he repudiated the liberal *maskilim* and Neolog, and also criticized other Hasidic groups such as Sadigora, whose leaders he accused of decadence and modernization.[24] Sandzer Hasidism epitomized the nineteenth-century alliance of Hasidism with Orthodoxy, and endorsed a "pre-Hasidic" ethos of Torah study and cultural insularity.[25] Through his association with Zilberman, Berish seems to have become linked with Sandzer Hasidism.

Berish's Sandzer affiliation is reflected in three aspects of his religious practice: his Torah study, his asceticism, and his charitability. Sandz Hasidism was particularly "rabbinic"; Halberstam was a prominent Torah scholar and halakhic authority, famous for his voluminous responsa, published as *Divrei Ḥayyim*.[26] Zilberman's scantier Talmudic writings were also compiled and published after his death. Berish apparently studied at Zilberman's yeshiva in Ratzfert, and in his later years continued to study both Talmud and kabbalistic texts in the small prayer hall, the *kloyz*, in Krakow. Berish's epitaph likewise notes that he studied both the "secrets of the Torah" and the Talmud with the traditional commentaries of Rashi and the Tosafists. Although Berish left no writings, he devoted many hours to traditional text study.

Berish also took on an intense ascetic praxis. The concept of penitence through suffering has rabbinic roots, but the medieval Ashkenazi Pietists elaborated a more active concept of *teshuvat ha-mishqal*, the "penitence of equivalence," according to which sinners should voluntarily cause themselves suffering to counterbalance the pleasures of sin.[27] By Berish's time, Jews around the diaspora had inherited an elaborate ascetic ideal, commonly including fasting and ritual immersions, inspired by both medieval pietism and early modern kabbalistic

---

23 Interestingly, Rumeld also reported about Halberstam's death, as mentioned by Meir Vunder, "*Kamah Shanim Ḥai Rabi Ḥayyim me-Sandz?*," *Ha-Ma'ayan* 14, no. 4 (1974): 44.

24 David Assaf, *Beguiled by Knowledge: An Anatomy of a Hasidic Controversy* [Heb.] (Haifa: University of Haifa Press, 2012); idem, "The Bernyu of Leova Affair and the Sandz—Sadigura Controversy: An Annotated Bibliography" [Heb.], *Jerusalem Studies in Jewish Thought* 23 (2011): 407–481.

25 David Assaf, "Sandz Hasidic Dynasty," in *YIVO Encyclopedia of Jews in Eastern Europe*, vol. 2 (New Haven: Yale University Press, 2008), 1661–1662; Benjamin Brown, "Substitutes for Mysticism: A General Model for the Theological Development of Hasidism in the Nineteenth Century," *History of Religions* 56 (2017): 253.

26 Benjamin Brown, "The Two Faces of Religious Radicalism: Orthodox Zealotry and 'Holy Sinning' in Nineteenth-Century Hasidism in Hungary and Galicia," *The Journal of Religion* 93 (2013): 350.

27 For analysis of the rabbinic sources, see "Expiation, Suffering and Redemption" in Pinchas Peli, *On Repentance: The Thought and Oral Discourses of Rabbi Joseph Dov Soloveitchik* (Northvale, NJ: Jason Aronson, 1996), 266–270.

ethics.[28] Although Hasidic thinkers often presented themselves as anti-ascetic, many *Ḥasidim* continued to embrace earlier forms of pietism.[29] Raphael Mahler notes Halberstam's frequent immersions in the *miqveh* and his endorsement of occasional fasting.[30] Zilberman also "fasted almost all his days. His favorite food was cold potatoes ... and he didn't want to derive pleasure from this world at all."[31] Rumeld writes as follows about Berish's asceticism:

> He constantly fasted. During the day he never tasted anything, only studied and prayed. He ate just one meal a day: at night. His meal was of meager vegetables, for since he repented no animal food entered his mouth, including eggs, milk, and butter. He slept infrequently on the ground, with a stone under his head. In the morning he woke up early and went to the river (in the winter he took with him an ax to split the ice ...), immersed himself in pure waters, came up and dried off and donned his black [mourner's] clothing and recited songs and praises to his Creator. Through all this, his body's build was mighty and solid like the bodies of the Gorales from his village.[32]

Bałaban demurs that this behavior was not in line with the instructions of his teacher; "even when the rebbe ordered him to behave like all other Jews, he didn't want to, and rather regularly 'fasted *hafsaqos*' from one Sabbath to the next and so he behaves until today." Yet even if Zilberman did object to Berish's excessive fasting, there was no problem among Sandzers with the practice of fasting per se. Berish was not entirely idiosyncratic, but rather emulated his Hasidic role models.

The distribution of alms also reflects the Sandzer ethos, for as Mahler emphasizes, Halberstam put great emphasis on charity.[33] Zilberman also "gave all he had to the poor," and wore such modest clothes that he was often mistaken for a

---

28 Jacob Elbaum, *Repentance and Self-Flagellation in the Writings of the Sages of Germany and Poland 1348–1648* [Heb.] (Jerusalem: Magnes, 1992), 13; Gershon David Hundert, *Jews in Poland-Lithuania in the Eighteenth Century: A Genealogy of Modernity* (Berkeley: University of California Press, 2004), 120–121.

29 Brown, "Substitutes for Mysticism," 267.

30 Raphael Mahler, "R' Ḥayyim Halberstam un Zayn Dor," in *Sepher Sandz: The Book on the Jewish Community of Nowy Sącz*, ed. Raphael Mahler (Tel Aviv: The Sandzer Society of New York, 1970), 255–256.

31 *Zikhron Naftali*, 7.

32 Rumeld, "Ba'al Teshuvah," part 3.

33 Mahler, "R' Ḥayyim Halberstam," 257.

poor, undistinguished Jew. Later in life, Berish's main occupation in Krakow was collecting charity for the poor: "On Friday he went around gathering together money for '*pidyon-mashkones*' in order to redeem the collaterals that poor Jews had pawned over the course of the week."[34] His dedication to charity, like that of his rebbes, performed a double function; not only did it help his fellow Jews, it kept him impoverished, which itself was considered a mode of humble piety. Until the end of his life, Berish remained committed to the Sandzer religious modes of perpetual study, asceticism, and charity.

IV.

Berish's whereabouts in the early twentieth century and during World War I remain a mystery, but he eventually married a woman named Ḥanah, daughter of Yeḥiel, from Maidan in western Galicia.[35] They settled in Krakow, and had two daughters. Surprisingly, the earliest literary reference to Berish in Krakow comes from 1924, in a chapter on Krakow in the travelogue of the German modernist writer Alfred Döblin.

> My companion is telling me—I lap up his stories—about a bizarre old man, Berishel, whom you encounter in the streets; he's covered with hair, like a mountain man. He used to be more liberal; now he eats no meat, wears prayer thongs [*tefillin*] and a prayer shawl outdoors, puts stones in his shoes. People are scared of him.[36]

As an assimilated Jew, Döblin came to Poland to observe the uncanny *Ostjuden*, the people to whom he ostensibly belonged.[37] Berish, the hairy old man with his atavistic rituals, is exactly the sort of anthropological object he sought.[38] Yet contrary to Döblin's romantic fetishization of Krakow's Jewish community,

---

34 *Zikhron Naftali*, 17.

35 Bałaban, "Der Rebbe R' Berish Ba'al-Tshuve fun Krakow."

36 Döblin, *Journey to Poland*, 191.

37 The classic treatment of this phenomenon is Steven E. Aschheim, *Brothers and Strangers: The East European Jew in German and German Jewish Consciousness, 1800–1923* (Madison: University of Wisconsin Press, 1982).

38 June J. Hwang, "Not All Who Wander Are Lost: Alfred Döblin's *Reise in Polen* [Journey to Poland, 1925]," in *Spatial Turns: Space, Place, and Mobility in German Literary and Visual Culture*, ed. Jaimey Fisher and Barbara Mennel (Amsterdam and New York: Rodopi, 2010), 255–274.

major religious and political shifts occured in the interwar years.[39] Among the Orthodox, Sarah Schnierer's educational revolution, the *Beis Ya'aqov* schools for Orthodox girls, is simply one example of these changes in traditional Jewish life.[40] Yet there is no indication that Berish took part in these controversies. He seems to have stayed put in Kazimierz, the center of the city's Orthodox and Hasidic population, where he acted out his penitential urges.

Döblin neglects Berish's humanity, but his text shows that, by 1924, Berish was a fixture of Kazimierz who attracted the attention of tourists and locals alike. In their articles, Rumeld and Bałaban sought to satisfy this curiosity:

> When you come, dear reader, to the city of Krakow, and you come to the Jewish suburb of Kazimierz, and you walk on "Jozef Street" and you see, behold, a man emerging from one of the alleys, and his appearance is very strange: long sidelocks and beard, down to his waist, and the color of his hair is light-yellow like a linen mat. In his arm, he carries a package of books: Talmuds, *Shulḥan Arukh*, and in his other hand, a cup of water... . He is adorned in his *tallis* and crowned in *tefillin*, and you ask one of the passersby: Who is this marvelous man? He answers and says to you: This is R. Berish'l *Ba'al Teshuvah*![41]

Berish's life must have been the subject of gossip. The Kazimierz native Sofia Rav Hon, for example, knew that he was "a secular *maskil* before he became a well-known man of Torah."[42] Mordekhai Lahav, who lived near Berish on Miodowa Street, remembered him as "not entirely clearheaded," and usually accompanied by one of his followers.[43] Berish had a complex relationship with these informal *ḥasidim*. Rumeld claims that he rejected the *qvittlakh*, the petitionary notes,

---

39 Rachel Manekin, "Orthodox Jewry in Krakow at the Turn of the Twentieth Century," *Polin* 23 (2011): 165–198.

40 Naomi Seidman, *Sarah Schenirer and the Bais Yaakov Movement: A Revolution in the Name of Tradition* (Oxford: Littman Library of Jewish Civilization, 2019). See also Vladimir Levin, "Denying Tradition: Academic Historiography on Jewish Orthodoxy in Eastern Europe," *Polin* 29 (2017): 255–284.

41 Rumeld, "Ba'al Teshuvah," part 3.

42 Sofia Rav Hon, "Zikhronot me-Qazimezh," in *Ha-Yehudim be-Qraqov: Ḥayeah ve-Ḥurbanah shel Qehilah 'Atiqah*, ed. Shlomo Lazar (Haifa: Va'adat ha-Hantzaḥah shel Yotz'ei Qraqov be-Ḥaifa, 1983), 209.

43 Mordechai Lahav, "Resisei Mare'ot me-Qraqov ha-Yehudit," in *Ha-Yehudim be-Qraqov: Ḥayeah ve-Ḥurbanah shel Qehilah 'Atiqah*, ed. Shlomo Lazar (Haifa: Va'adat ha-Hantzaḥah shel Yotz'ei Qraqov be-Ḥaifa, 1983), 203.

of the disadvantaged people who approached him: "the 'new *zaddiq*' expelled them from before him, declaring: 'Who am I to arouse for you the desire of the Blessed [God]? Behold: I also need compassion, atonement, and forgiveness, I the transgressor, the student who used to desecrate the Sabbath, etc.'"[44] Berish could not embrace a role as a *rebbe*; he still thought of himself as a penitent, as a sinner trying to return to God.

Shortly after the publication of Bałaban's article, Berish died, on July 24, 1931. On August 4 of that year, an advertisement ran in the Yiddish daily *Heint*, "concerning aid for the family of the deceased R. Berish *Ba'al Teshuvah* of blessed memory":

> We have received the following appeal from the committee to help the family of the deceased R. Berish *Ba'al Teshuvah* of blessed memory: The deceased R. Berish *Ba'al Teshuvah* of blessed memory in Krakow, who was strongly esteemed by the entire Jewish population, left behind him a wife and two daughters without any means to live. In order to help the orphaned family, a committee has been formed in Krakow with the Messrs. Hirsh Eisenstadt, M. Abrahams, and Israel Feingold at its head, with the intention to procure the necessary means. Until now they have collected, all together, 1,000 złoty. The collection will continue even further.

Berish's family had lived in poverty even during his life, largely due to his obsessive giving of charity—now it was their turn to receive support. Rav Hon remembered that "although he lacked means, he extended help to those poorer than him—which was not forgotten, for thousands accompanied him on his final way [to burial]." Berish's followers not only collected money for his family, they also financed the elaborate memorial, which I found, over eighty years later, still standing in the New Jewish cemetery on Miodowa Street. Only when I returned to his grave a second time that summer did I noticed a smaller plaque appended to the base of the stone. His wife and daughters had died "for the sanctification of God's name," murdered by the Nazis in 1942.[45]

---

44 Rumeld, "Ba'al Teshuvah," part 3.

45 Meir Vunder, *Me'orei Gaḷiziah: Enẓiklopediyah le-Ḥakhmei Gaḷiziah*, vol. 6 (Jerusalem: Makhon le-Hanẓaḥat Yahadut Gaḷiziah, 2004), 493.

V.

Berish's life continued to capture the Jewish literary imagination after World War II. Writing in New York, Menashe Unger included a chapter on Berish in his *Ḥasidus un Leben*. Published in 1946, the book was meant "to display the great changes, which Hasidism brought about in the day-to-day life of the Jews," that is, to describe Hasidism's social significance.[46] Unger was raised in a Hasidic family but had abandoned Orthodoxy; as Nathaniel Deutsch put it, Unger's approach to Hasidism was "socialist yet sympathetic."[47] The second half of *Ḥasidus un Leben*, in which Berish features, specifically focuses on the "folk-rebbes, who even in the much later times of Hasidism carried in themselves the glow of the Ba'al Shem Tov's Hasidism."[48] Unger claims to have heard about Berish from one of the latter's childhood friend, "an old Jew in Zakopane," but Unger actually adds nothing to—and borrows substantively from—Bałaban's account.[49] Unger's portrayal of Berish as an authentic example of the popular ethos of the Ba'al Shem Tov deemphasized Berish's asceticism. Nevertheless, the characterization of Berish as a "folk-rebbe" faitfully captures his role as a charitable benefactor.

The ultra-Orthodox world also preserved Berish's memory. Two brief Yiddish accounts of his life ran in the Jerusalem-based *ḥaredi* weekly *Yiddishe Likht*, one by M. Lebensohn in 1968, and one by A. Heilman in 1978.[50] The latter is particularly inventive; in Heilman's rendition, R. Berish grew up an orphan, among "Gypsies" on the Steppes. Then, on one fine day,

> the Kaiser Franz Josef, the last king of the Habsburg Dynasty, was visiting the mountains. When the Kaiser comes, there is an alarm, and from around come running the Gypsies to greet him. One greets the Kaiser with a dance. More than anyone, the little Jewish gypsy [Berish] danced. He sang with his pleasant voice beautiful Gypsy songs, and the Kaiser sat dumbfounded. It

46 For more on Unger's literary accounts of Hasidism, see Menashe Unger, *A Fire Burns in Kotsk: A Tale of Hasidism in the Kingdom of Poland*, trans. Jonathan Boyarin (Detroit, MI: Wayne University Press, 2015).

47 Nathaniel Deutsch, *The Maiden of Ludmir: A Jewish Holy Woman and Her World* (Berkeley: University of California Press, 2003), 39.

48 Menashe Unger, *Ḥasidus un Leben* [Yiddish] (New York: M. Unger, 1946), unpaginated introduction.

49 Ibid., 203.

50 M. Lebensohn, "Der Gevezener Pastukh un Student," *Das Yiddishe Likht*, May 31, 1968; A. Heilman, "Der Krakover Ba'al Tshuve," *Das Yiddishe Likht*, November 3, 1978.

> seemed to him that this is what the singing of the Levites in the Temple must have looked like.

In Heilman's account, the Kaiser decided to take Berish to Vienna, where he took the name "Bernard" and earned a doctorate. Bernard then journeyed to the Land of Israel, where he experienced a religious reawakening, which culminated with Yom Kippur in the holy city of Safed. In the synagogue of Isaac Luria, the tune of *Kol Nidrei* roused his soul, and he eventually returned to Europe, to the court of the Belzer *rebbe*. These fabrications entirely remove Berish from his context, and make every aspect of his life simultaneously bizarre and vague. For Heilman, the only message of Berish's life that mattered was that a lost soul can always come back to the fold.

VI.

While others have told the tale of Berish's migrations, he has remained nearly mute. One incident, however, gives him a last word. R. Yonah Furst (1916–1983), who reestablished the Slovakian Nitra yeshiva in the United States following the Holocaust, recounted the following story:

> I have already told that in Krakow there was a famous man who was called R. [B]erishel *Ba'al Teshuvah*, and he was a very great Torah scholar. He behaved as he had discerned for himself according to the *halakhah*; he prayed alone and even read Torah for himself alone. Once they remarked to him that the congregation talks while he reads from the Torah, and he is violating [the prohibition of putting a stumbling block] before a blind person. He answered that "If it is so, according to your logic, then at the hour when God gave the Torah to Israel, God violated [the prohibition of putting a stumbling block] before a blind person, since we see that there are those who don't behave according to the Torah—and it is obvious that it is not the case [that God was 'placing a stumbling block']."[51]

This anecdote partakes equally of sarcasm and Talmudic hermeneutics. Berish decided that he would pray and chant the Torah without a quorum. Someone

51 Yonah Furst, *Divrei Yonah*, vol. 1 (Monsey, NY: Tovia Avigdor Feldman, 2002), 93.

claimed that his practice violated the commandment "do not place a stumbling block before a blind person" (Lev. 19:14), which the rabbis interpret as a prohibition against causing another person to sin. Since Berish did not tell people when he was reading the Torah, he caused them to transgress the rule against speaking during Torah reading. Berish retorted by citing an analogous case: God gave the Torah, and yet Jews fail to follow its commandments. Since God cannot, presumably, be a sinner, God's action did not constitute "placing a stumbling block." This logic implies that the issue turns on the "blindness" of the masses; if they willfully misbehave, their sin is their own problem. Perhaps Berish was stating that his piety must be reckoned with; if others fail to acknowledge him, it is their problem. Yet the humor of his hermeneutic suggests that he knew he could make no demands of others. Berish's repentance, then, reflects an individualistic spirituality that could only exist in a world where traditional observance was no longer the (only) norm.

Bałaban wrote of Berish that the "details of his remarkable past ... show how many transmigrations [*gilgulim*] a person can pass through in their life." In his short life, Berish inhabited many of the social and religious positions—figuratively, the *gilgulim*—available to Jews in Eastern Europe in the late nineteenth century. Yet Berish displayed no internal conflict over his choice between secular life and piety. Most of his life was spent, rather, in an unflinching fight against the sins of his past. One hopes that Berish—the simple shepherd, the brilliant student, and the Sandzer Hasid—found his *tiqqun*, the mending of his being, through his perpetual penitence and acts of charity. He reminds us that understanding an instant of change can take a lifetime, or longer.

CHAPTER 20

Contemporary Israeli Explorations of Spiritual and Psychological Insights in the Tales of Rabbi Naḥman of Bratslav

David C. Jacobson

In an essay published in commemoration of the two hundredth anniversary of the passing of Rabbi Naḥman of Bratslav (1772–1810), the Israeli rabbi, poet, and editor Elhanan Nir writes with wonder about the emergence in recent decades of this Hasidic master as the culture hero of a wide variety of contemporary Israelis. "Rabbi Naḥman, who until recent years was the rabbi of a small group," he notes, "... became in a short time the guide of thousands of people ... [who are] completely different one from the other in all their life circumstances [and] who feel that somehow this ẓaddiq found them and opened them up to an entire world, and if not for him they would never have entered its gates."[1] Nir posits that Israelis are drawn to Naḥman because they sense in him a great capacity for empathy for them on a very personal level as they seek to cope with the psychospiritual issues that have been prevalent among people in the late

1 Elhanan Nir, "Keshe-Yehudi Medabber ʿal ʿAẓmo: Ha-Dimmui ha-ʿAẓmi ve Hashpaʿato al ha-ʿAmidah Nokhaḥ peney Hashem," in *Ḥay be-Emet: Ḥamishah Maʾamarim mi-Beit "Siaḥ Yiẓḥaq" be-Torat R. Naḥman mi-Braẓlav*, ed. Moshe Elyashiv Levin and Uri Lifshitz (Efrat: Yeshivat Siach Yitzhak, 2011), 69. For a detailed study of one of the central manifestations of the widespread popularity of Nahman of Bratslav in Israel, the mass pilgrimages of Israelis to pray at the grave of this Hasidic master in Ukraine, see Moshe Weinstock, *Uman: Ha-Masaʿ ha-Yisraʾeli le-Qivro shel Rabbi Naḥman mi-Braẓlav* (Tel Aviv: Yediʿot Aḥronot, 2011).

twentieth and early twenty-first centuries.[2] "The contemporary feeling among many," writes Nir, "is that only Rabbi Naḥman understands them, with the many upheavals of their souls and their many struggles, that he does not see each of them as just another person of a certain 'type' or from a whole 'society,' but rather as a specific manifestation ... that here is a great man who was in all places, the lofty and the lowly ones alike, 'who could make wondrous awesome teachings out of all that is in the world (*she-hayah yakhol la'asot torot nifla'ot ve-nora'ot mi-kol ha-devarim she-ba'olam* [*Ḥayyei Moharan*]).'"[3] Particularly attractive to people, observes Nir, is their recognition that Naḥman can teach them how within their deepest struggles they can discover the path to overcome them. "He wisely knew," writes Nir, "not to seek the solution but to transform the problem itself into a solution and thereby to solve it."[4]

In a similar vein, Jewish thought scholar Semadar Cherlow has declared that "[t]he drawing power of Rabbi Naḥman [among Israelis] is found ... in [his] 'words of advice' [*'eẓot*] that are needed by twenty-first-century people, whose distress is the distress of the heart and not philosophical confusion."[5] Naḥman's current popularity in Israel, she argues, stems from "the mutual echo between the psychological intuition embedded in his words of advice and psychological insights present in our current cultural landscape, such as those known to us from cognitive psychology as well as from psychological teachings inspired by teachings of [religious traditions of] the Far East."[6] Cherlow cites a number of examples of the striking congruence between Naḥman's teachings and those from other sources that have become popular in our time. By adapting the language of Naḥman's teachings, Cherlow suggests, those associated with Bratslav Hasidism who seek to draw Israelis to Naḥman as a spiritual leader are able to make his psychospiritual insights as accessible to them as currently popular psychospiritual teachings.[7] These currently popular psychospiritual teachings, Cherlow notes, "have the ability to direct [people] to discern the role that

---

2 In this article, I am using the term "psychospiritual" because I find it to be the best term in English to capture the way that Hasidic thought integrates the human dimensions of what is typically referred to as the psychological and the spiritual.

3 Nir, "Keshe-Yehudi Medabber 'al 'Aẓmo," 70.

4 Ibid., 72.

5 Semadar Cherlow, *Mi Heziz et ha-Yahadut Sheli? Yahadut, Postmodernizm ve-Ruḥaniyyut Akhshavit* (Tel Aviv: Resling, 2016), 185.

6 Ibid.

7 Ibid., 186. For a discussion of how Bratslav Hasidim who seek to draw Israelis to Nahman as a spiritual leader have adapted his teachings, see Tomer Persico, "Hitbodedut for a New Age: Adaptation of Practices among the Followers of Rabbi Nachman of Bratslav," *Israel Studies Review* 29, no. 2 (Winter 2014): 99–117.

our thoughts have in creating [our] suffering."[8] In the spirit of this insight, she observes, "Naḥman argues that fears are imaginary, and he declares that they play an important part in the interpretation we grant to events [in our lives]."[9] Cherlow argues that Naḥman's admonition to "cast oneself onto God blessed be He" (*lehashlikh aẓmo 'al ha-shem yitbarakh* [*Siḥot ha-Ran*]), resembles the contemporary psychospiritual advice "to cease sometimes making conscious efforts [to reach goals] or to limit the consciousness of [one's] responsibility."[10] Naḥman's teaching "not to confuse oneself with [thoughts] about what has happened and passed (*she-lo levalbel aẓmo be-mah she-kevar hayah ve-halakh* [*Siḥot ha-Ran*])," she argues, echoes the striving for what currently popular psychospiritual teachings refer to as a state of "'mindfulness,' the practice of which directs one to let go of inner thoughts and the cognitive mode [*ha-bilbulim* in Rabbi Naḥman's language] and simply connect with what is occurring around oneself and within."[11] In addition, she suggests, "the teaching of Rabbi Naḥman to prefer 'simplicity' [*temimut*] over abstract speculation or [his] teaching to have 'a settled mind' [*yishuv ha-da'at*]" correlate with the advocacy of currently popular psychospiritual teaching "to stop excessive activity and enable oneself to be fully present, and [Naḥman's] instruction to free oneself from seeking money or honor and to limit the ego echoes Buddhist approaches and psychospiritual teachings ... which direct one to let go of 'acquisitiveness' and 'desire' and the illusions of the ego and the attempt to control reality."[12] These contemporary psychospiritual teachings and those of Naḥman, Cherlow suggests, "differ significantly from "the modern Western Promethean ethos, which encourages people to challenge reality and to form it according to their will."[13]

Both Nir and Cherlow write of the widespread popularity of Naḥman Nahman primarily from their perspectives as Ashkenazic Religious Zionists who are attempting to explain why Naḥman has become so popular among the younger generation of Religious Zionists.[14] However, given the ways that they talk about Naḥman's appeal as a universal healer of psychospiritual suffering it is clear that

8 Cherlow, *Mi Heziz et ha-Yahadut Sheli*, 185.

9 Ibid.

10 Ibid., 186.

11 Ibid.

12 Ibid.

13 Ibid., 186–187.

14 This interest has been fostered in part by the increasing role of Hasidism in the curricula of Religious Zionist *yeshivot*, including Yeshivat Siach Yitzhak at which Elhanan Nir is a faculty member. See an analysis of this development and the negative reaction to it among some Religious Zionist rabbis in Nicham Ross, "Ha-Mitqafah 'al 'ha-Ḥasidut ha-Ḥadashah' be-Yeshivot ha-Ẓiyyonut ha-Datit," *'Iyyunim be-Tequmat Yisra'el* 7 (2014): 65–107.

they have in mind as well the wide appeal of Naḥman among Jews of other cultural identities, including Mizraḥi, traditionalist, and secular Jews.

In recent decades, during this popular spread of Bratslav Hasidism among many Israelis, a parallel phenomenon has emerged, in which an increasing number of Israeli writers who are not associated with the efforts of Bratslav Hasidism to present Naḥman as the healer of contemporary souls have engaged in the analysis of Bratslav texts from the perspectives of their professional orientations. Included in this trend are academics engaged in the study of Kabbalah, Hasidism, and other humanistic fields, as well as Religious Zionist rabbis and clinical psychologists. During the first two decades of the twenty-first century, a considerable number of books and articles have been published in Israel in which academics, rabbis, and psychologists have applied their conceptual systems and central concerns of their fields to interpretations of tales told by and about Naḥman. The result has been a fascinating dialogue between these writers' contemporary perspectives and those of Bratslav narratives, which yields new insights into these three fields as well as new insights into the meaning and significance of these narratives.[15] In this essay I will explore aspects of this phenomenon evident in essays written by three Israeli writers in which they present new readings of tales composed by Naḥman: Religious Zionist Rabbi Shimon Gershon Rosenberg, known by an acronym of his name, Rav Shagar (1949–2007); Eliezer Malkiel (b. 1957), a professor of philosophy; and Micha Ankori (b. 1938), a Jungian analyst.

Being Drawn to Naḥman

All three of these writers grew up at a time when Naḥman's writings were still a largely marginal phenomenon in Israeli culture. Rav Shagar was the first of them to discover Naḥman; as students of Rav Shagar, Eliezer Malkiel and Micha

---

15 A representative sample of essays by writers belonging to these three professional orientations and other categories of writers can be found in a collection of interpretations of Naḥman's tales by seventeen of these writers, Roee Horen, ed., *Ha-Ḥayyim ke-Ga'agu'a: Qeri'yot Ḥadashot be-Sippurei Ma'asiyyot shel R. Naḥman mi-Brazlav* (Tel Aviv: Yedi'ot Aḥronot, 2010). The active attempts by Bratslav *ḥasidim* to draw members of the Israeli public to a view of Naḥman as a culture hero is a new phenomenon in the history of Bratslav Hasidism. In contrast, the engagement in Bratslav literature by writers who do not identify with Bratslav Hasidism is not a new phenomenon. For over a century, there have been Jewish writers in the Diaspora and in Israel who have explored Bratslav Hasidism as a source on which to draw for the revival of Jewish culture and/or have engaged in the academic study of Bratslav Hasidism, including Hillel Zeitlin, Martin Buber, Joseph Weiss, Mendel Piekarz, Arthur Green, Zvi Mark, and others.

Ankori learned from him the significant ways in which Naḥman's writings can be seen as addressing psychospiritual issues. As a young Religious Zionist adult, Rav Shagar began to see Naḥman as a figure who could teach him how to deal with profound questions of faith with which he struggled in the aftermath of traumatic experiences he had fighting in the Yom Kippur War of 1973. During a battle on the Golan Heights the tank in which he was serving was hit by Syrian gunfire and set on fire, two of his fellow soldiers were killed, and he was badly wounded. Rabbi Yair Dreifuss, his close friend with whom he was the co-founder of Yeshivat Siach Yitzhak in Efrat, writes that Rav Shagar "described his faith in response to the [Yom Kippur] war as a shadow, a place in which God hid His face, and one of questions without answers."[16] Rav Shagar wrote that he was drawn to Naḥman's way of discovering faith from within religious doubt, "drawing his closeness [*devequt*] to God not from the presence of divine providence, but from its absence."[17] In showing Rav Shagar a path to the restoration of his religious faith, Naḥman also taught him how to transcend the despair that accompanied his crisis of faith, in the words of Rav Shagar's student Zohar Maor, "to turn pessimism and doubt into faith and deep joy."[18]

In his youth, Eliezer Malkiel was troubled by the fact that he felt compelled to question the Religious Zionist ideology in which he was being educated. He was concerned that his skepticism would prevent him from affirming clear truths that would serve as the basis for a coherent identity, that his freewheeling intellectual exploration would, in his words, lead him "in the direction of post-modernity, subjectivity, and relativism, in which everything comes apart."[19] As he began to study Bratslav Hasidism with Rav Shagar, Malkiel was relieved to learn that his teacher had found in Naḥman a way to resolve the conflict between skepticism and an identity based on commitment that so troubled Malkiel. In Naḥman's writings, Malkiel learned, "alongside the freedom and creativity and dismantling [and] a readiness to go to new places you find even so a very deep line of dedication and responsibility to something specific."[20] Later, when Malkiel entered the field of the academic study of philosophy he was drawn to the way that Naḥman's teachings and tales could serve as a mode of philosophical inquiry embodied in a form that was different from that of conventional philosophical

16 Yair Dreifuss, *Negi'ot be-Sefat ha-Lev* (Tel Aviv: Yedi'ot Aḥronot, 2013), 162–163.

17 Shimon Gershon Rosenberg (Shagar), *Shi'urim al Liqqutei Moharan*, vol. 2, ed. Netanel Lederberg (Alon Shvut: Makhon Kitvei ha-Rav Shagar, 2015), 469.

18 Zohar Maor, "Neshamot Nifgashot: Ha-Rav Shagar Qor'ei Rabbi Naḥman," *Ma'aseh Ḥoshev* 1 (2016): 236.

19 Interview of Eliezer Malkiel I conducted in Jerusalem in June 2017.

20 Ibid.

discourse, and as he explains, this discovery of the philosophical dimension of this Hasidic master's teaching is "evident every step of the way on my personal path to Rabbi Naḥman."[21] Malkiel was particularly attracted to the way that in his tales Naḥman conveyed his concerns with issues that could resonate with abstract philosophical concepts by means of concrete literary elements in his tales such as plot and characterization that could effectively capture what philosophy tries to contribute to human understanding.[22]

Unlike the Religious Zionists Rav Shagar and Eliezer Malkiel, Micha Ankori grew up as a secular Jew. In the course of his studies in the field of clinical psychology, he discovered in William James's classic work *Varieties of Religious Experience* a model of how religion and psychology could be connected. This discovery prepared him to begin to appreciate the degree to which one can discern the reflection of psychological issues in Kabbalah and Hasidism. With a group of fellow psychologists, he began to study kabbalistic texts with Professor Yoram Jacobson, a leading figure in that field of study at the time, and he also studied Hasidism, including the writings of Naḥman, with Rav Shagar.[23]

As a Jungian analyst Ankori discovered valuable psychological insights in the portrayal in Bratslav literature of "the agitation of Nahman's soul,"[24] which is evident in the many journeys Naḥman took and the mood swings he experienced.[25] In addition, Ankori was drawn to the fact that Naḥman's tales are replete with motifs found in myths and legends, which Jungian psychology considers to be an important source of knowledge about the human psyche. As Ankori explains, "motifs that recur in myths and legends actually represent personal psychic processes that are available for all people at all times. Jung assumed that there is a collective unconscious shared by human beings everywhere, and this dimension of human experience finds its expression in religion, legends, works of art, and dreams."[26] Naḥman's tales, Ankori found, are a treasure trove of such motifs with valuable spiritual and psychological significance for those seeking to understand the inner lives of humanity.

---

21 Eliezer Malkiel, *Masa' el ha-Sod: Be-'Iqvot Masa'o shel Rabbi Naḥman mi-Braẓlav le-Ereẓ Yisra'el* (Tel Aviv: Yedi'ot Aḥronot, 2007), 16.

22 Interview of Eliezer Malkiel I conducted in Jerusalem in June 2017.

23 Interview of Micha Ankori I conducted in his home in Nordia in June 2018.

24 Micha Ankori, *Me-Romei Reqi'im ve-Taḥtiyyot She'ol: Masa' ha-Nefesh shel Rabbi Naḥman mi-Braẓlav* (Moshav Ben-Shemen: Modan, 1994), 9.

25 Ibid., 11–12.

26 Micha Ankori, "Ga'agu'ei Nefesh be-Galutah: 'Al 'Ma'aseh Me'avedat Bat Melekh,'" in *Ha-Ḥayyim ke-Ga'agu'a: Qeri'yot Ḥadashot be-Sippurei Ma'asiyyot shel R. Naḥman mi-Braẓlav*, ed. Roee Horen (Tel Aviv: Yedi'ot Aḥronot, 2010), 108–109.

Pairs of Characters in Naḥman's Tales

The readings by these writers that we will consider are of the following tales, each of which was included in Naḥman's classic collection, *Sefer Sippurei Ma'asiyyot*: "The Tale of the Son of the King and the Son of the Maidservant Who Were Switched," interpreted by Rav Shagar in classes he taught at Yeshivat Siach Yitzhak in 2006;[27] "The Tale of the Wise Man and the Simple Man," interpreted by Eliezer Malkiel in a book he published in 2005 on the concepts of wisdom and simplicity in the writings of Naḥman;[28] and "The Tale of the Loss of the Princess," interpreted by Micha Ankori in a book he wrote on the relationship between Hasidism and analytical psychology published in 1991 and in an essay on the tale he published in 2010.[29] These tales have in common a pair of characters who are initially connected but become separated: baby boys born to a royal family and to a maidservant are switched by the midwife who delivered both of them and are raised according to the social status in which the midwife placed them; a wise man and a simple man grow up together but embark on very different life journeys; and a princess disappears from the royal palace, and the viceroy of the kingdom tries to find her and bring her home. As we will see, these writers devote much attention in their readings to what they perceive to be the relevance of the psychospiritual insights conveyed by Naḥman's tales to the inner struggles of people in the late twentieth and early twenty-first centuries, a characteristic of Naḥman's teachings that, according to Elhanan Nir and Semadar Cherlow, plays a central role in Naḥman's popularity in Israel as a healer of contemporary troubled souls.

Rav Shagar's Reading of "The Tale of the Son of the King and Son of the Maidservant Who Were Switched"

In "The Tale of the Son of the King and the Son of the Maidservant Who Were Switched," although the reader is told that the midwife switched the babies, no one in the kingdom portrayed in the story knows for sure whether she actually

27 Rav Shagar's oral presentation of this at Yeshivat Siach Yitzhak in 2006 was audio recorded, and a written version prepared by one of his students was subsequently posted at the website of the yeshiva. It was also published by the yeshiva under the title "Emunah be-'Olam le-lo Melekh: Hitbonenut be-Ma'aseh be-Ven Melekh u-Ven Shifḥah she-Nitḥalfu,'" in *Ḥay be-Emet: Ḥamishah Ma'amarim mi-Beit "Siaḥ Yiẓḥaq" be-Torat R. Naḥman mi-Braẓlav*, ed. Moshe Elyashiv Levin and Uri Lifshitz (Efrat: Yeshivat Siach Yitzhak, 2011), 11–34.

28 Eliezer Malkiel, *Ḥokhmah u-Temimut: Perush le-Khamah Torot ve-Sippurim shel Rabbi Naḥman mi-Braẓlav* (Tel Aviv: Yedi'ot Aḥronot, 2005).

29 Micha Ankori, *Ha-Lev veha-Ma'ayan: Ḥasidut u-Psikhologyah Analitit* (Tel Aviv: Ramot, 1991), 95–114; idem, "Ga'agu'ei Nefesh be-Galutah," 105–126.

switched them or if this occurrence is just an idle rumor. As a result, the true son of the king who was raised as the son of the maidservant is tortured by his inability to know for sure whether he is the natural born son of a maidservant or a prince robbed of his royal status. In his reading of the tale, Rav Shagar views the struggle of the true son of the king to determine his identity as a paradigm for the challenges facing moderns in discovering and committing themselves to a stable identity that would bring meaning to their lives. The true son of the king is unsure how to respond to the existential reality in which he finds himself. As Rav Shagar writes, "In the situation that was created the [true] son of the king has two options—to decline into depression and sadness in the wake of the extreme injustice that was done to him or to establish his identity as the son of the king precisely out of this reality."[30] Meanwhile, not knowing for sure if he actually is of royal blood, the true son of the maidservant who was raised in the royal family and is destined to become the king feels threatened by the proximity of the true son of the king to him, and so he pressures his potential rival to flee from their country.

In exile the true son of the king descends into a life of debauchery and despair. Rav Shagar reads the persistent identity confusion of the true son of the king as representing the inability of modern people to make an unequivocal commitment to an identity. As Rav Shagar writes, it is only when a person has a sense of a covenant (*berit*) with his life situation that he can arrive at his true identity. A sense of covenant, Rav Shagar explains, is "being at peace with myself, being one with myself."[31] The problem is, Rav Shagar argues, that "in effect one of the points that is most foreign to contemporary modern consciousness is the point of covenant—[like the true son of the king] almost always we are not at peace with ourselves, and we suspect that we are missing 'the real thing,' which is always occurring in another place." [32]

At one point in the tale, however, the true son of the king takes a walk by himself, contemplates his life while, in the words of the narrator of the tale, "being in the state of a settled mind" (*nityashev be-da'ato*), and he feels sorrow and regret for the way of life he has been leading.[33] Rav Shagar understands this description of the self-assessment by the true son of the king as a significant model of how moderns could develop a solid commitment to their life situations that they find so hard to embrace. "The way we conduct ourselves is generally very blind," writes Rav Shagar. "We mostly do not pay attention to what we do and

---

30 Shagar, "Emunah be-'Olam le-lo Melekh," 14.
31 Ibid., 23.
32 Ibid., 24.
33 Ibid., 21.

our thoughts run from one action that we must do to another. Stopping is paying attention to where I am going, where I am located."[34]

The story concludes when the true son of the king, who by then had been reunited with the true son of the maidservant, is crowned as the king of a country seeking to be led by a wise king. He demonstrates his wisdom by reordering elements in a garden that remains from the period when the last wise king ruled. Before entering the garden, he is warned that once he is in the garden it will be impossible for him to stay there because "when a person enters [the garden] he immediately feels that he is being chased and he cries out and he does not know and does not see who is chasing him, and thus they chase him until they force him to leave the garden."[35] Rav Shagar sees this image of the garden as representing the kind of severe psychological disturbance that is often experienced by moderns. "Before us," observes Rav Shagar," appears 'the garden of horrors': each person who enters the garden feels a strong 'dread of being chased' and runs for his life.... This is the situation of the modern world. Everyone has fears and a restlessness that pursue him. Actually, the person is chasing himself. In the modern era humanity loses its center. A person who does not have a direction, does not have an Archimedean point loses himself. The presence of a center in the life of a person is a necessary presence."[36]

When the true son of the king enters the garden, he discovers that he can transcend the terror that was experienced by others by standing next to a picture of the king in the garden, and he tells the officials of the country to put that picture in the center of the garden and from then on all would be able to enter the garden in peace. In this discovery by the true son of the king Rav Shagar sees the solution to fears that plague modern humanity:

> The way to solve the issue of the fear is to stop, to stand. Our fear is not real; we always live with the fear of what will be in the future.... Rabbi Naḥman is teaching that the present is not threatening and the fear exists only in thought, in the imagination of people. When a person lives in reality, in the present, the fear does not exist. The fear is the result of the distance between the person and something else. This distance is not real, and when a person becomes one with his present ... his fear is no longer experienced as threatening.[37]

---

34 Ibid.
35 Ibid., 31.
36 Ibid., 32.
37 Ibid.

Eliezer Malkiel's Reading of "The Tale of the Wise Man and the Simple Man"

In "The Tale of the Wise Man and the Simple Man," the two main characters begin with the same background and grow up together as loving friends. When both their fathers experience a decline in their economic status, which prevents them from being able to support their sons, the characters respond in very different ways. The simple man decides to support himself by becoming a shoemaker, but the wise man resists engaging in such a simple line of work. Instead, he decides to go out into the world and seek a way of earning a living that he might find to be more attractive. From a material point of view the simple man's life is rather limited. He never develops the skill of making shoes adequately, and so he is not able to charge much for them. Although he and his wife live a life of poverty, he is happy in his lot. In contrast, the more ambitious wise man is never satisfied with his life. He tries out various ways of making a living, each time moving on to a different kind of work, which he considers to be preferable. However, he is unable to commit himself to any decision he makes regarding work, because he keeps coming up with ideas about new occupations that would be more advantageous and in which he thinks he will avoid any possibility of failure.

In his interpretation of "The Tale of the Wise Man and the Simple Man," Eliezer Malkiel makes use of what he sees as fundamental differences between the thinking of the late eighteenth- and early nineteenth-century German idealist philosopher G. W. F Hegel and the twentieth-century French existentialist Jean-Paul Sartre.[38] In his analysis, Malkiel draws a contrast between how each of these thinkers views the possibilities and the limits associated with the formation of a person's identity. As Malkiel understands it, Hegel advocated striving for a balance between the objective circumstances of a person's life and the subjective aspirations he has. Both, he argued, can be used collaboratively by people in the formation of their identity. According to Hegel, Malkiel explains, the formation of identity involves sorting the definitions by others of my identity and deciding "which ones I am ready to adopt ... and which ones I reject."[39] It is by means of this process, according to Hegel, that a person arrives at what for him is an authentic identity about which he can declare, "Here I stand and

38 Malkiel makes the point that in his use of Hegel's thought he is taking a selective approach that does not take into account the full range of the philosopher's understanding of the nature of humanity: "I must emphasize, however, that my use of Hegel is selective and limited: he himself went far in his conception of humanity in different and some say strange directions that depart significantly from what I am suggesting here or wish to adopt." Malkiel, *Ḥokhmah u-Temimut*, 103.

39 Ibid., 105.

here I want to stand, this is the definition that expresses me, this is my purpose on this earth."[40]

Malkiel contrasts Hegel's understanding of how one can create an authentic identity with that of Sartre's. According to Sartre, argues Malkiel, the process of identity formation never allows for a satisfactory synthesis between the objective circumstances of a person's life and the subjective aspirations he has. The relationship between the two is always contradictory and unstable and can never be resolved. This is because there is no aspect of the objective circumstances of a person's life or the external definitions of who he is that cannot be completely undermined by his subjective desire to reject it and seek alternative forms of identity.[41]

Malkiel associates the portrait of humanity presented by Hegel with the character of the simple man in Naḥman's tale and the portrait of humanity presented by Sartre with the character of the wise man. Malkiel has a clear preference for the character of the simple man and suggests that this preference is shared by Naḥman. As Malkiel writes, the simple man lives a life in which he "cannot do anything in a complete manner, and despite this he is happy… . His completeness is within himself, in his full identification with what he does and who he is."[42] In effect, "he lives at peace with himself, with a feeling of satisfaction and fulfillment."[43] In keeping with the process of identity formation portrayed by Sartre, every element of the wise man's identity is always open to question; there is no element in his objective reality to which he is willing to make a commitment. Initially he approaches the world with self-confidence, and due to his abilities he succeeds.[44] However, his calculated approach to life is such that he is plagued by anxiety and alienation: "The wise man plans, studies matters from a wide range of perspectives, takes into account all possibilities, defends himself from all dangers … [and he sees the world as] material that he can form and maneuver in accordance with his skills and determination."[45] The price he pays for the wisdom he so exercises in which he is always considering alternatives, observes Malkiel, is "concern, worry, imagining the worst."[46] Malkiel points out how destructive to the wise man is the negativity with which he views the world: "The wise man, who lacks inner peace and is weak, wanders between perspectives and always finds the vulnerable spot; the point of view he adopts is always

---

40 Ibid., 106.
41 Ibid., 113.
42 Ibid., 30, 32.
43 Ibid., 37–38.
44 Ibid., 153.
45 Ibid., 152–153.
46 Ibid., 28.

that which negates and invalidates; he dismisses every accomplishment and is always filled with suffering."[47] Furthermore, "his constant refraining from trusting ... reflects life in an impersonal world; and even if this world is not hostile ... it is also not inviting, loving, and embracing; and it joins the position of the constant refraining, criticism, and suffering of the wise man who is not connected and does not identify with anything for even a moment."[48]

In the end, writes Malkiel, this alienated experience of the world destroys the wise man from within:

> Nothing penetrates the opaque screen that divides the wise man from the world and the wise man from himself.... Nothing pierces, excites, or moves in the reality of the life of the wise man.... When the world hides its inviting face from a person the personality collapses from a lack of caring or contact.... The response to a gray and meaningless world is apathy and boredom or frantic nervousness and generally the constant transition from one to the other.[49]

Micha Ankori's Reading of "The Tale of the Loss of the Princess"

In his second introduction to *Sefer Sippurei Ma'asiyyot,* Naḥman's disciple Nathan of Nemirov presents an interpretation of "The Tale of the Loss of the Princess" in which he explains that the attempt by the viceroy to restore the lost princess to her father the king refers to the kabbalistic image of the need to rescue the *shekhinah* from its exile from the primordial unity of God in order to bring about cosmic redemption. Ankori argues that when in this introduction Nathan understands the tale to be teaching that "every Jew must engage in this restoration [*tiqqun*] to raise the *shekhinah* from its exile ... searching for and seeking [*leḥappes u-levaqqesh*] the princess to restore her to her father," he is signaling that in telling this story Naḥman was not focusing on cosmic redemption, but rather on the efforts of each person to bring about the restoration (*tiqqun*) of his individual soul.[50]

This psychological process can be understood, writes Ankori, to be related to the Jungian concept of, "individuation, a process that characterizes the second half of life the main purpose of which is to include the various and contradictory

---

47 Ibid., 36.
48 Ibid., 154.
49 Ibid., 155.
50 Ankori, "Ga'agu'ei Nefesh be-Galutah," 106.

elements in the psyche to a complex and fruitful harmony."[51] Writing about individuation from a male point of view, Jung describes one of the central challenges of individuation as the striving of the male psyche to connect the masculine principle (the animus) to the feminine principle (the anima), a process that Ankori characterizes as providing "the gateway to the unconscious."[52] The journey of the viceroy to rescue the lost princess, Ankori writes, represents "the journey of the ego in search of a renewed connection with the feminine principle in its various aspects."[53] Ankori observes that in human psychology the disconnection of the male ego from the feminine principle leads to "a personality characterized by dryness, loneliness, and a feeling of emptiness."[54] He also writes that "the feminine principle... has a central role in the male psyche. When this principle is repressed there is a break in the personality. Such a situation is characteristic of men with ... inflexible and achievement-oriented personalities who are estranged from their emotional lives, held captive by ambition and aggression."[55]

In the course of the story, the viceroy finds the lost princess, who tells him that in order to rescue her from a palace in which she is being held captive, he must spend a year longing for her, and on the last day of the year he must fast and not sleep. On that last day, he finds a tree with appealing apples and he eats from one of the apples and falls asleep, breaking the conditions put forth by the princess and thereby preventing himself from being able to rescue her. The princess then tells him that in the coming year he must wait for her in longing and on the last day not drink wine and not sleep. However, on the last day of that year, he finds a spring flowing with wine and he drinks some of the wine and falls asleep, again preventing himself from being able to rescue the princess. In each instance of failure, after he awakens from his sleep the viceroy cries out to his servant, "Where am I in the world?" Ankori understands this to be the cry of a man who cannot find in his psyche the proper balance between the masculine and feminine principles.[56]

Ankori understands the tests of self-denial that the princess gives to the viceroy as representing truths embodied in Jungian psychological theory. "The ego is the center of conscious cognition, which includes knowledge, will, and choice, but there is a deeper level, which Jung called 'the Self.' ... 'The Self' represents

---

51 Ibid., 108.
52 Ibid., 109.
53 Ibid., 110.
54 Ibid.
55 Ankori, *Ha-Lev veha-Ma'ayan*, 99.
56 Ankori, "Ga'gu'ei Nefesh be-Galutah," 113.

the entirety of the psyche at all of its levels—conscious and unconscious."[57] The requirement of the viceroy to deny himself physical pleasures, according to Ankori, represents the need to engage in a

> sacrifice in a psychological sense, [that is] the self-denial by the ego for the sake of the deeper and more sublime dimension of the personality, the Self. The interests of the ego limit themselves for purposes that are more important than the satisfaction of the pleasure principle, and this self-denial is a necessary condition for the development of the ego. In the case [of the tale] this involves self-restraint, deferral of basic drives—a self-denial whose purpose is the return and inclusion of the feminine principle that was lost.[58]

The fact that the viceroy experiences delays in achieving this process is also, according to Ankori, true to human experience. While in life we experience disappointments that cause us suffering over lost opportunities, writes Ankori, "the yearning and the longing [to reach our goal] are revealed to us as of deeper value than the accomplishment itself, for the process of psychic development is nurtured by yearnings and longings more than by the fulfillment of desires.[59]

Conclusion

In comparing these three readings of Naḥman's tales, one is struck by the degree to which these writers, the Religious Zionist rabbi, Rav Shagar, the professor of philosophy, Eliezer Malkiel, and the Jungian analyst, Micha Ankori, discern in the tales contemporary patterns of psychospiritual suffering and insights about how to bring healing to the soul in our time. As Semadar Cherlow observed, Naḥman's popularity has stemmed from the reformulation of his teachings in a language that appeals to contemporary Israelis searching for psychospiritual insights that will serve as viable alternatives to elements of modern Western culture, which they see as responsible for the suffering of their souls. Similarly, in

---

57 Ibid., 110–111.

58 Ibid., 111.

59 Ankori, *Ha-Lev veha-Ma'ayan*, 114. Yearning is a human emotion, which plays a central role in the teachings and tales of Naḥman, as recognized by the title of Roee Horen's collection of contemporary Israeli readings of Naḥman's tales, *Ha-Ḥayyim ke-Ga'agu'a*.

the context of their professional identities, the writers whose interpretations of Naḥman's tales we have been considering discern in these tales insights about how one can transcend the psychospiritual wounding brought to Israelis under the influence of modern Western culture.

In a sense, when the viceroy in "The Tale of the Loss of the Princes," cries out, "Where am I in the world?" (*heikhan ani ba-'olam*?), he captures the existential disorientation of modern humanity represented by all three heroes of these tales. Rav Shagar describes this phenomenon as people not paying attention to what they do and filled with thoughts that run from one action that one feels compelled to do to another. These thoughts include suspecting that one keeps missing what is really important in life, as well as living in fear of what will be in the future. Similarly, Eliezer Malkiel identifies this existential disorientation as stemming from a tendency to continuously invalidate all life decisions as fatally flawed. In the spirit of Jungian psychology, according to Micha Ankori the challenge facing moderns is the lack of integration between the male and female principles in their psyches, which results in the emergence of what he refers to as "inflexible and achievement-oriented personalities who are estranged from their emotional lives, held captive by ambition and aggression."

The world that is experienced by the main characters in these tales is perceived by them and their modern counterparts as bleak, hopeless, and terrifying. In the words of Rav Shagar, this is a world in which "everyone has fears and a restlessness that pursue him." Malkiel portrays this experience of the world as "not inviting, loving, or embracing," as well as "gray and meaningless," producing within the souls of moderns "apathy and boredom or frantic nervousness." Ankori writes of "dryness, loneliness, and a feeling of emptiness."

In their analyses of how the Naḥman tales can be seen as portraying inner conflicts of people in contemporary times, these writers convey what they see as the way to form a stable identity that will bring peace to troubled souls. According to Rav Shagar, one needs to learn how to live in the present and discover that "the present is not threatening and fear exists only in thought, in the imagination of people." One may transcend the influence of this fear, Rav Shagar suggests, by engaging in a self-examination of where one is located in life and in what direction one is going. From this self-examination a person can develop an identity grounded in a "covenant" with one's situation, which will lead to being at peace with oneself.

Eliezer Malkiel presents the simple man as the model of how to arrive at an identity characterized by the certainty of knowing who one is: "His completeness is within himself, in his full identification with what he does and who he is." Furthermore, the simple man can arrive at a clear understanding of the nature of his identity and commit himself to it, a defined identity in which he can declare, "Here I stand and here I want to stand, this is the definition that expresses me, this is my purpose on this earth."

Micha Ankori sees the key to the healing of the soul to be the development of an identity based on the integration of contradictory elements, in particular the male and female principles, in one's soul. As Ankori states, the tale's references to the ongoing failures of the viceroy to effect that integration of the masculine and the feminine make clear that this integration is not easily achieved. Nevertheless, Ankori discerns in the story some degree of relief in the longing to accomplish that unity: "the yearning and the longing [to reach our goal] are revealed to us as of deeper value than the accomplishment itself, for the process of psychic development is nurtured by yearnings and longings more than by fulfilling desires."

In their readings of these tales, Rav Shagar, Eliezer Malkiel, and Micha Ankori have discovered a path to healing contemporary psychospiritual wounds that remarkably resembles the promise of healing by Naḥman that has transformed him into a popular culture hero in our time. This Hasidic master, who suffered from a marginalized existence in his life, has emerged in twenty-first-century Israel to provide insights on the psychospiritual crises of our time in the medium of popularized spirituality as well as in the more sophisticated language of rabbinic teachings, philosophy, and psychology.

CHAPTER 21

A Mystical Reunion in Manitoba: Howard Thurman and Zalman Schachter-Shalomi

Or N. Rose

Rabbi Zalman Schachter-Shalomi (1924–2014) was one of the most innovative and influential Jewish religious figures of the last several decades.[1] He is widely regarded as a learned and creative interpreter of Hasidism and Kabbalah, and a visionary spiritual leader. Not only did he found the Jewish Renewal Movement and mentor key figures in the (sibling) Havurah Movement,[2] but he also enriched contemporary Jewish life more broadly with a variety of creative (sometimes provocative) ideas and practices. Among Schachter-Shalomi's lasting contributions was his pioneering work as an interreligious practitioner. By the time of his death at the age of eighty-nine, he was considered a wise and erudite Jewish voice in international circles, participating in public and private gatherings with renowned figures such as His Holiness the Fourteenth Dalai Lama, Archbishop Desmond Tutu, and Father Thomas Keating.[3] Long before he grew into the role

---

1 See the extensive list of obituaries and memorials on the Yesod Foundation website, including pieces in *The New York Times*; *Huffington Post*; *Forward*; and *Jewish Telegraphic Agency*, http://www.yesodrzlp.org/blog-adirondack-2/2015/6/12/k78wh3obook2741ic6ueu10zadumg7.

2 See Shaul Magid, "Jewish Renewal Movement," *Encyclopedia of Religion*, 2nd ed. (Farmington Hills, MI: Thomson Gale, 2005), 7, cols. 4868–4874. See also idem, "Jewish Renewal: Toward a New American Judaism," *Tikkun* 21, no. 1 (January/February 2006): 57–60. On Ḥavurat Shalom, see Arthur Green, "Renewal and Havurah: American Movements, European Roots," in *Jewish Renaissance and Revival in America: Essays in Honor of Leah Levitz Fishbane*, ed. Eitan P. Fishbane and Jonathan D. Sarna (Waltham, MA: Brandeis University Press, 2011), 145–164.

3 See the collection of texts on Schachter-Shalomi's interreligious exploits in Zalman Schachter-Shalomi, *Rabbi Zalman Schachter-Shalomi: Essential Teachings*, ed. and intro. Or N. Rose and Netanel Miles-Yépez (Maryknoll, NY: Orbis Books, 2020), 176–203.

of Jewish sage and spiritual elder, however, Schachter-Shalomi began an idiosyncratic journey that took him from the world of Chabad-Lubavitch Hasidism[4] into dialogue with an array of practitioners from the world's religions.

One early influence along this winding trail was the distinguished African American teacher, preacher, and writer Reverend Howard Thurman (1899–1981). Schachter-Shalomi first met Thurman in 1955, when the young rabbi enrolled in a graduate program in the Psychology of Religion at Boston University (BU), where Thurman served as Dean of Marsh Chapel and Professor of Spiritual Disciplines and Resources in the School of Theology. It was this towering Baptist minister and his BU colleagues who provided Schachter-Shalomi with his first formal introduction to the modern study of religion, as well as to Christianity and other world religions (including several mystical works that were important to the young rabbi). More importantly, Thurman served as an important intellectual and spiritual model for the young rabbi and was among the first heterodox—non-Jewish or Jewish—religious leaders[5] with whom Schachter-Shalomi could identify personally and professionally, especially as someone who would serve as both a professor and Hillel professional (and part-time pulpit rabbi) in the immediate years after his time at BU. As Schachter-Shalomi remarked later in life, Thurman was a master of "applied religion,"[6] with an unusual breadth of talents and skills.

Like Schachter-Shalomi, Thurman was a self-described mystic[7] who placed great emphasis on personal religious experience. As such, he taught and wrote extensively on the use of prayer, meditation, and other spiritual disciplines in cultivating an awareness of God's loving presence in one's life.[8] The young rabbi was deeply moved to meet a learned, charismatic, and attentive teacher whose religious priorities were strikingly similar to those he valued and had cultivated through his Hasidic training. Schachter-Shalomi was especially impressed with

---

4 On Schachter-Shalomi's formative years in the Chabad-Lubavitch community, see Zalman Schachter-Shalomi, *My Life in Jewish Renewal: A Memoir*, with Edward Hoffman (New York: Rowman & Littlefield, 2012), 53–62.

5 See Gary Dorrien, "Howard Thurman," in his *The Making of American Liberal Theology; Idealism, Realism, and Modernity 1900–1950*, vol. 2 (Louisville, KY: Westminster John Knox Press, 2003), 359–365; and Luther E. Smith, *Howard Thurman: The Mystic as Prophet* (Washington, DC: University Press of America, 1981).

6 See Zalman Schachter-Shalomi, *Davenning: A Guide to Meaningful Jewish Prayer* (Woodstock, VT: Jewish Lights, 2012), 89.

7 See, for example, Howard Thurman, *Mysticism and the Experience of Love* (Wallingford, PA: Pendle Hill, 1961). See also Gary Dorrien, "True Religion, Mystical Unity, and the Disinherited: Howard Thurman and the Black Social Gospel," *American Journal of Theology and Philosophy* 39, no. 1 (January 2018): 74–99.

8 Howard Thurman, *Disciplines of the Spirit* (New York: Harper & Row, 1963).

Thurman's creative pedagogy, including his "labs" in which he made extensive use of music, poetry, and movement to help students open themselves to the types of religious experiences they were reading about in sacred texts and scholarly studies.[9] And like countless others, the rabbi was taken with Thurman's prowess as a preacher and ritual leader. It is no wonder that Schachter-Shalomi lovingly referred to Thurman as his "Black Rebbe."[10]

It is important to add that the relationship between these two men would not have blossomed had Dean Thurman not gone out of his way to welcome Schachter-Shalomi to the BU community and assure him that he had no interest in converting the rabbi.[11] As Schachter-Shalomi stated in an interview conducted in 2012: Thurman "wasn't interested in getting souls to Christ; like Jesus, he was interested in getting souls to God."[12] It was deeply moving for this emerging Orthodox rabbi and refugee from Nazi-occupied Europe to encounter such a passionate and talented Christian leader who regarded Judaism as an honorable and enduring tradition, and not primarily as a precursor to and/or outmoded version of Christianity. Finally, while neither man spoke at any length about issues of race or ethnicity in their relationship, I would imagine that they felt a certain kinship as members of two minority groups that had experienced significant oppression, including their own personal pain and loss.

This essay is dedicated to an exploration of an unpublished sermon Howard Thurman delivered at Marsh Chapel in July 1963 in which he describes in vivid detail a recent visit (February 1963) to Winnipeg for a lecture series. In this illuminating text, Thurman writes at length about his interactions with

---

9 Zalman Schachter-Shalomi, *My Life in Jewish Renewal*, 91.

10 See my 2004 interview with Schachter-Shalomi, "On the Growing Edge of Judaism: Reb Zalman at Eighty," in *Tikkun Reader: Twentieth Anniversary*, ed. Michael Lerner (New York: Rowan & Littlefield, 2007). Interestingly, the one other non-Jewish mentor that Schachter-Shalomi refers to in his memoir as a "rebbe" was the British-American polymath, Gerald Heard (d. 1971). See Schachter-Shalomi, *My Life in Jewish Renewal*, "Appendix A: Gerald Heard: My Irish *Rebbe*," 189–191.

11 On their first encounters at BU, see Zalman Schachter-Shalomi, "What I Found in the Chapel," in *My Neighbor's Faith: Stories of Interreligious Encounter, Growth, and Transformation*, ed. Jennifer Howe Peace, Or N. Rose, and Gregory Mobley (Maryknoll, NY: Orbis Books, 2012), 208. See also my analysis of these initial meetings in my essay "Howard Thurman's Mentorship of Zalman Schachter-Shalomi," in *Interreligious Studies: Dispatches from an Emerging Field*, ed. Hans Gustafson (Waco, TX: Baylor University Press, 2020), 228–235.

12 Unpublished interview with Zalman Schachter-Shalomi conducted by Peter Eisenstadt, June 28, 2012. My thanks to Dr. Eisenstadt for sharing his notes with me. Thurman famously spoke of Jesus as a Jewish holy man—and not God—who suffered mightily under the oppressive rule of the Roman Empire. As such, the ancient Galilean sage was an invaluable model for contemporary African Americans (and all others) seeking freedom and justice. See Howard Thurman, *Jesus and the Disinherited* (Nashville, TN: Abington Press, 1949).

Schachter-Shalomi.[13] At the time, the rabbi was serving as a professor in the department of Near Eastern and Judaic Studies and as director of B'nai Brith Hillel at the University of Manitoba. In fact, he helped bring his beloved mentor to the Canadian prairies through an academic travel grant from the Canadian government. This little-known document sheds light on the spiritual bond between these two outstanding American religious figures, on Thurman's mature understanding of the nature of religious experience, and on Schachter-Shalomi's budding ecumenical sensibilities. In exploring this sermon and other related sources, I am particularly interested in the ways in which it captures Schachter-Shalomi's movement from what he would later call his "restorationist" stance to one of "renewal."[14] This involved a gradual, sometimes jagged move away from his early professional efforts to faithfully transplant Eastern European Hasidism to North America, to crafting a vision of Jewish life that included robust engagement with non-Jewish religious and cultural traditions. As we will see, this also involved deliberate efforts to creatively apply ideas and practices from Hasidism to the interreligious realm, including his understanding of Thurman as a powerful spiritual guide or unlikely *rebbe* figure.

Setting the Scene: Brief Biographical Notes

When Schachter-Shalomi[15] first met Thurman in the fall of 1955, the veteran clergyman had already completed several chapters of his distinguished career. This included academic and ministerial roles at Morehouse and Spellman Colleges and Howard University. In 1935, Thurman and his wife, Sue Bailey Thurman, led a small delegation of African American Christian leaders to Ceylon, Burma and India to meet with Mahatma Gandhi (d. 1948) and other social activists and religious leaders. Upon his return to the United States, he helped introduce Ghandian non-violent resistance (*Satyagraha*) doctrine into the Civil Rights movement, inspiring many other colleagues, students, and admirers to follow suit, including the Reverend Dr. Martin Luther King, Jr.[16]

13 A version of this text can be found in *The Papers of Howard Washington Thurman*, vol. 5: *The Wider Ministry, January 1963–April 1981*, ed. Walter Fluker et al. (Columbia, SC: University of South Carolina Press, 2019), 14–18.

14 Schachter-Shalomi, *My Life in Jewish* Renewal, 104.

15 He was known at the time as Zalman Schachter. He added the name Shalomi ("of Peace") a decade later to balance his original family name—Schachter, "ritual slaughter" in Yiddish—and as a prayer for peace between Jews and Arabs.

16 See Luther E. Smith, "Introduction," Howard Thurman, *Howard Thurman: Essential Writings*, ed. and intro. Luther E. Smith (Maryknoll, NY: Orbis Books, 2006), 20–21. See also Quinton Dixie and Peter Eisenstadt, *Visions of a Better World: Howard Thurman's Pilgrimage to India and the*

This work led Thurman to write (among many other works) the influential book *Jesus and the Disinherited* (1949), widely considered a foundational theological text in the Movement. Thurman also served as co-pastor, with a white Presbyterian minister, of the Church for the Fellowship of All Peoples in San Francisco (1944–1953). This iconoclastic institution was one of the earliest racially integrated, intercultural churches in the United States. In moving to Boston in 1963, Thurman stated that this position offered him one final professional opportunity (he was fifty-two at the time) to spread the "contagion" of the Fellowship Church vision to a much larger audience of students, faculty, and laity.[17] He was, in fact, the first African American clergyperson to serve as dean of the chapel at a majority white university (and tenured faculty person at BU), where he reached large numbers of people both in Boston and throughout the country.[18] Thurman remained at BU until his retirement in 1965.[19]

Schachter-Shalomi arrived on the BU campus roughly ten years after beginning his career as a Chabad rabbi. He began his work in New Haven, Connecticut in 1946 (one year before his ordination), where he was dispatched by the sixth Lubavitcher rebbe, Rabbi Yosef Yitzchak Scheersohn (d. 1950), to help establish a Jewish educational program for youth in New Haven, Connecticut. In 1949, he and Rabbi Shlomo Carlebach became the first Chabad emissaries (*shlikhim*) to visit college and university campuses.[20] These educational forays were part of a broader coordinated effort by the Lubavitch leadership to reinvigorate traditional Jewish life in the aftermath of the Holocaust, an effort that was shot through with messianic yearning.[21] While Schachter-Shalomi

---

Origins of African American Nonviolence (Boston, MA: Beacon Press, 2011). Eisenstadt's more recent study, *Against the Hounds of Hell: A Life of Howard Thurman* (Charlottesville, VA: University of Virginia Press, 2021) is the most thorough biographical study of Thurman to date.

17 See Howard Thurman, "Letter to the Board of Trustees of Fellowship Church, 31 January 1953," in *The Papers of Howard Washington Thurman*, vol. 4: *June 1949–December 1962*, ed. Walter Fluker et al. (Columbia, SC: University of South Carolina, 2017), 55.

18 See Thurman, *With Head and Heart: The Autobiography of Howard Thurman* (New York: Harcourt Brace & Company, 1979), 168–169. By all accounts, Thurman transformed the moribund chapel into a lively hub for the BU community, Bostonians, and visitors from elsewhere. Additionally, his services were broadcast on local radio and television. He also wrote several books and spoke throughout the country during his time at the university.

19 Unfortunately, Thurman's tenure at BU ended with considerable disappointment, as he experienced increasing tension with university administrators and trustees about his vision for Marsh Chapel and its relationship to the greater Boston community. See Eisenstadt, *Against the Hounds of Hell*, "Chapter 12: Disciplines and Resources: At Boston University," 274–307.

20 See Schachter-Shalomi, *My Life in Jewish Renewal*, 65–70, 76–77, and Natan Ophir (Offenbacher), "Launching an Outreach Career," in his *Rabbi Shlomo Carlebach: Life, Mission, and Legacy* (Jerusalem: Urim, 2014), 60–76.

21 Schachter-Shalomi, *My Life in Jewish Renewal*, 65.

continued to identify as a Chabad Hasid for almost two decades,[22] his intellectual and spiritual curiosity led him to an intensive exploration of other religious and cultural traditions. This included eye-opening encounters with non-Jewish colleagues in New Haven, as well as a surprising ritual experience with Voodoo practitioners outside of Port-au-Prince, Haiti where he worked one summer as a Chabad representative.[23] Schachter-Shalomi entered the program at BU with the express permission of the seventh Lubavitcher rebbe, Rabbi Menachem Mendel Schneerson (son-in-law and distant cousin of his predecessor, d. 1994). At the time, Schachter-Shalomi was serving a small pulpit in New Bedford, Massachusetts. Part of his motivation for pursuing an MA was his desire to transition from congregational work to becoming a Hillel professional, for which he needed a graduate degree, since his rabbinic ordination was not from an accredited academic institution.[24]

"The Wider Ministry": Thurman's Trip to Winnipeg

In 1962 Howard Thurman gave up his role as Dean of Marsh Chapel, allowing him more freedom to speak and teach throughout North America and beyond.[25] It was in this context that he traveled to Winnipeg (after a visit with indigenous leaders in the province of Saskatchewan), where he gave several lectures and spent time with his former student. Thurman's arrival also coincided with the bar mitzvah celebration of one of the Schachter-Shalomi's children. While Thurman's public commitments did not allow him to attend the actual Sabbath morning service, he spent much of the preceding Thursday with the rabbi and his family. In Thurman's reflection on his time with Schachter-Shalomi, he describes a series of unusual devotional experiences that unfolded over the course of the day. Together, these anecdotes (and supporting documents) offer the reader a vivid and intimate portrayal of the reunion of these modern mystics.

---

22 He marked 1966 as the breaking point, as this was the year that Schachter-Shalomi spoke publicly about his experimentation with psychedelic drugs, and a Lubavitch spokesperson responded by stating that Schachter-Shalomi's rabbinic credentials were "questionable" in a newspaper article about the presentation. See Schachter-Shalomi, *My Life in Jewish Renewal,* 175–176.

23 Ibid., 83–84.

24 Ibid., 88–89.

25 See *The Papers of Howard Washington Thurman*, vol. 5: *The Wider Ministry, January 1963–April 1981*, ed. Walter Fluker et al. (Columbia, SC: University of South Carolina Press, 2019), 14–16. See also Eisenstadt, *Against the Hounds of Hell*, 303.

The first noteworthy occurrence Thurman describes—which serves as a preview of the rest of the day—took place soon after Schachter-Shalomi picked him up from his hotel:

> So, on Thursday he came to get me. I got in his automobile, one of those wonderfully sensitive automobiles that you have to know which thing to pull to get which response. And there is a bell hanging down from the top of it and every time the car moved, the bell would ring. And I said, what is this? And he said, "I'm going to give you one of those bells. I have it there because, every time the bell rings I am reminded that I am not as good as I ought to be."[26]

Clearly Thurman was intrigued by both the automotive technology and Schachter-Shalomi's idiosyncratic driving ritual. Characteristic of the rabbi, he was attempting to creatively fulfill the Hasidic imperative to remain *nokhaḥ penei ha-Shem*, truly in the presence of God (Lam. 2:19) as often as possible—even while navigating daily traffic![27] There are countless teachings in Hasidic literature about the need to remain connected to the divine even in the midst of mundane activities. If the Ba'al Shem Tov (d. 1760) sought to do so while riding on a horse-drawn carriage in Miedzybozh (located in modern Ukraine), then why not try to do so in a stick-shift car in Winnipeg?!

---

26 Howard Thurman, "The Wider Ministry and the Concept of Community" (unpublished sermon, July 28, 1963), 7–8. My thanks to Walker Fluker and Peter Eisenstaedt of the Howard Thurman Papers Project at Boston University for sharing a copy of this fascinating document with me.

27 In a revealing letter (June 6, 1964) to his Trappist friend Thomas Merton, Schachter-Shalomi further elaborates on his vehicular spiritual practices. He does so as a way of sharing with the monk his difficulty discerning what God desires of him in the midst of a hectic life as a professor and rabbi: "It is so difficult to think about G-d, always being His errand boy, then I say to myself: 'I didn't ask for the errand. It was sent to me. Maybe He wants my errands more than my meditations.' Even the time I used to have for intercession, while driving to and from campus, which is thirteen miles out of town, on my windshield visor there being a long list of people and I would glance up from time to time, and wherever I would feel for a moment arrested, I would take that name and offer a few rounds of favorite psalms or something from them, as well as make up my mind to offer charity on their behalf; but even this has been taken away from me. This little letter that I am dictating, is being done while I drive. So, I will pray for you and please pray for me, and we will keep in mind, won't we, that whatever curve we get pitched, we will try to bat. And after all, what is the business of the cross all about if not that." See Zalman Schachter-Shalomi, *My Life in Jewish Renewal*, 158. See also Edward Kaplan, "Personal Bridges, Spiritual Communities: The Correspondences of Thomas Merton and Zalman Schachter-Shalomi," *The Merton Annual: Studies in Culture, Spirituality, and Social Concerns* 26 (2013): 74–83.

Knowing that Thurman had a keen interest in the design of sacred spaces and religious pageantry more broadly,[28] Schachter-Shalomi proudly took his teacher to the Jewish chapel on campus:

> Then he took me over to the Hillel place and he wanted me to see the chapel; everything in the chapel except the pews had been done, created, made by the students or their families. All of the work in the room, even the curtains before the ark, was embroidered by one of the senior girls, and so forth and so on.[29]

This was a fitting first stop given the fact that the two men first met at BU's Marsh Chapel seven years earlier, when Thurman graciously arranged for a suitable worship space for his new Jewish student (including temporarily removing a large brass cross from the front of the room).[30] Seeing how Schachter-Shalomi engaged the students in a hands-on way in developing the chapel clearly impressed and gratified Thurman. Ever since his days at BU, the rabbi had been honing his "do-it-yourself" approach to Jewish religious life on campus and in other informal educational contexts. In so doing, he adapted various practices from Thurman, Catholic colleagues, and other contemporary cultural sources. Over time, Schachter-Shalomi's eclectic experiential methods would inspire a generation (or more) of younger Jewish seekers;[31] most of whom had no idea who Howard Thurman was or his influence on Schachter-Shalomi.[32]

---

28 For example, here is a description of the physical home he dreamed of creating for the Fellowship Church community in San Francisco: "My dream was to build a structure consisting of a sanctuary, a studio theater equipped both for electronic audiovisual presentations and for dramas, a dining room, parlors, and classrooms—and an inner court. This setting would contribute to a year-round program, integrating religion, art, and various cultures. The centerpiece of the building would be the sanctuary, and in it would be graphic designs in stone and wood, depicting the natural evolution of man's worship of God." See Howard Thurman, *With Head and Heart*, 165.

29 Ibid.

30 See Schachter-Shalomi, "What I Found in the Chapel," 208.

31 Among the many young Jewish seekers Schachter-Shalomi mentored were Richard Siegel, Michael Strassfeld, and Sharon Strassfeld, editors of the *Jewish Catalogue* series (Philadelphia: JPS, 1973, 1976, 1980). These "do-it yourself kits" (modeled after the iconic *Whole Earth Catalogue*) have had widespread influence in the North American Jewish community. See Jonathan Sarna, *American Judaism: A History* (New Haven, CT: Yale University Press, 2004), 318–323. Schachter-Shalomi wrote the final chapter of the first volume (adapted from his 1958 booklet, *The First Step*).

32 This is changing as scholars are increasingly interested in Schachter-Shalomi's place within North American religious life. Shaul Magid's work has been particularly important in this effort. See, for example, his book *American Post-Judaism: Identity and Renewal in a Postethnic Society* (Bloomington: Indiana University Press, 2013), especially chapters 2–5 and 8.

From the chapel, the rabbi took Thurman to a nearby common room to meet members of the rabbi's family, including his parents, who had traveled from Brooklyn to Winnipeg for the occasion:

> And he said, "My family will be coming, and I want you to meet them. My father is coming, he doesn't speak any English. He is from Galicia [located at the crossroads of Eastern and Central Europe], but I want you to see my whole family." So, they all came, and we sat around a table and had coffee and a sweet roll. And right in the middle of it, he said to his son, "Dr. Thurman is going to take you into the chapel and give you a blessing since he can't be here for the bar mitzvah." So, the three of us got up and went into the chapel and had the blessing.[33]

While Thurman did not comment on this experience further in the 1963 sermon, he did expand on it in an unpublished section of his autobiography (from which Schachter-Shalomi quoted in his own memoir):

> I'd never been in a position like that before, where the fact of being the instrumentality of a blessing was so personal and intimate and exclusive. It was not like saying a blessing with a group at a moment of some sort of celebration, but here was the celebration of a common religious experience and a friendship and an affection that existed between two men, each of whom came from a radically different tradition but had met in that zone in which there is no name or label. And standing there I bowed, and I prayed. I do not recall any words that were said, but what I do recall is the intensity of the religious experience when I opened my eyes and found that he from his kneeling position was looking up at my face.[34]

---

33 Ibid.

34 Schachter-Shalomi, *My Life in Jewish Renewal.* Thurman mentored other Jewish students and developed close relationships with Jewish colleagues, including rabbis Joseph Glaser and Dudley Weinberg of the Reform Movement. As Peter Eisenstadt notes, Thurman and Schachter-Shalomi shared specific spiritual and pedagogic affinities that led to a particularly intense connection. See Eisenstadt, *The Hounds of Hell,* 475–476, n. 134.

This unusual interreligious encounter, in which, according to Schachter-Shalomi, Thurman blessed both father and son,[35] left a significant impression on both men (alas, we do not know how the bar mitzvah boy felt about the experience!). The rabbi writes that this event "stayed with me intensely for over fifty years."[36] For anyone familiar with traditional Hasidic life, this scene is familiar from a typical meeting between a Hasid and his *rebbe* as the master is understood to be a person uniquely capable of channeling blessing.[37] Of course, in this case the Hasid made the request for blessing from his Baptist mentor. Clearly, Schachter-Shalomi held Thurman in high esteem, asking him for a *berakhah* (blessing) at this important intergenerational moment. Because these two men from "radically different" traditions shared in various religious experiments in Thurman's BU "laboratory," Schachter-Shalomi clearly felt that Thurman would understand and resonate with his request.

Following this intimate experience, Schachter-Shalomi took Thurman to his office. Commenting on the aesthetics of the space, Thurman stated that it was "a room that cannot be easily described" (also an apt description of this unusual rabbi!), as it overflowed with books, religious objects, and pictures of "individuals who have figured significantly in his life." Thurman was particularly taken by a large photograph of Schachter-Shalomi's Chabad master, Rabbi Yosef Yitzchak Scheersohn.[38] At that point, Schachter-Shalomi made another request for a blessing from his Christian master:

> ... I want you to sit in here for fifteen minutes without being disturbed, because I want you to open all the windows of your spirit so you can get a feeling of the place where I live and work and think, and then when you are away from here, the climate that you get now you can carry with you and you can put me in it and see me in my setting.[39]

---

35 According to Schachter-Shalomi Thurman "seemed surprised for a moment" but then proceeded to pray "wordlessly" placing a hand "on our shoulders." Schachter-Shalomi, *My Life in Jewish Renewal*, 91.

36 Ibid.

37 See Louis Jacobs, "Hasidism: Everyday Life," *YIVO Encyclopedia of Jews in Eastern Europe*, www.yivoencyclopedia.org/article.aspx/Hasidism/Everyday_Life, accessed October 1, 2018.

38 Rabbi Schneersohn welcomed and supported Schachter-Shalomi and his family into the Chabad community in Brooklyn, New York upon their arrival from Europe in 1940. As noted above, the elder Rabbi Schneersohn was succeeded by his son-in-law Rabbi Menachem Mendel Schneerson (d. 1994), with whom Schachter-Shalomi also had an intimate and increasingly complicated relationship.

39 Thurman, "The Wider Ministry and the Concept of Community," 8.

Thurman obliged his student, sitting down and taking in the scene so that he could keep him in heart and mind when he returned to Boston. Like the earlier request, this appeal makes it clear that Schachter-Shalomi regarded Thurman as a person of unusual spiritual power. The image of Thurman sitting at Schachter-Shalomi's desk offering a blessing with a picture of the sixth Lubavitcher Rebbe hanging before him dramatically captures the young rabbi's movement from "restoration" to "renewal," as he patched together his emerging identity as an unconventional mystical seeker and teacher.[40]

The visualization exercise Schachter-Shalomi invites Thurman to enact also reflects the rabbi's transitionary state as it seems to be a creative adaptation of a Hasidic meditation technique he wrote about in his very first publication, *The First Step* (1958), a brief manual on Jewish meditation for students and seekers,[41] which was inspired, in part, by Thurman's work on spiritual disciplines. There, he spoke about the Chabad technique of *ada'ata de-nafshei* (originally an Aramaic legal term denoting self-interest), in which the practitioner moves from contemplation of a lofty notion to visualizing herself in a particular situation in which the idea comes to life in a concrete manner. So, for example, one moves from thinking about God's *ḥesed* (love or mercy) as a general principle to how this virtue might be manifest in a specific moment of joy or pain. Borrowing a term from another spiritual mentor (and fellow Neo-Hasidic figure), Abraham Joshua Heschel (d. 1972), Schachter-Shalomi describes this contemplative exercise as "situational thinking."[42] In this case, Schachter-Shalomi asked Thurman to open

---

40 Interestingly, later that same year (December of 1963), Thurman made his one and only visit to Israel. In reflecting on the trip, he expressed significant disappointment that so many Israelis he met identified as ardent secularists and that the Hasidic and other ultra-Orthodox Jews he did encounter were highly conservative and uninterested in interreligious dialogue. As Peter Eisenstadt comments (*The Hounds of Hell*, 332–333), this was very different from his experiences with "free spirits" like Schachter-Shalomi. See, too, the quotation Eisenstadt brings (ibid., 333) from Thurman's Boston friend and colleague, Rabbi Roland Gittelsohn, who criticized the minister for setting out on the journey with an overly romantic vision of Jerusalem and the Holy Land based on popular American Christian teaching.

41 He first published this manual privately at the University of Manitoba (using his own second-hand printing device) and then through the B'nai Brith Hillel Foundation. Excerpts of it also appeared in the first *Jewish Catalogue*, reaching a much larger readership. There were subsequent adaptations of the text over the years. Recently, Schachter-Shalomi's close student and editor, Netanel Myles-Yépez, released a sixtieth-anniversary edition of the original booklet with minor corrections. See Meshulam Zalman Schachter, *The First Step: A Primer of Jewish Spiritual Life: 60th Anniversary Edition* (Boulder, CO: Albion-Andalus Books, 2020).

42 Schachter-Shalomi, *My Life in Jewish Renewal*, 15–22. See also his discussion of this topic in his later work, *Davening: A Guide to Meaningful Jewish Prayer* (Woodstock, VT: Jewish Lights, 2012), 170–175. He states there that this is a term he adapted from Abraham Joshua Heschel; see Heschel's *God in Search of Man: A Philosophy of Judaism* (New York: Farrar, Straus,

"all the windows" of his spirit, so that he could envision the rabbi in his daily work environment and send him good wishes from afar.

From Thurman's report, it seems that the minister was not taken aback at all by this second request. It may be that after the previous experience with the bar mitzvah boy, this seemed like a natural extension of the rabbi's previous wish. Further, Thurman was a person who believed deeply in the power of prayer and had a keen interest in shamanism, the occult, and other mystical-magical phenomena.[43] He seemed genuinely moved by the request of his Jewish student and believed that he could serve as an instrument of blessing.

If this was not enough spiritual intensity for one day, at Thurman's request Schachter-Shalomi took him on an outing to a Trappist Monastery on the outer edge of the city. This was a religious community that the rabbi visited many times and to which he took his university students,[44] as his interest in Catholicism and monasticism grew significantly in the late 1950s.[45] Upon their arrival at Our Lady of the Prairies, Thurman and Schachter-Shalomi were fed a vegetarian meal (honoring the rabbi's Jewish dietary needs), had a private conversation with the novice master (more on this below), and were invited to join the Vespers service. Thurman describes a moment late in the service that he experienced as revelatory:

> I don't know how I can say this to you. But there came a moment while one of the chants was being sung, when it seemed that I was moved out of my ... little space, and it was such a stirring thing—it seemed as if I was stripped to something very elemental in me, and I was not. It is the sort of thing that happens sometimes in prayer, when you are not you and you are not your

---

and Giroux, 1955), 5. For a detailed scholarly treatment of Schachter-Shalomi's approach to meditation, see Tomer Persico, "Jewish Meditation According to Rabbi Zalman Schachter-Shalomi," in his *The Jewish Meditative Tradition* [Heb.] (Tel Aviv: Tel Aviv University Press, 2016), 321–358.

43 See Mozella G. Mitchell, "'The Shaman's Doorway': Techniques of Myth and Ritual in Thurman," in *Debate & Understanding: A Journal for the Study of Minority Americans' Economic, Political, and Religious Development*, special edition, *Simmering on the Calm Presence and Profound Wisdom of Howard Thurman* (Spring 1982): 28.

44 Rabbi Jerry Steinberg, an undergraduate student of Schachter-Shalomi's at the University of Manitoba at the time, writes appreciatively about visiting the monastery with his teacher and mentor in his memoir, *Rogue Rabbi: A Spiritual Quest from Seminary to Ashram and Beyond* (Toronto, CA: ECW Press, 2012), 115–116.

45 See my forthcoming article, "Envisioning a *Jewish* Monastic Community: Zalman Schachter-Shalomi, Catholicism, and the B'nai Or Fellowship," in the *Journal of Christian-Jewish Relations* (2022).

> problem, but you are sort of laid bare, just the palpitation of your essential self, reduced to what is literal and irreducible in you in the presence of God. And when this happened, my eyes left the breviary, and I turned to him as he to me—our eyes met, this orthodox Jewish rabbi and I. And our eyes met and held.[46]

Embedded in this reflection are at least two related elements: First, Thurman describes an intense experience in which he is stripped to his essential self, to that which is "irreducible" beyond all personal concerns, in the presence of the divine. In the midst of this intensive journey he seems to lose himself momentarily in God. As he states, "I was not." Second, after emerging from this unitive (or deeply intimate) experience he raises his eyes and feels that he has connected in some unspoken, but profound way with his student. In fact, after briefly describing the rest of the events of that evening, including riding back to his lodging with Schachter-Shalomi in silence, Thurman ends his sermon with the following assertion and brief prayer:

> Experiences of unity are more compelling than all the concepts, ideologies, creeds, as important as they are, that divide. And if these can be multiplied all over the world, over a time interval of sufficient duration, there isn't any barrier between any of the children of God that cannot be removed. And if you believe this, then you will never close the door of your heart against any man, even though he may close the door of his heart against you.
>
> Accept, our Father, the offering of our faith and our words and our lives. Walk beside us as we go our way, tutor us in community, our Father.[47]

Reading these impassioned words, we learn just how meaningful this experience was for Thurman, and of his deeply held conviction that people from different religious traditions can share in transformative religious encounters. This coda also calls to mind Thurman's reflections on his voyage to South Asia almost thirty years earlier to meet with Mahatma Ghandi and other religious and civic leaders. While overseas, he had several encounters that convinced him that human beings from different religious and cultural contexts could join in

46 Howard Thurman, "The Wider Ministry and the Concept of Community," 8–9.
47 Ibid.

intensive spiritual experiences temporarily transcending (or letting go of) their differences.[48] Reflecting on this watershed experience overseas, he used the very same language as in his 1963 sermon, stating, "It became imperative now to find out if experiences of spiritual unity among people could be more compelling than the experiences which divide them." While articulated as a question in the mid-1930s, by the early 1960s this had become a cornerstone of his spiritual-ethical worldview and a central aim of his pastorate. At the same time, Thurman was also aware that even as people meet through such deep encounters, they enter and exit these meetings using different interpretative tools based on religious and other differences.[49] And yet, he insisted that such connections are real and offer seekers an important glimpse into the underlying unity of humanity and of life as a whole. The journalist Lerone Bennett, Jr. captures this tension in his oft-cited remark about the "Thurman synthesis":

> The Thurman synthesis includes and transcends at a higher level of integration all divisions—creedal, racial, sexual, and national. He believes "the highest act of celebration of the human spirit is the worship of God" and that in the act of worship there is "neither male nor female, Black nor White, Protestant nor Catholic nor Buddhist nor Hindu, but a human spirit laid bare, stripped to whatever there is that is literal and irreducible." But he contends that the experience of universality is only possible as a "derivative from the ground" of one's idiom.[50]

Significantly for our current discussion Bennett quotes Thurman as saying that it is in the experience of *worship* that a person is "laid bare" as he did in his later sermon.

What about Schachter-Shalomi? Clearly, he felt that he and Thurman, as different as they were, could share in transformative religious experiences together, otherwise he would not have asked his mentor to bless him and his child. Further, as a Chabad Hasid, he believed that the goal of the mystical quest is to cleave to God (*devequt*), and in peak moments of ecstasy or contemplation, to move into a state of *ayin* (literally "nothing") in which the devotee merges with the divine

---

48 Thurman, *With Head and Heart*, 129.

49 Idem, *Mysticism and the Experience of Love*, 21.

50 Leronne Bennett, Jr., "Howard Thurman: Twentieth-Century Holy Man," *Ebony* (February 1978): 69.

(as Thurman put it, "I was not").[51] The "place" to which the adept travels is also referred to as *ayin*, for it is in this mysterious, primordial realm that all of God's creative potential issues forth; it is a domain beyond all separation or individuation.[52] While Schachter-Shalomi did not actually comment on his experience of Vespers that evening, it seems clear that he felt that he and his mentor were not simply sitting side by side in the chapel, but were journeying together into a shared spiritual "zone." Exactly how he experienced his connection to Thurman, to the monks, and to God in this moment, we do not know.[53]

Dramatic as Thurman's Vespers reflection is, many years later, Schachter-Shalomi spoke enthusiastically about another component of their visit to the monastery: their discussion with the novice master, Brother Franciscus. As an educator and pastor, Thurman was interested in knowing about the struggles of new initiates to monastic life and how his host dealt with these challenges. The novice master replied that the most common complaint was from novices who felt that the long hours of disciplined prayer were unnecessary when they experienced much greater spiritual joy—"raptures"—while working in the fields (the monastery model was of *ora et labora*, "worship and labor"). Brother Franciscus went on to say that in response to such complaints he forbade them from coming to chapel, except for holidays and for Masses of obligation. Soon enough, the novices would come back to him and complain that they didn't join the monastery simply to be "farmhands." The novice master concluded his comments by saying that in this way the new monks came to realize that the hours they spend "on their knees in prayer" prepare them for the raptures in the fields—"Those who sow in tears, will reap in joy (Ps. 126:5)." Schachter-Shalomi recalled how much Thurman appreciated the novice master's response and how much he, as a young rabbi, appreciated his mentor's choice to engage their host in a conversation about their common work as spiritual guides. Given the limits of their visit,

---

51 See Rachel Elior, "Habad: The Contemplative Ascent to God," in *Jewish Spirituality from the Sixteenth Century Revival to the Present*, vol. 2, ed. Arthur Green (New York: Crossroad, 1987), 157–205.

52 Ibid. See also Daniel C. Matt, "*Ayin*: The Concept of Nothingness in Jewish Mysticism," in *Essential Papers on Kabbalah*, ed. Lawrence Fine (New York: New York University Press, 1995), 67–108.

53 This report on Vespers is illustrative of ongoing scholarly discussions about the nature of religious experience. Can individuals from different traditions meet in a common experiential zone, whether one defines it as "mystical" or otherwise? Are there practices—ecstatic or contemplative—that facilitate the shedding (even if temporary) of aspects of identity that usually prevent people from partaking of such unifying experiences? To what extent do reports by adepts from different traditions about similar experiences of interconnection and/or absorption in a greater whole impact this discussion? For a helpful discussion of these matters, see Catherine Cornille, *The Im-Possibility of Interreligious Dialogue* (New York: Crossroad, 2008).

Thurman wisely found a way to connect with, honor, and learn from Brother Franciscus.[54] Schachter-Shalomi's reflection demonstrates his keen interest in different facets of interreligious leadership and his attentiveness at this early stage of his career to the skill of cultivating fruitful relationships with the religious other.

"Little Islands of Thought": Schachter-Shalomi's Interreligious Journey Continues

While Schachter-Shalomi demonstrates uncommon openness to and reverence for Howard Thurman in the texts we have explored, it is also important to state that his development as an interreligious practitioner during the Winnipeg years (1956–1975) was gradual and involved a good deal of private and public experimentation. One can see this unfolding in his interactions with Thurman during this intense encounter in 1963 and in several other cases. For example, his meditation manual *The First Step* was clearly influenced by his experiences at BU, including the use of the term "spiritual disciplines and resources" in the opening sentence of the booklet.[55] This was the name of Thurman's signature course in which the rabbi participated in 1955. Still, Schachter-Shalomi also felt the need to state to his readers that if one is concerned that "the ideas and techniques" outlined in the primer "are taken from non-Jewish sources," they need not worry. He goes on to say, "The approach used here is that of classical Jewish mysticism, as refined by Chassidism, and in particular, by the Habad school."[56] He did so, in part, because he sought the approval of his Lubavitcher master, who carefully reviewed the text.[57] But he was also still very much trying to integrate his interreligious and cross-cultural experiences into an Orthodox framework. In a 2011 interview, Schachter-Shalomi spoke of his religious development

---

54 See Schachter-Shalomi, *Rabbi Zalman Schachter-Shalomi: Essential Teachings*, "Trade Secrets from the Monastery," 183–184.

55 Here is the opening to the primer: "This manual intends to give you practical information in the area of **spiritual discipline and resources** [bold added for emphasis]. I imagine you, the reader, in the following way: You are a 'seeker'. This means (to me) that you are trying to find a *way* to express some stirrings in yourself and to discover that holy source within you, so that it may begin to flow freely." A few lines later, he attempts to encourage the reader to take up the spiritual search in a disciplined manner using "Thurmanesque" language: "You need not have a clearly crystallized philosophy. All you need is a willingness to test some of your already held beliefs, and those which you wish to hold, in the **laboratory of your experience**." *The First Step*, 7–8. Schachter-Shalomi then proceeds to outline eight areas of traditional Jewish ideas and practices—shaped significantly by Chabad interpretations of them—designed to lead the seeker on a path of spiritual growth in relationship with God and community.

56 Ibid., 13–14.

57 My thanks to Netanel Miles-Yépez for confirming this fact. Apparently, the Lubavitcher Rebbe gave Schachter-Shalomi specific feedback, including suggestions on the bibliography.

during this time period as follows: "In those days these ideas were piecemeal, like little islands of thought; some of them were more psychological, some of them were more spiritual, some of them were more ecumenical."[58]

Schachter-Shalomi's worldview continued to evolve in the coming years based in large part on his encounters with non-Jewish and non-Orthodox Jewish religious and cultural figures.[59] This is evident from his contribution to the 1966 *Commentary Magazine* symposium on the "Condition of Jewish Belief," in which nearly forty leading Jewish figures reflected on a series of questions on theology, praxis, and politics.[60] While he still identifies himself as a Hasid and designates the seventh Lubavitcher Rebbe as "the repository" of his faith, Schachter-Shalomi also states that the most serious challenges to contemporary belief are "game theory and psychedelic experience"; while each challenges the contemporary seeker differently, both call into question a person's "ontological assertions."[61] However, he also asserts that psychedelics can serve to renew one's faith by disclosing that "all is one" and "God immanent surprises God transcendent." For Schachter-Shalomi this realization leads him back to a life of Torah, knowing that living in mundane reality requires one to "play this game or another," and that the Jewish game is the one he feels called to play.

In this light, he goes on to say that Jews must begin to reimagine their relationship with non-Jews, understanding that we are all playing different roles on

---

58 David Schneer, "Jewish Renewal and the Paradigm Shift: A Conversation with Reb Zalman Schachter-Shalomi," *AJS Perspectives: The Magazine of the Association of Jewish Studies* (Fall 2011), http://perspectives.ajsnet.org/the-religious-issue-fall-2011/jewish-renewal-and-the-paradigm-shift-a-conversation-with-reb-zalman-schachter-shalomi.

59 Schachter-Shalomi's interreligious and intra-Jewish explorations during this time period were interrelated, as he was meeting a variety of impressive figures from communities that he previously regarded as foreign, benighted, and/or dangerous. One such example was his decision to undertake doctoral studies at Hebrew Union College-Jewish Institute of Religion in 1963. While studying at the flagship center for Reform Judaism in Cincinnati, Ohio he also visited with his beloved friend Father Thomas Merton (d. 1968), who resided at the Abbey of Our Lady of Gethsemani near Bardstown, Kentucky (approximately a three-hour car ride from HUC-JIR).

60 See Zalman Schachter, "The Condition of Jewish Belief," *Commentary Magazine* 42, no. 2 (August 1966): 207–215. In the summer of 1963, Schachter-Shalomi made his first "trip" with Timothy Leary, then a research professor at Harvard University. See Schachter-Shalomi, *My Life in Jewish Renewal*, 141–154. One of Schachter-Shalomi's classmates in Thurman's course on spiritual disciplines and resources was Walter Pahnke (d. 1971), a prominent researcher on psychedelics and one of the organizers (along with Timothy Leary and Huston Smith) of the "Good Friday Experiment" that took place in the basement of Marsh Chapel at BU in April 1962. Apparently, Thurman gave his student permission to conduct the experiment while he led worship in the main sanctuary. See Eisenstadt, *Against the Hounds of Hell*, 297–301, and Paul Harvey, *Howard Thurman and the Disinherited: A Religious Biography* (Grand Rapids, MI: Eerdmans Publishing, 2020), 189–190.

61 *Commentary Magazine*, 42 no. 2 (August 1966), 213.

the cosmic stage.[62] In so doing, he raises the following question, which would preoccupy him for the rest of his life: "Is it possible to raise people to high levels of religious intensity without the accompanying fanaticism?" His answer is yes, "against all of the evidence of the past."[63] He further asserts that Jews have not historically developed a "viable theology of the Gentile," pointing briefly to the insufficiencies he finds in the apologia of such renowned thinkers as Judah Halevi (d. 1141) and Sampson Rafael Hirsch (d. 1888).[64] Still, Schachter-Shalomi argues that the language of chosenness remains important as it provides Jews and others the opportunity to openly disagree about substantive religious issues, guarding against a collapse of traditions into any form of homogenization. In so doing, he attempts to carve out a space for himself somewhere between "those liberals who do not want to maintain the distinction between Israel and the nations, and those archaics who take it too seriously."[65] There is, of course, ample room along this theological continuum, and Schachter-Shalomi would continue to explore his place on it over the next several decades, including the notion of chosenness.[66]

Conclusion

Howard Thurman and Zalman Schachter-Shalomi forged an uncommon bond in which the older African American Christian pastor served as a guide to and model for the emerging Hasidic rabbi. As we have seen, Thurman's visit to Winnipeg in the winter of 1963 left a lasting impression on both men for years to come. The groundwork for this memorable encounter was laid several years earlier when Schachter-Shalomi was a graduate student at BU (1955). As I have argued, part of what made Thurman such an attractive figure to

---

62 Ibid.

63 Ibid., 214.

64 Ibid. Interestingly, while he rejects Halevi's theory that the Jewish people are the "heart" of humanity (*Kuzari* II, 31:60), in his later "organismic" stage, Schachter-Shalomi consciously plays with the image of different religious communities together constituting a body. He does not have any interest in creating a detailed bodily mapping, but rather emphasizing the need for each individual "organ" and for the sharing of "vital nutrients." See his brief comments on Halevi's metaphor in Zalman Schachter-Shalomi and Daniel Siegel, *Credo of a Modern Kabbalist* (Victoria, British Columbia, CA: Trafford Publishing), 160–161.

65 Ibid., 215.

66 See, for example, Zalman Schachter-Shalomi, "Why Be Jewish," in Zalman Schachter-Shalomi and Joel Segel, *Jewish with Feeling: A Guide to Meaningful Jewish Practice* (Woodstock, VT: Jewish Lights, 2005), 181–221. See, also, Shaul Magid, "Rainbow Hasidism in America—The Maturation of Jewish Renewal," *The Reconstructionist* (Spring 2004): 48.

Schachter-Shalomi was the minister's ability to play multiple roles as a skilled teacher, preacher, writer, and counselor—a master of "applied religion." While a distinctly heterodox thinker, Thurman was also a rigorous intellectual, a charismatic public figure, and a self-described mystic—all hallmarks Schachter-Shalomi respected in his Orthodox Jewish mentors.

Thurman's unpublished sermon and related documents demonstrate the affection and affinities these men shared, including a desire to connect meaningfully with people from different religious backgrounds through dialogue, study, and ritual exploration. Further, the text sheds light on Thurman's mature vision of the possibility, even necessity, for shared religious experiences across lines of difference as a foundation for the cultivation of a pluralistic ethos. Finally, and most importantly for my ongoing study of Schachter-Shalomi's development as an interreligious practitioner, the texts we have examined offer a colorful and detailed snapshot of the young rabbi's evolving worldview, including his trust in and esteem for Thurman, whom he regarded as a potent spiritual adept and guide.

In closing this essay, I quote from a letter Schachter-Shalomi wrote to Thurman upon hearing that Thurman had transitioned from serving as the Dean of Marsh Chapel to "Minister-at-Large" at BU:

> I am greatly pleased with one thing. I've finally found out what you are. You have been, all the time, a minister at large, and no matter how wonderful and flexible the institution was, it could not quite contain you. I suppose this is what is meant to be in the image of one's Maker [see 1 Kgs. 8:27 and 2 Chr. 6:18], whom the heavens can't contain.[67]

As Schachter-Shalomi's colleagues and disciples would attest, "Reb Zalman" (as he was affectionately known) was very much a "rabbi at large," whose iconoclasm repeatedly challenged the bounds of institutional Jewish life. This involved an unfolding process of reimagining the relationship of Jews to people of other faiths and cultures. His intimate contact with Howard Thurman—his "Black Rebbe"—was one of the foundational experiences that inspired Schachter-Shalomi's decades-long involvement in interreligious efforts.

---

67 Zalman Schachter-Shalomi, personal correspondence, November 9, 1964. My thanks to Netanel Miles-Yépez for sharing a copy of this letter with me.

CHAPTER 22

"Kakha Zeh Ḥinukhi"—"That Makes It Educational": Parabolic Style in Kafka, Keret, and Castel-Bloom

Abigail Esther Gillman

I.

"Allakazeem, allakazam." The magic show always ends with the rabbit. The kids at the birthday party love it, and they get to pet the rabbit when it's over. And yet, laments the magician—the protagonist of Etgar Keret's story "Hat Trick"—[1] times are tough for magicians. Children mostly look at their phones.

One day, something unexpected happens. The magician puts his hand into the dark hat and pulls out the rabbit's bloody head! To his surprise, "the kids were ecstatic." He goes out and buys a new rabbit. When he returns home, the phone is ringing off the hook. He gets lots of bookings. But at the next performance, he puts his hand into the dark hole, and pulls out not a rabbit's head, but a dead baby. At this point, the magician gives up. He's terrified of what he might pick out of the hat next. "I don't perform at all any more… . I just lie awake and think about the rabbit's head and the dead baby. Like they're clues to a riddle; like someone was trying to tell me something, that this isn't the

1 Published in Etgar Keret, *The Girl on the Fridge* (New York: Farrar, Straus and Giroux, 2008). The story also appeared in the graphic novel collection by Actus Comics, *Jetlag: Five Graphic Novellas* (New York: Toby Press, 2006).

best time for rabbits, or for babies either. That this isn't really the right time for magicians."[2]

The magician's lament recalls the frustration of Franz Kafka's fasting artist: "We live in a different world now.... Just try to explain to anyone the art of fasting!"[3] But who is to blame for this tide of apathy? Is technology to blame? Is it a matter of the artist's self-doubt? Is it the fault of his audience—of what the Rabbis called ירידת הדורות, the decline of the generations? What factors link the plights of Franz Kafka, Prague Jew and exemplary modernist, and Etgar Keret, Israeli storyteller who has achieved global fame?

The difficulties of being a storyteller in an information age—an age of media oversaturation, disenchantment, and boredom—are woes that Israeli author Etgar Keret (b. 1964) indeed inherited from Franz Kafka (1883–1924). Keret claims to have discovered Kafka during his basic training in the Israeli army, finding himself in "a world that made no sense, and a system that had no logic."[4] This is also the universe that Keret's characters inhabit. Many of his stories portray banal occurrences or ordinary scenarios, which quickly escalate into absurdity, violence, evil, or just plain gruesomeness, leaving the characters at a loss and us readers scratching our heads. But something about Keret's tales compels us to put aside our revulsion and look for deeper meaning. In an interview, Keret commented, "I feel that 'Hat Trick' is not only a story about writing but one about the relationship between a writer and his reader."[5] Is the sequence of events in "Hat Trick" just a morbid attention-grabber? Is it possible that the baby and rabbit's head are "clues to a riddle"?

Before attempting to answer those questions, I turn to another contemporary text, which opens with the same surreal sequence of live animal, dead animal, and an (almost) dead baby, and which prefigures a plot as strange as any Keret story: Orly Castel-Bloom's novel *Dolly City*.[6] Keep in mind that this novel became so important in translation that it was designated by UNESCO as one of the best novels of the century.

---

2 Translation by Miriam Shlesinger. Also available in Etgar Keret, "Magic and Childhood," *Prospect Magazine* 131 (February 2007), https://www.theshortstory.org.uk/stories/downloads/keret.pdf.

3 Franz Kafka, *The Complete Stories*, trans. Willa and Edwin Muir (New York: Schocken Books, 1983), 268.

4 Marilyn Cooper, "Books That Shaped Great Authors," *Moment* 41, no. 4 (July/August 2016): 42–43.

5 Etgar Keret interview with Sophie Lewis, *Granta*, August 14, 2014, https://granta.com/interview-etgar-keret/.

6 Orly Castel-Bloom, *Dolly City*, trans. Dalya Bilu (Champaign and London: Dalkey Archive Press, 2010).

Dolly City opens with a mock "covenant between the pieces" (Genesis 15): protagonist Dr. Dolly is cutting up her dead pet goldfish on a marble kitchen counter. She inspects the pieces, noting, "In very ancient times, in the land of Canaan, righteous men would sacrifice bigger animals than this to God. When they cut up a lamb, they would be left with big, bloody, significant pieces in their hands, and their covenant would be a real covenant." But she is no Abraham. Her millimeter-wide slices of goldfish do not compare with the "big bloody significant pieces" in the Bible.[7] She burns them and then consumes them.

At once, she notices that her beloved dog is dying. After fifteen days, she draws on her medical knowledge to euthanize the dog. On the drive to bury him, sitting in the gravedigger's car, she spots a large black plastic bag. In the bag is a "blue, hungry baby."[8] Dr. Dolly brings the baby home and operates on him, hooking him up to an intravenous drip of drugs and minerals; she then injects herself with a sedative and goes out on the balcony to smoke a cigarette. "Instead of the voice of reason making itself heard, the situation took control of my eyeballs. They kept looking up, higher and higher, as if there was always something to see up there—more and more sky, a stairway of sky, a Tower of Babel of sky, instead of one deep, blue, unambiguous heaven"—but there is "nothing."[9] She realizes that the "infant's life was spared" and, having become an "unwilling mother,"[10] she begins to care for him, giving him the name Ben, "Son."

Castel-Bloom, in a newspaper article, identified the true story behind her novel's primal scene as a traumatic experience of trying to save her own baby from choking. Dolly's "passion for the Real," to use the phrase of literary scholar Ari Ofengenden, and arguably the novel as a whole, extends from the Israeli mother's desire to assert control over her son's body and her own mothering. Ofengenden argues convincingly that the space of *Dolly City* is the Real, as theorized by Lacan, Badiou, and Zizek.[11] Dolly's narrative attempts to "escape the stifling confines of the symbolic," including the Romantic, the sublime, and above all, the unbearable pressures of natural mothering.[12]

And yet, allusions to the divine, and to the Bible, pervade the novel, conveying that the symbolic still shapes its reality. Dolly's eyeballs look upward for something more than an "unambiguous heaven." She must reckon with the fact that

---

7 Ibid., 9.

8 Ibid., 14.

9 Ibid., 16.

10 Ibid., 17.

11 Ari Ofengenden, "Language, Body, Dystopia: The Passion for the Real in Orly Castel-Bloom's Dolly City," *The Comparatist* 38 (October 2014): 250–265.

12 Ibid., 255.

God is not around to help mothers protect their children, or to save children from their mothers.

> I had to keep him safe, keep the lightning and thunder from striking him and the earth from swallowing him up. I declared war to the bitter end: Dolly against the rest of the world. It was as if I said to God that if this child was my responsibility—then he was *my* responsibility. I didn't want favors from anyone, including His Holiness. I didn't want anyone else to do the job for me.[13]

In the absence of help from above, keeping Son alive becomes an *ideé fixe,* and Dolly's fanatical exploits to that end dominate the plot. "I would inoculate the child against as many diseases as possible. I ran out to buy vaccines against tetanus, whooping cough, diphtheria, polio, measles, jaundice, scarlet fever, smallpox, influenza, etc., and I gave them all to him at once—although I knew you shouldn't do this. I couldn't stop myself, I couldn't control my maternal instinct."[14] This futuristic satire targets not only the archetypal Jewish mother, but also "that most holy of institutions, the myth of motherhood—and its implications in the life of a nation," as the publisher's book blurb puts it.

In my description of the opening pages of *Dolly City,* I highlight how Castel-Bloom alludes to biblical mythology, to the domains of the symbolic and the significant. Before returning to Keret and Kafka, I shall explicate one biblical counter-text, the *'aqedah* (Gen. 22), which, like the novel, incorporates the plot elements of a parent's trial; an almost dead child; a dead animal; and a surprise intervention, which spares the child and (even more critically) saves the parent from his own impulses. In Genesis, where the backdrop is not a "blue, ambiguous heaven," God and the angel are pulling the strings, and the parent-protagonist knows exactly who is directing his actions. And yet, it is an understatement to say that the *'aqedah* poses more questions than answers. The fact that no explanation is given for the commandment to sacrifice a child lends the story a surreal and unreal quality. Abraham, with son, wood, and knife in tow, makes his way to the site. The lamb is present by omission. Abraham follows all the instructions, but as he lifts his hand with the knife to slaughter the child, an angel suddenly calls his name twice, and tells him not to harm the child, because "now I know that you fear God and did not withhold him from [God]." A long list of rewards follows. Whether out of gratitude, or catharsis, or a desire to seal the

---

13 Castel-Bloom, *Dolly City,* 22.
14 Ibid.

covenant, or because the altar built to receive the son needs to be put to some use, Abraham kills and sacrifices an innocent ram. Although the animal appears out of nowhere, this is no magic trick—the lamb and Isaac are saved, but, as Yehuda Amichai points out in his famous poem, the ram *must* die: "He didn't know about the conspiracy between the others."[15] Sacrifice is a necessity, if, in Dolly's words, this is to be considered a "real covenant."

Dolly City, a satire of Israeli (and also Jewish, Middle Eastern, universal?) motherhood, contains numerous allusions to the *'aqedah*. This places the novel within a wide-ranging tradition documented by Yael Feldman, Shalom Spiegel, and many others, of Israeli and Jewish literary, religious, and cultural responses to the story. My research takes a somewhat different approach, by reading the *'aqedah* as an early parable whose enigmatic message is that saving your child and risking your child's life are two sides of the same coin. This is the fine line, which Dolly walks throughout the novel. Nowadays, angels do not descend to save children from their parents, nor does the cutting up of an animal bring the efficacy of an animal sacrifice. But the inexplicable symbolic trial—the test of doing right by one's child, which brings parents to the brink of the unthinkable—somehow remains intact in modern times. The trial resembles the "inexplicable mass of rock," which is left behind for us to ponder once the legends of heroism and martyrdom about Prometheus have dissipated, according to Franz Kafka's parable "Prometheus." Like Dolly, and like Keret's forlorn magician, the modern individual does not stop looking for meaning behind such tests, despite the absence of a covenant. Although Dr. Dolly sees nothing at all when she turns her gaze heavenward, the realms of God and angels, heaven and hell, remain a powerful force-field, as they do in many of Etgar Keret's stories such as "Hole in the Wall," "Good Intentions," "Souvenir from Hell," "Pipes," and "Siren."

Keret's affinities with Kafka are frequently noted. Of Castel-Bloom, it is also said, "Kafka has come to Tel Aviv."[16] Dan Miron's verdict about Castel-Bloom echoes critical assessments of Keret. "Orly Castel-Bloom rejects any illusion of depth—in language, culture, human experience, the psyche, society, tradition, the past. She sees only a thin, shallow, insipid and lifeless reality, consisting of automatic existence with an abyss of chaos lurking underneath."[17] But Keret,

---

15 הגבור האמתי של העקדה היה האיל שלא ידע על הקנוניה בין האחרים. הוא כמו התנדב למות במקום יצחק.

16 "Nuits et jours d'Orly Castel-Bloom," *Le Monde*, March 13, 2008, https://www.lemonde.fr/livres/article/2008/03/13/nuits-et-jours-d-orly-castel-bloom_1022287_3260.html.

17 Dan Miron, "Mashehu al Orli Castel-Bloom," *Al ha-Mishmar*, June 16, 1989, 2. See also Avraham Balaban, "Biblical Allusions in Modern and Postmodern Hebrew Literature," *AJS Review* 28, no. 1 (April 2004): 189–204.

Castel-Bloom, and Kafka have not been juxtaposed in light of their uncannily similar responses to the Bible.

I propose that the writers' legacy from Kafka is not only absurdity and chaos; it is not only about powerless protagonists facing surreal trials and violent plots. It is also about the hermeneutic challenge, as it were, of solving an unnamed riddle; of finding a "way out" (see Kafka's "A Report to an Academy") and making meaning in the absence of a "real covenant." The challenge is older than Kafka: it originates in the genre of the Jewish parable, or *mashal:* a short story told by a prophet or teacher to convey a piece of wisdom about right action, whose authority derives from a higher power, to which Dolly refers as the "Tower of Babel heavens."

II.

This essay represents a chapter in a larger project about parabolic style in Jewish and Israeli literature. The project explores contemporary modes of reading, writing, and meaning making, which emerge out of the ancient *mashal* and share some of its features. My approach uses Franz Kafka's short stories as pivotal modern texts within the long tradition of parabolic writing.[18] The tradition of the Jewish parable reaches back to the Hebrew Bible; to Jesus's parables in the Synoptic Gospels; exegetical parables found in midrashic texts; and to Hasidic tales. The genealogy includes stories by Yiddish and Hebrew modernists, I. L. Peretz and I. B. Singer, and of course, S. Y. Agnon. Twentieth-century thinkers Martin Buber and Walter Benjamin engaged with storytelling on many levels—Buber's retellings of Hasidic tales in the early twentieth century can be counted here as well. Parables are found in postwar and post-Holocaust fiction (Elie Wiesel, Aharon Appelfeld). Parabolic style marks the writing of Israeli authors Etgar Keret and Orly Castel-Bloom, and the appeal of this style explains, I suspect, why those two have found a global readership in translation—why Castel-Bloom's 1992 novel *Dolly City* was selected to be a UNESCO "representative work," and why Etgar Keret's story "Outside" was featured in the *New York Times' Sunday Magazine* special issue, *Decameron Project,* of July 12, 2020, featuring twenty-nine short stories inspired by the COVID-19 pandemic of 2020. Last but not least, Israeli scholars and public intellectuals such as Ruth Calderon, Avivah

18 Here it is also appropriate to acknowledge that Kafka's stories were first identified as parables in a volume published by Schocken Books in Berlin in the 1930s; Nahum N. Glatzer edited a bilingual volume called *Parables and Paradoxes* (*Parabeln und Paradoxe*), which Schocken published in 1961.

Zornberg, and Haviva Pedaya, draw from this deep well of Jewish tales in myriad creative ways.

What do I mean by parabolic style? First and foremost, parables have a dual essence: they simultaneously provide access to wisdom, and bar direct access to that wisdom. I begin with two illustrations from Kafka, and one from the New Testament.

Franz Kafka's famous meta-parable "Before the Law" ("Vor dem Gesetz") stages a conversation between the man from the country and the doorkeeper. Like the door, which the man from the country seeks to enter, a parable is an undeniable entry-point—to the Law, Torah, or wisdom—designed to attract the unlearned and uninitiated. Like the doorkeeper, a parable keeps the wisdom at bay, preventing immediate entry. Instead of direct access, the one who approaches receives a riddle and a set of clues: shall I wait and keep trying to enter, or give up and leave? From the doorkeeper he also gets a little stool, so he can rest his body while trying to figure out the best approach.

Another of Kafka's meta-parables, "On Parables" ("Von den Gleichnissen"), begins: "Many complain that the words of the wise are always merely parables and of no use in daily life, which is the only life we have." Further complaints are raised. Why are parables so difficult to decipher? Are they worth the effort? Don't these cryptic texts merely *widen* the gulf between us and our teachers? A curious notion is floated: if we threw in our lot with those stories, in a leap of faith, could we escape our troubles altogether and *become parables*?

No less confusing is the characterization of the parable genre in the Gospel of Matthew 13, after Jesus recites the Parable of the Sower to a large crowd by the sea. Jesus's disciples ask, "why do you speak in parables?" The answer is long and complicated, but the essential point, made by way of allusion to Isaiah 6, comes in verse 13: "The reason I speak to them in parables is that 'seeing they do not perceive, and hearing they do not listen, nor do they understand.'"

But if people cannot hear the straight teaching, why tell them an enigmatic story?

Let us define a parable as a stylized short story, with scenic and dialogic structure, and two dimensions: in Hebrew, *mashal* and *nimshal*; in German, *Bildebene* and *Sachebene* (or *Deutungsebene*). Unlike an allegory, in which the plot points of the fictional tale clearly line up with those of the lesson, the two dimensions of a parable bear no natural resemblance to one another; rather, they are randomly "thrown together" (Greek *parabola*) in order to convince or "rule over" (Hebrew: *limshol*) the listener. The genre's power involves transporting the listener from one dimension to the other, from *Bild* to *Sache*, or, at the very least, sustaining her attention over the long haul. The transport sometimes occurs by way of a hook, or an unexpected twist, like the magic moment when the rabbit comes out of the hat.

I have found two different explanations of the parable's magic power. The first locates it in the ancient genre of the juridical parable. Such parables had a legal function.[19] A prophet presented listeners with a hypothetical legal case, and their "disinterest" enabled them to state an objective judgment and the proper penalty.[20] The hypothetical story had to be different enough from a real situation to enable one to listen objectively and arrive at a neutral verdict. A second explanation highlights not logos, but pathos—the story's emotional impact, akin to a seduction or manipulation, which circumvents reason altogether and appeals to the listener's passions. Both of these aspects converge in the famous scene of parable-telling in 2 Samuel 11–12, after Nathan the prophet recounts the tale of the poor man's ewe to King David. David first evinces pathos as he provides the correct assessment: "That man should be punished!" When the finger is pointed at him, he grasps the story's logic (logos): "I have sinned before God."

Gila Safran Naveh, in a fascinating book *Biblical Parables and their Modern Recreations,* argues that parables seduce the listeners by drawing them into a game of decoding, whereby the very *Unheimlichkeit* of the story entices them to follow the tale to its surprising conclusion and to buy in to the verdict.[21] David Stern, in his classic study *Parables in Midrash,* writes along similar lines that the parable "deliberately gives the impression of naming its meaning *insufficiently.* It uses ambiguity intentionally ... it artfully manipulates its audience to fill those openings so as to arrive at the mashal's correct conclusion."[22] This "artful manipulation" is precisely the magic that Keret's artist requires in order to succeed at his profession.

Do parables have a consistent theme? Let us say for now that parable plots entail, in the strict sense, a wise or philosophical verdict about good conduct: who is the best person, who is the best parent, who is a good son, who is a God-fearing person.

---

19 W. F. Albright, "Introduction," part 11: "Parables in Matthew," in *The Anchor Bible Matthew* (New York: Doubleday & Co. Inc, 1971), cxxxii–cxxxviii. See also Uriel Simon, "The Poor Man's Ewe-Lamb: An Example of a Juridical Parable," *Biblica* 48, no. 2 (1967): 207–242.

20 Albright, "Introduction," cxxxiv.

21 Gila Safran Naveh, *Biblical Parables and Their Modern Re-creations: From "Apples of Gold in Silver Settings" to "Imperial Messages"* (Albany, NY: State University of New York Press, 2000).

22 David Stern, *Parables in Midrash: Narrative and Exegesis in Rabbinic Literature* (Cambridge, MA: Harvard University Press, 1991), 15. Stern adds: "... Abby [sic] Warburg's famous saying [is] that God resides in the detail. In contrast, the mashal has God, or meaning, residing *between* its details, in the shifting sands that lie between the narrative and the nimshal, where story does not exemplify truth but simply alludes to it" (ibid.).

Parables stand "before the law" in the sense that they are literary offspring of scripture, Torah, religious wisdom, and most broadly, of the human-divine covenant. They are related to the religious homily, which openly delivers a religious message. They are also related to the fable, folktale, or exemplum (exemplary narrative, Heb. *ma'aseh*). By contrast, the exemplum "entails"[23] meaning directly: it speaks for itself through an epimythium, which is a moral saying appended to the story. In contrast, parables do not name their meaning. Ambiguity is part of their genetic makeup.

Perhaps their rhetorical power and hermeneutic versatility explains why exegetical parables (Heb. *mashal*) are found all throughout the midrash, rabbinic writings, the Gospels, philosophical texts such as Maimonides's *Guide for the Perplexed,* and Hasidic literature.[24] Jesus was a master of parables—a technique explicated in its historical context by Amy-Jill Levine in *Short Stories by Jesus: The Enigmatic Parables of a Controversial Rabbi.* Jesus was trying to overturn or invert people's assumptions about what constituted good conduct, about what God expects, about who should be punished and who is deserving of grace. In the parable of the Prodigal Son (Luke 15), a father suggests that the older son, who has been obedient and faithful day after day, is less favored than the younger son who spurned his inheritance, as he "was lost and then returned." Jesus's parables served the agenda of transporting his listeners into a whole new understanding of what God wants.

But wherein lies the appeal of the form to modernist and postmodern writers, whose universe is (otherwise) marked by boredom, obsessive-compulsive symptoms, violence, the grotesque, and theater of the absurd? Whose protagonists are mostly preoccupied with banal and surreal incidents of modern life? Who show again and again that the underside of the banal is the horrible, the grotesque, much as Gregor Samsa's insect-self is only one remove, one bad dream away, from his human life as a son, brother, and travelling salesman? Why do writers who resist metaphors, symbols, and the Romantic trope of surface vs. depth, and who favor of a "lean and apathetic literary style,"[25] employ parabolic style?

---

23 Susan Suleiman, cited in Stern, *Parables in Midrash,* 15.

24 See also Alan Appelbaum, *The Rabbis' King-Parables: Midrash from the Third-Century Roman Empire* (Piscataway, NJ: Gorgias Press, 2010). Parables are enormously important in rabbinic literature (Appelbaum counts 232 "king parables") where they served as homiletical and exegetical tools in the study house and in the synagogue the synagogue.

25 Dan Miron, cited in Zvia Ginor, "Involuntary Myths: Mania, Mother, and Zion in Orly Castel-Bloom's 'Ummi fi shurl,'" *Prooftexts* 25, no. 3 (2005): 235–257.

III.

I have suggested that presence of animals in Keret and Castel-Bloom (and Kafka) links them to the tradition of the biblical *mashal*. Throughout the Bible, animals are surefire intermediaries between humans and the Deity. A roasted animal is a sign of the covenant, which also protects the next generation. These functions are also pertinent within modern and postmodern parent-child parables.

To review: animals play a special role in the parable tradition. In fables and fairytales, by contrast, plants and animals may assume powers of human speech. Parables are constrained by realism. One might say that animals enter into the parables as trespassers, but once there, they develop a critical function, be that to secure the covenant, or to evoke pathos in the listener. In the story of the poor man's sheep in 2 Samuel 12, the sheep is the prized possession of a poor man who feeds and loves it. But the sheep is stolen and slaughtered by a rich man; and this fictional plot supposedly corresponds to King David's "real crimes"—against Bath Sheba whom he takes to his bed unlawfully; against her husband Uriah, whom he sends to the front lines to be killed (in order to protect Bath Sheba from being accused of adultery once she is found to be pregnant); and against the baby, the offspring of the adulterous union, who dies at God's hands as an explicit punishment for its parents' bad behavior.[26] It took a modernist poet, Yehuda Amichai, to express the role played by sheep in 2 Samuel in his poem titled "The Real Hero of the *'Aqedah*": "He didn't know about the conspiracy between the others."

הַגִּבּוֹר הָאֲמִתִּי שֶׁל הָעֲקֵדָה הָיָה הָאַיִל שֶׁלֹּא יָדַע עַל הַקְּנוּנְיָה בֵּין הָאֲחֵרִים.
הוּא כְּמוֹ הִתְנַדֵּב לָמוּת בִּמְקוֹם יִצְחָק

Like the poor man's poor sheep, the ram didn't know it was a test, a game; he was just in the wrong place at the wrong time "caught in the brush by its horns." In sum: animals in parables are mute, silenced, because parables refuse to name

26 See Joshua Berman's discussion of the parable and its biblical conventions, in "Double Meaning in the Parable of the Poor Man's Ewe (II Samuel 12:1–4)," *Journal of Hebrew Scriptures* 13, no. 14 (2013): "A careful examination of Nathan's censure in vv. 9–12 likewise reveals that there are two meanings to the parable and that they correspond to David's two sins. An understanding of a biblical convention is helpful here. In several other biblical passages a prophet issues a parable and then upon concluding the parable, immediately addresses the target audience, opening with the introduction, כה אמר יהוה, 'Thus says the Lord.' The formulaic introduction always represents the crossover from the parable to its mapping and the subsequent oratory points the target audience to the proper understanding of the parable (see, e.g., 1 Kgs 20:42; Jer 13:9; Ezek 24:6)."

their verdict. The next step is that they are slayed, sacrificed in the interest of the greater, divine-human game. At that point, they acquire a ritual function: they become literal scapegoats. (The scapegoat was invented in the book of Leviticus 16, in a parable of its own: lots are drawn over two goats: "And Aaron shall place lots upon the two goats: one lot 'For the Lord,' and the other lot, 'For Azazel,' for being cast out into the wilderness.) The *'aqedah* narrative may have been composed after such rituals of sacrifice and atonement had been codified.

The ram loses, but Isaac wins. Elie Wiesel offers a different interpretation: "Abraham won. That was why God sent an angel to revoke the order and congratulate him; He himself was too embarrassed."[27] Abraham plays along with the "test," carefully following the instructions, and so forces God's hand. It's not Abraham's faith that impresses God, but his perseverance: God blinks first. Abraham beats God at the game of parable.

What's at stake in what I am calling parabolic style is a not only a mode of writing, but also a mode of reading. Such texts engage the reader in a game of decoding, in which there are winners and losers. They point to, and reject, the top-down transmission of wisdom and values (from God to the parent to the child), purchased at the expense of loyalty. They require a test of faith (from child to parent to God), or between siblings (Cain and Abel; Jesus's Prodigal Son; Lessing's *Ringparabel*).

IV.

Etgar Keret's famous short story "Breaking the Pig" (לשבור את החזיר) offers the clearest reinterpretation of the *'aqedah* of the stories discussed thus far.[28] A father sets out to teach his son good values by giving him a test: the test involves saving up his shekels in a porcelain piggy bank; but the son, appropriately named Yoav ("God is my father"), outwits his own father. He rewrites the rules of the game, midway through. He saves the animal from being sacrificed. He proves that he, the child, is a better person than his own father, arguably a better father even than Abraham, even better than God. In so doing, he deflates the cliché, floated early on in the story, "it's educational."

---

27 Elie Wiesel, *Messengers of God: Biblical Portraits and Legends,* trans. Marion Wiesel (New York: Pocket Books, 1977), 105.

28 Etgar Keret, "Breaking the Pig," in his *The Bus Driver who Wanted to be God,* trans. Miriam Shlesinger et al. (New York: Riverhead Books, 2015). In Hebrew, this story has been published as Etgar Keret, "Lishbor et he-Ḥazir," in *Ga'agu'ai l-Kissinger* (Modiin: Kinneret Zmora-Bitan Dvir, 1994).

The story's first line uses an American pop cultural reference to throw the reader off the scent. Yoav asks his parents to buy him Bart Simpson on a skateboard; the father does not want to give the kid what he wants because he's "spoiled." Once the test is announced, the pieces fall into place. Father will teach his young son "the value of money" by making him earn the Bart Simpson skateboard. He buys him a porcelain piggy bank. The agreement is that each morning, if the son manages to drink a cup of hot cocoa with the skin on top, even to the point of vomiting, he will earn a shekel that he can drop into the piggy bank. "That way, it's educational." As in the *'aqedah,* there is a striking lack of correlation between the trial being imposed (drinking the nauseating drink, killing your promised, beloved son), and the lesson to be learned (the value of money, fear of God). Yoav's father proves to be not much brighter than Homer Simpson, after all.

Yoav does start to acquire values, but these have little to do with money or "education" in the patriarchal sense.

> Actually, the pig's cute, his nose is cold when you touch it, and he smiles when you push the shekel into his back and when you push in half a shekel too, but the nicest thing is that he smiles even when you don't. I gave him a name; I called him Pesachson, after a man who used to live in our mailbox—and my Dad couldn't peel off his label.

That Yoav sees a porcelain pig smile teaches us, first of all, that he probably doesn't see many smiles; that the pig smiles "no matter what I do" reveals the vapidity of the test. Strikingly, Yoav gives the pig an old-world name, learned from a former neighbor. This label stuck on the mailbox suggests the boy's affinity with old world values that will not go away. Pesachson, who "lived in the mailbox," was probably an elderly Holocaust survivor. It makes sense that Yoav names his pet after a dead survivor. The grandfather-survivor appears in other Keret stories such as "Shoes" and "Siren." Young protagonists, wise beyond their years, are drawn to elderly people and to old-world values; though they are prone to misinterpret those people and values—a consistent source of Keretian humor. Children instinctively know that they can "win" that way, by circumventing, as it were, the values of their peers, parents and teachers. Keret's children in "Pipes" and in "Hole in the Wall" turn the tables. But the name Pesachson has a deeper, biblical meaning: it means "son of Passover" and further evokes the paschal lamb. All of this makes sense in light of the fact that the boy's biblical name Yoav means "Yahweh is my father." Yoav is a father to his father, but also to a pig that becomes not only a pet and a friend but a "son." Finally, the son's declaration of unconditional love for the pet ("I love you more than mom and dad. I will love you no matter what") denotes authentic, "real" love that is not contingent upon the Symbolic, the Covenant, or any test.

When the piggy bank is ready to burst, Yoav's father brings out a hammer to crack the open. It is time to buy the Bart Simpson! He believes Yoav has learned *leha'arikh devarim*, "to value things"; he has acquired *muda'ut* ("awareness"). His father announces to the mother, "See, I was right … now he knows that things have value. Right, Yoavi?" This comment directly echoes Genesis 22:12: "… *For now I know* that you fear God … ." Unbeknownst to his father, Yoav has actually passed a different test, which is about feigning obedience to his father even as he unlearns his father's lessons.

> "Go on, break it. You've earned the Bart Simpson, you've worked hard enough for it." Pesachson smiled at me with the sad smile of a porcelain pig who knows his end is near. To hell with the Bart Simpson. Me hit a friend on the head with a hammer? "I don't want the Bart Simpson." I gave Dad the hammer back. "Pesachson is enough for me." "You don't understand," said Dad. "It's all right, it's educational, come on, I'll break it for you." Dad was lifting the hammer. Looking at Mom's crushed eyes [*shvurot*] and Pesachson's tired smile, I knew that it was up to me. If I didn't do anything, he was dead.[29]

Yoav grabs the hammer from his father, as surely as the angel stays Abraham's hand. But as he lives in a family that operates by trials and tests, he decides to trick his father, as well. He asks to stay the "execution" for one night, so that he can stuff in one last shekel in the morning. But Yoav and Pesachson leave together during the night, and Yoav returns him to his rightful habitat: a field with thorns.

> When they left the room I hugged Pesachson very tight and let the tears out. He didn't say anything, only trembled quietly in my hands. "Don't worry," I whispered in his ear, "I'll save you." That night I waited for Dad to finish watching TV in the living room and go to bed. Then I got up very quietly and sneaked out through the porch with Pesachson. We walked together [*be-yaḥad*] in the dark for a long time, until we reached a thorny field. "Pigs are crazy

---

29 Keret, "Breaking the Pig," 29.

> about fields," I told Pesachson as I put him down on the ground, "especially fields with thorns. You'll like it here." I waited for an answer, but Pesachson didn't say anything, and when I touched him on the nose to say good-bye he just gave me a sad look. He knew he'd never see me again.[30]

The last lines evoke the central *'aqedah* motifs of walking together, knowing, looking, and seeing. The father's comment "Now he knows ..." is revealed to be blindness: he misreads obedience for something he calls *muda'ut;* he mistakes a test for an education. The son's claim to "know" what the pig knows is both unreliable and true; he sees that Pesachson is no longer smiling. Because Yoav is a reliable/unreliable narrator, the pathos is all with him; the adult reader can see the naïve truth of the statement while still knowing it to be objectively false. But in both cases, the son's "knowing what the pig knows" repeats and exposes the absurdity of Yoav's father's knowledge about what his son has learned, and both knowings, in turn, shed new light on the dubious rhetorical assurance God gives Abraham: "now I know that you fear God." Abraham's action proves only his obedience, not what he feels. Though God in this test is purported to be omniscient, God is not so omniscient that God does not need to test Abraham in the first place. Does God really now know something about Abraham that he has not known before?

If the ram is the "real hero of the *'aqedah*" per Amichai, Pesachson the pig is the real hero of "Breaking the Pig." "Breaking the Pig" is an exemplary Keret parent-child parable. Keret's young protagonists are inevitably trapped in modern society, victims of their parents, teachers, school bullies, and school psychologists. They are incessantly seeking "a way out," and they instinctively gravitate to their grandparents, to old people, survivors, to animals, to fantasy life, play. The inanimate and the old is ultimately more humane, comforting, and real, than the contests and trials one encounters in day-to-day life. In Keret's parables, if not in life, children win and adults lose. Keret's tale qualifies as a meta-parable, in raising the questions of what is educational, and how one teaches "good values."

Conclusion: In Kafka's Light

The combination of magic; the *Unheimlichkeit* internal to the genre; and the need for forms suitable for transmitting wisdom in a secular world, have made

30 Ibid., 30.

parables popular in modernism and postmodernism. I have tried to show that one need not divide classic, didactic parables from modern, open-ended versions. Modern and postmodern writers evoke the texture or aura of the religious parables in order to create modern anti-parables for their times: in Kafka's case, for early twentieth-century Europe; in Castel-Bloom and Keret's, for post-Zionist Israel. These authors "break" the form of the biblical animal parable (from the *'aqedah* or the "Poor Man's Ewe Lamb" in 2 Samuel) associated with patriarchal religion, in order to coopt the power, play, and deep wisdom of the ancient genre for their own times and purposes.

Keret put his method and his motive into words on the occasion of receiving a major humanitarian prize, The Charles Bronfman Prize, in 2016:

> It is a great honor for me to be the 2016 recipient of The Charles Bronfman Prize. If I had the choice to either become a better writer or a better person, I would choose, with no hesitation, the latter option. I feel that The Charles Bronfman Prize sets the same priorities, being given not only for talent and excellence but more than anything, for the genuine attempt to make a change and shape the world we live in.

What is amusing here is that Keret gives a nod to the very tension in Kafka's parable, "On Parables." He asserts, if only in the subjective tense that parables—words of the wise—can be written in such a way that help people with their "daily cares." With this prize, Keret won in parable, and in reality. He adds:

> When I write, I try not to preach to my readers, but to put them in front of a text presenting an *incomplete* world, thus turning the reading process itself into a *ḥevruta* (fellowship) study. [...] The best way to learn a text is through arguing about its meaning with another person. The value of critical thought is of great moral importance. It doesn't excuse us at any moment from contemplating our decisions and assuming full responsibility for them."[31]

31 "Etgar Keret, Renowned Israeli Author, Wins $100,000 Charles Bronfman Prize," *Haaretz*, June 8, 2016, https://www.haaretz.com/life/books/etgar-keret-wins-100-000-charles-bronfman-prize-1.5393437.

Section III

STUDIES IN JEWISH EDUCATION

CHAPTER 23

Reading the *Sefat Emet* for Religious Consciousness: Modulations on *Or ha-Ganuz**

Elie Holzer

It is my view that Jewish thought and theology arise in the thickness of exegesis and are carried by its forms.

—Michael Fishbane, *Exegetical Imagination*[1]

The direct sensuous apprehension of thought.

—T. S. Eliot, "The Metaphysical Poets"[2]

וְלֹא נָתַן ה' לָכֶם לֵב לָדַעַת וְעֵינַיִם לִרְאוֹת וְאָזְנַיִם לִשְׁמֹעַ עַד הַיּוֹם הַזֶּה. (דברים כט:ג)

But God has not given you a heart to know, nor eyes to see, nor ears to hear, until today. (Deut. 29:3)

Introduction

For the *Sefat Emet*,[3] religious faith is far more than an epistemic state, denoting confidence in the truth of religious propositions. It is, rather, a mode of

* I am very grateful to Sari Steinberg for her comments and for improving my use of English in this article. Likewise, I am grateful to this book's editors for their detailed comments and suggestions.

1 Michael Fishbane, *The Exegetical Imagination: On Jewish Thought and Theology* (Cambridge, MA: Harvard University Press, 1998), 8.

2 T. S. Eliot, "The Metaphysical Poets," *Times Literary Supplement*, October 1921.

3 A rich collection of homilies by R. Yehudah Aryeh Leib Alter (1847–1905), the head of the Ger Hasidim and a leading figure among Polish Jewry, which were published by his son and

existence that reveals and actualizes the godly character of life, by way of attunement to seeing, to hearing, and to being responsive. This implies a particular relationship to religious language, praxis, and spiritual consciousness altogether. Consequently, I have come to view the *Sefat Emet*'s Hasidic homily as a central educational, formative, and transformative literary genre designed to inspire readers to encounter the divine presence through concrete forms of religious living.[4] As an educational scholar, I strive to conceptualize the progression from theory to pedagogical practice: I explore ways to engage the study of the Hasidic homily primarily as means of elevating religious consciousness, rather than as an epistemological activity designed only for attaining understanding, insight, or reflection. Using a phenomenological analysis of the "work of language" in the Hasidic homily, I seek to bring intentional modes of reading, of listening, and of presence to that "work," as well as design dynamic pedagogical activities conducive to the learner's religious growth.

In this article, I discuss theoretical foundations supporting this approach to the study of the *Sefat Emet*'s homilies and coin the concept of *poetic exegesis* regarding their potential formative and transformative effects. I then apply this concept in analyzing one such homily about the *or ha-ganuz* (the concealed light). I conclude with a pedagogical example for the study of this homily as a transformative practice. In connecting scholarship on the Hasidic homily with philosophical and pedagogical reflections, I am paying homage to Boston's Hebrew College. Throughout the hundred years of its existence, Hebrew College has served as an educational institution in two complementary ways: by promoting and yielding serious academic study of Judaism and by addressing, through teaching and learning, the broader Jewish community's continuous as well as newly emerging needs and challenges.

---

son-in-law shortly after R. Alter's death. Both the man and his homiletical oeuvre are known as the *Sefat Emet* (literally, "Language of Truth"). His books are studied in many sociological contexts, far beyond Hasidic circles. For selected translations of the *Sefat Emet*, see Arthur Green, *The Language of Truth: The Torah Commentary of the Sefat Emet* (Philadelphia: JPS, 1998).

4 Elie Holzer, "'*Sefat Emet*' Homilies in the Light of Paul Ricoeur's 'Work of the Text'" [Heb.], *Da'at, A Journal of Jewish Philosophy and Kabbalah* 81 (2016): 321–350; idem, "Prolegomenon to an Exegetical-Spiritual Pedagogy for the Study of Sfat Emet's Homilies: The Case of 'Self-Trust,'" in *The Oral and the Textual in Jewish Tradition and Jewish Education*, ed. Jonathan Cohen (Jerusalem: Magnes Press and the Jewish Theological Seminary Press, 2019), 139–164; idem, "Poetics of Exegesis in the Sefat Emet's Homilies: Semantic Innovations for Discernment and Disclosure," in *Be-Ron Yaḥad: Studies in Jewish Thought and Theology in Honor of Nehemia Polen*, ed. Ariel Evan Mayse and Arthur Green (Boston, MA: Academic Studies Press, 2019), 280–309.

Poetic Discourse

Poetic discourse is often believed to be essentially self-centered and non-referential. Philosophers such as Paul Ricoeur counter this conception by suggesting that second-degree reference, or *poetic reference,* is possible precisely when literal reference is suspended.[5] When engaging the *Sefat Emet*'s homilies through this lens, exegesis serves as far more than a means of legitimizing new ideas by grounding them in Scripture or traditional rabbinic texts. Where lived experiences and the work of language intersect, homiletics—their structure, discourse, and interplay with exegesis —evoke instances of the *Lebenswelt* (the world of lived experiences, as opposed to the conceptualized world), and their power of reference sets forth novel ontologies that reorient the reader by way of an ever-expanding vision of such reality.[6] Furthermore, innovative exegesis may enhance the learner's mindfulness and cultivate attunement to these lived experiences, at the core of which reside traces of the divine presence.

There are a number of ways to conceptualize how the encounter with texts contributes to selfhood and consciousness.[7] For Anthony Thiselton, along with the disclosure of cognitive content, Scripture has transformative purposes and entails a hermeneutics of transformation.[8] This implies that, rather than remaining in the realm of theory or merely satisfying curiosity, interpretation also can lead to a new understanding of the self's identity, responsibility, and potential

5 Paul Ricoeur, *The Rule of Metaphor: Multi-disciplinary Studies of the Creation of Meaning in Language* (Toronto, Buffalo, and London: University of Toronto Press, 1975), study 6. For Ricoeur, texts of a poetic character speak of a possible world and of a possible way of orienting oneself within it. For philosophical roots of this outlook, see Martin Heidegger's predicament, "Language Speaks" and "Language," in *Poetry, Language, Thought* (New York: Harper and Row, 2001), 185–202. For Heidegger, language is essentially not something that human subjects use instrumentally for the purpose of gaining conceptual control over their world. Rather, language is what *displays* human beings—to themselves and to others—as always/already in the world. It is through language that *disclosure* takes place.

6 This perspective is concurrent with the panentheistic principle that lies at the heart of Hasidic philosophies as expressed in a famous statement, "There is no place void of Him" (*Tiqqunei Zohar*, 112b).

7 Historically, the theory of interpretation (or "hermeneutics") began as critical reflection on the nature of textual interpretation. Yet, with the work of Friedrich Schleiermacher and especially Wilhelm Dilthey, hermeneutics also has embraced the interpretation and understanding of human beings, or of that which is "Other" in human life. Furthermore, philosophers such as Martin Heidegger, Hans-Georg Gadamer, and Paul Ricoeur understood hermeneutics as reflecting the essential interpretative character of human existence, to the point that reflection on the hermeneutics of texts has led to a hermeneutics of lived experience. Finally, in the work of Ricoeur, we reach a hermeneutics of selfhood and of human action.

8 Anthony Thiselton, *New Horizons in Hermeneutics: The Theory and Practice of Transforming Biblical Reading* (Grand Rapids, MI: Zondervan Publishing House, 1992), particularly 31–42.

for change and growth.[9] Notwithstanding the qualities of specific texts themselves, transformation hinges on the reader's intentional engagement with the texts' form and evocative content. Such conceptualizations have been creatively expanded in the Jewish context, particularly in Michael Fishbane's hermeneutical theology.[10]

Poetic Exegesis

Could it be that it is precisely what a person is used to seeing that prevents him from seeing?

"I am learning to see. I don't know why it is, but everything enters me more deeply and doesn't stop where it once used to. I have an interior that I never knew of," writes Rainer Maria Rilke.[11]

Broadly speaking, Hasidism's core mission is imbuing a person's consciousness and actions with a sense of, and a felt connection to, *devequt* (cleaving to the divine presence), that is, a mystical experience of the divine who is present everywhere.[12] In pre-Hasidic Jewish mystical literature, *devequt* denoted mainly an "objective" event in the world—"ontological *devequt*" in Jonathan Garb's terminology—while Hasidism added and emphasized the subjective dimension that accompanied it: "experiential *devequt*."[13]

The *Sefat Emet* presents a theology that Benjamin Brown has depicted as "dualistic monism." According to this view, the fundamental and real layer of the world dwells in the endless, invisible, and indivisible unity of God. Yet at a secondary, lower, and

---

9 Without going into further detail, these theoretical views extend to texts with the quality that Gadamer refers to as "classical," which captures the fundamentally unlimited "duration of a work's power to speak directly." H. G. Gadamer, *Truth and Method*, 2nd rev. ed., trans. Joel Weinsheimer and Donald G. Marshall (New York: Continuum, 2004), 285–290.

10 Michael Fishbane, *Sacred Attunement: A Jewish Theology* (Chicago: University of Chicago Press, 2008); idem, *Fragile Finitudes: A Jewish Hermeneutical Theology* (Chicago: University of Chicago Press, forthcoming). Both books are a very blessed source of inspiration and orientation in my own scholarly educational work. See also idem, *Jewish Hermeneutical Theology* (Leiden and Boston: Brill, 2015).

11 Rainer Maria Rilke, *The Notebooks of Malte Laurids Brigge*, trans. M. D. Herter (New York: Norton, 1964), 14.

12 See footnote 4.

13 Jonathan Garb, "On the Kabbalists of Prague" [Heb.], *Kabbalah: Journal for the Study of Jewish Mystical Texts* 14 (2006): 366. Let us recall that Gershom Scholem wrote about mysticism that "there are almost as many definitions of the term as there are writers on the subject" (Gershom Scholem, *Major Trends in Jewish Mysticism* [New York: Schocken, 1954], 3–4) and a somewhat milder version of that statement could probably be said about the meaning of *devequt*.

revealed layer—the realm of the human being—this unity cannot appear in full. In human experience, the divine's unity is intermittently more revealed or more concealed.[14] While the world's true nature is unity (hence *monism*), from the perspective of our lived experience, it operates in a constant dynamic between modes of revealed and concealed existence (hence *dualism*). The core of the *Sefat Emet*'s philosophy, the *'avodah* of the Jew, consists of spiritual-experiential achievement in this unredeemed world.[15] Thus, the idea of "drawing the light of unity" into the world of visibility and of plurality is essential in his homilies.[16]

This form of monism ascribes fundamental priority to the mental and the spiritual as it highlights the centrality of mindful awareness in daily life. Such integrated vision implies the cultivation of an inner disposition and a twofold seeing, open to glimpses of divine presence in and throughout concrete moments of life, requiring an acumen that lifts the veil of day-to-day routines and appearances. It is a non-dualistic consciousness, which transcends the separation between the visible and the invisible and between the inner and the outer: within oneself, in every creature, and in the world at large.[17]

This is to say that the orientations of the self toward inwardness and toward the surrounding world should not be perceived as dichotomized but rather as

---

14 This is a slightly refined description of Benjamin Braun's characterization of the *Sefat Emet*'s theology; see Benjamin Brown, "The Two Types of Unity: Maharal, Sfat Emet, and the Dualistic Turn in Late Hasidic Thought," in *Maharal: Overtones*, ed. Elhanan Reiner et al. (Jerusalem: Zalman Shazar Center, 2015), 411–448. I subscribe to this view as a central foundation of the *Sefat Emet*'s theology but definitely not as its exhaustive conceptualization. For instance, my sense is that at the heart of *Sefat Emet*'s theology, there is a threefold interplay between the revealed and the concealed, namely among the divine, the Torah, and the individual. See *Zohar* 3:73a.

15 The question of whether this goal should be understood as a form of mysticism remains open for exploration. In an instructive and enriching article, Benjamin Brown lists the *Sefat Emet* among those nineteenth-century Hasidic works that, according to his analysis, have substituted religious ideals and values from the first generation of Hasidism for the mystical ideals of these early Hasidic teachers. Benjamin Brown, "Substitutes for Mysticism: A General Model for the Theological Development of Hasidism in the Nineteenth Century," *History of Religions* 56, no. 3 (2017): 247–288.

16 *Meshikhat ha-or* in Hebrew. Needless to say, light is a central theme in Jewish mystical tradition. It is used as a way of describing metaphysical divine emanations and at times also evokes *ḥesed* (kindness, benevolence, goodness, charity, grace). Central in the *Sefat Emet*'s theology is the interplay of visibility and invisibility as expressed in Zoharic literature where "Let there be light" (Gen. 1:3) becomes "Let there be mystery/concealment," for *raz* (secret, hidden) and *or* (light) have identical numerical values; see *Zohar* 1:140a and *Zohar Ḥadash* on Gen. 8d.

17 Such is the main thesis of a book on the *Sefat Emet* that I am currently writing. As to the question of whether seeing, listening, and knowledge of the heart are merely avenues leading to *devequt* or also modes in which *devequt* is actualized, I tend toward the latter, as I will discuss in the book.

two poles of a continuum. A person does not merely oscillate between these axes; rather, a more complex dynamic between the two takes place, as is well reflected in Rilke's neologism *Weltinnenraum* (world-inner-space), indicating a retrieved unity through the abolition of inner and outer boundaries.

Thus, Hasidic life-thought cannot be satisfied with abstract articulations of philosophical inquiries. As noted by Nehemia Polen, the *Sefat Emet*'s interest is "more phenomenological than metaphysical, more a call to awareness than theological assertion."[18] In that regard, at least from a phenomenological perspective, the Hasidic homily—through its literary devices such as exegesis, composition, and structure—seeks to cultivate the reader's awareness of and spiritual response to the presence of divine manifestations in lived experiences. It is from this perspective that I conceptualize hermeneutical innovations, and their potential impact on the reader's hermeneutics of lived experiences, as a sophisticated use of language designed to be concurrently *revelatory* and *formative* for the learner's spiritual growth. Hence, my effort to conceptualize the study of the *Sefat Emet*'s homily as a spiritual practice.[19]

Philosophical Hermeneutics of Reading

Undeniably, the *Sefat Emet*'s homilies are characterized by their abbreviated form, their innovative and aphoristic interpretations of traditional sources, a subtle interplay between hermeneutic work and homiletical structure, and a profound understanding of sacred and religious life. Like other Hasidic masters, the *Sefat Emet* has a fondness for the polysemic nature of biblical and rabbinic language, its fortuitous ambiguities, and its perpetually surprising exegetical interconnections, which form the warp and weave of the semantic[20] web of his written homilies. In

---

18 Nehemia Polen, "Birkat Kohanim in the S'fat Emet," in *Birkat Kohanim: The Priestly Blessing*, ed. David Birnbaum, Martin S. Cohen, and Saul J. Berman (New York: New Paradigm Matrix Publishing, 2016), 263.

19 In this context, the relatively widespread term "spiritual practice" should be understood in the spirit of Pierre Hadot's use of "spiritual exercises," a translation of the Greek word *askesis*. See Pierre Hadot, *Philosophy as a Way of Life: Spiritual Exercises from Socrates to Foucault*, ed. A. Davidson (Oxford: Basil Blackwell, 1995), chapter 3; idem, *What Is Ancient Philosophy?* (Cambridge, MA: Harvard University Press, 2002), chapter 9. According to Hadot, ancient Greco-Roman schools of philosophy perceived their teachings as having to be accompanied by practical exercises of all sorts, with the goal of transforming the self so that it could both see and achieve its highest good and help people reach forms of consciousness that would reconcile them with the universe as a whole.

20 "Semantic" relates to meaning in language.

terms of their semantic content, these exegetical instances evoke an awareness of divine sparks in lived existence. Their referential capacity consists of setting forth novel ontologies[21] that reorient the reader by way of an ever-expanding vision of experienced life with a divine presence ("the innermost point") that is latent in all creatures yet essentially escapes a person's day-to-day gaze, listening, and consciousness.[22] Hence, exegesis becomes a form of *poiesis*—the act of producing something or making something appear through discourse.[23]

Paul Ricoeur's characterization of the poetic function of language further clarifies this point.[24] For example, metaphors generate semantic innovations[25] by bringing together and creating a tension between two unrelated and/or opposed semantic universes, causing the listener or reader to see something new.[26] "Things or ideas which were remote appear now as close," Ricoeur writes. Heuristically speaking,[27] the metaphor gives new meanings to conventional experiences, enabling the reader to see aspects or dimensions of life that usually are diminished by sensory perception or by conceptual and/or everyday language.[28] Ricoeur unearths the dynamics of poetic language not only in formal

---

21 Ontology is the branch of metaphysics concerned with the nature and relations of being.

22 For the meaning and the centrality of the "innermost point" in the *Sefat Emet*'s work, see Arthur Green, *The Language of Truth,* xxxii–xxxiii. Green offers two additional translations for the concept of the innermost point: "core of being" and "inward reality." See also Mendel Piekarz, "The Innermost Point in the Thought of Ger and Aleksander Teachers" [Heb.], in *Studies on Kabbalah in Jewish Philosophy and Moral-Ethical Literature: Dedicated to Isaiah Tishby,* ed. Yosef Dan and Yosef Hacker (Jerusalem: Magnes, 1985/1986), 617–660. The *Sefat Emet* repeatedly emphasizes the task of connecting with the "innermost point" or the "concealed light" in all realms of life. For example, "and our task is to find the concealed light and thus the truth will be revealed and everything will be subdued to God" (*Balaq* 5632 [1802], s.v. *va-yir'a Balaq*). This example is particularly interesting, as it seems to not entirely identify the inner/concealed light with the divine.

23 See Plato's definition of poetry: "whatever that passes from not being into being, the whole cause is composing or poetry." Plato, *Symposium,* 205b–c.

24 Ricoeur's bibliography shows that religious texts and topics have been the focus of much of his attention. See John W. Van Den Hengel, S.C.J., *The Home of Meaning: The Hermeneutics of the Subject of Paul Ricoeur* (Washington: University Press of America, 1982), 212.

25 The term "semantic innovation" refers to a new meaning attributed to language such as a word, a concept, or an expression.

26 See Paul Ricoeur, *The Rule of Metaphor,* 65–100. On the use of parables as a rhetorical device to transform the minds and the hearts of listeners in Hasidic teachings, see Ariel Evan Mayse, *Beyond the Letters: The Question of Language in the Teachings of Rabbi Dov Baer of Mezritch* (PhD diss., Graduate School of Arts and Sciences, Harvard University, Cambridge, MA, 2015), 465–471.

27 "Heuristic" indicates something that involves or serves as an aid to learning, by experimental methods.

28 Paul Ricoeur, "The Metaphorical Process as Cognition, Imagination and Feeling," *Critical Inquiry* 5, no. 1 (1978): 143–159. Poetic language discloses something about lived reality by

metaphors but in the use of symbols and narratives as well.[29] For him, these three forms of language are poetic first and foremost by dint of their heuristic effects. My sense is that the *Sefat Emet* makes use of a fourth form of poetic discourse in the service of spiritual-mental attunement: creative exegetical instances that serve as his homilies' organizing nuclei, hence my term, *poetic exegesis*.[30]

A Religious Hermeneutical Reading

When attending to the *Sefat Emet*'s exegetical constructs from a phenomenological perspective, we distinguish between the *revelatory* and *formative* effects of poetic exegesis. The *revelatory* effect awakens the reader in two complementary ways: the *semantic innovation* of the exegesis produces meaning (that is, an internal extension of language), and its *heuristic function* increases the unveiling power of language vis-à-vis novel and "extraordinary" or latent aspects of reality.[31]

Concurrently, the *formative* effect of poetic exegesis is its potential to mediate learners' cultivation of vision, listening, or knowledge of the heart, changing their day-to-day selves into transformed selves who are present to glimpses of divine presence.[32]

---

making reality appear different from that which is enabled by concepts or by sensory perception. The potential connection between such knowledge and the concept of *da'at* in the Kabbalistic tradition may be an interesting topic for further investigation. Hans Blumenberg writes extensively on the idea that we use metaphors when things are indiscernible within our conceptual categories. Hans Blumenberg, "Light as a Metaphor for Truth: At the Preliminary Stage of Philosophical Concept Formation," in *Modernity and the Hegemony of Vision*, ed. David Michael Levin (Berkeley: University of California Press, 1993), 30–86.

29 Paul Ricoeur, *The Symbolism of Evil*, trans. Emerson Buchanan (Boston, MA: Beacon Press, 1967).

30 On the visual nature of religious experience in Jewish spirituality, see, for example, Elliot R. Wolfson, *Through a Speculum That Shines: Vision and Imagination in Medieval Jewish Mysticism* (Princeton, NJ: Princeton University Press), 1994.

31 It should be noted that any separation between the meaning of language and all that is extra-linguistic, such as references to reality, is methodological at best, since no semantic innovation is possible without the heuristic function.

32 Paul Ricoeur's work on the prefiguration, configuration, and particularly re-figuration as three instances of the reading process are key for theorizing and for the articulation of pedagogical implications of such potential transformations through the reading of texts. Also, such a position begs broader epistemological and ontological questions as to the ability of language to lead beyond mere subjectivism. I cannot address these questions in this article. I do, however, note that we should resist being diminutive about "mere" poetic language. A lesson can be applied from Tillich, where to critics claiming that he thinks "God" is just a symbol, he exclaims that God is "not less" than a symbol: Paul Tillich, *The Dynamics of Faith* (New York: Harper and Collins, 2001).

The *Sefat Emet* makes no use of explicit persuasive rhetoric and avoids writing in the first person.[33] He thereby minimizes instructive discourse, which facilitates readers' adherence to the effects of poetic exegesis, while evoking their trans-subjective responses.

In the following section, I discuss instances of poetic exegesis around the theme of the concealed light (*or ha-ganuz*).[34] This *topos* of early rabbinic and medieval mystical literature is grounded in a midrashic interpretation of the light created on the first day of creation (Gen. 1:3–5). Similar to the very rich symbolism of light in other religious and spiritual traditions, in these bodies of Jewish literature, the primordial light operates as a metaphor for an ontological divine emanation that has been concealed and set apart for the righteous in the "time to come."[35] The metaphor of light, and particularly *or ha-ganuz*, plays an essential role in the *Sefat Emet*'s work, as expressed in the theme of "drawing the light" and the interplay between visibility and concealment in his theology, as indicated above.[36]

Three last methodological remarks before engaging in a close reading of the language at work in one of the *Sefat Emet*'s homilies:

My analysis comes through a phenomenological-hermeneutical approach, focusing on what the written homily "does" and enables the reader to see, as well as its potential effects on that same reader. I adopt Paul Ricoeur's approach

---

33 Unlike in his writings prior to becoming the leader of the Ger Hasidic group (1871): see Yosef Yakobson, "From Youth to Leadership and from Kabbalah to Hasidism: Stages in the Development of the Author of *Sefat Emet*" [Heb.], in *Many Voices: Memorial Volume for Rivka Schatz-Uffenheimer*, vol. 2, ed. Rachel Elior and Yosef Dan (Jerusalem: The Hebrew University, 1956), 429–446.

34 See *Bereshit Rabbah* 12:6; B. Ḥagigah 12a; *Zohar Ḥadash* on Gen. 1:20b; *Zohar Truma* 2:148b–149a; *Shemot Rabbah* 35:1; and *Psikta Rabbati* (ed. Ish Shalom) 36. The following is the version from *Bereshit Rabbah* 12:6 and B. Ḥagigah 12a: "And light was created on the first day? But it is written, 'and God set them in the firmament of the heaven' (Gen. 1:17), and it is written, 'and there was evening and there was morning, a fourth day' (Gen. 1:19). It is like R. Elazar. For R. Elazar said, 'The light which the Holy One, blessed be He, created on the first day, Adam saw through it from one end of the world to the other. When the Holy One, blessed be He, peered at the generation of the Flood and the generation of the Dispersion, and saw that their actions were destructive, He stood up and hid it from them, as it is said, 'And from the wicked their light is withheld' (Job 38:15). And for whom did He take it away? For the righteous of the time to come, as it is said, 'And God saw the light, that it was good' (Gen. 1:4), and good only refers to the righteous, as it is said, 'Say of the righteous, that he is good' (Isa. 3:10). Once He saw the light He hid away for the righteous, He rejoiced, as it is said, 'He rejoices at the light of the righteous' (Prov. 13:9)."

35 See footnote 14. See also Elliot R. Wolfson, "Hermeneutics of Light in Medieval Kabbalah," in *The Presence of Light: Divine Radiance and Religious Experience*, ed. Matthew T. Kapstein (Chicago: University of Chicago Press, 2004).

36 See footnote 14. A comprehensive analysis of the various ways by which *or ha-ganuz* is interpreted and contributes to the *Sefat Emet*'s theology will be discussed in a future article.

according to which we should "cease to ask the question of the inspiration of writings in the psychologizing terms of an insufflation of meaning to an author that projects itself into the text."[37] Rather, we turn to the text itself, and the referents inherent to the "world" described in the text. Only to the extent that we can imaginatively enter into this world does the text appear meaningful. Thus, in the context of the *Sefat Emet*'s homily, one must speak of *presentation* rather than *representation* because the agent of this showing is not Rabbi Alter but the homily itself. The author plays a maieutic role, a servant both of that which shows itself and of those who are helped to "see" its self-presentation.[38]

Rabbinic and Hasidic texts such as the homily discussed in this article often present ontological realities. Yet, I will intermittently analyze potential effects of the homily's "work of language" on the reader's consciousness. This is to say that the homily "demonstrates" only in the sense of showing what can be "seen." In the words of Heidegger: "to let that which shows itself be seen from itself in the very way in which it shows itself from itself."[39] Thus, light also evokes a person's visionary experience in which one not only "sees" those "places" but also encounters presences.[40] It is a perceived light due to its "weightiness," often described as divine glory, employing the Hebrew *kavod,* which refers to both glory and weightiness.[41] Such forms of transcendental consciousness-transformation are central in the *Sefat Emet*'s theology, particularly regarding Shabbat, as will be evident in the sample homily.[42]

Throughout my analysis, I pay attention not only to the *Sefat Emet*'s interpretations, but also to insertions and intertwinements of biblical and rabbinic citations, a central feature of his exegetical art. In the wake of the above, I do not relate to such insertions as "proof-texts," commonly understood as providing traditional authority or legitimation to the ideas discussed. Rather, I analyze them as a major key of *poetic exegesis* in both revelatory and potentially formative aspects within the reader's consciousness.[43]

---

37 Paul Ricoeur, "Philosophy and Religious Language," in *Figuring the Sacred: Religion, Narrative, and Imagination*, ed. Mark I. Wallace (Minneapolis: Augsberg Fortress, 1995), 44.

38 Of course, this does not apply to explicit biographical or historical references.

39 Martin Heidegger, *Being and Time* (New York: Harper and Row, 1962), 34.

40 See footnote 14.

41 See, for example, Isaiah 3:6: *male kol ha-areẓ kevodo.*

42 See Michael Fishbane, "Transcendental Consciousness and Stillness in the Mystical Theology of R. Yehudah Arieh Leib of Gur," in *Sabbath: Idea, History, Reality*, ed. G. Blidstein (Beersheba: Ben Gurion University of the Negev Press, 2004), 119–129.

43 Some scholars disagree on the value of exegesis in Hasidic homilies. Thus, for Louis Jacobs, exegesis is no more than a means to reach foregone conclusions and does not abide basic rules of language. See Louis Jacobs, *Their Heads in Heaven: Unfamiliar Aspects of Hasidism*

Sefat Emet, Shabbat Bereshit 5648 [1888]

I. Homiletic Exposition: Light, Face, and Shabbat

> *Section 1*: In the midrash on "And [God] blessed," He blessed it with the lights; the light of the human face is not the same during the week as it is on Shabbat.[44]

So opens the homily, reflecting the *Sefat Emet*'s common pattern of beginning with a biblical or midrashic source.[45] At first glance, this literary feature matches the convention of quoting the text that is about to be interpreted. Yet, from a phenomenological perspective, we notice that it is an abbreviated form of a longer text, implying that the reader is presumed to be fully acquainted with the midrash in question.[46] In addition, the *Sefat Emet* does not clarify what about the midrash triggers his interest or presents a textual challenge. Both the truncation and the omission of any such clarification compel readers to defamiliarize their earlier understanding of the midrash. Such a problematization of previous assumptions enhances a stance of wonderment, solicitude, and receptiveness.[47] This recurring pedagogical device in the *Sefat Emet*'s homilies can be labeled as "homiletic exposition." In this example, it makes the reader wonder about the nature of the light that emanates from the human face, as well as about the meaning of its intensification on Shabbat.[48]

(London: Vallentine Mitchell, 2005), 27. Norman Lamm downplays the importance of exegesis in favor of the homilies' ideas. It should be noted, however, that Lamm largely confines himself to writings of the first three generations of Hasidism. See Norman Lamm, ed., *The Religious Thought of Hasidism: Text and Commentary: Sources and Studies in Kabbalah, Hasidism and Jewish Thought*, vol. 4 (New York: Yeshiva University Press, 1999), xxx–xxxi. A refined analysis of the vast varieties of Hasidic homily oeuvres may indicate a significant disparateness in the roles played by exegesis.

44 *Bereshit Rabbah* 11:2.

45 The mode of the *Sefat Emet*'s selective citations at the opening of his homilies deserves a careful analysis, which is beyond the scope of this article.

46 The midrash renders: "The verse says: 'And God blessed the seventh day and sanctified it' (Gen. 2:3). By what has God blessed and by what has He sanctified the seventh day? He blessed it with the light of the human face: the light of the human face is not the same during the week as it is on Shabbat" (*Bereshit Rabbah* 11:2).

47 "Problematization" is widely discussed in the pedagogical philosophy of Paulo Freire. It is a pedagogical practice used to disrupt taken-for-granted truths and is thereby a foundation of critical pedagogy. See Paulo Freire, *Pedagogy of the Oppressed* (New York: Continuum, 2005).

48 From a theoretical perspective, for philosophical hermeneutics, a sentence or a text is meaningful if and only if it is an answer to a real (that is, asked) question. Gadamer writes: "One speaks with motivation, and does not just make a statement but answers a question," Hans-Georg Gadamer, "Language and Understanding," in *The Gadamer Reader: A Bouquet of the*

II. The Light of the Face

> *Section 2*: The meaning [of this light] is a disclosure of inwardness [*hitgalut ha-penimiyut*], as it is written: "A person's wisdom makes his face radiate" (Eccl. 8:1), thus referring to the disclosure of the expanded soul.[49]

We notice a twofold hermeneutic move: first, the *Sefat Emet* points to the light on the face as an expression of a person's invisible inwardness. This move is then further deepened by the insertion from Ecclesiastes, "A person's wisdom makes his face radiate." Again, at *prima facie*, the reader knows that in its biblical context, the word "wisdom" refers to a person's intelligence. Yet, the *Sefat Emet* reinterprets it to refer to the soul's radiance.

Both exegetical moves illustrate the revelatory function of poetic exegesis: they expand the meaning of the light that radiates from the human face to an impressionistic expression of a person's soul. Heuristically speaking, they orient the reader toward that "extraordinary" aspect of reality as a particular instance of wisdom showing on a person's face.

In terms of their formative function, these insights convey to readers the need to transmute their day-to-day (often objectifying, instrumental, or even scientific) gaze of human faces into a mindful "seeing" capable of sensing the presence of hidden inwardness[50] and capable of perceiving disclosure of the unseen soul.[51]

Later Writings, ed. R. Palmer (Evanston: Northwestern University Press, 1997), 104. Such implicit questions seem to answer, "What is this?" and, from a pedagogical perspective, "What sentence might help clarify the basic unit of language called 'this midrash'?" Brief utterances, whether written or spoken, do not yield meaning outside dialogue based on the dynamic of question and answer. See Gadamer, *Truth and Method*, 391. For the role of the historical context that has conditioned the genesis and the effect of the text, see Paul Ricoeur, *Time and Narrative*, vol. 3 (Chicago: University of Chicago Press, 1988), 174.

49 In this context, I translate the word *hitgalut* as "disclosure" rather than literally, as "revelation." The latter is identified as a central theological concept referring to God's revelation at Sinai. In contrast, in this context, *hitgalut ha-penimiyut* refers to the consciousness's awakening to the presence of something that was hidden. From that perspective, the term "disclosure" used in phenomenological/hermeneutic discourse seems more appropriate, as it also evokes appearance and being in the presence of.

50 In the words of the *Sefat Emet*: "The meaning [of this light] is a revealing of inwardness."

51 In the words of the *Sefat Emet*: "thus referring to the expanded soul's disclosure."

III. The Concealed Light in the World

The *Sefat Emet* carries the image of the light as a metaphor for disclosure of inwardness into the next section, this time to a new "place" and time: the all-encompassing world and the context of Shabbat.

> *Section* 3: And on the holy Shabbat, inwardness discloses itself in the entire world, as it is written, "And there was light" (Gen. 1:3), and our Sages explained that [the light] has been hidden away for the righteous.[52]

This section presents semantic innovations by creatively juxtaposing three separate units:

> Unit A: On the holy Shabbat, inwardness discloses itself in the entire world
>
> Unit B: as it is written, "And there was light" (Gen. 1:3),
>
> Unit C: and our Sages explained that [the light] has been hidden away for the righteous.

Most likely, unit A here is the outcome of the *Sefat Emet*'s interpretive move in sections 1 and 2. To recall, he first cites *Bereshit Rabbah* 11:2 about the light's radiance from the face during Shabbat (section 1). In section 2, he interprets that light as an expression of inwardness. Here (in unit A of section 3), the *Sefat Emet* combines the previous two ideas to say that inwardness discloses itself on Shabbat and, in addition, he expands the locus of that disclosure to the entire world by alluding to *Bereshit Rabbah* 11:2.

However, upon closer examination, we notice that the theme of primordial light is not associated with the idea of Shabbat in any of the major primary sources that discuss this theme.[53] It seems to be the *Sefat Emet*'s innovation to coalesce these two ideas through exegesis, the heuristic effect of which orients

---

52 Let us note that the literary/interpretive composition of sections 2 and 3 require further attention, which might also have poetic effects on the reader, who would be aware of the three observations that follow.

53 *Bereshit Rabbah* 12:6; B. Ḥagigah 12a; *Zohar Ḥadash* on Gen. 1:20b; and *Zohar Terumah* 2:148b–149a.

the reader toward a particular Shabbat consciousness, that is, an attunement to the presence of the inwardness of the world.[54]

Units B and C further reinforce that effect. As an entity, they reflect a succinct summary of the midrash about the primordial light.[55] However, unit A (the *Sefat Emet*'s own semantic innovation) has recontextualized the reader's imagination of the primordial light as belonging to a Shabbat consciousness.

Units B and C may also have a formative effect. In unit B, the *Sefat Emet* uses a Biblical quote: "And there was light." Again, we notice the absence of these words from Genesis in the primary sources that discuss the primordial light.[56] The *Sefat Emet*'s insertion of these particular words from Genesis 1:3 is almost certainly intentional. The reader may hear them as a call to attention for a visionary experience: "See! There is light. And yet, it has been concealed, waiting to be unveiled by your gaze."[57]

Finally, in unit C, the *Sefat Emet* paraphrases the midrash, saying "that [the light] has been hidden away for the righteous." We notice that he omits the end of the sentence in the midrash: "in the time to come." The heuristic effect of this

---

54 See Ezek. 46:1: "Thus said the Lord God: The gate of the inner court that looks toward the east shall be shut the six working days; but on the day of Shabbat it shall be opened, and on the day of the new moon it shall be opened." The *Sefat Emet* invokes this verse frequently and interprets the words "on the day of Shabbat it shall be opened" as a metaphor that indicates the inner gate, or the gateway to inwardness, implying that Shabbat is a time of access to the inwardness of oneself and of creation. For an example of the former, see *Sefat Emet, Shabbat Shuva Ha'azinu* 5636 [1875], and for the latter, see ibid., *Ha-Ḥodesh* 5657 [1897].

55 See footnote 32.

56 The first section of the *Zohar Ḥadash*, which discusses the topic of the concealed light, does begin by quoting, "Let there be light. And there was light," but this is not enough to account for the *Sefat Emet*'s selection in each of these two sections. Also, the story of the light's concealment in *Bereshit Rabbah* and B. Ḥagigah is associated with Gen. 1:4: "And God saw the light, that it was good," not with Gen. 1:3 as the *Sefat Emet* postulates in both sections. It goes without saying that one explanation of these discrepancies between the primary sources and the *Sefat Emet*'s homiletical composition in these two sections could be a lack of attention on the part of the author. Yet another possibility is that these are deliberate choices, designed to offer particular insights—as seems to be borne out by this and other similar instances in the *Sefat Emet*. In the *Book of the Zohar* 1:46a, Rabbi Yehuda emphasizes the presence of the word *va-yehi* rather than *ve-haya* (Gen. 1:3) as implying that this was not a new light but the retrieving of a light that had already been present. The *Sefat Emet* does not seem to relate to this view.

57 "Concealed" does not imply absent, nor inaccessible. Rather, it conveys that in order to be perceived, the light requires attention, seeking, and dispositions, among which is learning to see. See, for example, in *Zohar* Gen. 46:

רבי יהודה אומר, אם היה נגנז מכל וכל לא היה עומד העולם אפילו רגע אחד, אלא נגנז ונזרע כזרע הזה ועושה תולדות וזרעים ופירות, וממנו נתקיים העולם, ואין לך יום שאינו יוצא ממנו בעולם, ומקיים הכל, כי בו מזין הקב"ה את העולם, ובכל מקום שעוסקים בתורה בלילה יוצא חוט אחד מאור ההוא הגנוז, ונמשך על אלו שעוסקים בתורה, זה שאמר יומם יצוה ה' חסדו ובלילה שירה עמי.

omission is to situate the Shabbat consciousness as accessible by the reader in the *present* rather than in a utopian future.

IV. The Concealed Light in Each Creature

In the following section, we notice the *Sefat Emet*'s semantic innovation, which consists of focusing the reader's attention on the light concealed within each creature as it discloses itself on Shabbat.

> *Section 4*: And the saying "Let there be light" relates to each particular creature, because each shares in this light, yet it has been concealed and on Shabbat [some of it] is disclosed.

To that end, the *Sefat Emet* turns again to Genesis 1:3. Yet, unlike in the previous section, he inserts God's declaration, "Let there be light." A possible heuristic effect of this insertion is to cause "Let there be light" to resonate as a recurring call to readers. That is, it may awaken them to a state of consciousness, a felt visionary presence of this light in each creature. This possibility is reinforced by the fact that in this section, the *Sefat Emet* does not mention the ability of the righteous to access that light, which again, from a heuristic point of view, seems to allow all readers—even those who do not identify themselves as righteous—to hear the call.

V. Radiance, Dimmed Light, and Candlelight

> *Section 5:* And during the weekdays [that light is] like a speculum that does not radiate, and on Shabbat, like a speculum that illuminates. And thus the mitzvah of lighting Shabbat candles, to allude to the disclosure of this light on the holy Shabbat.

The concept of specula that do and do not radiate appears in talmudic literature to indicate different levels of intensity and clarity of prophetic visions.[58] The *Sefat Emet* introduces the concept as an image expressing the difference in the intensity of the primordial light on Shabbat (when the light discloses itself) and

58 See B. Yevamot 49b, *Zohar Ḥadash* on Genesis, *Midrash ha-Ne'elam* 17a. See also Wolfson, *Through a Speculum that Shines.*

during the weekdays (when it does not).[59] Let us note that unlike the term "concealed" or "hidden," this concept does not suggest absence of light but, rather, a dimmed light.[60]

The heuristic effect of this insertion is to emphasize for the reader the variable intensities of light's "presences" between weekdays and Shabbat. At this point, the *Sefat Emet* points to the lighting of the Shabbat candles, a ritual that both marks the threshold of the time at which the light of inwardness discloses itself and mirrors that extra light.[61]

The analysis of these five cumulative sections suffices to make visible the heuristic aspect of the homily's diachronic flow. Each of the sections orients the readers' attention to a place where their Shabbat consciousness should expand toward a "vision of the light." That is, it should give them a glimpse of the invisible unity of God that resides everywhere. Readers are first drawn to wonder about the textual imagery of the light that emanates from a person's face on Shabbat (section 1). From the visible human face, they then move toward an imagined vision of divine inwardness, evoked by that light (section 2). Next, they are oriented toward a more abstract focus of awareness, namely an imagined vision of the divine inwardness of the entire world (section 3). At this point, the homily turns back toward more tangible targets worthy of spiritual attention: the divine inwardness that can be envisioned in each distinct creature (section 4). Finally, the readers' attention is led to the concrete Shabbat candle, the kindling of which raises their awareness of the liminal moment beyond which the divine light discloses itself in all these different realms. At this point, most readers likely are refocused toward the light that radiates from a person's face.[62]

---

59 In the Hebrew, "weekdays" is rendered as *yemei ha-ma'ase*, days of "doing" or of action.

60 See footnote 55.

61 A comparison with the metaphor of a bright big light in the thought of René Descartes is in place. It stands for the bright light of reason, a light that doesn't leave much room for the imagination that is needed to allow for the interplay of presence and concealment in human beings as well as in the world around them. For a spiritual, non-religious contemplative approach to the flickering and vulnerable light of a candle, see Gaston Bachelard, *The Flame of a Candle* (Dallas: The Dallas Institute Publications, 1988). While operating on different ontological assumptions, Bachelard's work on reverie is worth putting into dialogue with *Sefat Emet*'s work on Shabbat consciousness, as both attend to the candle. For *Sefat Emet*, the light of the Shabbat candle marks the threshold to an expanded Shabbat consciousness, leading to *devequt*. Bachelard writes, "Reveries of faint light make the dreamer feel at home; the dreamer's unconscious becomes home for him. The dreamer, that twin of our being, that chiaroscuro of the thinking person, feels secure in his existence during this reverie in faint light." Bachelard, *The Flame of a Candle*, 4. For religious reveries focused on the flame of the Ḥanukkah candle, see *Sefat Emet, Ḥanukkah* 5632 [1871] and ibid., 5634 [1873].

62 The *Sefat Emet*'s homily continues by bringing forth additional aspects of such expanded Shabbat consciousness, which is beyond the scope of this article. Similarly, the theme of Shabbat's shining light, emanating from human faces, plays a central role in the *Sefat Emet*'s work.

Pedagogical Implications

Often, written and oral discourse about the study of Hasidic homilies focuses on content, with very little attention paid to the forms of engagement in studying. Yet, from a historical perspective, text study has served not only as a method of acquiring knowledge about the Jewish tradition, but also as a devotional activity believed to have a transformative impact on its practitioners' values and beliefs. People have studied traditional texts not only in order "to know," but also to be guided and inspired. Individuals also are likely more receptive to undergoing some type of transformation if they believe that these texts have metaphysical or inspired origins.[63] Today, however, individuals who identify as members of secular societies typically do not imbue traditional texts with metaphysical qualities nor with this type of visceral trust. Nevertheless, the concept of transformation continues to be associated with text study, primarily because of the transformative potential of readers' engagement with texts. This shift is, in part, a result of the "hermeneutic turn"—the growing awareness of the impact of processes of interpretation in literature and philosophy, emphasizing and inviting a refined attention to the *ways* people engage in meaning-making in general and with texts in particular.[64] Nicholas Davey's characterization of this shift aligns with my approach to the study of the *Sefat Emet*'s homily: "As encounters with texts (and others) are lived, learning from experience derives not just from that which is encountered but from the character of the encounter itself."[65]

One of John Dewey's important contributions to educational discourse is his conception of the pedagogical aspects of teaching as a focus of educational goals. According to Dewey, pedagogy should be evaluated on the basis of its educational impact on the learner and its direct relationship with the subject

---

63 The transformative effects of text study pertain to actions, beliefs, character development, etc. For examples in the Jewish tradition, see, for example, *Zohar* 2:99a–b; Moshe Idel, *Language, Torah and Hermeneutics in Abraham Abulafia* (Albany, NY: State University of New York Press, 1989). See also different meanings attributed to *Torah lishmah* study: Norman Lamm, *Torah Lishmah: In the Works of Rabbi Hayyim of Volozhin and His Contemporaries* (New York: Yeshiva University Press, 1989). Compare also to the concept of *lectio divina* in Christian traditions.

64 This is, of course, only one important change that has occurred. Broadly speaking, different literary and hermeneutical theories emphasize different foci, such as the text, the author's intention, the reader, and the reading process. See Thiselton, *New Horizons in Hermeneutics*. See also Wolfgang Iser, *The Act of Reading* (Baltimore, MD: Johns Hopkins University Press, 1978); Hans Robert Jauss, *Aesthetic Experience and Literary Hermeneutics* (Minneapolis: University of Minnesota Press, 1982); and idem *Toward an Aesthetic of Reception* (Minneapolis: University of Minnesota Press, 1982).

65 Nicholas Davey, *Unquiet Understanding: Gadamer's Philosophical Hermeneutics* (Albany, NY: State University of New York Press, 2006), 6.

matter.[66] This view obliterates the radical dichotomy of pedagogy and content (or means and ends), which characterizes major schools of thought in education as well as typical pedagogical habits of teachers of Hasidic texts.[67]

Thus, a deliberate decision to study the homily "on its own terms" may call for more refined attention to the pedagogical aspects of the study. What practical implications might such a view hold for teachers' pedagogical thinking and their design of practices for the study of Hasidic homilies? This article opens a discussion of this broad question by bringing an example from the *Sefat Emet*'s oeuvre. First, there is a need to conceptualize the theoretical foundations of the homilies' discourse—the "work of language"—involving engagement with fragmentary formulations and citations as instances of poetic exegesis. This was exemplified by a close reading of the homily using the lens of "innovative" and the "formative" effects. I now conclude with one practical implementation of the potentially transformative character of the study of this text, by means of taking the images that emerge from the content and engaging them contemplatively as figures of the heart.

Contemplative Application

The *Sefat Emet* aims to help readers develop an expanded Shabbat consciousness around different foci of spiritual vision. Our framing of the homily on the basis of Ricoeur's theory highlights the role of imagination as a venue for knowledge. Imagination suspends the first-order referential world and, as a result, brings to the fore a deeper attunement to *being*. As Ricoeur writes, poetic experience can "insert us within the world in a non-objectifying fashion," the self being reconstructed affectively, as a positive change of heart begins to emerge.[68] These foundations may open new possibilities for a re-evaluation of the role of imagination in the study of Hasidic language, its effects on inner transformation, and its connection with meditative practices of reading.[69]

---

66 John Dewey, *Democracy and Education* (New York: The MacMillan Company, 1906).

67 John Dunne, *Back to the Rough Ground: Practical Judgment and the Lure of Technique* (Notre Dame, IN: University of Notre Dame Press, 2001).

68 Ricoeur, "The Metaphorical Process," 157.

69 See footnote 17 about the role of "spiritual practice." On the cultivation of moral imagination, see Martha C. Nussbaum, *Poetic Justice: The Literary Imagination and Public Life* (Boston, MA: Beacon Press, 1995). According to Nussbaum, there is ethical value in emotions, and it is a mistake to ostracize them from the sphere of philosophical relevance. See also Elie Holzer, "Allowing the Text to Do Its Pedagogical Work: Connecting Moral Education and Interpretive Activity," *Journal of Moral Education* 6, no. 4 (2007): 497–514.

To implement this pedagogically, one may wish to allow for contemplative reading to be a significant component of the homily's study.

Transformative Awareness

When participants cultivate their inner depth, they may alter their attitude toward themselves and the world around them. The long-term goal of contemplative study of the homily is self-transformation: to go beyond learners' usual psychological patterns and structures of seeing and to help them awaken their own inner dimension.

Such study would be divided into two major rounds. In the first round, learners would merely conduct a close reading of the homily, figuring out its various parts and attending to the exegetical moves in particular. The latter implies paying close attention to the different forms of the *Sefat Emet*'s interpretive work, including the examination of biblical and rabbinic citations in their original context. The first round would end by making sense of the ideas discussed in the homily.

On this background, learners then would engage in a contemplative reading of the homily. To that end, each sentence or "section" of the text would be printed on a new line, which would be conducive to the learners' focused attention on each. This second round would begin with exercises designed to achieve a quiet and centered inner attitude, such as:

- An imagery exercise in which participants form in their minds an image of sitting in nature, together with their companions.
- A breathing exercise or a posture exercise in which the body is used as a metaphor for inner attitudes. The facilitator can provide instructions such as: "You are now in your body. Relax, step back from yourself, and open an empty space in your core."

At this point, each section is read aloud slowly. The purpose here is not to discuss the text but to carefully linger on the semantic innovations as well as on the image provided by the sections as whole. Thus, in the homily discussed above, participants would take time to silently process their wonderment about the image of the radiant face on Shabbat, described in the midrash. Subsequently, participants would engage in contemplative methods with each additional separate section, through a number of guided or evocative meditation techniques. Finally, participants would open an inner space of silence and would be attentive to the words that "want" to speak in them in that space, write them down, or share them aloud.

Needless to say, this kind of formative pedagogy, based on slow reading and deep attention to the work of language, is countercultural to institutionalized emphases on speed and efficiency. Yet, in a culture dominated by one-sided visibility,[70] this type of study of the *Sefat Emet*'s homily may hold particular promise for those who seeks to cultivate what Rilke has called a kind of "in-seeing":

> If I were to tell you where my greatest feeling, my universal feeling,
> the bliss of my earthly existence has been,
> I would have to confess: It has always, here and there,
> been in this kind of in-seeing,
> in the indescribably swift, deep, timeless moments
> of this divine seeing into the heart of things.[71]

70 The ideology of visual culture is an essential characteristic of contemporary culture: "In a society dominated by the production and consumption of images, no part of life can remain immune from the invasion of spectacle," (Christopher Lasch, *The Culture of Narcissism: American Life in an Age of Diminishing Expectations* [New York: W. W. Norton, 1991], 122). "The spectacle is the acme of ideology, for in its full flower it exposes and manifests the essence of all ideological systems: the impoverishment, enslavement and negation of real life," (Guy Debord, *The Society of the Spectacle* [New York: Zone, 1994], 151). For more recent and insightful discussions on the culture of spectacle and its deep connections to the philosophies and the ethos of cultural neo-liberalism, see Byung-Chul Han, *The Transparency Society* (Stanford, CA: Stanford University Press, 2015); idem, *Saving Beauty* (Medford, MA: Polity Press, 2018). In this context, the kind of vision promoted by spiritual works such as *Sefat Emet* should probably become a central topic of attention in contemporary Jewish religious educational thought and pedagogical practice—particularly by educators who seek to be inspired by Hasidic thought traditions. I am planning to discuss this topic in a future article.

71 Rainer Maria Rilke, *Rilke and Benvenuta: An Intimate Correspondence* (New York: Fromm International Publishing Corporation, 1987).

CHAPTER 24

Growing Up Jewish: Me'ah and American Jewish Adulthood

David B. Starr

In the 1990s the Boston Jewish community created and implemented the Me'ah program. An intensive curriculum-based two-year program built to make adults literate in Jewish history, texts, and ideas, Me'ah proposed to change people and institutions. The program became a school for adults, in the belief that education shaped and reshaped people and communities and cultures.

Me'ah emerged from the vision and commitment of the Combined Jewish Philanthropies (CJP) and Hebrew College, two Boston Jewish communal institutions. Designed to resonate with Boston's academic heritage, the best academics from the finest colleges and universities in the area taught in the program. They used state-of-the-art primary and secondary sources and they assigned homework to the students.

This initiative asserted that school could and should lead, not follow community; that education would create new Jews and new Jewish communities, in effect to reverse or to push beyond previous syntheses of American and Jewish life. And instead of creating a new future by a focus on children, this effort aimed at a new present by attacking the problem of adult Jewish illiteracy. This paper tells the story of that effort.

The origin of Me'ah began on a sunny day in June 1966, when Columbia historian Gerson Cohen delivered the commencement address at Hebrew Teacher's College in Brookline. He titled his talk "The Blessings of Assimilation in Jewish History." He told the audience that the history of the Jews revealed many and diverse aspects of assimilation. Those included the desire to erase one's Jewishness and to become something else. But on that bright day he celebrated assimilation for its complex and more often positive role in the survival of Judaism, by appropriating "new forms and ideas for the sake of growth and enrichment." Sectarian desires to withdraw to the cave offered poor chances for surviving, much less thriving. As scary as interaction with others might be, Jews historically understood engagement as the only real way forward.[1]

Cohen urged his audience to embrace both rich American and Jewish lives, a vision that required literacy in both traditions. That vision went beyond merely holding and balancing two different worlds. Instead he thought organically about the positive effects each civilization made upon the other: the "street" of the world enriched the "tent" of Jewishness, while Jewishness offered much in return to the world. If Jews rejected America or Judaism they risked short-changing both. Whether American Jews would make such an effort at synthesis remained to be seen.

Fast forward a quarter of a century later to the National Jewish Population Survey of 1990. It delivered the bad news of the negative type of assimilation of which Dr. Cohen spoke but in some ways optimistically chose not to highlight in 1966. Jews now intermarried with much greater frequency. Only a small percentage of Jews—mostly Orthodox—committed to Jewish parochial school or to retention of a traditional home observance including Shabbat and the dietary laws or to regular synagogue attendance. Statistically Jews—alone of all American religious groups—believed in and practiced a secular Americanism no matter how much they insisted that Judaism mattered. The organized community responded to such dire data by asserting the need for stronger Jewish education and by investing in old and new programs alike.

The Boston version of such efforts centered around two leaders at two institutions, both in the midst of change. David Gordis of Hebrew College (HC) and Barry Shrage of the Combined Jewish Philanthropies (CJP) came together for sole and shared purposes, both trying to reposition their institutions.

Though not necessarily obvious on the surface, Gordis and Shrage shared a central value that became a purpose. Gordis was a rabbi who wanted to shape communal policy, and Shrage made communal policy and cared deeply about Judaism. They both wanted to create an educated Jewish public. They both regarded as obsessive and short-sighted the community's emotional and programmatic commitment to nurturing Jewish children at the expense of investing in adults—the people who raised those young people like parents and teachers.

Jewish children needed Jewish adults who actually knew and expressed the culture that they then could organically pass on to children. No culture could survive without adults. Jewish culture was no longer organically accessible.

---

1 Gerson D. Cohen, "The Blessing of Assimilation in Jewish History," in his *Jewish History and Jewish Destiny* (New York: The Jewish Theological Seminary of America, 1997), 145–156.

The Jewish neighborhood, the Jewish street, Jewish vernacular languages, the entire notion of a mimetic Jewishness that held everyone in its embrace, gave way to more segmented Jewish life in suburbs like Brookline, Newton, and beyond.

Jewish community would have to be rebuilt, one that recreated Jewish adulthood. Gordis and Shrage gambled that a new kind of adult learning program could serve as a laboratory for this invention. If it worked, it would beget richer Jewish community. Rather than schools expressing culture, schools would create it. From that vision came Me'ah.[2]

Gordis came to Boston in January 1993 to take the helm of Hebrew College. Trained in the Conservative movement as a rabbi and holding a doctorate in rabbinics, Gordis possessed a *clal Yisra'el* vision. He believed that the Jewish community needed to focus on strengthening Jewish identity through modern learning methods applied to the entire corpus of Jewish cultural and civilization. He saw HC as pluralistic and transdenominational; partnering with, not opposing existing communal institutions.

Founded in 1921 as Hebrew Teachers College, HC faced a hard transition. It came into being to train teachers for the emerging network of Hebrew schools. At the same time it provided a basis from which to encourage Jewish higher education, a locus of Hebraism and Haskalah and Zionism. At a time when American colleges and universities remained indifferent or hostile to Jewish studies, the Hebrew colleges provided a haven for idealistic youth who wanted to continue their formal Jewish learning in an educationally organized manner, one not denominationally based or focused. From the 1930s through the 1960s, figures who became prominent in American Jewish life and scholarship, like Ben Halpern, Theodore White, Frank Manuel, Walter Ackerman, Arnold Band, Isadore Twersky, and Paula Hyman, all combined Harvard in the mornings and

---

2 Jonathan Sarna reminds us that American Jewish adult education innovations usually respond to crisis. See Robert Peers, *Adult Education: A Comparative Study* (London and New York: Routledge and Kegan Paul, 1958), as cited in Jonathan Sarna, "The Cyclical History of Adult Jewish Learning in the United States: Peer's Law and its Implications," in *Educational Deliberations: Essays in Honor of Seymour Fox* (Jerusalem: Keter, 2005), 207–222. On the historical implications of how culture produces education and vice versa, Bernard Bailyn argued that education needed to be viewed "not only as formal pedagogy but as the entire process by which a culture transmits itself across the generations" in its "elaborate, intricate involvements with the rest of society." Bernard Bailyn, *Education in the Forming of American Society* (Chapel Hill, NC: University of North Carolina Press, 1960), 14; Lawrence A. Cremin, *The Wonderful World of Ellwood Patterson Cubberley: An Essay on the Historiography of American Education* (New York: Bureau of Publications, Teachers College, Columbia University, 1965), 52; Alisdair Macintyre, "The Idea of an Educated Public," in *Education and Values: The Richard Peters Lectures*, ed. Graham Haydon (London: Institute of Education, University of London, 1987).

Hebrew College in the evenings, as they created a synthesis that Buber might have termed Hebrew humanism.[3]

Jewish studies arrived in the American university in the 1960s. That trend in American higher education siphoned off ambitious, talented students from the Hebrew colleges as they could now pursue both their general studies and their Jewish studies in more prestigious locales. The weakening of the five-day-a-week Hebrew school also contributed to a lowering of aspirations regarding Hebrew education. Perhaps most ironically, the birth of the state of Israel led to a decline in American Hebraism, as its most avid proponents tended to emigrate to the Jewish state, leaving a vacuum in their midst in the United States.

This shrinking of the College's role and status faced Gordis when he arrived in 1992 from the University of Judaism in Los Angeles. Traditionally a small, centralized institution that relied heavily on the CJP for its funding, Gordis grasped three realities about Hebrew College. The College must play a role in redefining the American Jewish agenda, which he thought demanded turning it away from peoplehood-centered externals like the Holocaust and Israel to questions of Jewish content and Jewish identity. The New Jewish Population Survey suggested the time for that sort of internal agenda had arrived. The College needed to emerge from behind its own walls, getting out into the community to deliver education. And the College needed to raise its own money if it wanted to cut its dependency on the CJP. Paradoxically, that required the CJP.[4]

Like many in the Federation movement, Barry Shrage hailed from a social work background. Raised in a traditional home and in an Orthodox day school in upper Manhattan, as an adult Shrage found his way back to Modern Orthodoxy. He considered himself in the Judaism business, rather than merely fundraising. He rebranded the Federation as centered on Torah and *ẓedeq*, Judaism as tradition and as social welfare.

Shrage viewed the Federation as a place from which communal strategy and energy could and should emerge, working in tandem with different agencies. Instead of the traditional emphasis on Jewish philanthropy as a foundation that raised money to be disbursed, Shrage defined the CJP as the nerve center of the entire community, the key body required to lead the transformation of Jewish life via the strengthening of Jewish identity and institutions. Education occupied a central stage in his worldview; he saw the individual and the community as

3 David Starr, "Hebrew College," in *Encylopaedia Judaica*, 2nd ed. (Detroit, MI: Macmillan Reference USA, 2007), vol. 8, 553–554; Walter Ackerman, "A World Apart: Hebrew Teachers Colleges and Hebrew-Speaking Camps," in *Hebrew in America: Perspectives and Prospects*, ed. Alan Mintz (Detroit, MI: Wayne State University, 1993), 105–128.

4 Interview with David Gordis, January 2007.

inextricably linked, either weakening or strengthening one another, depending on the state of affairs. He also believed that Bostonian Jews, traditionally careful with their dollars, might be willing to invest in an institution providing services that they came to value, in the realm of social services and in terms of their own Jewish identity. He said over and over again, in an echo of Ahad Ha'am, that Jewish thriving required cultural imitation and competition rather assimilation understood as the replacement of Jewish norms and values with universal ones. The Jews strive to study and value Maimonides and Shakespeare.

The Federation undertook two initiatives, one organizational and one programmatic. It created a Commission on Jewish Continuity (COJC). This invested in and to some extent centralized and coordinated content-oriented programming. It cooperated with local agencies like the religious movements and congregations, with the goal of strengthening those institutional communities. Shrage wanted to strengthen existing religious institutions even as he worried that they lacked the will and the right personnel (including the rabbinic leadership) to revision and reengineer themselves.

The Commission called its first major initiative Sha'arim (Gateways). It funded fifty percent of a new position in Jewish educational life, the family educator. Synagogues wanted to attract baby boom parents, practitioners of a new emphasis on child-centered parenting. The family educator bridged the domestic world of the family and the synagogue, traditionally focused on worship and children's education, but not families as units. This approach reflected the work of Marshall Sklare, who years before argued that most American Jews observed rituals most amenable to home observance, namely Hanukah and Passover. The family educator innovation sought to empower parents to learn and to practice Jewish rituals like *havdalah*, the ceremony marking the end of the Sabbath.[5]

The success of such family education initiatives encouraged Gordis and Shrage to think more ambitiously about adult Jewish empowerment. Models already existed that tackled this agenda. The Wexner Heritage and the Melton Mini-School existed as national models. Wexner grew out of the desire to Judaize lay leaders, in the wake of the Reaganomics boom of the 1980s. Unprecedented numbers of Jews in their thirties and forties accumulated great wealth, sometimes taking early retirement, searching for roles in non-profits and in public Jewish life. As the gap between funders and traditional leaders like rabbis and scholars widened, some felt the need to educate Jewishly the former. Wexner

---

5 Marshall Sklare, *Observing America's Jews* (Hanover, NJ: Brandeis University Press, 1993).

aimed at socializing Jewish leaders and at providing them a serious taste of regular Jewish study via text, history, and ideas of Jewish culture.

Melton grew out of the experience of one remarkable Ohio Jewish philanthropist, Florence Melton. A businesswoman and inventor, she tried to learn Hebrew as an adult, and wondered why no curriculum-based programs for adult Jewish learning or Hebrew existed. She urged and funded the Melton Centre for Jewish Education at the Hebrew University to develop a curriculum-based program that featured intensive learning and teacher training, to be delivered to as many diaspora communities as possible.

The program targeted not elites but underserved adult Jews, with no extrinsic agenda other than engaging them Jewishly via meaningful learning. The strategy aimed at market penetration via breadth rather than depth; the material and the instruction embraced the middlebrow. The highbrow might be bored, but better that marginal negative in the service of reaching everyone else. Meaning was key: the curriculum was thoroughly didactic and somewhat homiletic about asserting that history taught lessons, and should be integrated with the study of Jewish vocabulary, ideas, ethics, and rituals. It assumed a Judaism toward which people should be brought intellectually and personally.[6]

Shrage and Gordis differed in their evaluations of these programs. Shrage liked Wexner; he saw some of his funders galvanized by their experience of it, and he wanted to develop more like them. Issues of pedagogy and content concerned him less than habituating adult study and its impact on increasing the intensity of their Jewish identity and communal involvement. Gordis recognized that both programs grew out of a centralized national model and likely would leave little room for the College to play a major role, limiting its ability to project a new role in Boston. He also viewed Wexner and Melton as not quite academic: the former both educating and entertaining, the latter as not academic in nature. Melton failed in Boston to gain a foothold; Gordis deduced from that, too that the program made a poor fit with a more academically inclined community.

Someone once said that the aristocracy of New York rests on money, in Washington on power, in Boston on academics. Bostonians prided themselves on being the Athens of America, with more students and scholars per square foot than probably any other city. Boston, and its Jews, viewed their schools as part of their history, culture, lore, and inheritance. That reputational value remained paramount.

---

6 Lisa Grant, Diane Schuster, Meredith Woocher, and Steven Cohen, *A Journey of Heart and Mind: Transformative Jewish Learning in Adulthood* (New York: JTS, 2004); See the Mini-School's website for further details, http://www.fmams.org.il/.

Gordis knew that academic branding would be crucial to his vision for Hebrew College, and he determined that a successful Boston-based adult education program must try to create such a reputation for itself. The value of studying with a Harvard professor appealed to some enrollees; the substance of the curriculum appealed to others.[7]

Conversations began in 1993 to try something that combined all of these realities. The CJP and the Commission on Jewish Continuity partnered with Hebrew College to create a program that combined the elitism of the academy with the broad egalitarian outreach conducive to deep change in the community. The program bridged the cognitive and the affective dimensions of learning, by its academic nature and by its willingness to acknowledge the personhood of the learners. Building on the network of synagogues invested in the family educator program, the Commission reached out to these synagogues to become sites, and the College built and ran the program, overseeing its day to day management, its vision, curricular structure and content, and the selection and development of the faculty. The program consisted of two years of class sessions, long enough to feel sustained, not so long as to demand the impossible of adults.

Gordis suggested Me'ah—Hebrew for "one hundred"—as the title. The Hebrew name carried it with the ring of cultural seriousness and authenticity, but was not so onerous a term as to lead to near-certain linguistic paralysis. Students studied for 100 hours of classroom learning, one session a week, two-and-a-half hours per session, for forty sessions spread over two years.

Several principals sat in some or all of these early meetings: Gordis, Shrage, Carolyn Keller, director of COJC, and Annette Furst. A doctor and enthusiastic creator and participant in Jewish adult learning, Furst wanted the new program to be home-based, relying on networks of learners already engaged or those who more likely to engage in a domestic environment rather than a synagogue. Three location models emerged as possibilities: HC, synagogues, and the home. It was decided to roll out the program at both the College and in congregations.

Funding and infrastructure details followed suit. The Federation agreed to fund the program, both externally via grants to potential synagogue sites, and for the internal infrastructure needs of the College relating to program management. In addition to Bernice Lerner, already in place as the head of the College's Center for

---

7 I invoked these twin scenarios when speaking to a representative of an independent retirement community in which many affluent, well-educated Jews live in the South Shore. She expressed concern about the "Jewishness" of the program as a negative for many residents. I told her those people would respond positively to the institutional affiliations of the teachers, others to the contents. When I intoned the ineffable name of "Harvard" she agreed.

Adult Jewish Learning, the two agencies hired me to direct Me'ah as its academic head and to teach in the program. Previously, while in rabbinical school, I had gained invaluable experience working with the first Melton Mini-School site in New York. I arrived at Hebrew College in the summer of 1994, with the goal of creating the concept, building the program and launching it that fall.

I needed to create a program in less than three months. I knew for certain only two things. We planned to create two classes in two locations, and hired two teachers: biblical scholar Marc Brettler, then a professor at Brandeis University; and Ahuva Halberstam, a well-regarded Bible instructor in the community who taught, among other places, at Maimonides High School and the women's learning initiative Ma'ayan. The two locales reflected the institutional goals of sparking personal and synagogue transformation: one a joint class of two Lexington synagogues (Conservative and Reform); the other an open enrollment site to be at HC in Brookline. CJP subsidized the Lexington site at the rate of almost one hundred percent; participants needed to pay $100 per year, for two years. HC charged $1200 for the same course. The rabbis of the Lexington Reform and Conservative synagogues handpicked the students, drawing heavily on the already substantial amount of family and adult learning in their communities. The participants wrote essays sharing their stories—who they were and why they wanted to take the course.

These adults manifested a composite identity. Highly educated, they expressed skepticism about traditional religious truth claims at the same time as they searched from some sense of connection to something larger themselves. They identified family experiences as often religious, and they wanted to connect to Jewish peoplehood even as they maintained an ambivalence about Jewish tribalism. The essays they wrote stating their reason for enrolling showed a common thread: regardless of background, each person wanted to know how their Jewish story connected to the story of the Jews and of Judaism.

These learners therefore approached the prospect of serious adult learning with divided selves: one part highly self-aware and self-confident, one part ambivalent and self-conscious about their deficits. Their ignorance motivated them to learn; they perceived knowledge as helping them raise their children Jewishly, for example. They felt ready to learn. They took this trip alone. They might want to connect to a more observant partner or to children enrolled in day schools who knew more than they did, but this journey belonged to them. Most of them lacked Jewish role models: very few felt the impress of positive Jewish parental influence or of rabbis as mentors.[8]

8 On characteristics of adult learners, see Malcolm Knowles, *The Modern Practice of Adult Education: From Pedagogy to Andragogy* (Cambridge: Cambridge Book Co, 1988).

Many of these first students had studied as adults, and had enjoyed the experience of it, as far back as in college or recently in the synagogue. The COJC chose Lexington because of that track record. These students knew enough to know what they lacked: a base, a frame in which to situate ritual experiences, life cycle occasions, the random class.[9] No neat line separated cognitive goals from affective needs.[10]

This program aimed at education. It focused on teaching information and analytical problems, not on building skills like Hebrew language or learning how to read texts in the original. We hoped that by situating such education inside institutions those locales would change and become places of learning. Congregants would meet each other in class. They would get to know one another sharing an intense experience for two years. They would talk to each other after Shabbat services about their reading. They would develop, they would affect each other's development, and their shared community would develop through education and learning.

Behind curricular questions lay philosophical issues: what should be taught, the overall design, and the meta-rationalization of its purpose. David Gordis encouraged me to address explicitly the cognitive/affective relationship by creating parallel tracks. Gordis suggested that each module, beginning with Bible, feature two instructors. One would teach text and history, the *peshat* in effect, the other would teach the ideas emerging from the text. That would enable us to engage the texts horizontally and vertically, in context and in the chain of the Jewish tradition, ensuring an educational dialectic involving students, teachers, and multiple voices over time and place and sensibility. I rejected that model, partly on the grounds that it required recruiting and managing an even larger faculty, partly because I thought such a bifurcation artificial. I wanted to believe that critical learning should engage students ideationally and in some way sympathetically.

Instead we opted for a sequence that combined linearity with reverberating commentary. We framed each of the years around a core canonical text: year one the Bible, year two rabbinics. Those would be studied in the fall "semester." In the spring of each year commentaries on those texts would fill in the gaps: in year one modern texts would respond to the Bible, in year two medieval texts

9 Daniel Bell recounted an exchange with a Columbia student who in 1968 at the height of the student unrest on campus challenged him to justify why professors had the right to tell students what they should study and learn. To this Bell replied, "Because you don't know what you don't know. That's what I'm here for." Jonathan Dorman, *Arguing the World* (New York: Free Press, 2000).

10 Israel Scheffler, *In Praise of the Cognitive Emotions and Other Essays in the Philosophy of Education* (New York: Routledge, 2010).

would grapple with the legacy of the talmudic era. For example, in year one a biblical text might be Job, later that year in the course of considering modern history and thought, when the course reached Jewish existentialism Buber's essay on Job would introduce both the subject of German Jewish thought in the twentieth century and bring students back to the canonical text. Similarly, in year two a rabbinic text on sacrifice might find its counterpart later that year in a medieval text like the prayer book filled with *kinot* responding both to those rabbinic tonalities and to contemporaneous events like the Crusades. Each section enjoyed its autonomy, with instructors determining the trajectory of the subjects at the same time that each somehow connected to what came before it: biblical and modern; rabbinic and medieval.

Canonicity linked faculty and curriculum. The curriculum rested on the "sealed" Jewish canon, building on biblical and Talmudic foundations. Any instructor would have to work to include breadth and depth, covering not just their favorite verses or chapters of a favorite book or tractate, but giving students a sense of the breadth of history, text, and ideas.[11] In doing so the canonical books remained open, liable to the instructor's choices of particular texts and approaches to reading that text. Brettler taught the Bible via history and literature; Halberstam adopted the literary approach, utilizing both *peshat* and *derash*. Historicism taken seriously meant that anachronism, parochialism, evangelism, and intellectual isolationism must be avoided.[12]

The community took little notice of the new program. Carolyn Keller spent the spring of 1994 talking to the local branches of the United Synagogue and the UAHC (now URJ) encouraging them to support the venture and advocate for it with their rabbis and congregations. They greeted her with customary New England reserve, combined with political turf watching. One movement representative worried that a teacher from a different background might teach something in conflict with the worldview of the rabbi or his institution or congregants.[13]

That concern made clear to us what we faced. We needed, either covertly or overtly, to overcome the assumption that congregations owned learning for their congregants. How would congregants benefit from reading a text through a different lens, or by reading a new text? What would happen to the community if people confronted conflicts between institution-driven ideologies or their own views and those springing from academics teaching them? For that reason, and

---

11 Moshe Halbertal, *People of the Book: Canon, Meaning, and Authority* (Cambridge, MA: Harvard University Press, 1997).

12 Hans Meyerhoff, *The Philosophy of History in Our Time* (Garden State, NJ: Doubleday, 1957).

13 Interview with Carolyn Keller, February 2007.

inertia, most of the community adopted a wait-and-see approach to the appeal of a two-year course requiring classroom attendance and homework.

The first sites opened in the fall of 1994, in Lexington and at Hebrew College. Twenty-six people in each class took their seats. Rabbi Bernie Eisenman of Temple Emunah in Lexington remembered how strange it felt to walk past a classroom in his shul, look in the window, and see his congregants studying with another teacher. He would have to accommodate himself to energy, and to leadership models, not controlled by him or by the congregation.

Lessons to be learned from this pilot jumped out to us quickly. First and foremost, it was all about the teachers. If they were good at what they did, the students felt the excitement. This thrilled management even as we struggled to determine what it meant to be *good*. And what were we accomplishing in class other than engendering positive feelings? Were students gathering information? Were they doing something with that information?[14] Were they each in their own way imaginatively reacting to the class? Were they forming community in the classroom, a much more intense Jewish fellowship previously unknown to them? Were they learning how to think differently?

Those issues begged the question for me. Would the market determine our success, or were other measures equally if not more valid? What did we want to accomplish and why? How would we justify those aims to ourselves and to the other stakeholders?

One question I was faced with was how much free reign versus direct instruction to offer our teachers. Faculty enjoyed this teaching. They liked it not because it forced them to teach differently than in the university, to the contrary because they could teach the same materials the same way better here than there. Here they taught peers, not "thirteenth graders" as one instructor put it. They intuited there was something different about being Jewish, and teaching Jews, in a Jewish class, though that distinction remained unclear. What mattered most was teaching peers, students they need not baby. This constituted a significant revision to the attitudes regarding community and communal involvement in Gerson Cohen's day.[15]

---

14 Isadore Scheffler writes, "Cognitive perspective not only requires breadth; it demands also that the knowledge of the educated person be active. It must not simply be stored as information, but should enter into the educated person's perception and commerce with the environment." See "The Concept of the Educated Person: With Some Applications to Jewish Education," in *Visions of Jewish Education*, ed. Seymour Fox, Israel Scheffler, and Daniel Marom (Cambridge: Cambridge University Press, 2003), 221.

15 Cohen consciously or not revealed the ambivalence of Judaica scholars toward the community from which they came and upon which much of their support still depended when he

I chose not to impose my own pedagogical instincts on the faculty, even when I sometimes disagreed with their methods (for example, when teachers chose a lecture style, rather than a discussion style for their classes). I wanted to create a faculty culture of collegiality and shared investment in what I hoped would become a mission-driven enterprise. Who was I to tell them how to teach? The institutional culture reinforced this somewhat laissez-faire approach: we contracted with these instructors; they held full-time jobs elsewhere. At least initially we needed them more than they needed us. So I would speak my mind about strategy and practice; they would listen and decide what they wanted to do. The key lay in the faculty appreciating the similarities and differences between the university and the community: here they could and should value both cognitive and affective frameworks goals and outcomes.

That included a tone and culture of intellectual intensity and openness, and a sense that a covenantal relationship existed in the class between students and teachers, and between students. Teachers gave reading assignments that created a culture of seriousness. Students frowned on telling stories about personal identity and sharing Hebrew school horror stories; they wanted not to hear from their peers unless they had something important to say. They wanted above all not to be talked down to by the instructor. Encountering a textual difficulty in a biblical text, Halberstam tried passing off a *derash* as *peshat* and the students threw it back in her face, asking her for something more compelling.

The energy of a class when it worked felt palpable. One student told us, "I come here at seven PM tired from a long work day; I leave at ten energized. I can't sleep; I want to tell my husband everything I learned." Students pushed teachers and vice versa; community began to grow. At the end of the first year we sat with students and heard their reactions. Among other things we heard gender differences: women often liked to discuss and process information; men generally wanted to listen to the "expert." But these differences seemed less salient than excellence: the students valued high-quality instruction even if it came packaged in a fashion that didn't suit them perfectly.

Students got that in some ways the learning centered on them, in other ways it centered on the texts and the ideas. In other words they and Jewish learning each

---

noted: "Alas, the people of the book are today far more enchanted by *The Source* and *Goodbye, Columbus* than they are by the *Proceedings of the American Academy of Jewish Research* or the Yale Judaica Series. That, I suppose, is no more than we should expect from the vulgus, but it is not a situation that we can afford to watch complacently." Gerson Cohen, "An Embarrassment of Riches: Reflections on the Condiiton of American Jewish Scholarship in 1969," in *The Teaching of Judaica in American Universities: the Proceedings of a Colloquium*, ed. Leon A. Jick (Waltham, MA: Brandeis University Press, 1970), 135–150, here 149.

retained their autonomy even as they linked. Students also understood therefore that the learning ought to stimulate them precisely for its strangeness and difficulty. It was not supposed to feel good. One student told Brettler, "You took my view of the Bible away from me." That felt like a loss, and he still loved the learning. Another student, in the midst of a difficult medical situation, studied Job in class. She told the teacher that of all of the things she tried to cope with her personal life, that learning meant the most to her, even though she never referenced her situation in class. The learning mattered.

The rest is commentary. Boston is a small town in many ways, and secrets quickly leak out. We lacked a marketing campaign and elaborate materials. Marketing consisted of word of mouth, person to person, person to rabbi, rabbi to rabbi, professor to professor. Carolyn Keller and I went on the road and talked about the course; I would give sample classes we dubbed "Tastes of Me'ah." In spite of this no-frills strategy or maybe because we were so product-oriented, we grew from two to three to five eventually to twenty-some classes a year. We recruited dozens of faculty from the best universities in Boston, who in virtually all cases looked upon this as a contribution to the Jewish community as much as another source of supplemental livelihood.

What began as a small program in Boston grew at its peak to some forty classes a year including sites in metropolitan New York and Philadelphia, Cleveland, Baltimore, and Florida, and numbering several thousand graduates. The program became a brand, one identified with a certain quality of experience and benefit. People identified themselves as "a Me'ah graduate" as a way of articulating what sort of Jew they were and what sort of Jewish they did. Institutions changed as a result of Me'ah. Hebrew College grew enough in size and stature to relocate, raising the unprecedented sum for itself of $25,000,000, much of it from families connected with Me'ah. Increasingly the CJP became identified as a center for program and Jewish life as much as for fundraising. Synagogues—sometimes driven by the professionals and sometimes by laity—spun off all sorts of other adult learning. Hebrew College and the CJP developed pre and post-Me'ah programs. Students became leaders, they led sessions at their *tiqqun leil Shavu'ot,* they traveled differently, they sent children to day school, they enrolled in rabbinical school. The classrooms of Me'ah built communities within communities; in some cases cohorts continued studying together long after the two years commenced.[16]

---

16 Recall the historicist's credo *post hoc, ergo propter hoc.* A preceding B doesn't necessarily mean that A caused B. I present this sequence of Me'ah as antecedent to these manifold changes to suggest possible understandings of and reasons for results rather than asserting that I fully

Me'ah practiced two things that often might have felt contradictory. In formal terms the program taught in effect a sealed canon. A teacher, an expert in one's field, taught a fixed text, a discrete body of history or text or an idea, all of which involved strong claims about the truth of that subject. That suggested a process of *closing*. Yet as one analyst of the Me'ah classroom observed, the experience for the adult learners involved an *opening up*. One explored the self, one connected the class with contemporary matters, the atmosphere included students as well as the instructor and the material and the affective as well as the cognitive. Humor and tears and the full range of human emotions one could find there. All of that constituted a process of building community.[17]

Me'ah revealed what adult learners possess and lack, as they brought their childhoods with them and walked on their way. They carried a family legacy, an identity, a sense of curiosity about something deeply felt in spite of—or because of—lack of knowledge, much less understanding, of that heritage. At painful junctures like the loss of a parent, a young adult searched for God and sometimes failed to find not only God but even a trusted authority. No rabbi, no tradition, no family, no ritual, no book sat on one's shoulder or eased the way. The Me'ah classroom became a space for those who entered alone on a journey to some sort of community. That community shaped them even as they shaped it.

---

grasp the meaning of those changes or their causes. CJP surveys suggested increased levels in participants' observance and philanthropy; only possibly can we attribute these to Me'ah.

17 Rachel Bernstein, "Memo on Early Hunches/Codes/Themes" (seminar paper, Brandeis University, Waltham, MA, April 5, 2011).

CHAPTER 25

Striving for *Shlemut*: Navigating Explicit and Implicit Religiosity in Jewish Education

Michael Shire

Every student seeking matriculation into the master of Jewish education program at Hebrew College is asked to write a short essay on the following textual prompt from Proverbs 22:6: "Educate the child according to their way; even when they are old they will not depart from it." Many students, focusing on the first part of the verse, choose to write about the ways in which student-centered learning is a familiar and a predominant feature of modern American education. As one applicant wrote:

> The text is directing the educator to listen to and follow the minds of our young people—whoever they are and however they choose to express. This includes gender expression, creative expression, intellectual ability, and more. I believe this text's intention is to honor the innate person a student is and to teach them from there, to meet them where they are at rather than forcing in our mainstream education system.[1]

Students compare this to the so-called banking system of education, which assumes learners come as blank slates upon which to imprint the teacher's

1 Student A.

knowledge and wisdom.[2] The teacher takes on a pedagogic transmission role encouraging as much transfer of information as possible. Progressive education over the last century employs a different approach to education. It assumes that students have a wealth of experience and inherent motivation so that whatever material an educator presents is a complement to the already formed views and attitudes of the learners. The role of the teacher is to be a guide on a journey of learning to come into a deeper understanding of their lived experience:

> This text encourages us to let our young people be partners in learning, leading us towards the wells where they are most interested in exploring and from there, we educate.[3]

Others write about the nature of diversity of learners and the needs for identification and accommodation of children's different learning needs:

> To "educate a child according to his or her own needs and direction" means to me that I must keep "great minds do not think alike" in mind in everything that I do. It means designing curricula that have various modes of learning in each lesson in order to make sure that every student has an opportunity to understand the material. It means developing meaningful relationships and understanding children on a deeper level so that I can best provide what they need. It means recognizing that though there may be a shared destination or end goal, each child will have a different means of arriving at it. It is my responsibility, as an educator, to support every child on his or her path to that point, whether it is linear or not.[4]

As general education shifts from an identification of Special Needs in some learners to a wider more comprehensive notion of the overall neurodiversity of learning and a greater understanding of multiple intelligences, it emphasizes the need for teachers to come to know the complexities of the learning process and develop their practice to prepare and plan for it in real classroom settings with a diversity of learners. This is as true in Jewish educational settings as in general ones.

---

2 Paulo Freire, *Pedagogy of the Oppressed*, 30th anniversary ed. (New York: Continuum, 2006).

3 Student A.

4 Student B.

However, as if the Proverbs verse had two separate meanings, some students comment separately on "when they are old, they will not depart from it." The notion of lifelong Jewish learning beyond schooling points to a difference of purpose for religious education than for other forms of education and training. It suggests that Jewish education is an enrichment and life enhancement designed for thriving and flourishing with a thread of continuity over a lifetime:

> This creates an educational environment that students can connect to and thrive in—one they remember for years to come because it is connected to the direct experience of their lives.[5]

All of these themes mentioned by students—theories of student-centered learning, neurodiversity and multiple intelligences as well as lifelong learning and intergenerational education—are all key components of a Master in Jewish Education program. They are reflections of the current moment in Western education and as such their sources of theoretical origin derive from social science research, educational philosophy and secular educational theory and practice. However, these opening statements by matriculating students do not as yet reflect a more fundamental and vital aspect of becoming a Jewish religious educator. In order to understand the underlying assumptions of forming an approach to achieving the heart and soul of aJewish educator, we turn to sources within our own tradition.

In a remarkable, psychologically sensitive pedagogy, the Piaseczner *rebbe* Rabbi Kalonymos Kalmish Shapiro, as a pre-World War II ultra-Orthodox rabbi, offers a framework for a religious education grounded in traditional Jewish life yet open to the spiritual and emotional sensitization of the student on a pathway to an undivided self[6] or *shlemut*—wholeness.[7]

Rabbi Shapiro begins his treatise *Ḥovat ha-Talmidim*—The Students' Obligation—with a close and revealing interpretation of this very verse in Proverbs 22:6, "Educate the child according to their way; even when they are old they will not depart from it."[8] Focusing on the first word of the verse *ḥanokh*,

---

5 Student C.

6 A term used by Parker Palmer in his *Courage to Teach* to indicate integrity and coherence of the individual. See Parker J. Palmer, *The Courage to Teach: Exploring the Inner Landscape of a Teacher's Life*, 1st ed. (Hoboken, NJ: Jossey-Bass, 1998).

7 Michael J. Shire, "Torah Godly Play: An Innovative Approach to Religious Education for Shlemut." *Gleanings: A Dialogue on Jewish Education* 6, no. 2 (Summer 2019): 11–12.

8 Kalonymus Kalmish Shapira [Shapiro], *Chovas HaTalmidim—The Students' Obligation and Sheloshah Ma'amarim—The Three Discourses, Including a Biographical Sketch by Aharon Sorasky* (Spring Valley, NY: Feldheim, 2011), 3.

which is a form of the Hebrew word for education, *ḥinukh,* Rabbi Shapira derives a definition of religious education. Rather than viewing it merely as a matter of commandment (*ẓivui*) or of habituation into a tradition (*hergel*), Rabbi Shapiro emphasizes the concept of preparing and guiding a student to the realization of their latent potential that is inherent within them (*hoẓa'at ha-hakhsherah*). Noting that the word *ḥinukh* can also be used to describe the dedication of a house (*ḥanukat ha-bayit*), he applies the concept of education to the act of consecrating a newly built house that is to become a home. That is, the house is to be used for the purpose for which it was built for the first time. Rabbi Shapiro understands therefore that a religious education is for the person's actualization of their potential. It is a means to nurture the inherent qualities and dispositions of the child and provide a means for growth and development. This is the motivation to inspire a lifelong search for such potential.[9]

> When the word *chinukh* is used in the context of educating children it means to nurture the inherent character and talents that lie dormant within the child or only partially realized and develop them.... It is our responsibility to raise and teach him to discover it, to extract it and cause it to flourish. Only then will he become a devoted servant of God, he will develop a yearning for Torah that comes from within, and "even when he is old he will not depart from it."[10]

Rabbi Shapiro notes that a commanding or conditioning approach to education is no guarantee for this lifelong pursuit of meaning. He explains that such an approach, in common usage in prewar Polish *yeshivot,* is detrimental to the uncovering of potential of the child. Citing the first part of the Proverbs verse, "Educate the child according to their way," he rather exhorts the teacher to adapt his approach to each student who possesses an individual nature:

> If a teacher wants to discover his students' souls, their hidden inner reality—to nurture and inspire them to transcend the mundane so that their entire beings grow in sanctity and yearn for the

9 Social science research indicates that extrinsic motivations only work for students in the short term while intrinsic motivations have a long-lasting impact. See D. H. Pink, *Drive: The Surprising Truth about What Motivates Us* (New York: Riverhead Books, 2011).

10 Shapira, *Chovas HaTalmidim,* 7.

> transcendent, then he must be willing to be flexible. He must be willing to bend emotionally towards his students. He has to penetrate and move beyond their childlike nature until he reaches the hidden spark of their souls. Then he can bring out that spark, nurture it and make it grow.[11]

Rabbi Shapiro makes clear that the pedagogic tools for the cultivation of the mind and the acquisition of knowledge are not sufficient for this stated purpose of *ḥinukh*. Rather the teacher needs to enable students to flourish and grow holistically as a gardener tends and cultivates a garden. He is not however immune to the problems of closed hearts and minds and suggests channeling students' high spirits, anger or bad temper into positive traits just as a sour fruit ripens into a sweet one. He does warn teachers against blaming students for their inattention or lack of motivation in the light of the changing context of the community around them.

Rabbi Shapiro was a Hasidic *rebbe* of the Warsaw community before and during the Second World War. Born in Grodzisk, Poland in 1899, he was a scion of the Hasidic Kozienicer dynasty. Due to the early death of his father when Kalonymous was three years old, he was taken in and educated by his relative Rabbi Yerahmiel Moshe Hapstein of Kozienice whose daughter he eventually married. He was raised in an ultra-Orthodox environment though also obtained a modern Western education, learning German, science and even medicine and pharmacology.[12] He was therefore deeply steeped in the Hasidic ideology of mysticism and adherence to Jewish law while also coming to know of the content of Western education including psychology and social science.

In 1923 he founded the Dat Moshe yeshiva in Warsaw, which became a major educational institution attracting thousands of young students. However, Rabbi Shapiro lived in a fragmented community that was being threatened by external forces of assimilation and socioeconomic pressures. Young men were leaving the close confines of the ultra-Orthodox community and its way of life to opt for the open Western atmosphere of post-First World War Poland. Rabbi Shapiro was

---

11 Ibid., 9. The raising of sparks in an individual for Rabbi Shapiro is a reference to this concept in Kabbalah. However, it also is used in contemporary literature to suggest an inner potential to be realized by the student and drawn out by the educator. See Peter Benson and Michael Shire's application to Jewish Education in Peter Benson, *Sparks: How Parents Can Ignite the Hidden Strengths of Teenagers* (Hoboken, NJ: Jossey-Bass, 2013); Michael Shire, "Spark! Spiritual Engagement of Jewish Adolescents," *Reform Jewish Quarterly* (Fall 2015).

12 Nehemia Polen. *The Holy Fire: The Teachings of Rabbi Kalonymus Kalman Shapira, the Rebbe of the Warsaw Ghetto* (Lanham, MD: Rowman and Littlefield, 2004).

keenly aware of this tension in the lives of his students and the danger it posed to the viability of his community's future. *Ḥovat ha-Talmidim*, written in 1932, is therefore addressed directly to his students and those who would choose to find a means to bring fulfillment and meaning to the study of Torah and Jewish traditions even in changing times. It uses the language of emotion and personal growth to emphasize the potential of each student in striving for wholeness through learning and practice and the benefits that accrue in pursuing this goal. Understanding the pressures on students particularly in adolescence, he explicitly addresses the struggles with self-esteem, depression, anxiety, growing sexual awareness and worthiness. The book concludes with three separate discourses—*Sheloshah Ma'amarim*—written for older students with a view to integrating the earlier socio-emotional material with kabbalistic concepts that are foundational to Hasidic ideology including Torah study, prayer, singing and Shabbat observance.

Together *Ḥovat ha-Talmidim* and *Sheloshah Ma'amarim* make up the beginnings of a spiritual growth curriculum that will later include Shapiro's posthumously published writings *Hakhsharat ha-Avreikhim* for more advanced students. The text, again addressed directly to the students, emphasized their spiritual development, personal meaning in observance and practice including meditation and forming close relationships with teachers and fellow students. Through this series of educational treatises, Rabbi Shapiro provided a curriculum of religious growth connected to the study of Torah and Hasidic teachings and practice from a young age through adulthood. He initiated a new structure of formation, learning and enculturation albeit within a very traditional educational environment and as such offered a signature pedagogy that developed habits of the mind, soul and heart as well as offering organizing learning in a structured and scaffolded way to develop progression and sequence of learning.[13]

In developing this signature pedagogy, Rabbi Shapiro echoes the dimensions of religious education as described by Michael Rosenak in his distinction between *explicit* and *implicit* religion.[14] Explicit religion encompasses the beliefs and practices of the community; it defines the norms of those adhering to that religion.

---

13 Lee Shulman describes signature pedagogies as a means to organize the fundamental ways in which practitioners are educated for their future vocation. They incorporate surface, deep, and implicit structures in the pedagogy. See Lee Shulman, "Signature Pedagogies in the Professions," *Daedalus* 134, no. 3 (Summer 2005): 52–59.

14 Michael Rosenak, *Commandments and Concerns: Jewish Religious Education in Secular Society* (Philadelphia: JPS, 1987).

> The Religious experience that is to be transmitted and caught in explicit religious education is therefore faith in the Torah and in those who explain it and the trusting experience of being part of a faithful people. This faith-trust appears as a formal and social pattern of activities; specifically studying the Torah and carrying out the mitzvot, and doing this competently, together with other Jews who are similarly commanded. Explicit religious education is therefore socialization into the holy community.[15]

Implicit religion however denotes the search for meaning in an individual's life that poses questions of life's ultimate significance and its values meaning and purpose. The nature of explicit religion is one of acceptance of the norms of the community both past and present involving a rich use of religious language and symbol in an interpretive creative manner. The implicit approach involves personal struggle and individual choice in a mode of inquiry and discovery. Personal integrity is important, while becoming spiritual is considered paramount.

> Implicit religious faith is not assent to doctrines but an orientation to life and to the presence of God in and behind all things and events. Religious education is not a form of taming and training young people, rather it is making them sensitive to the presence of the unconditional in the life of each person indicating how it has been present in the life and memory of the historical community thus enabling the young people to encounter their own selves within this community.[16]

Rosenak understands the importance of both dimensions recognizing the tension that exists between religious belonging and religious becoming. He set three tasks for effective religious education: the socialization of the child into a religious community, fostering individuation as a religious person, and negotiating the tension between affirming a religious tradition on the one hand and affirming spiritual autonomy on the other. Each of these is also integral to Rabbi Shapiro's approach in *Ḥovat ha-Talmidim* with a focus on cultivating the dispositions necessary for the fostering a child's religious sensibility. However, his signature pedagogy is reliant on the correct relationship fostered by the teacher in navigating the tension between explicit and implicit religiosity.

---

15 Ibid., 140.
16 Ibid.

For Rosenak, the implicit is an integral and subsumed component of the explicit and has no independent existence of its own.[17] Rosenak maintains explicit religion can be performed without the implicit but then it lacks individual meaning and ultimate purpose. When the implicit is integrated with the explicit, a full religious experience is available, enhancing the religiosity of the individual within a religious tradition. The bringing together of these two aspects of personal search for meaning and the objective study of the phenomena of religion indicates how they might be integrated in religious education.

It is these two dimensions of religious education that Rabbi Shapiro describes when he formulates a pedagogic approach that emphasizes the deliberation and personalization of learning important in capturing the habits of heart, soul and mind of young people. His exhortation to focus on the implicit and inner convictions of the child is a means to open them to the explicit or normative aspects of religiosity. In this way he seeks to foster the cultivation of the potential inherent in the child, their distinctive spiritual signature and their ability to be self-authoring in their relationship to religious tradition.

Rabbi Shapiro's approach to education as the drawing-out (this is the literal meaning of the Latin word *educare*) of the child aligns itself with a progressive view of modern education. The notion of cultivating and drawing out the potential of the child in the process of education is a constant focus of this view of education. It was also held by another prominent educator living in the Warsaw Ghetto at the same time, Janucz Korczak.[18] It does seem evident from his knowledge of the psychology of learning that Rabbi Shapiro may have been familiar with some of the prominent progressive educators of the nineteenth and twentieth century such as Pesatalozzi, Steiner or Montessori or knew of their writings from secondhand sources. In his review of *Ḥovat ha-Talmidim* in 1932, Hillel Zeitlin particularly commented on this aesthetic approach, commending it as a means to stir up motivation, excitement and joy in the life of students. In light of the education being offered in *yeshivot* generally, Zeitlin is encouraged by Rabbi Shapiro's awakening of the unique soul rather than forcing conformity and memorization on the child.[19]

---

17 Michael Rosenak, "Zelophehad's Daughters, Religion and Jewish Religious Education," *Journal of Jewish Education* 71, no. 1 (Fall 2005): 3–21.

18 It is unknown whether Rabbi Shapiro and Janucz Korczak ever met or knew of each other's writings despite both being leaders of Jewish educational institutions in the Warsaw Ghetto.

19 See Ariel Evan Mayse, "Hasidic Renewal on the Brink of Destruction," *The Jewish Review of Books*, November 1, 2019; Hillel Zeitlin, "Hasidic *Rebbe*-Master Pedagogue" [Heb.], in his *Safran shel ha-Yeḥidim* (Jerusalem: Mossad ha-Rav Kook, 1979).

The notion of a spiritual signature of each child that is different from any other is seen explicitly here in Rabbi Shapiro's writings. The same notion is the subject of recent research by David Hay and Rebecca Nye, who develop this concept of a spiritual signature that is characterized by each child in their individual nature and character.[20]

Rabbi Shapiro's attempt to foster a spiritually rich and resonant implicit religiosity alongside a normative explicit religiosity offers contemporary Jewish education a means to further develop the thinking about Jewish education even in a postmodern world. Jewish education in the post-enlightenment age has mainly been about constructing the Educated Jew. In the nineteenth century, that meant a Jew educated in Western civilization in order to be modern, contemporary and enlightened. In the last generation constructing the educated Jew has come to mean something else: a Jew educated in their own forgotten heritage, reaffirming their identity that they hold amongst a series of identities in a postmodern world and engaging with a tradition and text and community that had been neglected. Michael Meyer calls for "Jewishly educated Jews" who are nurtured into an engagement and commitment to Jewish life and ongoing learning.[21]

But has Jewish education now to make another paradigm shift? As Jewish educators struggle with a sense of the purposes of teaching Torah in contemporary times, we must now ask: "what is the ideal outcome of Jewish schools"? Is it to affirm an identity, construct lenses to see the outside world, develop skills for Jewish competence, build pride and joy in being part of Israel—people, land, and destiny? The other side of the coin is missing here. How can Jewish education also awaken religious wonder and joy, foster religious growth, and find approaches to learning that foster *shlemut*—explicit and implicit connection to the holy, the spiritual, to God and personal faith?

Jewish education cannot be just about the technicality of the subject matter; it needs to cultivate students as co-learners with teachers attuned to the process of a dialogical relationship. This is a crucial element in Rabbi Shapiro's approach. The opening chapter of *Ḥovat ha-Talmidim* is addressed to teachers and parents, those whom Rabbi Shapiro most needs to convince of a change in the education of their students and children. He also needs to rely on their understanding and

---

20 David Hay and Rebecca Nye, *The Spirit of the Child*, rev. ed. (London: Jessica Kingsley Publishers, 2006), 94.

21 Michael A. Meyer, "Reflections on the Educated Jew from the Perspective of Reform Judaism," in *Visions of Jewish Education*, ed. Seymour Fox, Israel Scheffler, and Daniel Marom (Cambridge: Cambridge University Press, 2003), 152.

commitment to this navigation of explicit and implicit religiosity if he is to see wide scale change in Jewish education.

Describing rabbinic modes of relationships between teachers and their disciples, Elie Holzer refines the notion of attunement to mean navigating the tension of cultivating dispositions of caring and empathy while also grappling with a tradition of intellectual argumentation *maḥloket*. Holzer is careful to explain that building relationship without improving student learning does not constitute an effective Jewish education but that the converse is true as well.[22] The transformation of a learner requires a reconstitution of meaning as the teacher needs to pay attention to all aspects of the teaching relationship; subject matter, student, and self, reflecting David Hawkins's instructional triangle and the interrelationship between its elements.[23] To this end, the teacher needs to understand her own beliefs and attitudes alongside her commitment to the tradition as well to the student and their growth.

A new paradigm of Jewish education needs to address questions of meaning and probes these issues of the spirit. Baḥya ibn Pakuda in his eleventh-century treatise *Duties of the Heart* was open to understanding a quest for a holistic Judaism when he described the duties of the heart as the primary factor for Jewish spiritual growth. Knowledge of Torah and the performance of mitzvot may bring a sense of accomplishment, but it cannot refresh the soul, deepen sensitivity to life, or help see reverence in daily life. Professor Eugene Borowitz wrote that we need to find a way to take people "beyond immanence" in religious education to balance their religious commitments with religious devotion.[24] As an early advocate of a pietistic Reform Judaism, he proposed three ways that educators might foster this spiritual quest: through the tradition of marking moments in time with the recitation of *berakhot*; through the powerful meanings expressed in Psalms; and through verbal and nonverbal expressions of our spiritual and religious yearnings. Almost half a century later, we have yet to see compelling pedagogical models to use these rich traditional tools in Jewish education to inculcate spiritual awakening and building a Jewish spiritual practice for our young.

The challenge of religious education is how to induct young people into a 4,000-year-old tradition and to inspire them to carry it forward, shaped by their own life experience. Jewish education has sometimes struggled with success

---

22 Elie Holzer, *Attuned Learning: Rabbinic Texts on Habits of the Heart in Learning Interactions* (Boston, MA: Academic Studies Press, 2016).

23 Hawkins's instructional triangle of teacher, student, and subject matter is commonly used to describe the interrelationships fostered in learning environments. See "I, Thou, It," Hawkins Centers of Learning, accessed June 21, 2021, http://www.hawkinscenters.org/i-thou-and-it.html.

24 Eugene Borowitz, "Beyond Immanence," *Religious Education* 75, no. 4 (Summer 1980): 387–408.

in doing both. There is a shift now toward the personalization of tradition and religious values and practices that is called *shlemut*—wholeness.[25] This call for a new paradigm shift in religious education needs to find expression in educational strategies and practices that intentionally cultivate and foster personal meaning-making, while at the same time embed spiritualized ritual practice, Judaism's value claims, and most importantly, a sensing and knowing beyond self to community and obligation. It is a call for a pedagogy that fosters deep religious experiences, to grapple with life's essential and enduring questions of meaning and purpose and to recognize what it might mean to encounter the presence of the divine.

What is more is that this combination of inner, personal meaning-making and outer expression of practice and values has to be formed individually but fostered and sustained communally for Jewish education to be deemed successful. It is as if the very goal of religious education is, in the words of religious educator Dr. Bob Pazmiño, to become "who you are and whose you are."[26] We will only know that, if a generation finds that the traditions they have inherited and shaped is the very one that gives them meaning and purpose and to which they offer their loyalty and commitment sustained in communities of practice.

Rabbi Shapiro somehow survived the experience of the Warsaw Ghetto and its uprising and final liquidation. However, he was then transported to the Trawnicki concentration camp where he was killed in 1943. Realizing that the situation was extremely precarious, he had managed to bury his teachings and sermons delivered in the ghetto for them to be found and published after the war under the title *Esh Qodesh*—Holy Fire. His works continue to inspire Torah students within and beyond the Hasidic community. *Ḥovat ha-Talmidim* is used extensively in *yeshivot* as a text for study with students, and Rabbi Shapiro's approach to a combination of explicit and implicit religion in Jewish education is re-examined in the light of twenty-first-century learning needs. The actualization of potential in *ḥinukh* as a soulful approach to the religious growth of each Torah learner is a legacy that endures. As a dedicated educator and spiritual mentor, he provides a summary of his pedagogy when he says, quoting the *Zohar* 3:13, "Look at this child whom I have placed before you."

---

25 The components of educating for *shlemut* consist of authoring the self, cultivating dispositions, being in relation to community, repairing the world, presencing the divine, and practicing Jewish. See Bill Robinson, "Striving for Shlemut: An Emerging Approach to Jewish Education," *Gleanings: A Dialogue on Jewish Education* 6, no. 2 (Summer 2019): 4–6; see also Shire, "Torah and Godly Play."

26 Robert W. Pazmiño and Michael Shire, "A Curriculum for Interfaith Study and Teaching," *Journal of Interreligious Studies* 15 (2014).

Contributors

Rachel Adelman

Rabbi Dr. Rachel Adelman is associate professor of Hebrew Bible at Hebrew College. She holds a PhD in Hebrew Literature from the Hebrew University of Jerusalem, and is the author of *The Return of the Repressed: Pirqe de-Rabbi Eliezer and the Pseudepigrapha* (Brill, 2009) and *The Female Ruse: Women's Deception and Divine Sanction in the Hebrew Bible* (Sheffield Phoenix, 2015). Rachel is currently working on a new book project: *Daughters in Danger from the Hebrew Bible to Modern Midrash.* In June of 2021, she was ordained as a rabbi at Hebrew College. When not writing books, papers, or *divrei Torah,* it is poetry that flows from her pen.

Arnold J. Band

Dr. Arnold J. Band was born in Boston in 1929. He graduated from the Boston Latin School in 1946, and holds degrees from Boston Hebrew College (1949), Hebrew University (1949–50), Harvard College (1951), and University of Paris (1953). Arnold earned his PhD from Harvard University in 1959. He served as an assistant professor at Boston Hebrew College (1954–59), and as Professor of Hebrew and Comparative Literature at UCLA (1959–2005). Arnold's published works include *Hebrew Poetry* (1963), *Nostalgia and Nightmare: Study of S.J. Agnon* (1968), *Tales of Nachman of Bratzlav* (1974), and over 100 articles in Hebrew and English. He has resided in Silver Spring, MD since 2017.

Sharon Cohen Anisfeld

Rabbi Sharon Cohen Anisfeld became president of Hebrew College in July 2018, after serving as dean of the Rabbinical School from 2006 to 2017. Sharon graduated from the Reconstructionist Rabbinical College in 1990, and subsequently spent fifteen years working as a Hillel rabbi at Tufts, Yale, and Harvard universities. She has been a regular summer faculty member for the Bronfman Youth Fellowships in Israel since 1993 and is coeditor of two volumes of women's writings on Passover, *The Women's Seder Sourcebook: Rituals and Readings for Use at the Passover Seder* (2002) and *The Women's Passover Companion: Women's*

Reflections on the Festival of Freedom (2002). Her sermons, poems, and essays have been published widely.

Michael Fishbane (Editor)
Dr. Michael Fishbane is the Nathan Cummings Distinguished Service Professor of Jewish Studies at the University of Chicago. A native of Boston, he was profoundly influenced by carrying a "double load" in high school and college, when he also attended the Prozdor and the Hebrew Teachers College. He was honored several years ago with an honorary doctorate from Hebrew College, and regards this as a treasured gift. Building on his HC background, he has gone on to write many scholarly books on the history of Jewish thought, from the Bible to contemporary theology, and has devoted himself to works for the larger community and its education as well.

Abigail Esther Gillman
Abigail Esther Gillman, PhD is professor of Hebrew, German, and comparative literature in the Department of World Languages and Literatures at Boston University, and Core Faculty at the Elie Wiesel Center for Jewish Studies. She is the author of two books: *Viennese Jewish Modernism: Freud, Hofmannsthal, Beer-Hofmann and Schnitzler* (Penn State Press, 2009) and *A History of German Jewish Bible Translation* (University of Chicago Press, 2018). Her current research pertains to the *mashal* in Jewish literature, Aharon Appelfeld, and Jewish translation history. At Hebrew College, she has taught courses on Hebrew language, Jewish literature, and Israeli cinema.

Arthur Green (Editor)
Rabbi Arthur Green, PhD is the Irving R. Brudnick professor of Jewish philosophy and religion at Hebrew College. He also serves as Rector of the Rabbinical School, which he founded in 2003. Art is also professor emeritus at Brandeis University, where he occupied the distinguished Philip W. Lown professorship in Jewish Thought. He is both a historian of Jewish mysticism and a theologian. His most recent writings include *Judaism for the World* (Yale, 2020) and a translation and commentary to the Hasidic classic *The Light of the Eyes* (Stanford, 2021).

Melila Hellner-Eshed
Dr. Melila Hellner-Eshed is a senior research fellow at the Shalom Hartman Institute in Jerusalem. She has taught Jewish mysticism and Zohar for the past 25 years at the Hebrew University in Jerusalem, and serves on the faculty of the

Institute of Jewish Spirituality. She teaches and works with Jewish communities around the world. Her publications include *A River Flows from Eden: The Language of Mystical Experience in the Zohar* (Stanford University Press, 2009), and her new book, *Seekers of the Face: The Secrets of the* Idra Rabba *in the Zohar* was published September 2017 (English translation forthcoming, Stanford University Press, 2021). Melila is active in *Sulha,* a reconciliation project that brings together Israelis and Palestinians.

Elie Holzer

Rabbi Elie Holzer, PhD is a practice-oriented philosopher of Jewish education. Elie heads the Ochs Chair for Teaching Religious Studies and serves at the School of Education at Bar Ilan University, and on the North American Mandel Teacher Educators Institute's faculty. He authored, with Orit Kent, *A Philosophy of Havruta: Understanding and Teaching the Art of Text Study in Pairs* (2014 USA National Jewish Book Award) and *Attuned Learning: Rabbinic Texts on Habits of the Heart in Learning Interactions.* He works on spiritual pedagogies for teaching Hasidic homilies and *niggun* and on Hasidism as a venue for a post-critical Jewish religiosity.

David C. Jacobson

David C. Jacobson is professor of Judaic studies at Brown University. He is the author of *Modern Midrash: The Retelling of Traditional Jewish Narratives by Twentieth-Century Hebrew Writers; Does David Still Play before You? Israeli Poetry and the Bible; Creator, Are You Listening? Israeli Poets on God and Prayer; Beyond Political Messianism: The Poetry of Second-Generation Religious Zionist Settlers;* and *The Charm of Wise Hesitancy: Talmudic Stories in Contemporary Israeli Culture.* He is currently writing a study of contemporary Israeli interpretations of the tales of Rabbi Naḥman of Bratslav. He holds a BJEd degree from Hebrew Teachers College.

Daniel Judson

Rabbi Dan Judson is the dean of graduate leadership programs at Hebrew College. He received his doctorate in Jewish history from Brandeis University. His book *Pennies for Heaven: A History of American Synagogues and Money,* was a finalist for the National Jewish Book Award. Dan's research on synagogue finance has been featured in The New York Times, The Boston Globe, and NPR. He was the rabbi of Temple Beth David in Canton, MA for ten years and coauthored a number of books on Jewish rituals for Jewish Lights Publishing.

Jane Kanarek

Rabbi Dr. Jane Kanarek is associate professor of Rabbinics and associate dean of academic development and advising at Hebrew College. She is the author of *Biblical Narrative and the Formation of Rabbinic Law* and the coeditor of *Learning to Read Talmud: What It Looks Like and How It Happens* and *Motherhood in the Jewish Cultural Imagination*, both of which were finalists for the National Jewish Book Award.

Judith A. Kates

Dr. Judith Kates received her PhD in comparative literature from Harvard University in 1971, and a DHL *honoris causa* from Hebrew College in 2017. She served as a professor of Jewish women's studies at Hebrew College from 1992 until her retirement in 2018. As a founding member of the Hebrew College Rabbinical School faculty, Judith taught Tanakh, midrash, and medieval and modern biblical commentary. She has also taught widely in programs of adult learning. Judith is coeditor (with Gail Twersky Reimer) of two pioneering volumes of women's biblical commentary, *Reading Ruth: Contemporary Women Reclaim a Sacred Story* (1994) and *Beginning Anew: A Woman's Companion to the High Holy Days* (1997).

Daniel Klein

Rabbi Daniel Klein is the dean of students for Hebrew College's graduate leadership programs. Since his youth, many of Daniel's formative Jewish educational experiences have been with Hebrew College. A graduate of Prozdor, Daniel also spent many summers as a camper and counselor at Camp Yavneh. He was ordained by and received a Master's in Jewish Education from Hebrew College in 2010. Prior to his current role, Daniel oversaw admissions and student life for Hebrew College's ordination programs from 2011 to 2020.

Anne Lapidus Lerner

Dr. Anne Lapidus Lerner received a BJEd and an MHL at Hebrew College, where she also taught, and her BA, MA, and PhD from Harvard University. She has been a member of the Jewish Theological Seminary faculty since 1969 and was the first woman to serve as a JTS vice chancellor. She served as dean of the Albert A. List College of Jewish Studies, and as associate dean of its Graduate School. Lerner founded the JTS Jewish women's studies program and the Paula E. Hyman memorial mentoring program at the Association for Jewish Studies. She was a research associate at the women's studies in religion program at Harvard and scholar-in-residence at the Hadassah-Brandeis Institute.

She has published a book on Saul, and *Eternally Eve,* and a classic study of the rise of Jewish feminism. Her honors include an Honorary Doctorate from Hebrew College and the Mathilde Schechter Award from Women's League for Conservative Judaism.

Ariel Mayse

Rabbi Ariel Evan Mayse, PhD, is an assistant professor of Religious studies at Stanford University and the rabbi-in-residence at Atiq: Jewish Maker Institute (atiqmakers.org). Previously he was the director of Jewish studies and visiting assistant professor of modern Jewish thought at Hebrew College. Ariel holds a PhD in Jewish Studies from Harvard University and rabbinic ordination from Beit Midrash Har'el in Israel. His is the author of *Speaking Infinities: God and Language in the Teachings of Rabbi Dov Ber of Mezritsh* (University of Pennsylvania, 2020), and, with his teacher Arthur Green, editor of *A New Hasidism: Roots and Branches* (Jewish Publications Society, 2019).

Nehemia Polen

Rabbi Nehemia Polen, PhD is professor of Jewish thought at Hebrew College, where he has taught since 1988 and has been on the Rabbinical School faculty since its inception. His areas of teaching and research include Bible (especially the Book of Leviticus) and Hasidism. His publications include *The Holy Fire: The Teachings of Rabbi Kalonymus Shapira, the Rebbe of the Warsaw Ghetto* and *The Rebbe's Daughter,* a translation and analysis of the Hebrew memoir of Malka Shapira, daughter of the Kozienicer Rebbe, which focuses on the spiritual lives of women in early twentieth-century Hasidic Poland.

Shayna Rhodes

Rabbi Shayna Rhodes was a member of the first graduating class of the Hebrew College Rabbinical School, and is currently codirector of the Beit Midrash and a member of the faculty. She teaches Talmud, Tanakh, and *halakhah.* Raised in an Orthodox home, Shayna attended Bais Yaakov of Baltimore through high school. She earned a degree in European History from Barnard College where she met her husband, Jonathan. After completing a master's degree in computer science from City University, and raising a family of five children, she continued a family legacy of rabbinical training and Torah study that stretches back centuries.

Ira Robinson

Professor Ira Robinson, who holds a PhD in Judaic studies from Harvard University, spent forty-two years at Concordia University in Montreal, many of them as professor of Judaic studies and chair of the Department of Religions and Cultures. His most recent book is entitled *A Kabbalist in Montreal: The Life and Times of Rabbi Yudel Rosenberg*. He graduated from the Hebrew College Prozdor (Worcester Branch) in 1969.

Or N. Rose

Rabbi Or Rose is the founding director of the Miller Center for Interreligious Learning and Leadership of Hebrew College. Before assuming this position, he held several other posts within the institution, including as an associate dean of the Rabbinical School. Or is the author or editor of both scholarly and popular works on Jewish spirituality and interreligious and cross-cultural engagement.

Michael Rosenberg

Rabbi Michael Rosenberg, PhD is a member of the faculty at Hadar Institute in New York. Previously, he served as associate professor of Rabbinics at Hebrew College for nearly a decade. He is the author of *Signs of Virginity: Testing Virgins and Making Men in Late Antiquity*, and the coauthor, with Ethan Tucker, of *Gender Equality and Prayer in Jewish Law*.

Shani Rosenbaum (Managing Editor)

Rabbi Shoshana (Shani) Rosenbaum is a faculty member at the Rabbinical School of Hebrew College. She holds a BA in Near Eastern and Judaic Studies from Brandeis University and received rabbinic ordination from her teachers at Hebrew College. Shani has studied at Midreshet Lindenbaum, Matan, Beit Midrash Har'el, Yeshivat Hadar, and in the Pardes Kollel and has taught Talmud, *halakhah*, and midrash through Hebrew College's Open Circle. She has served on the programming teams at Jerusalem-based non-profits Encounter and OLAM, and at T'ruah: The Rabbinic Call for Human Rights.

Jonathan D. Sarna (Editor)

Dr. Jonathan D. Sarna (Prozdor '70, HTC '74) is University professor and Joseph H. & Belle R. Braun professor of American Jewish history at Brandeis University, where he directs its Schusterman Center for Israel Studies. He also is a past president of the Association for Jewish Studies and chief historian of the National Museum of American Jewish History in Philadelphia. A fellow of the American Academy of Arts and Sciences and of the American Academy of Jewish Research, he has written, edited, or coedited more than thirty books on American Jewish history and life, including *American Judaism: A History*.

George Savran

George Savran, PhD studied at Brandeis University with Professor Nahum Sarna and Professor Michael Fishbane. He has taught at Wellesley College, Indiana University, Hebrew College, Hebrew Union College (Jerusalem), and the Hebrew University of Jerusalem. He was director of biblical studies at the Schechter Institute for Jewish Studies in Jerusalem for twenty-five years. His books include *Telling and Retelling: Quotation in Biblical Narrative* (1989) and *Encountering the Divine: Theophany in Biblical Narrative* (2005). He is presently at work on a study of identity formation in the Jacob narrative in Genesis.

Michael Shire

Rabbi Michael Shire is the academic director of the master's degree in Jewish education and chief academic officer at Hebrew College. Previously, he served as vice-principal of Leo Baeck College in London. He is the author of several works on spiritual growth in Jewish education, including the entry on "Spiritual Education" in the International Handbook of Jewish Education (Springer), and four books of illuminated and creative Jewish liturgy. He teaches courses at the College and is the founder of a Jewish spiritual pedagogy named Torah Godly Play.

David Starr

Rabbi Dr. David Starr is the executive director of Tzion, a program for Israel literacy, and a research associate of the Tauber Institute for the Study of European Jewry, Brandeis University. He teaches in the faculties of Hult International Business School, Hebrew College, and the Wexner heritage program, and served as scholar in residence for Israel Education and Programs at Gann Academy. He was the founding dean of *Me'ah* and vice-president at Hebrew College. David is currently writing a biography of Solomon Schechter and a study of education and its impact on the religious life of Jewish adults. He holds a doctorate in history from Columbia University and rabbinic ordination from JTS.

Avinoam J. Stillman

Avinoam J. Stillman is a doctoral candidate and research associate at Freie Universität Berlin. After completing his BA at Columbia University, he pursued his MA at Ben-Gurion University under the supervision of Professor Jonatan Meir. His thesis focused on the Korets printings of kabbalistic and Hasidic books in the late eighteenth century. Avinoam's current research explores the history of Lurianic kabbalah in the Ottoman Empire and East-Central Europe in the early seventeenth century. Although never formally affiliated with Hebrew

College, he grew up in Brookline in the orbit of (neo-)Hasidic academia, and his mother, Naomi, worked at the College.

Ilan Troen

Dr. Ilan Troen is professor emeritus on the Lopin Chair of Modern History at Ben-Gurion University and the Stoll Family Chair in Israel Studies at Brandeis University. He was dean of Humanities and Social Sciences (BGU), founding director of the Ben-Gurion Research Institute for the Study of Israel and Zionism (Sde Boqer, Israel) and the Schusterman Center for Israel Studies at Brandeis, as well as the president of the Association for Israel Studies. Ilan authored and edited numerous books in American, Jewish and Israeli history and is founding editor of *Israel Studies*. He is a graduate of Prozdor (1958) and Hebrew College (1962) and received the Benjamin Shevach Award for Distinguished Achievement in Jewish Educational Leadership in 2012. He made *aliyah* in 1975.

Index

www.ingramcontent.com/pod-product-compliance
Lightning Source LLC
Chambersburg PA
CBHW070407100426
42812CB00005B/1660